THE PROPHET
Isaiah

A COMMENTARY

VICTOR BUKSBAZEN

The Friends of Israel Gospel Ministry, Inc.
P. O. Box 908, Bellmawr, NJ 08099

THE PROPHET ISAIAH: A Commentary
By Victor Buksbazen, Th.D.

Copyright © 2008 by The Friends of Israel Gospel Ministry, Inc.
P.O. Box 908, Bellmawr, NJ 08099
www.foi.org

First Printing   2008

Original copyright © 1971 by The Spearhead Press, an imprint of The
Friends of Israel Gospel Ministry, Inc.

Translation of Isaiah from Hebrew to English by Dr. Victor Buksbazen.
All Scripture other than Isaiah is quoted from *The New Scofield Study
Bible*, Authorized King James Version, Oxford University Press, Inc., 1967.

ISBN-10: 0-915540-05-3
ISBN-13: 978-0-915540-05-1
Library of Congress Catalog Card Number: 2008920340

Cover Design by Waveline Direct, Inc., Mechanicsburg, PA

when we attempt to penetrate any other ancient literary document, such as Homer, Plato, or Sophocles. There is a divine reality in prophecy which defies mere literary or historical analysis, because here is a spiritual phenomenon which goes beyond any other human experience.

In the final analysis, the book of Isaiah, like all other prophetic writings, can be only spiritually comprehended. The study of Isaiah calls for a sense of awe and the need for divine guidance, which alone can unlock the mystery of prophecy and revelation.

Strangely enough, in spite of the great importance of the book of Isaiah, the average Bible reader is, apart from a few isolated Messianic passages, hardly familiar with this sublime prophetic document, or with the regal personality of the man behind the book. In the fourth century, St. Jerome called Isaiah "Not so much a prophet as an evangelist."

And yet, Isaiah was even more than that. He was the voice of God speaking to Israel, addressing their immediate and desperate predicament, and also proclaiming those timeless, eternal truths which carry a message for men of every generation. Isaiah was the writhing and lashing conscience of his people, a vital link in the chain of prophets whom God, from time to time, sent unto Israel, lest they perish completely.

> Howbeit I sent unto you all my servants the prophets, rising early and sending them, saying, Oh, do not this abominable thing that I hate. But they hearkened not, nor inclined their ear to turn from their wickedness, to burn no incense unto other gods. Wherefore my fury and mine anger was poured forth, and was kindled in the cities of Judah and in the streets of Jerusalem; and they are wasted and desolate, as at this day (Jer. 44:4-6).

As we become familiar with the historical circumstances of Isaiah's prophetic ministry, we begin to grasp that which is eternally significant and relevant in his message, and that which applies in a special way to our own confused and turbulent times, when men, as in the days of the prophet, have made their motto: "Let us eat and drink; for tomorrow we shall die" (Isa. 22:13).

Basically, apart from the external trimmings and trappings of our contemporary civilization, the world of the prophet was very much the same as ours. Essentially man is always the same, a rebel facing a holy and outraged God. And yet, the marvel of it all, this God is nevertheless a God of mercy.

Sometimes the line of demarcation between the prophetic message directed to his own generation and that which pierces the veil of a distant future, is not sharply delineated. Often the prophet seems to speak to his own time, but his message applies equally to generations yet unborn, and lifts the veil of God's redemptive design for the human race.

The same timeless voice of God which spoke through Isaiah to the

Preface

It is with fear and trembling and with great diffidence that we approach this study.

The grandeur of the man, the sublimity of the subject and the magnitude of the task are awe inspiring. They bring to mind God's word to Moses: "Draw not nigh hither: put off thy shoes from off thy feet, for the place whereon thou standest is holy ground" (Ex. 3:5) .

Perhaps no other book of the Bible, with the exception of the Pentateuch, has suffered so much from destructive criticism as the book of Isaiah. For nearly two centuries it has been the fashion among critics to break up this book into small units, and to attribute its authorship to various unknown writers.

J. Skinner, who is fairly representative of this school, begins the introduction to his commentary on Isaiah, chapters 40-66 in this fashion: "The last twenty-seven chapters of the book of Isaiah are an anonymous prophecy, or series of prophecies which all critical writers agree in assigning to an age much later than the time of Isaiah."*

Modern critics divide the book of Isaiah into First Isaiah (chapters 1-39) , the Second or Deutero—Isaiah (chapters 40-55) , and the Third or Trito—Isaiah, (chapters 56-66) , Even these portions of the book have been further broken up into fragments, to the point where there is hardly any part of Isaiah the authenticity of which has not been questioned at one time or another. Most of the assumptions and arguments behind this fragmentation of Isaiah are unwarranted and specious, sometimes to the point of being almost frivolous.

We shall later examine these arguments more closely, and will make an effort to substantiate our position with regard to the integrity and unity of the book of Isaiah.

Apart from the question of the unity of the book, there are many other important problems which call for answers. One of the questions which must engage the mind of every serious student of Isaiah should be: "What were the historical circumstances under which the prophet exercised his ministry?" It is obvious that the prophet did not labor in an historical or spiritual void but amidst constantly and swiftly changing events which had a profound effect upon his people during his life time (app. 765-685 B.C.) . Isaiah is the divinely appointed prophet who brings the mind of God to bear upon these events and their outcome.

It would be impossible to understand the real significance and meaning of the prophet's message without understanding what was happening in Israel and the world in which Isaiah lived.

And yet, important as such historical knowledge might be, this alone would still be entirely inadequate for the proper grasp of his prophetic message. For in dealing with Isaiah, we are in a different position from

Foreword

The Book of Isaiah is the longest of the prophetic anthologies which have come down to us. Its author was a person of unusual spiritual insight whose perception of the divine revelation was reflected in writings of great poetic beauty. His prophetic ministry seems to have been of long duration, and was also rather out of the ordinary in that it attracted a small group of disciples. The teachings and writings of Isaiah were voluminous, as the canonical book indicates, and dealt in one way or another with all the important Near Eastern nations. Isaiah's lofty conception of God was matched by a pressing concern for the ethical outworking of the covenantal responsibilities among the Chosen People. More than most prophets, he was concerned to apply the concept of divine holiness to political affairs, and his contacts with the royal court afforded him opportunities for influencing the domestic and international policies of the southern kingdom.

The author of this two-volume work has made a commendable effort to catch the significance of Isaiah's life and thought in the larger pattern of divine self-disclosure. This is far from easy to accomplish, since although the Hebrew text of the prophecy has been comparatively well preserved, as the Dead Sea Isaiah manuscripts indicate, there are certain rather obscure allusions in the writings which are difficult to comprehend. Dr. Buksbazen has made his own translation from the Hebrew, and this, with the accompanying explanatory comments, throws new light upon the meaning and emphasis of the original. As a well-known Hebrew Christian, the author quite rightly sees Jesus Christ foretold in the Messianic utterances of the prophet, and he expounds these sections with great spiritual awareness and sensitivity.

To render the Hebrew of Isaiah into English in such a way that it reflects accurately the nuances of the thought and expression of the original author is a very difficult undertaking. Dr. Buksbazen, however, has the decided advantage of being able to bring the profound spiritual traditions and insights of God's ancient people to his task of translating and commenting upon the writings of Isaiah. The result is a challenging rendering and exposition of the literary deposit of an outstanding Hebrew prophet which merits the serious attention of all students of the Word of God.

R. K. Harrison

Wycliffe College,
University of Toronto.

2

Acknowledgements

A number of persons have helped in preparing the manuscript of this work for printing. To all of them I am deeply indebted.

I am most grateful to Dr. R. K. Harrison of Wycliffe College, Toronto, Canada, for his kindness in writing the foreword to this book, and to those who helped him prepare the indexes. My thanks also to Mr. H. L. Ellison, noted English Bible scholar and author, who has contributed some helpful suggestions.

A special word of appreciation is due to Dr. Mary Bennett for her valuable help in reading the manuscript and correcting the proofs.

For the unceasing encouragement of my beloved wife Lydia and the painstaking typing and retyping of the manuscript I am profoundly grateful.

Finally, I wish to express my filial gratitude to the memory of my departed father, Abraham Joseph, son of Isaiah Buksbazen, at whose feet I learned the rudiments of the Hebrew language and a love for Israel's great heritage—the Scriptures.

Victor Buksbazen

Collingswood, New Jersey

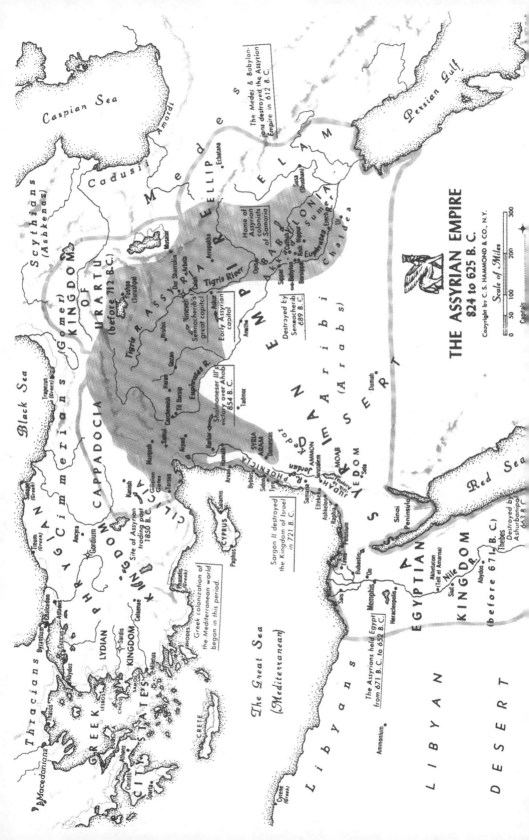

Page

Introduction to Isaiah Part II 323
Jewish Tradition Concerning the Book of Isaiah
Translation and Commentary
Chapters 40   Israel's Hour of Deliverance has Arrived 330
         41   God Holds the Destiny of the Nations
Chapter 42   The Servant in Whom the Lord Delights 343
Chapter 43   Jehovah's Abiding Love for Israel 349
Chapter 44   Repentant Israel Promised the Spirit 354
Chapter 45   Cyrus to Deliver Israel 360
Chapter 46   The Idols Contrasted with Jehovah 367
Chapter 47   The Humiliation of Babylon 370
Chapter 48   An Exhortation to the Captivity 374
Chapter 49-51   Prophecies About the Servant 379
Chapter 51   A Message of Hope 391
Chapter 52:1-12   Jerusalem the Holy City 397
Chapter 52:13-   The Suffering of the Servant of the Lord
         53:12   and His Future Glory 400
Chapter 54   Zion's Glorious Feast 423
Chapter 55   An Invitation to a Spiritual Feast 428
Chapter 56-58   Messages of Encouragement and Rebuke 433
Chapter 59   Sin has come Between Israel and her God 448
Chapter 60   The Glory of the New Jerusalem 454
Chapter 61   The Messiah's Mission and Israel's Destiny 460
Chapter 62   Jehovah Will not Rest Until Zion
                      is Redeemed 465
Chapter 63   Israel's Avenger and Redeemer 469
Chapter 64-65   Israel's Plea and Jehovah's Answer 476
Chapter 66   A Man-Made Temple Cannot Hold an
                      Infinite God 488

Postscript 498
General Index 501
Index of Biblical References 503
Bibliography 509

Contents

Page

Acknowledgements 1

Foreword 2

Preface 3

The Prophets of Israel 9

The Life and Work of Isaiah 37

Who Wrote the Book of Isaiah? 47

The Critics of Isaiah 55

The Indivisibility of Isaiah 63

The Message of Isaiah 71

The Major Themes of Isaiah 77

Some Problems of Biblical Chronology 81

Chronological Tables of the Kingdoms of Judah and Israel 87

Synopsis of Chapters 1-39 91

Translation and Commentary

Chapters   1-6   Prophecies Concerning Judah and Jerusalem .. 95

Chapters   7-12   The Book of Immanuel 145

Chapters 13-23   Oracles Concerning Israel's Neighbors 189

Chapters 24-27   The Apocalypse of Isaiah 235

Chapters 34-35   The Book of Woes 247

Chapters 34-35   The Doom of Edom and the Return
                            of the Redeemed 275

Chapters 36-39   Historical Events 281

SUPPLEMENT – Some Guidelines to the Interpretation
                            of Prophecy 299

General Index 305

Index of Biblical References 309

Bibliography 319

people of Judah and to Ephraim in the 8th century B.C., is still speaking to us today. We may ignore this voice, but only at the peril of suffering the same catastrophe which ancient Israel and Judah had to experience.

Isaiah lived during a crucial period in the history of Israel. The two feuding kingdoms of Samaria and Judah, the Palestine of Isaiah, were caught in the jaws of a giant nutcracker consisting of the two rival empires of Assyria and Egypt, each bent on liquidating and absorbing the other. Tiny Israel and Judah were in their path, an enclave of monotheism (at least officially) in a pagan world.

Beside the military conflict between the two giants of the Fertile Crescent, there was also an unceasing war between their gods and the God of Israel. On the one hand there was Jehovah, "The Holy One of Israel" as Isaiah delighted to call Him, and arrayed against Him was the vast pantheon of the cruel, sensual, blood-thirsty and greedy gods of Israel's neighbors. Some of these "gods" were more blood-thirsty and debauched than their human worshippers.

While the God of Israel was calling His people to a holy and righteous life, the gods of Israel's neighbors, personifying the untamed and blind forces of nature, the gods of fertility and conquest, were constantly tempting and alluring Israel to make a religion out of their sensual appetites and baser instincts.

And yet when the Israelites compared their own national weakness with the might of their neighbors, they were often tempted to follow those gods, in the belief that only they were powerful enough to assure them survival, prosperity and victory over their enemies.

A classic example of this fatal fascination of the alien gods for Israel during the days of Isaiah was Ahaz himself, the king of Judah:

> And in the time of his distress did he trespass yet more against the Lord: this is that king Ahaz. For he sacrificed unto the gods of Damascus, which smote him: and he said, Because the gods of the kings of Syria help them, therefore will I sacrifice to them, that they may help me. But they were the ruin of him, and of all Israel (2 Chr. 28:22, 23).

Ahaz may strike us as being not only wicked, but foolish. And yet are we really so very different from Ahaz and the people of his day? Is not man still tempted to serve the same old gods of lust and power which his ancestors worshipped in the long ago, under a different guise and different names?

The archeological discoveries in the Near East during the past century have enormously increased our knowledge of the Biblical world and of its long forgotten peoples. As a result of this, the Bible has emerged a much more historically reliable document than many of its critics were willing to credit it only a few decades or even a few years ago.

Cities, temples, palaces, nations, documents, humble and great per-

5

sons of whom we knew little or nothing, have suddenly come to life. Again the stones and ruins speak to us with a mighty voice. Archeology has repeatedly authenticated the Bible as a trustworthy book, and added a new dimension to our understanding of the Scriptures and Biblical history.

Yet in spite of all this new evidence, the heart of the prophetic message still remains a "sealed book" to many, because "the natural man receiveth not the things of the Spirit of God: for they are foolishness unto him: neither can he know them, because they are spiritually discerned" (1 Cor. 2:14).

It is surprising how little has been written about Isaiah in our century. Most of the major works on Isaiah, as Drechsler, Alexander, Ewald, Hengstenberg, Duhm, Keil, Delitsch, Barnes, G. A. Smith, Skinner, Driver, to mention just a few, were written in the nineteenth century, and are now either out of print, or need to be brought up to date, in line with our more recent comprehension of the history, the religions and the languages of the peoples of the Bible lands and the findings of archeology. Unfortunately some of the above works were permeated with the spirit of negative criticism, so that the reader instead of gaining a clearer understanding of Isaiah was left more confused and bewildered than before. Doubt was instilled in the mind of the student, so that, like the serpent of old, he was made to wonder "Hath God said?"

There is a further consideration which prompted us to attempt the study. Every great prophet, and especially Isaiah, must be presented to each generation in the context of its own experiences and its own peculiar insights. Only thus can the eternal and unchangeable Word of God be appropriated by each succeeding generation.

It is in the hope of making even a modest contribution toward a better understanding of Isaiah, the greatest of all the writing prophets, and in reliance upon God, that we venture upon this study.

Our study was not written for Old Testament specialists, but rather for all those who seek to gain a more meaningful and well balanced understanding of that great prophetic book of Isaiah, and to bring into clearer focus the world in which he lived.

In translating the book of Isaiah from Hebrew into English, the author has followed closely the Massoretic text, yet seeking to avoid being too literal, which would make our translation sound stilted or unnatural. We have, of course, diligently consulted most of the existing translations of the Old Testament, beginning with the incomparable but unfortunately antiquated King James Version, and ending with the smooth-reading English version of the Jerusalem Bible, which, however, is often more of a paraphrase than a true translation.

We have kept our comments brief, frequently letting the prophet speak for himself where the text was clear and self-explanatory. On the other hand, where the meaning of the Hebrew was uncertain, or the various historical allusions and peculiarities of Isaiah's style called for it, we have provided more detailed explanation. Our comments generally are exegetical rather than homiletical, in the belief that when once the reader has grasped the true sense of "the vision of Isaiah, the son of Amoz," the Holy Spirit will enable him to apply the prophetic message to his individual needs, and to his circumstances; for through Isaiah God spoke not only to the prophet's contemporary generation in Judah and Jerusalem, but to all of humanity, of every generation and in all places. Through His servant Isaiah, the Eternal God revealed eternal truth, and heralded the coming of Him who is "the way, the truth, and the life."

Today many of those who study Isaiah are in a position somewhat similar to that of the Ethiopian eunuch, who was so puzzled about the meaning of what he was reading. When the early disciple of Christ, Philip, approached him and asked: "Understandest thou what thou readest?" the wise and humble Ethiopian answered: "How can I, except some man shall guide me?" (Acts 8:31).

We can only pray that the same Spirit of God who guided Philip may also help us to a more complete and satisfying understanding of the great prophet Isaiah, the herald of the Kingdom of God and of the King-Messiah.

We trust that our effort will be a joint venture of spiritual discovery and enrichment for both writer and reader.

*The Book of the Prophet Isaiah, Chapters XL-LXVI, page IX, in Cambridge Bible, Revised edition 1917.

The
Prophets
of Israel

Before we proceed with our study of the prophet Isaiah, it is necessary that we consider first of all, that unique Old Testament phenomenon — prophetism. Underlying much of the destructive criticism of the Scriptures in general, and of the book of Isaiah in particular, are certain false assumptions concerning the nature of Biblical prophetism. These have distorted the understanding of the Bible in the minds of many.

What then is prophetism? What distinguished the Hebrew prophet from other men? What were his functions? How does the Old Testament prophet differ from the pagan "prophets" and diviners? How do we know whether he is a true messenger of God? What was the role of the prophet in the history of salvation? Did the prophet address himself mainly to his own generation and to contemporary events, or was his message predictive of the future? We believe that to all these, and to many related questions, the Scriptures themselves can give us adequate answers.

First of all, let us consider the meaning of the term "prophet." It comes from the Greek word *Prophetes,* the root of which is a composite verb *pro-phemi,* which means "to speak in advance" or "to speak for another person." The prophet did both. He was a spokesman for God in His relationship with Israel, and he predicted coming events.

The first Biblical reference to the term "prophet" (in Hebrew *nãbi*) is found in connection with an incident in the life of Abraham, when God commanded Abimelech to return Sarah to her husband Abraham.

> Return the wife of this man for he is a prophet and he will pray for thee and thou shalt live, But if thou wilt not return, know that thou wilt most certainly die and all that is thine (Gen. 20:7).

Here the prophet is presented as a man under God's special protection. He is an effective intercessor. To harm him in any way is to provoke divine wrath and retribution.

The Titles of The Prophets

The various titles by which the prophets were known, give us some insight into the meaning of prophetism. The most general and best known Hebrew term for prophet is:

1. *Nãbi*. This word is derived from a root which means "to well up," "to speak forth," consequently, "to make solemn pronouncements in the name of God."

Some believe that the word *nãbi* is probably related to the Accadian root which means "a man who is called" or "a man who calls" i.e. in the name of God.[1]

Both the Hebrew and the Accadian derivations clearly suggest that the prophet is "a spokesman for God."

The classic passage which describes the prophet in such a capacity is Exodus 7:1-2b: "And Jehovah said unto Moses, Behold I have set thee as God (Elohim) to Pharaoh, and thy brother Aaron shall be thy prophet. Thou shalt say all that I will command thee and thy brother Aaron shall speak to Pharoah."

Here the function of the prophet is precisely indicated; God speaks to the prophet, who in turn communicates His message to the proper addressee. This is the main function which the Old Testament assigns to the prophets. They are God's messengers and spokesmen.

In addition to the term *Nãbi* the prophets were also known by a number of other appellations.

2. The prophet is frequently called "The Man of God" — *Ish Elohim*. "And there came a man of God unto Eli and said . . . " (1 Sam. 2:27a).

Occasionally the prophet is referred to as "the holy man of God" (2 Ki. 4:9).

3. *Abodai ha-nebiim*. When God speaks of the prophets he sometimes refers to them as "My servants the prophets."

However, Jehovah warned Israel and Judah through every prophet and every seer, saying: Turn back from your evil ways and observe my commandments and my statutes according to the law which I commanded your fathers, and which I sent to you by my servants the prophets. (2 Ki. 17:13).

4. *Ro'eh*. Among the oldest designations of the prophet is the term "seer" from the Hebrew root *ra'ah* — to see. The *locus classicus* for this term is 1 Samuel 9:9:

In former times in Israel when a man went to inquire of God he would say 'let us go to the seer' [*ro'eh*]. For the one who is now called prophet' [*nãbi*] was formerly called 'the seer'.

5. *Hozeh*. There are two distinct Hebrew words which are translated

into English as "The Seer." The first is *ro'eh* — seer. The second is *hozeh*, also translated "seer." No doubt there was a difference between the two kinds of "seers" but the distinction became obliterated in the course of time.

The Hebrew verb *ra'ah* — "to see" is generally applied to physical sight. In this sense *ro'eh* would be a person to whom the Lord has granted the gift of seeing certain things which would otherwise remain unseen to the natural eye.

On the other hand the term *hozeh* from the verb *haza* — "to see" (Amos 1:1), seems to indicate an inward vision or an extra-sensory perception which God gives to His chosen messengers, the prophets, to enable them to see that which the physical eyes or mind cannot see. Isaiah speaks of "the valley of vision" — *gai' hizzaion* (22:1).

The distinction between the three different terms: the seer — *ro'eh,* the seer — *hozeh,* and the prophet — *nābi* is clearly marked in the Hebrew text of the following passage:

> The acts of David the King, from the beginning to the end, these are recorded in the chronicles of Samuel the Seer [*Ro'eh*] and in the chronicles of Nathan the prophet [*Nābi*] and in the chronicles of Gad the seer [*Hozeh*] (1 Chr. 29:29).

All three terms, *ro'eh, hozeh* and *nābi* eventually became interchangeable, and the term *nābi* became the usual designation of a prophet.

The Prophet Par Excellence

In the Pentateuch Moses is presented as the model prophet and as the pattern for all later prophets. In some ways the relationship between the apostles and Christ parallels the relationship between the prophets and Moses. Jewish tradition refers to Moses as *Moshe Rabbenu,* — "Our Master Moses." Just as the genuineness of the apostolic doctrine was measured by its harmony and conformity to the gospel of Christ, so the teaching of the prophets could only be judged by its conformity to the Law of Moses. The final authority of every prophet was the Word of God as revealed in the Torah — the Law of Moses.

> And when they (the false prophets) say to you, consult them that have familiar spirits and the wizards who mutter, should not a people rather consult their God. Should they consult the dead for those who are alive? *To the law* (Torah) and to the testimony! If they speak not according to this word it is because there is not a glimmer of light in them [lit. "no dawn"] (Isa. 8:19-20).

The Reluctant Prophet

Every prophet must resemble in some of his essential features the characteristics of his prototype Moses. And what were the characteristics of Moses?

Let us consider some of them. First of all the prophet had to be a man called of God. Such a man was Moses. He did not appoint himself as a spokesman for God, on the contrary he strenuously resisted the divine call, but in the end God prevailed. This was true not only of Moses (Ex. 3:1-4) but also of Amos (7:14-15), of Isaiah (ch. 6), of Jeremiah (1:4-19) and of Ezekiel (1:28, 3:16-17).

It is the mark of the true prophet that he is genuinely reluctant to become an intermediary between God and His people. There are many reasons for this reluctance. Every true prophet is deeply aware of his own inadequacy, and feels crushed under the burden of responsibility laid upon him. He shrinks from the negative reception which he knows awaits him and he seeks to escape the embarrassments to which he will inevitably be exposed as a prophet. Being human, he endeavors to avoid the heartache and the anguish of the prophetic calling. However, in the end he must submit to the overwhelming power of God's presence and calling. Try as he may, he cannot escape the divine compulsion. And yet, contradictory as this may sound, the prophet is nevertheless a free agent. He may choose to reject his call, but if he did that, he could no longer live with himself or face his God.

> Then I said, I will not make mention of him, nor speak any more in his name. But his word was in mine heart as a burning fire shut up in my bones, and I was weary with forbearing, and I could not stay (Jer. 20:9).

The apostle Paul was also deeply conscious of such inner compulsion. "Woe is me if I preach not the Gospel" (1 Cor. 9:16[2]).

Prophetic reluctance is best demonstrated by the experience of Moses as related in Exodus (3:11, 4:10). We shall analyze it in some detail.

In Exodus 3:2-6 we have a description of the divine manifestation granted to Moses in the burning bush. This is followed by his commission to go to Pharaoh with God's command "let my people go," (Ex. 3:10). However Moses objected strenuously: "Who am I, that I should go to Pharaoh, and that I should lead forth the children of Israel from Egypt?" (Ex. 3:11). Moses' first reaction is an overwhelming sense of unworthiness and inadequacy.

In answer God gave Moses the assurance that He would be with him and that after He would bring them forth from Egypt, "the children of Israel will serve God upon that mountain" (3:12[3]).

Moses raised still another objection; "the children of Israel do not know God's name." In Biblical language that means that the Israelites did not know the true nature and power of God. To this God answered:

> Say to the children of Israel 'I AM THAT I AM' (Hebrew: 'I will be that I will be') sent me, the God of Abraham, the God of Isaac, and the God of Jacob sent me, this is my name forever (Ex. 3:14-15).

Ehye-asher-ehye — "I AM THAT I AM" — expresses the deepest truth about God, He is the ultimate reality, which underlies all reality (cf. Acts 17:28).

Jehovah is not only the essence of all existence, but He is the God who made Himself known to the fathers, and dealt with them graciously. This emphasis upon God's revelation in history was common to all the prophets.

Moses continued to object. This time he claimed lack of proper credentials as God's messenger, and the people's unbelief. "Behold they will not believe me and will not listen to my voice, for they will say: 'Jehovah has not appeared unto thee' " (Ex. 4:1).

Now God assures Moses that He will enable him to perform miracles which will authenticate him before the people as a messenger of God.

Finally Moses makes known another and perhaps the real cause of his reluctance: his physical handicap, a speech impediment.

> And Moses said to Jehovah, please Lord, I am not a man of words, either heretofore, or since thou hast spoken to thy servant. I am heavy of mouth and tongue. Then the Lord said to him Who has made man's mouth, who makes him dumb, or deaf, or seeing, or blind? Is it not I, Jehovah? Now therefore, go, and I will be with thy mouth and teach thee what thou shalt say (Ex. 4:10-11).

Consistently God uses the weak and the handicapped, so that His servants may learn to depend on Him and not on their own strength. Jehovah will not be deterred by any of man's excuses. When everything else failed, Moses finally blurted out: "Please Lord, send somebody else" (Ex. 4:13).

At last "God's anger was kindled against Moses" (vs. 14). He then gives Moses his brother Aaron for a spokesman. "He shall speak for you to the people and he shall be a mouth for you, for you shall be to him as God" (vs. 16).

This passage may be considered as describing the essential relationship between God and prophet. What Moses was to Aaron, God was to Moses. The prophet acts as God's mouthpiece.

We have dwelt in some detail upon the call of Moses because it illustrates dramatically the prophet's reluctance to accept his call and the divine compulsion under which all the prophets labored. This divine compulsion was beautifully expressed by Amos: "The lion has roared, who will not be afraid? The Lord Jehovah has spoken, who will not prophesy?" (Amos 3:8).

The Prophet's Anguish

Closely related to the prophet's reluctance is his anguish. The prophet is by the very nature of his calling a tragic personality. He is a man caught in the middle, between a Holy God and a rebellious people. He lives in constant tension between a love for his people and a love for his God, torn between his loyalties to and sympathies for God and also for Israel. In a sense every prophet had to bear a cross, to which he was nailed by his love for his people and his even greater love to Jehovah.

The prophet is the sympathetic nerve of his people and responds with utmost sensitivity to every shock, to every disease or pathological condition of his community. Yet as keenly as he may sense the ailments of his people, he is even more keenly in sympathy with the disappointment and frustration, if the word may be so used, of God. Jehovah's disappointment and frustration are so beautifully expressed in Isaiah's song of the vineyard, where the prophet depicts God as a husbandman who has planted a pleasant vineyard and expected good and wholesome fruit but instead is reaping wild grapes (Isa. 5:1-3).

To his people the prophet often appears as a relentless and even ill-tempered accuser. His words smart and lash. But in the presence of his God the prophet is an intercessor and pleader on behalf of his rebellious people.

> And it came to pass on the morrow, that Moses said unto the people, Ye have sinned a great sin: and now I will go up unto the Lord; peradventure I shall make an atonement for your sin. And Moses returned unto the Lord, and said, Oh, this people have sinned a great sin, and have made them gods of gold. Yet now, if thou wilt forgive their sin—; and if not, blot me, I pray thee, out of thy book which thou hast written (Ex. 32:30-32).

Perhaps no other prophet has expressed this anguish more dramatically than Jeremiah,

> My anguish, my anguish, I writhe in pain.
> Oh the walls of my heart! My heart is beating wildly.
> I cannot keep silent.
> For I hear the sound of the trumpet,
> The call to war.
> For my people are foolish. They know not me.
> They are foolish children. They have no understanding.
> Expert in doing evil but to do good they know not how.
> (Jer. 4:19-22).

It is the destiny of every prophet to be hated and condemned by his people. His constant rebukes and predictions of God's judgment to come upon the nation sting like a whip applied to a lacerated body. Amos complained: "They hate him that rebuketh in the gate, and they abhor him that speaketh uprightly" (Amos 5:10).

The royal priest Amaziah complained that the land could not stand the predictions of doom by Amos (7:11). Jesus Himself was deeply conscious of the prophet's tragedy when He said: "O Jerusalem, Jerusalem, thou that killest the prophets, and stonest them which are sent unto thee—" (Mt. 23:37a).

14

Prophetic Pathos

The prophet is a man of deep pathos in the classic sense of the word, which means "suffering." He suffers with his people, for his people and because of his people. Above all he suffers with God and for God, because sin and unrighteousness alienate the people from their holy God. Isaiah cries:

Woe is me, for I am lost,
For I am a man of unclean lips and I dwell amidst a people of unclean lips
For my eyes have seen the King, The Lord of Hosts (Isa. 6:5).

The prophet does not speak or write like an orator who chooses his words carefully and arranges them into a well organized topical argument. The prophet does not address himself to the rational mind of his people in the manner of the Greek philosophers or Roman orators. The Hebrew prophets appeal to the hearts and to the conscience of their people. Because of this their words often sound harsh and even violent. The prophets' anguish and pathos often lends to their words the quality of great poetry.

Note 1. *The New Bible Dictionary* article "The Prophets and Prophecy"—
Intervarsity Fellowship

Note 2. Plato in his "Crito" speaks of the condemned-to-death Socrates as telling his disciple that he was controlled by a higher power, the "voice of God" which he dared not disobey. However, this "voice of God" is Socrates' way of describing his own conscience. It was not a positive message from God, but the restraining influence of his conscience.

Note 3. It should be noted here that one of the proofs of the genuineness of Moses' calling was the fulfilment of a future event.

The True and the False Prophet

Beside those who were the authentic messengers of God, there were also counterfeit prophets. It was not always easy to distinguish between the two.

The true prophet can be best understood when compared with his counterpart, the false prophet.

There are three major passages in the Scriptures which deal in some detail with this subject:

1. Deuteronomy 13:1-5

2. Deuteronomy 18:9-22

3. Jeremiah 23:9-33

Let us consider these passages briefly.—

1. If there arise among you a prophet, or a dreamer of dreams, and giveth thee a sign or a wonder, And the sign or the wonder come to

pass, whereof he spake unto thee, saying, Let us go after other gods, which thou hast not known, and let us serve them; Thou shalt not hearken unto the words of that prophet, or that dreamer of dreams: for the Lord your God proveth you, to know whether ye love the Lord your God with all your heart and with all your soul. Ye shall walk after the Lord your God, and fear him, and keep his commandments, and obey his voice, and ye shall serve him, and cleave unto him.

And that prophet, or that dreamer of dreams, shall be put to death; because he hath spoken to turn you away from the Lord your God, which brought you out of the land of Egypt, and redeemed you out of the house of bondage, to thrust thee out of the way which the Lord thy God commanded thee to walk in. So shalt thou put the evil away from the midst of thee (Deut. 13:1-5).

Not the performance of a sign or miracle, nor even the fulfilment of a predicted prophecy, but complete faithfulness to Jehovah is what marks the authentic prophet. In all his actions, the true prophet is motivated by a wholehearted loyalty to God, regardless of consequences.

On the other hand, if the prophet's message leads to apostasy, this would brand him as a false prophet.

2. In Deuteronomy 18:9-22 the children of Israel were given the following indications to help them to recognize a false prophet.

A prophet in Israel must not be like the pagan diviners, soothsayers, augurs, sorcerers, wizards or necromancers. Such practices were an abomination to Jehovah (Deut. 18:9-14).

But the prophet, which shall presume to speak a word in my name, which I have not commanded him to speak, or that shall speak in the name of other gods, even that prophet shall die.

And if thou say in thine heart, How shall we know the word which the Lord hath not spoken?

When a prophet speaketh in the name of the Lord, if the thing follow not, nor come to pass, that is the thing which the Lord hath not spoken, but the prophet hath spoken it presumptuously: thou shalt not be afraid of him (Deut. 18:20-22).

The ancient religions of the Semites, of the Egyptians and later of the Hellenic-Roman civilizations were replete with the practice of divinations, prognostications and with black and white magic. Black magic was used for the purpose of causing harm to one's enemies, as in the case of Balaam, who was requested by Balak to curse Israel (Num. 22:5,13). White magic was exercised in order to obtain deliverance from disease, from demons and other malevolent forces.

Archeologists have found in the ancient temples of Babylon and Egypt clay models of sheep livers from which prognostications were made concerning future events. Auguries were also made from the flight of birds, or from the position of heavenly bodies (astrology), or through contacts with the spirit world (the witch of Endor, 1 Sam. 28:7), or pagan deities (diviners). All these practices were a basic part of the religions of Israel's neighbors. Significantly even the Hebrew word for magician — *hartom* (Ex. 7:22) is apparently of Egyptian origin.

The book of Daniel mentions these various forms of soothsaying and sorcery as common Babylonian practices. "Then the king commanded that the magicians, the enchanters, the sorcerers and the Chaldeans (astrologers) be summoned to tell the king his dreams" (Dan. 2:2).

Greek and Roman literature tells us that the *mantis* (prognosticator) and the augur or diviner, played an important part in the affairs of their peoples. Statesmen consulted these prophets in matters of state. Generals waged wars only when the augurs and diviners assured them that conditions were "auspicious." Even in our times, astrology, chiromancy, spiritism, etc. play an important part in the beliefs and conduct of some people. All these practices were severely condemned by the prophets. The true prophet's communion was only with God and his message was God inspired.[1]

3. Isaiah accuses the false prophets that they speak to the people "smooth things," that which they like to hear (Isa. 30:10). Jeremiah charges that the false prophets give aid and comfort to those who despise the Word of God by saying to them: "It shall be well with you and no evil shall come upon you" (Jer. 23:17).

Of such "prophets" Jeremiah says that they did not stand "in the counsel of the Lord" (literally in Hebrew "in the secret of Jehovah") (23:18). These are self-appointed "prophets" but not God's messengers.

> I did not send these prophets, but they ran: I did not speak to them, yet they prophesied. But if they had stood in my counsel, they would have proclaimed my words to my people. They would have turned them from their evil way, and from their wicked doings (Jer. 23:21-22).

For these "prophets" Jeremiah has deep contempt, because instead of delivering to the people "the burden of the Lord" (that is God's message), they are in themselves a real burden. "If the people shall ask you, or a prophet, or a priest 'What is the burden of the Lord?' say to him, 'You are the burden'" (Jer. 23:33).[2]

The true prophet speaks what God commands him to say, whereas the self-seeking prophet is a man-pleaser, a demagogue and a hireling. Perhaps the best example of the difference between the true and the false prophets is the story of the encounter between Micaiah the son of Imlah and the four hundred false prophets (1 Ki. 22:6-28). God's verdict about all these deceitful prophets is contained in these words:

> Behold, I am against the prophets, saith the Lord, that use their tongues, and say, He saith. Behold, I am against them that prophesy false dreams, saith the Lord, and do tell them, and cause my people to err by their lies, and by their lightness; yet I sent them not, nor commanded them: therefore they shall not profit these people at all, saith the Lord (Jer. 23:31-32).

Was the Prophet a Professional Preacher?

It has been suggested that the false prophet was a professional, whereas the true prophet was not.[3] However, there is nothing in the Scriptures to support this position. Some prophets were "professional preachers of righteousness" while others would be termed today "laymen." There were prophets whom God raised up for a specific occasion or situation, like Jonah.

Amos might be considered among such "occasional" prophets. When he was accused by the high priest, Amaziah, of prophesying for a living, Amos protested that he was "not a prophet, nor the son of a prophet." By this he apparently meant that he was not a prophet by profession, and that he had not been trained in the school of the prophets, as some others were.

It is generally assumed that "the sons of the prophets (1 Ki. 20:35, 2 Ki. 2:3,5,7,15) were young men in training for the prophetic ministry under the supervision of an experienced prophet, who acted as their master and dean. The prophet Elisha and probably Elijah before him acted in such a capacity (2 Ki. 2:1-18).

Of course, nobody could be "trained" to become a prophet who was not called of God. The office of the prophet was "charismatic," that is, by divine endowment; only Jehovah could call a man to be His messenger and mouthpiece. However, once a prophet was thus called by God, an apprenticeship under an experienced servant of God might conceivably be of great benefit to the incipient prophet. In any event, it would appear that the major prophets of Israel, such as Isaiah, Jeremiah and Ezekiel dedicated their entire lives to the prophetic ministry. In this sense they were professional prophets. Every other aspect of their lives was subordinated to their highest calling, that of being a prophet of God.

The Message of the Prophets

The Hebrew prophet was God's messenger to God's people in a specific historical context. Therefore, in order to appreciate the full significance of the prophet's message, it is essential that we make an effort to understand, as much as this is possible, after a lapse of 2500 - 3000 years, the circumstances under which any particular prophet was performing his divine errand.

Moses was God's messenger to the Hebrew people in Egypt and on their way to the Promised Land.

Elijah was the mouthpiece of God during the dark period of Ahab and Jezebel.

Amos, Hosea, Isaiah and Micah fulfilled their prophetic calling under the sinister shadow of the approaching Assyrian invasions of Israel and Judah.

Jeremiah was the voice of God to Judah just before and during the Babylonian exile. Ezekiel shared the fate of his fellow exiles in Babylon during the captivity.

All the prophets spoke in the name of Jehovah concerning the specific events and situations which confronted them and their people. However this message reached out beyond their own times, foretelling what God purposed to do in the future in order to accomplish His great design of redemption.

The Prophet as Preacher, and Messenger of Things to Come

The prophetic message has two basic ingredients, the exhortative or the ethical, and the predictive. Both these aspects of prophecy must be fully considered and appreciated. Neither of these should be unduly emphasized at the expense of the other. It is wrong to look upon the prophets as merely preachers and teachers of "the good way of life," as some do. It is also misleading to consider the prophets merely as predictors of distant events in the eschatological future. Liberal theologians generally dwell upon the ethical element in prophecy, ignoring the predictive. On the other hand, the more conservative tend to emphasize the predictive, not giving due weight to the ethical. Neither of these aspects of prophecy can be divorced from the other. Exhortation and prediction form the warp and the weft of prophecy.

The Jewish scholar, Abraham J. Heschel, in his thought-provoking book, *The Prophets of Israel*, dwells on the ethical character of the prophetic message. It is, however, most significant that in his extensive study of the prophets he manages to avoid the word "Messiah" or "Messianic," —a most remarkable feat. This position is quite typical of the thinking which makes the word "prophetic" practically synonymous with ethical teaching.

On the other hand, there are those who look upon the prophetic books as being mostly a collection of Messianic and eschatological prophecies. It is only as we give to both the ethical and the predictive elements, to the exhortative and the eschatological aspects their rightful place, that we may reach a reasonable and sane understanding of the prophets and of their message. The lack of proper balance in the interpretation of the prophet is responsible for much harm and mischief.

Nowhere is this more apparent than in the history of the interpretations of Isaiah.[4]

In our study we shall therefore consider the prophets in their dual capacities of "forthtellers," that is, preachers of righteousness, and "foretellers," that is, men divinely inspired to predict future events in God's grand design for the redemption of Israel and mankind.

The Ethical Element

The ethical element plays a most important part in all prophetic writings. This could hardly be otherwise, for unlike the pagan deities, Jehovah is above all else a holy and righteous God. Over the whole Scripture is written in flaming letters the message: "Ye shall be holy: for I the LORD your God am holy" (Lev. 19:2). The prophets were men who were extremely conscious of the holiness of God. Because of this they were also agonizingly aware of the exceeding sinfulness of their own people.

> Then said I, Woe is me! for I am undone; because I am a man of unclean lips, and I dwell in the midst of a people of unclean lips: for mine eyes have seen the King, the Lord of hosts (Isa. 6:5).

Modern man has become so inured, so callous to every manifestation of wickedness and moral depravity, that he either does not react to it at all, or if he does, his reactions are dulled. Not so the prophet. Every act of unrighteousness hits him like a sledgehammer. The prophet looks upon sin as an outrage against God and the very cosmic order of things, (Isa. 1). He considers unrighteousness not merely as a moral shortcoming, but as a wanton and impious insult hurled in the face of the majesty and holiness of God. It makes the prophet writhe with a sense of indignation and outrage, to the point where he seems to be beside himself, as when Isaiah prayed to God against his own nation "forgive them not" (Isa. 2:9).

God's Angry Men

The prophets were God's angry men, heartbroken over the apostasy of their people. Their denunciations of Israel were often harsh and even violent. But almost invariably there was also a compassion and tenderness which made their plaintive pleadings deeply moving. At times their words almost sounded like those of a modern day anti-Semite. However, there is one basic difference between the prophet and the anti-Semite. The scorching words of the prophet came from a broken heart, which was torn between the love of God and an anguished concern for his kinsmen. They were the words of a father to his wayward children, or of a brother pleading with his brothers to repent and turn to God.

While the anti-Semite delights in malicious faultfinding, the prophet agonizess over the sins of his people and is shamed by their failings. His minatory oracles are designed to bring about repentance and to avert the wrath of God and His judgment. Threatenings, exhortations and prayers for Israel's repentance often follow one another in rapid succession. They all come from the overburdened hearts of the prophets.

Condemnation and consolation, judgment and the promise of redemption, all these constitute an integral part of the same prophetic message. Without understanding of the place of predictive prophecy, there can be no understanding of prophecy.

Notes: 1. For a detailed discussion of pagan practices of divination and augury see the article "Magic & Sorcery" in *The New Bible Dictionary* Inter-Varsity Fellowship.

2. The Septuagint and the Vulgate read *Attem ha-massah* — "You are the burden," instead of the Massoretic reading *Et mah-Massah* — "What burden?"

3. Jakob Jocz: *The Spiritual History of Israel,* page 106.

4. Edward J. Young: *Studies in Isaiah.*

Predictive Prophecy

One of the primary aspects of Old Testament prophecy was prediction of future events. It was one of the marks which authenticated the genuine prophet.

> When a prophet speaketh in the name of the Lord, if the thing follow not, nor come to pass, that is the thing which the Lord hath not spoken, but the prophet hath spoken it presumptuously: thou shalt not be afraid of him (Deut. 18:22).

Prophetic prediction was not mere prognostication, as practiced by pagan soothsayers and diviners in order to satisfy the morbid curiosity of certain individuals, or to help kings and captains in the conduct of military campaigns. Biblical prediction served a spiritual and moral purpose; to warn men of divine wrath and judgment to come upon all unrighteousness and sin; to call men to repentance, and to the ways of righteousness.

In times of national disaster and despair, predictive prophecy served to comfort and to encourage the nation with a promise of divine deliverance and restoration on condition of repentance (Jer. 18:9, 26:13).

Predictions were not always of a vague or general character but were sometimes specific and detailed. The Assyrian invasion, the fall of Samaria and later Jerusalem, the Babylonian captivity, were events predicted in advance. The appearance of certain important historic personalities was foretold and some were even mentioned by name.

In 1 Kings an unnamed prophet to Jeroboam:

> . . . . . O altar, altar, thus saith the Lord; Behold, a child shall be born unto the house of David, Josiah by name; and upon thee shall he offer the priests of the high places that burn incense upon thee, and men's bones shall be burnt upon thee (13:2).

This prediction was made about 300 years before its fulfilment, which was later recorded in 2 Kings 23:15, 16.

Probably the best known and most hotly disputed prediction of a future event, concerns the prophecy in Isaiah 44:28 and 45:1, where the future deliverance of the Jews from Babylonian captivity by Cyrus the Mede is foretold. This prophecy was made more than a century and a half before it came to pass. We intend to discuss this prophecy in detail later on.

The Scriptures of the Old and New Testaments abound in predictions, which later were remarkably fulfilled. In Isaiah there is the striking prophecy concerning the future desolation of Babylon and the prediction that this proud metropolis shall never be inhabited again (Isa. 13:19-20).

In the days of Jeremiah when many Jews sought refuge in Egypt from deportation to Babylon, the prophet predicted that the enemy's hand would overtake them even in Egypt (Jer. 43:8,13; 44:24-30; Ezk 29:19-30; 30:10; 32:11).

Historical and archeological evidence have amply confirmed these prophecies. There are also numerous predictions in the New Testament. In the Gospel of Matthew (11:20-23) Christ predicted the desolation of Chorazin, Bethsaida and Capernaum at a time when those places were still flourishing towns, teeming with people. Today their ruins bear mute testimony to the fulfilment of the prophecy.

The Parting of the Ways

It is exactly at the point of predictive prophecy that conservative and liberal theology come to a parting of the roads. Conservative scholars accept the record of Scripture as factual and historically trustworthy. On the other hand liberal scholars generally assume an a priori position that predictive prophecy is an impossibility because it is contrary to the laws of nature and experience. They therefore consider the prophetic predictions as *vaticinia post eventum*—or predictions after the foretold events have already taken place. To put it bluntly, according to these scholars, wherever prophetic predictions occur these must be treated as highly suspect, and their authors viewed as "pious frauds."

Many of the arguments against the authenticity of the book of Isaiah and of other Biblical documents are based on such assumptions. We expect to deal with this when discussing the unity of Isaiah.

But let it be said here and now, to assume such a negative position in relation to prophetic prediction is to deny the omnipotence and omniscience of God, and His ability to impart to His chosen servants, the prophets, the knowledge of certain future events.

These critics, while arrogating to themselves an almost superhuman ability to discern the genuineness or otherwise of Scriptural texts, words, or even single letters, show a remarkable lack of criticism in relation to their own methods. However, with the passing of time, many of the theories and criticisms have been shown to have been based on unsupported speculation. Recent archeological discoveries and the finding of ancient, hitherto unknown documents, such as the Ugaritic Tablets and the Dead Sea Scrolls, have tended to lift Biblical research from the level of mere textual and literary criticism and speculation to the more realistic and verifiable area of historical data.

We hold, that the burden of proof concerning the reliability of predictive prophecy is not upon those who accept the Biblical record as they find it, but upon those who deny it. To do otherwise is to stultify every attempt at a true understanding of the Scriptures, and of those men who were called of God to write them down.

The prophets were not merely sagacious men of extraordinarily keen perception and insight, but holy men of God who stood "in the secret of the Lord."

Amos expresses trenchantly this peculiar "confidential" relationship between God and the prophet: "For the Lord Jehovah does not do a thing without revealing His secret to His servants the prophets (Amos 3:7).

Prophetic Inspiration and Communication

We shall never be able to comprehend fully the mystery of communication and converse between God and prophet. Sometimes, we are informed, the prophet hears God speaking, sometimes he sees visions, and sometimes God comes to the prophet in a dream.

Isaiah relates how and upon what occasion he saw the Lord:

In the year that king Uzziah died *I saw* also the Lord sitting upon a throne . . . (6:1a).
Also, *I heard* the voice of the Lord, saying, Whom shall I send, and who will go for us? Then said I, Here am I; send me (6:8).

There are occasions when God speaks to the prophet in dreams.

And he said, Hear now my words: If there be a prophet among you, I the Lord will make myself known unto him in a vision, and will speak unto him in a dream (Num. 12:6).

Although the word "inspiration" does not appear in the Hebrew or the Greek texts of the Scriptures, yet its meaning is clearly implied.[1]

Concerning the seventy men whom Moses selected at the command of the Lord to assist him in his work, we read:

And the Lord came down in a cloud, and spake unto him, and took of the spirit that was upon him, and gave it unto the seventy elders: and it came to pass, that, when the spirit rested upon them, they prophesied, and did not cease (Num. 11:25).

Obviously these seventy were ordinary men, who prophesied "when the spirit rested upon them."

The expression "thus saith the Lord" appears 359 times in the Old Testament. There are many other phrases to the same effect which occur in the Bible.

The word of the Lord came unto me . . . (Jer. 36:27).
The hand of the Lord was upon me . . . (Ezk. 3:22).

In a similar way Christ in His prophetic capacity professed that He spoke the message given to Him by His Father: "Jesus answered them and said, My doctrine is not mine, but his that sent me" (John 12:49).

Every book of the Bible bears witness explicitly or by implication, "Thus saith the Lord."

The Interaction between God and Prophet

Although God is the primary author of every book of the Bible, the literary form of the Scriptures reflects the diverse personalities and characters of its human authors. God inspired the prophets but did not violate their personalities which were nevertheless completely yielded to God. How this interaction between God and man was accomplished, we do not know. This is part of the mystery of inspiration. The prophet was not a mechanical device through which God spoke but a living personality completely yielded to and in absolute sympathy with the purpose and will of God. Inspiration does not obliterate the human personality. Consequently each book of the Bible bears, so to speak, the fingerprint of its human writers.

Amos was as different from Hosea, and Isaiah from Ezekiel, as human beings can possibly be.

Inspiration might be compared to a line of communication between God and the prophet, who in turn communicates the divine message to the people or to an individual recipient.

The result of inspiration is revelation, which is God's disclosure of Himself and of His plans to the prophets. Through revelation God makes known His purpose and will and what part the prophet is to have in its accomplishment.

In contrast to the pagan diviners and soothsayers, especially in Syria and Canaan, who in order to "foretell" usually worked themselves up into a state of ecstasy and frenzy by wild gyrations of their bodies, accompanied by sex and alcoholic orgies, the prophets of Israel were in complete possession of their mental faculties during their state of inspiration.[2]

What the Apostle Paul said concerning the New Testament prophets also applies to those of the old dispensation.

And the spirits of the prophets are subject to the prophets. For God is not the author of confusion, but of peace . . . (1 Cor. 14:32-33).

Revelation is not just an imparting of reliable information otherwise not available to human beings, but a personal disclosure of God and of His nature. Each divine self-disclosure is a personal coming of God to man.

In this sense all prophecy is Messianic in character.

The full and final self-disclosure of God, the fulness of His manifestation was in the Lord Jesus Christ: "Who is the image of the invisible God . . . For it pleased the Father that in him should all fulness dwell" (Col. 1:15-19).

Contents of the Prophetic Message

Although each individual prophet differed from all other prophets in his message and emphasis, yet there are certain elements which are common to all of them. These elements of the prophetic message could be summed up under the following headings:

1. Reaction to historic events or situations

2. Denunciation of sin

3. Pronouncement of divine judgment

4. Call to repentance

5. Promise of deliverance

6. The vision of the Messiah and the Messianic Kingdom

7. Eschatology or the ultimate triumph of God

Some prophets deal with only a few of these subjects, others with all. In Isaiah all aspects of prophecy are most fully developed.

The Prophetic Methods of Communication

Every prophet was conscious of the fact that he was a messenger of God's Word or oracle.

What the prophet had to say was *Debar Elohim* — the Word of God. This "Word" the prophet couched in the spoken, written or acted-out form.

Sometimes these oracles took on the form of parable or allegory. The parable is a short descriptive story designed to illustrate a particular truth or point. The allegory is a more elaborate story which fits in many details the situation which the prophets seek to illuminate.

Parables and allegories are in some respects similar to object lessons. However their purpose is not merely to appeal to the physical senses, but to stir up the spirit and the deepest emotions of the listeners.

A typical parable is found in 2 Samuel 12:1-9 where the prophet

Nathan brought home to King David the heinousness of the sin which he had committed with Bathsheba. Another example of a poetic parable is Isaiah 5:1-7, where Israel is compared to a vineyard upon which God has bestowed much labor and love with such disappointing results.

The parable and allegory have always been a favorite and dramatic form of teaching used with telling effect by the prophets of the Old Testament (Ezk. 17:1-10) and in the New Testament by Jesus Himself (Mt. 13). The Hebrew term for parable is *Mashal*. When the parable was couched in poetic form it was sometimes referred to as *Shir*—a song (Isa. 5:1-7). When the parable was particularly puzzling it was called *Chidah* literally a "puzzle."

The Acted Parable

Among the most dramatic means of conveying the prophetic message was the acted parable. Thus when the kingdom of Israel was to be divided into two, the prophet Ahijah was commanded to tear his garments into twelve pieces, and to give ten to Jeroboam (1 Ki. 11:29-30). Isaiah walked naked and barefoot as a sign that the king of Assyria would lead away as prisoners naked and barefoot the Egyptians and Ethiopians, in whom the Israelites trusted (Isaiah 20).

To demonstrate Israel's unfaithfulness to God, the prophet Hosea was commanded to marry the lewd woman Gomer (Hos. 1:2-3).

Sometimes the prophet uses symbolic names which vividly depict a situation or condition. Hosea's children are called *Lo-ruhamah*—"Unpitied" and *Lo-ammi*—"Not My People" as a sign that God will have no mercy on unrepentant Israel, and that they are "not His people" (Hos. 1:6-9).

Isaiah's sons are called *Shear Yashub*—"A Remnant Shall Return" and *Maher-Shelal-hash-baz*—"Hasten-Spoil-Hurry-Loot," to express hope for the future and impending disaster.

A favorite way of driving home their point was the use of alliteration and the play on words, which are generally lost when translated from Hebrew into any other language. Isaiah is particularly fond of this literary device. Here is an example:

> For the vineyard of the Lord of hosts is the house of Israel, and the men of Judah his pleasant planting and he expected *justice* but behold, *bloodshed,* for *righteousness,* but instead there is *crying* (Isa. 5:7).

In Hebrew the words "justice" and "bloodshed" are an alliteration and also a play on words:

             Mishpat—justice   —— *Mispach*—bloodshed
similarly — *Tsedakah*—righteousness —— *Tseakah*—crying

Or Isaiah 7:9 "If you will not believe, you will not prevail." Note the play on words in Hebrew: *Thaaminu*—believe, *Thaiamainu*—prevail.

Here is an example from Amos:

Thus hath the Lord God shewed unto me: and behold a basket of summer fruit. And he said, Amos, what seest thou? And I said, A basket of summer fruit. Then said the Lord unto me, The end is come upon my people of Israel; I will not again pass by them any more (Amos 8:1-2).

In Hebrew the word for "a basket of summer fruit" is *Klubh Kaits*. The word for "an end" in Hebrew is *Kaits*.

The prophets generally delivered their messages orally in the hearing of the people (Isa. 1, Jer. 7:1-2, Ezk. 17:1-2).

Sometimes the message of the prophets was written down (Jer. 30:2; Isa. 30:8; Hab 2:2).

We know that the prophet Jeremiah, while imprisoned by the king, employed Baruch the scribe to write down God's message (Jer. 30).

It is entirely possible that some of the messages which the prophets delivered first orally were later written down by them for posterity. Other prophetic messages were collected either by contemporaries or later editors into one book which became known by the name of the prophet. Such books or collections of oracles were apparently known already in Isaiah's time (Isa. 29:11-12).

The reference to "the book of Jehovah" in Isaiah 34:16 is of special significance, because it clearly points to the existence at that time of such an authoritative book, most likely the Pentateuch.

Search out the book of Jehovah and read, none of these prophecies shall fail, none shall be without her match (fulfilment) for his mouth has commanded and his spirit has gathered them.

The Prophetic Style of Delivery

It would be of considerable interest to know the manner in which the prophets delivered their messages. A possible clue to this, we believe, is found in Ezekiel 33:30-33:

Also, thou son of man, the children of thy people still are talking against thee by the walls and in the doors of the houses, and speak one to another, every one to his brother, saying, Come, I pray you, and hear what is the word that cometh forth from the Lord.
And they come unto thee as the people cometh, and they sit before thee as my people, and they hear thy words, but they will not do them: for with their mouth they show much love, but their heart goeth after their covetousness.
And lo, thou art unto them as a very lovely song of one that hath a pleasant voice, and can play well on an instrument: for they hear thy words, but they do them not.
And when this cometh to pass, (lo, it will come,) then shall they know that a prophet hath been among them.

The words "thou (the prophet) art unto them as a very lovely song of one that hath a pleasant voice, and can play well on an instrument . . ." might indicate that the prophet delivered this message in a sing-song voice, as is the custom even today among Oriental people. It is a special kind of preaching and exhorting voice, calculated to stir the emotions of the hearers, and to convey to them either the feeling of impending doom and judgment, or to stir their consciences to repentance. Those who are acquainted with the style of the traditional Eastern-European Jewish preacher, the *maggid,* would probably have an approximate idea of the style of delivery of the prophets.

The prophets were not classic orators in the style of Demosthenes or Cicero. They were simple men with a burning message from God in their hearts. But such was the power behind their word and the pathos of their message that inevitably their voices and gestures gave expression to what was stirring their souls.

Now thundering and threatening when proclaiming the wrath of God, now pleading and plaintive when calling to repentance, now tender and lyrical when depicting the mercies of God and the glory of His future reign. To see and listen to a prophet in action must have been a profound and never-to-be-forgotten experience.

Notes: 1. The word "inspiration" in the King James translation is used twice, Job 32:8 and 2 Timothy 3:16, but in the original texts the term "inspiration" does not occur.
Job says: "But there is a spirit in man: the inspiration of the Almighty giveth them understanding" (Job 32:8).
"The inspiration of the Almighty" in Hebrew *Nishmath Shaddai* literally "the breath of the Almighty."
Paul writes to Timothy: "All Scripture is given by inspiration of God." (2 Tim. 3:16).
In Greek the word for "inspiration of God" is *Theopneustos* literally "God-breathed."

Notes: 2. For an interesting discussion of ecstasy induced by alcohol and sex orgies and its place in pagan prophecy, see *The Prophets* by Abraham J. Heschel, chapters 19-21.

The Role of the Prophets in the Theocracy of Israel

It was Josephus, the famous first century historian, who, in order to describe Israel's system of government, coined the term "theocracy."

There is endless variety in the details of the customs and laws which prevail in the world at large. To give but a summary enumeration: some peoples have entrusted the supreme political power to monarchies, others to oligarchies, yet others to the masses. Our lawgiver, however, was attracted by none of these forms of polity, but gave to his constitution the form of what — if a forced expression be permitted — may be termed a "theocracy," placing all sovereignty and authority in the hands of God.[1]

Since Israel, ideally speaking, was a "theocracy" where every aspect of life was under "the sovereignty and authority of God," there was hardly any event in the life of Israel or any national institution which did not come under the searching scrutiny, and when necessary, under the scorching denunciation of the prophets.

The prophets were especially incensed by a ritualism, which, while making a show of piety, was devoid of spiritual insight and moral value. Because of their negative attitude toward a sterile ceremonialism, many contemporary scholars, both Jewish and Christian, have concluded that the prophets were basically opposed to the whole system of sacrifices and to the numerous ritual observances which ancient Israel practiced.

In reality the prophets represented the inherent conflict between popular religiosity and a spiritual concept of the genuine worship of God. To the average Israelite, religion meant the rite of circumcision, the temple, the priesthood, sacrifices, the Sabbath, the feasts, and the numerous ordinances based on the Law of Moses. As long as the Israelite conformed visibly to the demands of this Law, and performed its verifiable injunctions, or avoided its prohibitions, he was satisfied that he was serving God and doing His will. Even if he missed the goal of holiness and righteousness which was the very heart of the Law, yet the very performance of his "religious duties," even if it was mechanical, gave the Israelite a sense of security and of being right with God. In the mind of many, the religious act had, as it were, a magical efficacy. The medieval theologians later called this *Opus Operatum*—the religious act, which is automatically efficacious and pleasing to God, regardless of the spiritual or moral condition of the worshipper, or his motivation.

This form of worship devoid of holiness, of righteous living and mercy in daily conduct, was to the prophets an abomination. Samuel, one of the oldest of the prophets, sought to impress upon his people that "to obey is better than sacrifice" (1 Sam. 15:22).

As spokesmen for God the prophets were bound to look upon all religious practices from the divine standpoint. If they were to be faithful to their prophetic calling, "to root out, to pull down, to destroy . . . to build and to plant" (Jer. 1:10), the prophets were bound to condemn a religion, which in their judgment, had become perverted and had degenerated into a mere system of ritualism. To the prophets, true and acceptable worship of God meant the imitation of God in His holiness, righteousness and in His boundless mercy.

> And the Lord said, because this people draws near to me with his mouth, and honours me with his lips, but his heart is far from me, and their fear of me is a precept taught by men;
> Therefore will I continue to perform a marvelous work among this people, a real marvel; the wisdom of his wise men shall perish and the intelligence of their men of intellect shall become obscured (Isa. 29:13, cf. Mt. 15:8-9).

The religious act, without the deed of mercy, was to them so much sham and hypocrisy.

Hosea the contemporary of Amos expressed the same thought in these words: "I desire kindness (*hesed*) and not sacrifice, a knowledge of God rather than burnt offerings (Hos. 6:6).

The great prophet Isaiah found the practice of ritualism, side by side with moral decay and heartlessness in daily conduct, a nauseating spectacle in the sight of God (Isa. 1:10-17).

The chasm between "mere religion" of endless rituals and ceremonies and God's true requirements of man, is a recurrent and favorite topic of the prophets. Perhaps no other prophet has expressed it more poignantly than Micah:

How shall I approach the Lord
And bow down before God on high?
Shall I approach him with burnt offerings or yearling calves?
Does the Lord require thousands of rams and endless rivers of oil?
Shall my first-born atone for my transgressions,
The fruit of my body for the sin of my soul?
Thou hast been informed, O man, what is good
What the Lord desires from thee—
Only to practice justice to love kindness and
To walk in humility with thy God (Mic. 6:6-8).

There was no aspect of the national life, no institution, no matter how sacred, which escaped the scrutiny of the prophets. Not even the temple itself, that hallowed center of national worship, where Jehovah was presumed to dwell in person, could escape prophetic condemnation when it became a place of mere ritualism, providing the people with a false sense of security, or even with an excuse for ungodly conduct (Jer. 7:4-16).

Even the sacred rite of circumcision, that visible sign in the flesh of the covenant relationship between God and Israel, could not escape prophetic scorn when its true significance became obscured. Jeremiah predicted equal judgment to come upon Jews and Gentiles alike.

Behold the days come that I shall visit judgment upon all who are circumcised, together with the uncircumcision:
Upon Egypt, Judah, the children of Ammon and Moab and upon those who live in the most remote corners and in the wilderness.
For all these nations are uncircumcised in the flesh,
But the house of Israel is uncircumcised in the heart (Jer. 9:25-26).

Being a "theocracy," that is, a God-ruled nation, ancient Israel knew no division between sacred and secular, holy and profane. All life was indivisible and subject to the will of God, as enjoined by divine commandments and ordinances. The kings of Israel were not mere secular rulers, or heads of state, but God's chosen servants anointed to their office by His prophets (1 Ki.1:34, 1 Chr. 29:29). The anointed king was the prototype of the ideal king, the Messiah. The kings of Israel, no less than the priests and all other religious institutions, came under the searching scrutiny and judgment of the prophets. We remember the dramatic confrontations between the prophet Nathan and King David, (2 Sam. 12:1) ; between Elijah and Ahab (1 Ki. 18:17, 18; 1 Ki. 21:20) and between Isaiah and Ahaz (Isa. 7:3-25) .

The prophets themselves, as an integral part of the theocratic system, subjected their own activities to God's lofty standards for the prophetic ministry (See The True and The False Prophets page 15).

And yet in spite of the strongly negative attitude of the prophets to all that which, in their time and later, commonly passed for religion, it would nevertheless be a mistake to think that the prophets were on principle opposed to the religious establishment of Israel. Their true opposition was directed against the paganization of Israel's worship. They were against treating Jehovah as if He were some kind of pagan deity, just another Baal, who could be bribed with a fat sacrifice. They were against turning worship of the living God into magic. In paganism the worshiper did certain things for his deity, such as sacrificing to him. In return the deity assured his devotee long life, prosperity or victory over his enemies. The pagan cults of Israel's neighbors made few or no demands on the spiritual and moral life of the worshiper. He could be as base as possible as long as he performed his "religious" duties.

It was to this debasement of the religious life and its divorce from practical holiness, from righteous conduct and loving kindness, to which the prophets so violently took exception. The prophets, like Jesus in later times, were absolutely persuaded that the act of worship and the righteous deed cannot be divorced from each other. They must go together (cf. Amos 5:21-25 with Mk. 7:9-13) . Only a holy people, which practices righteousness and lovingkindness, can serve the Lord acceptably.

The prophetic message must be read in the context of the moral and spiritual decadence which the prophets witnessed. When Jesus said: "Think not that I am come to destroy the law, or the prophets: I am not come to destroy, but to fulfill" (Mt. 5:17) . He was continuing and confirming the spiritual direction which the prophets had given to Israel's religion. The rejection of Jesus by His generation was no mere coincidence. It was completely in line with the reception which the prophets experienced in their time.

To the priest, to the ruling princes and frequently to the man in the street, the prophet was often an unbearable busybody and gadfly, a man who refused to mind his own business, but kept telling people how to live their lives and run their business, when all they wanted was a comfortable religion and not a constant challenge and a lacerated conscience.

The trouble was that the prophets were deeply persuaded that the way Israel lived or worshipped God *was their* most important *business*. The prophets of Israel were the God-appointed keepers of the national conscience. Here was the crux of the tragic conflict between the prophet and his people. A violent clash was inevitable. It led to persecution and death. The path of the prophets led to Jesus and to Calvary.

The New Testament Prophets

It is generally assumed that the activities of the Old Testament prophets came to an end long before the New Testament times. However, on closer investigation one finds that there were prophetic personalities in Israel all through the period both between Testaments and in the New Testament times.

The book of Revelation is a prophetic document. At the very outset of the New Testament period we have the striking prophetic figure of John the Baptist, of whom Jesus said: "For all the prophets and the law prophesied until John" (Mt. 11:13). Not only was John the Baptist a prophet but so was his father Zacharias before him (Lk. 1:67-79).

There are also several women mentioned in the Gospel of Luke, who appear in a prophetic capacity: Anna the prophetess (2:36-38), Elisabeth the mother of John the Baptist (1:42-45), and Mary herself, the mother of Jesus (1:46-55).

The stern message and severe manner of John the Baptist were reminiscent of the earlier prophets, especially of Elijah. Like his predecessors, John preached the wrath of God to come and called to repentance (Lk. 3:3-7). He identified Jesus as being the long expected Messiah (John 1:29). He died a prophet's death (Mt. 14:1-11).

The ministry of John the Baptist was not an isolated instance, but rather a part of the vigorous stream of prophetic activities which characterized the period. The well-known church historian, Adolf Harnack, thus describes these activities:

Josephus, the historian, played the prophet openly and successfully before Vespasian. Philo called himself a prophet, and in the Diaspora we hear of Jewish interpreters of dreams, and of prophetic magicians. What is still more significant, the wealth of contemporary Jewish apocalypses, oracular utterances, and so forth shows that, so far from being extinct, prophecy was in a luxuriant bloom and also that prophets were numerous. From its earliest awakening, then, Christian prophecy was no novelty, when formally considered, but a phenomenon which readily coordinated itself with similar contemporary phenomena in Judaism.[2]

Although from time to time there appeared among the Jews men who laid claim to the gift of prophecy, yet once the canon of prophetic Scripture was completed around the year 200 B.C. the line of succession of universally recognized prophets was broken. However, prophecy as such had not disappeared.

Christ Himself was a prophetic personality par excellence. For not only did He personify the prophetic vision of the Messiah, but His whole life and ministry were prophetic in character. Many of His contemporaries looked upon Him as "the Prophet" (John 7:40).

Jesus looked upon His disciples as continuing the prophetic tradition and predicted that they would be persecuted in a similar manner as were the ancient prophets:

> Wherefore, behold, I send unto you prophets, and wise men, and scribes: and some of them ye shall kill and crucify and some of them shall ye scourge in your synagogues and persecute them from city to city (Mt. 23:34).

We know from the Acts of the Apostles and from later history how literally this prophecy came to pass.

Not only were the apostles active in a prophetic capacity, but many Christians were endowed with the gift of prophecy. One of them, Agabus, is mentioned by name (Acts 11:27-28). The daughters of Philip were known as "prophetesses" (Acts 21:8-9).

Prophecy was a gift which the Holy Spirit endowed upon believers in the early church, both men and women (1 Cor. 11:4-5).

In 1 Corinthians, chapter 14, the functions of the New Testament prophet are described. Their purpose was "edification, exhortation, and for the comfort" of believers (1 Cor. 14:3). The message of the New Testament prophet was designated as a "revelation" (1 Cor. 14:30).

The gift of prophecy was distinct from "the speaking of tongues": "He that speaketh in an unknown tongue edifieth himself, but he that prophesieth, edifieth the church" (1 Cor. 14:4).

The New Testament prophets were a unique order of men within the early church. Their office differed from that of the apostles and from the teachers: "And God has appointed in the church first apostles, second prophets, third teachers, then workers of miracles, then healers, helpers, administrators, speakers in various kinds of tongues" (1 Cor. 12:28 R.S.V.).

The position of the prophets in the early church was second only to the apostles, yet more important than that of teachers. The difference was mainly this, that teachers taught already revealed truths and doctrines, whereas the prophets had a personal revelation directly from God (1 Cor. 14:30). However, this revelation was subject to the approval of the apostles and of the assembly of believers.

The Apostle Paul insisted on order in the Church and on self-control on the part of the New Testament prophets:

> Let the prophets speak two or three, and let the other judge.
> If anything be revealed to another that sitteth by, let the first hold his peace.
> For ye may all prophesy one by one, that all may learn, and all may be comforted.
> And the spirits of the prophets are subject to the prophets.
> For God is not the author of confusion, but of peace, as in all churches of the saints (1 Cor. 14:29-33).

Just as the message of the Old Testament prophets had to be in keeping with God's revelation to Moses, so the message of the New Testament prophets had to be in harmony with that of the apostles. The Apostle Paul insisted that: "If any man think himself to be a prophet, or spiritual, let him acknowledge that the things that I write unto you are the commandments of the Lord" (1 Cor. 14:37).

We have now considered the origins, the nature and the significance of prophetism. It was a spiritual phenomenon peculiar to Israel, unique and without parallel. In spite of superficial similarities between prophetism and pagan divination, the similarity is more apparent than real. The soothsayers of Mari, Assyria, Babylon, Egypt and Greece were individuals who in a state of frenzy or ecstasy divined in the name of their tribal or national gods in the interest of certain rulers or important persons. There was little or no moral content in their divination.

On the other hand, the prophets of Israel were the spokesmen of the living God, maker of heaven and earth. While this God, Jehovah, was in a peculiar way the God of Israel, He was nevertheless the God of all nations. He was a holy and righteous God who hates iniquity. The prophets were God-inspired and directed preachers of righteousness. They demanded repentance, predicting judgment on the unrepentant and promising redemption and mercy to those who would turn to God.

The prophets of Israel looked for a new earth and a new heaven and a renewed human race (Isa. 2:2-4).

Although their activities covered a period of more than six centuries from Samuel to Ezra, and sporadically even well into New Testament times, nevertheless their message was in its essentials of the same moral and spiritual fabric and fiber. "A holy God can only be worshipped in spirit and in truth" (John 4:24).

The prophetic message pointed to One who personified all their holiest aspirations and longings, the Messiah of Israel. In this respect Jesus and the Talmud, while differing in their interpretations of the prophets, both agreed that the prophetic message was essentially Messianic. To His disciples the risen Christ said:

These are the words which I spake unto you, while I was yet with you, that all things must be fulfilled which were written in the law of Moses and in the prophets, and in the Psalms concerning me (Lk. 24:44).

In a later time the Talmud expressed a similar conviction:

Kol Ha-neviim lo hithnabu eila al yemoth ha-mashiach All the prophets prophesied only concerning the days of the Messiah (Sanhedrin 99a).

The prophets were the eternal rebels against the established order of things whenever this order deviated from the Word and will of God. They were in continuous conflict with all the sacred taboos and popular shibboleths dear to the hearts of many. This made them despised and rejected by their own community and people. They became the proto-types of the Great Sufferer, the Servant of God.

Every individual in every generation, who for the sake of divine truth and righteousness endures ridicule and persecution, falls heir to the heritage of the prophets.

> Blessed are ye, when men shall revile you, and persecute you, and shall say all manner of evil against you falsely, for my sake. Rejoice and be exceeding glad: for great is your reward in heaven; for so persecuted they the prophets which were before you (Mt. 5:11-12).

Israel's prophets form the true link between the Old Testament and the New, not only because so many of the Messianic predictions were fulfilled in the person of Jesus, but more importantly, because the New Testa-ment more than any other religious tradition, carried forward the genu-ine spirit of the prophets. To no other historic personality are the words of the great prophet so relevant as they are to the person of Jesus.

> Behold, I have given him for a witness to the people, a leader and com-mander to the people.
> Behold, thou shalt call a nation that thou knowest not, and nations that knew not thee shall run unto thee because of the Lord thy God, and for the Holy One of Israel; for he hath glorified thee (Isa. 55:4-5).

We have to agree with the statement: "Humanly speaking, without the prophets, there would be no New Testament, no Church, no Salva-tion."[3]

In the course of five millennia of our civilization the human race has produced a legion of great leaders and lawgivers, of thinkers and teachers, of poets and philosophers. Many of them have left the imprint of their footsteps, for good or for ill, upon the records of history. Yet none of them have so profoundly affected the minds and hearts of men as did the prophets of Israel. They brought to men an exalted vision of a holy, righteous and merciful God, a God who abhors sin and evil and demands that those who worship Him should live holy and righteous lives.

The prophets had a horror of all sham and hypocrisy in religion and in daily life. They set up standards of right and wrong which have eternal validity. Their vision of God and of His kingdom forever continues to draw men, even when they fail to recognize the source of their dreams and aspirations.

They were the royal heralds of the bright dawn when the government of God, the true theocracy shall be established in all the earth. They saw a chastised and repentant Israel at last walking in the light of God and the nations submitting themselves to the law of God and "neither shall they learn war any more" (Isa. 2:2-5).

Like shining stars in a dark night, they have helped men find their eternal bearings and have guided the wayfarers in the paths of truth to the City of God. In this prophetic firmament Isaiah was a star of the first magnitude. It might be said of him, as it was later of John the Baptist, that "he was not that Light, but was sent to bear witness of that Light" (John 1:8).

NOTES:

1. *Josephus*—H. St. J. Thackeray, M.A. Published by Harvard University Press, Cambridge, Mass. Against Apion II. 165 page 359.

2. *The Mission and Expansion of Christianity in the First Three Centuries,* page 332, Adolf Harnack.

3. *The Spiritual History of Israel by* Jakob Jocz, page 123.

The Life
and Works
of Isaiah

The Man Called Isaiah

Halfway between Moses the Lawgiver and Jesus the Messiah stands the towering figure of Isaiah the son of Amoz, a contemporary of the prophets Amos, Hosea and Micah. In Isaiah prophecy found its most sublime and majestic expression. The Book of Isaiah is undoubtedly the high-water mark of prophetic vision and thought.

Not many details are known about his life. The ancient Jewish tradition that Isaiah's father Amoz was a brother of King Amaziah has no historical foundation. Isaiah was apparently a resident of Jerusalem and a member of a prominent family. We know that the prophet was a married man and referred to his wife as "the prophetess" (Isa. 8:3).

Isaiah's two sons are mentioned by name (7:3, 8:1-3). The name of the first was *Shear-Yashub*—"A Remnant-Shall-Return"; the second son was called *Maher-Shalal-Hash-Baz*—"Hasten-to-Spoil-Hurry-to-Prey." Thus the two sons of the prophet became the living symbols of the twin themes of Isaiah's message: Divine mercy and wrath.

We do not know whether the word "prophetess" indicates that Isaiah's wife was a prophetess in her own right, or whether this was merely a title of honor. Both alternatives are possible. We know from the Old Testament that there were women in Israel who prophesied, for instance Miriam, the sister of Moses, Deborah, Huldah and others.

Whatever the meaning of the term "prophetess," it is apparent that Isaiah's family was completely united and dedicated to the service of God and that their lives were subordinated to the prophetic vocation of the head of the household. Together they stood as a living testimony to the truth which God had entrusted to Isaiah. The prophet himself was apparently deeply conscious of this:

Behold, I and the children whom the Lord has given me are signs and portents in Israel from the Lord of hosts who dwells on Mount Zion (Isa. 8:18).

It is quite possible that Isaiah, who was so keenly aware of the symbolism of names, may have seen in his own name not a mere coincidence, but divinely appointed significance. For the name "Isaiah" in Hebrew *Yeshayahu*, or abbreviated *Yeshaiah*, is a composite one which means "Jehovah is salvation." A study of Old Testament personal names reveals that names, as a rule, were not given to children as a mere distinguishing label, but rather as a testimony to the faith and the hope which animated the parents.

The faith expressed in Isaiah's name was at the very heart of all his prophecies—"Salvation is in Jehovah." It is interesting to note that the name "Jesus" (Hebrew *Yeshua*) is a later variant of the same name and also means "Jehovah is salvation," or "Jehovah saves" (Mt. 1:21).

Like Elijah before him, and John the Baptist later, Isaiah normally wore a garment of hair cloth or sackcloth around his loins, and sandals on his feet. This was the customary garment of a prophet. However, at the Lord's command and in order to drive home the point about the futility of Judah's reliance on Egypt against Assyria, Isaiah walked about naked for a period of three years (except for a loin cloth) (Isa. 20:2-6).

No doubt the prophet's behavior must have appeared eccentric and bizarre in the eyes of his contemporaries just as it would to us today. Indeed most prophets were considered by their contemporaries "queer" if not plain crazy. We know that some people contemptuously called the prophet Elijah *meshugah*, a "mad fellow" (2 Ki. 9:11). On the other hand we also note that godly men like Obadiah, treated the same prophet with extreme deference and respect, addressing him as "my lord Elijah" (1 Ki. 18:7).

The dates of Isaiah's birth and death are a matter of conjecture and of internal Scriptural evidence. It is characteristic of the Scriptures that the limelight is usually focused on the message rather than on the messenger, on the prophecy rather than on the prophet. Only those personal details were mentioned which were considered essential for the understanding of the message. There are no biographies in the Bible, in the modern sense of the word. Biblical personalities are as a rule presented as instruments in God's hand to reveal His purpose or to help in its accomplishment. They appear on the stage of history for a God-appointed purpose and then disappear.

From Isaiah 1:1 we may conclude that the prophet's ministry must have covered at least a part of the reign of Uzziah during the period of his leprosy and separation when his son Jotham was co-regent and later king (2 Ki. 15:5, 2 Chr. 26:21), and all of Ahaz's and of Hezekiah's reigns. Ancient tradition holds that Isaiah lived long enough to witness the early part of Manasseh's reign of terror and was finally murdered by that ungodly king.

The following dates which should be considered as approximate, give us a chronological framework for the life-span of Isaiah.[1]

Uzziah or Azariah	
co-regent 791-767	767-740 B.C.
Jotham	
co-regent 750-740	740-735 B.C.
Ahaz	
co-regent 744-735	735-715 B.C.
Hezekiah	
co-regent 729-715	715-687 B.C.
Manasseh	687-642 B.C.

The statement in Isaiah 6:1 "In the year that King Uzziah died I saw also the Lord . . ." is generally ..cepted as the date of Isaiah's original call to the prophetic office and the beginning of his ministry. However this assumption is unwarranted and contradicts the obvious sense of the opening passage of the book of Isaiah:

> The vision of Isaiah the son of Amoz, which he saw concerning Judah and Jerusalem in the days of Uzziah, Jotham, Ahaz and Hezekiah, the kings of Judah (1:1).

Here is an explicit statement that Isaiah "saw" or was already an active prophet "in the days of Uzziah." Therefore Isaiah chapter 6 does not record the prophet's original call, but his reconsecration and rededication to the prophetic ministry after the death of Uzziah. The vision in the Temple of the thrice Holy God in a time of national crisis resulted in a rededication of the prophet as God's messenger to Israel to warn the nation of approaching judgment and disaster, (Isa. 6:9-12), and also of the subsequent redemption awaiting a repentant remnant (vs. 13).

There are numerous indications in the Old Testament that the prophets were usually called to their public ministry in their youth. It is therefore reasonable to assume that Isaiah was at the time of Uzziah's death (740 B.C.) not older than about 25-30 years. This would give us an approximate date for Isaiah's birth around the year 770-765 B.C., give or take a few years.

Like the date of Isaiah's birth, so also the date of his death poses a problem. A strong clue relating to this matter is provided in the Second Book of Chronicles:

> Now the rest of the acts of Hezekiah, and his goodness, (or kindly acts) behold, they are written in the vision of Isaiah the prophet, the son of Amoz, and in the book of the kings of Judah and Israel (32:32).

This statement would indicate that Isaiah outlived Hezekiah (687 B.C.) and recorded his life and "his kindly acts" in a book called "The Vision of Isaiah," which was later included in the book of "The Kings of Judah and Israel." Thus the closing years of Isaiah's life are brought into the reign of the wicked king Manasseh (687-642). This brings up the question, how long did Isaiah live? Jewish and Christian tradition both assume that Isaiah died a martyr's death under king Manasseh.

The tradition that Isaiah was murdered by Manasseh may contain some historical substance and was apparently based on 2 Ki. 21:16a "Moreover he (Manasseh) shed very much innocent blood till he filled Jerusalem from one end to another."

Some of the early church fathers (e.g. Jerome) saw in the statement of Hebrews 11:37 "they were sawn asunder" a reference to the manner of Isaiah's death. If credence is to be given to the ancient tradition that Isaiah lived to the advanced age of 92 years, 7 years of which were under the reign of Manasseh, this would give us a date for his death around the year 680 B.C. Thus, both on the basis of internal Scriptural evidence and of ancient tradition, which seem to be in substantial harmony with each other, we arrive at an approximate life span of ninety years or more for Isaiah, covering the period between 770 or 765-680 B.C.

The chronological references in Isaiah 1:1 apparently apply only to the years of the prophet's public life and do not include the years of his semi-retirement under Manasseh, when Isaiah, due to advanced age, may have confined himself mostly to literary activities. Many conservative scholars (Alexander, Keil, Hengstenberg and more recently Oswald T. Allis and Edward J. Young) believe that during that period the prophet wrote the second part of his book (ch. 40-66) in anticipation of the Babylonian exile and Israel's future deliverance.

In addition to his prophetic activities Isaiah was apparently also a prominent historian. In 2 Chronicles 26:22, we read: "Now the rest of the acts of Uzziah, first and last, did Isaiah the prophet, son of Amoz, write."

In addition to this monograph about King Uzziah, there was also another historical work by Isaiah, dealing with the life of Hezekiah. This apparently contained some prophecies because in 2 Chronicles 32:32 this book is referred to as "The Vision of Isaiah." Both these historical works were lost. It is possible that the most important events and prophecies contained in those two works were incorporated in the books of Chronicles and in Isaiah chapters 36-39.

The Stature of Isaiah

There was a regal grandeur about Isaiah. The man who saw Jehovah in the holy temple in all His awesome and exalted majesty could no longer be overawed by mere mortal, whether king or commoner. Isaiah's scorching denunciation of the vices and follies of the inhabitants of Judah had the effect of a branding iron upon the naked flesh. He exposed the avarice and the injustice of the rich, and thundered against the smug self-indulgence of Jerusalem's aristocracy. He confronted the idolatrous

King Ahaz with the disastrous consequences of his foreign alliances and practices. He was nauseated by the spectacle of a religious ritualism, utterly devoid of holiness and justice, and scorned the dizzy flirtatiousness of the fashionable high society ladies of Jerusalem. Those who once heard Isaiah knew that "there was a prophet in Israel."

However, Isaiah was not just another voice, however powerful and eloquent, against the besetting sins and corruption of his nation. Isaiah was above all, the prophet of undaunted faith and undying hope in God's redemptive purpose for Israel and for all mankind. It was his vision of the kingdom of God under the rule of the Messiah, which left its most indelible imprint upon his own contemporaries and subsequent generations.

In his God-given wisdom and prescience, he counseled Israel not to rely on the arm of the flesh, nor to become entangled in foreign alliances with rapacious and ruthless neighbors, but rather to put their trust in Jehovah. "In quietness and in confidence shall be your strength" (Isa. 30:15b).

There were numerous historical circumstances which served to enhance the stature of Isaiah. He lived in a most perilous time, when the very physical, national and spiritual survival of Samaria and later of Judah was at stake. During Isaiah's lifetime the ruthless power of Assyria swept down from the North and put an end to the kingdom of Samaria, and all but wiped out Judah. Isaiah clearly foresaw the imminent disaster. He kept warning the blind rulers, the pleasure-seeking princes and aristocracy and "the people laden with iniquity" about the approaching day of judgment and wrath. However, they preferred to trust in foreign alliances rather than in God (Isa. 30:16).

The prophet Isaiah was God's man of the hour. His burning words were destined to provoke either livid rage or repentance. "Hear the word of the Lord, ye rulers of Sodom; give ear unto the law of our God, ye people of Gomorrah" (Isaiah 1:10).

Of one thing we can be sure: Isaiah was not the most popular citizen of Jerusalem. His people were in no mood to have their conscience constantly bruised and lacerated. They preferred a man who would soothe their feelings and lull them into satisfied somnolence. How well aware of this was the prophet these words bear witness: "... this is a rebellious people ... which say to the seers, See not; and unto the prophets Prophesy not unto us the right things. Speak unto us smooth things, prophesy deceits" (Isa. 30:9-10).

Isaiah's range of vision, his far-sighted thought and depth of feeling were unsurpassed by any other prophet. This is the way the German theologian Ewald characterized Isaiah:

> While no thought is too high or too far off for him, neither is there any
> phenomenon of his age which is beyond the range of his eye, or is too

difficult for the strength of his prophetic arm, every topic of prophetic discourse and teaching being commanded by him from his regal position. As a watchful, far seeing guard and watchman of his age, standing as it were in the center of the Hebrew world and of genuine religion, his eyes take in and command from his position everything that can provoke a prophet to speech and action. There is nothing that escapes the truth of his thought or the wrath of his words.[1]

Isaiah was endowed with a superb mastery of language, which was concise, colorful, harmonious and effective. Filled with holy indignation his words lashed and seared as they fell upon the ears of his listeners: "Ah sinful nation, a people laden with iniquity, a seed of evildoers, children that are corrupters: they have forsaken the Lord, they have provoked the Holy One of Israel unto anger, they are gone away backward" (Isa. 1:4).

There was bitter irony in his words as he painted a vivid picture of the fashionable ladies of Jerusalem and predicted their approaching disgrace:

Moreover the Lord saith, Because the daughters of Zion are haughty, and walk with stretched forth necks and wanton eyes, walking and mincing as they go, and making a tinkling with their feet: Therefore the Lord will smite with a scab the crown of the head of the daughters of Zion, and the Lord will discover their secret parts (Isa. 3:16, 17).

In vain did the prophet try to warn his people. But they in their blindness, instead of repenting, were banqueting and fattening themselves up like dumb animals before the slaughter:

And in that day did the Lord God of hosts call to weeping and to mourning, and to baldness, and to girding with sackcloth: And behold joy and gladness, slaying oxen, and killing sheep, eating flesh, and drinking wine: let us eat and drink; for tomorrow we shall die (Isa. 22:12, 13).

Isaiah took no delight in prophesying doom. His tenderness and love for Israel always came through clearly. He, himself, described so movingly his own state of mind when he saw the day of wrath fast approaching:

Therefore said I, Look away from me; I will weep bitterly, labor not to comfort me, because of the spoiling of the daughter of my people. For it is a day of trouble and of treading down, and of perplexity by the Lord God of hosts in the valley of vision, breaking down the walls, and of crying to the mountains (Isa. 22:4, 5).

He was a man of great sensitivity. His moods and words changed with every changing circumstance. At times he almost sounded like Jeremiah, the weeping prophet of exile. On other occasions he reminds us of Hosea the tragic prophet of the northern kingdom.

And now, O inhabitants of Jerusalem, and men of Judah, judge, I pray you, betwixt me and my vineyard. What could have been done in it?

Wherefore, when I looked that it should bring forth grapes, brought it forth wild grapes? (Isa. 5:3, 4).

Isaiah's Hebrew style is characterized by a fondness for the play on words and alliterations, which are almost invariably lost in most translations. To emphasize a particular thought or point he often uses parables and allegories. With the talent of a great master, he always manages to make his visions or thoughts come to life with vivid and bold strokes. No other prophet was able to conjure up before the eyes and ears of his listeners such a vivid sense of the awesome majesty of God's presence as did Isaiah (chapter 6). Comparing the omnipotence of Jehovah, the creator of the universe and the God of history with the *Elulim*, "the nothingness" of man-made idols, his voice rings with sheer contempt and scorn (Isa. 30:22; 31:7).

Isaiah's vision is not confined to the destiny of Israel alone, but embraces all of mankind in the wideness of God's mercy. Even such ancient and traditional foes as Egypt and Syria are included in the blessing of the future kingdom of God:

In that day shall Israel be
The third with Egypt and with Assyria,
Even a blessing in the midst of the land;
Whom the Lord of hosts shall bless, saying,
Blessed be Egypt my people, and Assyria the work of my hands,
And Israel mine inheritance (Isa. 19:24, 25).

Isaiah is justly considered the greatest of all the writing prophets. Abraham the patriarch, Moses the lawgiver, David the king and Isaiah the prophet, these are the towering and luminous figures of the Old Testament. No other book of the Old Testament with the possible exception of the Psalms, contains such a wide sweep of far-sighted vision, of penetrating insight into the heart of man or foreknowledge of future events, as the book of Isaiah. It should however be remembered that whereas the book of Psalms is a collective work, the book of Isaiah was the message of one man, notwithstanding the widely held opinions of many theologians to the contrary.

The range of his visions, the variety of his emotions and moods might be compared to those of a great cathedral organ played upon by a master. At times one may hear the tempestuous, passionate chords of a Beethoven symphony or the majestic notes of Bach, or the solemn message of redemption and triumph of Handel's "Halleluiah." Now and again we may hear the plaintive and lyric tones reminiscent of a Grieg or Chopin. However behind it all is the Holy One of Israel, the God of Isaiah, the one who infused the song and the message into the heart of the prophet.

Isaiah has impregnated the hearts and minds of men with lofty vision of final redemption as no other prophet before him. He left an indelible impact upon his contemporaries and later generations. It is almost certain that Jeremiah and Ezekiel were familiar with the prophecies of Isaiah. It is more than likely that Micah the contemporary, though younger, prophet of Moresheth, a small town only about 20 miles southwest of Jerusalem, was a personal friend of Isaiah, with whom he cooperated. This would explain the identity of Micah 4:1-3 and Isaiah 2:2-4.

According to the testimony of Josephus (*Antiq.* 11:1,2) Cyrus the Great, the conqueror of Babylon was so impressed by the prophecies of Isaiah which mentioned him by name (Isa. 45:1), that in 538 B.C. he permitted the Jews to return to Jerusalem.

The Synagogue and the Church have made extensive use of the book of Isaiah in their liturgies and prayers. His prophecies, although variously interpreted by Jew and Christian, continue to "speak comfortably to their hearts" in the hour of personal or national perplexity. No other prophet was quoted so frequently by Christ and His apostles as Isaiah. Indeed it would be impossible to understand the New Testament truly without the knowledge of Isaiah.

So heart-searching and pregnant with hope for all mankind has been the prophecy of Isaiah, the seer of the small mountain kingdom of Judah in the 8th century B.C., that his oracles have become a part of man's ultimate hope of redemption for himself and for mankind.

Throughout the ages, Isaiah, probably more than any other prophet, has fascinated the minds of the humble and the learned, and has stirred the hearts of teachers and preachers, of poets and artists, and of those who saw great visions for the human race.

Ignored and often forgotten, Isaiah, God's voice crying in the wilderness of men, could not stay forgotten. The man who heard the imperious voice of God: "Whom shall I send and who shall go for me?" not only answered for himself: "Here am I, send me," but also ignited a fire in the hearts of countless men, thrusting them forth as God's messengers on seemingly hopeless errands to succeeding generations of blind and willful men.

The message of Isaiah spans all generations and bridges the chasm between time and eternity. More than any other prophet Isaiah brought to mankind the transcendent image of the Messiah in the dual role of God's Anointed King and Suffering Servant who poured out his life for the redemption of many.

St. Augustine called Isaiah "Not so much a prophet as an evangelist." The book of Isaiah has often been referred to as "the Fifth Gospel" or "the Gospel according to Isaiah."

Isaiah's God was no mere tribal deity, but the Creator of heaven and earth, and the God of all nations, a holy and righteous God who abhors evil whether committed by His chosen people Israel or by any other nation:

> Come near ye nations to hear; and hearken, ye people:
> Let the earth hear, and all that is therein;
> The world and all things that come forth of it.
> For the indignation of the Lord is upon all nations,
> And his fury upon all their armies (Isa. 34:1, 2).

Beyond the day of divine wrath and judgment Isaiah looked to the day when nations shall at last attain peace, when the knowledge of God shall cover the earth "as the waters cover the sea." The Messiah and His kingdom were the woof and warp, the heart and the core of Isaiah's vision.

> And there shall come forth a rod out of the stem of Jesse, and a Branch shall grow out of his roots:
> And the spirit of the Lord shall rest upon him, the spirit of wisdom and understanding, the spirit of counsel and might, the spirit of knowledge and of the fear of the Lord; And shall make him of quick understanding in the fear of the Lord; and he shall not judge after the sight of his eyes, neither reprove after the hearing of his ears: But with righteousness shall he judge the poor, and reprove with equity for the meek of the earth: and he shall smite the earth with the rod of his mouth, and with the breath of his lips shall he slay the wicked.
> And righteousness shall be the girdle of his loins, and faithfulness the girdle of his reins. The wolf also shall dwell with the lamb, and the leopard shall lie down with the kid; and the calf and the young lion and the fatling together; and a little child shall lead them.
> And the cow and the bear shall feed: their young ones shall lie down together: and the lion shall eat straw like the ox.
> And the suckling child shall play on the hole of the asp, and the weaned child shall put his hand on the cockatrice' den.
> They shall not hurt nor destroy in all my holy mountain:
> For the earth shall be full of the knowledge of the Lord, as the waters cover the sea (Isa. 11:1-9).

This vision is a part of the legacy which Isaiah bequeathed to mankind. It still fills the hearts of men with hope and faith. It has exercised through the ages a more effective influence than all the transient forces of the passing centuries.

NOTES:

1. Due to difficult problems connected with the dating of Biblical kings most chronological tables vary slightly from each other. We have generally followed *The Chronology of the Kings of Judah and Israel* by E. R. Thiele in *Journal of Near Eastern Studies,* July 1944.

2. G. H. Ewald, *Commentary on the Old Testament Prophets,* English Translation. Volume 2, page 6.

Who Wrote
The Book
of Isaiah?

Who wrote the book of Isaiah? Is it really important to find an answer? There are those who question whether Isaiah actually did write all of the book named after him. There are others who say: "What difference does it make who wrote the book of Isaiah, as long as we believe that what is written there is the Word of God?"

But can we really believe that the book of Isaiah is the Word of God if we cannot believe the claim which the book makes for itself at the very beginning, that it is "the vision of Isaiah the son of Amoz"?

And if we cannot believe this, can we believe similar claims in the books of Amos, Hosea, Micah, Joel, Jeremiah, Ezekiel and all the other prophets? Were they really the authors of the books named after them? If that is not true, how can we rely on other historical statements made in the same books? And if we cannot depend on the prophetic books as being historically reliable, how can we accept their message as being inspired by the Holy Spirit? Are the prophetic books truly the living Word of God, or are they a collection of "pseudepigraphical documents" which cannot truly be regarded as Holy Writ? These are far reaching and essential questions which make us realize how important it is to find the right answer to our initial question "Who wrote the book of Isaiah?"

The question goes even futher than we have already indicated, if we remember that the Lord Jesus Christ Himself, and His apostles, repeatedly quoted from different parts of Isaiah, always attributing them not to some unknown prophet or to a disciple of Isaiah, or to a group of unknown writers, but to Isaiah himself. If we accept the theory of the majority of critics, that the book of Isaiah is a compilation of oracles first pronounced or written down by a number of unknown authors, then we are forced to admit that Christ and His apostles, lacking the "advantage" of modern scholarship, were sadly mistaken. It is no use to evade the issue, as some do, by saying that Christ really did not say anything about the authorship of the book, and that he merely referred to the book of Isaiah regardless of who wrote it. If words mean what they say, our Lord was obviously convinced that Isaiah wrote the book of Isaiah, when he said "Isaiah says," or "Isaiah said" or "Isaiah crieth."

How important and far reaching the question "Who wrote Isaiah?" is. The fact is that for two and a half millennia both the Synagogue and the Church believed that Isaiah was the author of all sixty-six chapters of the book named after him. Were they all mistaken? We are persuaded that they were not, in spite of all self-assured and haughty claims to the contrary by a great many modern critics.

A careful examination of the internal and external evidences pertaining to the subject leads to the conclusion that the book of Isaiah was written by the prophet Isaiah by inspiration of the Holy Spirit. In the next chapters we shall seek to substantiate this with considerable evidence before proceeding with our study of Isaiah.

For more than two millennia there was a general consensus among Jews and Christians that the book of the prophet Isaiah was written by one man, known as Isaiah the son of Amoz. Toward the end of the 18th century this unanimity gradually began to change. A new type of negative Biblical criticism emerged which questioned the authenticity of the existing Hebrew and Greeks texts of the Scripture and the authority of the Bible as the Word of God.

Among the early forerunners of our modern textual criticism (sometimes also referred to as "higher criticism") there was the famous commentator, Abraham Hin Ezra (1092-1167) who questioned the Mosaic origin of certain parts of the Pentateuch.

The Birth of Modern Criticism[1]

The Dutch Jewish philosopher Benedict Spinoza (1632-1677) published in 1670 his famous work *Tractatus Theologico-Politicus* in which he expressed critical views about the origin of the Bible. In Spinoza's pantheistic philosophy which equated God with nature, (*Deus sive natura*), there was no room for a personal God, for revelation or miracles. He insisted that the Bible must be judged by the same criteria as any other literary document. Thus Spinoza was in a sense the father of Biblical criticism.

Modern Biblical criticism however began in earnest in the 18th century. Before we review briefly the development of Biblical criticism, it is well to take a look at the intellectual atmosphere which prevailed in Western Europe (and to a lesser degree also in America) during the second half of the 18th century and later.

The Climate Which Produced Biblical Criticism

The 18th century was an age of intellectual, political and spiritual ferment. It was the age of "deism," a philosophy which assumed that God was a kind of absentee landlord, who, having created the world, endowed it with certain unalterable laws, and left it to run its course in conformity with these laws. This philosophy was particularly strong among English theologians of the 17th and 18th centuries. The deists attacked the traditional view concerning the authorship of the Scriptures and denied the possibility of miracles in an orderly world. To them reason was the sole instrument of acquiring and evaluating what is true. The deists and the rationalists considered human reason as the supreme authority.

The 18th century was an age of rationalism and humanism. God was dethroned in favor of omnipotent rational man. Rationalism was one of the main forces behind the French Revolution.

The 18th and 19th centuries were also an age of philosophical materialism which assumed that only that is "real" which can be perceived by the senses and evaluated by the rational human mind.

It was an age of scepticism which queried man's ability to know at all. It questioned even reason itself. In his *Critique of Pure Reason*, Kant taught that man can never know what "things in themselves" are (*Das Ding an sich*), but only as these things appear to us through the medium of our minds. All the time-honored basic assumptions, theories and principles of our Western civilization were subjected afresh to the questioning mind of man.

The 19th century was an age of ethical scepticism, as distinguished from philosophical or epistemological scepticism. Its high priest was Frederick Nietzsche, the sworn enemy of Biblical ethics which he considered as "slave morality," suitable only for slaves and weaklings and not for "supermen." Nietzsche's philosophy later appealed to Hitler in a special way. The philosophies of Fichte, Hegel, Feuerbach, Schopenhauer, Nietzsche, Karl Marx, Charles R. Darwin (*The Origin of Species*), profoundly influenced the thinking of the 19th century. They created an intellectual and spiritual climate which directly or indirectly deeply affected also the study of the Scriptures.

In literature it was fashionable to debunk the historicity of some of the luminaries of the ancient classics. Among the first who were submitted to this debunking type of literary criticism was the blind Greek poet Homer. Some scholars of classical literature maintained that the *Iliad* and the *Odyssey* were not the works of Homer at all, but a compilation by later writers or editors, who collected the heroic sagas of prehistoric Greece into two epic poems. Other works of antiquity were in a similar manner subjected to destructive literary criticism.

Even some authors of comparatively modern times, such as Shakespeare, (1564-1616), did not escape this type of debunking criticism. His works became the subject of a heated controversy as to their true authorship, a controversy which still continues. No less than 57 different persons have been suggested as "the real" authors of Shakespeare's works. The best known among these were the contemporaries of Shakespeare, Sir Francis Bacon and Christopher Marlowe.

It is inevitable that in the intellectual atmosphere of rationalism and humanism, the standards of literary criticism should also be applied to Biblical research.

In 1753 the French physician Jean Astruc, considered the father of modern Biblical criticism, propounded the theory that Moses composed Genesis from two main sources, "The Elohist" and "The Yahvist" or "Jahvist," ("E" and "J"). According to Astruc the characteristic feature of the first source was the use of the word *Elohim* for the name of God. This source he named "The Elohist." The second, which used *Yahveh* as the name of God, he called "The Yahvist." In our study we will continue to use the traditional and more euphonius "Jehovah" which is a combination of the sacred tetragrammaton "YHWH" or "JHWH" and the vowels of the word *Adonai* — Lord. This was introduced by 7th century A.D. Jewish scholars known as "the Massoretes," who provided the Hebrew text of the Old Testament with the appropriate vowels, which were absent from the original manuscripts.

Astruc's theory was further developed by J. G. Eichhorn in his *Introduction to the Pentateuch,* in 1780-1783.

The Documentary Theory

Other scholars such as DeWette, H. Ewald and especially K. H. Graf, 1866, followed in the footsteps of their predecessors. This type of Biblical criticism became known as "the documentary theory."

It was Julius Wellhausen who in his publications (1876-1884) gave the documentary theory its most developed and complete form. His theory reduced the patriarchs to legendary figures. Even Moses himself became a nebulous, if not legendary, personality. Wellhausen maintained that since, during the times of Moses, writing was hardly known among the Hebrews, he could not have been the author of the Pentateuch, which he considered as a compilation of several documents. The first document he called "J" for *Jahwist* (around 850 B.C.), the second was "E" for *Elohist* (750 B.C.), "D" for Deuteronomy (c. 621 B.C.), and "P" for Priestly Code, (about 500-450 B.C.).

These documents, according to Wellhausen, were finally collected, edited and fixed in their present form by an unknown "redactor" or "redactors" around the year 400 B.C. Because of constant overlapping of the so-called sources (*Elohim* used in "J" source and *Jahwe* in "E" source) the documentary theory underwent further fragmentation and refinement at the hands of later scholars.

On closer investigation the documentary theory turns out to be mostly conjecture based on unproven assumptions, or on an incomplete knowledge of the cultural history of Israel and the Near East. Archeology has, since the days of Wellhausen and his associates, brought to light important documents and artifacts which prove that writing was not only well-known and widely used among Semitic peoples of that period, but also cast new light on the history and the languages of the whole Near East. To a remarkable degree archeology has confirmed the historical reliability of the Bible. In the light of this more complete knowledge, some of the critical theories of earlier days have had to be either abandoned or substantially modified.

Even before the documentary theory, (also known as the Graf-Kuenen-Wellhausen theory) became dominant among Old Testament scholars, there emerged a strongly conservative school of thought which defended the traditional views about the authorship of the Bible and the inspiration of the Scriptures. Among the conservative scholars were E. W. Hengstenberg (*Dissertations on the Genuineness of the Pentateuch,* translated into English in 1847), C. F. Keil and W. H. Green (*The Higher Criticism of the Pentateuch,* 1895), Friedrich Delitzsch (*Commentary on the Old Testament*), and James Orr, (*The Problem of the Old Testament,* 1900).

Early in the 19th century the book of Isaiah became the demarcation line between conservative and liberal Biblical scholarship. Among those who staunchly defended the unity of Isaiah was the outstanding American scholar and oriental linguist Joseph Addison Alexander (*Commentary on the Prophecies of Isaiah,* 1847). His book is of considerable value even today. The only drawback to it is that Alexander tends to confuse historical Israel with the Church of Christ. This was due to an understandable lack of historical perspective, which is sometimes shared even today by some otherwise outstanding scholars.

The Isaianic authorship of chapters 40-66 was also advocated by the learned Hebrew Christian scholar Moritz Drechsler (*Der Prophet Jesaiah,* 1849) and the Italian rabbi, Samuel Luzatto (*Le Profeta Isaia,* 1855).

Among contemporary defenders of the unity of Isaiah are the Americans, O. T. Allis (*The Unity of Isaiah,* 1950) and Edward J. Young in his valuable *Studies in Isaiah* (1954), and *Who Wrote Isaiah?* (1958). The renowned Bible scholar Franz Delitzsch in his *Commentary on Isaiah* took a cautious position, on the whole leaning toward the unity of Isaiah. Delitzsch after reviewing the arguments of those who see in the book of Isaiah the work of several authors and pointing out the serious difficulties which these arguments involve, said:

And yet much seems to be better explained when chapters 40-66 are regarded as testamentary discourses of the one Isaiah and the entire prophetic collection as the progressive development of his incomparable charism.[2]

Some of the contemporary Hebrew scholars in Israel, Yehezkiel Kaufmann,[3] and Rachel Margalioth,[4] have recently joined in the defense of the conservative position and made some valuable contributions.

Among English-speaking people, the Wellhausen position was first popularized by W. Robertson Smith and by S. R. Driver. Today the documentary theory has lost much of its original influence, and has been seriously undermined by Scandinavian scholars who emphasize the reliability of ancient oral traditions (Engnell and especially E. Nielsen *Oral Tradition* published in 1954).

What Wellhausen did to the Pentateuch, Bernhard Duhm, born in 1847, a disciple and personal friend of Julius Wellhausen, did to the book of Isaiah with his work *Das Buch Jesaia* (1892).

Duhm argued that since the passage in 2 Chronicles 36:22 (cf. Ezra 1:1-4) which deals with the decree of Cyrus permitting the Jews to return from Babylon to Jerusalem to rebuild the temple, mentions Jeremiah, therefore Isaiah 40-66 must have been written later than the book of Jeremiah. Isaiah 1-39, Duhm designated as the "First Isaiah," assigning chapters 40-66 to later unknown writers.

Duhm proceeded further to dismember Isaiah 1-39, especially those prophecies which predict the downfall of Babylon as *"vaticinia ex post eventu."* By the time he was through there was little left of the book of Isaiah which he considered as genuinely Isaianic.

The second part of Isaiah, Duhm further subdivided into chapters 40-55 and 56-66.

Chapters 56-66 (with the exception of the so-called Servant Songs 42:1-4, 49:1-6, 50:4-9 and 52:13-53:12), Duhm attributed to a writer whom he designated as Trito-Isaiah or "The Third Isaiah." The whole book of Isaiah became a hodgepodge of supposedly anonymous collections, which were later loosely put together by anonymous editors into what became known as the book of the prophet Isaiah. The invention of a Third Isaiah was the major accomplishment of Duhm.

Bernhard Duhm's position was later popularized among English-speaking people by J. Skinner in his *Commentary of Isaiah* (2 volumes in the Cambridge Bible).

Today the position almost universally held by the critics is that the book of Isaiah is a composite work written by at least three and probably more unknown authors. They divide the book into three main parts:

First Isaiah—chapter 1-39
Second Isaiah—chapters 40-55 (Deutero-Isaiah)
Third Isaiah—chapter 55-66 (Trito-Isaiah)

Once the process of fragmentation was started, it continued *ad infini-tum*. Only about 11 chapters of the book of Isaiah are generally recognized by the critics as genuine, and hardly any of the critics agree with each other. In his Commentary on Isaiah, Delitzsch remarks:

> Wilful contempt of external testimony and frivolity in the treatment of historical data have been from the very first the fundamental evils apparent in the manner in which modern critics have handled the question relating to Isaiah. These critics approach everything that is traditional with the presumption that it is false, and whoever would make a scientific impression upon them, must first declare right fearlessly his absolute superiority to the authority of tradition.[5]

According to these critics the question of the unity of Isaiah has been definitely settled in their favor. To reject their position is, in their view, a mark of intellectual and scholastic backwardness which can only be looked down upon with amused condescension.

Thus R. H. Kennett (1909) at the very start of his lectures on the composition of the book of Isaiah, declared that "To argue at length that the book of Isaiah is not all the work of Isaiah the son of Amoz, but is a composite document, would be but to slay the slain."

We shall now review briefly the position of those who argue against the unity of Isaiah, and then proceed to explain why we believe that the book of Isaiah was written by one man, known in history as the prophet Isaiah, the son of Amoz.

NOTES: 1. The term "criticism" is in itself not something negative or condemnatory. "Criticism" is derived from the Greek verb *krinein*—to judge, to assess, to evaluate. There is a positive type of criticism which seeks to understand and evaluate properly a given document or text. Criticism becomes a negative exercise when it is based on preconceived notions or unwarranted assumptions.

2. Quoted in *Studies in Isaiah*, p. 31, by E. J. Young.

3. Yehezkiel Kaufmann, *Toldoth Emunath Ha-Israelith*, vol. III, Tel Aviv, 1948.

4. *The Indivisible Isaiah* by Rachel Margalioth (Sura Institute for Research, Jerusalem) .

5. Delitzsch, *Biblical Commentary on the Prophecies of Isaiah*, p. 59.

The
Critics
of Isaiah

Two basic assumptions underlie the negative approach to prophecy; first that anything which cannot be explained in a rational way is not real, hence miracles do not exist, and second, that predictive prophecy, in the true sense of the word, does not exist.

According to this school of negative criticism, Biblical prophecy is essentially a form of ethical exhortation, and the prophets were teachers of moral conduct. Predictive prophecy is explained by them either as a retrospective glance into the past *(vaticinium ex eventu)*, or else a sagacious appraisal of current events and a reasonable forecast of their inevitable consequences. They consider the prophets as merely well-informed interpreters of contemporary history. Any claim to God-imparted precognition is considered by them as suspect *per se*. It goes without saying that to the Bible-believing person this position is completely unacceptable and even repugnant. To deny that an omnipotent and personal God could or would reveal to His chosen servants future events which are veiled to mortal eye, comes little short of denying God Himself.

A naturalistic approach to prophecy had to reject *a priori* as ungenuine, the predictive prophecy about Cyrus (Isaiah 44:28-45:1) made nearly two centuries before the actual event. However, to Isaiah himself, this very prophecy was an authenticating proof of its divine origin and genuineness. It was a testimony that "the Holy One of Israel" alone is able to foretell the future, long before it comes to pass.

Thus saith the Lord, your redeemer, the Holy One of Israel; For your sake I have sent to Babylon, and have brought down all their nobles, and the Chaldeans, whose cry is in the ships. I am the Lord, your Holy One, the creator of Israel, your King (Isa. 43:14, 15).

For Jacob my servant's sake, and Israel mine elect, I have even called thee by thy name: I have surnamed thee, though thou hast not known me (Isa. 45:4).

The utter "nothingness" of idols is made manifest by the fact that they cannot do this. And so Isaiah challenges "the gods" to prove their power by foretelling future events, just as Jehovah does:

> Show the things that are to come hereafter, that we may know that ye are gods: yea, do good, or do evil, that we may be dismayed, and behold it together. Behold, ye are of nothing, and your work of nought: an abomination is he that chooseth you. I have raised up one from the north, and he shall come: from the rising of the sun shall he call upon my name: and he shall come upon princes as upon morter, and as the potter treadeth clay (Isa. 41:23-25).

The Cyrus prophecy was the starting point for the theory of two Isaiahs, which was later increased to three or even more Isaiahs.

The Arguments against the Unity of Isaiah

The arguments against the unity of Isaiah are divided into three main groups.

1. That the internal evidence of chapters 40-66 points to the period in which they were written, namely at the end of the Babylonian exile (about 546-539 B.C.). Cyrus was then already on the horizon, as a rising, military star about to conquer the Babylonian Empire (Driver). Others attributed the second part of Isaiah to an even later post-exilic period (George A. Smith, Gunkel, Skinner and others.)

2. That the literary style and language of Isaiah 40-66 differs substantially from that of the first part of Isaiah.

3. That the theological ideas expressed in chapters 40-66 differ considerably from those of chapters 1-39. S. R. Driver, one of the more moderate among the critics wrote:

> It need only be added (for the purpose of precluding misconception) that this view of its date and authorship in no way impairs the theological value of the prophecy, or reduces it to a *vaticinium ex eventu:* on the other hand, the whole tone of the prophecy shows that it is written prior to the events which it declares to be approaching; on the other hand it nowhere claims to be written by Isaiah, or to have originated in his age. Nor upon the same view of it is any claim made by its author to prevision of the future disallowed or weakened.[1]

Let us now take a closer look at the above arguments.

1. Internal Evidences:

Those who favor the composite authorship of Isaiah claim that chapters 40-66 reflect a Babylonian background, and that the unknown prophet addressed himself to his fellow exiles, seeking to comfort them. Yet a closer analysis of chapters 40-66 does not support this claim. Neither does the prophet address himself chiefly to the yet unborn deportees in Babylon.

It is significant that the word "Babylon" occurs only four times in Isaiah, part II, 43:14, 47:1, 48:14, 20; whereas in the first part, Babylon is mentioned nine times (13:1, 19; 14:4, 22; 21:9; 39:1, 3, 6, 7).

Actually the prophet Isaiah addressed himself to his contemporaries to whom he had already previously predicted deportation to Babylon (39:6-7).

The opening words of Isaiah chapter 40 are a natural sequence to the preceding gloomy prediction of deportation. Now Isaiah sought to comfort his people "the mourners of Zion" with the message of their future deliverance.

Comfort ye, comfort ye my people, saith my God.
Speak ye comfortably (or "speak to the heart") to Jerusalem ....
(Isa. 40:1, 2).

That the prophet himself was located outside Babylon is evident from the words "Depart ye, depart ye, go out from thence" (52:11a). The word "thence" (in Hebrew *mishsham*) clearly indicates the prophet's geographical location outside Babylon. This is also implied in the following passage:

Thus saith the Lord, your Redeemer, the Holy One of Israel; For your sake I have sent to Babylon, and have brought down all their nobles, and the Chaldeans, whose cry is in the ships (43:14).

The passage: "I have set watchmen upon thy walls, O Jerusalem" (62:6a) would indicate that the walls of Jerusalem were still standing when the prophet wrote down those words.

It is only when one assumes that chapters 40-66 were not written by Isaiah, that numerous passages, which in themselves are vague and indefinite, can be interpreted to have a much later background. But this is a case of proving a proposition with "evidence" which is itself completely unproved.

Another contention of the critics is that since the prophet predicted the restoration of Jerusalem and the cities of Judah, without previously predicting exile, the prophet must have lived himself during the period of exile, when the destruction of Jerusalem was already an accomplished fact. In support of this argument, the following passage is quoted:

That confirmeth the word of his servant, and performeth the counsel of his messengers; that saith to Jerusalem, Thou shalt be inhabited; and to the cities of Judah, Ye shall be built, and I will raise up the decayed places thereof. (Isa. 44:26).

First of all this passage does not prove that at the time when Isaiah pronounced this particular oracle, Jerusalem and the cities of Judah were already destroyed and uninhabited. The prophet looked upon the future destruction and exile as already accomplished in the purpose of God.

Furthermore if we accept (as we do) the traditional position concerning the unity of Isaiah, then it follows that the prophet had already in the past foretold the approaching disaster and exile: 3:24-26, 5:5-6, 13: 17-22, 32:11-14, 39:6-8. (We realize that some of these passages are disputed by the critics on the same inadequate grounds on which the whole theory of the composite authorship of Isaiah is based.)

We need to remember that the threat of exile as punishment for disobedience to God is one of the recurring themes of the prophetic message, beginning with Moses (Lev. 26:23, Deut. 28:64, etc.). In Israel's political situation, invasion and exile were a constant and ever-present peril. We know from modern history many instances of nations who are always exposed to the peril of invasion chiefly due to their geographical situation.

Likewise the prediction of future restoration following national repentance was also a recurring theme in prophecy, long before the Babylonian exile (Lev. 26:27-45). Even during the most prosperous and glorious period of the monarchy under Solomon, the possibility of exile always loomed large before the eyes of the leaders of Israel. Solomon prayed:

When thy people Israel be smitten down before the enemy, because they have sinned against thee, and shall turn again to thee, and confess thy name, and pray, and make supplication unto thee in this house:
Then hear thou in heaven, and forgive the sin of thy people Israel, and bring them again unto the land which thou gavest unto their fathers
(1 Ki. 8:33, 34).

Amos, the older contemporary of Isaiah, predicted the restoration of Israel before he ever predicted an exile:

And I will bring again the captivity of my people of Israel, and they shall build the waste cities, and inhabit them; and they shall plant vineyards, and drink the wine thereof; they shall also make gardens and eat the fruit of them (Amos 9:14).

Micah, Isaiah's younger contemporary, predicted specifically the Babylonian exile to be followed by restoration:

Be in pain, and labour to bring forth, O daughter of Zion, like a woman in travail: for now shalt thou go forth out of the city, and thou shalt dwell in the field, and thou shalt go even to Babylon; there shalt thou be delivered; there the Lord shall redeem thee from the hand of thine enemies (Mic. 4:10).

We therefore conclude that the previously quoted passage of Isaiah 44:26, does not in any way militate against its genuine Isaianic character.

As we have already mentioned, one of the chief arguments against the genuineness of Isaiah 40-66 is the specific mention by name of Cyrus. This, the critics say, is supposed to be unparalleled in prophecy and supposedly unworthy of prophecy, making it too much like pagan soothsaying.

Yet we recall how an unnamed prophet predicted some 200 years before the event took place, the action of a yet unborn king, whose name was to be Josiah:

> And he cried against the altar in the word of the Lord, and said, O altar, altar, thus said the Lord; Behold a child shall be born unto the house of David, Josiah by name; and upon thee shall he offer the priests of the high places that burn incense upon thee, and men's bones shall be burnt upon thee (1 Ki. 13:2).

To argue that this prediction is also a later interpolation, is another instance of trying to prove one unproved assertion by another of the same kind. This is known as reasoning in a vicious circle.

Biblical prophecy is a unique phenomenon, which in order to be understood, must be considered on its own terms. Even if the Cyrus prediction should be a singular and unparalleled instance, it would still not be proof against its authenticity. There is always the possibility of a first time, of a singular and unique occurrence. Must we limit God to our preconceived notions about what He can or will do under certain circumstances?

Far from indicating a Babylonian background, the internal evidence in Isaiah 40-66 points to the existence of the temple and to an active sacrificial cult: "And Lebanon is not sufficient to burn, nor the beasts thereof sufficient for a burnt-offering" (Isa. 40:16). The people are rebuked for not bringing the appointed sacrifices into the temple. "Thou hast not brought me the small cattle of thy burnt offerings; neither hast thou honored me with thy sacrifices" (Isa. 43:23a). The well known repugnance of Isaiah to a sacrificial cult divorced from godly conduct, is clearly evident in the following passage:

> He that killeth an ox is as if he slew a man; he that sacrificeth a lamb, as if he cut off a dog's neck; he that offereth an oblation, as if he offered swine's blood; he that burneth incense, as if he blessed an idol. Yea, they have chosen their own ways, and their soul delighteth in their abominations (Isa. 66:3).

Instead of pointing to a Babylonian background for chapters 40-66, the internal evidence indicates one which is consistent with that of Isaiah.

2. The Argument from Literary Style:

Much has been made by the critics of the supposedly marked differences in style and language between the first and second parts of Isaiah. In the opinion of Driver, "the subject of chapters 40-66 is not so different from that of Isaiah's prophecies against the Assyrians, as to necessitate a new phraseology and rhetorical form; the difference can only be explained by the supposition of a change of author."[2]

Some twenty words and phrases in chapters 40-66 have been singled out in support of the contention that these prophecies came from an author (or authors) other than Isaiah. However, some of the same words which are supposedly characteristic of the Second Isaiah are also found in those parts of Isaiah which are admittedly genuine.

For instance the word "to break forth" (into singing, Hebrew *parats*), in 44:23, also occurs in Isaiah 14:7. (On the genuineness of chapter 14 we will have something to say later.) "The whole earth is at rest and is quiet: they 'break forth' into singing." Another instance, "rejoice" (Hebrew *sōs*) "I will greatly rejoice in the Lord" (Isa. 61:10, 62:5), "The wilderness shall rejoice [the same Hebrew verb] (Isa. 35:1, 10).

And if some of the words in the second part of Isaiah do not occur in the earlier chapters, this in no way indicates a change of authors. A change in theme, situation, even mood, will often dictate the choice of words. This is true not only of Isaiah, but of other prophets and of writers in every age.

Thus the expression "the vengeance of the Lord," *(nikmath Jehovah)*, occurs only in two chapters of Jeremiah, and nowhere else in that whole book (50:15, 28; 51:6, 11). Or the expression "slain by the sword" is found only in two chapters of Ezekiel and nowhere else in that book (31: 17, 18 and 32:20, 22, 25, 28, 31, 32). Does Jeremiah 50 start a Second Jeremiah or Ezekiel 30 begin a Second Ezekiel? Similar situations where a prophet uses certain expressions only in one section of his writings could be multiplied from other prophetic books.

As far as the book of Isaiah is concerned, there is an overwhelming similarity or identity of words and phrases which strongly point to the fact that the man who wrote the first part of Isaiah is the same whom the critics call the Second or Third Isaiah. It is a much safer procedure to accept the same authorship for the whole book of Isaiah than to launch out on the uncertain seas of literary speculation and guesswork.

3. The Assumed Difference in Theological Ideas:

According to the critics there is a divergence in theological concepts between the first and second parts of Isaiah. Thus the First Isaiah emphasizes the majesty of God (Isaiah 6), whereas the Second Isaiah emphasizes the infinity of God, the creator and sustainer of the universe, the author of history, the first and the last, the God beyond comprehension (Isa. 40:12-18, 28; 41:15, 18; 48:15, etc.).

Another point of assumed difference is the doctrine of a faithful remnant, so prominent in First Isaiah, but less in evidence in the second part (59:20; 65:8). The figure of the Messianic King is a distinctive feature in the first section of Isaiah, while in the second part the Messianic

King is replaced by "the righteous servant" (42:14; 49:1; 50:4-9; 52:13, 53:12; 61:1-3).

When we analyze the above differences, we find that they do not support the weight imposed upon them by the critics. Of course, there is a difference of imagery and symbolism, but these differences are not contradictory or mutually exclusive. The majesty of God described in Isaiah chapter 6 is in complete harmony with the infinitude of God, described in 40:12-18; they are complementary aspects of the divine.

Similarly the difference between the idea of the King Messiah and the Servant of God is a difference of imagery but not as regards their ultimate purpose, as the divinely appointed instrumentalities for the accomplishment of God's will. There is an inner harmony between the Messiah, who is the "rod out of the stem of Jesse" (Isa. 11:1), and the servant of God as described in Isaiah 61:1, 2.

> And there shall come forth a rod out of the stem of Jesse,
> and a Branch shall grow out of his roots:
> And the spirit of the Lord shall rest upon him, the spirit
> of wisdom and understanding, the spirit of counsel and might,
> the spirit of knowledge and of the fear of the Lord;
> And shall make him of quick understanding in fear of the Lord:
> and he shall not judge after the sight of his eyes,
> neither reprove after the hearing of his ears;
> But with righteousness shall he judge the poor and reprove
> with equity for the meek of the earth: and he shall smite
> the earth with the rod of his mouth, and with the breath
> of his lips shall he slay the wicked.
> And righteousness shall be the girdle of his loins, and
> faithfulness the girdle of his reins (Isa. 11:1-5).

> The Spirit of the Lord God is upon me; because the Lord hath anointed me to preach good tidings unto the meek; he hath sent me to bind up the brokenhearted, to proclaim liberty to the captives, and the opening of the prison to them that are bound:
>
> To proclaim the acceptable year of the Lord, and the day of vengeance of our God; to comfort all that mourn (Isa. 61:1-2).

Similarly the idea of a remnant while not conspicuous in the second part of Isaiah is not altogether absent there. The prophet refers to the remnant either directly or by implication. "And I will bring forth a seed out of Jacob, and out of Judah an inheritor of my mountains: and mine elect shall inherit it, and my servants shall dwell there" (Isa. 65:9). The idea of the remnant is also implied in Isaiah 56:8, 66:19.

The contempt for idols, so characteristic of Isaiah, is conspicuous in both parts of the book.

> Their land is full of idols [vanities]; they worship the work of their own hands, that which their own fingers have made.
> And the common man bows down, and the man of stature abases himself, therefore forgive them not (Isa. 2:8-9).

The same theme appears repeatedly in a more elaborate form in the second part of Isaiah—(40:18-20; 44:12-19; and 46:5-7).

Incidentally the very frequent denunciation of idols, is in itself an indication of the pre-exilic origin of these passages. After the Babylonian exile, idolatry, at least, in its more primitive and crass form, was no longer the peculiar national sin of the Jews, as it was before the exile.

The more polished and reflective style in the second part of the book is due, no doubt, to the fact that whereas in the earlier part the prophet dealt with the immediate daily problems of his time and mostly orally, in the streets of Jerusalem. In the later prophecies, when the prophet withdrew from the public arena to the privacy of meditation and reflection, he could write down in a more leisurely fashion what the Spirit of God conveyed to him.

Behind all the oracles of the book of Isaiah, there is the same man with the same message: God's wrath and mercy, sin and judgment, exile and restoration. His message throughout the whole book is radiant with the vision of the Messiah, the anointed Servant of God, His exalted and redemptive life and vicarious death . (52:13; 53:1-13) and the final triumph of His glorious kingdom (2:2, 4; 9:7; 11:6-9; 60:1-22; 65:17-25) .

NOTES:

1. S. R. Driver, *An Introduction to the Literature of the Old Testament* (1897), page 243.

2. Driver, *Op. cit.,* page 238.

The
Indivisibility
of Isaiah

We have already discussed the arguments of those who hold that the book of Isaiah is a composite work resulting from a fusion of several smaller fragments. Let us now consider the arguments in favor of the unity of Isaiah.

1. The strong similarity of language and style in the first and second parts of Isaiah

2. The significance of chapters 36-39 in relation to the unity of Isaiah

3. The heading of the book of Isaiah

4. The evidence of the Septuagint and the Dead Sea Manuscripts

5. The testimony of Ecclesiasticus

6. The unbroken chain of 25 centuries of tradition

7. The testimony of the New Testament

1. Similarity of Language and Style

Much has been made by the critics of Isaiah of the supposed difference in language between what they consider to be the genuine Isaiah and the so called Second and Third Isaiahs. We have previously mentioned some of the differences.

Let us now consider a number of expressions and turns of speech which occur almost exclusively in Isaiah, but rarely if ever, in any other prophetic writings:[1]

> a. "For out of . . . shall go forth the law"
> For out of Zion shall go forth the law (2:3).
> For the law shall go forth out of me (51:4).

b. **"Law and judgment for the nations"**
For out of Zion shall go forth the law ...
And he shall judge among the nations (2:3b, 4).
He shall bring forth the judgment to the nations ...
the isles shall wait for the law (42:1-4).

c. **"They shall see the glory of the Lord"** (35:2).
"And the glory of the Lord shall be revealed and all flesh
shall see it together" (40:5).
"They shall come and see my glory" (66:18).

d. **The wolf, the lamb and the lion.**
"And the wolf shall dwell with the lamb and the lion shall
eat straw like an ox, they shall not hurt or destroy in all my
holy mountain" (11:6-9).
"The wolf and the lamb shall feed together ... and the
lion shall eat straw like the bullock. . . . They shall
not hurt nor destroy in all my holy mountain" (65:25).

e. **"I delighted not"—(*lo hafatzti*). In Isaiah only.**
"I delighted not in the blood of bullocks" (1:11).
"But ye did that which was evil ... wherein I delighted
not" (65:12).
"But they did that which was evil in which I delighted
not" (66:4).

f. **"Your hands are full of blood."**
"Yea, when you make many prayers, I will not hear; your
hands are full of blood" (1:15b).
"Your hands are defiled with blood" (59:3).

g. **"That we may know." No other example in all of the
Old Testament.**
"And let the counsel of the Holy One of Israel draw nigh
and come, that we may know it" (5:19).
"Tell the things which are to happen hereafter that we may
know that ye are gods" (41:23).
"Who hath told in advance that we may know" (41:26).

h. **"They shall not rise" (*bal-yakumu*). In Isaiah only.**
"They shall not rise and inherit the earth" (14:21).
"They shall not rise" (43:17).

i. **"To mourn as a dove."**
"I did mourn as a dove" (38:14).
"And mourn sore like doves" (59:11).

j. **"To turn every man" (*Ish Panah*) No parallel elsewhere.**

And as sheep that no man taketh up; they shall every man turn to his own people" (13:14).

"All we like sheep did go astray; we have turned everyone to his own way" (53:6).

k. **"And I have brought down"** *(Ve-orid)* **An expression used exclusively by Isaiah.**
"And I have brought down the inhabitants" (10:13).
"And I have brought down their life blood on the earth" (63:6).

l. **"Branch"** *(Netzer)*
"The branch of my planting" (11:1 and 60:21).

m. **"Nothingness"** *(Tohu)*—**Other than in Isaiah appears only once in the prophetic writings (1 Sam. 12:21).**
"The city of nothingness (24:10).
"With a thing of nothingness" (29:21).
"The line of nothingness" (34:11).
"Things of nothingness" (40:17).
"As a thing of nothingness" (40:23).
"Wind and nothingness" (41:29).
Also 44:9; 45:18; 49:4;

n. **"The Lord reigneth in Zion"** **Peculiar to Isaiah and some Psalms—Psa. 99 and 102.**
"For the Lord of hosts reigneth in Mount Zion" (24:23).
"That saith unto Zion: Thy Lord reigneth" (52:7).

o. **"The Holy One of Israel"** *(K'dosh Israel)* **The Holy One of Israel, as a designation of God, is peculiar to Isaiah. It appears twelve times in the first part of Isaiah and thirteen in the second part.**
Part 1—1:4; 5:19; 5:24; 10:20; 12:6; 17:7; 29:19; 30:11, 12, 15; 31:1; 37:23
Part 2—41:14, 16, 20; 43:3, 14; 45:11; 47:4; 48:17; 49:7; 54:5; 55:5; 60:9, 14;
Also once **"The Holy One of Jacob"** (29:23).

Isaiah's vision in the temple of the thrice Holy God apparently so impressed itself upon the mind of the prophet that the designation of God as "the Holy One of Israel" became his distinctive mark. Some have called it the signature of Isaiah.

p. **"Nations" - "Peoples"** — *(Goiim - Le-ummin).*
"Come near ye nations, to hear; and hearken ye people" (34:1).

"Let all the nations be gathered together and let the peoples be assembled" (43:9a).

q. **"Deaf — Blind"**

"In that day shall the deaf hear—and the eyes of the blind shall see" (29:18).

"Hear ye deaf, and look ye blind (42:18).

"Who is blind but my servant or deaf as my messenger" (42:19).

r. **"The Lord will say"** *(Yomar Jehovah* instead of *Amar Jehovah)* **No other example in prophetic writings.**

future in the sense of the past (Isa. 1:11, 18; 33:10; 40:1, 25; 44:21; 66:9).

Many more phrases and expressions peculiar to Isaiah and to his individual usage of Hebrew could be quoted. However, the above quotations taken from every section of Isaiah make it clear that all the sixty-six chapters of Isaiah came from the same mind and from the same pen as directed by the same Holy Spirit of God. The phraseology, the individual expressions, the language pattern throughout the book are such as to preclude the possibility of imitation. They are like the whorls of a fingerprint, which match beyond any peradventure. From the beginning to the end, the book of Isaiah bears the fingerprints of one and the same man, Isaiah, the son of Amoz.[2]

2. The Significance of Chapters 36-39

Another indication pointing strongly to the unity of Isaiah is the position of the historical section of Chapters 36-39, which forms a link between the first and the second parts of the book. These four chapters, with the exception of Hezekiah's prayer, are repeated almost verbatim in 2 Kings 18:13—20:19. The statement of 2 Chronicles 32:32 clearly implies that chapters 36-39 were written by the prophet Isaiah:

"Now the rest of the acts of Hezekiah, and his goodness, behold, they are *written in the vision of Isaiah the prophet,* son of Amoz, and in the book of the kings of Judah and Israel" (cf. also 2 Ki. 20:20).

Chapters 36-37 conclude that part of Isaiah which dealt chiefly with the Assyrian menace and God's miraculous deliverance of Jerusalem and Judah from the attempted invasions, first by Rezin of Damascus allied with Pekah of Samaria, and later by the army of Sennacherib.

In chapters 38-39 the prophet relates certain events during the reign of Hezekiah which he foresaw as being a prelude to the future disaster—the Babylonian captivity. Chapter 38 describes the story of Hezekiah's sickness, his prayer for healing, and the answer to his prayer.

The story of Hezekiah's folly is related in chapter 39. In his foolish pride, King Hezekiah showed off his treasures to the Babylonian delegation which presumably came to congratulate him upon his recovery, but in reality to enlist Hezekiah's aid in a revolt against Assyria. After this event Isaiah predicted the tragic end of the house of Hezekiah in Babylonian captivity (39:5-8).

Thus Isaiah 39 forms a natural link between the first and second parts of Isaiah. The Assyrian menace fades away. From now on it is Babylon which casts her grim shadow upon the future destiny of Judah.

3. The Heading of the Book of Isaiah

The vision of Isaiah the son of Amoz which he saw concerning Judah and Jerusalem in the days of Uzziah, Jotham, Ahaz, and Hezekiah, kings of Judah (Isa. 1:1).

The importance of this heading lies in the fact that all the fifteen prophets which are designated in the Hebrew Bible as "the latter prophets" beginning with the book of Isaiah and ending with the book of Malachi, start with a heading in which the name of the prophet is clearly indicated. Sometimes the name of the prophet's father is also mentioned, as in the case of "Isaiah, the son of Amoz" and "Joel the son of Pethuel." Sometimes the period of the prophet's ministry is also indicated, as in the case of Amos, Hosea, Isaiah, Micah and Jeremiah. There is no prophetic book without a heading in which at least the name of the author is clearly mentioned. Even such a tiny, one-chapter book as Obadiah states the name of its author.

Is it then conceivable that a book as extensive and important as Isaiah 40-66 should not mention the name of its author? How could "the Great Unknown" as the critics have called the author or authors of the second part of Isaiah have written the most important prophetic document in all of the Bible, without anybody knowing his name or their names?

To assume that this is exactly what has happened is to add confusion to a mystery. It is preposterous to assume that a people who has so jealously guarded and preserved its sacred Scriptures would include in its canon a book of a completely unknown prophet. Historically and psychologically this is incredible.

4. The Evidence of the Dead Sea Manuscripts

In 1947 in a cave near the Dead Sea among many other manuscripts two complete scrolls of Isaiah were found.

In the opinion of competent scholars these oldest manuscripts of Isaiah originated about 150 B.C. In those manuscripts there is no lacuna or gap between the end of chapter 39 and the beginning of chapter 40. If Isaiah 1-39 were a complete book in itself and chapters 40-66 a later addition, one would naturally expect such a gap. The lack of any hiatus or separation between chapters 39 and 40 proves that the ancient scribe was not aware of any change in authorship or of a break in the continuity of the scroll.

Similarly the Septuagint, the Greek translation of the Old Testament which was begun in the third century B.C. and was obviously based on a much older Hebrew manuscript, does not indicate any discontinuity between the first and second sections of Isaiah.

5. The Testimony of Ecclesiasticus

In the extra-canonical book of Ecclesiasticus (C. 180 B.C.) we find this significant testimony concerning Isaiah:

> For Hezekiah did that which pleased God, and walked valiantly in the way of David his father, which Isaiah the great prophet and faithful in the sight of God, had commanded him. In his days the sun went backward, and he lengthened the king's life.
> With a great spirit he saw the things that are to come to pass at last, and comforted the mourners in Zion. He showed what should come to pass for ever, and saw things before they came (Ecclesiasticus 48:25-28).

Jesus ben Sirach, the author of Ecclesiasticus, alludes to several references in the first and second parts of Isaiah, and attributes them all to the same author, namely Isaiah.

The reference to "the sun went backward" is recorded in Isaiah 38:7,8. The words of Ecclesiasticus "and he comforted them that mourn in Zion" point to the opening words of Isaiah 40:1 "Comfort ye, comfort ye my people" and also to the words in 61:2b, 3—"to comfort all that mourn, to appoint unto them that mourn in Zion, to give unto them beauty for ashes, the oil of joy for mourning, the garment of praise for the spirit of heaviness."

The words of Ecclesiasticus 48:27 "with a great spirit he saw the things that are to come to pass at last," obviously allude to the words "I have even from the beginning declared it to thee: before it came to pass I showed it to thee" (Isa. 48:5a) and to similar passages in 48:3 and 6.

It is apparent that the author of Ecclesiasticus, Jesus ben Sirach, considered chapters 40-66 as well as the preceding chapters as coming from the prophet Isaiah.

6. The Evidence of an Unbroken Tradition

For twenty-five centuries Jewish and Christian tradition were unanimous in attributing the whole book of Isaiah to one person only, Isaiah the son of Amoz. Some scholars have in the past argued that Ibn Ezra, the famous 11th century Jewish Bible commentator had considered Isaiah chapters 40-66 as a post-Isaianic document. However, Ibn Ezra himself seems to contradict this. Commenting on the words 41:14: "I helped thee," (past tense), Ibn Ezra explains:

Here a verb in the past is employed instead of one in the future — the reason being that all decrees to take place in the future are regarded as though they were already in operation. Futhermore the past and future utterances concern human creatures only [and not God].

On Isaiah 45:4, "I have called thee by thy name; I have surnamed thee, though thou hast not known me." — Ibn Ezra comments: "He speaks to one not yet created." It is therefore evident that Ibn Ezra did not attribute chapters 40-66 to a "Second Isaiah."[3]

The theory of the composite nature of the book of Isaiah started about 150 years ago, and has no support in ancient tradition which unanimously attributed the whole book to one and the same author.

7. The Testimony of the New Testament

To the Bible-oriented Christian the evidence of the New Testament, especially of Christ Himself, is final and conclusive, and that for two reasons:

a. Primarily because of the inspired and authoritative character of the New Testament.

b. Because the testimony of the New Testament concerning the unity of Isaiah forms an additional strong link in the unbroken tradition jointly held by Christians and Jews. Even Jewish scholars point out this fact in support of the unity of Isaiah.[4] The New Testament quotes more frequently from the book of Isaiah than from all other books of the Old Testament put together. Invariably Christ Himself and His apostles quote from Isaiah with such introductory formulas as: "Isaiah the prophet," "The prophet Isaiah," "Isaiah prophecied," "Isaiah says," "Well spake the Holy Ghost through Isaiah the prophet," etc.

The New Testament refers in twenty-one places to the book of Isaiah, mentioning the prophet by name:

Matthew - Isaiah		Mark - Isaiah	
3:3	40:3	1:2-3	40:3-5
8:17	53:4	7:6	29:13
12:17, 18	42:1		
13:14	6:9, 10		
15:7, 8	29:13		

Luke - Isaiah		John - Isaiah	
3:4	40:3-5	1:23	40:3
4:17	61:1, 2	12:38	53:1
		12:39, 40;	6:9, 10
		12:41	6:1

Acts - Isaiah		Romans - Isaiah	
8:28-33	53:7, 8	9:27	10:22, 23
		9:29	1:9
		10:16	53:1
		10:20	65:1

In addition there are numerous indirect references or allusions to the book of Isaiah which have not been included in the above list.

It is clear that Christ and the apostles, as well as the Jews of that time, were convinced that the book of Isaiah was composed by the prophet Isaiah and inspired by the Holy Spirit.

There are additional weighty arguments in favor of the unity of Isaiah, but what has been said already should be sufficient for any unprejudiced student of the subject.

Notes: 1. Where the text differs from the King James Version, it has been translated by the author from the Hebrew.

2. The Israeli scholar Rachel Margalioth in her study *The Indivisible Isaiah* (published in 1964 by Sura Institute for Research, Jerusalem) has presented an excellent analysis of the language of Isaiah.

3. See the *Bulletin of the American School of Oriental Research*, No. 110.

4. Rachel Margalioth, *op. cit.*, page 13.

The
Message
of Isaiah

The Historical Background

The message of Isaiah is best understood in the context of the place and times in which the prophet lived. Isaiah grew to manhood during the long reign of King Uzziah (792-740 B.C.), who is described as a "good king." However, Uzziah's weakness was his overweening pride and rashness (2 Ki. 15:1-7; 2 Chron. 26:1-23).

A successful ruler and administrator, Uzziah, also known as Azariah, restored the Red Sea port of Elath to Judah. He subdued the Ammonites and the Philistines and developed the agricultural and domestic industry of Judah, and expanded her trade with foreign lands. During his reign Judah prospered, economically and politically. However, the spiritual climate and the moral health of the nation declined, due to religious formalism and ritualism, the corruption of the luxury-loving patricians and the insatiable greed of her merchants and landed gentry. The city laborers and tenant farmers were poor and exploited. Conditions in Judah were similar to those in her sister state of Samaria, as reflected in the books of Amos, Hosea and Micah, and in the historical records of that period.

Outwardly, religion prospered, but the spiritual and moral vigor of the nation was seriously undermined by the corrupting forces within and the paganizing influences from without. At the same time, in spite of all the corroding forces and influences there was in Judah a healthy national core—"the remnant." Isaiah looked upon this spiritual remnant "the holy seed," as the hope of Israel's regeneration and revival (Isa. 6:13, 1 Ki. 19:18, Rom. 11:5).

The military and material success and the economic prosperity of Judah apparently went to the head of Uzziah. Not satisfied with his exalted position as king, he sought to usurp the functions and prerogatives of the priestly office. "But when he was strong, his heart was lifted up to his destruction; for he transgressed against the Lord his God, and went into the temple of the Lord to burn incense upon the altar of incense" (2 Chron. 26:16).

For this sacrilegious act the king was smitten with leprosy. The last years of his life Uzziah lived in isolation, in a specially built small mansion on the outskirts of Jerusalem.[1]

During that period Jotham, the heir apparent, became the actual ruler of Judah, and upon his father's death in 740 B.C. succeeded to the throne.

Some time toward the end of Uzziah's life and during the regency of Jotham, Isaiah entered upon his prophetic mission. We have no clear indication concerning the exact date of this event. Biblical men were not nearly so history-conscious as we are today. Isaiah's consecration, or rather confirmation as prophet (Isa. 6:1) took place the year Uzziah died, probably some time after his entrance upon his ministry (Isa. 1:1).

Judah's political independence and economic prosperity up to the time of Uzziah's death were made possible by Assyria's preoccupation with the military problems to the north and the east of her borders. This political situation gave a number of smaller kingdoms of the Fertile Crescent, including Syria and Palestine, a breathing spell from the ruthless military pressure of Assyria, which sought to consolidate all the lands between the Euphrates and the Nile into one world empire. However, when Tiglathpileser III (745-727) became master of Assyria the situation changed completely. In the Bible Tiglathpileser is also called by his native name Pul (2 Ki. 15:19; 1 Chron. 5:26).

A man of obscure and humble origin but adventurous spirit, Tiglathpileser usurped the throne and managed to vanquish his neighbors to the north and south of the Assyrian empire. This enabled him to turn his attention to the kingdoms of west Asia adjacent to his territories. Before he could realize his ambition to create a great world empire, Tiglathpileser had to vanquish all those independent kingdoms which lay in his path. Among the most important of these were Hamath and Arpad in Northern Syria, Damascus, Sidon, Tyre, Samaria, Judah, the city-kingdoms of the Philistines, Moab, and above all the famed ancient kingdom of Egypt.

After defeating Hamath and Arpad, Tiglathpileser subdued Rezin of Damascus (750-732 B.C.), and his ally Menahem of Samaria (752-742). The two were permitted for a time to retain their kingdoms as vassals of Assyria. Menahem was compelled to pay Tiglathpileser 1000 talents of silver (2 Ki. 15:19). In his annals Tiglathpileser boasted:

> As for Menahem (Mennihimmu) terror overwhelmed him . . . He fled and submitted to me. Silver, colored woolen garments, linen garments . . . I received as his tribute . . . I returned him to his palace and imposed tribute upon him.[2]

The Assyrians were skillful and ruthless warriors who kept all their neighbors in terror. However, their great weaknesses, which eventually caused their downfall, were their extreme cruelty to the vanquished, and their lack of administrative skill. Everything rested on sheer brute force without any consideration for the suffering or the outraged dignity of the defeated. Consequently the vassal provinces and tributary kingdoms were restless and rebellious, always on the lookout for an opportunity to cast off the yoke of their hated masters. They plotted and combined in ineffective alliances, which in turn provided the Assyrians with further excuses for renewed invasions and annexations of the rebellious kingdoms. Fierce warlords, the Assyrians were poor diplomats and administrators. In this respect the Babylonians, the Persians and later the Greeks and the Romans were much superior to them.

During the reign of Pekah of Samaria (740-732) Tiglathpileser dismembered the kingdom of Samaria, annexing Galilee and Gilead, and deported the tribes beyond the Jordan into Assyria (2 Ki. 15:27-31).

When Ahaz succeeded to the throne (735-715) Rezin of Damascus, in alliance with Pekah of Samaria, invaded Judah (2 Ki. 16:5-6, Isa. chapters 7-8), probably in the hope of forcing Ahaz into a coalition against the Assyrians.

Frightened out of his wits, Ahaz made the fatal mistake of asking help from Tiglathpileser—"the lamb" was inviting the tiger to save him from the wolves! To purchase this assistance Ahaz even made the Assyrian a present of the gold and silver which belonged to the house of God. Yet, as the Biblical chronicler later tersely recorded "but he (Tiglathpileser) helped him not" (2 Chron. 28:21). In 732 Tiglathpileser took Damascus, and according to the custom of that period, deported its population into Assyria.

When later Hoshea, the last king of Samaria (732-722 B.C.), failed to pay his annual tribute to Assyria and conspired with Egypt, Shalmaneser (727-722) laid siege to Samaria for a period of three years. The city was eventually captured by his able successor, Sargon II in 722. Thus the independent kingdom of Samaria, which lasted a little over 200 years, (930-722 B.C.) came to a tragic end (2 Ki.17:4-6).

The Samaritans

Many of the most prominent inhabitants of Samaria (according to Assyrian records, 27,290 Samaritans) were deported to the northern provinces of Assyria. In their place Sargon sent some of his conquered subjects to repopulate Samaria. The newly-arrived colonists retained their own native gods, but also accepted the Law of Moses and the worship of Jehovah. They also introduced certain changes into the Pentateuch, asserting that Mt. Gerizim and not Jerusalem was the God-appointed center of worship. Eventually they became a schismatic group, half Israelitish, half pagan.

So these nations feared the Lord, and served their graven images, both their children, and their children's children: as did their fathers, so do they unto this day (2 Ki. 17:41).

In time the newcomers intermarried with the still numerous Israelites who were never deported from Samaria (Jer. 40:7; 41:5), and formed a new nation, known to this day as the Samaritans. Samaria was a fertile ground for the development of a schismatic people, because there were ancient traditions of rivalry between the northern tribes and the inhabitants of Judah, who naturally considered themselves as the guardians of the temple and of the holy city Jerusalem.

The new Samaritan nation with their rival cult and center of worship, Mount Gerizim, from the very beginning became a thorn in the side of the Jews. The hostile relations between the Samaritans and the Jews are reflected in the book of Nehemiah and especially in the Gospels (John 4:9; 8:48; Lk. 9:51-53).

A small remnant of the Samaritans, about 300 people, have survived to the present day, and live in Israel, around Nablus. They have preserved their own ancient scrolls of the Law, a Samaritan priesthood and some of the Biblical sacrifices and ceremonies. Even as in the days of Christ (John 4:9), they still do not mingle with the Jews.

Long before Samaria ceased to be an independent people, they became morally corrupted and spiritually corroded, until the judgment of God fell upon that hapless nation.

Summing up the cause of the downfall of the northern kingdom, the Biblical historian records:

> For the children of Israel walked in all the sins of Jeroboam which he did; they departed not from them; until the Lord removed Israel out of his sight, as he had said by all his servants the prophets. So was Israel carried away out of their own land to Assyria unto this day (2 Ki. 17:22-23).

With the fall of Samaria the fate of Judah was sealed. It was only a question of time. Nevertheless the inhabitants of Judah carried on as if the day of judgment would never come. Isaiah expressed the mood of the people in these never-to-be-forgotten words: "Let us eat and drink; for tomorrow we shall die" (Isa. 22:13).

Looking back at the events in the divided kingdom during the lifetime of Isaiah, we are amazed at the lack of insight and statesmanship on the part of the leaders of Israel. However, the history ot many nations shows the same shortcomings leading to the same disastrous consequences. Unfortunately Israel, in spite of her sacred heritage, was no exception. Practical politics was substituted for divine guidance and wisdom. Only Spirit-filled men like Amos, Hosea, Isaiah and Micah were granted a clear understanding of their times. They warned their people about the coming day of judgment and called to *teshubah* — a complete turnabout in every area of national and personal life. But the prophets remained "a voice crying in the wilderness." Isaiah was the angry prophet of an outraged God. But he was also the prophet of hope, of divine compassion and redemption.

With respect to national politics Isaiah and later Jeremiah counseled against foreign entanglements. He warned his people that Israel's salvation can only come from her God and not from foreign alliances. Earlier in his prophetic ministry Isaiah severely rebuked Ahaz for calling upon the Assyrian to rescue him from his adversaries, Rezin of Damascus and Pekah of Samaria. In the eyes of the prophet this was an act of impiety and a vote of "no confidence" in Jehovah (Isa. 8:5-8). Later the prophet Isaiah was just as outspoken an opponent of an alliance between Judah and Egypt against Sennacherib of Assyria:

> Woe to them that go down to Egypt for help; and stay on horses, and trust in chariots, because they are many; and in horsemen, because they are very strong; but they look not unto the Holy One of Israel, neither seek the Lord! . . . Now the Egyptians are men, and not God; and their horses flesh, and not spirit. When the Lord shall stretch out his hand, both he that helpeth shall fall, and he that is holpen shall fall down, and they shall fail together . . . Turn ye unto him from whom the children of Israel have deeply revolted (Isa. 31:1,3,6).

Only the Lord Himself could deliver Judah, was the cry of Isaiah: "For through the voice of the Lord shall the Assyrian be beaten down, which smote with a rod" (Isa. 30:31).

But the rulers of Israel and Judah looked upon Isaiah as a visionary and a meddler. They were "the practical politicians." So they did what statesmen and politicians always do; they looked to their military defenses and made alliances with their neighbors, according to what, in their view, the political situation required. The disastrous and short-sighted foreign policies of the divided kingdoms were only a complement to the moral decay which was wasting the national health of Israel. Seemingly a deeply religious people, their national conduct amounted to practical atheism or paganism.

In vain did Isaiah pour out his heart warning his people. His words fell upon deaf ears which could not hear, and upon fat-encrusted hearts which could not or would not perceive. Judah's punishment was that God sent upon his people a judicial hardening of heart so that repentance and healing became impossible. The nation had to go through the cleansing experience of divine judgment: "Make the heart of this people fat, and make their ears heavy, and shut their eyes; lest they see with their eyes, and hear with their ears, and understand with their heart, and convert, and be healed" (Isa. 6:10).

Israel's doom, and later Judah's, became inevitable. However, the prophet's earnest pleading stayed the hand of God for yet another century, and so Jerusalem was spared from being ravaged by Sennacherib in 701 B.C.

And yet even amidst Isaiah's gloomiest predictions of judgment and doom, there was always in his message a bright ray of hope. That hope was centered around a faithful remnant and the God-given redeemer who would grow out of the stem of Jesse. Upon these rested the prophet's faith in Israel's restoration and in the final establishment of the glorious Kingdom of God.

In the meantime the history of Judah was running its natural course. It alternated between a few godly rulers and many evil ones "who did not that which was right in the sight of the Lord."

The reign of the ungodly and wicked Ahaz, who hastened the downfall of Judah, was followed by the rule of the God-fearing, but rather weak and imprudent king Hezekiah. Under his reign Sennacherib's army invaded Judah and captured most of her fortified cities with the exception of Jerusalem. The Assyrian annals thus recorded the situation of Judah at that time from the standpoint of Sennacherib:

> As for Hezekiah the Jew, who did not submit to my yoke, 46 of his strong walled cities, as well as the smaller cities in their neighborhood . . . I besieged and took . . . Himself like a caged bird I shut up in Jersusalem, his royal city . . . As for Hezekiah, the terrifying splendor of my majesty overcame him . . . and his mercenary troops deserted him.

In answer to the prayers of Isaiah and Hezekiah's humbling of himself, God miraculously delivered Jerusalem and destroyed the Assyrian army by sending a plague upon them (701 B.C.). Yet Hezekiah's fatal weakness, his imprudent pride, was his undoing, even as it was of his great-grandfather, Uzziah, about half a century before.

> But Hezekiah rendered not again according to the benefit done unto him; for his heart was lifted up: therefore there was wrath upon him, and upon Judah and Jerusalem. Notwithstanding Hezekiah humbled himself for the pride of his heart, both he and the inhabitants of Jerusalem, so that the wrath of the Lord came not upon them in the days of Hezekiah (2 Chron. 32:25, 26).

For another century Judah was able to preserve a precarious semblance of independence. It came to an end when Babylon, once a province of Assyria, became master of the vast empire of Mesopotamia stretching from the Gulf of Persia almost to the banks of the Nile.

Isaiah, Israel's prophet par excellence, for over half a century, was an eyewitness and participant in many of these events. What his physical eyes could not see, the Spirit of God revealed to him in remarkable detail. The oracles and prophecies of Isaiah were in an astonishing manner confirmed by subsequent history.

Notes: 1. Israeli archaeologists recently uncovered in Ramath Rahel, a suburb of Jersusalem, a small mansion suitable for a single person's residence. It is believed to have been the home of the leper king Uzziah.
2. D. D. Luckenbill, *Ancient Records of Assyria and Babylonia* Volume I (Chicago, 1926), section 772.
3. Luckenbill, *op. cit.*, Volume II, Section 240.

The Major
Themes
of Isaiah

Most of the major prophetic themes find a forceful and majestic expression in the book of Isaiah.

1. There is the frequent indictment of the nation's sinful condition, reflected in her religious and moral decay.

2. Israel's unfaithfulness to God will bring about divine chastisement in the form of a foreign invasion and captivity. The prophet refers to this chastisement as "the day of the LORD" (2:12, 13:6, 9 etc.).

3. The neighbors of Israel whom God is using as an instrument of punishment, will in turn be judged for their arrogance and cruelty (1:24; 10:5-13; 13:11-13).

4. Behind God's judgment there is also His eternal love and the gracious purpose of the restoration of Israel (4:5, 6; 24:23; 25:10; 26:1; 31:5; 32:6).

5. Israel's national survival and regeneration will come through a "holy seed" — the faithful remnant (6:13; 8:18; 10:20-22).

6. The Messiah and His Kingdom. "In the latter days" God will raise up a Messianic King, "a branch of the stem of Jesse, upon whom shall rest the spirit of the Lord" (11:1-10). This Messianic King will be the divinely ordained Prince of Peace, the ruler over the Kingdom of God (2:1-3; 9:5,6; 25:3).

In the second part of Isaiah the Messianic King takes on the character of the suffering and obedient Servant, who is contrasted with Israel, God's disobedient and blind servant.

7. Eschatological and apocalyptic prophecies concerning the ultimate triumph of the Kingdom of God. The vision of a redeemed Israel, and

of a regenerated humanity, serving Jehovah and living in peace with one another.

These varying strands of prophecy are woven with great force and sublime faith into the message of Isaiah. For sheer beauty of language and eloquence, Isaiah has no peer among the prophets. In his notes on Isaiah, Barnes wrote: "No man can be a close student of Isaiah and remain an infidel; no man can study his writing with prayer, who will not find his faith confirmed, his heart warmed, his mind elevated and purified, and his affections more firmly fixed on the everlasting beauty of God."[1]

Isaiah's language is terse, his metaphors and similes are most appropriate to the occasion. He exhibits a marked fondness for alliterations and for the play on words, most of which are unfortunately lost in translation. As much as possible, we shall seek to draw the attention of the reader to these characteristics of the book.

In Isaiah Biblical prophecy reached its inspired climax. What Demosthenes was to Greek oratory, Isaiah was to Hebrew prophecy. He was God's voice to Israel, the conscience of the nation, the herald of the Messiah and of His universal Kingdom. Isaiah's vision burst asunder the narrow confines of national Israel and bequeathed to all of mankind a sacred and enduring patrimony.

For many centuries Isaiah has been known as "the Old Testament evangelist" and his prophecies have been described as "the Gospel according to Isaiah." The prophet Isaiah was more often on the lips of our Lord and of His apostles than any other prophet.

Hebrew Parallelisms

Each of the prophecies of Isaiah is a complete oracle in itself, fashioned in the characteristic form of Hebrew poetry — the parallelism, which is a unit of thought. Parallelisms are either synonymous or antithetic. In the synonymous parallelism, the thought of the first line is amplified in the second line:

And I will give children for their princes
And babes shall rule over them (Isa. 3:4).

In the antithetic parallelism, the thought of the first line is a pair of contrasting ideas paralleled in the second line by another pair of contrasting ideas.

Woe unto them that call good evil, and evil good
That put darkness for light and light for darkness (Isa. 5:20).

Classic Hebrew poetry does not use rhyme, but employs rhythm and meter. Several verses, usually two or more, form one strophe. This strophic system of Hebrew poetry is sometimes helpful in the understanding of the text where the meaning may not be quite clear.

The Hebrew Text of Isaiah

In spite of minor differences in the ancient manuscripts of Isaiah, the Hebrew text has been preserved with remarkable fidelity. The slight variations which exist are chiefly due to the error of copyists.

However, Biblical scribes or copyists, "the *Sopherim*", have always been (and still are today) highly trained and dedicated professional men who did their work with great care and painstaking devotion. They considered their occupation as a sacred trust. One error in transcription might render a whole book unfit for public use in temple or synagogue.

Thus the Jews have proved themselves as faithful guardians of the Old Testament Scriptures, meriting the gratitude of all who cherish the Word of God as their most precious spiritual heritage.

It is interesting to note that the two manuscripts of Isaiah recently (1947) discovered in the Qumran caves, which are over a thousand years older than any previously known text of Isaiah, are essentially the same as the Massoretic text (916 A.D.) The two Qumran texts of Isaiah known as 1QIsaᵃ and 1QIsaᵇ go back to the first century B.C.

In this study of Isaiah we plan to make our own translation of the book and to provide suitable explanations and comments, which will be exegetical and not homiletical in character.

We shall follow closely the traditional Hebrew text of Isaiah, seeking to avoid either extreme of a literal but stilted translation, or the pitfalls of a loose paraphrase which sometimes, instead of illuminating the original meaning of the text, may obscure it by substituting the translator's own interpretation. We shall seek to recapture not only the original sense of the words of Isaiah, but as much as this is possible, also the mood, and the spirit of the prophet's message.

Note 1. *Notes on the Old Testament — Isaiah* Vol. I by Albert Barnes, Baker Book House, Grand Rapids, Mich., page 2.

79

Some Problems
of Biblical
Chronology

What sinews are to the body, chronology is to history. It binds the disjointed events of history into one integrated and intelligible whole. Chronology tells us not only *when* certain historical events took place, but may also help us understand *why* these events occurred. To the student of Biblical history and the prophetic writings, the knowledge of chronology is essential.

The very first verse of Isaiah immediately poses the question of chronology. "The vision of Isaiah the son of Amoz, which he saw concerning Jud. and Jerusalem in the days of Uzziah, Jotham, Ahaz, and Hezekiah kings of Judah" (Isa. 1:1).

Right away we have to answer the question, when did these kings reign?

As soon as we seek to answer this question we are confronted with the fact that we do not have sufficient data in the Bible for a satisfactory answer. What is even more disconcerting is that the data which we have, if not studied carefully seem to be contradictory. Nowhere in the Old Testament do we have one absolute date from which we might be able to start our calculations either backward or forward.

It is only as we cross-check the chronological data of the Scriptures with those of Israel's neighbors that we are enabled to arrive at a fairly accurate chronology of Biblical events.

For the period of the divided kingdoms of Israel and Judah, most of the chronological data are recorded in the books of Kings and Chronicles, and in the historical portions of the prophets. However this information is not complete or precise. When, for instance, we read about the beginning of the reign of Azariah-Uzziah we are at once confronted with a multitude of unanswered questions which need to be carefully considered.

> In the twenty and seventh year of Jeroboam king of Israel began Azariah son of Amaziah king of Judah to reign.
> Sixteen years old was he when he began to reign, and he reigned two and fifty years in Jerusalem (2 Ki. 15:1,2).

Here are some of the intricate questions which these two verses pose:

1. When exactly in the twenty-seventh year of Jeroboam's reign over Israel did Azariah-Uzziah become king of Judah? Was it during the first month of Jeroboam's reign over Israel, or during any of the subsequent months of that year? If we multiply the potential difference by the twenty-three kings who ruled over Judah, that may add up to a considerable number of years.

"The Accession Year" System

2. The second question is how did the kings of Israel and Judah count their regnal years? Was it the same in both countries? We know now that this was not the case. In Israel they used a system of reckoning which is called "the accession year system." This meant that the first year of a king's reign was counted, not from the year he became king, but from the beginning of the new year after he became king. Thus a king's reign in Israel might be counted in his land as five years, but in Judah where the regnal year began from the day when the king came to the throne, the same five years would be counted as six.

3. Which system did the Biblical historians of the books of Kings and Chronicles employ when relating the regnal years of the kings of Israel and of Judah? Apparently they used both systems, depending on whether the king in question reigned over Israel or Judah, and on the system which at a particular time was used in that kingdom.

When the two different systems of regnal years, the accession and the non-accession system, were employed over a long period of time. The result was a considerable difference in the combined number of years attributed to the reigns of the kings of Israel and the kings of Judah as recorded in the book of Chronicles and in the book of Kings respectively.

The official record for Judah was "the book of the chronicles of the kings of Judah" (1 Ki. 14:29; 15:7, 23; 2 Ki. 8:23; 12:19, etc.).

For Israel the official record was "the book of chronicles of the kings of Israel" (1 Ki. 14:19; 15:31; 16:5, etc.).

Later after both kingdoms came to their unhappy end, both records were combined into one history of the Hebrew kingdoms called "the book of the kings of Judah and Israel" (2 Chron. 16:11; 25:26; 27:7; 28:26, etc.).

4. "Sixteen years old was he (Uzziah) when he began to reign" (2 Ki. 15:2). We are not informed whether Uzziah-Azariah was exactly sixteen years old, or sixteen years and a certain number of months. The difference multiplied by the number of kings who reigned in Judah as we have previously mentioned could amount to a considerable number of years.

The Question of Co-Regency

5. "He reigned fifty-two years in Jerusalem." Again we are not told expressly whether or not the fifty-two years covered the whole period of his reign including the last years when he was smitten with leprosy "unto the day of his death, and dwelt in a separate house. And the king's son was over the house, judging the people of the land" (2 Ki. 15:5).

Apparently Jotham took over the duties of kingship during the last years of Uzziah as co-regent and became king upon the death of his father. In other words, the question of co-regency and its effect on the chronological records of the Old Testament is not completely clear. However, in this particular case it is obvious that the fifty-two years of Uzziah's reign included the period of Jotham's co-regency.

The Different Calendars of Israel and Judah

6. Another question which needs to be answered is this: Were the years of the northern kingdom identical with those of Judah? There are numerous indications that they were not. In Israel the new year began in the spring, the first day of the month of Nisan and lasted to the beginning of the next Nisan (March/April). It was a Nisan-Nisan year.

In Judah the year started in the fall, the first day of Tishri and lasted to the beginning of next Tishri (September/October), a Tishri-Tishri year.

7. Another question is: How does the Biblical year compare with our own year?

The Hebrews following the Assyrian and the Babylonian calendar used the lunar year, consisting of twelve lunar months. Each month which began with the new moon, until the next new moon, lasted 29 days, 44 minutes, 2.8 seconds. To compensate for the difference between the lunar year and the solar year of 365 days and 6 hours and some minutes, an extra month was intercalated usually every seven years. That extra month was called "the second Adar." The Jews of today still use the same calendar.

We have analyzed the brief passage concerning the reign of king Uzziah, during whose reign Isaiah grew up (2 Ki. 15:1-5; 2 Chron. 26:1-3), in order to demonstrate some of the problems which are inherent in Biblical chronology. The further we go back into the distant past, the more uncertain Biblical chronology becomes.

Fortunately the difficulties of Biblical chronology have been greatly eased by the archeological discoveries of the past 150 years, which have enabled us to correlate Biblical data with the historical records of the Assyrians, the Babylonians, and the Egyptians.

The Eponym Lists

Of special importance to the historian are the so-called Assyrian eponym lists. The Assyrians had a custom of naming each year after some high government official, an outstanding priest, governor of a province, or the king himself. This would be similar to an American system which would count the years by her prominent public figures. Under such a system we might have had, "the year of George Washington" "the year of Benjamin Franklin" or "the year of Abraham Lincoln."

Such public figures in Assyrian history were known as eponyms or limmu. A considerable number of eponym lists have been preserved to the present time. The oldest of these eponym lists go back to the 10th century B.C.

The Canon of Ptolemy

Another important help for establishing the exact dates of many ancient events in the Near East is the Canon of Ptolemy. Ptolemy (70-161 A.D.) was an outstanding Greek scholar, an astronomer, geographer and historian. His famous Canon starts with the reign of Nabonassar in Babylon, 747 B.C. It continues with the reigns of the rulers of Babylon, of Persia, of the Greeks and the Romans up to the time of Emperor Antoninus Pius, 138-167.

In this Canon Ptolemy records over eighty solar and lunar eclipses and planetary positions which make it possible to establish with complete accuracy when those astronomical phenomena took place. A key date in the Canon of Ptolemy is the eclipse of the sun which took place in the month of Simanu, in the eponym of Bur-Sagale, which according to astronomical calculations, took place June 15, 763 B.C. With this date fixed with absolute accuracy it has been possible to provide a reliable chronology for the various eponyms from 891 B.C.-648 B.C. It then became possible to establish dependable Biblical chronology by synchronizing certain events recorded in the Old Testament and referred to in the historical records of the Assyrians.[1]

One such important date was that of the capture of Jerusalem, which according to the records of Nebuchadnezzar, took place the second day of Adar; this corresponds to March 16, 597 B.C.[2] However, the precise date of the final destruction of Jerusalem and of the Holy Temple has not been fixed with complete certainty. Jewish tradition dates this event the 9th of Ab (July/August) 586 B.C. Many scholars accept this date (e.g. Thiele), while William F. Albright and others calculate the destruction of the Temple to have occurred one year earlier.[3]

Because the Biblical year overlaps our calendar year, Old Testament events are often dated in dual form, for example: Destruction of the

Temple 587/86 B.C. For the sake of simplicity we have retained the single form of dates. Example: "Temple destroyed - 586 B.C."[4]

Notes:
1. For a detailed discussion of the involved problems of Old Testament chronology we highly recommend the important work of Prof. Edwin R. Thiele: *The Mysterious Numbers of the Hebrew Kings*, Eerdmans Publishing Co., Grand Rapids, Michigan. Revised edition 1965.

2. Thiele — *op. cit.* p. 196.

3. W. F. Albright "The Chronology of The Divided Monarchy of Israel," Bulletin of the American Schools of Oriental Research 100, 1945, pp. 16-22. Also W. F. Albright, *Archeology of Palestine*.

4. For further study of Old Testament chronology we also suggest the following works: The articles about Biblical Chronology, Assyria, Babylonia, Persia, and The Old Testament Calendar in the *New Bible Dictionary* New edition Intervarsity Fellowship, London, 1962. D. J. Wiseman *Chronicles of Chaldean Kings*, 1956.

Chronological Tables
of The Kingdoms
# of Judah and Israel

(Approximate dates)

Before the Division

Saul   1025 - 1010 B.C.

David   1010 - 971 B.C.

Solomon 971 - 931 B.C.

THE DIVIDED KINGDOMS

ISRAEL		JUDAH		DAMASCUS		ASSYRIA	
Jeroboam 931-910 B.C.		Rehoboam		Rezon	935 B.C.	Ashurnasirpal	
Nadab	910-909		931-913 B.C.				883-859 B.C.
Baasha	909-886	Abijah	913-911				
Elah	886-885	Asa	911-870				
Zimri (7 days)	885	Jehoshaphat	870-848				
Tibni	885-880			Benhadad I—880-843		Shalmanesser III	
Omri	880-874						859-824 B.C.
Ahab	874-853						
Ahaziah	853-852	Jehoram	848-841			Shamsi-Adad V	
Jehoram	852-841	Ahaziah	841				823-810 B.C.
Jehu	841-814	Athaliah	841-835	Hazael	843-796	Samimuramat 810-805	
Jehoaz	814-798	Joash	835-796			Adadnirari III 805-782	
Jehoash	798-782	Amaziah	796-767	Benhadad II-796-760			
Jeroboam II	782-753	Uzziah	Azaria			Shalmaneser IV	
Zachariah	753-752		767-740				781-772
Shallum 752		(Co-regent from				Ashurdan III, 772-755	
	(1 Month)	791)				Ashurnirari V 754-745	
Menahem	752-742	Jotham	740-735	Rezin	760-732	Tiglathpileser III	
Pekahia	742-740	(Co-regent from 750)					745-727 B.C.
Pekah	740-732	Ahaz	731-715	Damascus Captured		Shalmaneser V	
Hoshea	732-722						727-722 B.C.
Samaria captured	722				732	Sargon II	722-705
by Assyrians		Hezekiah	715-686			Sennacherib	705-681

JUDAH		ASSYRIA	
Manasseh	686-642	Esarhaddon	681-669
Amon	642-640	Ashurbanipal II	696-627 B.C.
Josiah	640-609	Ashuretililani	627-620
Jehoahaz	609	Assyrians driven out from	
		Babylon	625 B.C.
Jehoakim	609-597	Sinshariskun	620-612
		Fall of Assur	614
Jehoachin	597	Ashuruballit II	612-610
Jerusalem captured by Nebu-		Fall of Nineveh	612 B.C.
chadnezzar 597 (March 15)		End of Assyrian Empire 609 B.C.	

KINGS OF BABYLON AND PERSIA

Nabopolassar	625-605 B.C.
Nebuchadnezzar	604-562
Evil Merodach or Amel Marduk	561-560
Nergal-shar-usher	559-556
Nabonidus	556-539
Cyrus captures Babylon	539
End of Babylonian Empire	
Cyrus	539-530
Cambyses	530-522
Pseudo-Smerdis	522-521
Darius I	521-486
Xerxes I	486-464
Artaxerxes I	464-423
Darius II	423-404
Artaxerxes II	404-359
Ochus	358-338
Arses	337-336
Darius III	335-332
Alexander the Great of Macedonia	333-323

MAJOR EVENTS FROM ISAIAH TO THE RETURN FROM EXILE

Isaiah's Consecration	740 B.C.
Judah invaded by Rezin of Damascus and Pekah of Samaria	735
The Tribes Beyond the Jordan carried away by the Assyrians	734
Damascus captured by Tiglathpileser	732
Samaria captured by Sargon and the deportation of Israelites to Assyria	722
Sennacherib's Siege of Jerusalem	701

Isaiah's death (approximately) 686-85
Egypt Conquered by Esarhaddon 676
Fall of Nineveh 612
End of Assyrian Empire 609
Daniel Taken to Babylon by Nebuchadnezzar 605
Jerusalem captured by Nebuchadnezzar
Many Jews including Jehoachin and
Ezekiel exiled .... 597, March 16
Destruction of Jerusalem and Temple
More Jews exiled 586
Cyrus Captures Babylon 539
Cyrus permits Jews to rebuild Jerusalem 538
Zerubbabel returns to Jerusalem 538
Rebuilding of Temple started 537
Temple Completed 516
Ezra Goes to Jerusalem 458
Nehemiah in Jerusalem 445-433

Synopsis
of Chapters 1-39

SECTION I

Chapters 1 - 12   PROPHECIES CONCERNING JUDAH AND
JERUSALEM
Chapter   1: 1   Heading of the book
    2-31   A General Introduction to the book of Isaiah,
Jehovah's Indictment of His People
Chapter   2: 1-5   The Messianic Kingdom
    6-22   Idolatrous Israel will be Judged
Chapter   3: 1-15   The Lord about to Judge the Corrupt Rulers,
Who Oppress the People
    16-26-   The Frivolous and Luxury Loving Women of
Chapter   4: 1   Jerusalem Will Be Humiliated
    2-6   A Messianic Prophecy: A Remnant Will Experi-
ence the Protection of Jehovah
Chapter   5: 1-7   The Song of the Vineyard
    8-23   Six Woes against Common Evils
    24-30   God's Judgment Will Come in the Form of a
Terrible Invasion
Chapter   6: 1-4   Isaiah's Vision of God in the Temple
    5   The Prophet's Confession of his Unworthiness
    6-13   The Consecration and Commission of Isaiah
Chapters 7 - 12   THE BOOK OF IMMANUEL
Prophecies During the Reign of Ahaz
Chapter   7: 1-9   Isaiah's Confrontation with Ahaz
    10-16   The Immanuel Prophecy
    17-25   Invasion Predicted
Chapter   8: 1-4   The Birth of Maher-shalal-hash-baz
    5-22   Prediction of Assyrian Invasion
Chapter   9: 1-7   The Prophecy concerning the Prince of Peace
    8-21   Samaria's Pride and Self-Deception

Chapter 10: 1-6   Woe to the Unrighteous, They Will Soon Be
                       Judged
           5-19   The Arrogant Assyrian, God's Rod of Anger
                       Will Soon Be Broken
           20-27   A Remnant To Be Delivered
           28-34   The Assyrian Invasion Visualized
Chapter 11: 1-16   The Messianic King and His Kingdom
Chapter 12: 1-6   The Song of Redeemed Israel

SECTION II

Chapters 13 - 23   ORACLES CONCERNING ISRAEL'S
                       NEIGHBORS
Chapter 13: 1-22   The Future Destruction of Babylon
Chapter 14: 1-8   Israel's Deliverance and Universal Peace
            9-17   A Taunting Song against Lucifer in Sheol
            18-27   Joy among Captive Nations
                       over Assyria's and Babylon's Downfall
            28-32   The Burden of the Philistines
Chapter 15: 1-7   The Burden of Moab
Chapter 16: 1-5   Moab Exhorted To Show Compassion for Zion
            6-12   Lament over Moab
            13-14   The Prophecy concerning Moab To Be Fulfilled
                       within 3 Years
        17: 1-14   The Burden of Damascus
        18: 1-8   Woe to "the Land beyond the Rivers of
                       Ethiopia"
        19: 1-20   The Burden of Egypt
            21-25   Egypt's and Assyria's Future Partnership,
                       with Israel
        20: 1-6   Assyria To Overrun Egypt and Ethiopia
        21: 1-17   A Series of Burdens against "the Desert,"
                       Dumah and Arabia
Chapter 22: 1-16   The Burden of the Valley of Vision—the Prophet
                       Weeps over Jerusalem's Blindness
            17-25   The Message to Shebna the King's Steward
Chapter 23: 1-18   The Burden of Tyre

SECTION III

Chapters 24 - 27   APOCALYPTIC PROPHECIES
Chapter 24: 1-23   Universal Judgment Prophesied
Chapter 25: 1-12   The Believer's Refuge in Time of Storm
Chapter 26: 1-21   Redeemed Israel's New Song of Praise
Chapter 27: 1-11   An Apocalyptic Vision
            12-13   Israel's Regathering

SECTION IV

Chapters 28 - 35   THE BOOK OF WOES
Chapter 28: 1-13   Prediction of Ephraim's Captivity
         14-28   A Warning to the Inhabitants of Jerusalem
Chapter 29: 1-8   A Message of Woe for Ariel (Jerusalem)
         9-16   Jerusalem Smitten with Blindness and a
                  Perverse Wind
         17-24   A Promise of Healing for the Repentant
Chapter 30: 1-33   Warning against an Alliance with Egypt
Chapter 31: 1-9   The Prophet's Appeal: "Turn ye unto Him
                  from whom the children of Israel have deeply
                  revolted" vs. 6.
Chapters 32-34   A Series of Warnings and Promises of Deliverance
Chapter 35: 1-10   A Vision of Israel's Deliverance and Return from
                  Exile

SECTION V

Chapters 36 - 39   HISTORICAL EVENTS
Chapter 36: 1-3   The Assyrian Invasion during the Reign of
                  Hezekiah
         4-21   Rabshakeh's Blasphemous Threats
         22-
Chapter 37: 4   Hezekiah's Dismay
         5-7   Isaiah's Message to Hezekiah
         8-13   Sennacherib's Arrogant Message to Hezekiah
         14-20   The Prayer of Hezekiah
         21-35   The Lord's Answer
         36-38   Sennacherib's Army Smitten
Chapter 38: 1-22   The Illness and Recovery of Hezekiah
Chapter 39: 1-2   Merodach-Baladan's Embassy and Hezekiah's
                  Folly
         3-8   Isaiah Predicts a Tragic End to Hezekiah's
                  House in Babylonian Captivity

Prophecies Concerning
Judah and Jerusalem

A Corrupt Nation Faces an Outraged God

Isaiah, Chapter 1

Verses 1-9

1. The Vision of Isaiah, the son of Amoz, which he saw
   Concerning Judah and Jerusalem in the days of Uzziah,
   Jotham, Ahaz and Hezekiah, kings of Judah.

2. Hear, O heavens, give ear, O earth
   For the Lord has spoken:
   I have reared sons and raised them up,
   But they have rebelled against me.

3. The ox knows his owner,
   The ass the crib of his master,
   Israel does not know,
   My people do not understand!

4. Ah, sinful nation, a people laden with iniquity,
   Seed of evildoers, sons of corrupters!
   They have forsaken the Lord,
   They have despised the Holy One of Israel,
   They have turned backward.

5. Upon which place will you yet be smitten?
   You will still continue to rebel,
   The whole head is sick,
   The whole heart is diseased.

6. From the sole of the foot even to the head
   There is not a sound spot,
   Only bruises, stripes and running sores,

Not pressed out, nor bound up
And not softened with oil.

7. Your country is devastated, your cities burned with fire,
Your land in your very presence is devoured by aliens
And utterly ruined in the customary manner of aliens.

8. And the daughter of Zion is left
Like a hut in a vineyard,
Like a shack in a melon field
Like a city under siege.

9. Except the LORD of Hosts
Had left us some survivors,
We would have been almost as Sodom
We would have been like Gomorrah.

Analysis of Chapter I.

The first chapter is an introduction to the whole book of Isaiah. It forms a prologue to the whole collection of Isaiah's messages.

Verse 1. The Heading of The Book

Verses 2-9. The nation is charged with gross ingratitude to Jehovah, with apostacy and complete moral corruption.

Verses 10-31. Israel's worship of God is hypocritical and an attempt to cover up her moral perversion and iniquity. There follows a call to repentance before the wrath of God will come upon the whole nation in judgment. Only a repentant remnant shall escape destruction, but the rebels and sinners shall be consumed.

General Comment to Chapter 1

"The vision of Isaiah the son of Amoz, which he saw." In Hebrew the words *"haza"*—to see, and *"hazon"* vision, are expressions which describe spiritual perception. The root is a technical term which refers to a revelation imparted by God to His chosen servants, the prophets. Therefore in our text "the vision of Isaiah" means the revelation which God vouchsafed to the prophet Isaiah. Its meaning is similar to the expression in Revelation 1:1 "The revelation of Jesus Christ which God gave unto him (John). . . ."

"Concerning Judah and Jerusalem." As a native of Jerusalem and citizen of Judah, Isaiah's prophecies are directed primarily to his own native land Judah and its spiritual and political capital Jerusalem. Looking out from the lofty position of the Holy City, Isaiah perceived the destiny of Judah and of her sister state Samaria.

However, Isaiah's vision ranged far beyond the borders of the two states of Judah and Israel and included all mankind as seen from the standpoint of God's eternal purpose and of His future Kingdom.

Nevertheless Israel's ultimate destiny was always in the center of Isaiah's vision. He saw the restoration and redemption of Israel as having redemptive significance for all nations.

This is why Isaiah is important, not only for Israel or for the generation of the prophet, but for all nations and all times.

However, in order to understand correctly the message of Isaiah, we must give full weight to its historical setting and context. To ignore this must inevitably lead to all kinds of distortions and misleading interpretations.

Already the early church fathers tended to spiritualize and to allegorize the prophetic Scriptures, appropriating all the promises of divine favor and blessing to the Christian Church, and leaving the predictions of divine wrath and dire punishment for the Jews. This approach to the Scriptures has for centuries colored the thinking and the beliefs of Christian people in relation to the Jews and their place in the divine economy of redemption. The Church became "the new Israel" or "the true Israel." The Jews became spiritually disinherited.

Here is a typical example of misleading interpretation of prophecy, which unfortunately is still common among Catholic and Protestant theologians. The eminent 19th century Old Testament scholar, Joseph Addison Alexander, in his *Commentary on the Prophecies of Isaiah*, published in Princeton in 1847, expounded that the Israel of the Old Testament was merely the temporal embodiment of the Church. Consequently Isaiah was not addressing himself to historical Israel or Judah, but to the Christian Church of the future! Alexander even rebuked those who dared interpret prophecy in its obvious sense, with these words:

> If this be a correct view of the structure of these prophecies, nothing can be more erroneous or unfriendly to correct interpretation, than the idea which appears to form the basis of some expositions, that the primary object in the Prophet's view is Israel as a race or nation, and that its spiritual or ecclesiastical relations are entirely adventitious and subordinate. The natural result of this erroneous supposition is a constant disposition to give everything a national or local sense. This is especially the case with respect to the names so frequently occurring, Zion, Jerusalem and Judah, all of which, according to this view of the matter, must be understood as meaning nothing more than the hill, the city, and the land, which they originally designate. *This error has even been pushed by some to irrational extreme of making Israel as a race* the object of the promises after their entire separation from the church and their reduction, for the time being, to the same position with the sons of Ishmael and of Esau.[1]

This position, which allocates to Old Testament Israel the same place as Ishmael and Esau has been typical of many Christian scholars for nearly nineteen centuries, and has not been completely overcome even today. This is a part of the heritage which the Roman Catholic Church has bequeathed to the Reformation. First, Israel was politically disinherited by Rome, and later spiritually by the church of Rome. Here lies one of the deep roots of so-called "Christian" anti-Semitism. This misreading of the Old Testament Scriptures has had a baneful effect on Jewish-Christian relations even to the present day.

It was against this attitude of mind that St. Paul, with prophetic foresight, so earnestly pleaded with the early Christians of Rome: "Boast not against the branches, but if thou boast, thou bearest not the root, but the root thee. . . . Be not highminded, but fear" (Rom. 11:18, 20.)

This age-old misinterpretation and misapplication of Scripture has profoundly affected and distorted the thinking of Christians in vital areas of faith, doctrine and conduct. To be properly understood, the Bible must be interpreted in its primary sense wherever this is the obvious meaning, and not spiritualized. Where Isaiah speaks of Judah and Jerusalem, he means Judah and Jerusalem; where he speaks of Israel, he means Israel; where the prophet speaks of the restoration of Israel, he means the restoration of Israel, and not of the Church.

The Word of God is able to stand on its own feet without any support by means of exegetical gymnastics, even when this is supposed to be in the interests of the Bible or of the Church.

There is, however, a true and legitimate link between Israel and the Church; this link is the Messiah of Israel who is also the Head of the Church. The prophetic vision of the Kingdom of God embraces both the Jews and the nations, and Isaiah speaks about it in many places.

It will be our endeavor to interpret the prophecies of Isaiah in their primary sense and obvious meaning, just as they were directed by the prophet to the people of Judah and to all of Israel.

The God of Isaiah and of the prophets is also the God and Father of our Lord Jesus Christ, of whom Isaiah prophesied. This will be our standpoint in the interpretation of the prophecies of Isaiah.

Let us now briefly digress to discuss the manner in which the prophecies of Isaiah were gathered together into one book and later transmitted to posterity. Calvin in his *Commentary on Isaiah,* explained it in the following way:

> After delivering his message orally, the prophet (Isaiah) would compose a written draft of it, and post it on the gates of the Temple where all might become more familiar with it. This written draft would then have been taken by the priest, who preserved it for posterity, despite their ofttimes conflict with the prophets. They would have been the ones responsible for prefixing the title to the book.[2]

However, in view of the well-known conflict between prophet and priest, which sometimes amounted to open hostility (Amos 7:10-13), it seems to us unlikely that the priests would be interested in preserving the writings of the prophets, especially of a prophet so critical as Isaiah. It is more likely that either the prophet himself, or some of his disciples or his close friends collected the orally delivered or written prophecies of Isaiah, which were later published in one scroll. Either Isaiah himself, or one of the later editors also arranged the prophecies in a more or less chronological order, digressing only from this arrangement where other important considerations made it desirable.

We cannot be certain to which period of Isaiah's ministry chapter 1 of his book belongs. The searching and impassioned denunciation of Judah, and the stern call to repentance before the approaching day of divine wrath may have been selected either by the prophet himself or by one of his associates as a fitting introduction to the whole book.

In Isaiah 1:7a ("Your country is devastated, your cities burned with fire, your land is devoured by aliens"), there is a possible clue as to the historical situation of Judah at that time. There were several such situations which fitted Isaiah's description of Judah during that particular period.

There was the terrifying foray of Tiglathpileser into northern Israel in 738 B.C. A few years later (735 B.C.) there was the joint campaign of Rezin of Damascus and of Pekah of Samaria against Ahaz of Judah. Then there was the most devastating invasion of Judah by Sennacherib and his famous siege of Jerusalem in 701 B.C. described by Isaiah himself (Isa. 37:36-38). The last event seems best to fit into Isaiah's picture of Jerusalem at that time.

> And the daughter of Zion is left
> Like a hut in a vineyard
> Like a shack in a cucumber field,
> Like a city besieged   Isaiah 1:8.

This also fits in well with Sennacherib's own account of his invasion of Judah and the siege of Jerusalem.

> As for Hezekiah the Judean, who had not submitted to my yoke, forty-six of his strong cities together with innumerable fortresses and small towns which depended on them, by overthrowing the walls and open attack, by battle engines and battering rams, I besieged, I captured, I brought out from the midst of them and counted as a spoil 200,150 persons, great and small, male and female, horses, mules, asses, camels, oxen and sheep without number. Hezekiah himself I shut up like a bird in a cage in Jerusalem his royal city. . . . The fear of the greatness of my majesty overwhelmed him, even Hezekiah, and he sent after me to Nineveh, my royal city . . . he sent his ambassadors to offer homage.[3]

The above Assyrian record is most enlightening, not only in what it says, but also in that which it passes in silence. There is no hint in the Assyrian record of Sennacherib's hasty retreat from Jerusalem and return to Nineveh. However, Isaiah tells us about the disaster, probably in the form of a plague which befell the hitherto invincible armies of Sennacherib, from which he never recovered (Isa. 37:36-38).

Only divine intervention could have lifted the Assyrian siege of Jerusalem. Consequently the date of 701 B.C. appears to be the most likely time for the prophecy contained in Isaiah chapter 1.

The words "In the days of Uzziah, Jotham, Ahaz and Hezekiah, kings of Judah" (verse 1), give us the approximate length of the prophet's ministry. Assuming that Isaiah began his ministry shortly before the death of Uzziah, 740 B.C. (not after his death, as most commentators maintain) and lasted until the end of Hezekiah's reign (685 B.C.), we arrive at a period of approximately 55 years.

2   The Lord appears as plaintiff against His people Israel charging them with rebellion.

Hear, O heaven, give ear O earth,—in Hebrew
Shimu shamaim, ve-hazini eretz.

These are alliterative words, skillfully employed by the prophet to heighten the sense of outrage. Israel's sin is so enormous, and so disturbing to the divine order of the universe, that no lesser witnesses than heaven and earth will do. This passage reminds us of the song of Moses recorded in Deuteronomy 32:1. It begins in a similar manner:

Give ear, O ye heavens, and I will speak,
And hear, O earth, the words of my mouth.

Both in form and substance Deuteronomy 32 and Isaiah 1 have much in common. In both sections Israel is charged with gross ingratitude, spiritual perversion and iniquity.

The thread of stern rebuke and of constant call to repentance weaves throughout the Old Testament from Moses to Malachi. It is also carried over into the New Testament.

Isaiah makes it emphatically clear that his words are not his own, but those of the Lord Himself. Heaven and earth must listen "for the Lord has spoken."

The charge against the nation is rebellion:

I have reared sons and raised them up
But they have rebelled against me.

The two verbs *"giddalti ve-romammti"* have a dual meaning. They describe the process of bringing up children to full maturity, but they also mean "to make great and of high stature."

Israel's claim to greatness is based not on her own merit or intrinsic greatness, but on what the Lord Jehovah has done for her.

But they have rebelled against me—*"poshu be."*

The words mean literally "transgressed against me," but are often used in a political sense, as when a subject becomes disloyal to his sovereign lord, or a subject nation to its overlords or masters. It should however be noted, that in spite of their rebellion and disloyalty to Him, God still calls them "sons."

3 Even the proverbially dumb animals, such as the ox and the ass, have sufficient sense to understand who is their master and who provides them with their daily food and shelter. By contrast:

Israel does not know,
My people do not understand

Israel lacks both in basic intelligence, such as exhibited even by the ox and the ass, and does not possess their sense of gratitude.

Although Isaiah is chiefly the prophet of Judah, yet he addresses himself on behalf of Jehovah to all of Israel, that is to the whole nation north and south. Divided politically for over two centuries and often fighting against each other, they were nevertheless always conscious of the fact that the division was artificial, and that spiritually they were one nation—Israel. In spite of their rebellion, base ingratitude and sinfulness, God still calls them *"ammi"*—my people. Behind divine indignation there is also a glimmer of His mercy.

4 In verses 2, 3, Jehovah Himself appears as the accuser of His people; now it is the prophet who presses home the charge of rebellion (4-9).
"Hoi Goi hoteh"—Ah, sinful (literally "sinning") nation—
"Hoi Goi" is another of those numerous and favorite alliterations highly favored by Isaiah in order to express outrage or exasperation.

This nation is not only sinful, but has made sinning a habit. Instead of being a *"Goi kadosh,"* a holy nation, they are a *"Goi hoteh"*—a sinful nation, a people weighed down, or laden with iniquity which is pulling them down into an abyss.

The sinful condition of Israel was not just the condition of the prophet's own generation, but resulted from the cumulative effect of long generations of sinners. They were the seed of evildoers, sons of corrupters. They had forsaken Jehovah, they had despised the Holy One of Israel.

Their sin was not merely the result of spiritual indolence, or a passive drifting away from God, but a positive act of defiance and despising "the Holy One of Israel." For the first time we now meet with Isaiah's favorite designation of God, as "the Holy One of Israel," which with a few exceptions, (in Jeremiah and some Psalms), is the peculiar mark of Isaiah. It is quite possible that even the above noted exceptions may have been due to Isaiah's influence.

They have turned backward. Instead of going forward in spiritual growth and maturity they have actually regressed. This nation so singularly privileged and chosen to be *"am segulah"* — a chosen people, instead of growing in the knowledge of their Lord, have gone back to their pagan origins.

In verses 5 and 6 the nation is viewed collectively as a highly diseased body. There is not one sound place left in the whole national body, and yet in their blindness they continue to rebel—inviting further disasters.

5   The King James Version reads:

Why should ye be stricken any more?
Ye will revolt more and more.

Many ancient and modern translators have rendered this passage in a similar fashion. However the Hebrew word *"al-me"* is best *translated* "upon which place" or "where else," because Isaiah views the whole nation as one body. "Why" would have been more naturally expressed in Hebrew with the word *"Lamah,"* as in Isaiah 1:11.

6   The head and the heart are sick, the whole body from head to foot is without a sound spot. It is completely covered with old sores and freshly inflicted running wounds, but still the nation continues to revolt against God.

In this verse we have an interesting bit or *ars medica,* the medical art, as practiced in the days of Isaiah. Bruises, sores and fresh wounds were pressed out to remove dirt and pus, then after being treated with oil to soften swelling and as a soothing agent, the affected part of the body was bound up or bandaged.

7   Having dramatically described in considerable detail the critical condition of the nation, the prophet now proceeds to give us a picture of the tragic situation of the country. It is a land which has been devastated by the repeated invasions and incursions of foreigners, and has in recent years experienced the terrible depredations inflicted by ruthless and powerful neighbors. We have already indicated that verse 7 seems to fit the situation of Judah in the days of Hezekiah soon after Nebuchadnezzar due to divine intervention, withdrew from Jerusalem in 701 B.C., but not before he inflicted upon Judah terrible blows. Many fortified cities were taken by the Assyrians and a great multitude of important people were carried away into captivity. These were blows from which Judah never completely recovered and eventually, after a little more than a century, she succumbed completely to the successors of the Assyrians, the Babylonians. The prophet describing the national catastrophe uses the term *"K'mah-pecheth zarim"*—"Like the overthrow of strangers (or aliens) ,[4] a word which to the Hebrew ear would at once bring to memory "the overthrow of Sodom" (Gen. 19:25-30) . "The overthrow of strangers (or aliens) " was so thorough as to be comparable to that of the cities of the plain.

8   Deprived of her surrounding strongholds and the supporting cities of the Judean kingdom, not to mention the already captured sister state of Samaria, she was isolated and apprehensive about her future.

The daughter of Zion is left
Like a hut in a vineyard
Like a shack in a cucumber field (or melon field)
Like a city under siege.

Isaiah's picture of Jerusalem's helpless situation is striking and vivid. Her strength is no greater than that of a flimsy hut erected for the watchmen of a vineyard or that of a shack in a melon or cucumber field, a common sight in the Holy Land even today.

9   The prophet identifies himself with his own nation saying:

Except the Lord of Hosts
Had left us a few survivors

The King James Version translates the Hebrew word *"sarid"* with "remnant." However, *"sarid"* (sometimes used with a companion word *"pleita"*—fugitives) applies to those who have survived a disastrous battle or a catastrophe, even as Lot and his family survived after the destruction of Sodom and Gomorrah.

The prophet Isaiah used quite a different word for the term "remnant," in Hebrew *"shear"* (Isa. 10:21, 22; 11:11, 16). Isaiah named his own son *"Shear-Yashub"* "A Remnant Shall Return" (Isa. 7:3).

10   Hear the word of the Lord you chieftains of Sodom
Give ear to the law of our God, you people of Gomorrah!

11   What need have I of the multitude of your sacrifices? saith the Lord
I am replete with burnt offerings of rams,
With the fat of fattened animals.
The blood of oxen, of lambs and goats, I desire not.

12   When you come to appear before my face
Who asked you to trample my courts?

13   Bring no more vain offerings,
Incense is an abomination to me.
The new moons and the sabbaths,
The calling of assemblies, I cannot endure.
Iniquity and festive crowds I cannot bear.

14   The new moon, the sabbaths, I cannot stand,
Iniquity and your calling of assemblies my soul hates.
They have become a burden to me,
I am weary from bearing them.

15   When you spread forth your palms [in supplication]
I shall hide my eyes from you.
Even when you do much praying
I do not hear—your hands are full of blood.

16   Wash yourselves, cleanse yourselves,
Remove the evil of your deeds from my sight,
Cease to do evil.

17 Learn to do good, seek judgment,
Restrain the oppressor, do justice to the orphan.
Plead the cause of the widow.

In the Hebrew text, between verses 9 and 10 there is a small open space which is called *"piska"* or a pause. It indicates the end of a passage *"parashah"*. When the next passage begins on the same line following a *piska* this is called a closed *parashah*. When the passage begins on the next line, it is an open *parashah*.

Comment:
10 The verse begins with the same word as verse 2, "hear." In the face of God's anger and approaching judgment, the people are solemnly summoned to hear "the word of the Lord" and "the law of our God." "The word of God" and "the law of God" are equated. The Hebrew word *"Thorah"* usually translated "the law" is more than merely "the law." It is the full revelation of God's will given to Moses and the prophets.

The so-called "Law of Moses" was composed of ritual and moral ordinances, designed to regulate all of a man's life, his relationship to God and to his fellow men. However, man whether ancient or modern, was always inclined to make the ritual and ceremonial aspects of "the law" the center of his religion, ignoring the moral and spiritual intent of "the law." This was true, not only of Israel, but of all religious men in every generation. The prophet's anger was not directed against the religious cult as such, but rather against a mechanical and superficial observance of a ritual without aspiring to conform to the holiness and righteousness of God.

Isaiah previously compared Jerusalem (v. 9) to the desolate cities of Sodom and Gomorrah. Now the prophet compares Jerusalem's spiritual and moral condition to that of those two degraded cities. The rulers and the people of Judah were as sinful and wicked as the people of Sodom and Gomorrah.

Not since the time of Moses had any prophet dared to address himself to his people in such scathing and insulting terms. Isaiah's indictment was designed to cut to the quick, and to challenge their self-esteem and pride. A people whose conscience had been seared by generations of habitual sinning and smug self-satisfaction, had to be made aware of their apostasy and of the wrath of their God. About a century later, the prophet Ezekiel, in a similar manner, compared Jerusalem with Sodom and Gomorrah: "This was the iniquity of thy sister Sodom, pride, fulness of bread and abundance of idleness was in her and in her daughters, neither did she strengthen the hand of the poor and needy" (Ezk. 16:49).

These words have a strangely modern ring to them. They point to Israel's arrogance, overweening pride, to the corrosive influence of too much affluence and leisure, and to the callous indifference of the rich to the plight of what we today would call "the underprivileged" and "the have-nots." Israel's condition was in many respects similar to that of our modern society. Can we escape the destiny of Jerusalem, seeing that the God of Israel is also our God?

11-15 The prophet anticipates the hurt and outraged reaction of his people. He knows that they will point with pride to their religious orthodoxy; to their diligence in offering all the required sacrifices; to their painstaking observance of the sabbath and the feasts; to their faithful participation in the Temple worship, and their numerous prayers. However, the prophet declares that all this has become repugnant to Jehovah. He cannot endure religious orthodoxy and moral depravity. Verses 13-14 seem to be repetitious but their apparent redundance is deliberate. It serves to emphasize how tedious and insufferable all their endless sacrifices, their festive assemblies and even their prayers have become to God.

We would be in error if we assumed that all the religious people of Isaiah's time were hypocrites, or that their prayers were insincere. Their problem went much deeper than that. They had come to believe, just as many other "pious" people in every generation have, that being "religious" and "observant" could replace a holy and humble walk with God, or a righteous and compassionate relationship to their fellow-men, especially to the poor and needy. "Even if you do much praying I do not hear— your hands are full of blood" (v. 15).

The usual stance of the Israelite at prayer was to spread forth his hands, palms upward. However, when these praying hands were covered with blood, God could not hearken to their prayers, but only see innocent blood dripping from their palms. Their very display of piety with blood-stained hands, was itself blasphemy. By their "pious activities," they were unconsciously seeking to reduce Jehovah to the level of the deities of their pagan neighbors, who were as immoral and unconcerned about righteousness as their devotees. All these gods expected of their worshipers was bloody sacrifices and homage. Not so the God of Israel. He who would approach Him must do so only with clean hands and a pure heart.

Up to this point Isaiah was telling his people what the Lord did *not* require of them. Now his approach becomes positive, making clear what God *does* require of them.

16 "Wash yourselves, cleanse yourselves" are synonymous expressions, although each has a somewhat different connotation. *"Rahatzu"*—wash yourselves, refers to physical cleanliness. Here metaphorically speaking, it refers to the removal of the filth of wickedness. The second expression *"hizzaku"*—cleanse yourselves, signifies inward cleanliness. A godly Israelite is one who not only refrains from evil deeds, but one who is also inwardly clean.

17 True righteousness must be expressed in acts of righteousness. Goodness has to be learned and practiced, so that it becomes second nature.

The word for justice employed here is *"mishpat"*—literally "judgment." It is more than mere legal and formal justice, it is the justice which springs from a heart which has been cleansed by the Spirit of God. The oppressor must be restrained and not allowed to become a law unto himself. Only thus can justice prevail. In the Scriptures, the orphan, the widow and the stranger always personify those who in a special way need the protection and compassion of the community. They are the poor, the needy and the helpless. The nation's moral health or sickness could be judged from the way they were treated. The Law of Moses from the very beginning inculcated compassion for them.

Thou shalt neither vex a stranger, nor oppress him;
For ye were strangers in the land of Egypt.
Ye shall not afflict any widow or fatherless child.
If thou afflict them in any wise, and they cry at all unto me,
I will surely hear their cry and my wrath shall wax hot (Ex. 22:21-24).

Just as Isaiah sternly rebuked "the pious" men of his day for their sham piety, so did Jesus seven centuries later accuse "the religious" men of His day:

Ye pay tithe of mint and anise and cummin and have omitted the weightier matters of the law, judgment, mercy and faith.
These ought ye to have done, and not to leave the other undone (Mt. 23:23).

Men have always found it easier and more pleasing to their vanity to comply with ceremonial rites and thé external aspects of their religion than to conform to God's purpose. Justice and compassion can never be replaced by religious orthodoxy. Only when the people will seek to conform to the moral intent of the law can God deal with them in mercy.

18 Come now and let us reason together, saith your Lord.
   If your sins be like scarlet,
   They shall become white as snow.
   If they be red as crimson,
   They shall become as wool.

19 If you consent and obey,
   You will eat the good of the land.

20 But if you refuse and resist—the sword will eat you,
   For the mouth of the Lord has spoken it.

In their present state of disobedience and rebellion, Israel's covenant relationship with God had been deeply disturbed. However, the prophet holds out to his people the bright hope of reconciliation with God, on condition that they will repent and cease from their evil ways.

Comment:

18 "Come now"—*"Lehu-na-"*, this is the usual formula of appeal and encouragement. "Let us reason together." Assuming a change of heart,

God would be willing to deal with them as a Father with His children, not on the basis of retributive justice, but of grace, and would forgive them freely.

Their forgiveness would not be based on their merit. However their change of conduct would be an indication of their sincere desire to be reconciled to God. Such a change would be a sinful people's first step towards a waiting Father, who is willing to meet His prodigal people more than halfway and to forgive them.

Scarlet and crimson are two shades of deep red, symbolic of sin. Red is the color of blood. It also symbolizes sin which leads to bloodshed and death. To overcome sin, God provided the blood of atonement for reconciliation. However, a sacrifice must never degenerate into an *opus operatum*, a mechanical or magical device which automatically secures forgiveness, regardless of the sinner's hardness of heart, and without his sincere repentance.

White is the color of innocence, of sins forgiven. Here we have an example of the symbolism of colors frequently encountered in the Scriptures.

19-20 The prophet offers Israel a choice between life and death.

If you consent and obey
Ye shall eat the good of the land.
If you refuse and resist — the sword will eat you
For the mouth of the Lord has spoken it.

We are reminded of the words of Moses: "I call heaven and earth to witness this day against you, that I have set before you life and death, blessing and cursing. Therefore choose life, that both thou and thy seed shall live" (Deut. 30:19). The choice is up to Israel, either obedience to God and blessing ("eat the good of the land"), or disobedience and then "the sword will eat you." They may experience divine favor or be consumed by the consequences of their own rebellion against God.

Verse 20 is followed by another pause of reflection. In view of the nation's long history of defiance against God, the prophet mournfully concluded that a thoroughgoing spiritual change was not to be. This caused him to reflect about Israel's glorious past and her lamentable present moral decline.

21 How has the faithful city become a harlot?
She was full of justice.
Righteousness dwelt in her,
But now—murderers.

22 Your silver has become dross,
Your wine diluted with water.

23 Your leaders are misleaders and companions of thieves.
Everyone loves a bribe and chases after rewards.
Orphans they do not judge,
The widows' cause they champion not.

Comment:

21 *"Eihah"*—"How" is a word which sounds like a sigh. It is the opening word of Jeremiah's Book of Lamentations. In a similar manner Isaiah's mournful *"eihah"* starts his lament over Jerusalem. The memory of her glorious past and her wretched present condition evokes unspeakable sadness in his heart. No other city has been wept over so much by the prophets and by Jesus Himself, as this city of Jerusalem.

How has the faithful city become a harlot?
She was full of justice.
Righteousness dwelt in her
But now — murderers

Faithfulness and harlotry are mutually exclusive. Alas for Jerusalem who has become a harlot! The expression "dwelt in her"—*"yalin bah"* literally means "used to spend nights there." Righteousness was once at home in that city but now it has become the home of murderers. The word *"merachetzim"* is a very strong term and means "professional murderers" —killers for hire. This is how low Jerusalem has fallen.

22 The figure of silver turned into worthless dross, which is usually thrown away, and of wine made insipid by excessive dilution, presents a vivid metaphor of Jerusalem in her fallen condition.

23 The prophet now leaves the picturesque metaphor in order to give us a chilling description of Jerusalem's terrible reality.

"Your leaders are misleaders and companions of thieves." Here is another example of Isaiah's favorite alliteration, which is lost in the English translation. In Hebrew it is: *"Saraih—sorrerim"*—"your princes are, rebels," which we have translated "Your leaders are misleaders and companions of thieves."

The terrible charge here is of collusion which exists between the ruling spheres of Jerusalem and the criminal elements of the city, the professional thieves *("gannavim")*.

"Everyone loves a bribe." The King James Version renders this incorrectly. "Everyone loveth gifts." The Hebrew term is *"shahad"*—"a bribe"—not a gift. It is the illegitimate "gift" for the purpose of perverting justice. Bribery was a crime against which the law of Moses specifically warned with farsighted wisdom. "Thou shalt not accept a bribe, because a bribe blinds the shrewd, and distorts the word of the just" (Ex. 23:8). Where justice can be bought, there can be no justice.

The expression "chases after rewards" is of particular interest. It is another of those literary allusions in which Isaiah abounds. The word for "peacemaker" in Hebrew is *"rodeph shalom,"* literally "one who chases after peace." However, the leaders and judges of Israel, instead of being *"rodephei shalom"*—peace-makers—are *"rodephei shalmonim"*—"chasers after rewards." They are men who are willing to sell out justice to the highest bidder.

Reading Isaiah, especially verses 21-23, one cannot escape the impression that the prophet was not indulging in rhetoric, but that he was describing a real live situation which he knew from personal experience and observation. Jerusalem was a city full of bribery and corruption, of organized crime, and of "justice" for a price. It was a place where collusion between civic leaders and the criminal element was a frequent occurrence, where killers could be had for hire. It was a situation similar to that which exists in many of our large cities today. Is it any wonder that Isaiah the prophet of the Holy God of Israel was outraged to the innermost depths of his being?

Somehow modern man has lost his capacity for righteous indignation. Crime and sin have become so commonplace that he is hardly able to react to it with burning wrath. Modern man has become casehardened. Not so the prophets, they were livid with indignation. They were God's angry men, consumed with righteous indignation, crying out against all injustice and pretense. They were the living conscience of the nation, who rebuked with stinging, slashing words which cut to ribbons all sham and make-believe. Behind their rebuke there was the full force and authority of an outraged God.

Here a word of caution might not be out of place: let no man dare to assume the mantle of the prophet to criticize and to rebuke God's people unless he has agonized over their sinfulness (Isa. 6:5).

24 Therefore, this is the pronouncement of the Lord Jehovah of Hosts,
The Mighty One of Israel
Oh, I will vent my wrath upon my foes
And avenge myself upon my enemies.

25 I will turn my hand against you
And purge your dross in the furnace
And remove all your alloy.

26 Then will I restore your judges as at first
And your counselors as in the beginning.
After that you shall be called
The city of righteousness, the faithful bastion.

27 Zion shall be redeemed through judgment,
And her penitent ones with righteousness.

Comment:

24 "Therefore," the situation being such as the prophet has depicted,

there was only one course left open to a Righteous and Holy God—to execute judgment. This then is the declaration of "The Lord Jehovah of Hosts, the Strong One of Israel." The Hebrew word *"neum"* means a solemn declaration or decree.

Nowhere else in Isaiah do we find such an accumulation of the names of God as here. The prophet sought to bring to bear upon the situation the full weight of divine authority and His determined will. The God of Israel is the Lord *(Adon)*, He is Jehovah, the Eternal One, the very Essence of Reality. He is the God of heaven and earth, the Strong One of Israel *(Abir Israel)*, who has consistently proved His power in mighty acts of deliverance throughout the history of Israel. He is the God who is able to redeem, as well as to execute judgment. This God was now full of wrath against His chosen people, whom He had so signally favored in the past, but who now have become unfaithful and ungrateful. In their present condition, He can only deal with them as His "foes and enemies."

Although the prophet speaks of God venting His wrath and avenging Himself upon His enemies, this wrath and vengeance of God are not purely punitive, but have a saving purpose. This is made clear in the following verses.

25   Alloys are removed from metals by smelting in fire. So Israel too will undergo a most painful process of purging through internal corrosion and external fires.

26   When once the moral gangrene and the dross of corruption have been removed, then the Lord will restore His people to their pristine condition of righteousness and God-given wisdom. After that will the harlot Jerusalem (verse 21) again become a city of righteousness, a faithful bastion just as in those old days when there were true judges and counselors in Israel.

One might ask, when did such a condition of pristine purity ever exist in Israel? Perhaps the prophet had in mind the golden era of David or Solomon, perhaps it was his personal vision of Jerusalem, so deeply embedded in his heart and soul, perhaps he was thinking of "Jerusalem the Golden" which will one day yet become a blessed reality (Isa. 66:10-12).

27   There is hope for Zion and for her penitent ones who will be redeemed with justice and righteousness. Here Zion stands for redeemed Israel or her penitent remnant. *"Shoveiha"*—this is a word with a dual meaning: 1, those who will return (from exile), and 2, the repentant remnant, which will survive the divine judgment and indignation. The very act of divine judgment which will come upon Israel as punishment for her unfaithfulness will, in the end, also be the means of her redemption.

28   But the rebels and the sinners
       Shall be destroyed together,

And those who forsake the Lord
Shall be consumed.

29 For they shall be ashamed of the oaks
In which you have taken delight,
And blush for the gardens
Which you have chosen.

30 For they shall be like the oak
Whose leaf has wilted,
And like a garden which has no water.

31 And the strong one shall be as tow,
And his work as a spark
Both shall burn together
And none shall quench them.

Comment:

28 In the closing passage of his grand indictment of Israel, the prophet deals with that part of the nation which will continue in her rebellion against God. These rebels and sinners shall be destroyed and consumed together. Here is a picture of a bonfire, as when the master of the house breaks up all the unwanted and useless objects in his household which clutter up his place, and consigns them all to a fire.

29 In the day of God's judgment, when the utter uselessness and futility of their oaks and gardens, the objects of their idol worship, shall be exposed as false and futile, those who delighted in them shall blush with shame. They will realize that they have put their trust in vanities.

30 The worshipers of the oaks (another play on words—*"Eilim"* means both oaks or terebinths, and idols) these worshipers of man-made idols and the groves where they worship, shall become like a naked and barren oak, an oak without a leaf, and a parched garden without water, a picture of utter desolation.

31 "The strong one" *(hosen)*, the man who makes the idol, "and his work," the idol itself, shall both burn together without anyone able to quench the conflagration. The implication here is that sin carries within itself its own final destruction. "The wages of sin is death" (Rom. 6:23b) .

The first chapter was placed at the beginning of the book of Isaiah as a suitable introduction to the rest of his prophecies. From now on we shall see all the themes touched upon in this first chapter repeated and more fully developed in all the messages of this greatest of prophets.

Notes: 1. Joseph Addison Alexander, *Commentary on the Prophecies of Isaiah*, page 71. Reprinted by Zondervan.

2. Edward J. Young, *The Book of Isaiah*, Volume 1, page 28: Eerdman's Publishing Co., 1965.

3. D. D. Luckenbill, *Ancient Records of Assyria and Babylon*, Vol. II, Sect. 240.

A Collection of Early Messages
during the Reign of Uzziah-Jotham

ISAIAH Chapters 2 - 5

Chapter   2:1   Subheading of the collection

Verses   2-4   Zion the future center of light and truth for all
                    nations

           .5   An appeal to Israel to walk in the light of the Lord

           6-11   Israel's besetting sins: idolatry, her reliance on
                    wealth and military strength

           12-22   The day of the Lord is fast approaching.

Chapter   3:1-7   Judah to experience foreign invasion, followed by
                    hunger and anarchy

           8-15   Judah's brazen sins and oppression of the poor are
                    hastening the judgment of God.

           3:16-   The fashionable and self-indulging daughters of Zion
           4:1   to experience extreme humiliation.

           2-6   The prophecy concerning the Branch of the Lord

Chapter   5:1-7   The song of the vineyard

           8-23   The message of woes against Israel

           24-30   The Lord's anger is kindled against His people

                    A merciless invader will ravish the land and the
                    nation

Chapter 2

2:1 The Word which Isaiah the son of Amoz saw concerning Judah and Jerusalem.

"The word which Isaiah . . . saw" sounds strange to our ears. However the Hebrew term *"davar"* has a broader meaning than the English term "word." *"Davar"* often means "a matter," "an event," "a deed" or "a record." The Book of Chronicles is called in Hebrew *"Divrei ha-yamim,"* literally "the words of the days."

In our text "the word which Isaiah saw" means "the vision which Isaiah saw." This vision, like all of Isaiah's prophecies, concerns the future of Judah and Jerusalem. When the prophet speaks about other nations or events he does so because it has a direct bearing upon the destiny of Judah or Israel.

"The word which Isaiah saw" is in the prophetic past tense. The prophet sees the future as if it had already taken place. Isaiah 2:2-4 is a prophecy about the glorious future of Zion as the center of the Kingdom of God. The same prophecy is repeated, almost verbatim, in Micah 4:1-4. Here are the two parallel passages:

Isaiah 2:2-4	Micah 4:1-4
2 And it shall come to pass at the end of the days that the mountain of the house of the LORD shall be established on the top of the mountains and will be lifted up above the hills, and unto it shall stream all the nations.	1 And it shall come to pass at the end of the days that the mountain of the house of the LORD shall be established on the top of the mountains and will be lifted up above the hills and unto it shall stream peoples.
3 And many people will go forth and will say: Let us go and ascend to the mountain of the Lord, to the house of the God of Jacob, and he will teach us of his ways, and we will walk in his paths. For out of Zion shall go forth the Law and the word of the LORD out of Jerusalem.	2 And many nations shall go forth and will say: Let us go and ascend to the mountain of the LORD and unto the house of the God of Jacob, and he will teach us of his ways and we will walk in his paths. For out of Zion shall go forth the Law and the word of the LORD out of Jerusalem.
4 And he shall arbitrate between the nations and he shall decide for many peoples: and they shall beat their swords into plowshares and their spears into pruning knives: Nation shall not lift up sword against nation and they shall not learn war any more.	3 And he shall judge between many peoples and will decide for strong and distant nations; and they shall beat their swords into plowshares and their spears into pruning knives. Nation shall not lift up sword against nation and they shall not learn war any more.
	4 But every man shall sit under his vine and under his fig tree, without anyone to make him afraid. For the mouth of the LORD of hosts has spoken it.

Comment
Verses 2-4

The relationship between the two parallel passages of Isaiah and Micah have long intrigued Biblical scholars. Which of the two passages is older? Which prophet borrowed from the other? Opinions have been sharply divided, some holding that Isaiah's was the older and original prophecy, others Micah's. Some scholars suggest that both prophets quoted an old and well-known prophecy.

On the whole we favor the position that Isaiah was the original author of the prophecy for the following reasons:

A. Because a careful analysis of the Hebrew text indicates that the language of Isaiah 2:2-4 is peculiarly Isaianic.[1] The passage also fits in well with the context.

B. Micah, in chapter 4:4 elaborates in greater detail about the conditions which will prevail after his prophecy will have become a reality. It may be assumed that the less elaborate form of prophecy is the original one.

C. The fact that Isaiah was the older of the two prophets would tend to favor the assumption that he was the author of the prophecy under discussion.

As for the view that both prophets quoted an already existing prophecy, perhaps Joel, there is nothing really to substantiate this position. It is also conceivable that both prophets received the same prophecy independently of each other.

2 "And it shall come to pass." These six English words render one Hebrew word *"Ve-haiah,"* which literally means "and it came to pass." Although the verb is in the past tense, the context clearly indicates that the prophet speaks of the future.

"At the end of the days" or "in the last days," in Hebrew *"be-aharit ha-yamim,"* is an expression which, as a rule, refers to the Messianic times. The word "eschatology" is derived from the Greek word *"eschaton"*—"the last," which, in turn, is a translation of the above Hebrew phrase.

The end of the days is that period of time which closes human history. It is the era which inaugurates the Kingdom of God, when the Lord Himself will rule the nations, as well as the hearts and minds of men. It will be the realization of true theocracy, not the rule of priests or religious functionaries, but of God Himself. The end of times bridges time and eternity.

"The mountain of the house of the Lord."

This is not Mount Zion as a geographical location, but the very center of God's government over the nations of the world. Zion will at the end of the days be not merely the center of Israel's national worship, but the very fountain of spiritual life for all nations. The same thought was expressed again by Isaiah later, when he said: "For mine house shall be called an house of prayer for all people" (Isa. 56:7).

We recall that these were the words which Jesus later quoted adding reproachfully: "but ye have made it a den of iniquity" (Mt. 21:13).

From time immemorial certain mountains have been associated with the worship of national deities (Olympus, Parnassus, Mount Seir, Gerizim, the Hill of Mars, etc.). When human history shall have run its course, Zion, the habitation of the God of Jacob, will tower above all other mountains where all other national deities are worshiped. In the end Jehovah alone will be exalted above all gods.

When once the nations shall recognize Jehovah as the only true God, "they shall stream"—unto Zion. Like a river glorious, nations, small and great, near and distant, highly civilized and primitive, shall stream toward the house of the God of Jacob on Mount Zion.

3 "Many peoples shall go." The King James Version uses the singular for "people," but in the Hebrew text the word is *"ammim"*—"peoples." Although "peoples" and "nations" appear to be complementary or even synonymous terms, there is however a difference: *"Goy"*—nation, is a term applied to a people who have already achieved a true sense of their identity, whereas *"am"* refers to a people still in its formative stage, preceding nationhood. Yet the distinction is not always clear or definite; it is possible that the prophet visualized both the highly advanced and civilized nations, as well as the less developed peoples of the earth, who will at the end of days flow to Zion to draw spiritual sustenance and light from Jehovah.

"And he will teach us of his ways and we shall walk in his path."

Even as once Israel heard the voice of God thundering from Sinai, and responded by saying: "We shall do and obey"—so in that glorious future, nations will spontaneously and willingly learn from the Lord's Word and also walk in the paths of God. This will not be mere intellectual assent, or knowledge of right and wrong, but a spontaneous and sincere desire of the nations to know the will of God, and to walk in His ways.

"For out of Zion shall go forth the Law and the Word of God from Jerusalem." Here "the Law" is not the ritual or ceremonial law of Moses, but "the law behind the law," the Law of God's light and truth. This Law is also the Word of the LORD, the eternal Logos, the Way, the Truth and the Life.

Although the Messiah is not specifically mentioned in this passage, the prophet will have many opportunities to introduce us to Him, describing in great detail His glorious reign and character.

4 "And he shall arbitrate between the nations and decide for many peoples."

In that glorious future nations will not resort to force of arms to decide their clashing interests, but the Lord Himself will be the judge between nations, and He Himself shall render His decision for many peoples. The King James Version translates this passage "will rebuke many people." However, the Hebrew word *"ve-hohiakh"* means "one who renders a final decision in a dispute"—an arbiter. When once God shall assume the government over the nations, any resort to force of arms will become altogether unthinkable. The ancient dream of mankind of total disarmament and peace among the nations which, so often, has gone aglimmer, will at last become a glorious reality, not because of men's efforts but because the Spirit of God will at last indwell the hearts and minds of men.

"They shall beat their swords into plowshares and their spears into pruning knives."

The sword and the spear symbolize man's weapons of destruction, from the ancient bow and arrow to modern nuclear implements of death. The plowshare and the pruning knife are man's agricultural or constructive implements. The prophet sees the time coming when the instruments of death and destruction shall be turned into constructive tools for the benefit of all mankind.

"Nation shall not lift up sword against nation and they shall learn war no more."

All arsenals of war, all military academies, all military camps, and training fields will go out of business and will cease to exist. The prophet sees this as a glorious finale to history, when the Lord Himself shall rule over the hearts and minds of people and over the affairs of all nations.

No prophet, lawgiver or great teacher has ever expressed more poignantly or movingly man's ancient yearning for peace. After twenty-five centuries Isaiah's vision still remains an unfulfilled dream. So long as God is defied or ignored in the affairs of men, and the Prince of Peace is rejected, there can be no real peace. "But the wicked are like the troubled sea, when it cannot rest, whose waters cast up mire and dirt. There is no peace, saith my God, to the wicked" (Isa. 57:20, 21).

2:5 Having presented Zion as the future habitation of God's Word and the focus of His Light to which all nations shall one day stream for light and guidance, the prophet now appeals to his own people:

116

"House of Jacob let us walk in the light of the Lord."

The appeal is charged with great emotional intensity. In the original Hebrew it comes through loud and clear in the beseeching *"Lehu ve-neilhu"*—

"Do let us go and let us walk."

In his appeal Isaiah includes himself with his people. It is always "Let us go" and "let us walk." The sins of Israel are his sins, their failures his failures. This identification of the prophet with Israel will come through time and again, as in his famous confession: "Woe is me! for I am undone; because I am a man of unclean lips, and I dwell in the midst of a people of unclean lips" (Isa. 6:5a).

It is this identification with "the house of Jacob" which authenticates the true prophet. Those who only harp and carp upon the sins of Jacob, without being heartbroken and without sharing in the tragedy of their own people, are not bona fide servants of God, but enemies of Israel.

It is possible that Isaiah uses the phrase "house of Jacob" to emphasize the condition of his people in their unrepentant state, who still need to obtain victory in order to become "Israel"—"a prince with God."

6 For thou hast forsaken thy people, the house of Jacob,
  Because they are full [of customs] from the East,
  And of soothsayers like the Philistines,
  And they shake hands with foreigners.

7 And their land is replete with silver and gold,
  And there is no end to their treasures.
  Their land is filled with horses,
  And there is no end to their chariots.

8 Also their land is filled with idols;
  They worship that which their fingers have made.

9 And the common man bows down,
  And the prominent man humbles himself,
  Forgive them not!

10 Enter into the rock, and hide thyself in the dust
   Before the terror of the Lord,
   And from the glory of his majesty.

11 The arrogant eyes of the ordinary man shall be humbled,
   And the haughtiness of men of stature shall be brought low,
   And only the LORD himself shall be exalted in that day.

Comment

Verses 6-11

In the above passage the prophet deals with those evils which have caused Jehovah to forsake the house of Jacob. First among the evils is that the nation has become paganized. Their land is "replenished from the east." As our context indicates, this is a reference to the oriental superstitions and idolatry which have flooded the whole country. It is full of soothsayers and they "shake hands with foreigners,"—a reference to close commercial and cultural relations with idol-worshiping foreigners, which has resulted in the paganization of Israel.

7 Another evil which affects the nation is its great affluence. "The land is filled with silver and gold, and there is no end to their treasures." Not only great poverty, but riches and affluence can destroy a nation, when they bring in their wake a reliance, not on God, but on self, or on the military power and prowess of the nation.

"The land is full of horses, and there is no end to their chariots."

Horses and chariots were at that period of military history the latest advance in the art of warfare. The land is also filled with idols produced locally which the common people and their leaders worshiped. Wealth has induced a false sense of security and boosted their national pride.

9 The prophet reaches the climax of outrage when he cries out in an apparent fit of anger and frustration "Forgive them not!" Somehow the human quality of the prophet comes through to us very clearly in spite of the twenty-six centuries which separate us from his times. This momentary lapse of Isaiah's usual compassion for his people can only be explained by the depths of the prophet's anguish as he looked on helplessly at the growing spread of injustice, idolatry and the corroding influence of wealth, side by side with the increasing arrogance and smug self-assurance of the leaders of Judah.

However all their false pomp and glitter is destined to come to a fearful end. Therefore the prophet counsels his people to hide themselves in the rock and in the dust from before the terror of the Lord and His majesty which will soon be made manifest. Then will the arrogance of small and great, of the common people and the prominent men be humbled.

In the end, when all man's proud achievements will have turned into dust and ashes, Jehovah alone will be exalted.

Several times in verses 9, 11 and 17, Isaiah uses two different expressions for "man" or "men": "adam" is man whom God made out of dust, the word "ish" is man in his full human dignity and valor (cf. the Latin "homo" and "vir"). In verse 9 we have sought to indicate this difference by translating "adam" as "common man" and "anashim" (the plural of "ish") by prominent men.

From verses 12-22 the prophet gives us a glimpse of the terrors of "The day of the Lord." It is a day of universal judgment, which will affect all of mankind, all of man's civilization, and all nature.

12 For the day of the Lord is upon all which is proud and lifted up.
And upon all that which is high,
It shall be brought low.

13 Upon all the cedars of Lebanon, the tall and lofty,
   And upon all the oaks of Bashan

14 Upon all the high mountains and upon all the lofty hills.

15 And upon every high tower and upon every fortified rampart.

16 And upon all the ships of Tarshish,
   And upon all stately vessels.

17 And the arrogance of man shall be brought low,
   And the pride of men shall be humbled
   And only the Lord himself shall be exalted on that day.

18 But the idols shall cease altogether.

19 And they shall enter into the caves of the rocks,
   And into the holes of the dust,
   From before the terror of the Lord and the glory of his majesty,
   When he arises to terrify the earth.

20 In the day men shall cast away
   Their idols of silver and idols of gold
   Which they have made for themselves to worship,
   To the bats and the moles.

21 To enter the clefts of the rocks,
   And the fissures of the crags,
   From before the terror of the Lord,
   And from the glory of his majesty,
   When he arises to terrify the earth.

22 Cease ye from man, whose breath is in his nostrils,
   For of what account is he?

Comment

16 "Tarshish"—Tarseus or Carthage, was a city at the western end of the Mediterranean, hence "the ships of Tarshish" is a metaphor for all ocean-going ships. The terrifying vision of the Lord's Day brings to mind a world-wide earthquake of unprecedented intensity.

21 When the Lord shall arise to terrify the earth, man's civilization and proudest accomplishments shall collapse and crumble into dust. Only God shall remain supreme and exalted.

22 In view of all this, the prophet appeals to the house of Jacob to give up their trust in man. For when all is said and done: "of what account is he?"

Chaos and Breakdown of Government

ISAIAH, Chapter 3:1-15

1 For behold, the Lord Jehovah of Hosts,
Is about to remove from Jerusalem and Judah the stay and staff,
The whole stay of bread and the whole staff of water.

2 The mighty man and the man of war,
The judge and the prophet, the diviner and the elder.

3 The commander of fifty and the dignitary,
The counselor, the skilled magician and the expert enchanter.

4 And I will give them youngsters for their princes,
And youthful pranksters shall rule over them.

5 The people shall oppress one another, every man his neighbor.
The boy will be insolent to the old man,
The base fellow to the respectable man.

6 When a man shall ake hold of his brother in his father's house:
"You have a mantle, you shall be our ruler,
And let this ruined heap be under your hand."

7 But in that day he will remonstrate saying:
"I will not be a healer,
Nor is there bread nor a mantle in my house,
You will not make me a ruler of the people."

8 For Jerusalem has stumbled, and Judah has fallen
because their tongues and their deeds are against the LORD,
To defy his glorious Presence.

9 The look in their faces bears witness against them,
And their sins they declare just like Sodom,
They hide it not.
Woe to their souls, they have done wrong to themselves.

10 Say to the righteous, it is well;
For they shall eat of the fruit of their deeds.

11 Woe to the wicked, it shall be ill with him
According to the work of his hands, he shall be recompensed.

12 As for my people, youngsters are their oppressors,
And women rule over them.
O my people, your leaders mislead you,
And confuse the direction of your paths.

13 The LORD has taken up a position to contend,
    He is standing up to judge the people.

14 The LORD will enter into judgment
    With the elders of the people, and with their princes
    "It is you who have devoured my vineyard,
    The spoil of the poor is in your houses."

15 What right have you to crush my people,
    And to grind the faces of the poor?
    This is the solemn message of the LORD of Hosts.

Comment

Verses 1-15

Continuing the message of God's wrath and judgment which will soon be manifested, Isaiah predicts that the Lord is about to remove all those resources which gave the people under the reign of Uzziah and Jotham a false sense of security, of great prosperity and of orderly, undisturbed government.

1 "The Lord Jehovah of Hosts," this is a solemn appellation of God, who is about to remove from the land "the stay and staff of bread and water," the very essentials of survival and well-being.

2-3 The Lord will also remove all military and civil authority, whether duly appointed, or even unlawfully established. The work of the Lord will be so complete in its devastation that it will reach down to the lowest ranks of the military establishment and civil authorities.

"The commander of fifty" is the equivalent of a junior officer or sergeant in our modern military order. The judge and the prophet and the elder represent established and legitimate authority; the diviner, the skilled magician and the expert enchanter, are the popular but forbidden and unlawful counselors to whom the mass of the people have so frequently resorted, in defiance of Jehovah Himself, and of His Law (Deut. 18:9-14).

4-5 The result of the total collapse of authority will be that the young, the inexperienced and the lawless element, shall rule the nation. They will be mere *"naarim"* and *"taalulim"* — youngsters and pranksters. This will lead to widespread oppression of the people by the people and to disrespect and defiance of all authority.

6-7 Such conditions will produce anarchy and a desperate effort to establish some kind of orderly government. Yet contrary to the usual inclination of men to grasp at any opportunity to exercise power and authority, there will be none willing to assume the responsibility of feeding, clothing and ruling the frantic and destitute masses, and their ruined land which the prophet scornfully calls "the heap."

8-9 The approaching disaster of Jerusalem and Judah is so grievous, because it will be self-induced, and will be the result of their wicked tongues and acts which defy "the glorious presence of the Lord" (lit. the eyes of His glory). The practice of sin has left its stigma upon their faces, which gives them away just as the sins of Sodom could not be hidden. The prophet cries out in anguish: "Woe unto their souls, they have done harm to themselves!" This is one of those sudden exclamations, which seem to illuminate the soul of the prophet and to reveal his deepest emotions.

10-11 Yet God is just and rewards men according to the intents of their hearts and according to their deeds. The apostle Paul later expressed the same truth: "Be not deceived, God is not mocked, for whatsoever a man soweth, that also shall he reap" (Gal. 6:7).

12 Now the prophet addresses himself to the contemporary situation of his people. They are oppressed by juveniles and ruled by women. It is a situation which is so strongly reminiscent of conditions in our modern society. All this brings forth a cry from within the prophet's tormented heart:

"O, my people, your leaders mislead you, and confuse your paths."

13-15 The moral condition of the nation having reached such depths of depravity, the Lord is about to assume the role of Judge and to pronounce judgment on His people. First to be judged will be "the elders and the princes of the people." The elders represented the elected leaders of the nation, "the princes" were the hereditary rulers. Both are equally guilty in the eyes of God. The charge against them is plunder of the nation which has been entrusted to their rule: "You have devoured my vineyard, the spoil of the poor is in your houses."

The prophet speaking for the Lord, seems to be almost livid with outrage and indignation. He cries: *"Mahlahem?"*—"By what right?" "What do you mean that you crush my people and grind the faces of the poor?"

Here we have a very striking metaphor, tellingly employed by the prophet. Just as the stones of a mill crush grain and then grind it to fine flour, later to be baked and eaten as bread, so the leadership of Jerusalem and Judah crush and grind the faces of the people in order to devour them completely.

Having dealt with the leaders of the nation, the prophet now turns his attention to the elegant ladies of Jerusalem, whom he apparently had in mind when he said that women rule over the people (v. 12).

From 3:16 to 4:1 the prophet foretells the fate of those fashionable ladies of Jerusalem and their approaching doom.

122

The Haughty and Pampered Women of Jerusalem
Will Come To A Terrible End.

Isaiah, Chapter 3:16-4:1

16 The Lord also said,
Because the daughters of Zion are haughty,
And walk about with outstretched necks
And ogling eyes,
Mincing along as they go,
Making a tinkling noise with their ankles

17 The Lord shall inflict with a scab
The heads of the daughters of Zion,
And the LORD shall uncover their secret parts.

18 In that day will the Lord take away the adornments
Of their ankle clasps, the head bands,
The moon-shaped pendants and the scarves,

19 The earrings, the armbands and the veils,

20 The diadems, the stepping-chains, the girdles,
The perfume bottles and the amulets

21 The signet rings and the nose rings

22 The gala dresses, the cloaks and the handbags

23 The metal mirrors, the fine linen garments,
The turbans and the outer veils.

24 And this is what shall happen:
Instead of perfume, there shall be a stench,
Istead of a girdle, a rope,
Instead of well-groomed hair, a bald head,
Instead of a fine robe, a sack,
Branding, instead of beauty.

25 Thy men shall fall by the sword,
And thy heroes in battle.

26 And her gates shall mourn and wail.
And utterly bereft, she shall sit upon the ground.

4:1 In that day shall seven women take hold of one man saying:
We will eat our own bread and wear our own clothing,
Only let us be called by thy name; take away our disgrace.

Comment

3:16-4:1

Having condemned the leading men of Judah for their greed and oppression of the poor, (3:13-15), the prophet now turns his attention to their women, the fashionable ladies of Zion. With profound scorn Isaiah describes their arrogant demeanor and provocative attire.

16 They walk about with "outstretched necks and ogling eyes," or as J. B. Phillips paraphrases this passage, "walking with their noses in the air and flirting with their eyes."

17 These "daughters of Zion" do everything possible to attract attention to themselves. They parade along the streets with short mincing steps and make sure that everybody notices their feet, which are decorated with tinkling stepping-chains attached to their ankles. One can almost see these extravagantly attired ladies on a Sabbath evening or a feast day, as they parade up and down the main promenade of Jerusalem, their noses in the air, casting long side glances as they pass by.

18-23 There is profound scorn in the prophet's detailed enumeration of all these twenty-one items of feminine finery. He sees in this self-indulgence and display of luxury a visible sign of their inner emptiness and callous disregard of all the suffering and injustice in their midst. Their whole bearing and appearance proves that they are the proper wives, sisters and daughters of those arrogant and wicked men of Jerusalem who grind the faces of the poor (v. 15).

24-26 In terse and staccato phrases Isaiah describes the disaster which will befall these heartless and snobbish daughters of Zion. He ends with a moving description tinged with compassion for the utter misery which will come upon them. Her mighty men and war heroes slain, she herself will sit on the ground, dejected and bereft of all her pride, her beauty and her loved ones.

Living in the shadow of an ever-present menace of hostile invasions, Isaiah foresaw the inevitable calamity which eventually was to destroy both kingdoms. His predictions were tragically fulfilled in the history of Israel on numerous occasions, especially the Babylonian invasion of 586 B.C. and the final Roman captivity.

When Jerusalem was captured and leveled to the ground by the Romans in 70 A.D., the emperor Titus struck a commemorative medal, depicting the daughter of Zion sitting on the ground under a palm, mourning. The inscription on the medal was "*Judea Capta.*" Titus may have had the words of Isaiah 3:26 in mind when he struck that medal.

4:1 This verse describes the situation which will prevail in Jerusalem after the men of Judah shall fall in battle. So few eligible men will be left, and women will be so desperate to marry, that seven of them (or any large number) will take hold of any surviving man, imploring him to marry them, even if they should have to support themselves, in order to avoid the disgrace of spinsterhood and childlessness.

This verse parallels Isaiah 3:6, where the men of Jerusalem were described as being so desperate, that they offered the rule to anyone who had something to eat and a garment to put on. Here the women are presented in a similar plight, ready to thrust themselves upon any man who will offer them his name.

Note: 1. *The Indivisible Isaiah,* by Rachel Margalioth, pages 36, 77, 105, 106, 107.

The Branch of the Lord

Isaiah, Chapter 4:2-6

2   In that day shall the branch of the LORD
Be beautiful and glorious,
And the fruit of the land the pride and glory
For those of Israel who escaped.

3   And it shall come to pass that he who will be left in Zion
And he who will remain in Jerusalem shall be called holy,
All those who are inscribed for life in Jerusalem.

4   This will come to pass when the Lord shall wash away
The filth of the daughters of Zion, and will remove from Jerusalem
The bloodstains in her midst
With the spirit of judgment and the spirit of fire.

5   Then will the Lord create above all the habitation
Of Mount Zion and upon her assemblies
A cloud and smoke by day
And a bright flaming fire by night,
And over all this glory there will be a canopy.

6   And there shall be a pavilion for a shade by day from the heat,
And a refuge and a shelter from the storm and the rain.

Comment

Verses 2-6 After a severe indictment of the sins of his people and a prediction of divine judgment, the prophet now completes his message with a glorious vision of Israel's redemption, after the time of her punishment and purging is completed.

2 Israel's redemption will come through "the branch of the LORD," in Hebrew *"Tsemah Jehovah,"* or sometimes *"Tsemah David." "Tsemah"* means growth or vegetation in general, or a sprout, a plant, a branch. When used in conjunction with Jehovah or David, it has a Messianic connotation, and refers to the Messianic King who is a branch of the stem of Jesse (11:1).

There are two passages in Jeremiah which speak of "the branch":

1) Behold the days come saith the LORD that I will raise unto David a righteous Branch and a King shall reign and prosper and shall execute judgment and justice in the earth. In his days Judah shall be saved and Israel shall dwell safely; and this is his name whereby he shall be called; the LORD OUR RIGHTEOUSNESS *Jehovah Tsidkenu* (Jer. 23:5-6).

The second "Branch" prophecy in Jeremiah reads:

2) In those days and at that time will I cause the branch of righteousness to grow up unto David and he shall execute judgment... (Jer. 33:15).

Two more "Branch" prophecies are recorded in Zechariah:

1) Behold I will bring forth my servant the Branch (Zech. 3:8).

2) Behold the man whose name is the Branch (Zech. 6:12).

The prophecy in Isaiah 11:1 is another of the "Branch" prophecies: "And there shall come forth a rod out of the stem of Jesse, and a Branch shall grow out of his roots."

All "the Branch" prophecies have a strong Messianic content. "The Branch" is a rod of the stem of Jesse, that is a descendant of King David (Isa. 4:2, 11:1). His mission is to save Judah. This divinely appointed king-Messiah is referred to by Jeremiah as "the Branch of righteousness." He is endowed with divinity, so that the prophet calls Him *"Jehovah Tsidkenu"*—The LORD our Righteousness (Jer. 23:5-6).

Zechariah calls Him "my servant the Branch" (Zech. 3:8) or the man whose name is "the Branch."

Although there were a number of good kings in Israel since the days of Isaiah (Hezekiah, Josiah, Zedekiah) none of them came near the fulfillment of the prophetic vision of the Messianic king. It is therefore understandable that the earliest Jewish commentators always interpreted the term "Branch" as a reference to the Messiah. In fact one of the many rabbinic names for the Messiah is *"Tsemah"*—"branch." The Hebrew prayer book is replete with references to the Messiah who is called *"Tsemach David"*—the Branch of David.

The ancient Chaldee paraphrase of Isaiah 4:2 translates "the Branch of Jehovah" as *"Meshicha d'Jah"*—the Messiah of Jehovah. "In that day," that is, when this prophecy shall be fulfilled, then shall "the Branch of Jehovah" (that is the Messiah) be beautiful and glorious in the eyes of redeemed Israel. "And the fruit of the land their pride and glory." Here is an allusion to the dual nature of the Messiah: As "the Branch of the LORD," He is of divine origin, as "the fruit of the land," He is also human. "Inscribed for life," the Targum paraphrases as those who are written for "eternal life" (See also Ex. 32:32; Dan. 12:1; Rev. 13:8).

3 "He who will be left in Zion, and he who will remain in Jerusalem, shall be called holy." Only a holy remnant will live to enjoy the glorious days of the Messiah.

4 This remnant will be made up of men and women purged of all filth and innocent blood by the Spirit of fire and judgment.

5-6 Over this cleansed and sanctified assembly the Lord will spread a supernatural pavilion symbolic of His protection.

The prophet goes back to Israel's experiences in the wilderness when the Lord surrounded His people with His personal protection, guiding them with a cloud of smoke by day and a shining flame of fire by night. We have a vision of perfect fellowship and harmony between the Lord and His people, unmarred by sin or evil. Hosea, Isaiah's contemporary prophet, described in similar terms the restored relationship between the Lord and His people, speaking of Israel as the bride of Jehovah:

> And I will betroth you to me in righteousness and in justice,
> In steadfast love and in mercy.
> I will betroth you to me in faithfulness,
> And you shall know the LORD (Hos. 2:19, 20).

The Song of the Vineyard

Isaiah, Chapter 5:1-7

1 Let me sing of my beloved
A song of my friend about his vineyard.
My beloved had a vineyard
On a most fertile hill.

2 And he dug up the ground and cleared it of stones,
And planted it with choicest vines.
He also built a watchtower in the midst of it,
And he looked forward that it should bring forth grapes,
But it brought forth wild grapes.

3 And now, O citizen of Jerusalem, and you, men of Judah,
Judge between me and my vineyard:

4 What could have been done for my vineyard,
And I have not done it?
Why then, when I expected it to produce choice grapes,
Did it bring forth wild grapes?

5   And now, I will tell you,
    What I will do to my vineyard;
    I shall remove its hedge,
    And it will be eaten up.
    I shall tear down its fence,
    And it will be trodden down.

6   And I will turn it into a wasteland.
    It shall not be pruned, nor hoed
    And briars and thorns will come up.
    I will also command the clouds,
    that they rain no rain upon it.

7   For the vineyard of the LORD of hosts is the house of Israel
    And the men of Judah the plant of his delight,
    And he looked for justice, and behold bloodshed,
    For righteousness, and behold, a screaming!

Comment

Verses 1-7   This is a most exquisite elegy. It is a parable in the form of a plaintive song concerning "my beloved and his vineyard." In the days of Isaiah the stony hills of Judea were beautifully terraced and planted with choice and delightful vineyards. Every citizen of Judah was well acquainted with these lovely vineyards which produced luscious grapes. He knew how much toil, care and love had gone into the making of one of these vineyards, and how much hope the hardworking husband-man invested in it. Every Judean could easily understand the frustration and the heartache of the owner, when all his labor produced was sour, misshaped *"b'ushim"*—inferior, unripe little berries or wild grapes. This song is a parable which clearly and plainly explains its meaning.

> For the vineyard of the LORD of Hosts is the house of Israel,
> And the men of Judah the plant of his delight,
> And he looked for justice and behold bloodshed,
> For righteousness, but behold, a screaming! (v. 7).

What a terrible disappointment to Jehovah has the house of Israel turned out to be. Instead of the delightful grapes of justice, she yielded the wild grapes of wrath and bloodshed. Instead of being a land of righteousness, there is the cry of the oppressed and wronged.

No translation can do justice to the prophet Isaiah's superb choice of Hebrew words. In verse seven there are two pairs of alliterations:

1. *Mishpath - mispach*, justice - bloodshed
2. *Tsedakah - tseakah*, righteousness - a cry, or scream of anguish

The very sound of Isaiah's words most emphatically pronounce the truth that in the sight of God, Israel, upon which He has lavished so much love and labor, has become a great and bitter disappointment. There was therefore nothing left for Jehovah to do but to tear down the fences of the vineyard, and to let it be trampled and destroyed, until the time of chastisement and purging would be completed.

The Message of Woe

One of the forms of stern rebuke frequently used by the prophets, especially by Isaiah was the cry of "woe!" This exclamation begins an impassioned denunciation of some common evil observed by the prophet among his people. It usually ends with the pronouncement of an inexorable retribution which the Lord will bring upon His people, unless they repent, and set a particular wrong right.

It is interesting to note how often the Lord Jesus Himself used the cry of "woe" to denounce prevailing evils or spiritual perversions which were common in His day (Mt. 11:21; 23:13-20; Lk. 6:24-26, etc.).

A careful analysis of the Gospels clearly indicates that among the favorite Scriptures of the Lord Jesus, in addition to the Pentateuch, were the Psalms and Isaiah. From these books He quoted repeatedly and often alluded to them.

Isaiah 5:8-23 In this passage Isaiah denounces six different types of evildoers. His message is obviously based on personal observation and his knowledge of the Judean scene.

Although Isaiah's wrath is directed against wicked persons and evils of his own generation, it is frightening to contemplate how his words apply poignantly also to our own times and our own situation.

Verses 8-10   The First Woe: Against the Greed of the Rich

8 Woe to them that join house to house,
And connect field with field,
Till there is no more room left,
So that you alone may dwell in the land.

9 Into my ears the LORD of hosts [has whispered]:
Many houses shall become desolate,
Yea, large and goodly ones, for lack of inhabitants.

10 For ten acres of a vineyard shall yield only one bath
And the seed of an homer will yield an ephah.

Comment

5:8 The first woe is directed against the insatiable greed of some rich landlords and plantation owners, who mercilessly oppressed their poorer neighbors. The conditions of which the prophet Isaiah speaks are also described in the writings of other contemporary prophets like Amos,

Hosea, Micah, and are reflected in the historical writings of that period. Apparently men of wealth were quite ruthless in their acquisition of property, squeezing out the poor and the helpless from their homes and depriving them of their small lots. A classic example of this kind of ruthlessness is described in the story of King Ahab who coveted the vineyard of his neighbor Naboth (1 Kings, chap. 21).

9 Isaiah announces that he received a message which the Lord has spoken or whispered into his ears, that these grand mansions so wickedly acquired, will be deserted and without residents, as a result of enemy invasion of the land.

What one such invasion did to Judah in the days of Ahaz is described in 2 Chronicles 28:5-8. Just in one day 120,000 men were killed by Pekah of Samaria, and 200,000 people, men, women and children were carried off into captivity.

10 As another punishment for their greed, the Lord will send upon their fields a failure of harvest resulting in famine.

Ten acres of vineyard will yield one ephah, which is approximately four gallons of wine, an extremely low yield. A homer of seed, which is equal to forty-eight gallons, will produce one bath, or one tenth of an homer, a disastrous result.

What Isaiah is saying to these greedy men is: Your wicked acquisitions will bring you no blessing, but a curse.

Verses 11-17   The Second Woe: Against
                        Drunkards and Merrymakers

11 Woe to them that rise up early in the morning
    To run after strong drink,
    Who linger late into the night,
    Till wine inflame them!

12 And there are the harp and the viol, the drum and the flute
    And wine at their drinking banquets,
    But the work of the Lord they regard not,
    Neither do they consider the actions of his hands.

13 This is why my people have gone into captivity,
    For want of knowledge;
    And their honorable men are famished,
    And their multitude parched with thirst.

14 Therefore has sheol enlarged her desire
    And opened her yawning jaws beyond measure.
    Down go their glory and their tumult
    And he who rejoiceth among them.

15 And the plain man is bowed down
   And the man of stature is humbled
   And the eyes of the haughty are cast down.

16 But the LORD of hosts shall be exalted in judgment,
   And God, the Holy One shall be sanctified through righteousness.

17 And the lambs shall graze, as if in their pastures,

   And strangers shall eat in the ruins of the fat.

Comment:

11-17 In this second woe Isaiah's ire is turned against those whose chief aim in life seems to be drinking and having a good time. Those were the "good time Charlies" of Isaiah's day. Their constant imbibing and carousing so dulled their moral and spiritual sensibilities that they no longer gave any thought to God nor to His mysterious weaving of the strands of history, which will in the end completely obliterate all their pomp and glory.

14 *"Sheol"* incorrectly translated in the King James Version as "hell," is the land or abode of the dead. The prophet presents *sheol* symbolically, as some great monster with yawning jaws waiting to swallow up the whole nation, all those mindless merrymakers and the multitudes of the people, the guilty with the innocent. They shall either perish or go into captivity, mainly for lack of knowledge of God's will and purpose (v. 13-15).

16 When all this work of punishment is completed, the LORD of hosts alone will remain exalted and sanctified in His work of judgment and righteousness.

17 The once beautiful, cultivated and rich land now ravaged by the enemy will become an uncultivated heath where stray lambs shall graze and roaming strangers shall scavenge in the land which once was so rich and prosperous.

Verses 18-19   The Third Woe: Against Those Who Deliberately Provoke God

18 Woe unto them who drag iniquity as with cords of vanity,
   And sin as if with cart ropes

19 Who say: Let him make haste
            And hurry up his work
            That we may see it.
            And let the counsel
            Of the Holy One of Israel
            Draw near and come,
            That we may know it.

Comment:

18-19 In this woe the prophet deals with those who deliberately commit iniquity in order to force God's hand. They blasphemously challenge God, either because they deny His very existence, or because they think that He does not care. A similar thought was expressed by the Psalmist (53:1): "The fool has said in his heart There is no God."

20   The Fourth Woe: Against Spiritual and Moral Perversion

Woe to them who call evil good and good evil,
Who make out darkness to be light,
And light darkness,
Sweet to be bitter, and bitterness sweet.

Here the prophet singles out the morally degraded and perverted who no longer know or care about what is right or wrong, fair or foul, good or evil. All moral values have undergone a complete perversion.

21   The Fifth Woe: Against the Clever Fools

Woe to them who are wise in their own eyes
And in their own sight are very clever.

In this fifth woe Isaiah speaks about a common type known in every generation, and in every place. Having lost their way to God, the fountain of true wisdom, they appear to be wise *(chachamim)* in their own estimation and consider themselves very clever *(nevonim)*. In fact they are conceited fools, easily recognizable by the smirk of self-congratulation on their faces due to their assumed superior wisdom and pity for those who do not possess their great intelligence. Elsewhere Isaiah referred to this same type of people in these words: "Therefore behold I will proceed to do a marvelous thing among the people . . . for the wisdom of their wise men shall perish and the understanding of their prudent men shall be hid" (29:14).

The Apostle Paul speaks about those who are wise in their own eyes in this way: "But God hath chosen the foolish things of this world to confound the wise; and the weak things of this world to confound the things which are mighty" (1 Cor. 1:27).

Without God, man with all his wisdom is doomed to remain a clever fool, because: "The fear of the LORD is the beginning of wisdom" (Prov. 9:10).

Verses 22-23   The Sixth Woe: Against the Heroes of the Bottle

22   Woe to them who are heroes to drink wine
And great warriors in mixing strong drink.

23 Who justify the wicked for a bribe
And take away the justice from the just.

Comment

22 For the second time Isaiah returns to the evil of strong drink, apparently a widespread habit of the idle rich of his day. In the second woe (v. 11-17) Isaiah dealt with the evil of alcoholism and its degenerating effect upon the nation as a whole. History has confirmed the truth of Isaiah's warning, not only in the experience of Israel, but also of many nations and mighty empires. Drunkenness and unbridled luxury are the sure sign of a decaying civilization, which is doomed to perish in the end.

23 However in this sixth woe the prophet deals with one particular aspect of alcoholism; its perverting effect upon the rulers and the judges of a people. Alcoholism undermines their sense of justice and fairness. It makes them an easy mark for bribery and corruption. The heroes of drinking wine and "mixing strong drink" (the cocktail parties) are the same who:

Justify the wicked for a bribe,
And take away the justice from the just.

Verses 24-25   The Reason Why The LORD'S
Anger Is Aroused

24 Therefore, just as a tongue of fire devours the stubble
And the chaff is consumed by the flame,
So shall their roots be as rottenness,
And their blossom shall go up like dust,
For they have rejected the law of the LORD of hosts,
And despised the word of the Holy One of Israel.

25 Because of this is the anger of the LORD kindled against his people
And he stretched forth his hand and smote them.
And the hills trembled,
And their carcasses were as refuse in the streets.
For all this, his anger is not turned away,
And his hand is still stretched forth.

Comment

24 In the message of the six woes (8-23) Isaiah laid bare some of the evils which were sapping away the moral strength of the nation. Now he sums it all up by saying that this people is rotten from the root to its blossom, its superficial prosperity and outward glitter is ready for the fire, just like so much stubble and chaff.

25 The cause of Israel's depravity lies in her rejection of and contempt for the Holy One of Israel and of His Word. For this reason, God's awesome anger has been aroused against His people, so that even the hills will tremble when He executes judgment.

Although the prophet uses the past tense, he obviously predicts punishments which are yet to come. This will come in the form of a terrible invasion.

Verses 26-30   An Enemy Army as the Instrument of Divine Anger

26   And he will give a signal to nations from afar,
And he will whistle to them from the end of the earth,
And behold they will come speedily, quickly.

27   None shall be weary, none shall stumble,
None shall slumber nor sleep;
Not a belt shall be loose,
Not a shoe latch shall be broken.

28   Their arrows are all sharp,
Their bows all bent.
Their horses' hoofs are as hard as flint,
Their wheels like a whirlwind.

29   His roar is like a lion's,
They shall roar like young lions and snarl.
He will take hold of his prey and make off,
And there will be none to rescue.

30   In that day he will roar against them,
       like the roar of the sea,
And looking at the land, it is darkness and misery,
The light has become dim in the cloudy skies.

Comment
Verses 26-30

Here is one of the most awesome descriptions of an immense hostile army on the march. But the invisible Commander-In-Chief is the Lord Himself.

He gives a signal to distant nations, and whistles for them and they come running. Nothing can stop them. Disciplined and hardened, they are an awesome army, relentlessly pushing forward, like a tidal wave, on their mission of conquest and destruction.

They descend upon the hapless nation like roaring lions, killing and carrying off their prey. The whole land and the sky is dark from the smoke and the fire of burning cities and villages.

Such was one of the frightening visions which Isaiah presented to his people in flaming words. It was a prophecy which was fulfilled during and long after the lifetime of the prophet, when first Samaria and later Judah were carried off into captivity.

The Vision of the Lord in the Temple

The Prophet Commissioned

Isaiah, Chapter 6

Verses   1-4   The vision of the Lord in the Temple.

           5-8   Isaiah's confession and cleansing.

           9-10   The prophet called to a mission of hardening and seeming failure.

           11-13   The ultimate outcome; devastation of the land, exile and survival of "a holy seed."

Verses 1-4

1   In the year when King Uzziah died I saw the Lord sitting upon a throne, high and lifted up, and the train [of his garment] filled the temple.

2   Seraphim stood above him, each had six wings; with twain he covered his face, with twain he covered his feet, and with twain he did fly.

3   And they cried to each other and said:
Holy, holy, holy is the Lord of Hosts.
The whole earth is full of his glory.

4   And the foundations of the thresholds shook at the voice of them that cried. And the house was filled with smoke.

Some General Observations

The sixth chapter of Isaiah, which describes a theophany and the commissioning of a prophet, is one of the most majestic and awe-inspiring passages in all the Old Testament.

Actually any theophany, that is God's manifestation of Himself to man, is a voluntary limitation on the part of God of His divine nature in order that men might be able to experience His awesome presence without perishing. The enormous energy produced at an electric power station must first be transformed into such a form of electricity as will enable the consumer to use it without being himself consumed.

The question whether this chapter records the original call of Isaiah or whether he was commissioned while he already exercised his prophetic ministry, is a matter of debate, which cannot be answered with complete certainty. The majority of commentators favor the first assumption.

On the other hand ancient rabbinical tradition, followed also by some early Christian commentators, holds that Isaiah was already a prophet when he "saw the Lord" (v. 1). The rabbis maintained that the gift of prophecy was withdrawn from Isaiah when he failed to rebuke King

Uzziah for his presumptuous attempt to offer incense in the Temple (2 Chron. 26:16-21). In keeping with this view they translate verse 5a "Woe is me because I was silent," instead of "I am undone."

It is clear that Isaiah's vision and commission took place in the year of Uzziah's death, presumably soon after that event, apparently during his early ministry (cf. Isa. 1:1 with 6:1).

Another point of debate concerns the position of chapter six: why was it placed in its present position and not at the very beginning of the book, where the call of other prophets was usually recorded? (Jer. 1:4-10, Ezk. 1:1-28, Hos. 1:1-2).

It is generally agreed that the first chapter of Isaiah is an introduction to the whole book. Chapters 2-5 present a collection of prophetic messages covering the earliest period of Isaiah's ministry during the reign of Uzziah and Jotham, approximately from 740-735 B.C.

During that period in spite of the solemn warnings of Isaiah, and his predictions of approaching disaster, the people continued to sink deeper in their disobedience and defiance of God, with resulting moral decay. Meanwhile Israel's enemies were forging an ever tighter noose around Israel and Judah, menacing the very existence of the two divided and feuding kingdoms. No doubt Isaiah must have been asking himself why his nation was rushing so blindly toward its own doom. The prophet found the answer to his painful query in recalling the commission which the LORD of Hosts gave to him early in his ministry.

He remembered that he was called to speak to a people who would neither hear nor heed his message. Now things were coming to pass exactly the way the Lord said they would. The political and moral situation of Israel served to confirm the prophet, that he was called to a frustrating and apparently useless ministry, described in chapter 6:9, 10. Isaiah's call was further confirmed by later events during the disastrous reign of Ahaz. These events are reflected in the prophecies of chapters 7-12. The placing of chapter 6 in its present position, therefore, appeared to be natural and logical, serving to clarify the past as well as future events.

Comment

Verses 1-4   The year when Uzziah died. This was approximately the year 740 B.C. Uzziah died after a reign of fifty-two years. In many ways Uzziah was a good and successful king. He subdued most of the hereditary enemies of Judah. He turned Jerusalem into a fortified bastion and equipped the city with the most modern weapons of war of his day. He also helped to develop the agriculture and the commerce of the nation. Under him Judah became a prosperous nation (2 Chron. 26:6-15). However, Uzziah suffered from a common human failing; success went to his head. One incident in particular led to Uzziah's tragic downfall. It is described in 2 Chronicles 26:16:

But when he was strong, his heart was lifted up to his destruction: for he transgressed against the Lord his God, and went into the temple of the LORD to burn incense upon the altar of incense.

For this act of hubris the king was smitten with leprosy and was compelled to spend the rest of his life in an isolated house built especially for him. His son Jotham became prince regent and ruled over the nation about twelve years before his father died.

Five years before Uzziah died Tiglathpileser III (745-727 B.C.), the ambitious warrior king of Assyria, suddenly appeared on the horizon of the Near East. His grand design was to conquer all the kingdoms between the Euphrates and the Nile and to establish in their place one great Assyrian empire. Naturally all the conquered or imperiled kingdoms seethed with apprehension and revolt, forming alliances against the Assyrians and plotting political intrigues and rebellions. The kingdoms of Samaria and Judah were tottering on the brink of doom, not only because of the foreign menace, but primarily because of their spiritual and moral decay.

However, instead of repenting and turning to God, as Isaiah and other prophets had urged, the people were caught up in a frenzy of self-indulgence, dissipation and mutual harrassment and oppression. This is how Isaiah saw the contemporary scene:

And in that day did the Lord God of Hosts call to weeping, and to mourning. . . .
And behold joy and gladness . . . eating flesh, and drinking wine; let us eat and drink; for tomorrow we shall die (Isa. 22:12, 13).

Such was the situation of Jerusalem and Judah in the year when King Uzziah died.

No wonder that Isaiah felt depressed and apprehensive about the future of his people. It was a time of crisis for Israel and for the prophet himself. Was there any hope for his nation?

It was during this time of crisis and distress that Isaiah went to the holy Temple in order to meditate and to seek guidance and instruction from his Lord.

He went into the temple in humility of heart, deeply conscious of his own unworthiness, and the Lord deigned to reveal Himself to him, and to commission him as His messenger. The long-lived King Uzziah was dead, but Isaiah saw that the Eternal and Holy God of Israel lives and reigns in all His awesome majesty and glory.

I saw the Lord. . .

Numerous passages in the Scriptures tell us that man cannot see God and live (Ex. 33:20, John 1:18). Is there then a contradiction between Isaiah's statement "I saw the Lord" and those passages? Of course not! Man cannot see God as He truly is, but God may and did reveal Himself to some of His chosen servants, in such a way that they knew that God did appear to them.

To Abraham, the Lord appeared in the plains of Mamre in the form of three men, one of whom he addressed as "My Lord" (Gen. 18:1-3). To Jacob God appeared in the form of a man with whom he wrestled for a blessing till dawn. Then he called the name of the place Peniel, "for I have seen God face to face and live" (Gen. 32:24-30). To Moses the Lord appeared in the burning bush (Ex. 3:4), and to Isaiah the Lord manifested Himself as the eternal King enthroned in His holy Temple, surrounded by fiery angels, while His glory filled all the earth.

When the eternal God manifested Himself in Christ, "He made himself of no reputation and took upon him the form of a servant and was made in the likeness of men" (Phil. 2:7).

In a sense every theophany is a manifestation of Christ, because God condescends and limits Himself in order to manifest Himself in such a form as man can comprehend and endure. This is why John the evangelist referring to Isaiah's vision states that Isaiah spoke of Christ (John 12:41), high and lifted up. Some scholars (Delitzsch, Slotki, Kissane, Phillips) apply the words "high and lifted up" to the throne, and not to God Himself. However, these words are attributes of God and not of His throne. His train (that is the hem of His royal robe), flowed over and filled the Temple. Some interpreters understand that the word Temple *(Heichal)* refers to the heavenly·Temple sometimes mentioned by the Psalmist (Psa. 11:4, 18:6, also in Mic. 1:2). However the reference to certain physical aspects of the Temple such as the foundations of the thresholds (v. 4), and the altar with its several implements (v. 6), indicates that Isaiah had in mind the earthly Temple in Jerusalem. Nevertheless Isaiah's awesome vision of the Lord in all His majesty seemed to break down all the physical dimensions and limitations of a man-made structure and to take on the aspects of the heavenly Temple, which encompasses and fills all the earth.

2 Seraphim, plural of "seraph"—a fiery angel. From Isaiah's description of these angelic beings they appeared to be in the form of man but with three pairs of wings. One pair of wings covered their faces so that they should not see the Lord, two of their wings covered their feet, in a gesture of reverence and modesty, and one pair of wings they used to fly and to hover as "they stood" in attendance upon Jehovah. The plural noun "seraphim" does not indicate clearly whether there were only two angels or a host of angels.

3 From Isaiah's description of the seraphim, we gather that their function was to serve God, to worship Him and to execute His will (v. 6). Their adoration of God consisted in a continuous chant:

138

Holy, holy, holy is the Lord of hosts
The whole earth is full of his glory.

The essence and supreme attribute of God, according to this vision of God, is His holiness, which expresses His perfection, His purity, and His absolute "otherness" and "aboveness" over all His creation. The glory of God which fills the whole earth, or as some have translated this passage "the fullness of the earth is His glory," is the reflection and manifestation in the universe of the holiness of God.

The thrice repeated holy, holy, holy, *(trisagion)* expresses emphatically the absolute holiness of God. Some Christian commentators see in this an allusion to the Trinity of God, but Calvin was of the opinion that the doctrine of the Trinity cannot be deduced from this particular passage. The vision of the thrice holy God became so central to our prophet's experience that his description of Him as "the Holy One of Israel" became the hallmark and seal of Isaiah's writings. The expression "the Holy One of Israel" occurs twelve times in the first part of Isaiah (1-39), and seventeen times in the second part (40-66). Chief rabbi Luzzato of Rome years ago made this observation: "The prophet as if with a presentiment that the authenticity of the second part of his book would be disputed, has stamped both parts of his book with the name of God 'the Holy One of Israel,' as if with his own seal." The only other passages where "the Holy One of Israel" occurs are in the Psalms, three times; (71:22, 78:41, 89:19) and twice in Jeremiah (50:29, 51:5).

4 The effect upon the Temple of the angelic chant: "Holy, holy, holy, the whole earth is full of his glory" was like the eruption of a volcano; the foundations of the thresholds of the Temple shook and "the house filled with smoke." Smoke and fire often signify the presence of God, as at Mount Sinai, or during the wilderness wanderings of the children of Israel (Ex. 19:18). Elsewhere Isaiah prophesied that after the cleansing and restoration of Israel the LORD would create over all the habitation of Zion and over all her assemblies "a cloud and smoke by day, and the shining of a flaming fire by night" (4:5).

Verses 5-8   Isaiah's awareness of his sinful condition, followed by his cleansing and call.

5 And I said:
   Woe is me for I am undone,
   For I am a man of unclean lips,
   And I dwell amidst a people of unclean lips,
   For mine eyes have seen the King
   The LORD of Hosts.

6 Then one of the seraphim flew unto me,
 And in his hands was a glowing stone,
 Which he took with the tongs from off the altar.

7 And he touched my mouth and said:
 Behold this has touched thy lips,
 And thine iniquity is taken away,
 And thy sin is atoned.

8 Then I heard the voice of the Lord, saying:
 Whom shall I send,
 And who will go for us?
 Then said I, Here am I, send me.

Comment

5 The effect upon Isaiah of the presence of the thrice Holy God and of His ministering angels was such that he felt "undone." In Hebrew *"nidmeithi,"* which is derived from the verb *"dum."* In the passive form this means "to be lost," to perish, or to be annihilated. As we have mentioned before, some of the ancient Jewish commentators confused the verb *"dum"*—"to be undone" with *"dumam"* which means "to be speechless" or "silent." On the basis of this they understood that the Lord withdrew from Isaiah the gift of prophecy when he failed to rebuke Uzziah for his presumption.

Isaiah himself explains why he felt "undone":—

 a. Because of his own and his people's sinfulness.
 b. Because "my eyes have seen the King, the LORD of Hosts."

No one can stand in the presence of a holy God without becoming profoundly and devastatingly aware of his sinful condition. Only the wicked, or those who are completely deprived of spiritual insight can think well of themselves. To see the Lord is to have a most humbling experience. Isaiah's realization of, and identification with "a people of unclean lips" only added to his sense of unworthiness. Another reason why Isaiah felt "undone" was because as an Israelite he knew well God's Word to Moses: "Thou canst not see my face, for there shall no man see me and live" (Ex. 33:20).

6-7 However, as soon as Isaiah confessed his own sinfulness and unworthiness, the Lord provided a remedy: one of the seraphim, at the command of the Lord, touched his mouth with a glowing stone (or burning coal), which he took from the altar, and pronounced that his iniquity was removed and his sin atoned.

Years before Uzziah had entered the Temple of God in the pride of his heart and been stricken with leprosy (2 Chron. 26:16-21).

Now Isaiah came into the Temple in great humility, deeply conscious of his sinfulness and unworthiness, and received a new vision of God, forgiveness of his sins and atonement.

8 Then I heard the voice of the Lord, saying:
Whom shall I send, and who will go for us?

Only the man whose sins have been forgiven is worthy and able to hear the voice of God, and to obey Him. The Lord did not address Himself directly to Isaiah, but spoke, as it were, impersonally. There was no compulsion or pressure. Those who would go on the Lord's errand must do so voluntarily.

It is interesting to note that the Lord uses the plural "Who will go for us?" Some commentators have called this and also Genesis 1:26 "the plural of majesty." The use of the plural here is striking. While we do not wish to stress unduly the Trinitarian interpretation of this passage, the least that can be said is, that the teaching about the Triune God is not inconsistent with the Old Testament Scriptures, but in complete harmony with them.

Isaiah's response to God's call is brief and definite: "Here am I, send me." The Hebrew is even more concise: *"Hinneni, shlahani."* It might be well to remember the two words: *Hinneni, shlahani*—Here am I, send me.

Verses 9-10   The Prophet's Commission

9 And he said: Go and tell this people,
   Hear indeed, but understand not;
   And see indeed, but perceive not.

10 Make the heart of this people fat,
   And their ears heavy,
   Paste down their eyes,
   Lest they see with their eyes
   And hear with their ears,
   And understand with their heart
   And then turn and be healed.

Comment:
9-10   And He said, go and tell this people.

Note the words "this people" and not the usual "my people," indicating the Lord's intense displeasure with Israel. No other prophet has ever been called to a more heartbreaking and frustrating mission than Isaiah, a completely negative errand. In effect the prophet was to tell his people:

to hear but not to understand
to see without being able to perceive
to make their hearts insensitive, and unresponding to God's will.

The prophet is commanded to smear (or to paste), their eyes shut, lest they repent and be healed. He is to preach his people "callous, deaf and

141

blind." Such a commission sounds extremely harsh and cruel. And yet it corresponds to a terrible reality of the human spirit. A deliberate and continued refusal to perceive what God is doing or to hear His voice must eventually result in blindness and deafness; a deliberate refusal to respond to the promptings of His Spirit must make one's heart hard and callous, until the point is reached where there is no return and no cure.

11-13 Israel's callousness to last until the land has become devastated and the people exiled. Yet "a holy seed shall remain."

11 And I said, "How long, O Lord?"
And he answered:
Until cities become devastated and without inhabitant,
And houses without men
And the land become utterly waste

12 And the Lord has removed men
And the desolation in the midst of the land
Shall be very great.

13 And if there be a tenth which shall return, it too shall
Be consumed; like the terebinth and the oak when they
Cast off [their acorns], their substance remains:
The holy seed is her substance.

Comment:
11-12 And I said, "How long, O Lord?"

The prophet was dismayed, not because he was sent on such a thankless mission, but because of what his commission held out for the future of his people. From the depths of his heart came the agonized cry, "Lord, how long?" How long will Israel's condition of spiritual blindness, deafness and callousness continue? Isaiah's question sums up the cry of all the prophets.

The Lord's answer to Isaiah was in effect "Until their cities be destroyed, the people removed from their land and the country ravaged and devastated." Before there can be any hope of healing and restoration, Israel must first drink the cup of defeat, of total devastation and of exile.

"The Holy Seed"

13 Verse 13 is characteristic of the whole message of Isaiah. In spite of all his predictions of gloom and disaster, there is a bright glimmer of hope for Israel's future, the rainbow of promise, after the violent storm of destruction has passed.

For a while the message of gloom continues without relief: Even if a tenth of the people should survive and come back from exile, that small survivorship will again be consumed, just as when the terebinth and the oak in the fall shed their leaves and are burned. Yet all is not lost, the stump of the tree remains and shall live again. One day it will cover itself with leaves as with a new glory. Verse 13 is difficult to translate because the Hebrew words lend themselves to differing interpretations. The word "leaves" is not expressly in our Hebrew text, but seems to be implied. Others translate "like the terebinth and the oak whose stump remains standing when it is felled," (R.S.V.). However the basic thought remains the same. The Hebrew word *"matseveth"* can be translated either as "a stump" or "substance."

The doctrine of "the holy seed" belongs to the heart of Isaiah's message. In one form or another the prophet alludes to it in all of his oracles. "The holy seed" is not just a mere survivorship, who will come back from exile. Those who later returned from Babylon were not all faithful to the Lord; not all of them belonged to "the holy seed." Only those who truly repented and believed in the Lord and did His will were of "the holy seed." The Apostle Paul later called them: "a remnant according to the election of grace" (Rom. 11:5). In this holy seed was vested the hope of Israel's redemption. Out of this "holy seed" was to come the Messiah Himself who would be the Redemption and the Redeemer of Israel. Thus in a real sense Isaiah 6:13 is a Messianic prophecy.

The sixth chapter of Isaiah contains the kernel of all that Isaiah ever prophesied: The vision of the thrice holy Lord, a deep awareness of his own and his nation's sinful condition, his call to prophecy to a disobedient and unresponsive people, to predict the approaching disaster and exile, and the return of a small survivorship, out of which shall come forth "a holy seed," a faithful remnant, and the Redeemer.

To this divine commission which "the Holy One of Israel" entrusted to the prophet, Isaiah remained faithful throughout his long and dedicated life. Like the Apostle Paul, eight centuries later, Isaiah could have said: "Whereupon, O King . . . I was not disobedient unto the heavenly vision." (Acts 26:19).

The Book
of Immanuel

Prophecies during the Reign of Ahaz (735-715 B.C.)

Isaiah, Chapter 7

Verses	1, 2	Rezin of Damascus and Pekah of Samaria plan to capture Jerusalem.
	3-9	Isaiah brings Ahaz a message of reassurance from the Lord.
	10-13	Ahaz disbelieves the prophet and rejects the offer of a sign.
	14-16	Nevertheless, the Lord gives the house of Judah a sign: The birth of Immanuel.
	17	Judah's real peril not Rezin and Pekah, but the Assyrian king.
	18-25	The Assyrian invasion will result in extreme desolation.

Verses 1, 2

1 It came to pass that in the days of Ahaz, the son of Jotham, the son of Uzziah, the king of Judah, that Rezin, the king of Syria and Pekah, the son of Ramaliah, went up to Jerusalem to war against it, but could not subdue it.

2 When the house of David was informed that Syria was encamped in Ephraim, his heart and the heart of his people trembled, as the trees of the forest tremble before the wind.

A few Observations concerning Isaiah, Chapter 7

This chapter contains a pivotal Messianic prophecy (v. 14) which is crucial to the understanding of the whole message of Isaiah. This is why next to chapter 53, Isaiah 7 has been one of the most contested parts of the book.

Isaiah 7:14 is a watershed which separates conservative Biblical scholarship from the so-called liberal school of Old Testament exegesis. It is our opinion that the conservative position, which interprets this prophecy Messianically, is more consistent with the Hebrew text and the sense of this oracle than the position of those who take a contrary view.

Comment:

1 In the days of Ahaz . . .

Of all the kings of Judah, Ahaz was one of the most sinister, debased and disastrous rulers in the history of his people. His idolatrous proclivities and lack of true statesmanship brought irreparable harm to Judah. In appealing to Tiglath-pileser for help against Samaria and Syria, Ahaz invited the wolf to protect the sheep. This misguided act of so-called "practical politics" eventually sealed the doom not only of Israel but also of Judah.

Apparently the purpose of the Syro-Ephraimitic expedition against Ahaz was to force him into an alliance against Assyria, or failing this, to put on the throne of Judah a collaborator, an unknown person called "the son of Tabael" (v. 6). Incidentally, Isaiah and Ahaz provide us with a fascinating study in diametrically contrasting characters, in faith and unbelief, in far-sighted vision and wisdom, contrasted by moral decadence and political obtuseness.

2 And the heart of Ahaz and the heart of his people trembled

Had the two northern confederates succeeded in their plan, they would have wiped out the whole Davidic dynasty of which Ahaz was, at that particular historical point, the degenerated and unworthy representative. Ahaz had ample reason to be in terror of the two kings. Only recently each of them had in turn inflicted a terrible holocaust upon Judah and decimated her people. (2 Chron. 28:5-8). Ahaz and the house of Judah had ample cause to tremble "like trees of the forest before the wind."

Verses 3-9

3   Then said the LORD to Isaiah, go out to meet Ahaz, you and your son Shear-Yashub, to the end of the aqueduct of the upper pool, to the road of the fuller's field.

4   And say to him: take heed and keep calm, do not be afraid, and let not your heart melt before these two stumps of smouldering firebrands, before the fierce anger of Rezin and Syria, and of the son of Remaliah.

5 Because Syria, Ephraim and the son of Remaliah have designed an evil plan against thee, saying:

6 Let us march against Judah and harass him, and we will set up a king in their midst, namely the son of Tabael:

7 Thus saith the Lord Jehovah, It will not happen, nor come to pass.

8 For the head of Syria is Damascus, and the head of Damascus is Rezin, and within sixty-five years Ephraim will be broken in pieces, so that it will be a people no more.

9 And the head of Ephraim is Samaria, and the head of Samaria is the son of Remaliah. If you will not believe, you will certainly not survive.

Comment:

3 The Lord sends Isaiah to Ahaz with a message of reassurance.

At this time when Ahaz was completely dismayed and frightened, the Lord was still mindful of His promise to David (2 Sam. 7:12-16), and sent Isaiah accompanied by his son Shear-Yashub (A-Remnant-Shall-Return), with a message of reassurance. The presence of Shear-Yashub was to serve both as a warning of impending disaster and also as an assurance that even in the wrath of God there is mercy. It may be surmised that Ahaz went out to the city aqueduct to inspect the water supply of Jerusalem before the expected siege.

4-7 Take heed and be quiet . . .

"Do not panic, but trust in the Lord," this in essence, was the prophet's counsel for Ahaz. Under similar circumstances at a later time, when Hezekiah was considering an alliance with Egypt against Sennacherib, Isaiah also warned the king against it. "In quietness and in confidence shall be your strength," (30:15) was the prophet's advice.

What seemed a terrible menace to Ahaz in reality was only a passing dark cloud, Rezin and Pekah were just "two smouldering firebrands" about to burn out.

The term "the Lord Jehovah" (v. 7) emphasizes the absolute sovereignty and omnipotence of God.

8, 9 Within sixty-five years Ephraim will be broken in pieces.

8 The prophet sets a definite time limit for the end of Ephraim as a people, namely a period of sixty-five years. Subsequent history confirmed Isaiah's prediction in a remarkable way.

The chronological order of events after Isaiah's prediction was this.:

734 B.C. Isaiah met Ahaz (Isa. 7:3).

732 B.C. Damascus was captured and Rezin killed (2 Ki. 16:9).

722 B.C. Samaria was captured and a large part of her population carried off into captivity (2 Ki. 17:4-6).

669 B.C. Esar-haddon, king of Assyria, put a complete end to Samaria by carrying off the rest of the ten northern tribes to Assyria and resettling Samaria with colonists from the Assyrian provinces, who became known as "Samaritans" (2 Ki. 17: 22-24).

Thus the period of sixty-five years, (734-669 B.C.) predicted by Isaiah was literally fulfilled and Ephraim ceased to be a separate and distinct people.

Because of its preciseness some critics have called this particular prophecy a *vaticinium ex post eventu*—a prophecy made after the event had already taken place. However, this type of criticism only proves the critic's blind spot in refusing to accept the possibility of predictive prophecy, while expecting others to accept his unbelief as an article of faith.

9 If you will not believe, you will not survive . . . [or remain].

The prophet again uses his favored method of the play on words, which in the Hebrew original reads:

"*Im lo taaminu - lo teamenu.*" The alliteration escapes us in the English translation. Luther skillfully translated this into German:

"*Glaubt ihr nicht, so bleibt ihr nicht.*"

Isaiah was telling his people that in order to survive they must believe.

Verses 10-16 The Sign of The Virgin

10 And the Lord spoke again to Ahaz, saying:
below or in the height above.

11 Ask thee a sign from the LORD thy God, either from the depth

12 But Ahaz said: "I shall not ask, nor will I tempt the LORD."

13 And he [Isaiah] said: Hear ye now, O house of David, is it not enough that you weary men, will ye also weary my God?

14 Therefore the Lord himself shall give you a sign, behold the virgin shall conceive and bear a son, and shall call his name Immanu-el [God-With-Us].

15 Butter and honey shall he eat till he knows to refuse evil and to choose good.

16 For before the boy shall know to refuse evil, the land of whose two kings thou art in terror shall be forsaken.

17 The LORD will bring upon thee and upon thy people a day, such as has not come since the day when Ephraim seceded from Judah, that is the king of Assyria.

Comment:

10   The Lord spoke again to Ahaz . . .

In verse 3, the Lord spoke to Isaiah. Here He addresses Himself directly to Ahaz. This is a classic example of the close identification between the prophet and God; when the prophet speaks, God speaks through him. God's word and that of His prophet are inseparable.

11   Ask thee a sign from the LORD, thy God . . .

The Lord offered to give Ahaz any sign which he might ask whether down below on earth or above in heaven. In spite of the rank apostacy of Ahaz and his gross disloyalty, the Lord still calls Himself "thy God," perhaps in order to stimulate any latent faith within the soul of Ahaz.

12   However Ahaz conveniently assuming the mantle of "pious scruple" refused "to tempt God." He probably had already decided to ask Tiglath-pileser for help.

In reality Ahaz was not tempting God, but disobeying Him. It is true that Deuteronomy 6:16 enjoins: "Ye shall not tempt the LORD your God." When the devil tempted Jesus to cast Himself down from the top of the Temple, Christ quoted to him that very commandment. However, in the case of Ahaz it was the LORD Himself who commanded him to ask for a sign, which he hypocritically refused to do.

A sign, in Hebrew *oth,* may be an event or a symbolic action, which serves to authenticate the prophet's word as God's message. The predicted event may or may not be a miracle, and may come to pass immediately, or in the distant future. Sometimes the person to whom the sign was given did not live to see it come to pass. The sign was given in order that when it came to pass, future generations might know that the God who spoke also fulfilled the promise which He made.

13   It is not enough that you weary men . . .

After Ahaz refused the offered sign, the prophet addressed himself not only to Ahaz but to all the household of David. In the past the kings of Judah had often wearied God by refusing to believe His messengers. Now Ahaz and the whole house of David were wearying the Lord by refusing to believe Him.

14   Behold therefore the virgin shall conceive and bear a son and shall call his name Immanuel.

The Meaning of Almah in The Old Testament

Before we can profitably discuss the significance of this key Messianic prophecy, we must first understand the meaning of the word *"almah."* Etymologically *"almah"* is derived from the verb *"alam,"* "to hide," or "to conceal," an apt term for the nature of virginity. However the meaning of words cannot always be fully established by their etymological derivation alone. In this particular case it is also necessary to determine the Old Testament usage of the word *"almah,"* which appears first in connection with Rebekah, the future bride of Isaac. In Genesis 24:43 we read: "Behold I stand by the well of water, when the virgin [*almah*] cometh to the well to draw water."

In the same chapter Rebekah was previously described in this manner "And the damsel [*naarah*] was very fair to look upon, a virgin [*bethulah*], neither has any man known her" (v. 16).

Thus Rebekah is referred to in the same chapter of Genesis as "a damsel"— *naarah*; a virgin—*bethulah*; and *almah,* another term for virgin, or a young unmarried woman of good repute. The term *"almah"* is never applied to a married woman.

Altogether the word *"almah"* and its plural *"alamoth"* occurs seven times in the Hebrew Scripture:

Genesis 24:43—applied to Rebekah, the future bride of Isaac

Exodus 2:8—applied to Miriam, the sister of Moses

Psalm 68:25—translated "damsels" playing with timbrels in King James Version (plural *"alamoth"*)

Song of Solomon 1:3 and 6:8—virgins (of the royal court)

Proverbs 30:19—King James Version—"The way of a man with a maid" *(almah)*

Isaiah 7:14—"Behold the virgin. . . ." *(ha-almah)*

In every instance the context decidedly favors the translation "virgin."

It is interesting to note that until comparatively recent times, before the word *"almah"* became a key issue, it was always translated "a virgin" by Jewish and Christian scholars.

Almah in the Septuagint and in the New Testament

In the 3rd century B.C., long before there ever was a Christological controversy between Jews and Christians, the Jewish translators of the Septuagint rendered the word *"almah"* with the Greek term for virgin *"parthenos."* Matthew in 1:23, quoting Isaiah 7:14 from the Septuagint used the same term *"parthenos."*

The Testimony of Rashi

The most famous medieval Jewish Bible commentator, Rashi (1040-1105), known for his determined opposition to the Christian interpretation of the Old Testament, made this astounding comment concerning the meaning of *almah*:

"Behold the almah shall conceive and bare a son and shall call his name Immanuel. This means that our Creator shall be with us. And this is the sign: the one who will conceive is a girl *(naarah)*, who never in her life has had intercourse with any man. Upon this one shall the Holy Spirit have power."[1]

150

Rashi's comment is remarkably reminiscent of Luke 1:35: "The Holy Ghost shall come upon thee and the power of the Highest shall overshadow thee. . . ."

Likewise in his comment on The Song of Solomon 1:3, Rashi frankly explains that *"alamoth"* the plural of *"almah"* means *"betuloth"* — "virgins."

Almah in Ugaritic Literature

In the Ugaritic literature, discovered in 1927, a language closely related to Hebrew, the term *almah (glmt)* refers to an unmarried woman.[2]

Almah in Modern Hebrew

It is interesting to note that in modern Hebrew the word "virgin" is rendered either as *"almah"* or *"bethulah."* Thus the English-Hebrew Dictionary, (Efros, Kaufman, and Silk, Tel-Aviv) translates the word "virgin" into Hebrew with *"almah,"* or *"betulah."* Reuben Alcalay, (chief of the Translation Department of the Prime Minister's office of Israel) in *The Complete English-Hebrew Dictionary,* translates the word "miss" as *"almah."*

It is therefore clear that etymologically, contextually and historically the word *"almah"* means "a virgin," and is correctly so translated in the King James Version. The translation of *"almah"* as a "young woman" in the Revised Standard Version is ambiguous and therefore misleading.

The question has been asked why did not Isaiah choose the common noun *"bethulah"* for virgin, instead of *"almah."* The answer is: the term *"bethulah"* while often used in the Old Testament in the sense of "a virgin," sometimes also refers to "a married woman," for instance:

Lament like "a virgin" *(bethulah)* girded with sackcloth for the husband of her youth (Joel 1:8).

Obviously the *bethulah* in this passage was a married woman, who lost her husband and therefore was not a virgin. On the other hand *almah* always refers to an unmarried woman.

Likewise in Deuteronomy 22:19, a married woman, after the wedding night is described as *bethulah*—a term which supposedly applies exclusively to a virgin. Therefore, we conclude that of all possible terms which Isaiah might have used to describe a virgin *"almah"* was the best and least ambiguous.

The Meaning of the Sign

Let us now consider the meaning of Isaiah 7:14. How did Ahaz understand the words of Isaiah, and what did they mean to the prophet himself?

Jewish, and some Christian commentators maintain that if the sign

151

was to have any meaning to Ahaz and his household, it had to be relevant to their immediate problem. The birth of a Saviour some seven centuries later would have meant little to them.[3]

However, it is our understanding that "the sign" which the Lord gave to the house of Judah was relevant both to the current situation of Ahaz, as well as to the more basic predicament of Judah, namely her apostate condition and the need of redemption for all of Israel.

The disbelieving and idolatrous Ahaz was bound to understand the sign offered to him through Isaiah, in its most commonplace and literal sense, namely that he was being offered an assurance that he need not fear his two mortal enemies who were threatening his reign and the future of his dynasty. In token of this assurance, a virgin will conceive and bear a son and will call his name "Immanuel." This will be a sign that "God is with us."

By the time this child would be old enough to say "Daddy and Mummy," the two kings who were at present threatening his life and his kingdom, would be no more. The idolatrous Ahaz was completely incapable of comprehending the full significance of the sign given to him by God, and its implications for the future destiny of Israel. But even on this pedestrian and literal level Ahaz was not willing to receive the assurance given to him by God.

But what did the sign mean to Isaiah himself? No one was more deeply aware of Israel's real peril than Isaiah. The menace to Israel did not come from "the two smouldering firebrands," and in the final analysis, not even from the unspeakable Assyrian, terrible as he later proved to be. To Isaiah Israel's malaise was much deeper. His people were perishing from a moral disease, from a cancer of the soul. Its "head" represented by wicked Ahaz was mortally sick. The nation was covered with festering sores from head to toe. Only God could save His people, and He would do this in sending a divine Redeemer, who would be an offspring of the stem of Jesse (11:1). This was the heart of Isaiah's expectation for the destiny of Israel. It was the Messianic hope. To miss this point is to miss the whole thrust of Isaiah's message.[4]

A careful analysis of Isaiah's prophecies makes it clear that the prophet expected such a God-given supernatural Redeemer. Isaiah 7:14 predicts His birth. Isaiah 9:6,7 describes His birth and Divine character, while chapter 11:1-5 describes His glorious reign.

The expectation of this God-anointed Redeemer also runs through all other prophetic Scriptures, beginning with Genesis 3:15, which has been called "the protoevangelion," or the first Messianic prophecy, to the last book of the Old Testament, Malachi. (3:1).

Therefore, Isaiah 7:14 should be considered not as an isolated prophecy, which deals only with a specific historical situation, but as a link in a whole chain of Messianic prophecies, the sum total of which was intended to convey to Israel a clear presentation of the person and the mission of the coming Messiah. Isaiah was assuring the house of David and all the people of Israel that the dynasty of David, imperiled by foreign powers and debased by such rulers as Ahaz, would nevertheless not perish, but that God would send a Saviour, of the line of David, born of a virgin, who would establish the glorious and everlasting kingdom of God (Isa. 9:6).

The Meaning of Immanuel

It was one of the central doctrines of the Hebrew Scriptures that God was present with His people, watching over their destiny. He was with the patriarchs (Gen. 26:3; 28:15; 39:2,3). He was with Moses (Ex. 3:12) and with His people as a national entity (Ex. 3:16; 33:15-17).

The Tabernacle in the wilderness (and later the Temple in Jerusalem) was a material and physical symbol that God was amidst His people. This Presence was visible to the children of Israel in the cloud which filled the Tabernacle by day, and the pillar of fire which rested over it by night, or went before them as they journeyed in the wilderness (Ex. 40:38).

The very word for "tabernacle" in Hebrew *Mishkan* is derived from the root *shachan*—to dwell, to rest, to abide, the same root from which the word *"Shechinah"* is derived.

Isaiah was now prophesying that the birth of that wonder child, whom the virgin will call "Immanuel," "God-Is-with-Us," shall be a visible manifestation in flesh and blood, that God is truly among His people, in a manner more real and more intimate even than the Tabernacle or the Temple.

The apostle John understood this when he wrote:

And the Word was made flesh, and dwelt among us, (and we beheld his glory, the glory as of the only begotten of the Father), full of grace and truth. John 1:14

It was this certainty of the Presence of God among His people which allowed Isaiah to defy all the hostile forces of the nations assembled against Israel. Take counsel together and it shall come to nought, speak the Word and it shall not stand, for "God is with us" [*Immanu-el*] (Isa. 8:10).

The prophet's faith in the coming of the Messiah was the very foundation of his confidence in Israel's future triumph and redemption.

What kind of redeemer did Isaiah think that Immanuel would be? Isaiah gives an answer to this in chapters 9:6,7 and 11:1-10 where he describes Immanuel's glorious reign. The three prophecies, Isaiah 7:14; 9:6,7; and 11:1-10, are closely related and should be studied together. The name Immanuel, just as the four names in Isaiah 9:6, was not meant as a proper name, but rather as a description of the person and character of the Messiah.

Did Isaiah have any specific person in mind when he spoke of the coming Messiah? Some Jewish commentators have sought to identify the child with Hezekiah, or even with Isaiah's second son, Maher-shalal-hash-baz. Chronological and other considerations must exclude Hezekiah completely. As for Isaiah's son, it is clear that the prophet would never have referred to his wife as *"ha-almah"*—"the virgin," a term never applied to married woman, especially since "the prophetess," that is Isaiah's wife, was already the mother of his first son Shear-Yashub. Apart from this neither Hezekiah nor Isaiah's son resembled even approximately the exalted figure of the Redeemer so majestically depicted by Isaiah. In short, Isaiah spoke of the coming Messiah, without knowing, who ultimately He would be, or when He would come. This the Lord withheld from the vision of Isaiah, as He did from Old Testament saints (1 Pet., 1:10-12).

Looking at the person of Jesus in the light of the New Testament we realize that when Isaiah prophesied the coming of a divine deliverer of Israel, he described Him in such a way that it could apply only to Him. The portrait of the Messiah presented by Isaiah fits only the Christ of the New Testament.

15-16 Butter and honey shall he eat . . .
A reference to the primitive conditions which will prevail during the early life of Immanuel (cf. verses 21-22).

Verse 17 The LORD will bring upon thee and upon thy people and upon thy father's house days which have not come, from the day when Ephraim seceded from Judah, that is the king of Assyria.

Comment:
Having assured Ahaz that the cause of his fear will soon pass away, the prophet now points out that a far greater menace to the king and to his people was the very person whom he so foolishly invited to rescue him from his enemies, namely Tiglath-pileser, the king of Assyria. The disaster which the ferocious Assyrian will inflict upon Judah will be such as had never happened before, since the secession of the ten tribes of Israel from Judah.

Verses 18-25 The Approaching Assyrian Invasion and Its Aftermath
18 And it shall come to pass in that day that the LORD shall hiss for the fly which is in the remote regions of the rivers of Egypt, and for the bee which is in the land of Assyria.

154

19 And they shall come and rest all of them in the rugged valleys, and in the clefts of the rocks, and upon the thorns and upon all the pastures.

20 In that day shall the LORD shave with a razor hired beyond the river, that is with the king of Assyria, from head to the feet and also the beard.

21 And it shall come to pass in that day, that a man shall keep alive a young cow and two sheep.

22 And it shall be that from the abundance of milk he shall eat butter; indeed butter and honey shall everyone eat, that will remain in the midst of the land.

23 And so it shall be that in the place where there were a thousand vines worth a thousand pieces of silver, it shall become briers and thistles.

24 One shall come there with arrows and bow:
for all the land shall become briers and thistles.

25 And all the hills which are digged with hoes, thou shalt not go there, for fear of briers and thorns. It shall be a place to send oxen, and for sheep to trample.

Comment:

18-25

18 Previously (5:26) Isaiah predicted that the Lord would whistle for distant nations which would descend upon Judah to loot and to despoil her. Now he identifies those nations as Egypt and Assyria, the hereditary enemies of Israel. Egypt is syymbolized by the pestiferous fly which infested the Nile Delta, and Assyria as the stinging bee, symbolic of the cruel nature of the Assyrians.

19 "The Egyptian fly" and "the Assyrian bee" later clashed when Necho of Egypt and Nebuchadnezzar of Assyria fought against each other for the possession of the important key city of Carchemish on the Euphrates. Josiah, the king of Judah became involved unwisely in this conflict and was killed in 609 B.C. Carchemish was finally captured by Nebuchadnezzar in 605 B.C. From then on Judah's doom was sealed. In 587-86 B.C. Jerusalem was captured and the people led into the Babylonian captivity.

20 "The Assyrian razor" from beyond the Euphrates whom Ahaz had foolishly hired, will shave Judah from top to toe, including the beard. To an Israelite the beard was the emblem of his manly dignity. Isaiah predicted that the land would be shaven clean of man and of all his treasured possessions, and that the unfortunate survivors would undergo the most cruel treatment and indignities. This was exactly what happened later under Sennacherib who in 701 invaded Judah, destroyed 46 cities and led 200,000 people of Judah into captivity.

21-22 A young cow and two sheep . . .

Here Isaiah gives a graphic description of the condition which will prevail in Israel and Judah after the enemy will have done his worst. The pitiful few survivors left after the invasion and deportation, will live on milk and honey, the spontaneous products of a wild and uncultivated land, just as one might live in a primitive jungle.

The once choice and valuable vineyards, which used to be worth a thousand pieces of silver, that is a sizable fortune, will become a wilderness overgrown with briers and thistles. The hills once so carefully and lovingly hoed and terraced, which used to be a joy to the eye, (even as they are today in some parts of Israel) will become a jungle of impassable and unsightly growth, suitable only for wildlife hunting and the grazing of oxen and trampling of sheep.

Notes: 1. Rashi, Mikraoth Gedoloth on Isaiah 7:14.

2. Edward J. Young, *The Book of Isaiah*, Volume 1, page 287.

3. This position is taken, among others, by Rabbi Dr. I. W. Slotki in his *Isaiah*.

4. Professor Abraham J. Heschel of the Jewish Theological Seminary of America in his book *The Prophets* (The Jewish Publication Society of America) manages to discuss Isaiah on almost a hundred pages without even once mentioning the word "Messiah" or "the Messianic hope," a truly remarkable feat.

The Prophet Receives an Ominous Command

Isaiah, Chapter 8

Verse 1   And the LORD said unto me: "Take thee a large tablet and write upon it with a common writing stylus concerning *Maher-shalal-hash-baz* — the spoils speeds, the booty hastens!

2   So I took unto me reliable witnesses, Uriah the priest and Zechariah the son of Jeberechiah.

3   Then I drew near the prophetess, after which she conceived and gave birth to a son and the LORD said: Call his name Maher-shalal-hash-baz.

4   For before this boy will know how to call "My father and my mother" the wealth of Damascus and the spoil of Samaria shall be carried away to the king of Assyria.

Comment:

Verses 1-4   An Ominous Sign

The Lord commands Isaiah to take a large tablet and inscribe upon it words which predict that "Soon there will be spoil and booty" *(Lemaher-shalal-hash-baz)*. The inscription is to be made with the writing stylus commonly used by ordinary people *(behereth enosh)*.

This inscription is to be authenticated by the witness of two well-known men of his day. Later when Isaiah's wife gave birth to a son, he was to call him Maher-shalal-hash-baz, the very name which God told him to write down on that tablet. The actual fulfilment of the prophecy took place when Damascus was captured by the Assyrians in 732 B.C. and Samaria ceased to be a kingdom in 722 B.C. From this point on to chapter 39, Isaiah deals chiefly with the Assyrians as the primary menace to Judah.

Verses 5-8   A Further Warning to Judah

5   And the LORD continued to speak to me further saying:

6   Since this people despises the waters of Shiloah which flow softly and take pleasure in Rezin and in the son of Remaliah,

7   Now therefore will the Lord bring upon you the waters of the river [Euphrates] which are mighty and many, that is the king of Assyria and all his pomp: and he shall overflow all his channels and go over all his banks.

8   And he shall sweep over Judah overflowing as he passes through and reaching up to the neck; and the spread of his wings shall fill the width of thy land, O Immanuel.

Comment:

5-8

The people of Judah, witnessing the defeat of Rezin of Damascus at the hands of Tiglathpileser, were apparently delighted. However, Isaiah warns them that their contempt for "the quietly flowing waters of Shiloah," a brook at the foot of Mount Zion which symbolizes divine protection and help, relying instead on Assyrian help, will bring them grief and disaster. Instead of the quiet waters of Shiloah, the gentleness of God's mercy, they will now experience the vehemence of the flood of waters of the mighty Euphrates, the destructive power of the Assyrians which will soon submerge the whole land.

The prophet gives us a very dramatic picture of the flooding of the land by the forces of Assyria which will sweep away everything in their path. Then he changes the metaphor rapidly, to an eagle with outspread wings, hovering over his helpless prey, Israel and Judah. At this point there comes from the heart of Isaiah the cry: "Immanuel," an appeal to the divine Saviour whose coming he previously predicted, as if imploring him to come quickly and save His people.

Verses 9-10 The Prophet defies Israel's enemies in the name of Immanuel

9 Make an uproar, you peoples, and be broken in pieces; and hear, all you distant lands. Arm yourselves and be smashed in pieces; arm yourselves and be smashed in pieces.

10 Plot your plots, they shall come to naught,
Scheme your schemes, they shall not stand;
for with us is Immanuel [God is with us].

Comment:

9-10 The Invocation of Immanuel

The very thought of Immanuel, the Redeemer of Israel, brings renewed confidence to the prophet so that he defies all hostile nations assembled against God's people. Whatever their wicked plans or schemes, they shall come to naught because with us is God, Immanuel, the promised redeemer.

Verses 11-15 The Prophet Warned Not to Submit to Popular Pressures

11 For the LORD has spoken to me with a forceful hand and has forbidden me to walk in the way of this people, saying:

12 Say not "treason" to all that which this people calls "treason." Do not fear their fears nor dread their terrors.

13 Only the LORD of hosts alone, him shall you sanctify. Let him be your fear and your dread.

14 And he shall be for a sanctuary [to you], but for a stumbling stone and a rock of offense to both houses of Israel, for a trap and a snare to the inhabitants of Jerusalem.

15 And many of them shall fall, and shall be broken, they will be snared and will be taken.

Comment:

Verses 11-15

The Lord addresses himself to Isaiah and to those in Judah who are faithful to Him, not to share the popular prejudices and not to submit to the pressures of the people or their leaders. Apparently Isaiah's warning to the king not to enter into an alliance with Assyria was considered by many as *kesher,* an act of treason or conspiracy. "Fear the Lord and you need fear no man," was the prophet's counsel.

Verses 16-18 Isaiah's Meditation

16 Bind up the testimony, seal this instruction among my disciples.

17 And I will wait for the LORD, who hides his face from the house of Jacob and I shall hope for him.

18 Behold, I and the children which the LORD has given me shall be for signs and wonders in Israel from the LORD of hosts who dwells in Mount Zion.

Comment:

16-18

16 Isaiah prays that God may bind up the testimony which He entrusted to him and seal His instruction in the hearts of his disciples. Apparently there was a group of faithful disciples around Isaiah who followed him closely and preserved his message in their hearts, and probably wrote them down for posterity. This is the only passage where Isaiah alludes to his disciples.

17-18 Isaiah and his two sons are to be living "signs and wonders" in Israel. The very names of the prophet and his two sons, which had a symbolic and prophetic significance, were a living confirmation of God's message to His people.

The name Isaiah, in Hebrew *Yeshaiahu*, means "The Lord will save" or "salvation is of the Lord." It was a testimony to all the people of Israel that their salvation did not depend upon Assyria or Egypt, nor upon any political alliance, but only upon the Lord of hosts.

The names of Isaiah's sons also carried an unmistakable message. *Shear-Yashub*—"A Remnant Shall Return," was a living prophecy of approaching exile and of divine deliverance to follow. The name implied not just physical survival and a return from exile, but a return to God.

Maher-shalal hash baz—literally "Speed - Spoil - Hasten - Booty." The name was meant to be a living prediction that an invasion of Israel and Judah by the Assyrian plunderer was imminent and sure to come. In addition to their prophetic names, Isaiah and his two sons were living "signs and wonders" because of their stand against the official policies of the king and public opinion, which was considered unpatriotic or even treasonous by the majority of the people.

Verses 19-22   Isaiah's Instructions to His Disciples

19 And when they shall say to you: Consult them who have familiar spirits and the wizards who chirp and mutter. Should not a people rather consult their God? [Should they consult] on behalf of the living, the dead?

20 To the law and to the testimony! If they speak not according to this word, there is no dawn in them.

21 And they shall pass through, afflicted and hungry, and when they

shall be hungry, they shall fret themselves and they shall curse their king and their God, as they turn their faces upward.

22   And they shall look at the earth, and behold distress and darkness, the gloom of anguish and widespread dimness.

Ch. 9:1   Nevertheless there shall be no lasting gloom to her, who was in anguish. As in the former days he brought reproach upon the land of Zebulun and the land of Naphtali, so in the latter times shall he glorify the way of the sea, beyond the Jordan, Galilee of the nations.

Comment:

A Warning against the Practice of Pagan Superstitions
19-22   Side by side with the true worship of God as taught by Moses and the prophets, there was in Israel a widespread popular cult which had its roots in pagan practices. It consisted of black magic, necromancy and witchcraft. All this was strictly forbidden by the Law. Many people, while paying lipservice to God, still practiced idolatrous rites and superstitions. The prophets often had to contend with all these insidious practices and demoralizing rites.

Isaiah warns his disciples and followers not to give any heed to those who invoke familiar spirits *(oboth)* or to the wizards *(Yiddonim)* "the knowing ones." These practitioners of the black arts chirped and muttered their incantations in order to impress their clients. A classic example of such illicit practices is recorded in the story of the witch of Endor, who, at the request of Saul, invoked the ghost of the prophet Samuel (1 Sam. 28:7-25).

The true worshipper should seek guidance and instruction only from the Lord and not from ghosts and wizards.

20-22   To the Law and to the Testimony

Isaiah counsels his disciples not to be misled by any man's words. The only way they can verify the teachings of men is by comparison with "the Law and the testimony"—*le-torah veli-theudah.* Here the Law means God's revealed will through His servant Moses as confirmed by the testimony of His prophets. If men contradict God's Word, it is because they have no dawn in them, that is not even a glimmer of light.

Those who rely on them shall in times of distress and hunger, become utterly despondent and frustrated and in their misery they will curse their king and their God, which is a thoroughly familiar mood. ("It's the government's fault," "Curse God"—"How could God do such a thing to me?")

As they turn their faces upward—In the past they either defied God, or ignored Him, but now in their utter misery they look up to God for

160

help. But heaven is brazen and God does not answer, for He does not hear the unrepentant.

22 And they shall look to the earth— Verse 22 is very similar to Isaiah 5:30 where the prophet in almost identical terms, describes the utter gloom and despondency of men, after the enemy has done his worst.

Ch. 9:1 This verse is actually the last verse of chapter 8 and is so arranged in the Hebrew text.

Nevertheless there shall be no lasting gloom to her who was in anguish. This is a reference to the heritage of the tribes of Zebulun and Naphtali in northern Galilee. Time and again it was exposed to the ravages of enemy invasions. Only recently (734 B.C.), it was afflicted with an invasion by Tiglath-pileser (2 Kings 15:29). But now there is to come a new dawn upon these very regions who suffered the reproach and shame of enemy oppression. These same regions will be the first to experience divine deliverance. To this very region shall come the divinely appointed Deliverer of Israel.

The Way of the Sea,— known in later centuries as the *Via Maris,* was the road which led from Egypt by way of Acco (Acre) to Damascus, along the shores of the Sea of Galilee.

Galilee of the Nations,— Hebrew *Gelil-haggoim,* literally "the circuit of the nations," was so called because this northernmost part of ancient Israel was the gateway through which gentiles entered the land of Israel either as invaders or traders. Here the foreign influence was very strong. The two tribes of Zebulun and Naphtali were closely associated as neighbors, and dwelt in this part of the country which was known as Upper Galilee (Jud. 4.6).

The Birth of Immanuel

Isaiah, Chapter 9

Verses 2-7

2 The people who walked in darkness
Have seen a great light.
They that dwell in the land of the shadow of death
Upon them a light hath shined.

3 Thou hast made the nation great,
Thou hast increased their joy.
They rejoice before thee according to the joy of harvest,
As they rejoice when they divide the spoil.

4 For the yoke of his burden
And the staff of his shoulder,

The rod of his oppressor,
Thou hast broken as in the day of Midian.

5   For every boot which tramples in fierce battle,
And the cloak rolled in blood
Shall be committed to burning
To feed the fire.

6   For unto us a child is born,
Unto us a son is given.
And the government shall be upon his shoulder,
And his name shall be called
Wonderful Counselor, Mighty God,
Everlasting Father, Prince of Peace.

7   Of the increase of his government,
And of peace there shall be no end.
Upon the throne of David and upon his kingdom
To establish it and to uphold it
With judgment and with righteousness
From henceforth even forever.
The zeal of the LORD of hosts shall accomplish this.

Comment:

Verses 2-7   The Birth of the Messianic King

2   Isaiah looks into the future and sees the people, who for a long time walked in darkness and in the shadow of death, suddenly illumined by a great light, a light which will set them free and break their yoke of bondage, physical as well as spiritual.

3   Before we can understand this verse properly, we must explain some peculiarities of the Hebrew text and the somewhat misleading translation of this passage in the King James Version which reads:

> Thou hast multiplied the nation
> and not increased the joy

While the Hebrew word *hirbitha* can be translated "thou hast multiplied" a more suitable translation would be "thou has magnified" or "made great," as indicated by the context and the parallelism of the two lines.

Another misunderstanding is due to an unfortunate misspelling by some ancient scribe of the Hebrew word *lo,* which, spelled one way, *(lamed alef)* means "no," but spelled another way *(lamed vav)* means "him." In our passage the second spelling is obviously the correct one. The massoretes, who noticed the misspelling, inserted in the Hebrew text a sign called *keri* which gives the passage a positive sense:

Thou *hast* increased their joy.

God has honored the nation of Israel by sending through them the light of the world. Their joy is great as that of reapers at harvest time; as they who divide rich spoil after the enemy has been defeated.

4-5 These two verses explain the cause of the joy.

4 The yoke of the burden, the enslaving staff around the neck, and the punishing rod of the enemy have at last been broken.

"As in the day of Midian," is a reference to the days of Gideon when the Israelites were sorely afflicted by the Midianites. It was then that Gideon and his chosen three hundred warriors, separated by the Lord Himself, obtained a signal victory over their enemy (Jud. 7).

5 For every boot which tramples in fierce battle . . .

Every last vestige of war symbolized by the heavy military boot of the trampling soldier and his blood-soaked cloak shall be burned. The thought expressed here complements the vision of the Messianic Kingdom which the prophet previously described in chapter 2:2-4.

6-7 The Messianic age will be inaugurated by the birth of the wonder child. His advent is described in jubilant tones.

6   **For unto us a child is born,**
                  Unto us a son is given.

In chapter 7:14 the birth of Immanuel was previously announced. Now the miracle child who will bring redemption is introduced in greater detail.

His birth as a child indicates His humanity. That He is given "unto us" *(lanu)* as a son, emphasizes the fact that He is God's gift to His people. His supernatural character is further indicated by the fact that "the government shall be upon his shoulder," that in a peculiar way God has entrusted to Him the rule over His people.

The Names of the Miracle Child.

The peculiar double-membered four names given to the child underline His divine character.

And his name shall be called Wonderful Counsellor,
Mighty God, Everlasting Father, Prince of Peace.

Contemporary Jewish and Christian scholars differ sharply on the interpretation of these names.

Jewish commentators did not dispute at all the Messianic nature of this prophecy until modern times, when the Christological controversy became very heated. The ancient (first century B.C.) Aramaic *Targum Jonathan* paraphrased this passage:

> And there was called His name from of old,
> Wonderful, Counsellor, Mighty God, He who

163

lives for ever, the Messiah in whose days
peace shall increase."[1]

This paraphrase presents the ancient, authentic and traditional interpretation of this passage. Later Jewish commentators, strenuously seeking to avoid the Christian interpretation, gave it a different meaning.

The renowned medieval Jewish commentator Kimchi rendered this passage:

The God who is Wonderful, Counsellor,
the mighty God, the eternal Father, calls
His name the Prince of Peace.[2]

This translation is from the standpoint of grammar, construction and context untenable, because the names would then refer to God and not to the expected child. The extent of embarrassment of modern Jewish translators with regard to this passage is indicated by the fact that Rabbi Israel W. Slotki in his commentary on Isaiah (Soncino Press) refused altogether to translate the names into English and simply transliterates them:

And his name is called Pele-joez-el-gibbor-Abi-ad-sar-shalom[3]

Among Christian commentators there is some difference of opinion as to the proper division of the names. The King James Version divides the names into five members translating Wonderful, Counsellor, the Mighty God, the Everlasting Father, the Prince of Peace. However, the massoretic accentuation supports the division into four names, each consisting of two members:

Pele Yoetz, El Gibbor, Abhi Ad, Sar Shalom

Pele Yoetz—Wonderful Counsellor—Actually the word *"pele"* is not an adjective but a noun, literally translated this means Wonder Counsellor.

The word first occurs in connection with the appearance of the Angel of God to Manoah, the father of Samson:

And Manoah said to the angel of the LORD What is your name?
And the angel of the LORD said to him: Why do you ask my name seeing that it is secret [Peli] . . .
And Manoah said to his wife, we will surely die because we saw God (Jud. 13:17-18, 22).
For their fathers he did wonders [pele] in the land of Egypt, in the field of Zoan (Psa. 78:12; also Psa. 88:12).

The word *"pele"* therefore indicates a wonder, a mysterious act of God, beyond human grasp. *Pele* wonderful or mysterious is an attribute of God, like holiness. *Pele Yoetz* therefore means a wonderful counselor who partakes of the very nature of God.

Elsewhere Isaiah wrote:
This also cometh from the LORD of Hosts who is wonderful in counsel and great in deliverance (Isa. 28:29).

Thus the first name of the child clearly indicates His divine character.

El Gibbor—Mighty God

Elsewhere Isaiah calls God *El Gibbor* (10:21): "A remnant shall return, a remnant of Jacob, to the mighty God [*El Gibbor*]"

Jeremiah refers to God: "The God who is great and mighty [*Ha-El Ha-gibbor*] his name is the LORD of hosts" (Jer. 32:18).

Here the Messiah is called the mighty God, the same name as God, thus clearly bearing witness to the divinity of the Messiah. Some translate *El Gibbor,* God-like hero, but in view of Isaiah 10:21 this is not satisfactory.

Abhi ad—The Everlasting Father

Literally the Father of eternity. In Isaiah 63:16b the prophet approaches God in these words: "Thou O Lord art our father, our redeemer, from everlasting is thy name." Here the father aspect in relation to His people is emphasized. He acts in relation to His people with paternal compassion. "Like a father pitieth his children, so the Lord pitieth them that fear him" (Psa. 103:13).

We are reminded of the words of Matthew 9:36 concerning Jesus: "But when He saw the multitudes, he was moved with compassion on them. . ." Some commentators who sought to diminish the implication of divinity in this name of the Messiah, translated *Abhi ad* - the father of booty or spoil, which neither grammatically nor contextually is admissable. The name means that the Messiah is eternal and paternal in relation to His people.

Sar Shalom—The Prince of Peace

On another occasion Isaiah prophesied that the Messianic kingdom will be a kingdom of universal peace and harmony. Now the prophet presents the Messiah as the Prince of Peace, the King of the Messianic Kingdom. The Messiah is the King of Peace. The Hebrew word *shalom* has a much wider meaning than our term "peace." Shalom is not merely absence of war and strife but prosperity, well-being, harmony within and without, peace in one's heart and peace with God, it is the perfect state of man.

Taken together the four names of the coming Messiah are an extension of the name Immanuel. They are not names in the modern sense, but rather attributes of the one to whom they are given.

7 Of the increase of his government and peace, there shall be no end upon the throne of David.

Since this Messianic Kingdom has its origin in the eternal purpose of God and is established on the dual foundation of justice and righteousness, it will increase and last forever. Justice is righteousness applied in life, righteousness is the divinely revealed and implanted knowledge of right and wrong, which motivates the man of God. The kingdom of righteousness and peace is also human. The King shall be of divine origin as well as heir of the line of David. The zeal of the Lord is that holy, determined will of God which ever strives to perform His redemptive purposes in the history of His people.

The zeal of the Lord of Hosts shall perform it.

Most Jewish commentators and some others believe that Isaiah expected Hezekiah to be the Messianic King of his prophecy. This however completely contradicts the exalted divine personality the prophet visualized as the Messiah and is in stark contrast to the life of Hezekiah, who was a man of war and not a prince of peace.

In this connection there is a peculiar sidelight on this matter in the Babylonian Talmud: "Bar-Kafara says that God intended Hezekiah to be the Messiah and Sennacherib to be Magog, but Hezekiah was unworthy of this honor."[4]

This indicates that the passage was interpreted by the ancient rabbis Messianically, and that Hezekiah was considered as a possible fulfillment of this Messianic prophecy, but rejected as unsuitable. No other historical personality fits the prophet's vision of the Messiah Jesus, the son of David and the Son of God.

9:8-10:4 The Lord's Unrelenting Wrath is Provoked by the Nation's Wickedness and Arrogance
Verse

8 The Lord sent a word to Jacob
   and it lighted upon Israel.

9 And all the people shall know,
   Ephraim and the inhabitant of Samaria,
   They who in the pride and arrogance of heart say:

10 The bricks are fallen, but we will build with cut stones,
   The sycamores are cut down, but we will replace them with cedars.

11 Therefore the LORD will set up high the oppressors of Rezin,
   And spur on his enemies.

12 Syria from the east and the Philistines from the rear
   And they will devour Israel with a full mouth.
   For all this his anger is not turned away
   And his hand is outstretched still.

13 Yet the people do not turn to him, who smites them
   Nor do they seek the LORD of hosts.

14 Therefore will the LORD cut off Israel head and tail,
   Palm branch and rush, in one day.

15   The elder and the man of prominence, he is the head,
      The prophet and the teacher of lies, he is the tail.

16   For they who lead this people cause them to go astray
      And they who are led by them are swallowed up.

17   Therefore shall the Lord have no joy in their choice young men.
      Nor shall he have compassion upon their orphans and widows.
      For everyone of them is a hypocrite and an evildoer
      And every mouth speaks abomination.
      For all this his anger is not turned away.
      And his hand is stretched out still.

18   For wickedness is burning like a fire,
      It consumes briers and thorns,
      It sets on fire the brushwood of the forest
      And it goes up in billows of smoke.

19   The land is burned by the wrath of the LORD of Hosts
      And the people have become like the food of fire.
      No man has pity on his brother.

20   He snatches on the right side and is hungry.
      He gobbles on the left but is not satisfied.
      Everyone devours his own flesh.

21   Manasseh against Ephraim, Ephraim against Manasseh,
      And both together against Judah.
      For all this his anger is not turned away
      And his hand is stretched out still.

Isaiah, Chapter 10

Verses 1-4

1   Woe to them who decree iniquitous decrees
     And to the writers who legislate trouble.

2   To deprive the poverty-stricken of a fair verdict,
     And to rob the poor of my people of justice,
     So that widows may become their spoil
     And to make orphans their loot.

3   And what will you do on the day of visitation?
     And in the day of ruination, which will come from afar?
     To whom will you run for help?
     And where will you leave your [vaunted] glory?

4   Nothing will remain, except to crouch under the captives.
     And fall under the slain.

For all this his anger is not turned away
And his hand is stretched out still.

Comment:

Verses 9:8-10:4   The Wrath of Jehovah Against His People

This section is divided into four harmonious strophes of about the same length, each ending with an ominous refrain which expresses God's unrelenting anger and determination to continue punishing Israel until they have learned their lesson. The four times repeated refrain reads:

For all this his anger is not turned away,
And his hand is stretched out still (9:12, 17, 21 and 10:4).

Strophe 1, 9:8-12   The Arrogance of Samaria

8   The Lord sent a word to Jacob

Here "a word" means God's message to His people, which He sent to them through His servants the prophets in the course of many generations.

9-10   When the Lord's Word which He now sends through Isaiah will come to pass the whole nation of Ephraim (the northern ten tribes) will then know that God has spoken. At the present moment they are blinded by their pride (gaavah), and by their arrogance, which makes them boast that they can easily replace their brick houses with the more expensive houses of quarried stones, and the cheap sycamore wood with expensive cedar.

11-12   Because of their arrogance the LORD will help the enemies of Rezin and Samaria and will entice them to attack all of Israel.

Syria from the east, the Philistines from the rear.

The Philistines never waged war against the northern kingdom but only against Judah. This is a further indication that the prophet uses here the word "Israel" in its larger sense, referring to both divided kingdoms.

Strophe 2,   v. 13-17   The Wicked Leaders of the Nation Shall Be Destroyed.

13-15   Since the nation persists in its arrogant rebellion against their Lord, the LORD will bring disaster upon their leaders, "and cut off head and tail." Isaiah himself explains what he means by "head and tail." "The elder and the prominent man," the official leaders of the nation, these are the head. The unofficial but popular (false) "prophets" who are synonymous with "the teacher of lies"—they are the tail.

16   The charge that the false prophets and teachers lead the people astray is a familiar one in Isaiah (3:12).

17   Just as these wicked leaders had no compassion on the orphans and widows, so will God take no pity on their choice young men (*bahurim*). For everyone of them is a hypocrite and evildoer and every mouth speaks abominations.

The word "hypocrite" *(honef)* primarily means "a flatterer."[5] The false prophet and lying teacher always flatters his audiences, telling them the things which they like to hear, that they are not as sinful as the true prophets of God would have them believe, and that their grim predictions will not come to pass. By flattering their people they mislead them.

Every mouth speaks abominations.

Because their hearts are wicked, their mouths are also full of folly and abominations.

Strophe 3, v. 18-21—Wickedness and Insatiable Greed Will Destroy the Nation

The land and its people are consumed by their own wickedness and the wrath of God. The social and moral conditions prevalent in Isaiah's time are frighteningly reminiscent of the moral situation of our own times.

There is snatching and grasping right and left, a ruthlessness even toward one's own flesh and blood. The more they snatch and grab the more unsatisfied and insatiable they become.

This ruthlessness is expressed not only in personal but also in national affairs. Manasseh and Ephraim, two of the most closely related tribes are always at each other's throat. The only time they join forces is to plot and to attack their brothers from the South, Judah. Here is a picture of a nation where everybody is against everybody, thus bringing down the wrath of God upon all of them.[6]

Strophe 4, Isaiah 10:1-4 Corrupt Lawmakers Make Corrupt Laws

10:1-2 The prophet denounces the lawmakers who decree iniquitous decrees in order to deprive the poor, the needy and the helpless of justice, in order to enrich themselves.

3-4 The denunciation is followed by a few searching questions which hardly need further elucidation. He predicts that God is about to visit the nation with His judgment in the form of a devastating invasion by a distant enemy, the Assyrians. Since they have not repented nor turned to God, to whom will they turn for help in the hour of judgment, and where will they leave all their "glory?" The word "glory" here is used ironically and applies to their pride in their cherished possessions and wealth (Isa. 9:10). They will eventually go into captivity as miserable and crushed prisoners or will fall among the slain.

The arrogant Assyrian shall be destroyed
Isaiah, Chapter 10:5-19

Verses 5-19

5   Woe Assyria, the rod of mine anger,
     The staff in their hands is my indignation!

6   I will send him against an hypocritical nation,
     And against a people of my wrath will I give him a charge,
     To take spoil and to take plunder,
     And to tread them down like the mire of the streets.

7   However he does not mean it so,
     Nor does he think so in his heart.
     But it is in his heart to destroy,
     And to cut off nations not a few.

8   For he says:
     Are not my princes all of them kings?

9   Is not Calno as Carchemish?
     And Hamath as Arpad?
     Is not Samaria as Damascus?

10   As my hand has reached the kingdoms of these idols,
     Whose graven images excel those of Jerusalem and Samaria,

11   Shall I not, as I have done to Samaria and to her idols,
     Do the same to Jerusalem and to her graven images?

12   Therefore it shall come to pass when the Lord shall perform
     His whole work upon Mount Zion and Jerusalem that he will
     Punish the fruit of the arrogant heart of the king of Assyria
     And the pride of his haughty looks.

13   For he has said: I have done this by the strength of my hand,
     And by my wisdom, for I am clever.
     I have removed the boundaries of people,
     And plundered their stored up treasures,
     I have brought down the inhabitants like a valiant man.

14   My hand has found, like a nest, the riches of peoples,
     And as one gathers abandoned eggs,
     So have I gathered all the earth,
     And there was none that fluttered a wing,
     Or opened his mouth and chirped.

15   Should the axe boast against him who hews with it?
     Should the saw exalt itself against him who moves it?
     As if a rod should move them who lift it,
     Or a staff lift up him who is not wood.

16   Therefore will the Lord,
      The LORD of hosts send leanness upon his fat ones.
      And under his glory there shall be kindled a burning,
      And it will crackle with the crackle of a crackling fire.

17   And the Light of Israel shall be a fire, and his Holy One a
      flame,
      It will burn and consume his thorns and briers in one day.

18   The glory of his forest and of his fruitful land,
      He will consume soul and body
      And he will become as a sick man, who is wasting away.

19   And the remnant of the trees of his forest shall be few in
      number
      So that a child will be able to write them down.

A Few Observations Concerning Assyria

According to the Biblical account Ashur, the firstborn son of Shem,
was the progenitor of the Assyrian people (Gen. 10:22). He was the
founder of Ninevch, Rehoboth and Calah in the land of Sumer (Biblical
Shinar, Gen. 10:10-11). Their country was situated along the banks
of the Upper Tigris and its tributaries, in northern Mesopotamia. The
Assyrians were of Semitic origin, while the Babylonians to whom they
were related in language, religion and history were of Hamitic background (Gen. 10:6-10). Both nations inherited the highly advanced
Sumerian civilization, which they adapted to their own national needs.

Of all the nations which inhabited ancient Mesopotamia, the Assyrians
were the most warlike and ruthless. They lived for war and gloried in
their military exploits and cruelty. They developed a highly advanced
war machine and used naked terror as a means of conquest and as a
method of holding their defeated enemies in abject fear and submission.

The Assyrians were apparently among the first in history to apply psychological warfare. Approaching the walls of a city which they were
about to attack, they would address the defenders in their native tongue,
demanding their surrender. Just such an incident is vividly described in
Isaiah 36:4-21. If the defenders refused to surrender, the Assyrians would
then lay siege to the city and attack the walls with battering rams, or
dig tunnels underneath, or kindle huge fires under the city gates and
walls until they collapsed. After the capture of the city, the Assyrian king
would sit upon his throne at the gate of the city, surrounded by his
resplendent court.

The conquered population was marched before him, headed by their
king or ruler. Most of the captives, young and old, would then be killed,
or burned alive as a sacrifice to the national god of Assyria, Assur. Sometimes the captives would be flayed alive, or blinded, or would have their

heads impaled on sharp stakes. Those who were not massacred would be driven into captivity, sometimes with hooks in their noses. The city itself would be plundered and its accumulated wealth carried away into Assyria.

Early in their history the Assyrians were subject to the Babylonians. However in time they gained strength and carved out an empire of their own, which by the time of Tiglath-pileser I (1115-1077 B.C.) reached from the valley of the Tigris to the shores of the Mediterranean Sea. After the death of Tiglath-pileser I the Assyrians went into decline and were forced to defend their lands against the rebellious mountain tribes of the northeastern and northwestern regions. It was during this period that the kingdom of Israel under David and Solomon experienced its golden age of growth and prosperity.

During the ninth century B.C. under Ashurnasirpal (885-860 B.C.), the Assyrians resumed their forward sweep toward the west and south. Their great ambition was to create an empire which would include all the vast territories between the Persian Gulf and the Nile Valley. Tiny Israel and Judah were caught in the middle between the Assyrian hammer and the Egyptian anvil. The prophetic books of Isaiah, Nahum, Micah and Jeremiah reflect this situation.

With the accession of Tiglath-pileser III (745-727 B.C.) the Assyrian wars of conquest reached Samaria and Judah, aided by the short-sighted policy of Ahaz who invited the Assyrian king to help him against the coalition of Damascus and Samaria.

Isaiah, whose life was spent in the ominous shadow of the Assyrian menace, had an intimate and accurate knowledge of their overweening arrogance and unspeakable cruelty. His messages reflect the keen insight of a firsthand observer. It is quite possible that the prophet saw multitudes of panic-stricken refugees fleeing from their plundered and burned villages and towns as they sought shelter in Jerusalem, and he may have received from them firsthand reports.

Even surpassing Isaiah's intimate knowledge of the Assyrians was his amazing foreknowledge of the doom which the Lord had in store for that overbearing and blasphemous people which was so intoxicated with its own strength, and respected neither God nor man.

Isaiah's prediction of Assyria's downfall was fulfilled when in 612 B.C. the combined force of the Babylonians, the Medes and the Scythians, captured Nineveh, the enormous and opulent capital of Assyria. After that Nineveh became a desolate ruin and a pasture for flocks, just as the prophets predicted long before.

In 609 B.C. the Medes and the Babylonians again jointly attacked what was left of the once mighty Assyrian empire and carved it up among themselves.

The prophet Nahum, a contemporary of Isaiah, left a striking description of the Assyrian lust for blood and predicted the destruction of their capital, Nineveh.

> The lion did tear in pieces enough for his whelps
> and strangled for his lionesses. He filled his
> holes with prey, and his dens with ravin.
> Behold I am against thee, saith the LORD of hosts . . .
> Woe to the bloody city! It is full of lies and
> robbery; the prey departeth not . . .
> And it shall come to pass, that all they that look
> upon thee shall flee and say, Nineveh is laid waste,
> who shall bemoan her? (Nah. 2:12, 13; 3:1, 7).

In less than a century the predictions of the prophets concerning the fall of Assyria were completely fulfilled. By 609 B.C. Assyria was no more.

Comment:

5 Woe Assyria . . .

The same God who through His messenger Isaiah scourged Israel and warned that He would punish them for their sins now predicts that Assyria, the very instrument of His indignation, will also be judged by Him. The Holy One of Israel is no respecter of persons. Israel which received the Law of God and defied it, shall be punished according to the Law, but Assyria which knew not the Law of Jehovah, was nevertheless guilty, because she broke the natural law of justice and compassion which the Creator imparted to the conscience of all men. The apostle Paul later emphasized this principle of divine justice:

> For there is no respect of persons with God.
> For as many as have sinned without law shall also
> perish without law: and as many as have sinned in
> the law shall be judged by the law . . .
> For when the Gentiles which have not the law, do by
> nature the things contained in the law, these having
> not the law, are a law unto themselves (Rom. 2:11, 12, 14).

It was God who used Assyria as an instrument of His wrath to punish Israel, and commissioned them to do this. Without His permissive will, they could not have done what they did.

6 For many centuries the Lord had spoken to His people, through His servants the prophets. Yet they disobeyed them and defied the One who sent them. Now as a last resort God was sending their pitiless enemy, the Assyrian, with a charge to plunder Israel and to tread them down like the mire of the streets.

7 However he does not mean it so:

In her overweening arrogance, Assyria did not consider herself as an instrument in God's hand, to serve His purposes, but was driven by her insatiable lust for blood, plunder and power.

Assyrian records are replete with revolting descriptions of massacres of defeated enemies. Here is a typical record left by Sargon II (722-705) : "The Thamudites, the Ibadites, the Marsimanates, the Khapayans, distant Arab tribes, who inhabit the desert, of whom no scholar, or envoy knew and who never brought tribute, I slaughtered in the service of Assur, and transported what was left of them to Samaria."[1]

8 Are not my princes all of them kings?

The kings of Assyria of that period gave themselves the title of "the king of kings." In one of the Assyrian records, Esarhaddon (681-669) gloats:

I am powerful, I am all powerful, I am gigantic,
I am colossal, I am honored, I am magnificent,
I am without an equal among all the kings.

Many of the generals of the Assyrian armies were former kings or princes of the defeated nations.

9 Is not Calno as Carchemish? Is not Hamath as Arpad? Is not Samaria as Damascus?

The cities mentioned here help to establish an approximate date of Isaiah's message. Damascus fell to Assyria in 732 B.C., Samaria in 722, Carchemish the Hittite capital on the Euphrates was captured by Sargon, in 717 B.C.

Since Isaiah obviously delivered his message before the Assyrians, under Sennacherib, laid siege against Jerusalem in 701 B.C. (v. 28-34), this must have occurred sometime between 717-701 B.C., probably at the end of the reign of Ahaz (735-715).

10, 11 In comparing the pagan idols with the God of Israel, Jehovah, the Assyrian blasphemed the living God. To him all "gods," including Jehovah, were *"Elilim"*—"nonentities," or *"pesilim"*—"graven images," who could not help anyone. This was exactly the line of reasoning which Sennacherib displayed, when he demanded that the inhabitants of Jerusalem surrender to him (2 Ki. 19:8-13; 2 Chron. 32:17-19; Isa. 36:14-21).

12 However, the Lord will not be mocked forever, and when the Assyrian has served God's purpose against Judah, his turn will come. This is the way the Lord deals with nations or individuals when their overweening pride reaches the limit.

13, 14 The Assyrians attributed their great military success to their own valor ("by the strength of my hand have I done it") and to their superior wisdom and cleverness. By normal human standards the Assyrians were indeed a highly intelligent people. Their magnificent cities and edifices, the ruins of which were excavated within the last century or so, their imposing high temples known as ziggurats, after which the tower of Babel was patterned, their exquisitely wrought fine arts and highly sophisticated civilization and their military organization, all these bear witness to their intellectual vigor.

And yet in spite of all this, they were not a wise people, and unwittingly prepared for themselves their own doom, which they so richly deserved. Their basic weakness was their overbearing arrogance and their complete lack of compassion for their vanquished enemies. This gross inhumanity called down upon their heads the wrath of God and man. Their victims were always on the lookout for an opportunity to wreak vengeance upon their tormentors. This lack of true wisdom was a most important factor in the final downfall of the Assyrians, and nobody wept at their funeral.

More than a century before Nineveh fell, the prophet Nahum asked: "Nineveh is laid waste, who shall bemoan her?" (Nah. 3:7).

14 So have I gathered all the earth.

These words, which Isaiah attributes to the Assyrians, accurately describe their policy of worldwide conquest.

My hand has found the riches of the people like a nest and as one gathers eggs that have been forsaken.

The expression "none fluttered a wing or opened his mouth to chirp" is reminiscent of a favorite Assyrian boast, found in their records, concerning their defeated enemies who "fled like a young pigeon."

The word "chirped" in Hebrew *"metzaftzef,"* is an onomatopoetic one which imitates the sound of a chirping bird. Every word, every metaphor and figure which Isaiah employed bears witness that he was truly the great master of the Hebrew language.

15 Should the axe boast against him who hews with it?

In a series of incisive questions the prophet exposes the preposterous presumption of Assyria's pride. Instead of realizing that they were merely instruments in the hands of a higher power, they acted as if they themselves were gods. They were like the axe or the saw which boasts against them who use it, or like a rod made of wood which exalts itself against him "who is not wood," that is the man who uses it.

16-19 When once the Lord completes his purpose concerning Israel, the utter hollowness of the Assyrian conceit shall be exposed and punished.

"Their fat ones," those who fattened themselves on loot and the misery of nations, shall experience "leanness," that is extreme want, perhaps Isaiah had in mind a wasting disease, such as consumption.

16 "Under their glory" refers to the shakiness of the whole structure of the Assyrian empire which was based merely on brute force. Once the Lord kindles a fire under it, it will burn and crackle like crackling fire fed by dry thorns and briers. Isaiah uses three onomatopoetic Hebrew

175

sounds to suggest the crackling of a fire: *"Yekad, yikod kikod"* — "Will crackle with the crackle of a crackling fire."

The God who is the Light of Israel, will be a consuming fire to the Assyrians, and will consume the flimflam glory of a wicked empire, and, (changing the metaphor) will turn it into a sick and fast wasting body (v. 18).

19 When the Lord was done with the Assyrians even a little boy was able to write down on a school tablet what was left of them.[2]

Verses 20-27 A Chastened Remnant Will Return to the LORD

20 And it shall come to pass in that day,
That the remnant of Israel,
And the escaped of the house of Jacob
Shall no longer lean upon him who smote them,
But shall lean upon the LORD,
The Holy One of Israel, in truth.

21 A remnant shall return, a remnant of Jacob,
To the mighty God.

22 For though thy people, O Israel, be as the sand of the sea,
Only a remnant within it shall return.
A destruction is determined, overflowing with righteousness.

23 For a determined end,
Shall the Lord, the LORD of Hosts,
Make in the midst of all the earth.

24 Therefore thus says the Lord, the LORD of hosts,
Be not afraid of Assyria,
O my people, that dwells in Zion,
He will smite you with the rod and will lift up his staff
Against you, in the manner of Egypt.

25 For yet a little while and the indignation shall end,
And my anger shall be to their destruction.

26 And the LORD of hosts shall stir up against them a scourge,
As the smiting of Midian at the rock of Oreb,
And his rod shall be over the sea, in the manner of Egypt.

27 And it shall come to pass in that day
That his burden shall be put aside from his shoulder,
And his yoke from his neck.
And he shall burst his yoke because of fatness.

Comment:

20-22 In this section the remnant of Israel or Jacob occupies the center. The term *"shear"* — a remnant, is used four times, either in combination with Israel (v. 20), or in combination with Jacob (v. 21), and once *"pleitah beth yaakob"* — "the survivors of the house of Jacob," with emphasis on the physical aspect of the survival.

However, the center of this passage is the spiritual remnant, which will no more rely for help on the very enemies who sought to destroy them, that is on Assyria or on Egypt, but will return to *El Gibbor,* the Mighty God. Twice Isaiah uses the term *"Shear-Yashub,"* A-Remnant-Shall-Return, the very name of his first-born son, while *El Gibbor* — Mighty God, is the very name by which the Messiah was called in chapter 9:6.

The parallel to *El Gibbor* — Mighty God, is *Kadosh Israel* — "the Holy One of Israel" (v. 20), which is an implied identification of the Messiah with God, since both God and the Messiah are referred to as *El Gibbor,* and *Kadosh Israel.* Not all of Israel shall return to God, but only a remnant within Israel (v. 22).

23 God's righteous judgment, which He will visit upon the nations of the world, will not leave Israel unscathed. Only a remnant will survive. It is to this remnant that Paul refers when he says that "all Israel shall be saved" (Rom. 11:26). There is nothing automatic about salvation, it does not come by virture of race but by grace, and God is no respecter of persons.

24-26 Since the main purpose of Isaiah's message was to comfort Israel who faced the Assyrian invasion with trepidation, so he now reminds them that their present gloomy prospect will soon come to an end.

In tender terms he reassures them:
Be not afraid, O my people, of Assyria,
He will smite you with the rod . . .

However this affliction will not last very long. Assyria under Sennacherib indeed soon grievously afflicted Judah, devastating her cities, occupying most of her land and laying siege to Jerusalem.

26 After the manner of Egypt is a reference to the bitter experience of Israel centuries before in Egypt. But the Lord's indignation which until now was directed against Israel will soon be turned against Assyria. However in her case it will lead to her complete destruction (v. 25).

The Lord will stir up against Assyria a scourge. That scourge will be Babylon, who in time became powerful enough to destroy their former Assyrian rulers and oppressors. It is important to notice that Isaiah looked beyond the contemporary Assyrian menace and predicted their defeat by the Babylonians, more than a century before it happened.

26 As the smiting of Midian at the rock of Oreb
This is a reference to the Midianite defeat under Gideon's three hundred chosen warriors (Jud. 7:16-25).

Previously it was Israel who was afflicted by Assyria in the Egyptian manner, now it will be Assyria which will be smitten by God in the manner of Egypt at the Red Sea.

27 The Assyrian burden will depart due to divine intervention from without. The yoke will also burst from Israel's neck, because of God's grace which will produce regeneration within Israel itself, so that the yoke will not be able to hold the neck in submission.

Verses 28-34 The Assyrian March Against Jerusalem

28 He is come to Aiath,
 He is passed through Migron,
 To Michmash he entrusts his baggage.

29 They have crossed the pass,
 They lodge for the night in Geba.
 Ramah trembles, Gibeah of Saul has fled.

30 Shriek with a shrill voice, O daughter of Gallim!
 Listen Laish, alas poor Anathoth!

31 Madmenah is running away,
 The inhabitants of Gebim flee for cover.

32 This very day he shall halt at Nob,
 He will shake his fist at the mountain of Zion's daughter,
 The hill of Jerusalem.

33 Behold the Lord, the LORD of hosts,
 Shall lop off the boughs with terrifying power,
 And those who are of high stature shall be chopped down,
 And the lofty one shall be laid low.

34 And he shall cut down the thicket of the forest with iron,
 And Lebanon shall fall by a mighty one.

Comment:

28 Isaiah visualizes the inexorable Assyrian march against Jerusalem. He sees them in a vision, as they approach Jerusalem from the north, coming closer and closer to the holy city.

Actually when Sennacharib besieged Jerusalem in 701 B.C., he took a different route from the one described by Isaiah. He approached the city from the south, after taking the fortress city of Lachish and numerous other fortified places. However, Isaiah describes the regular, anticipated line of march to Jerusalem from the north. Isaiah's description of the Assyrian advance, as they plunder and destroy city after city, and the flight of their terror-stricken populace, is unsurpassed for vivid stark reality.

Isaiah sees the enemy entering Aiath about thirty miles northeast of Jerusalem, the first city within the kingdom of Judah.

In order to take Jerusalem by surprise, the enemy bypasses the normal route of advance, marching through difficult valleys. He leaves his encumbering equipment in Michmash, causing panic wherever he goes.

The prophet's heart goes out in compassion to the panic-stricken refugees, as they flee from their merciless enemy. Those of us who in recent years observed the peoples of Europe and Asia fleeing from their enemies for dear life, will readily understand the terror and misery of the Judean people, as they ran from the armies of Sennacherib, seeking shelter in their Holy City, Jerusalem. Yet with every hour, the Assyrians came closer and closer to Jerusalem. Finally they reached Nob, a hillside town north of Jerusalem within sight of the city. Now Zion was almost within their grasp, and the Assyrian in a gesture of menace and defiance was shaking his fist at it (v. 32).

At this point of extreme peril, when Jerusalem appeared to be doomed, the Lord of hosts would come to the rescue of His people.

33 The exclamation **"Behold"** marks the dramatic moment of divine intervention, and the appellation of God as "the Lord, the LORD of hosts" *(ha-adon Jehovah Tsebaoth)* emphasizes the absolute sovereignty and power of Jehovah. Assyria will come up against Jerusalem like a marching forest of mighty men, but God will suddenly lop off its boughs and branches and will lay low those who, in their great conceit considered themselves so high and mighty. As if with an iron axe God will cut down the thicket of the mighty forest of Assyrian forces.

34 Lebanon shall fall by a mighty one.

Lebanon, famous for its mighty cedars, symbolizes the mighty forest of the Assyrian armies.

Jewish commentators saw in the words "a mighty one" an allusion to the angel of God, who destroyed the armies of Sennacherib at the walls of Jerusalem:

> And the angel of the Lord went forth and slew in the camp of the Assyrians 185,000 men, and when the men woke up in the morning behold they were all dead carcases (Isa. 37:36).

Notes: 1. *The Targum of Isaiah* with English Translation, Oxford Press, 1945.

2. David Kimchi, *Commentary on Isaiah,* by Louis Finkelstein, page 62.

3. Israel W. Slotki, *Commentary on Isaiah,* Soncino Press, page 44.

4. B. Sanhedrin 94a.

5. In referring to some of the Pharisees as, "hypocrites," Christ had this passage of Isaiah as a precedent. In the 4th century B.C., Socrates and Plato, called the sophists, who were manipulators of ideas and words in order to mislead people, *kolax* — flatterers. Dante places "flatterers and hypocrites" in "nether hell." Dante, *Inferno,* Canto XVIII.

6. In recent times some Jews called the New Testament anti-Semitic, because of a few unfavorable references concerning some of the Jewish people or their practices. On the same basis the prophets would have to be considered "anti-Semitic." In fact some chapters of Isaiah contain more "anti-Semitism" than all of the New Testament. Yet neither the prophets nor the New Testament writers had anything to do with "anti-Semitism," but spoke from burdened hearts as brothers to brothers and as messengers of God concerning the evils and sins of their nation.

7. A. H. Sayce, *Assyria*, p. 179.

8. In the year 538 B.C. when Cyrus permitted the Jews to return to Jerusalem and to rebuild the Temple, he, in accordance with his humane policies, also gave leave to the Assyrian remnant to return to their ancient homeland. But unlike the Jews, the Assyrians never again played a role in the history of the nations.

The Messianic King and His Kingdom

Isaiah, Chapter 11

Verses 1-5   The Davidic Origin of the Messiah and His Character

1   There shall come forth a shoot
From the root stock of Jesse,
And a twig out of his roots shall bear fruit.

2   And the spirit of the LORD shall rest upon him,
The spirit of wisdom and understanding,
The spirit of counsel and might,
The spirit of knowledge and the fear of the LORD.

3   And his delight will be in the fear of the LORD,
He shall not judge after the sight of his eyes,
Neither decide after the hearing of his ears.

4   But with righteousness shall he judge the poor,
And will decide with equity for the meek of the land.
And he shall smite the earth with the rod of his mouth,
And with the breath of his lips shall he slay the wicked.

5   And righteousness shall be the girdle of his loins,
And faithfulness the girdle of his waist.

Comment:

1   In the last verses of chapter 10 Isaiah predicted that the mighty Assyrian empire would come down with a crash like the forest of Lebanon, never to rise again. In complete contrast to Assyria the fallen house of David which had come upon such evil days, would again sprout a new twig which would grow and bear fruit.

2 The **new Twig** would be the Messianic king upon whom the spirit of the LORD would rest. This spirit of the LORD would manifest itself in a sixfold way, forming together as it were a seven branched candlestick. Each of the branches is inter-related with and indivisible from the central stem, which is the Spirit of the Lord.

This **Spirit** is simultaneously the spirit of wisdom and of understanding, of counsel and of might, of knowledge and the fear of the LORD.

Wisdom, like holiness, righteousness and love, is the very essence of God. It is by His wisdom that God planned and created the universe — (Prov. 8:22-30). This wisdom is identical with the Word of God and the incarnate Word, Christ (John 1:1-14, see also Gen. 1:4-26).

Understanding is the obverse side of wisdom: it makes possible the comprehension of the true nature of things. Understanding is applied wisdom.

The Spirit of the LORD is also the spirit of **counsel and might.**

Previously Isaiah (9:6) called the Messiah "wonderful counselor." Here He is described as possessing the spirit of counsel and might, which is the power to counsel or plan wisely and to execute His plans.

The Spirit of knowledge and the fear of the Lord.

True knowledge is humble because it has its roots in the fear of the Lord. The fear of the Lord is the beginning of knowledge (Prov. 1:7). There can be no ultimate knowledge without the knowledge of God. The fear of the Lord is not abject terror before God, but that holy reverence which stands in awe before the infinite wisdom, majesty and holiness of God.

"Woe is me," cried Isaiah, "for I am undone; because I am a man of unclean lips, for my eyes have seen the King, the Lord of Hosts" (6:5).

3 Endowed with the fullness of the Spirit of the LORD, the Messiah "delights" to see others fear the Lord. The Hebrew word for "delights" is *"haricho."* Literally it means "to inhale with delight," like the fragrance of a sweet smelling offering (Lev. 3:5, 16).

Thus filled with the Holy Spirit, the Messiah will not depend upon fallible human senses such as sight or hearing to render righteous judgments and decisions, but will have perfect knowledge from within His inner self. John said of Christ: He "needed not that any should testify of man, for he knew what was in man" (John 2:25).

4 **With righteousness shall he judge the poor.**

It is most characteristic of the prophets that they always displayed a profound concern for the welfare of the poor, the humble, the dispossessed and the helpless. The Messiah of Isaiah's vision is endowed with this quality of justice and mercy in a supreme measure: "He will judge with righteousness the poor and decide with equity for the meek."

He shall smite the earth with the rod of his mouth.

His message will be so absolutely just and right that all evil or sin will be completely exposed in His holy presence. All that which is sinful and wicked shall stand condemned in the light of His Word.

5 Righteousness shall be the girdle of his loins.

To gird one's loins is a Scriptural figure which represents a man's readiness to do battle with his adversary.

The apostle Paul describes the girdle as an essential part of the believer's armament (Eph. 6:14).

The Messiah in His warfare against darkness and sin shall be girded with righteousness and faithfulness. The Hebrew word *"emunah"* "faithfulness," may also be translated "faith." The Messiah does not depend on the sword or any other lethal weapon, but on the power of the Spirit. Righteousness and faithfulness are His weapons and His faith in God gives Him the certainty of the ultimate victory of His work of redemption.

Verses 6-9   The Transformation of the Animal World under the Messiah's Reign

6 And the wolf shall dwell with the lamb,
   And the leopard shall lie down with the kid,
   And the calf and the young lion and the fatling shall lie down
      together,
   And a little child shall lead them.

7 The cow and the bear shall graze,
   Their young ones shall lie down together,
   And the lion shall eat straw like the ox.

8 The suckling shall play on the hole of the viper
   And a weaned child shall put his hand upon the adder's den.

9 They shall not hurt nor destroy,
   In all my holy mountain.
   For the earth shall be filled with the knowledge of the LORD,
   Even as the waters cover the sea.

Comment:

Verses 6-9

The advent of the Messiah will result not only in a complete change of human behavior, but will also profoundly affect the nature of the fiercest animals. Isaiah gives a most enchanting vision of such a transformation in the animal kingdom. The most ferocious beasts are presented as living side by side with the most defenseless domestic animals in perfect harmony and amity, the wolf with the lamb, the leopard with the young goat, the calf and the fatling flank a young lion, and all of them are led by a little boy *(yeled)*.

What an enchanting vision, what a hope! But is it realistic? To this question the prophet answers: "yes," because in the holy mountain of God there will be no hurting and no harming. The holy mountain of God stands for the dominion of God under the Messiah King. This Messianic hope is based on the conviction that under the reign of the Messiah the earth will be filled with the knowledge of God even as the waters cover the sea.

Bible commentators differ as regards the proper interpretation of this vision. Is this prophecy to be understood literally or figuratively? Does the prophet speak of real wolves and lambs, lions and calves, bears and cows or are they mere symbols of the ferocity of men? Calvin holds to the latter position, and sees in this prophecy a prediction of a change in human nature, so that the human wolves and lions and snakes will no longer harm the human lambs and kids. In Isaiah 65:25 the prophet expresses the same hope. Likewise in Isaiah 55:12b we find a similar thought expressed that somehow nature is deeply involved in the redemption of man. There is a profound interdependence between the destiny of man and nature:

The mountains and the hills shall break forth before you in singing
And all the trees of the field shall clap their hands.

In the Old Testament Scriptures there is an undercurrent of thought reflected also in the New Testament, that ever since man through his disobedience to God brought sin into the world, all of nature has become deeply involved in man's sin, and that all of creation anxiously awaits the redemption of the children of man.

After Adam disobeyed God, the Lord said to him: "...cursed is the ground for thy sake; in sorrow shalt thou eat of it all the days of thy life" (Gen. 3:17b).

With this in mind the Apostle Paul writes: "Because the creature itself also shall be delivered from the bondage of corruption into the glorious liberty of the children of God. For we know that the whole creation groaneth and travaileth in pain together until now" (Rom. 8:21,22).

So Isaiah's vision of the restored harmony and peace within the animal kingdom, and between the animal world and man, is probably more than a mere figure of speech, but rather a keen anticipation of a return to that pristine condition which existed in the Garden of Eden. Of course the prophet believed that before this could take place, man himself must cast off his sinful nature and take on the glorious nature of his Redeemer, the Messiah. This vision of Isaiah 11:6-9 was the prophet's way of expressing his faith in the transforming and regenerating power of the Messiah. Underlying this transformation of all creation will be a new intimate and profound personal knowledge of the LORD by a redeemed race.

Verses 10-16   Israel under the Reign of the Messiah

10 And it shall come to pass in that day the root of Jesse
That stands as a banner of the peoples,
Unto him shall the nations seek,
And his place of rest shall be glorious.

11 And it shall come to pass in that day,
That the Lord will again set his hand the second time
To gather the remnant of his people,
That which is left from Assyria and from Egypt,
And from Patros, and from Cush and from Elam,
From Shinar and Hamath, and from the isles of the sea.

12 And he will lift up a banner to the nations,
And assemble the dispersed of Israel,
And gather together the scattered of Judah
From the four corners of the earth.

13 And the jealousy of Ephraim shall depart,
And they that harass Judah shall be cut off.
Ephraim shall no more be jealous of Judah
And Judah shall not vex Ephraim.

14 And they shall swoop down
Upon the shoulder of the Philistines toward the sea
Together they shall spoil the children of the East;
They shall put forth their hand upon Edom and Moab,
And the children of Ammon shall obey them.

15 And the Lord will dry up the gulf of the Sea of Egypt,
And will wave his hand upon the river with his scorching wind,
And will smite it into seven streams,
And cause men to cross it dryshod.

16 And there shall be a highway for the remnant of his people,
Who will remain from Assyria,
Like as it was for Israel,
In the day when they came up from the land of Egypt.

Comment:

10 The root of Jesse, or the shoot of the stock of Jesse (11:1) are the established designations of the Messiah. Formerly unknown among the nations, He will grow in stature and universal respect, so that His personal divine rule shall become a banner under which the nations will rally. His place of rest *(menuchah)* applies to Jerusalem, or the Mount of Zion as the focus of His glorious reign. The Vulgate understands the word *"menuchah"* to refer to the sepulchre of Christ, which is incorrect.

11 The Second Time.

The first time the Lord delivered His people with a strong hand out of Egyptian bondage. Now the Lord is about to do it again and will deliver the remnant of His people from the lands of their future dispersion. In addition to Assyria and Egypt, Isaiah mentions other places of Israel's dispersion: Pathros is Upper Egypt, Cush is Ethiopia, Elam is the land in the southern part of Media, Shinar or Sumer is the land between the lower Euphrates and the Tigris in Babylonia, Hamath was a great city on the Orontes in northern Syria, between Arpad and Damascus. The "isles of the sea" are the coastlands on the Mediterranean.

Some commentators have argued that this passage did not come from Isaiah's pen because at that time (715 B.C.) Israel's dispersion was not so extensive. This objection is not valid as we do not know how extensive the Jewish Israelite-Judean dispersion was at that time. It should also be remembered that Isaiah speaks prophetically concerning Israel's distant future, reaching out beyond the Assyrian and even beyond the Babylonian exile.

12 He will lift up a standard for the nations (the alliterative *"ve-nasa nes"*). Once Israel is reconciled to God, those very nations which brought about Israel's exile and dispersion will be used by the Messiah to help assemble His people from the four corners of the earth. The expression "the dispersed of Israel and the scattered of Judah" indicates that Isaiah had in mind a worldwide dispersion.

13-14 Ever since Israel seceded from Judah there had been fierce jealousy and bloodshed between the two sister kingdoms. Isaiah bitterly deplored this condition (9:20), but now under the rule of the Messiah the former jealousy and rancor will vanish, and the much hoped for unity of all Israel will become a blessed reality.

Thus united and redeemed, Israel will find a new security against her ancient foes, and the enemies of the Lord.

15-16 Just as at the exodus from Egypt, the Lord prepared for His people a dry path through the Red Sea, so will He again destroy or dry up *(heherim)* the Gulf of Suez, and a pathway through the River Euphrates, so that the remnant of Israel may return to their homeland on a highway prepared by the hand of God.

The Song of Redeemed Israel

Isaiah, Chapter 12

Verses 1-6

1 In that day thou shalt say:
   I thank thee, O LORD,
   That though thou hast been angry with me,
   Thine anger is turned away and hast comforted me.

185

2 Behold, the God of my salvation;
  I will trust and not be afraid.
  For the Lord God is my strength and my song,
  And he has become my salvation.

3 Therefore with joy shall ye draw waters
  From the wells of salvation.

4 And in that day ye shall say:
  Give thanks unto the LORD, proclaim his name
  Make known his deeds among the nations.
  Cause them to remember that his name is exalted.

5 Sing unto the LORD for he hath done glorious things,
  Let this be known in all the earth.

6 Cry out and shout, O inhabitant of Zion,
  For great in thy midst is the Holy One of Israel.

Comment:

Verses 1-6

When the Lord delivered Israel from their bondage in Egypt, Moses and the children of Israel intoned a triumphant song of praise extolling the mighty deeds of God (Ex. 15:2-18).

Now that the Lord is about to deliver His people for the second time the prophet puts in the mouth of redeemed Israel a new song, similar in character to the former song, which they sang after they left Egypt.

The new hymn of Israel is divided into two strophes (not into two separate hymns as some maintain). The first verse 1-3, is a psalm of praise, extolling God's compassion, expressing a renewed confidence in the Lord, as the fountain of their salvation.

The second strophe (v. 4-6) exhorts God's people to declare among the nations His great salvation and the presence in their midst of the Holy One of Israel. The whole hymn is saturated with an exuberant and joyful missionary spirit.

1 **"In that day"**—is a much favored Isaianic expression, used by the prophet in connection with God's mighty acts of redemption. "That day" is "God's D Day."

Many ancient and modern commentators have applied this hymn of praise to the Church, which they have substituted for Israel. But this is doing violence to the Scriptures and the obvious sense of our text.

This hymn like so many other prophecies and oracles of the Hebrew Scriptures may legitimately be applied to all those who are a part of the people of God, regardless of national origin, so long as we understand clearly that the prophet speaks primarily to Israel and of Israel.

1 **I thank thee, O Lord.**

Israel as a nation will experience her redemption in a personal way.

Thou wert angry, but thine anger is turned away.

God's anger will become a thing of the past, and Israel will exult in His forgiveness and comfort.

2 Behold, the God of my salvation.

Having experienced salvation Israel shall be filled with new confidence and a new song. The word salvation, *"Yeshuah"*, occurs three times in verses 2 and 3, and is the central theme of this passage. Here "salvation" implies not mere release from physical bondage, but a renewal of the spirit, resulting from Messiah's reign and a true knowledge of God.

It is no sheer accident that the Messiah of the New Testament is called *"Yeshua"*— (anglicized "Jesus"), which in Hebrew means salvation, or the Lord's salvation: ". . . thou shalt call his name Jesus, for he shall save his people from their sins" (Mt. 1:21b).

Apparently Jesus Himself was fully aware of the significance of His name, when He declared in the home of Zaccheus: "This day is salvation come to this house . . . For the son of man is come to seek and to save that which was lost" (Lk. 19:9, 10). Thus salvation, according to Isaiah, is inextricably inherent in the very name and mission of the Messiah.

3 Ye shall draw waters with joy from the wells of salvation.

To Biblical man so dependent for his very life and sustenance upon the abundance of water, it frequently symbolized the life-giving power of the Word of God. This is reflected in such passages as Isaiah 55:1, Jeremiah 2:13, 17:13, Ezckiel 36:25, John 3:5, 4:14. In the days of the Messiah, Israel shall draw with joy the life-giving waters of salvation from the wells of salvation, and not from empty cisterns of brackish waters (Jer. 2:13).

4-6 The second strophe of this remarkable hymn of the redeemed is imbued with a deep missionary spirit.

4 Having experienced God's great salvation Israel cannot remain silent. Israel will feel impelled to proclaim His name and to make known the Lord's great work of salvation among the nations of the world.

This impulse to bear witness to the Lord, springs from a sense of deep gratitude to God for what He has done. The proclamation of "the good news" is never selfish or nationalistic, it is not small-hearted, nor narrow-minded. It is carried on a surge of joy and thanksgiving to the Lord. It is directed toward all people and therefore is "ecumenical" in the purest and best sense of the word. The people of God, having tasted the salvation of God sing about it, and are exhorted to make it known "in all the earth," to use a Greek phrase, to shout salvation to all the *"oikumene"* —the whole inhabited world.

6 The inhabitant of Zion, the citizen of the Kingdom of God, is encouraged to shout jubilantly, because the Holy One of Israel, her Lord and Redeemer is great in her midst. In the person of her Messiah, the presence of God will at last become a reality. Immanuel will at last be exalted and praised among His people. On this note of triumph the prophet closes the book of Immanuel.

Oracles Concerning
Israel's
Neighbors

A Special Note: This section of Isaiah contains a series of oracles which are called "burdens," and deal with Israel's neighbors. The term "burden," "*massa,*" is derived from a verb which means "to lift up," in this case, to lift up one's voice or spirit, that is to prophesy, or to have a vision. The burdens are mostly predictions of divine judgment and punishment for the sins of the nations against Israel.

These are the contents of Isaiah 13-23:

Chapter	13:1—14:27	Against Babylon
"	14:28-32	Against Philistia
"	15, 16	Oracle and Lament for Moab
"	17	Against Damascus
"	18	Against Ethiopia
"	19	Against Egypt
"	20	Prophecy about Egypt and the Capture of Ashdod
"	21:1-10	Oracle concerning the wilderness of the sea (Babylon)
"	21:11-12	Concerning Edom
"	21:13-14	Concerning the Arabs
"	22:1-14	Oracle against Jerusalem
"	22:15-23	Against Shebna, the unfaithful steward
"	23	Against Tyre and Sidon

There is a similar group of oracles in Jeremiah (chapters 46-51), and in Ezekiel (chapters 25-32). A close analysis of the text indicates that Jeremiah was acquainted with Isaiah chapter 13 and not the other way around, as some have maintained.

The Authorship of Isaiah Chapters 13-14

The authenticity of these two chapters has been questioned by some critics who regard them as written, or at least heavily edited, by later compilers of the book of Isaiah, perhaps shortly before the end of the Babylonian exile, around the year 540 B.C.

The main argument for their position is that during the lifetime of Isaiah, Babylon was not the dominant world power, but Assyria, which crushed Samaria and was a constant menace to Judah. The critics therefore assume that Isaiah either did not write these two chapters, or if he did write the gist of them, he must have referred to Assyria, but later editors, before or during the exile, changed the text to make it apply to Babylon.

Against this argument it should be pointed out that the heading of the oracle claims Isaiah himself as its author:

The burden of Babylon which Isaiah the son of Amoz saw (13:1)

To assume that this heading is a forgery, is to attribute complete lack of honesty to the unknown editors of the book, without any compelling evidence, simply because the critics do not believe in predictive prophecy. Isaiah, and other prophets, as we have previously indicated, were indeed in the habit of predicting future events. He foretold the utter annihilation of the Assyrian empire more than a hundred years before this happened, and that in a prophecy which most critical scholars consider as genuine (10:12-19). More than a century before it happened Isaiah also predicted the Babylonian exile (39:6-8).

To substitute mere conjecture and speculation for the evidence of the Hebrew text, handed down to us without significant changes through the centuries, is to abandon chart and compass for mere guesswork.

Another argument against the authenticity of Isaiah 13 and 14 advanced by some, is the supposed difference in language and style of the two chapters from those parts of the book which the critics accept as genuine.

However, a careful analysis of the two chapters reveals at least 52 expressions and turns of speech, which are found nowhere else but in Isaiah, and in a few verses in Jeremiah, (40:39; 50:16) where he obviously relies on Isaiah as his original source. These peculiarities of speech are inherent in Isaiah's style, but not in Jeremiah's.[1]

A Prophecy against Babylon
Isaiah, Chapter 13

Verses 1-22

1   An oracle about Babylon, which Isaiah the son of Amoz saw.

2 Hoist a banner on a bare mountain,
   Raise your voice to them,
   Wave the hand and they will come
   To the gates of the nobles.

3 I have commanded my consecrated ones,
   And I have also summoned my warriors for my wrath,
   My proudly exulting ones.

4 Hark, the tumult in the mountains,
   Like as of a great people.
   Hark, the roar of assembled kingdoms of nations,
   The Lord of hosts is mustering an army of battle.

5 They come from a distant land,
   From the ends of the heavens.
   The LORD and the instruments of his indignation,
   To ruin all the land.

6 Howl, for the day of the Lord is near,
   It shall come as a devastation from the Almighty.

7 Therefore all hands shall be limp,
   And every human heart shall melt.

8 They shall be terrified; pangs and pains shall seize them,
   They shall writhe in pain like a woman in labor:
   They shall look aghast at each other.
   Their faces as faces of flame.

9 Behold, the day of the LORD is coming,
   Cruel, full of wrath and fierce anger.
   To make the earth desolate;
   And to destroy the sinners from it.

10 For the stars of the heavens and their constellations
   Shall not give their lights,
   The sun shall be dark as it rises,
   And the moon shall not cause her light to shine.

11 And I shall visit upon the world its evil,
   And upon the wicked their iniquity;
   And I will put an end to the arrogance of the presumptuous,
   And the pride of the tyrants I will lay low.

12 And I will make a common man more precious than fine gold,
   And a human being more valuable than the gold of Ophir.

13 Therefore will I make the heavens to tremble,
   And the earth shall be shaken out of her place,
   Because of the wrath of the LORD of hosts,
   And in the day of his fierce anger.

14   And it shall be like a doe when chased,
      And as a sheep that no one gathers in;
      Each man shall turn to his people,
      And every man shall run to his country.

15   Everyone that shall be found shall be pierced,
      And everyone caught shall fall by the sword.

16   Their babies shall be dashed to pieces before their eyes,
      Their homes shall be plundered, their wives raped.

17   Behold, I will stir up the Medes against them,
      Who think not of silver
      And take no pleasure in gold.

18   Their bows shall dash their boys to pieces;
      And will have no pity on the fruit of the womb,
      Their eyes will not spare children.

19   And Babylon, the glory of kingdoms,
      The proud ornament of the Chaldees,
      Shall be as when God overturned Sodom and Gomorrah.

20   It shall not be inhabited forever,
      Neither dwelt in from generation to generation.
      No Arab shall pitch his tent there,
      Neither shall the shepherds make their flocks to lie down there.

21   But wild beasts of the desert shall lie down there;
      And their houses shall be full of jackals,
      And satyrs shall carouse there.

22   Hyenas shall howl to each other in their palaces,
      And jackals in their luxury mansions.
      Her time is about up,
      And her days shall not be prolonged.

Comment:

Verses 1-22

Isaiah 13 is the first of a series of prophecies dealing with the approaching judgment of the nations adjacent to Israel. The series begins with Babylon, the center of the proud, God-defying pagan world.

1   This is the title of this particular "burden" or oracle. It claims Isaiah as its author, in flat contradiction of those who would classify this prophecy as non-Isaianic.

2   **Hoist a banner on a barren hill.** This is typical of Isaiah's imagery, familiar to us from other parts of his book (5:26; 11:10; 18:3). A barren hill is a most suitable place to signal to distant places for armies

to gather for war. As the warriors come closer to the hill they are beckoned by hand and called by voice to come "to the gates of the nobles," a figure of speech which stands for Babylon. Some commentators think that there actually was a gate in Babylon called "the gate of the nobles."

3-5 The prophet introduces the LORD of hosts Himself, as the commander-in-chief of the armies, assembled for the overthrow of Babylon. The warriors are called "my consecrated ones," that is the ones whom the Lord has singled out for the special task of destruction. They are also called "the warriors for my wrath," and "my exulting ones." It is an enthusiastic army, an army made up of the victims of Babylon's rapacity and cruelty, an army, which will execute the divine wrath with alacrity and joy.

6-22 The theme of this passage is "the day of the LORD," in which the prophet describes in terrifying detail the punishment which the LORD is about to visit upon Babylon. This is a subject oft repeated by Isaiah and was first applied to Israel (2:12; 4:1; 5:1-30). Now the day of the LORD is predicted as a punishment for Babylon, the successor of wicked Assyria.

The day of the LORD is described as "a devastation from the Almighty," a typical Isaianic alliteration, *k'shod mi-Shaddai*—a destruction from Shaddai (v. 6). In the face of God's wrath, men are helpless, their hands tremble, their hearts palpitate. They are in pain like a woman in labor, they pale, or alternately are flushed (v. 7, 8).

The LORD'S day is a cruel visitation. It is *"dies irae et calamitatis,"* a day of wrath and calamity. The Lord will devastate the earth and destroy its sinners (v. 9).

When God judges the earth all of nature is involved, even the stars, the constellations, the sun and the moon (v. 10). When God shall finish with sinful, wicked and arrogant humanity, only a remnant will survive, so that a common man *(enosh)*, and an ordinary human being *(adam)* will be more precious than fine gold or the gold of Ophir, (a place located in South Arabia and famous for its gold, 1 Ki. 10:11, Psa. 45:9).

The LORD'S day will cause universal panic, especially among the foreign merchants who used to throng to Babylon, the center of world commerce. Each foreigner will seek to flee to his own country (v. 14), and those caught will be mercilessly butchered. Even their children will not be spared and their women shall be ravished (v. 14-16).

The invaders of Babylon are now mentioned by name as the Medes, a barbaric nation from southeastern Mesopotamia, who together with the Persians under Cyrus the Great of Persia conquered the Babylonian empire in 539 B.C. Cyrus himself was of Median descent, and therefore could be considered a Mede.

The Medians were motivated by a fierce desire of revenge for past humiliations inflicted upon them by Babylon, so that the prospect of plunder of silver and gold held no attraction for them (v. 17).

19-22 This is the heart of the prophecy concerning the ultimate fate of Babylon, which was so remarkably fulfilled. Beautiful Babylon, the pride and glory of the Chaldees will become like Sodom and Gomorrah, never to be inhabited again, not even by the wandering Arab, but shall become the eerie haunt of all kinds of spooky desert beasts.

Just as Isaiah predicted, Babylon became a heap of ruins and was never inhabited again. The ruins of ancient Babylon were excavated in the 19th century in the neighborhood of the city of Mosul, in modern Iraq.

> Note: 1 For a detailed discussion concerning the genuineness of Isaiah chapters 13 and 14, from the standpoint of language and style and Jeremiah's reliance on the above chapters, see Rachel Margalioth, *The Indivisible Isaiah*, pages 22-28.

Restored Israel Will Triumph Over Her Enemies
Isaiah, Chapter 14

Verses 1-2

1　For the LORD will have mercy on Jacob,
　　And will again choose Israel, and cause them to rest upon their
　　　land:
　　And the stranger shall join them, and they shall attach themselves
　　To the house of Jacob.

2　And the people shall take them and bring them to their place:
　　And the house of Israel shall take possession of them
　　In the land of the LORD
　　For servants and for handmaids, and they shall take captive their
　　　captors.

Comment:

1 Following God's judgment of Babylon which will result in her complete obliteration, the LORD will show mercy to His people Israel and restore them to their land. He will also vindicate His people so that "the stranger" shall join them. The term *"gair"* means "a resident alien," a sojourner. In later rabbinical literature *"gair"* was the technical term for a gentile who became a Jew by faith. This idea is apparently inherent in our text and finds expression in the phrase "they shall attach themselves to the house of Jacob." It means that they shall voluntarily become a part of the house of Jacob, of their faith, and of their destiny. The word "again" signifies a new era in the relationship between the LORD and Israel. As He once brought them back from Egypt to their promised land, so will He do it again and bring them back from Babylon.

2 On the face of it, this prophecy sounds rather vindictive when it speaks about taking captive their former captors and ruling over the former oppressors of Israel. In reality Isaiah is merely enlarging in a somewhat different form his former prophecy concerning the nations who during the reign of the Messiah shall stream to the mountain of the Lord to learn there to walk in His ways (2:2-4).

The prophet had in mind not a physical but a spiritual conquest of the peoples of the world. Politically speaking, this prophecy was never fulfilled to any significant or lasting degree. However, in a spiritual sense it was an integral part of Isaiah's Messianic hope and that of the other prophets (Isa. 2:2-4; 52:10; 54:2-5; 55:5; Mic. 4:1-4; Zech. 8:2-23).

Concerning Isaiah 14:1-2 Delitzsch says: "We have here *in nuce* (in a nutshell) the comforting substance of chapters 46-66. Babylon falls that Israel may rise."[1]

Verses 3-23 A Taunt Song Against the King of Babylon

3   And it shall come to pass in the day when the LORD shall give thee rest from thy toil and from thy disturbance and from thy hard labor which was imposed upon thee.

4   Then shalt thou raise this parable against Babylon and shalt say:
How has the oppressor ceased! ·
The insolent city has ceased!

5   The LORD has broken the staff of the wicked,
The scepter of the rulers,

6   Which smote peoples in wrath,
With an incessant stroke
And ruled the nations in anger,
With unsparing persecution.

7   At rest and quiet is the whole earth,
They break forth into singing.

8   Even the cypresses rejoice at thee, the cedars of Lebanon; saying
"Since thou art laid down,
The feller shall not come up to cut us down."

9   Sheol from down below is astir because of thee,
To meet thee at thy arrival.
The feeble ones are stirred up for thee
Even the [leading] he-goats of the earth,
It raises from their thrones all the kings of the nations.

10   With one accord they will answer and say to thee,
"Art thou also made feeble as we are?
Art thou become like us?

11   Thy pomp is brought down to Sheol,
       The noise of thy harps.
       The maggot is spread under thee,
       And the worms cover thee."

12   How art thou fallen from heaven,
       Thou star of light, son of dawn,
       Thou hast been hurled down to the earth,
       Thou who has weakened nations.

13   And thou hast said in thy heart:
       "I will ascend into heaven,
       I will exalt my throne above the stars of God,
       I will sit down upon the mount of the assembly [of gods]
       In the uttermost parts of the north.

14   I will ascend above the heights of the clouds
       I will be like the Most High."

15   However thou wilt be cast down to Sheol,
       Into the uttermost parts of the pit.

16   They that see thee shall look at thee attentively,
       And will consider thee thoughtfully, [saying:]
       "Is this the man who made the earth tremble?

17   Who turned the world into a wilderness and razed its cities,
       And did not release his prisoners to return home,
       Who made kingdoms shake?"

18   All the kings of the nations repose in honor,
       Everyone in his home.

19   But thou, thou art cast out from thy grave,
       Like a despised branch,
       In the raiment of the slain, who are thrust through with the
         sword,
       That go down to the stones of the pit, like a trampled carcass.

20   Thou shalt not be united with them in burial,
       Because thou hast destroyed thy land,
       Thou has killed thy people,
       Let not the seed of the evildoers be named for ever.

21   Prepare a place of slaughter for his sons,
       For the iniquity of their fathers,
       Lest they rise up and inherit the earth
       And replenish the face of the earth with cities.

22 And I will rise up against them, is the decree of the LORD of
    hosts,
    And I will cut off from Babylon name and remnant, shoot and
    sprout.
    This is the decree of the LORD of hosts.

23 And I will make it into a possession of the hedgehogs,
    And into marshes of water,
    And I will sweep it away with the besom of destruction.
    This is the decree of the LORD of hosts.

Comment:

2-3 This is an introduction to "the parable," *(mashal)* or taunt song
against the king of Babylon, which ransomed Israel shall raise, after
their deliverance from bondage.

Apparently "the king of Babylon" is not any particular historical figure, but the personification of all the wickedness, arrogance and cruelty
of the Babylonian empire. We might even go a step further and say that
the king of Babylon personifies all the self-deification and self-glorifica-
tion of the godless governments of all ages. The word "parable,"
"mashal," is a short dramatic poem or lament over a fallen hero. In our
case the parable could best be described as a taunt song.

4b-23 The scene of the taunt song is set in Sheol, the dim netherworld
of the departed who are called *"rephaim"* — "the feeble ones." They lead
a shadowy existence reminiscent of the inhabitants of Hades, described
in Homer's *Odyssey* and in Virgil's *Aeneid.*

The departed spirits are all agog with excitement when they hear,
that their former tormentor, the king of Babylon is dead, and has
arrived in Sheol.

4b They greet him with mocking words:

How has the oppressor ceased!
How has the city of torment ceased![2]

6 This is an accurate description of the harsh and merciless rule of
Babylon.

7, 8 The demise of the Babylonian tyrant has brought peace to the
whole world. In verse 8 there is one of those characteristic touches of
Isaiah, his keen interest and love for trees, so often referred to in his
writings (1:29, 30; 2:13 6:13; 9:10; 10:18; 17:7; 32:15; 41:19; 55:13) .

These trees have cause to rejoice, because with the destruction of
the Babylonian empire there is no more need for the endless felling
of cypresses and cedars, which were used for the vast armies and navies
and for other military purposes (bridges, roads, etc.) .

9-11 "The feeble ones" and "the he-goats" (the leaders of the nations) together with the dead kings exult that at last their slayer is dead and has become just like one of them, with maggots for his bedding and worms for his cover.

12-14   How art thou fallen from heaven!
   Thou star of light, son of dawn!

The King James Version translates the Hebrew phrase *"helel ben shachar"* as "Lucifer, the son of the morning." *"Helel"* means the shining one, or the morning star, and *"ben shachar"* literally "the son of dawn." Isaiah calls the king of Babylon "star of light and son of dawn" because in his boundless conceit he regarded himself as a celestial being. This thought is further expanded in verse 13-14. In his blasphemous pride the fallen king sought to ascend above the stars and take his seat among the gods of the Babylonian pantheon, which according to their mythology was located on a far northern mountain. Like Satan himself he aspired to be like the Most High. Some of the Church fathers and later commentators saw in this passage a description of Satan's revolt against God, and of his downfall. Whenever man seeks to deify himself, it ends in disaster.

15-17   However thou shalt be cast down to Sheol.

Here is the contrast between the insatiable ambition of mortal man and the overruling power of God. Instead of being "like the Most High," the king of Babylon was hurled down to the deepest pit (v. 15). The man who once was the object of awed adulation, before whom nations trembled, who razed cities and held captive countless people, suddenly became the object of scorn and headshaking.

The Psalmist expresses a similar thought, when he speaks of the prosperous wicked, whom God in a moment will hurl down from their exalted positions of pride and power to complete oblivion:

How are they brought into desolation, as in a moment they are utterly consumed with terror (Psa. 73:19).

18-23   The prophet continues to describe the inglorious, but once powerful tyrant, personified by the king of Babylon. His end will be in a nameless pit, flung there by his own enraged subjects and removed from his honored burial place.[3] He was cruel not only to foreign nations, but slaughtered even his own people (v. 20).

Prepare a place of slaughter for his sons.

His subjects are determined that his dynasty should not be perpetuated, lest the evils of their father be continued by his sons (v. 21). The Lord Himself solemnly declares that He is against that wicked kingdom and will sweep it away as a woman sweeps out her home with a broom, and will not leave a remnant or a living vestige to perpetuate Babylon. Their country will be turned into an eerie wasteland of hedgehogs and marshes. Twice Isaiah uses the most solemn form of affirmation *"neum Yehovah Tsebaoth"*—"the solemn decree of the LORD of hosts."

The subsequent history of the empires of Assyria and Babylon is a confirmation of the dependability of God's promises. The once mighty and beautiful metropolis Babylon, with its fabulous royal palaces and mansions, the sky reaching ziggurats, (tiered temples) the hanging gardens, its artificial canals, the work of highly skilled engineers and architects, which seemingly made that magnificent city an impenetrable fortress, was conquered by Cyrus the Méde, and eventually demolished, never to be rebuilt. Babylon literally became a habitation for hedgehogs and porcupines. For many centuries nobody was even sure exactly where Babylon once was. Desert sands covered the ruins of the once proud and beautiful city. Only in the last century archeologists have uncovered the ruins of Babylon, near Mosul in Iraq. Out of the depths of the archeological mounds numerous artifacts and documents emerge which bear eloquent witness to the glory that once was Babylon. The name Babylon in the Scriptures itself became a synonym of all that which is ungodly and wicked, of all the powers and human institutions which defy God and exalt themselves against Him (Rev. 14:8).

Verses 24-27   The LORD Has Decided to Break Assyria

24   The LORD has sworn saying:
Surely as I have thought, so shall it come to pass,
And as I have purposed, so shall it take place;

25   To break Assyria in my land,
And upon my mountains will I tread him under foot.
Then shall his yoke depart from them,
And his burden shall depart from his shoulder.

26   This is the purpose that I have purposed over the whole earth
And this is the hand,
That is stretched over all the nations.

27   For the LORD of hosts has purposed
And who shall bring it to naught?
His hand is stretched out,
And who shall turn it back?

Comment:

24-27   The prophet now returns from the yet remote future when divine judgment will fall upon Babylon, to Israel's immediate peril—Assyria. The Lord has sworn to break Assyria "in my land," that is in the land of

Israel. This prophecy alludes to the disastrous Assyrian campaign against Judah, when Sennacherib's army was smitten by the angel of the Lord under the walls of Jerusalem (701 B.C.). From then, until 609 B.C. the story of Assyria was one of gradual disintegration and final defeat.

In verses 26, 27 Isaiah's vision of God's judgment widens to encompass not only Assyria but all the nations of the earth. God's determined purpose cannot be annulled, nor can His hand, stretched out in punishment, be turned back by any human power.

Verses 28-32 Oracle against Philistia

28 In the year when king Ahaz died was this burden.

29 Rejoice not, O Philistia, all of thee,
    That the rod which smote thee is broken.
    For out of the serpent's root shall come forth a viper,
    And his fruit shall be a flying snake.

30 And the first-born of the poor shall feed,
    And the needy one shall lie down in safety,
    But I will kill thy seed with famine
    And thy remnant shall be slain.

31 Howl, O gate, cry, O city.
    Thou wilt melt away, O Philistia, altogether.
    For out of the north comes a smoke
    And there is no straggler in his ranks.

32 And what shall one answer the messengers of the nations?
    That the LORD has established Zion
    And that the afflicted of his people shall take refuge in her.

Comment:

28 The date of this oracle is given as the year when Ahaz died, approximately 715 B.C.

29 Rejoice not Philistia. It is not completely clear from out text whom the prophet described as "the rod which smote the Philistines but is now broken." Some think this is a reference to the death of Ahaz, others to Tiglathpileser who died in 727 B.C. or his successor Shalmaneser. From the vocabulary which the prophet employed: the serpent's root, the viper, the flying snake, it is more likely that he had in mind the Assyrian rulers, who harrassed the Philistines and plundered them repeatedly.

Who were the Philistines? According to Genesis 10:14 (also 1 Chronicles 1:12) they were a Hamitic people. Some time during the second millennium B.C. they came to Canaan from Caphtor, (Crete), in the

Aegean Sea, and settled along the southwestern coast, below the territory of Judah. The land which they inhabited was called Philistia (in Hebrew *Palesheth*), from which the name "Palestine" is derived.

When the Israelites came out of Egypt, they were commanded by the Lord to bypass the coastal area inhabited by the Philistines (Ex. 13:17). For centuries the Philistines remained the hereditary enemies of Israel. Samson's exploits, and David's fight against Goliath are two of the best-known incidents in the conflict between the Israelites and the Philistines.

Eventually the Philistines were subdued by David and forced to pay him tribute. However, later they frequently revolted against Judah and raided their cities. In the Assyrian records there are frequent references to the Philistines as a tributary but rebellious people.

30 Isaiah contrasts the ultimate destiny of Judah with that of the Philistines. Judah though poor and needy, shall be fed by the hand of the Lord and attain ultimate safety, however "the root and remnant" of Philistia, (note the alliterations in Hebrew and in English) shall perish.

31 Howl, O gate, Cry, O city.

This is a lament over Philistia the powerful federation of five separate cities: Ekron, Gath, Ashdod, Ashkelon and Gaza. The prophet addresses himself to the whole federation, as if they were one city. Although their contemporary enemy was dead (whoever he might have been), all of Philistia will eventually be dissolved. Their destruction will come like a pillar of smoke from the north, by a determined invader, in whose ranks there shall be no straggler. This description of the enemy is similar to that which the prophet used about the Assyrian army on the march (5:26, 27).

Zechariah, the post-exilic prophet, mentions the Philistines for the last time (9:6), in the Old Testament, predicting their doom. From then on we never hear about them again in the Scriptures. Isaiah's prophecy about their disappearance from the pages of history without a trace, became a reality.

32 Apparently in their hour of peril, the Philistines sent an embassy to Judah pleading for an alliance against a common enemy. The prophet was against such an alliance with a pagan people, and instead counseled his nation to trust in the Lord, who had established Zion. In the God of Zion is Israel's true refuge and safety.

Notes: 1. Delitzsch, *op. cit.,* Vol. I page 306.

     2. "The City of Torment" in Hebrew *"madhevah"* is a unique word of uncertain derivation and meaning. It occurs only once in the Hebrew Scriptures and is variously translated. The King James Version renders it as "the golden city"; the Revised Standard Version as "the insolent fury." The Jerusalem Bible, a new Roman Catholic version translates it as "a place of insolence." The recently discovered Dead Sea Scroll of Isaiah

1QIsaᵃ reads *"marhevah"* instead of *"madhevah"* as in the accepted Masoretic text, and would therefore mean "a place of insolence." We have followed the traditional Hebrew text and translated *"madhevah"* as "a city of torture or torment."

3. Isaiah's description of the end of the Babylonian tyrant reminds us vividly of the end of Hitler and Stalin, and of many wicked rulers before them.

Lament Over Moab

Isaiah, Chapter 15

Verses 1-9

1 The Burden of Moab.
Because in the night that Ar is laid waste,
Moab is ruined.
Because in the night that Kir is laid waste,
Moab is ruined.

2 He goes up to the temple and to Dibon
To weep in the high places.
On Nebo and Medeba Moab howls;
On every head there is baldness,
Every beard is slashed.

3 In their streets they gird themselves with sackcloth;
On her rooftops and squares everybody howls.
They are overcome with weeping.

4 Heshbon cries, and also Elealeh,
Their voices are heard as far as Jahaz.
Even the warriors of Moab cry aloud,
Their souls distressed within them.

5 My heart cries out for Moab;
His fugitives flee to Zoar, to Eglath-Shelishiah,
They who ascend to Luhith, go up weeping,
On the road to Horonaim a pitiful cry is raised.

6 For the waters of Nimrim shall become desolate;
The grass shall wither, the herbs shall wilt,
Nothing green shall grow.

7 And so the abundance which they have stored up,
And the provisions which they have laid up,
Will they carry away across the brook of the willows.

8 For their cry has gone around the borders of Moab;
The wail reaches Eglaim, the wail reaches Beer-elim.

9   Because the waters of Dimon shall be filled with blood;
    For I shall lay upon Dimon an addition [of trouble],
    A lion for those of Moab who shall escape,
    And for the remnant of the land.

Comment:

Verses 1-9

In chapters 15 and 16 the prophet Isaiah predicts the downfall of Moab, a people descended from Lot and his eldest daughter (Gen. 19:31-37). Their land was east of the Dead Sea, between the city of Jaazer in the north and the Wadi Zered in the south, a territory now part of Jordan. The Moabites worshipped Chemosh and Baal-Peor, to whom they offered human sacrifices, and practiced a licentious cult.

Although closely related to each other by descent and language, there was bitter enmity between the Moabites and Israel. During the Egyptian exodus, when Israel asked permission to pass through the land of Moab, their request was refused (Jud. 11:17).

Balak, king of Moab, fearing the growing strength of Israel, hired Balaam to curse them (Num. 22-24). Later, the Israelites were seduced by the Moabite women (Num. 25).

Because of their unfriendly spirit and acts, the Ammonites and the Moabites were excluded from the community of Israel (Deut. 23:3, 4).

During the days of the Judges, Eglon, king of Moab, invaded Israelite territory, as far as Jericho, and oppressed the land for eighteen years, until he was assassinated by Ehud the Benjaminite (Jud. 3:12-30).

Nevertheless, there apparently was some sporadic contact between the two neighboring peoples.

Elimelech of Bethlehem emigrated to Moab, and his sons married Moabite women, one of whom, Ruth, later married Boaz and became the ancestress of King David (Ruth 4:18-22, Mt. 1:5-6).

In the year 1868 a German missionary in Southern Palestine came across one of the most important archeological finds in history, the so-called Stone of Mesha. It was a slab of stone three feet ten inches high and two feet across, containing thirty-four lines of writing, relating the triumph over Israel by Mesha, son of Chemosh, king of Moab. The inscription recorded how Mesha threw off the yoke of Israel and built a high place as an expression of gratitude to Chemosh. The inscription reads in part: "As for Omri, king of Israel, he humbled Moab for many days, for Chemosh was angry at his land. And his son followed him, and he also said: 'I will humble Moab—but I have triumphed over him and Israel perished for ever.' "[1]

The Moabite Stone dates back to about 830 B.C. and covers a period during the reign of Ahab of Israel, and of his son Joram (2 Ki. 1-3).

Moab was frequently invaded by the Assyrians, the Babylonians, the Persians, and later by various Arab tribes. In the early part of the 6th century B.C. the Moabites lost their national independence, but survived as a separate people until the 2nd century B.C. when they were subdued by Alexander Jannaeus. After that they disappeared from the scene of history.[2]

Thus the prophecy of Isaiah and of the later prophets concerning the national extinction of Moab was literally fulfilled.

In chapter 15:1-9 Isaiah describes with deep compassion the pending disaster of Moab:

My heart cries out for Moab (v. 5a)

There is no malicious joy in the heart of the prophet as he describes Moab's approaching calamity.

The plight of the bewildered and sorely stricken Moabites stirs the prophet's heart to great compassion. Isaiah sees the helpless Moabites go up to their temples and to their high places to weep and to lament, putting on sackcloth and disfiguring their beards in the accepted signs of mourning (v. 1-3).

Even the hardened warriors are deeply affected by the grief of their people as they flee to the high places in search of refuge (v. 4). The King James Version translates *"Eglath Shelishiah"* as "a heifer of three years old," a possible reference to the strength of Zoar (v. 5). It is, however, more likely that *Eglath Shelishiah* is the name of some forgotten city. Altogether Isaiah mentions in his lament over Moab about a dozen localities, some of which are still in existence today, and others of which no longer exist.

The once lush fields and gardens, now neglected, lie abandoned and desolate (v. 6). The refugees carry off their accumulated stores and wealth to "the brook of the willows" (v. 7). It is not clear whether this is the name of a place, or a description of any brook overgrown by willow trees, where the fugitives might reasonably hope to find shelter from their pursuers.

And still their misery is not at an end. Upon the remnant of the Moabites God will send a lion (v. 9), obviously a reference to the numerous foreign intruders which successively harassed the land and the people of Moab.

The Burden of Moab continued

Isaiah, Chapter 16

Verses 1-14

1   Send tribute to the ruler of the land,
From the crags which face the wilderness
To the mount of the daughter of Zion.

2   As a wandering bird cast out from her nest,
So shall the daughter of Moab be at the fords of the Arnon.

3 Give us counsel, render a decision.
   Make your shadow like the night in the midst of noontime,
   Hide the outcasts, do not betray the wanderers.

4 Let my outcasts dwell with you;
   Be a hiding place to Moab from the spoiler;
   For extortion is at an end,
   And they that trample shall cease to be in the land.

5 And a throne shall be established in loving-kindness;
   And upon it shall sit in truth, in the tent of David,
   One who judges and seeks justice,
   And one alert to righteousness.

6 We have heard of the pride of Moab; he is very proud,
   His haughtiness, his pride, his wrath,
   His boastings are vain.

7 Therefore let Moab wail for Moab,
   Everyone shall wail, sorely stricken
   For the raisin cakes of Kir-hareseth.

8 For the fields of Heshbon languish, and the vine of Sibmah;
   The lords of the nations have struck down her choice plants,
   Which reached to Jazer and stretched into the wilderness;
   Her branches were spread abroad, and passed the sea.

9 Therefore will I weep with the weeping of Jazer;
   I shall water with my tears the vine of Sibmah,
   Of Heshbon and Elealeh,
   For upon thy summer fruit and upon thy harvest,
   The shout of battle has fallen!

10 And joy and gladness are taken away
   From the fruitful field;
   In the vineyard there shall be no singing,
   There shall be no shouting;
   The treader shall not tread out wine in the presses;
   The exuberant shout of the vintage has ceased.

11 Therefore do my bowels moan for Moab like an harp
   And my soul for Kir-heresh.

12 And it shall be that when Moab presents himself,
   And has wearied himself upon the high places,
   When he shall come to his temple to pray,
   It shall be of no avail.

13 This is the word which the LORD spoke concerning Moab long
   ago,
   But now the LORD says:

14 In three years, like the years of an hireling,
    The glory of Moab shall become contemptible,
    In spite of all her great multitude;
    And the remnant shall be small and without strength.

Comment:

Verses 1-14

The prophet continues to describe the unhappy plight of Moab after their defeat, when they were forced to flee from their native land.

1, 2 In their despair, the once proud and arrogant Moabites, who now wander around like birds, cast out from their nests, decide to send emissaries with tribute to the Temple of God on Mount Zion, in order to seek protection from the once despised Israelites.

3-5 Give counsel, render a decision . . .

In these lines the prophet puts into the mouth of the Moabite emissaries the words of their petition, as they plead for protection from their enemies, and for asylum for their fugitives. Having in the past committed numerous hostile acts against Israel, they now seek to gain their favor with high sounding flattery.

4 Be a hiding place to Moab from the spoiler

We do not know who in this instance is referred to as "the spoiler." It might have been any of the numerous invaders, who, from time to time, harassed Moab, while Israel yet remained free.

5 And a throne is established in loving-kindness . . .

To secure the favor of the Judean ruler, the Moabites describe in most flattering terms the reign of justice and righteousness prevailing in Judah, in contrast to the lawlessness and injustice which at that time was rampant in Moab.

It is not quite clear whether the Moabite delegation, in their flattering speech, described the actual conditions prevailing in Judah at that time, or whether they were speaking of the future.

In any case, it is significant that the Moabites use terms which strongly reflect the Messianic expectations, nurtured by the faithful remnant in Israel and by Isaiah himself, centering around the Messianic king, who will sit upon the throne of David and execute justice and righteousness.

6 We have heard of the pride of Moab . . .

The prophet counsels his people not to trust the honeyed but insincere words of the Moabites, and to remember their long history of pride, arrogance and implacable wrath.

7 Therefore let Moab wail for Moab . . .

Unrelieved by Judah, the Moabites continue to bewail their bitter fate.

The raisin cakes of Kir-Haresheth

Apparently these raisin cakes were a specialty of that Moabite city, and symbolized to the exiled Moabites the fondly remembered luxuries of home, a typical human trait of refugees who recall the good things once taken for granted, but now so sorely missed by them.

8-11 For the fields of Heshbon languish . . .

A further description of the desolate land, once so rich and prosperous, but now plundered by "the lords of the nations" and forsaken by her own inhabitants.

Again and again the innate tenderness and compassion of Isaiah breaks through as he laments over Moab—

Therefore will I weep with the weeping of Jazer,
I will water with my tears the vine of Sibmah (v. 9)

or

My bowels moan for Moab like an harp
And my soul for Kir-heresh. (v. 11)

The harvest has ceased, the exuberant shout of the harvesters *"Heidad,"* which may mean "Oh joy" or "Glory be" has stopped, silenced by the noise of battle (v. 10) .

There is something of the nature of the Messiah Himself in the prophet Isaiah as he weeps with the weeping, and his heart goes out in compassion to poor stricken Moab.

12 Smitten by their enemies, driven from their homes, denied refuge by Israel, because of their past treacheries, the Moabites now turn to their gods for mercy—"but to no avail."

13, 14 The reason why all this misery has come upon Moab is because God has so determined long ago.

Now the LORD has confirmed His decree that all this should come to pass within three years.

. . . like the years of an hireling

Just as the hireling who is hired for a period of three years, will not work a moment longer after his term is finished, so shall Moab not escape her destiny which is to become a small, insignificant remnant after the appointed time of three years has run out.

It is not clear from our text when the three years predicted by Isaiah began or when they came to an end, but from that time onward Moab's decline started and "her glory became contemptible." In due course Moab, like the rest of the nations against whom Isaiah raised his lament, ceased to be a nation.

Oracles Concerning Damascus and Ephraim

Isaiah, Chapter 17

Verses 1-14

1 The oracle of Damascus.
Behold, Damascus is removed from being a city,
And has become a heap of ruins.

2 The cities of Aroer are forsaken;
They shall be for flocks,
They shall lie down, and none shall make them afraid.

3 And the fortress shall cease from Ephraim,
And the dynasty from Damascus,
And the remnant of Aram shall be like the glory of Israel,
This is the decree of the LORD of Hosts.

4 And it shall come to pass in that day,
The glory of Jacob shall be made lean,
And the fat of his flesh shall shrink.

5 And it shall be as when the harvester gathers the standing grain,
And his arm reaps the ears;
And it shall be as when one gleans the ears
In the valley of Rephaim.

6 And there shall be left in it gleanings,
As when the olive tree is shaken, two or three berries
On top of a high branch,
Four or five in the fruitful tree
Says the LORD of Hosts.

7 In that day shall man regard his Maker,
And his eyes shall look at the Holy One of Israel.

8 And he shall not regard the altars, the work of his hands,
And that which his fingers have made shall he not fear,
The Asherim and the incense altars.[3]

9 In that day shall their fortified cities be like that which is
forsaken,
In the wooded place and in the high branches
Which the children of Israel have long forsaken,
And it shall be a desolation.

10 For thou hast forgotten the God of thy salvation
And the Rock of thy stronghold thou hast not remembered,
Because of this you will plant pleasant plants
And set it with an alien slip.

11 In the day of the planting you will make it grow,
   And in the morning you will cause your seed to blossom.
   Yet it will be a harvest heap and a tormenting pain
   In the day of reaping.

12 Woe, the uproar of many people,
   Like the roaring of the seas,
   The rushing of nations,
   Like the rushing of mighty waters.

13 The nations shall roar like the roar of mighty waters,
   But he will rebuke and they shall flee far away,
   And he will chase them like the chaff on the mountains
   Before the wind,
   Like the whirling dust before the storm.

14 Behold at even time, turmoil;
   But before the morning they are no more.
   This is the portion of those who despoil us,
   And the lot of those who plunder us.

Comment:

Verses 1-14

This prophecy goes back to the earlier times of Isaiah's ministry, probably around 738-35 B.C. Damascus and Israel who lost their independence, in 732, and 722 B.C. respectively, were still free when Isaiah delivered this oracle concerning Damascus.

      1-3   Prediction of the downfall of Damascus

      4-6   The downfall of Israel

      7-9   Israel's repentance

  10, 11   The cause of Israel's disaster; her turning away from Jehovah

  12-14   Prediction of the downfall of Assyria

1-3 Damascus the mistress of Syria, is doomed and will soon cease to be a city. The cities under her dominion will be forsaken and become pasture land. The doom of Damascus will also bring about the downfall of Ephraim who allied herself against her own kinsmen of Judah. This is the unalterable decree of the Lord (*neum Yehovah Tsebaoth*).

4-6 The glorious and prosperous kingdom of Israel shall come upon lean times. After the Lord has completed His judgment, few of her inhabitants will be left, as when a reaper leaves a few ears of corn at harvest, or when a few olives are left behind in the tall branches, after the olive tree has been shaken. This prophecy harks back to chapter 7 and the events described there.

7-9 However, when the day of judgment shall come, Israel shall turn away from her idolatry, from the worship of the Asheroth, that is the sacred poles and images representing Ashtarte, the semitic Aphrodite, the goddess of love, and from the incense altars (v. 8). This shall come to pass when the strong cities of Israel shall have become wild forest thickets or like the forests in the high inaccessible mountains (v. 9). The Septuagint follows a reading which gives the sense of the deserted places of the Hittites and the Amorites.

10, 11 The root cause of Israel's disaster is in her forsaking of her Maker. She has planted for herself pleasant, but alien plants, a figure of speech descriptive of the worship of alien gods.

For a while these alien plants looked pleasant, but their end was a harvest of grief and torment.

12-14 The instrument of the divine wrath shall be the Assyrians, who are not mentioned by name, but alluded to in the same terms as the prophet did in chapters 8:5-8, 10:5-7, 24-26. Yet a glimmer of hope is implied in this prediction of pending judgment. In the evening there shall be turmoil, but before dawn comes, the nightmare of oppression will be gone (cf. Psa. 73:16-20). Thus the prophet holds out the hope of the preservation of a remnant who will return to God, and bring healing and restoration to Israel.

Notes: 1. The Stone of Mesha is in the British Museum.

2. Josephus Antiq. XIII, 5.

3. Recent archaeological discoveries in the Holy Land have at last clarified the correct meaning of the Hebrew term "hammanim" which means "incense altars."

Imperilled Ethiopia seeks Allies

Isaiah, Chapter 18

Verses 1-7

1   O, land of the buzzing of wings,
    Which is beyond the rivers of Ethiopia

2   That sends ambassadors by the sea,
    In vessels of papyrus upon the face of the waters.
    Go, ye swift messengers,
    To a nation tall and smooth,
    To a people feared near and far,
    To a mighty nation and victorious,
    Whose land rivers divide.

3 All ye inhabitants of the world,
   And ye who dwell on the earth,
   When you see a standard raised on the mountains, look!
   And when the trumpet is sounded, listen!

4 For thus said the LORD unto me:
   I will be quiet and look on in my abode,
   Like the bright heat in the sunshine,
   Like a cloud of dew in the heat of harvest.

5 For before the harvest, when the blossom is ended,
   And the bud becomes a ripening grape,
   He will cut off the shoots with pruning knives,
   And the branches he will take away and lop off.

6 They shall be left together to the birds of prey of the mountains,
   And to the beasts of the earth;
   And the birds of prey shall feed on them in the summer,
   And the beasts of the earth shall feed on them in the winter.

7 At that time there shall be brought gifts to the LORD of hosts,
   From a people tall and smooth, and from a people feared near and
      far;
   From a nation mighty and conquering, whose land the rivers
      divide,
   To the place of the name of the LORD of hosts, Mount Zion.

Comment:

Verses 1-7

Chapters 18-20 form a remarkable prophecy which deals with the destiny of Ethiopia, Egypt, Assyria and Judah. Here Isaiah reaches the pinnacle of prophetic universalism, unsurpassed anywhere else in the Old Testament. Isaiah foretells the downfall of Israel's hereditary enemies, Egypt and Assyria, but goes on to predict that in the end both nations shall come to know the LORD, and together with Israel they shall worship Him and be reconciled to Him and to each other. This prophecy is particularly striking in the light of the ongoing and unresolved conflict between contemporary Israel and the successor nations of ancient Assyria and Egypt, which form the bulk of the Arab lands of today.

The historical background of chapters 18-20 is set against the political events of the last two decades of the 8th century B.C.

Around the year 720 B.C., Ethiopia, taking advantage of the internal problems of Egypt, conquered that land and became master of the Nile Valley for the next sixty years. Shabaka, the Ethiopian ruler of Egypt (circa 716-701 B.C.), expecting an Assyrian invasion of the Nile Valley, sent ambassadors to the various provinces of Egypt and to neighboring kingdoms, seeking to enlist their support against Assyria in the event of war.

1, 2 The people who sent their ambassadors in search of allies are not specifically mentioned by name. We are only informed that they lived beyond the rivers of Ethiopia, or along the valleys of the Blue and White Nile. It is the land of "the buzzing of wings." The Hebrew word *"tsilsal"* —to "buzz"—has suggested to most commentators the deadly "tsetse" fly, in which the area "beyond the rivers of Ethiopia," that is the Upper Nile and its tributaries, abound. Today this area forms a part of modern Egypt, Sudan and Ethiopia.

The ambassadors travel in light and swift papyrus boats along the tributary rivers of the Nile, which in Egyptian literature is sometimes called "the sea." The destination of the ambassadors is to a people described as "tall and shining," or "of smooth skin" who inspire great fear among their neighbors. Many commentators understand this to be a reference to the tall and well built Nubians, or the Watusi tribes, which inhabited the regions of the Upper Nile.

3 The ambassadors are to alert these people to be ready for an outbreak of hostilities between the Ethiopia-Egyptian dominion and the Assyrians.

Some Jewish commentators believed that the Ethiopian ambassadors were actually sent to Jerusalem in search of military help. However, our text does not warrant this conclusion.

4-6 Isaiah, addressing himself to the ambassadors, and indirectly to Israel and the nations of the world, makes known what the Lord Himself had revealed to him concerning the impending Assyrian invasion. The Lord will, for a time, hold His peace and permit the situation to take its natural course. But when the Assyrians will seem to have victory in their grasp, He will suddenly and violently destroy their evil power. The seeming inaction of God does not indicate His indifference, but that He is waiting for the situation to mature and then His terrible judgment will certainly follow.

The prediction of the downfall of Assyria may be related to the disaster which befell Sennacherib in 701 B.C. at the siege of Jerusalem, as described in Isaiah 37:36-38.

7 When the LORD manifests His power over Assyria, Ethiopia and the very people to whom she sent ambassadors to seek their support, will recognize that their ultimate salvation must come from Jehovah, the LORD of all nations. Ultimately to Him alone will all people bring their gifts of adoration, to Him who dwells on Mount Zion.

Isaiah gives expression to his faith that Jehovah is the supreme ruler of all nations, and not alone of Israel, and that at the end every knee shall bow before Him in worship and adoration.

On the level of practical politics Isaiah remains faithful to his God-centered view of history and so counsels his people to abstain from foreign alliances, no matter how attractive these may seem at the moment, but to look to Jehovah Himself for their protection and ultimate redemption.

Isaiah 18 thus forms an introduction to chapter 19, which deals with the future destinies of Egypt, Israel and Assyria and their mutual relationship to one another and to the LORD Himself.

Judgment upon Egypt and her Redemption

Isaiah, Chapter 19

Verses 1-15 Egypt Shall Be Torn by Civil Strife and Ruled by a Foreign Tyrant

1 The burden of Egypt.
Behold the LORD rides upon a swift cloud
And is coming to Egypt.
And the idols of Egypt will shake at his presence,
And the heart of Egypt shall melt within it.

2 And I will incite Egypt against Egypt
And a man shall fight against his brother,
And a man against his neighbor,
City against city, kingdom against kingdom
And the spirit of Egypt shall be confused within her
And I will confound their counsels.

3 And they shall consult idols and wizards,
The ghosts and the familiar spirits.

4 And I will deliver Egypt into the hand of hard masters,
And a cruel king shall rule over them.

5 And the waters shall fail from the sea,
And the river drained dry.

6 And the canals shall become foul,
And the river branches of the Nile shall dwindle and dry up,
The reeds and the rushes shall wilt away.

7 The meadows by the Nile, at the edge of the Nile,
And all that which is planted by the Nile,
Shall dry up, shall be driven away and be no more.

8 And the fishermen shall lament,
And all they that cast the hook in the Nile shall mourn,
And they that spread nets upon the waters shall languish.

9 They that work in combed flax and weavers of cotton
   Shall be confounded.

10 And the foundations shall be crushed,
    And the wage earners shall be grieved in spirit.

11 Mere fools are the princes of Zoan!
    The wise counselors of Memphis give foolish counsel.
    How say you to Pharaoh:
    "I am the son of wise men, the son of ancient kings"?

12 Where then are thy wise men?
    Let them tell thee now, let them inform thee,
    What the LORD of hosts has purposed against Egypt!

13 The princes of Zoan have become fools,
    The princes of Memphis are deceived.
    They have led Egypt astray,
    They who are the cornerstone of the tribes.

14 The LORD has poured out in her midst a spirit of confusion,
    They have caused Egypt to stagger in all her doings,
    As a drunk staggers in his vomit.

15 And there shall be no work which Egypt can do,
    For head or tail, of palm branch or rush.

Comment:

Verses 1-15

In this prophecy which indicates an intimate knowledge of Egypt, Isaiah predicts the judgment which is about to come upon this land, in whom the politicians of Judah put so much confidence to help them against their common enemy, Assyria.

1 Behold the LORD rideth upon a swift cloud . . .

A figure of speech indicating that God is about to perform judgment. At His Presence, all the idols of Egypt, which, in fact, are *"elilim"*—"contemptuous nothings"—will be shaken and toppled. This will result in public confusion and widespread civil war.

2 I will incite Egypt against Egypt, a man against his neighbor—

Normally, the two main parts of Egypt, Upper and Lower, were under the same ruler, Pharaoh, but now there will be chaos, anarchy and civil strife.

3 The traditional form of religion shall fail. The people will resort to magic, wizardry, spiritism, those dark forms of superstition which always lurk in the background of popular feelings, ready to take over, whenever the established form of religion fails.

4 As a result of Egypt's internal chaos, she will fall prey to a cruel, foreign taskmaster. It is difficult to establish whom Isaiah had in mind as "the harsh foreign king." Esarhaddon (681-669), Cambyses (530-522) and others have been suggested. It is possible that the prophet did not allude to any specific foreign invader, but to the eventual decline of Egypt as a world power.

5 The worst of Egypt's plagues which the Lord has in store for this unhappy land will be the failure of the river Nile, the fountain spring of Egypt's economy, to provide her life-giving waters. The results of this natural calamity are described in the following lines, which bring to mind the plagues of Egypt in the days of Moses: first, the river Nile, referred to as "the sea," shall dry up.

6 Then the streams and the canals shall become putrid.

7 All the vegetation which depends on the Nile waters shall dry up and vanish.

8 The whole fishing industry, by hook or by net, shall cease, bringing hunger and dismay to the fishermen and to the whole population.

9 The famous linen and cotton industry of Egypt which provided the finest woven manufactures of the ancient world shall come to a standstill, causing dismay among the combers and weavers (and incidentally to the shipping industry engaged in export).

10 The foundations of the land—the rich land owners and industrialists and the common wage earners—shall be grieved in spirit.

11-14 Isaiah taunted those vaunted wise men of Egypt, the counselors of Pharaoh who advised him on the affairs of state. Why did they not inform the king what God had planned for their land? Those wise men of Zoan (ancient Tanis in the Nile Delta and Memphis, were the representative cities of Egypt), turned out to be mere fools (v. 11).

12 Why did they not inform the king about Jehovah's purpose for Egypt? Because they did not know. Isaiah apparently alludes to other days, and to another man, who did know and who was able to give the king right counsel. He was the Hebrew slave Joseph, who had the spirit of true knowledge and prophecy and so could advise Pharaoh to take the right steps to forestall disaster.

13 However, the present leaders of Egypt lead Egypt astray.

14 Because the Lord has poured out upon them, not a spirit of wisdom and knowledge, but of utter confusion. When disaster strikes, they stagger and wallow in their own vomit, the excretion of their own deluded minds.

15 There shall be no work in Egypt. This sums up the magnitude of the calamity which shall befall Egypt. This total economic stagnation and lack of productive work will affect all the classes of Egypt. The rich and powerful is "the head"—the unskilled laborer who depends on his daily wages to survive is "the tail." There simply will not be any material to work with—palm branch or rush.

The conditions described in this passage are strikingly analogous to the situation which prevails from time to time in some of our own industrial countries, causing grave economic crises and general dismay.

Verses 16-25   The LORD Shall Smite

16 In that day shall Egypt be like women, and it shall tremble and be afraid because of the shaking of the hand of the LORD of hosts which he shakes over them.

17 The land of Judah shall become a terror to Egypt, every one to whom it will be mentioned shall be afraid because of the purpose of the LORD of hosts which he purposes against it.

18 In that day there shall be five cities which will speak the language of Canaan and swear to the LORD of hosts, one of these shall be called the City of the Sun.

19 In that day there shall be an altar to the LORD in the midst of the land of Egypt, and a pillar to the LORD at the border.

20 And it shall be for a sign and a witness to the LORD of hosts,
And when they shall cry to the LORD of hosts because of oppressors,
He will send a Saviour, who will defend and deliver them.

21 And the LORD shall make himself known to Egypt and the Egyptians shall know the LORD in that day and they shall worship him with sacrifice and offering and they shall vow unto the LORD and shall perform it.

22 And the LORD shall smite Egypt, smiting and healing, and they shall return unto the LORD and he will be entreated of them and will heal them.

23 In that day there shall be a highway out of Egypt to Assyria, and the Assyrians shall come into Egypt and the Egyptians to Assyria. And the Egyptians shall worship with the Assyrians.

24 In that day shall Israel be the third with Egypt and with Assyria, a blessing in the midst of the earth.

25 Whom the LORD of hosts shall bless, saying: Blessed be my people Egypt and Assyria, the work of my hands, and Israel my heritage.

Comment:

Verses 16-25

In this passage we hear echoes of the exodus story; when the Lord sent plagues upon Egypt in order to deliver His people Israel. However, this time God will smite Egypt in order to heal her and to make her together with Assyria and with Israel His very own people. Here Isaiah reaches the pinnacle of prophetic vision which embraces the redemption not only of Israel but also of those nations which in the past were the enemies of God and of His people. In Isaiah 2:2-4 the prophet gave us a grand vision of the nations walking in the light of Israel's God. Here the ancient enemies of Israel and of Israel's God are depicted as coming into a close relationship with Jehovah and together with Israel, fellow-heirs of the Kingdom of God.

The process of Egypt's conversion is gradual: At first, Egypt trembles like women before the extraordinary acts of Jehovah (v. 16). Because Judah is the land of His visible habitation and presence, it becomes the object of fear. No doubt, the memory of what the Lord did to Egypt many centuries before when He delivered Israel is an element in this fear (v. 17).

18 Five cities in Egypt shall speak the language of Canaan . . .

According to the Greek historian, Herodotus, there were no less than 20,000 cities in densely populated Egypt. The five cities speaking "the language of Canaan," which later became the language of Judah, and of true worship, indicates that a small part of Egypt will turn to the Lord and worship Him. "To swear to the Lord" is a term indicative of allegiance to and faith in Jehovah.

One of these cities shall be called the City of the Sun. In Hebrew, it is *Yir-ha-heres,* which the King James Version translates "the city of destruction." Many ancient Hebrew manuscripts read "the City of the Sun" *(ha-cheres),* which is Heliopolis, one of the oldest cities in the Nile Delta. To refer to "the City of the Sun" as "the City of Destruction" is typical of the prophets as a mark of their contempt for the heathen idols. Hosea called Bethel—"The House of God"—*Beth-aven*—"The House of Iniquity" (Hos. 4:15).

19 The altar in the midst of Egypt dedicated to the worship of the Lord and the border pillar also dedicated to Jehovah will be clear signs that Egypt belongs to the God of Israel.

Josephus reports that the priest Onias IV in the year 154 B.C. built a temple in Leontopolis dedicated to the worship of Jehovah which rivalled in magnificence the Jerusalem Temple.[1] Onias and the Egyptian Jewish colony justified their action on the basis of Isaiah 19:19.

20 When they shall cry to the Lord because of oppression . . .

Long ago, Israel was oppressed in Egypt and they cried unto the Lord because of oppressors. Then He sent a Saviour to deliver them. Now Egypt will be oppressed in her own land and the Lord will send her a Saviour to deliver her, just as He once delivered Israel.

21 Even as Israel came to know the Lord as a result of her deliverance, so Egypt too will come to know the Lord. This time Egypt will serve the Lord with sacrifice and offering, and will also keep her vows to the Lord. This will be in contrast to former days when Egypt vowed to the Lord to set Israel free, but did not keep her vows.

22 The LORD shall smite Egypt and heal her.

In former days Egypt was smitten, but she was not healed. Now her affliction shall lead to repentance and to healing.

23-25 Here is one of the most sublime visions ever predicted by prophet and seer. In verse 23, the two rival empires and enemies of Israel, which throughout their history sought to swallow up each other and to impose their will upon each other, will become reconciled and close partners in commerce and in worship of the Lord. The highway from Egypt to Assyria is symbolic of their new relationship to each other and to the Lord.

24 Israel shall be a third with Egypt and Assyria.

Little Israel caught between the Egyptian anvil and the Assyrian hammer was the perennial victim of the depredations of both powers. Isaiah sees the time coming when Israel will be a partner and ally of her former foes, and together, they will become a blessing to all the inhabitants of the earth. The promise which the Lord once made to Abraham will at last be fulfilled, "and in thee shall all the families of the earth be blessed" (Gen. 12:3b).

25 This is one of the most glorious lines in all of the Old Testament Scripture: pagan Egypt is to become just like Israel **"my people"**—God's people. Assyria, the most bloodthirsty, ferocious kingdom which human cruelty has ever established, shall become a nation of whom a Holy God will be able to say with joy: **"the work of my hands."** As for Israel, she will at last be what God always intended her to be: **Israel my heritage,** the inheritor and the blessed carrier of His holiness, His righteousness and His love for all of mankind.

Obviously, this sublime prophecy has not yet been fulfilled. Assyria, as a nation, has completely disappeared from the historical horizon. The Egypt of modern times is only very remotely related to the Egypt of antiquity. Can this prophecy ever be fulfilled? God's promise through His prophet Isaiah answers emphatically, "yes."

While ancient Assyria and Egypt have disappeared, the successor nations of those two empires which embrace much of the contemporary Arab and Muslim world are still alive, and are, together with Israel, in the very center of this troubled and perplexed world. After three millennia, they are still engaged in bitter conflict with one another. However, this glorious and, as yet, unfilled promise holds out a bright hope of eventual reconciliation to the nations of the world under the King Messiah. One day the God of Israel will be the God not only of the Arab and Jewish nations, but of all the peoples, who dwell on earth. Such is the vision of the prophet.

For this prophecy to become a reality, another prophecy of Isaiah concerning the Prince of Peace must first be fulfilled. He must sit upon the throne of His father, David, and establish His glorious kingdom of justice, of righteousness and peace (Isa. 9:6, 7).

For the fulfillment of Isaiah's vision, our torn and tortured humanity is still longingly waiting.

Note: 1. Josephus, *Jewish Wars* X, 3.

Isaiah walks the streets of Jerusalem naked

Isaiah, Chapter 20:1-6

Verses 1-6

1   In the year that Tartan came to Ashdod, when Sargon, king of Assyria sent him, and he fought against Ashdod and subdued it.

2   At that time the LORD spoke through Isaiah the son of Amoz saying: "Go and loosen the sackcloth from off thy loins and thy shoe from off thy foot." And he did so, walking naked and barefoot.

3   And the LORD said: Even as my servant Isaiah walked naked and barefoot for three years as a sign and a wonder against Egypt and Ethiopia

4   So will the king of Assyria lead away the captives of Egypt and the exiles of Ethiopia, the young and the old, naked, barefoot and with uncovered buttocks, to the shame of Egypt.

5   And they shall be dismayed and ashamed because of Ethiopia their expectation and of Egypt their glory.

6   And the inhabitants of this coast land shall say in that day: Behold such is our expectation, to whom we fled for help to be delivered from the king of Assyria: and how shall we escape?

Comment:

1-2   Presents the historical circumstances of Isaiah's astonishing action in walking about publicly naked and barefoot for a period of three years.

It happened when Tartan (which is not a name but the title of the chief of staff of the Assyrian forces) was sent by Sargon (722-702 B.C.), king of Assyria, to subdue the Philistine city of Ashdod, after they refused to pay the annual tribute. This took place in 711 B.C. The conquest of Ashdod, an exceedingly strong fortress, was also to be a preliminary campaign in Sargon's plan to conquer Egypt. The fall of Ashdod and the close proximity of a mighty Assyrian army sent shivers down the spine of Hezekiah, king of Judah. He, therefore, was considering an alliance between Judah and Egypt, then ruled by an Ethiopian dynasty, under Pharaoh Shabaka, against their common enemy, Assyria.

At that time the Lord gave Isaiah the strange command to take off his coarse sackcloth coat and sandals, the usual garment of mourners (1 Ki. 21:27, 2 Ki. 6:30), and of prophets (2 Ki. 1:8; Zech. 13:14; Mt. 3:4).

3 Walking naked and barefoot.

It was usual for mourners to wear under the sackcloth some sort of shirt, so that stripping oneself of the sackcloth did not mean complete nakedness, but only comparatively speaking. The Lord would never have commanded His prophet to walk about "stark 'naked," since this would be an indecent act. Yet for Isaiah to walk about publicly in his undershirt called for a great measure of self-humiliation, especially for a prominent person of Isaiah's stature and aristocratic background.

Isaiah's "nakedness" was to be a sign and wonder, that is, a symbolic act of what the Lord had purposed for Egypt and Ethiopia: defeat and extreme humiliation.

4 Defeated and disgraced, the Egyptian and Ethiopian captives shall be dragged into captivity in the usual degrading manner of the Assyrians, even less attired than "naked" Isaiah.

5-6 The sight of the wretched captives would cause Judah to realize how illusory was their expectation to be rescued from Assyria by Egypt and Ethiopia.

In Sargon's palace in Khorsobad, an inscription was discovered in which the Assyrian king boasted that he fought against Sebech (Shabaka, the Ethiopian ruler of Egypt) and forced him to pay tribute.

Apparently Isaiah's symbolic action drove home his point and Hezekiah, in spite of all allurements, did not ally himself with Egypt.

Once more Isaiah was able to save his people, at least for a short period of time, from putting their trust in the broken reed, Egypt.

A prediction about the Fall of Babylon
Isaiah, Chapter 21:1-10

Verses 1-10

1 The oracle concerning the wilderness of the sea.
   As whirlwinds in the Negev, sweeping on,
   It comes from the desert, from a terrible land.

2   A grievous vision is declared to me:
The spoiler spoils, the destroyer destroys.
Go up, Elam! Besiege, O Media!
All the sighing I have caused to cease.

3   Therefore are my loins filled with convulsion,
Pangs have taken hold of me, like the pangs of a woman in birth.
I am so contorted that I cannot hear,
So dismayed that I cannot see.

4   My heart beats wildly, terror has gripped me,
The darkness which I craved has turned for me into trembling.

5   They prepare the table, spread the cloth,
They eat, they drink.
Arise, you princes, anoint the shield!

6   For the Lord has thus said to me:
Go and set a watchman, what he will see, let him declare.

7   And he saw riders, horsemen in pairs
Riders upon donkeys, riders upon camels,
And he listened keenly, very keenly.

8   Then he who saw cried.
Upon a watchtower I stand, O Lord, all day long.
And am set upon my watch all the nights.

9   And behold riders are coming, horsemen in pairs.
And he shouted and said "Fallen, fallen is Babylon!"
And all the graven images of her gods,
He has dashed to the ground.

10   O, my threshed ones, and child of my threshing floor,
That which I have heard from the LORD of hosts,
The God of Israel, that have I declared to you.

Comment:

Isaiah chapters 21 and 22 record a series of four oracles which deal with the downfall of Babylon (21:1-10), of Edom (v. 11, 12), of Arabia (v. 13, 14), and of Jerusalem (22:1-14). This is followed by a prediction against the arrogant and self-seeking king's steward, Shebna (v. 15-25).

The authenticity of chapter 21, just as of many other parts of Isaiah (chapters 13, 14, 40-66), has been questioned, mainly because of its predictive character. However, we have already indicated that the foretelling of future events is an integral part of the prophetic message.

1 Isaiah is fond of symbolic names and descriptions which dramatize his messages. "The wilderness of the sea" is a symbolic name for Baby-

lonia, a land floating as it were, amidst the marshes and waters of the lower Euphrates. Jeremiah (51:13) calls Babylon "a land which dwells upon many waters." When the Euphrates flooded the land, Babylon was indeed like a land in the sea.

Just as the whirlwinds in the Negev or the south swept with violent force northward, so also will the armies assembled against Babylon sweep out with devastating force from the south and east beyond the Euphrates. This event actually took place during the reign of Cyrus, who in 539 B.C. brought to an end the Assyro-Babylonian empire.

2 A grievous vision. . . There is an innate gentleness in Isaiah, which shrinks with horror at the sight of carnage and destruction, even when its victims are the enemies of Israel.

The spoiler spoils, the destroyer destroys. This refers to the ravaging actions of the armies of Elam and Media, who were part of the forces of Cyrus. Their victory will put an end to all the sighing of the oppressed nations.

3, 4 Describe in vivid detail the effect of the terrible vision upon the sensitive spirit of the prophet.

The darkness I longed for. . . Normally night brings soothing sleep to the anguished soul, but to the prophet the darkness only brings acute disturbance and nightmares.

5 The scene changes. The prophet is transported in spirit to Babylon, where he sees the nobles assembled for feasting, unaware of and not caring about their mortal danger.

Herodotus, the Greek historian of the 5th century B.C., describes in detail the enormous fortifications of Babylon, which, in addition, was also protected by a wide artificial moat, made by the famous Queen Semiramis, who diverted the course of the Euphrates, making it run in serpentine fashion between the walls of the city.

But Cyrus' engineers drained the moat by turning its waters into a nearby marshland. Thus the Persians were able to enter the city unawares, walking along the former river bed straight into the city, while the Babylonians were feasting and dancing. Herodotus adds that the city was so immense that those in the center did not even realize that the enemy was already in their midst. Isaiah addresses himself to the banqueting princes to arise and prepare for battle against the approaching enemy.[1]

6-9 In contrast to the careless watchmen set by the carousing Babylonians, who failed to warn their masters, God has set His own faithful watchman, the prophet himself, to look into the approaching events with all the keenness of his spirit and his senses. The prophet stands on watch day and night, giving faithful warning about everything that the Lord has shown him.

He sees the approaching enemy, riding on horses, camels and asses, animals, which were used not only as mounts for the cavalry, but for carrying equipment and also to cause confusion in the ranks of the enemies. The prophet-watchman sees the enemy cavalcade entering the city, then emerging with the triumphant shout: "Fallen, fallen is Babylon!" This triumphant shout was later echoed by John: "Babylon the great is fallen and is become the habitation of devils and every foul spirit" (Rev. 18:2). Already in Isaiah's vision, Babylon is the symbol of universal tyranny and injustice, under which all the nations groan and languish.

In the book of Revelation, Babylon symbolizes the wicked world powers, which openly defy God and His Anointed, and which eventually will be crushed by the Son of God.

10   With infinite compassion the prophet turns to his people, whom he calls "my threshed ones and child of my threshing floor," with the assurance that their tormentors, who threshed them so long, will themselves be destroyed and that a new dawn will soon come for them. He assures his people that his vision is from God, and not the product of his own fond hopes.

Verses 11, 12   The Oracle concerning Edom

11   The oracle of Dumah. Someone calls to me from Seir:
Watchman! How far is it into the night?
Watchman! How far in the night?

12   The watchman says:
The morning is coming, and also night.
If you will inquire, inquire. Return, come!

Comment:
Verses 11-12

This brief, rather enigmatic oracle deals with the land of Edom, called here Dumah, a word with a double meaning. First, Dumah was a region of Idumea, or Edom, near the mountain of Seir. *Dumah* also means "silence," or "a place of silence." Dumah therefore symbolizes the destiny of Edom, the hereditary enemy of Israel. It will one day become a silent, forsaken and forgotten place. The old abandoned city of Petra, built by the Nabateans in the last two centuries B.C., was located in ancient Edom. An eerie, haunted, silent place—Dumah.

The prophet hears a voice coming from Seir with the anxious query: Watchman, how far is the night spent? When will morning come? The watchman, who is the prophet himself, answers: The morning will come, but then night will fall again.

The prophet uses two words which are not Hebrew but Aramaic. They are *"atha"*—"come"— (as in *Maran-atha*—Lord come), and *"Thibayun,"* —"inquire". It is related to the Hebrew *"shuv"*—to "return."

Aramaic, a language closely related to the Babylonian and other Semitic tongues, was the *lingua franca,* the common language of the Middle East. Perhaps the prophet was hinting that the downfall of Edom will be at the hands of an Aramaic speaking people.

The sense of the prophet's answer is: The night of your present turmoil will end, and a new day will follow, but soon another night will come. If you seek a comforting answer to your anxious inquiries, you must first "return," a word which also means "to repent." Only then will the answer be such as you hoped for; the night of your suffering will come to an end, and a new bright morning of deliverance will dawn upon you.

The Edomite inquirer voices man's eternally agonizing question: "How long will the night of suffering and violence last; how soon will day come?" It has a universal significance. It is the cry of mankind in the midst of a nightmare of mutually inflicted torment and endless horror. The prophetic answer given to the Edomites and to every passing generation is still the same. If you seek a solution to your problems, you must come back to God, *"shuvu"*—return and repent. Otherwise there can only be one dark night of horror followed by another, with only brief intervals between.

Verses 13-17   The oracle concerning Arabia

14   In the thickets of Arabia shall you spend the night, you caravans of the Dedanites. Bring water to meet the thirsty ones. The inhabitants of the land of Teman will bring bread for the fugitives.

15   For they fled from swords, from drawn swords and from the bent bow.
   From the hardships of war.

16   For thus did the Lord say to me, In a year's time, like the year of a hireling, and all the flower of Kedar will fade away.

17   And the remnant of the numbers of archers, the mighty men of Kedar, shall be slight, for the LORD God of Israel has spoken.

Comment:

Verses 13-17

Another enigmatic oracle concerning an Arab merchant tribe, the Dedanites, a people living in the brushland wilderness of Arabia.

14, 15 The word "Arab" in Hebrew has a double meaning, depending on which vowel signs are used, it may mean either "Arab" or "evening." Thus "The oracle concerning Arabia," may also mean "The oracle concerning the evening." Evening is approaching for the Dedanites. The enemy, probably the Assyrians or the Babylonians, will cause them to flee from their native land east of Edom and to seek shelter in the vast desert of Arabia. There, their kinsmen, the Arabs of Yemen, will give them bread and water to help them survive.

16 This prophecy will come to pass in exactly a year ("as the year of a hireling" which means not a day less or more).

The glory of Kedar. Kedar is an Arab tribe of northern Arabia. Together the Dedanites and the Kedarites represent all of the inhabitants of Arabia, from south to north. Their glory or pride was in their military prowess, especially in their excellent archers. This glory will soon disappear because the God of Israel has so decreed.

The basic thought which the prophet voices is that the destiny of all peoples, regardless how strong, is in the hands of the God of Israel, and what He has decreed for their future must come to pass.

1. Herodotus, *The Histories,* Book One, 193.

A Lament Over Jerusalem

Isaiah, Chapter 22:1-14

Verses 1-14

1   The oracle concerning the valley of vision.
     What is it with thee now,
     That all of thee has gone up to the rooftops?

2   Thou art full of uproar, a boisterous city,
     A proud citadel.
     Thy slain ones were not slain by the sword,
     And were not killed in battle.

3   All thy leaders have fled together,
     They were fettered without bow,
     All who were found of thee were bound together,
     They fled far away.

4   Therefore said I, look away from me.
     I will weep bitterly.
     Press not upon me consolation
     For the spoiling of the daughters of my people.

5   For it is a day of trouble, of trampling down and perplexity
     From the Lord, the LORD of hosts, in the Valley of Vision.
     A breaking of the wall, and of crying, echoing against the mountains.

6   And Elam bore the quiver,
     With chariots of men and horsemen
     And Kir uncovered the shield

7   And it came to pass in that day,
     That the choicest valleys were full of chariots
     And the horsemen set themselves in array against the gate.

8 And he laid bare the covering of Judah,
And in that day thou didst look
To the armament in the forest house.

9 And didst see the breaches of the city of David,
That they were many, and you gathered together

10 The waters of the lower pool. And you numbered the houses
And you broke down the houses to reinforce the wall.

11 And you made a reservoir. between the walls
For the waters of the old pool.
But you looked not to him who has done this,
Neither did you regard him, who fashioned it long ago.

12 And in that day, did the Lord, the LORD of hosts, call
To weeping and to mourning
To baldness, and to girding of sackcloth.

13 And behold joy and gladness,
Slaughtering of oxen and killing of sheep,
Eating of flesh and drinking of wine.
"Let us eat and drink,
For tomorrow we shall die"

14 And the Lord, the LORD of hosts, has revealed
Himself in my ears:
"Surely this iniquity shall not be expiated for you,
Until you die, saith the Lord, the LORD of hosts."

Comment: Introductory remarks:
Verses 1-14

The exact historical circumstances of this prophecy are difficult to establish, but it appears to relate to that period when the Assyrian armies under Sennacherib made an unsuccessful attempt in 702, 701 B.C. to take Jerusalem. The city was spared, because of divine intervention, but not before the invading Assyrian armies had captured many other cities in Judah, and thousands of the defenders were carried away into captivity.

The prophet saw that the deliverance of Jerusalem from Sennacherib was merely a reprieve, and that the final calamity was only a matter of time, unless her people repented and turned to God.

But, instead of repenting, Jerusalem went on a wild spree of orgies, of eating and drinking, "for tomorrow we shall die" (v. 13).

For such defiant and incorrigible refusal to repent, there can be no expiation, but only death, physically and eternally.

1-4   The Valley of Vision

Jerusalem was built on several hills, with valleys running between them. The city is surrounded by high mountains. In relation to these mountains, Jerusalem appeared to be in a valley. It is quite possible that Isaiah himself lived in one of the valleys in the city, where the Lord vouchsafed to him the visions and prophecies recorded in his book.

What is it with thee now?

Such is the literal translation of the Hebrew and not as in the KJV "What ails thee now."

The problem of the Jerusalemites was that they did not discern any cause for apprehension or alarm. Nothing ailed them. Their mood was one of joyful celebration, because the Assyrians unexpectedly departed from the gates of the city. Isaiah shows us the citizens of Jerusalem on the flat rooftops of their homes going wild with shouting and jubilation (v. 1). The prophet expresses amazement at their short sightedness and their lack of humble thanksgiving to God for their narrow escape. So he reminds them that far from having experienced a victory, they were, by the mercy of God, merely spared complete disaster.

Her leaders were captured and killed, or were taken prisoners as they were trying to escape, and not in honorable battle.

4, 5   Therefore said I, look away from me.

What a dramatic contrast between the foolish inhabitants of Jerusalem, celebrating their momentary reprieve, completely unmindful of God, and the prophet, whose heart is breaking because of the folly of his people and the awesome future which he foresees.

Isaiah, weeping bitterly over Jerusalem, reminds us of Jesus weeping over that city as He sees her terrible future (Lk. 19:41-44).

Jerusalem has frequently been the cause of tears and heartbreak to her prophets.

5   For it is a day of trouble, of trampling and perplexity from the Lord.

Isaiah foresees the day of disaster, the siege, the breaking down of the walls, the cry of misery and anguish echoing back from the hills.

6   Elam and Kir, two Eastern provinces of Assyria. Their horsemen and bowmen were dreaded by all.

7, 8   The invading armies which filled the valleys of Judah laid bare the weakness of her fortifications. It was then that the leaders of Jerusalem took stock of their armament, stored up "in the forest house" —the armory of Jerusalem.

9-11 The military leaders noticed the weak parts of the city walls and took steps to correct the situation by tearing down some of the houses to obtain materials for the reinforcement of the fortifications.

The water supply was augmented by certain engineering projects and by providing Jerusalem with an adequate water supply from a reservoir located between the city walls.

These plans, anticipated by the prophet, were actually carried out by Hezekiah, perhaps at the behest of Isaiah himself (2 Ki. 20:20 and 2 Chron. 32:30).

The prophet was not opposed to any sensible military precautions which the defenders of Jerusalem undertook to protect their city. He was merely outraged by the fact, that in all plans and precautions the inhabitants of Jerusalem gave no thought to their outraged God, who brought upon them their predicament:

12 When the inhabitants of Jerusalem were going wild in a frenzy of celebrations because of their supposed victory, that was "that day" when the Lord gave them another opportunity to go into deep mourning and of pleading with Him for mercy.

13 But instead Jerusalem indulged in a riotous orgy of gorging themselves with meat and wine.

These words express the mood of the godless masses: "Let us enjoy ourselves while we can, tomorrow we shall die anyway."

14 The Lord has revealed it in my ears. This expression provides us with an interesting insight into the way the Lord sometimes conveyed His message to the prophets. Sometimes He whispers His message into the ear of the prophet, as the still small voice. Sometimes He speaks audibly, as in Isaiah 6:8a.

And I heard the voice of God saying

Surely this sin will not be expiated.

The Hebrew word for "expiated" has the same root as the word *"Yom Kippur"*—"The day of atonement."

Their sin was willful and defiant disregard of God. This sin shall not be atoned for. Those who sin in this manner shall die.

The Targum, the ancient Aramaic paraphrase of this passage renders it "till ye die the second death"—that is, eternal death.[1]

---

1. Quoted by Delitzsch Vol. I p. 397.

The Arrogant Royal Steward

Isaiah, Chapter 22:15-25

Verses 15-25

15 Thus says the Lord, the LORD of hosts:
Go, get thee to that steward, to Shebna
Who is over the house

16 What hast thou here, and whom hast thou here,
That thou hast hewn for thyself a tomb high up,
And carved out a mausoleum for thyself in the rock?

17 Behold the LORD will fling thee away,
With the flinging of a [powerful] man,
And will twist thee round and round

18 And toss thee away like a bundle,
Like a ball [tossed] into an open land.
There will you die and there will be
The chariots of thy glory.
You who are the disgrace
Of your master's house

19 And I will thrust thee from thy position,
And I will pull thee down from thy station.

20 In that day it shall come to pass,
That I will call my servant Eliakim
The son of Hilkiah.

21 And I will invest him with thy robe,
And I will bind him with thy girdle.
And thy government will I commit into his hands,
And he will be a father to the inhabitant of Jerusalem,
And to the house of Judah

22 And the key of the house of David I will put on his shoulder,
He will close and none will open, and he shall open and none will
close,

23 And I will fasten him as a peg in a sure place,
And he shall be for a throne of honor to his father's house

24 And they shall hang upon him all the glory of his father's house,
The offspring and the offshoots, all the small vessels
From the cups to all the vessels of flagons.

25 In that day, saith the Lord of hosts, will the peg
Fastened in a sure place give way, and it shall be
Cast down and fall, and the burden which was upon
It shall be cut off; for the LORD has spoken.

Comment:

Verses 15-25

Judging from his Aramaic name, Shebna was an alien who settled in Jerusalem, without roots in the country or among the aristocracy of Judah (v. 16). Apparently, through innate shrewdness and ruthlessness, he attained the highest position in the land, as steward and head of the royal household. It was a position roughly equivalent to prime minister, personal confidant of the king and chief administrator of the royal household. This gave Shebna almost unlimited powers which, unfortunately, he did not use in the best interest of his master, nor of the nation, but for self-aggrandizement and enrichment. Isaiah bluntly called him "a disgrace to his master." Incidentally, such an insult against the highest official in the land, indicates the fearlessness of the prophet, as well as the measure of freedom which the prophets were able to exercise in ancient Judah, until the times of Manasseh.

Inordinately ambitious, Shebna sought to perpetuate his name by carving for himself a choice burial place in a high rock of Jerusalem, where the aristocracy and the kings were buried (v. 16).

Now the Lord commanded Isaiah to declare to Shebna, that he will be cast down violently from his high position and tossed into exile into a wide-open country, probably Babylon. The Lord will entrust his office and powers to Eliakim, a more worthy person who, in contrast to Shebna, will be like a father to the people of Jerusalem and Judah (v. 21).

The robe and the girdle were emblems of high office as right-hand man to the king.

The key of the house of David was probably a real key which went with the office of royal steward, but was also a symbol of his powers to open the treasury of the king, and of his favors. Any promotion in the king's service was dependent on him (v. 22).

This misused position of great power and honor shall be entrusted to a more worthy servant of God, namely Eliakim (v. 23, 24).

However, in this grand prophecy, couched in Messianic terms, there is an air of foreboding: Eliakim, who is likened to "a sure peg" in the kingdom of his master, upon which all kinds of honorable and dependable service hinge, will in time become an abused peg, upon which all his children, grandchildren, distant relatives and friends shall fasten themselves (the small vessels and the large flagons of v. 24), until they will pull down the peg and fall down together with its overload. Isaiah foresees that nepotism will cause the downfall of Eliakim's house.

There is a warning which applies to every generation and time. On the one hand, there are the wicked and self-seeking stewards, like Shebna, and on the other, there are the stewards like Eliakim, who, honorable and good themselves, allow unworthy relatives or friends to abuse their trust, bringing disaster upon themselves and their benefactor.

The book of Isaiah does not inform us about the final destiny of Shebna or of Eliakim. Both are mentioned again in Isaiah 36:22 and 37:2. Eliakim apparently became head of Hezekiah's household in place of Shebna who held the less important position of scribe. It is even possible that Shebna later repented.

The Decline and Fall of the Phoenician Cities

Isaiah, Chapter 23:1-14

Verses 1-14

1 An oracle concerning Tyre.
   Wail, you ships of Tarshish,
   For it is destroyed, so that there is no home to enter.
   This was revealed to them from the land of Cyprus.

2 Be still, you inhabitants of the coast,
   And you seafaring merchants, their suppliers.

3 Who ply many waters, with the sowing of Shichor
   Whose revenue is the harvest of the Nile,
   And the trade with nations.

4 Be confounded, O Sidon, thou stronghold of the sea,
   For the sea has said:
   I have not travailed, nor given birth,
   I have not raised young men,
   Nor brought up young maidens.

5 When this report reached Egypt,
   They were distressed on hearing about Tyre.

6 Cross over to Tarshish,
   Wail, you inhabitants of the coast.

7 Is this your proud city,
   Whose origin is in antiquity,
   Whose feet carried her to distant places to settle?

8 Who has purposed this against Tyre,
   The dispenser of crowns,
   Whose merchants were princes,
   And her traders the nobles of the earth?

9 It is the LORD of hosts who purposed it,
   To demean the pride of all glory,
   To bring into contempt the nobles of the earth.

10 Overflow your land like the Nile,
    Thou daughter of Tarshish, there is no haven any more.

11 He has stretched forth his hand upon the sea
    He stirred up the kingdoms,
    The LORD has commanded concerning Canaan,
    That her strongholds should be demolished.

12 And he said: be proud no more,
    Thou oppressed virgin daughter of Tyre.
    Rise up and cross over to the land of Cyprus
    Yet even there no respite awaits thee.

13 Behold the land of the Chaldees,
    A people that once was not,
    The Assyrians turned her
    Into a habitation of desert creatures,
    They have set up their siege towers,
    They have destroyed her palaces, they made her a ruin.

14 Wail, you ships of Tarshish,
    For your stronghold is ruined.

Comment:

Verses 1-14

Isaiah 23 is the last chapter in the cycle of oracles against the nations which surrounded Israel (13-23). It began with a prophecy about the downfall of Babylon, the great power of the 7th and 6th centuries B.C. The cycle ends with an oracle concerning the decline and eventual fall of Tyre and her Phoenician colonies, the greatest maritime and trading empire of antiquity.

Babylon represents the corruption and wickedness of brute military power, Tyre symbolizes the international trade and commerce which does not seek to serve God or humanity, but is merely interested in selfish accumulation of wealth.

Tyre with her international trade and world-wide connections reminds us of medieval Venice or of Great Britain in more recent times. Phoenicia and her colonies were the trading people, par excellence, of the ancient world.

The Phoenicians gave the European nations their alphabet, which is of Semitic origin. A highly talented people, they nevertheless brought no blessing to the nations because they lacked spiritual motivation.

Isaiah's vision reaches out beyond the fall of Tyre and of her trading empire to the times when all commerce and industry will serve the Lord and the people "who dwell before the face of the Lord."

This is a pregnant prophecy, which starts from a concrete historical situation and culminates in a vision of the latter days, when the kingdoms of the earth shall become part of the Kingdom of God and of the Prince of Peace.

1 Wail, you ships of Tarshish

Isaiah opens the oracle by giving us a glimpse of a Phoenician fleet returning to their home port in Tyre from a distant journey. Upon reaching Cyprus, they are informed that Tyre has been destroyed and they have no port to go back to.

2-5 When this report reaches the cities of the coastland and Egypt, they are all numbed into silence by fear. Sidon, the parent city of Tyre, is horror-stricken (Shichor is the upper Nile, v. 3). The sea taunts Sidon that she is like a bereaved mother without sons or daughters, that is all the cities and colonies which she has once established.

6-9 The prophet counsels the inhabitants of the coast to cross over to Tarshish, a colony of Phoenicia in Spain, to seek refuge there. Upon seeing the downfall of Tyre, people ask: Is this the proud trading city of antiquity, who once crowned kings and established colonies. Who has purposed this destiny for Tyre, the dispenser of crowns? It is the Lord who did this to demean and to bring into contempt all the pride of men.

10-14 Overflow the land

Now that Tyre has fallen, her daughter Tarshish is like a ship without a haven.

Be proud no more (v. 12). The KJV translates this: "Thou shalt no more rejoice." The Hebrew word *"aliza,"* usually translated "rejoice," has the nuance of joy springing from haughty self-confidence.

The inhabitants of Cyprus, a colony of Tyre, were not anxious to receive their erstwhile rulers and oppressors.

Behold the land of the Chaldees . . .

Isaiah calls the Babylonians by their archaic name Chaldees (see also Isa. 47:1), who originally inhabited the northeastern mountains of Mesopotamia. They were later driven out by the Assyrians and forced to settle along the lower Euphrates, the land which became known as Babylon. This is why they are called by Isaiah "a people that was not," that is a people who were once obscure, who will, with their huge war machines and siege towers, in the future, destroy Tyre.

Actually, Nebuchadrezzar of Babylon besieged Tyre for 13 years (587-574 B.C.) and forced Tyre into submission. This was the beginning of the decline. Although Tyre survived and later regained some of her old trade and stature, she eventually succumbed to Rome together with her colonies. The last Phoenician colony which was razed by the Romans was Carthage; on the north coast of Africa, destroyed in 146 B.C.

Wail, you ships of Tarshish The oracle ends in the same way as it starts.

Verses 15-18   Tyre Forgotten and Restored

15   And it shall come to pass in that day
       That Tyre shall be forgotten for seventy years,
       As the days of one king, but at the end

Of seventy years she will fare as in the song of the harlot:

16 Take a harp, go round the city
Thou harlot, long forgotten!
Play sweetly, keep on singing,
That thou mayest be remembered

17 And at the end of seventy years,
The LORD will visit Tyre
And she will return to her trade
And will play the harlot
With all the kingdoms of the world,
That are on the face of the earth.

18 And her commerce and gain
Shall not be hoarded nor stored up,
But shall be for the people
Who dwell before the face of the LORD,
That they may eat to satiety
And for stately attire.

Comment:

15 When Cyrus the Great conquered Babylon in 539 B.C., Tyre and many other subject peoples were set free together with Israel. After a time, Tyre regained some of her former international position in world trade. We do not know exactly which year Isaiah had in mind as the start of "seventy years."

"The years of one king" refers to the unchangeable order of things which prevails under the reign of one and the same king.

16 After seventy years, Tyre will seek her former customers. Isaiah compares Tyre to a pathetic old harlot, who forced by poverty and old age, goes out into the streets to ply her former trade. The song of the harlot gives us a curious sidelight on certain aspects of life in the great cities of the ancient world.

17 Isaiah compares selfish trade, without the redeeming feature of service to God and to His people, to harlotry.[1]

18 After that, the profits from Tyre's commerce shall no more be hoarded for selfish gain, but shall be used for the service of "the people who dwell before the face of the Lord," a reference which primarily applied to Israel, but embraces all God's people.

On this sublime note, that one day all gain of trade and commerce will be employed for the service of God, the great prophet Isaiah closes his series of oracles concerning the nations.

Note: 1. It should be noted that in the days of Isaiah, Israel was chiefly a farming and pastoral people. Trade in Israel was largely internal, and played a minor role in the national economy. It was only during their exile that the Jews were forced to become a trading people.

The Apocalypse
of Isaiah

The Final Judgment
Isaiah, Chapter 24

Verses 1-23

1 Behold the LORD makes the earth empty and makes it waste,
He mars its face and scatters its inhabitants;

2 Priest and people all alike,
Servant and master,
Maid and mistress,
Buyer and seller,
Lender and borrower,
Creditor and debtor.

3 The earth shall be utterly emptied and utterly despoiled,
For God has spoken this word.

4 The earth mourns and pines away,
The haughty people of the earth wither away.

5 The earth is defiled under her inhabitants,
For they have transgressed the laws,
They have violated the eternal covenant.

6 Therefore a curse is devouring the earth,
And they that dwell therein are desolate.
This is why the inhabitants of the earth are burnt up,
And few are the men left.

7 The new wine is failing, the vine is withering,
All the merry-hearted groan.

8 The merry tambourines have ceased,
The noise of the revelers has stopped,
The merry harp has ceased.

9 They drink wine without a song,
Strong drink has become bitter to its drinkers.

10 Broken down is the city of chaos,
The entrance to every house is shut up.

11 There is crying in the streets amidst wine,
All the joy is darkened, mirth is banished from the land.

12   Desolation is left in the city
And the gate is smashed and destroyed

13   For thus shall it be in the midst of the earth,
In the midst of the peoples.
As at the shaking of an olive tree, as at the gleaning,
When the vintage is done.

14   They shall lift up their voices, they shall sing joyfully
For the majesty of the LORD, they shall shout from the sea.

15   Therefore glorify the LORD in the sunlit places,
In the isles of the sea glorify the name of the LORD, the God of
     Israel.

16   From the uttermost part of the earth have we heard songs:
"Glory to the righteous one."
But I said: I am desolate, I am desolate, woe is me!
The traitors betray, the traitors treacherously betray.

17   Terror, the pit and the snare are upon thee,
O inhabitant of the earth.

18   And it shall come to pass that he who will escape the voice
Of terror, shall fall into the pit.
And he who climbs out of the pit shall be taken by the snare.
For the windows from above shall open,
And the foundations of the earth shall shake.

19   The earth splitting will split,
The earth crumbling will crumble,
The earth tottering will totter.

20   The earth will reel like a drunk,
It will sway like a shack,
Its transgressions will weigh it down,
It will fall never to rise again.

21   And it shall come to pass on that day,
That the LORD will punish the hosts on high, that are on high,
And the kings of the earth on the earth.

22   And they shall be gathered together like prisoners in the pit,
And they shall be shut up in prison.
And after many days they shall be punished.

23   And the moon shall be confounded and the sun shall be ashamed,
For the LORD of Hosts shall reign on Mount Zion and Jerusalem,
And before his elders there shall be glory.

Comment:
Verses 1-23

Isaiah Chapters 24-27 are frequently referred to as "the little apocalypse." This section deals with the final judgment of all humanity and the universe itself, and is interspersed with hymns of supplication and praise.

It is a grand finale to Chapters 13-23, in which Isaiah prophesied concerning the ultimate destiny of the nations surrounding Israel.

24:1-23 Universal Judgment
1-5 Behold the Lord makes the earth empty

In language replete with assonances and alliterations, so typical of Isaiah but almost impossible to reproduce in translation, the prophet describes the terrors of God's judgment which will come upon the world and its inhabitants. None will be spared, regardless of position. This judgment will come upon the earth because it has become defiled by her inhabitants, as once Sodom and Gomorrah were defiled and brought down upon themselves divine wrath.

Men have transgressed "the laws"—*(toroth)* the universal laws of moral conduct and the covenant which God once made with mankind after the flood (Gen. 9:1-17).

Paul refers to these universal laws which are inscribed in the conscience of all men, and to which they have failed to live up (Rom. 1:18-22).

6 Because of this a curse is devouring the earth

One of the themes of the Old and the New Testaments is the interrelationship between man's spiritual condition and nature. Before his fall, man lived in a perfect environment, in paradise. But when he disobeyed God and sinned, a curse came upon the earth: "Cursed is the ground for thy sake" (Gen. 3:17).

The apostle Paul declares:
For we know that the whole of creation
Groaneth and travaileth in pain together until now (Rom. 8:22).

The Hebrew verb *"haru"* translated in the KJV as "They are desolate" means to be burned or charred. In our nuclear age, this term sounds frighteningly realistic and beyond the imagination of earlier commentators.

7 The merry-hearted groan . . .

From verse 7-13 Isaiah describes in dramatic detail the effects of God's judgment upon men while they are preoccupied with senseless revelling and drinking.

14 They shall lift their voices, they shall sing joyfully

In verses 14-16a the prophecy of gloom and doom is interrupted by the sound of a distant song of praise by a redeemed remnant. It comes from the sea, that is from the west and "the sunlit places" (Hebrew—*Urim*)—poetic for "the east."

"Glory to the Righteous"

Some understand "the righteous" as referring to God Himself. However since God is nowhere else called *"Tsadik"*—"the righteous one," it therefore means "the righteous people of God," or His faithful remnant.

16b-23 But I said: I am desolate, I am desolate, woe is me

In the midst of the songs of the redeemed, there is a sudden cry of deep distress which comes from the heart of the prophet, as if he suddenly realized that his vision is something that is still in the distant future, but at present he is confronted by wicked men and traitors who deal in an exceedingly treacherous manner. And so Isaiah continues with his description of the final judgment to come which will shake and sway the whole universe like a flimsy shack in an orchard (v. 20).

The earth will fall under the weight of her iniquity. God will punish the heavenly host above and the kings of the earth (v. 22). Divine judgment will extend to the world of invisible powers on high, which exercise a pernicious influence on all the rulers of the earth. A passage which is closely related to our text is Ephesians 6:12, where Paul writes:

> For we wrestle not against flesh and blood, but against principalities, against powers, against the rulers of the darkness of the world, against spiritual wickedness in high places.

23 In the face of all the wickedness which the judgment shall reveal, the moon itself shall be confounded—or blush, and the sun shall pale with shame.

In the end the LORD of hosts, that is the God who reigns supreme over all the powers of heaven and earth shall have His visible seat on Mount Zion, and before His "elders," that is before His redeemed saints who have always trusted in Him, there shall be glory (v. 23).

A Hymn of Praise
Isaiah, Chapter 25

Verses 1-12

1 O LORD, thou art my God
I will extol thee, I will praise thy name,
For thou hast done wonders,
Counsels of old in faithfulness and truth.

2 For thou hast made of a city a heap,
Of a fortified bastion a ruin,
A castle of strangers to be no city,
It shall never be rebuilt.

3 Therefore shall the strong people glorify thee,
The bastion of the violent nations shall fear thee.

4 For thou hast been a stronghold to the poor,
A stronghold to the needy in his distress,
A shelter from the storm, a shadow from the heat,
For the blast of the violent ones
Was like a storm against the wall.

5   Like the heat in a dry place thou didst subdue
   The uproar of the strangers,
   Like the heat in a shadow of a cloud
   The song of the strangers was brought low.

6   And the LORD of hosts shall make a feast in this mountain
   A feast of fat things for all the peoples
   A feast of clear wine,
   Of fat things full of marrow, of clear wine well refined.

7   And he will destroy upon this mountain
   The face of the covering which is cast upon all peoples.
   And the veil which is spread over all the nations.

8   He will swallow up death forever,
   And the Lord God shall wipe away tears from all faces;
   And the reproach of his people will he take away from off all the
     earth,
   For the LORD has spoken.

9   And it will be said in that day:
   Lo, this is our God, we have waited for him,
   And he will save us.
   This is the LORD, for whom we waited,
   We will be glad and rejoice in his salvation.

10   For in this mountain will the hand of the LORD rest,
   And Moab will be trodden down under him,
   As the straw is trodden down in the dung-pit.[1]

11   And he will spread out his hands in the midst of it,
   As the swimmer spreads out his hands to swim
   And his pride shall be brought down low
   Together with the skill of his hands.

12   And the high fortress of thy walls
   He will bring low, lay low,
   And bring it down to the ground, to the dry dust.

Comment:

Verses 1-12

Isaiah chapters 1-12, the so-called book of Immanuel, ended with a hymn of praise. Chapters 13-23, which deal with the future destiny of the nations surrounding Israel are followed by the final judgment of all mankind (24), and in a similar way end with hymns of praise and prayer by redeemed Israel (25, 26).

1 O LORD, thou art my God, I will exalt thee. . . . Having witnessed the wonders *(pele)*, which God has performed and His faithfulness in the fulfillment of His ancient plans, redeemed Israel now extols Jehovah as their God.

2   For thou hast made of a city a heap . . .

No specific city is mentioned by name. The prophet might have had in mind any of the great centers of the arrogant and oppressing powers, such as Nineveh or Babylon.

3   God has turned these proud cities into a heap of ruins with the result that they now must recognize the sovereignty of the Lord and worship Him.

4, 5   The triumph of Jehovah over the pagan powers has brought deliverance to Israel, just as a shadow provides relief from the heat, or a wall protects against the storm.

6a   And the Lord shall make in this mountain a feast . . .

Isaiah sees God's judgment upon mankind not as a mere penal measure, but as a means of their conversion. Once the nations shall turn to Him in humble faith and obedience, the LORD will receive them as His returning prodigals and prepare a feast for them. These are echoes of Isaiah's grand vision of the nations streaming to Zion to worship the God of Israel and to walk in His ways (Isa. 2:2-4). The theme of the Messianic feast to which Isaiah alludes here frequently occurs in later rabbinical literature.

7   The prophet sees the day coming when the veil of ignorance which blinds all nations and causes them to reject this rule will ultimately be removed from all faces.

8   He will swallow up death forever . . . and wipe away the tears from all faces and the reproach of His people from all the earth.

Here is one of the most glorious visions which the Scriptures hold out to men. Victory over death and cessation of all evil and injustice which dim the eyes of men with tears.

Just as the entrance of sin has brought death into the world, so victory over sin will bring triumph over death and an end to all the misery and suffering resulting from sin.

In 1 Corinthians 15:54-57 the apostle Paul quotes this text of Isaiah, which is also echoed in Revelation 21:4.

An integral part of the vision of God's triumph over sin is the vindication of God's people Israel, whose reproach will be removed forever. As long as the forces of evil are triumphant in this world, God's people will always be despised and put to shame.

9   And it will be said in that day:
   LO, this is our God

The vision of divine victory over sin and wickedness and the vindication of His people fill the prophet's heart with a song of praise. Verse 9 is like a shining pearl of a psalm, set within the center of a hymn.

10-12 In this mountain will the hand of the LORD rest upon Moab
In spite of the cataclysmic judgment which God shall visit upon the nations, not all of them will repent. Some will remain obdurate and unrepentant to the very end. Moab, the ancient enemy of God's people, appears in this passage not only as a historic neighbor of Israel, and a thorn in her flesh, but also symbolizes that part of humanity which will remain God-defying to the very end. Their destiny is to end up on the dung-pit of history! No skills or craft will save them, even as a swimmer cannot swim in a dung-pit, they and all their vaunted civilization will end up in dust and ruins.

> Note 1. Dung-hill or dung-pit, in Hebrew Madmenah is probably a play of words on the Moabitish city "Madmen," mentioned in Jeremiah 48:2.

A Song of Praise
Isaiah, Chapter 26

Verses 1-21

1 In that day shall this song be sung in the land of Judah:
We have a strong city,
Salvation has he set for walls and bulwarks.

2 Open the gates, that a righteous nation,
Which keeps faith may enter in.

3 Thou shalt keep in perfect peace the mind which is steadfast,
Because he trusts in thee.

4 Trust you in the LORD forever,
For in Jah, the LORD [is] an everlasting Rock.

5 For he has brought down them who dwell on high,
The lofty city he laid low, laying it low to the ground,
Bringing it down to the dust.

6 The foot shall tread it down,
The feet of the poor, the steps of the needy.

7 For the righteous the way is straight.
He makes plain the path of the righteous.

8 Verily in the way of thy judgments,
Have we waited for thee, O LORD,
The longing of our soul is toward thy name and thy remembrance.

9 With my soul have I desired thee in the night,
And with my spirit within me have I sought thee before dawn,
For only when thy judgments are in the earth,
Shall the inhabitants of the world learn righteousness.

10 Let favor be bestowed upon the wicked,
Yet will he not learn righteousness,
And will not perceive the majesty of the LORD.

11 LORD, when thy hand was lifted up, they did not see it.
But they shall see and be ashamed, because of thy zeal for thy
people.
Yea, a fire shall devour thy enemies.

12 LORD, thou wilt establish peace for us,
For thou hast also wrought all our works for us

13 O LORD our God, [other] lords have had dominion over us,
But only by thee do we make mention of thy name.

14 They are dead, they shall not live,
They are shades, they shall not rise;
To this end dost thou visit and destroy them,
And make their memory perish.

15 LORD, thou hast added to thy nation,
Thou hast added to thy nation, thou art glorified,
Thou hast enlarged all the borders of the land.

16 LORD, in trouble they sought thee,
Silently they poured out [their hearts]
When thy chastening was upon them.

17 As a pregnant woman about to give birth
Is in pain and cries out in her pangs,
So have we been before thy Presence, O LORD.

18 We have been pregnant, we have been in pain,
We have, as it were, brought forth wind,
We have not wrought salvation in the land,
Neither have the inhabitants of the world fallen.

19 Thy dead shall live, together with my corpse shall they rise,
Wake up and sing, you who dwell in the dust.
For thy dew is the dew of light, and the earth shall cast up her
dead.

20 Come my people, enter thy chambers, and shut the door behind
thee,
Hide thyself for a brief moment,
Until the indignation shall pass.

21 For, behold, the LORD will go forth from his place
To visit upon the inhabitant of the earth his iniquity,
And the earth shall disclose her blood,
And shall no more cover her slain.

Comment:

Verses 1-21

Isaiah Chapter 26 is a hymn of redeemed Israel. It alternates between praise, and prayerful reflection. Like Chapter 27 it begins with the phrase, "in that day," a term which signifies the opening of a new dispensation in God's dealing with His people, or with mankind.

1-6   A Song of praise for divine protection.

1 Israel, which has witnessed God's judgment upon the proud and unrepentant nations, having experienced salvation, now sings a song of praise. Jerusalem shall be a strong city not because of her fortifications, that is, her walls and bulwarks (the outer walls of a fortress), but because of the salvation of her God.

2 Jerusalem shall become an abode fit for a people faithful to God and to His word.

3, 4 The mind which is completely stayed upon Jehovah experiences "perfect peace" (in Hebrew *Shalom, shalom*—peace, peace). Therefore let all the faithful trust in *"Jah,"* a' poetic abbreviation for Jehovah, for He is the Eternal Rock. All else may give way and vanish, only the LORD remains everlasting.

5, 6 The prophet sees "the proud city," the symbol of God-defying arrogant power, vanquished and humbled to the dust, trodden down by the feet of God's poor and needy. To this faith Christ gave expression in the Sermon on the Mount, in these words: "Blessed are the meek, for they shall inherit the earth" (Mt. 5:5).

7, 8 The just man finds God's way straight and plain for he longs to do the will of God, and craves for God and His presence.

10, 11 But the wicked do not learn justice, nor see the hand of God, even when the Lord is good to them. They have no eye for the majesty of God, nor for His manifestation in history. Only as they become aware of the Lord's zeal for His people, in preserving them from their wicked designs will they be covered with shame, that is, with intense embarrassment and confusion.

12 A humble prayer for establishment of God's peace in view of all the acts of mercy and favor which He has performed on behalf of His people in the past.

13-15 A reflection upon the fact that so many "lords," that is, tyrants and "gods" have claimed dominion over Israel, nevertheless, Israel has remained faithful only to His name (v. 13).

All those enemies of God are now dead and gone, even their memory shall perish (v. 14).

243

Yet in spite of persecution and trouble Israel has increased, has enlarged her borders and faithfully continues to honor her God (15).

16-18 In times of trouble the people of God have sought Him and silently poured out their hearts before Him. They were like a woman in pain about to give birth. They knew the pains and pangs of childbirth, yet without obtaining that salvation, for which they had hoped.

20-21 Come my people enter into thy chambers.

In view of God's wrath, which is about to be poured out on the disobedient and rebellious nations, Isaiah counsels his people to wait patiently and in quiet seclusion for the wrath of God to pass. Then all the shed blood of the innocent victims will be vindicated and the identity of all those who were slain in secret or unknown to men, shall be revealed. Isaiah is saying in essence: those who died in faith, even if they are unknown to men, are known to God.

God's Judgment upon the World Empires
Israel Will Be Punished in Measure, Then Redeemed
Isaiah, Chapter 27

Verses 1-13

1 In that day will the LORD
   With his heavy, great and strong sword
   Punish the leviathan, the swift serpent,
   And leviathan, the sinuous serpent,
   And he will slay the dragon which is in the sea.

2 In that day: A pleasant vineyard, sing you to it.

3 I the LORD guard it, I water it every moment,
   Lest it be hurt, I watch over it night and day.

4 Wrath have I none,
   Would that I had briers and thorns before me
   I would step out and burn them altogether.

5 Or else let them take hold of my strength,
   And make peace with me, let them make peace with me.

6 In days to come Jacob will take root,
   He will blossom and bloom,
   And fill the face of the earth with fruitage.

7 Has he smitten him as he smote those who smote him?
   Or was he slain as they were slain who slew him?

8 When he cast him out,
   This was the full measure of his punishment
   He sifted him with his violent breath
   In the day of the east wind.

9   Therefore by this shall the iniquity of Jacob be atoned:
    When he will put away the stones of the altar,
    Like chalkstones which are ground to pieces,
    So that the images of Astarte, and the incense altars
    Shall rise no more.

10 For the fortified city has become solitary,
    An abandoned habitation and a forsaken wilderness:
    Where the calf feeds and where it lies down
    And browses on the branches.

11 When the boughs are withered, they shall be broken,
    Women shall come and use them for firewood.
    For this is a people of no understanding,
    Therefore will their Maker have no compassion on them,
    And he who formed them will show them no favor.

12 In that day it shall come to pass,
    That the LORD shall thresh from the stream
    Of the River Euphrates to the brook of Egypt
    And you shall be gathered one by one, O sons of Israel.

13 And it shall come to pass in that day,
    That a great trumpet shall be sounded,
    And they shall come who were lost in the land of Assyria,
    And they who were dispersed in the land of Egypt,
    And they shall worship the LORD,
    In the holy mount in Jerusalem.

Comment:

1   Isaiah continues the theme of the last chapter which is the impending judgment of the nations, especially of the three world powers: Assyria, Babylon, and Egypt. Leviathan the "swift serpent," an aquatic monster of mythical origin, represents Assyria, situated along the banks of the swift river Tigris. Babylon, the great empire along the winding Euphrates, is described as "the leviathan, the sinuous serpent," and Egypt is called "the sea dragon." Divine judgment upon these three proud nations is indicative of God's judgment upon all the world powers. Their destiny is to be obliterated by His "heavy, great and strong sword."

2-5   A song in praise of Jehovah, the keeper of His vineyard—Israel. It is reminiscent of a similar song of the vineyard, in Isaiah 5:1-6.

2   **A pleasant vineyard, sing you unto it.** The KJV following the commonly accepted Hebrew text *"kerem herem"* translates it "a vineyard of red wine." However, the Septuagint and the Aramaic Targum follows a variant reading *"kerem tsemed,"* preserved in a number of

Hebrew manuscripts, and translates this as "a pleasant vineyard." In our opinion this seems to be the better text and corresponds more closely to the song of the vineyard of chapter 5:1-6.

3 Here also Isaiah expresses God's disappointed love for His vineyard —Israel, in view of all the care and labor bestowed upon it.

4 Nevertheless the Lord does not deal with His people as if they were worthless briers and thorns which He would burn in one wrathful gesture.

5 Oh, if only Israel would repent and make her peace with God.

6 The day will come when she will do so. At that time Jacob will take root and flourish and blossom and fill the earth with her fruit. Here is one of the most beautiful promises concerning Israel's future to be found anywhere in the Scriptures.

We are reminded of the apostle Paul's prediction that Israel's spiritual restoration will be "the riches of the Gentiles" (Rom. 11:12).

7-13 God's dealing with Israel is basically different from the way He has dealt with other nations. He punishes His people in moderation.

7 Has he smitten him, as he smote those who smote him?

In this rhetorical question Isaiah draws the attention of his people to the fact that even in wrath God has shown mercy toward Israel.

8 The full measure of His punishment of Israel was only exile and dispersion, and not total extinction which was the destiny of many mighty nations.

9 . . . by this shall the iniquity of Jacob be atoned.

Israel must abandon her idolatry and destroy the idols devoted to the cult of the licentious goddess Astarte and to the worship of the sun. The altars of these idols must be ground to pieces, like soft chalkstones.

10, 11 The fortified city shall be solitary . . .

Isaiah dramatically depicts Jerusalem as destroyed and abandoned by her enemies, her streets overgrown with wilting leaves and branches, which women gather for firewood, and calves browsing in the midst of the destroyed city, which has become like a wilderness. All this will be the result of Israel's lack of spiritual comprehension and insight into the ways of her God.

12,13 Isaiah looks beyond the punishment and sees the day of Israel's restoration.

One by one the LORD will bring back the exiled from their dispersion. He will gather them like hand-picked fruit, after the shaking of the trees is over. The LORD will cause a great trumpet *(shofar)* to be sounded and they shall come streaming back from their exile in Assyria and Egypt to Jerusalem, where they will worship their Lord.

The Book
of Woes

In this group of oracles, each beginning with the exclamation, "Woe," Isaiah warns the leaders of Jerusalem against relying upon Egypt for military help against Assyria. That wicked empire will be destroyed, not with the sword of man, but through divine intervention.

The first which is also the oldest oracle in this group (chapter 28:1-6) is directed against "the drunkards of Ephraim." It is a warning to the rulers of Jerusalem to repent and to mend their ways lest they share the fate of Samaria.

The last woe of the series (33:1-12) is directed against Assyria. Most of the oracles, with the exception of the first were apparently delivered during the reign of Sennacherib (705-681 B.C.), before his disastrous attempt to capture Jerusalem in 701 B.C.

Isaiah, Chapter 28

Verses 1-6   An oracle against Samaria

1   Woe to the crown of pride of Ephraim's drunkards,
    And to the fading flower of his splendid beauty,
    Which is at the head of the lush valley,
    You who are struck down by wine!

2   Behold the LORD has a mighty and strong one,
    Like a hailstorm, a destroying tempest,
    He will throw down to the ground with the hand.

3   He will trample them with the feet,
    The crown of pride of the drunkards of Ephraim.

4   And the fading flower of his splendid beauty,
    Which is at the head of the lush valley,
    Shall be like the early ripe fig before summer,
    Which, whoever sees it, as soon as it is in his palm gulps it down.

5   In that day shall the LORD of hosts be for a crown of glory,
    And for an ornament of beauty to the remnant of this people.

6 A spirit of justice, to him who sits in judgment,
  A spirit of courage, to them who turn the battle away from the
    gate.

Comment:

1 Woe . . . to Ephraim's drunkards

Isaiah denounces the proud rulers of Samaria as irresponsible and ungodly drunkards.

2, 3 They will soon experience the wrath of God through the terrible power of mighty Assyria, who will trample them under foot and gulp them down like a sweet early fig. Since Samaria fell to the Assyrians in 722 B.C., this prophecy must have been pronounced shortly before that date, but it is inserted here as a timely warning to the rulers of Jerusalem.

5, 6 In that day . . .

This phrase usually indicates the beginning of a new era. Here it inaugurates the time of Israel's repentance and restoration to God.

Verses 7-13 Against the drunken priests and prophets

7 And these too, are reeling with wine,
  And stagger from strong drink.
  Priest and prophet are reeling from strong drink,
  They are confused with wine,
  They stagger from strong drink,
  They reel in vision, they stumble in judgment.

8 For all tables are covered with filthy vomit,
  There is not a clean place left.

9 "Whom does he teach knowledge?
  Whom is he making understand his message?
  Babies weaned from milk?
  Babies taken from the breast?

10 With this: '*Tsav, latsav, tsav latsav,*
        Kav lakav, kav lakav
        Zeir sham, zeir sham' "
  [Precept upon precept, precept upon precept
  Line upon line, line upon line
  Here a little, there a little].

11 Verily through stammering lips, and an alien tongue
  Shall he speak to this nation,

12 To whom he once said: "Here is rest for the weary,
  And this is the refreshing,"
  But they would not listen.

13 So the word of the LORD shall be to them:
"*Tsav latsav, tsav latsav*
Kav lakav, kav lakav
Zeir sham, zeir sham"
So that they may walk and fall backwards and be broken
And snared and taken captive.

Comment:

7, 8   There are few passages in the prophetic writings which express so vehemently Isaiah's profound disgust with the nation's depraved priests and prophets. Instead of being mediators between the people and their God, instead of teaching them the Word of their God, they are so degraded by their filthy orgies, and so overcome by alcohol that they reel, stagger and mumble, even while performing their prophetic and priestly functions.

9, 10   When Isaiah attempts to bring them to their senses they scoff at him and mimic his words in the senseless fashion of drunks. In verse 10, the prophet reproduces the actual mimicry and mockery of his words by the drunkards. In effect they say to him, whom do you think you are lecturing? Are we babies just weaned from our mothers' breasts? Stop your foolish babbling.

11   In answer the prophet says: Since you consider my words strange, and unintelligible babbling, the Lord will speak to you through the strange and unintelligible sounds of Assyrian soldiery.

We can imagine how harsh anl uncouth the language of the Assyrian invaders must have sounded to the Hebrew ear. Although both languages were of Semitic origin, they differed vastly, especially when spoken by the coarse Assyrian soldiers. Each sounded to the other as if he were being mocked. In a deeper sense, the whole misery of the Assyrian depredations was an unintelligible mystery to the Jews.

12, 13   Since they would not listen to God who offered them peace and security, they will have to learn the message of the invaders and spoilers brought to them in the barbarian language and strange sounds.

Verses 14-22   Against the ungodly rulers of Jerusalem

14   Therefore hear the word of the LORD, you scornful men,
You rulers of this people which is in Jerusalem,

15   Because you have said we have made a covenant with death,
And have come to an understanding with Sheol,
When the sweeping scourge shall pass
It will not overtake us,
For we have made the lie our shelter,
And falsehood our hiding place.

16 Therefore thus says the Lord God:
Behold I lay a stone in Zion,
A tested stone, a precious and sure corner stone.
He who believes shall remain steadfast.
And I will make justice the measuring line,
And righteousness for a plummet.
And the hail shall sweep away the sheltering lies,
And the waters shall overflow the hiding place.

18 And your covenant with death shall be cancelled,
And your agreement with death shall be voided.
And when the scourge shall pass
It will crush you.

19 As often as it passes it will sweep you away,
For it will pass morning after morning,
By day and by night,
It shall be sheer terror to understand the message.

20 For the bed is too short to stretch in it,
And the blanket too narrow to cover oneself.

21 For the LORD will rise up as in Mount Perazim,
He will bestir himself as in the valley of Gibeon,
To do the deed, his strange deed,
To perform his work, his amazing work.

22 So now, cease your scoffing,
Lest your bonds become even tighter,
For I have heard from the Lord God of hosts,
A complete and determined plan of destruction
Upon all the land.

Comment:

14 Having previously pronounced the doom of Samaria and of her inebriated rulers, both civil and religious, Isaiah now addresses himself to the scornful men and rulers of Jerusalem. *"Anshei latzon"*—scornful men, is probably derisive play on words for *"anshei Zion"*—men of Zion. This would parallel closely the next line, "You rulers of this people, which is in Jerusalem."

15 In their conceit and self-deception they are like their brethren of Ephraim, who were also not afraid of death, nor of Sheol, nor of the sweeping scourge.

They rely on lies and duplicity; while playing their political intrigue with the Egyptian, they pretend loyalty to the Assyrian; while pretending to be loyal to Jehovah, they flirt with the pagan deities of their neighbors, frequently called by the prophets "a lie," or "falsehood."

16-20   This passage is the *apodosis* (counterpart) to verses 14, 15.

16   Behold I lay in Zion a stone—
Apparently a reference to the Messiah (not to Hezekiah as some commentators have maintained, nor to the Temple in Jerusalem), who is
the tried and true cornerstone of God's kingdom (Psa. 118:22). He that
believes in Him shall remain steadfast regardless of all disasters and
trials.

17   In the Kingdom of the Messiah justice shall be the measuring line
and righteousness the plummet, instruments by which one measures the
true and straight line of any structure.

18, 19   Using the very terms previously used by the scoffers of Jerusalem, the prophet predicts that they will become the victims of death
and Sheol and of the sweeping scourge (epidemic diseases), the companions of devastating war and will know the misery of exile. It shall be
sheer terror to understand the meaning of the message, (in Hebrew
"shemua," hearing or report, the same term which Isaiah used in 53:1).
    The very report of the disaster will strike terror into the hearts of the
believers.

20   For the bed is too short to stretch in it,
   And the blanket too narrow to cover oneself.
   This is a proverbial description of an impossible situation.

21   Just as the Lord fought on the side of David against the Philistines
at Mount Perazim (2 Sam. 5:20), and with Joshua in the valley of Gibeon (Josh. 10:10), so will He now do the strange thing of fighting against
the very same people whom He had previously helped.

22   So now, cease your scoffing
   Isaiah concludes his address to the haughty rulers of Jerusalem: "Stop
your scoffing, you will only hurt yourselves more. God is about to devastate the whole land."

Verses 23-29   The parable about the plowman

   23   Give ear and hear my voice
        Attend and listen to my speech:

   24   Does the plowman keep on plowing in order to sow?
        Does he [constantly] open up his ground and harrow it?

   25   Is it not so, that when he has levelled its surface,
        Does he not scatter the black poppy seed and cummin,
        And put in wheat in rows,
        And barley in the appointed places,
        And spelt in its border?

   26   He has been instructed aright,
        His God has taught him.

27 For black poppy seed is not threshed with a threshing sledge,
    Neither is the cartwheel rolled over the cummin,
    For the black poppy seed is beaten with a flail,
    And cummin with a rod.

28 Does one crush breadgrain?
    No, he will not forever keep threshing it,
    And though the wheels of his wagon and his horses
    Roll over it, he will not crush it.

29 This too comes from the LORD of hosts
    Wonderful is his counsel, great is his wisdom.

Comment:

Verses 23-29

Isaiah uses the *mashal*—the parable, of which he was such a master. To illustrate God's remarkable way of dealing with His people, he compares God's actions with those of a farmer, whose wisdom is also God-given. God is the great plowman, Israel His soil—He breaks up His ground, He furrows it just enough to make it ready to receive the seed, that is the Word and the Wisdom of God (v. 23, 24). The black poppy seed and the cummin are used in oriental cooking and baking, as condiments or spices.

The farmer plants his grain in its appointed places (v. 25). He knows how to cultivate his soil, because he has been instructed by God Himself; he employs the right instruments and methods to accomplish his task (v. 26-28). How much more does the Lord God Himself know how to deal properly with His soil—Israel? As the prophet considers the wonderful ways of God, he ends with an exclamation of adoration:

Wonderful is his counsel,

Great is his wisdom!

The word employed by Isaiah for "wisdom" is *"tushiah,"* which is practical wisdom in action.

God's Purpose for Jerusalem
Isaiah, Chapters 29 and 30

Isaiah 29:1-8

1 Woe Ariel, Ariel, the city where David encamped,
   Add year to year, let the feasts come around!

2 Then will I distress Ariel,
   And there shall be moaning and groaning,
   And she shall become to me Ariel—a hearth of God.

3 And I will encamp against thee round about,
   And will lay siege against thee with a mound,
   And will raise siege against thee.

252

4   And brought low, thou shalt speak from the ground,
    And from the dust thou shalt mutter thy speech.
    And thy voice shall be like that of a ghost from the ground.
    And out of the dust shall thou hiss thy speech.

5   And the multitude of thy foes shall be like fine dust,
    And the multitude of the oppressors like the driven chaff,
    It shall come to pass in an instant, suddenly.

6   Thou shalt be visited by the Lord of hosts,
    With thunder, with earthquake and with a great roar,
    With whirlwind, with tempest and with the flame of a consuming
        fire.

7   And it shall be like a dream, like a nightmare,
    The horde of nations that war against Ariel,
    And that distress her.

8   And it shall be as when the hungry man dreams that he eats,
    But when he wakes up and behold, his soul is empty.
    Or when the thirsty man dreams that he drinks
    But when he wakes up and behold, his soul is parched with thirst.
    So shall the multitude of nations be,
    That war against mount Zion.

Comment:

1   Woe Ariel, Ariel!

Jerusalem is poetically called "Ariel," a compound word which means "the hearth of" (*ari*) and "God" (*El*). It is "the hearth of God" because here was the temple and the altar of God where sacrifices were brought to Him.

The city where David encamped. . . .

Jerusalem was the city which David conquered and fortified, and which was named after him "the City of David." Here he achieved his great victory over the Jebusites, and laid the foundation of his kingdom.

Add year to year, let the feasts come around. . . .

Year after year passes and Jerusalem continues to celebrate her perennial feasts without caring about the future.

2   But the Lord is about to distress Ariel—the altar of God. Then there shall be moaning and groaning everywhere. Only then will Jerusalem become "Ariel," a true altar of God.

3-5   Isaiah describes the pending siege and humiliation of Jerusalem by a horde of hostile invaders, which will be as thick as fine dust. The city, once so joyful and full of clamor and noise, will whisper from the ground as if it were a habitation of ghosts.

253

6-8 But when all will appear lost and the proud city about to be violated by the invaders, God will visit Jerusalem with thunder and earthquake. In the hour of their seeming triumph, the enemies of Zion shall wake up as if from a bad dream. Their expectation of victory shall turn into a nightmare.

Verses 9-12 The incredible obtuseness of the people of Jerusalem who fail to understand the Lord's repeated warnings.

9 Be amazed and bemused,
    Shut your eyes and be blind,
    You who are drunk but without wine,
    Who stagger, yet without strong drink.

10 For the Lord has poured out upon you
    The spirit of deep sleep and has closed your eyes.
    The prophets and your heads, the seers, has he covered.

11 And the vision of all this has become to you
    Like the words of a sealed book,
    Which when given to one who is learned,
    And he says please read this, he replies,
    "I cannot because it is sealed."

12 Then the book is given to one who is unlettered,
    Saying please read this, and he says,
    "I cannot because I am not learned."

Comment:

9-12 The prophet decries the astounding and willful obtuseness of the people. They have shut their eyes to the truth and behave like drunkards without actually being drunk (v. 9). Isaiah concludes that this state of mind is the result of God's punishment. He has sent a deep hypnotic sleep *("tardemah"*—the same word appears in Genesis 2:21) upon the prophets and the leaders of Jerusalem. The word "seer" is synonymous with "prophet," and is used here for emphasis. The "heads" are the rulers of the people. This spiritual blindness has affected both the educated and the uneducated. The educated man is unwilling to read the signs of the times, and refuses to break the seal of the book or scroll, which the prophet offers him to study, while the uneducated man is unable to read. One way or the other both are blind, with a blindness which is either self-imposed or God-inflicted as a punishment for their insincerity and hypocrisy. Since at the time when the prophet wrote the above oracle the Old Testament was not yet completed, it must be assumed that Isaiah was referring either to his own book of prophecies, or to the books of Moses.

Verses 13, 14   The piety of the people is superficial and mechanical, not from the heart.

13   And the LORD said, because this people draw near to
Me with their mouth and honor me with their lips,
But their heart is far removed from me,
And their fear of me is a man-made commandment,
Learned by heart.

14   Therefore will I do a marvelous work with this
People, wonderfully and wondrously,
And the wisdom of their wise men shall perish,
And the insight of their prudent men shall become obscured.

Comment:

13, 14   When men willfully blind themselves to God and their worship becomes mere ritual, without heart or soul, He imposes upon them the penalty of their superficiality and insincerity. Their wisdom ceases to be wisdom and their insight or intelligence *(binah)* is darkened. This is the remarkable and astonishing work of God. From the perspective of twenty-five centuries, the modern reader of Isaiah can only stand amazed at the truth of these words, which apply with equal force not only to ancient Israel but to the human race in every generation.

Verses 15-24   The evil counselors shall fail because of their perversity.

15   Woe to them that search deep to conceal their plan from the
LORD,
Who work in the dark and say:
"Who sees us and who knows us?"

16   Oh, your perversity!
Should the potter be considered the same as the clay?
Should the thing which was made say of its maker,
"He made me not"?
Or a thing framed say of him that framed it,
"He has no understanding"?

17   Is it not so that in a very short time
Lebanon shall be turned into a fruitful field,
And the fruitful field shall be considered as a forest?

18   In that day shall the deaf hear the words of a book,
And the eyes of the blind shall see out of obscurity
And out of darkness.

19   And the humble shall increase their joy in the LORD,
And the needy among men shall rejoice in the Holy One of Israel

20 For the tyrant shall come to nought,
   And the scoffer shall cease,
   And they that watch for iniquity shall be cut off.

21 Who condemn a man for a word,
   Who lay a snare for him, that reproves in the gate,
   And turn aside the cause of the just man with a hollow excuse.

22 Therefore thus says the LORD to the house of Jacob,
   He who has redeemed Abraham,
   Jacob shall no longer be ashamed,
   And his face shall no longer grow pale.

23 For when his children shall see the works of my hands,
   They shall hallow my name.
   And they shall sanctify the Holy One of Jacob,
   And stand in awe of the God of Israel!

24 And they who err in spirit shall come to understanding,
   And the murmurers shall learn instruction.

Comment:

15 Woe to them that seek to conceal their plans from the LORD.
A powerful group, probably closely linked to the political and military leadership of Judah, was apparently pressing king Hezekiah to ally himself with Egypt against the Assyrians. Aware that Isaiah was strongly opposed to their plans, these leaders sought to arrange the Egyptian alliance in secret. The prophet as the official spokesman of the LORD considered their machinations an attempt to conceal their plans from the LORD Himself.

16 Oh, your perversity!
Isaiah disdains and ridicules such efforts, as an attempt by the clay vessel to be wiser than the potter, or the creation than the Creator Himself. Their perversity consists in seeking to outsmart and outwit their God.

17 . . . in yet a little while . . .
This is a recurrent refrain in the prophetic message. "Of what value are all your clever little plans and stratagems when soon the LORD Himself will intervene to subdue the tyrants and to punish the wicked?"

Lebanon shall be as a fruitful field
God's intervention will affect both nature, and the nature of men.

18 The deaf shall hear . . . the blind shall see

19 It is characteristic of the prophets and especially of Isaiah, that when God intervenes, He always does so on behalf of the meek, the

humble and the poor. Behind the Sermon on the Mount there is much
of the prophetic vision and message of Isaiah and of the other prophets.

20 . . . The tyrant shall be brought to nought . . .
. . . The scoffer shall cease.

The tyrant is the foreign oppressor. The scoffer is the home-grown,
ungodly cynic.

21 . . . Who condemn a man for a word
And lay a snare in the gate.

This whole passage is directed against the perverse judges and officers
of the law, who, instead of protecting the innocent and the just, seek
to entrap them by clever legalistic devices and hollow pretexts, founded
on nothing (Isaiah uses the word *"tohu"*—that which is without substance, nothing).

22-24 Jacob shall no longer be ashamed.

God will not forever countenance these iniquitous conditions, and no
longer shall the house of Jacob need to be ashamed because of foreign
oppression and domestic injustice.

23 For when his children shall see the works of my hands.

The Hebrew construction of this phrase is not quite clear. The KJV
translates: "When he seeth his children." The translation which we suggest seems to provide a more satisfactory reading.

The prophet is saying in effect: "You may not understand God's dealings with you now, but your children looking back from the perspective
of generations, will hallow the name of God and stand in awe before His
amazing providential guidance. Even they who are spiritually most re-
calcitrant and the murmurers shall then come to understanding and will
be willing to receive divine instruction, unlike the present-day scoffers,
who refuse the counsel of God and of His appointed servant, the prophet.
Some of the older commentators, in line with their theology which identified the Church with "the New Israel," saw in this reference to "his children" an allusion to the spiritual children of Israel, the Gentiles, in contrast to the physical descendants of Abraham and Jacob. However, this is
a tortured exegesis, unsubstantiated by the plain sense and the context
of Isaiah's words.

Isaiah, Chapters 30-31

The main theme of the two chapters is Judah's sin of seeking an alliance with pagan Egypt, rather than trusting the LORD to deliver them
from Assyria.

Isaiah 30:1-7

The clandestine efforts of the rulers of Judah to make an alliance
with Egypt is denounced by the prophet.

1 Woe to rebellious sons, says the LORD,
  To take counsel, but not of me,
  To form alliances but not of my spirit,
  To heap sin upon sin.

2 That are going down to Egypt,
  Yet have not sought counsel from my mouth;
  To seek refuge in the stronghold of Pharaoh,
  And to take shelter in the shadow of Egypt.

3 Therefore will the stronghold of Pharaoh become your shame,
  And the shelter in the shadow of Egypt, your disgrace.

4 For his princes have arrived in Zoan,
  And his ambassadors have reached Hanes.

5 But they shall all be ashamed of a people who will not help,
  Or profit them, but cause shame and reproach.

6 The burden of the beasts of the Negev.
  In a land of trouble and anguish,
  From whence the lioness and the roaring lion come,
  The rattlesnake and the flying serpent.
  They carry their wealth on the shoulders of young asses.
  And their treasures upon the humps of camels,
  To a people who will not profit them.

7 For the help of Egypt is vain and empty
  Therefore have I called her: "The Reclining Sea-Monster."

Comment:

1 Isaiah denounces the secret political maneuvers afoot in certain political circles to form an alliance with Egypt. In the eyes of the prophet such plans were sinful and contrary to the will and spirit of God.

2-5 That are going down to Egypt . . .

Apparently a Judean delegation was already on its way to seek an alliance with Pharaoh, and had reached Zoan and Hanes, the two great cities in the Nile Delta. Isaiah predicted that the help of Egypt would be of no avail, and would only cause shame and disgrace.

6, 7 The prophet visualizes the caravan of the Judean ambassadors passing through the wild and eerie land of the Negev, inhabited by lions and all kinds of snakes. The fauna of the Negev, since the time of Isaiah, has changed considerably, but snakes still infest some parts of it. The caravan of camels and asses is loaded down with rich presents for the rulers of Egypt. However, all this will be of no avail since Egypt will not help Judah. Isaiah calls Egypt "The Reclining Sea-Monster" (*Rahab-hem-shabeth*), literally "the Sitting Rahab." *Rahab* (Sea-Monster) is the name applied to Egypt elsewhere (Isa. 51:9, Psa. 87:4, 89:10, etc.) .

Verses 8-17 A scathing denunciation of the people is recorded for a testimony to future generations.

8   Now come, write it for them on a tablet
    And inscribe it in a book,
    That it may be to the last day,
    For a witness forever:—

9   This is a rebellious people!
    Lying sons, sons who refuse to hear the instruction of the LORD.

10 Who say to the seers: See not,
    And to the prophets: Do not prophesy to us right things,
    Speak to us flattering things, prophesy delusions!

11 Turn aside from the way,
    Leave the path,
    Cause the Holy One of Israel to cease from before us.

12 Therefore thus says the Holy One of Israel:
    Because you despise this word,
    And you would rather trust in oppression and crookedness
    And depend on them

13 Therefore shall this iniquity be to you,
    As a breach about to fall, as a bulge in a high wall,
    Whose collapse will come suddenly, in an instant.

14 And he will break it as the potter's vessel is broken,
    Shattering it without pity,
    So that not a shard shall be found in the wreckage
    To scoop up fire from the hearth, or to draw water from the
        cistern.

15 For thus says the Lord God, the Holy One of Israel:
    In sitting still and in rest shall be your salvation.
    In quietness and in confidence shall be your strength.
    But you would not!

16 And you said: Not so, for we will flee on horses
    And we will ride upon the swift.
    Therefore your pursuers shall also be swift.

17 One thousand shall flee at the threat of one,
    At the threat of five shall you flee,
    Until you will be left like a flagstaff on the top of a mountain,
    And like an ensign on a hill.

Comment:

8   In view of Judah's stubborn refusal to trust the Lord, Isaiah is commanded to inscribe a denunciation of the people in a book, as a permanent record for all times. Evidently Isaiah possessed an extremely keen sense of history, and an awareness that he prophesied and wrote not only for his own generation, but also for generations yet unborn.

9-11 This is one of the most severe indictments of Israel, ever uttered by a prophet.

Israel is a rebellious and deceitful people which refuses to listen to God's teaching (the Torah) and which seeks to silence or subvert the prophets, forbidding them to speak the truth. They prefer to listen to flatteries and deceitful assurances, rather than to listen to that which is right.

Only a true and fearless man of God would dare to fling such harsh accusations in the face of his people. One can well imagine how they must have been livid with rage on hearing Isaiah's words.

12-17 Because of their rebellious spirit and their rejection of divine protection, the prophet warns his people of the approaching ruin. They were like a bulging wall about to collapse (v. 13). When that happens, nothing will be left—"not a shard to scoop up fire cinders or to draw a little water" (v. 14).

Israel might have had safety and salvation if only they had trusted the Lord and allowed Him to fight their battles, but they would not (v. 15). This verse sums up best Isaiah's conviction about Israel's foreign policy.

Now the prophet in turn ridicules the military concepts of the leaders of Judah, with the alliterative phrase: *"Al sus nanus"*—"We will flee on horses." He warns the leaders of Jerusalem that this strategy will end in complete disaster (v. 17).

Verses 18-26 In spite of Judah's rebellion, the Lord is nevertheless waiting for repentance, so that He may be gracious to her.

18 And yet the LORD is waiting to be gracious to you,
And yet the LORD will rise up that he may have compassion on you.
For the LORD is a God of justice
Blessed are all who wait for him.

19 For the people in Zion shall dwell in Jerusalem,
Thou shalt weep no more.
He will be most gracious unto you at the voice of thy cry,
When he will hear, he will answer.

20 And the LORD will give you bread in distress,
And water when it is scant.
And thy teacher shall no more hide himself
But thine eyes shall see thy teacher

21 And thy ears shall hear a word behind thee saying:
"This is the way, walk you in it,
When you turn right or left."

22 And you will defile your graven images overlaid with silver,
    And your molten images covered with gold,
    You will thrust them away as a filthy rag,
    And say to it: "Begone!"

23 And he will give rain for thy seed to sow in the ground,
    And bread of the produce of the land,
    And it will be plentiful and rich.
    In that day shall thy cattle feed in broad pastures,

24 And the oxen and young asses, that till the ground,
    Shall eat tasty fodder
    Which has been winnowed with shovel and fork.

25 And upon every high mountain,
    And upon every lofty hill,
    There shall be streams and watercourses,
    On the day of the great slaughter, when the towers shall fall.

26 And the light of the moon shall be as bright as the light of the
        sun,
    And the light of the sun seven times as bright,
    As the light of seven days.
    On the day when the Lord shall bind up the breach of his people,
    And will heal the stroke of his wound.

Comment:
Verses 18-26

The usual pattern of threat is followed by the promise of restoration, on condition that the people will return to God, who is anxiously waiting to be gracious to them (v. 18).[1]

19, 20 Bread in distress and water when it is scant . . .

The Lord will not permit His people to perish altogether, but will provide them with the essentials of life, when they will cry to Him in their anguish.

20 Thy teacher shall no more hide himself . . .

The only passage where God is called a "teacher." The Hebrew construction permits it to be read as either singular "teacher" or plural "teachers." The first seems to be preferable, and may have Messianic implications.[2]

22 You will defile your graven images.

It is apparent that in the days of Isaiah, even under such a godly king as Hezekiah, crass idolatry was still deeply rooted among the people. The prophet detested this with all his soul, and referred to it with the obnoxious word *"davah"*—a filthy or abominable rag.

22-26 When once Israel shall uproot her idolatry, then the LORD will again bless the land and its people. Abundant rain, rich crops for men and beasts, streams of water even in arid hills, the destruction of the enemy and his war engines, these will be the future blessings.

26 . . . the light of the moon as bright as the sun

A metaphoric picture of the great joy of the people after the Lord shall have healed their grievous wounds. Light is often the symbol of salvation.

As we have frequently pointed out, in Isaiah's vision of redemption, all of creation is somehow deeply involved with the destiny of man. It is blessed when man is blessed, and suffers under the curse of sin. How true this is in our own time when man is threatened with extinction by the pollution of his ecological environment.

Verses 27-33 The sudden appearance of the Lord in awesome splendor and indignation to punish Assyria.

27 Behold the name of the LORD comes from afar,
    Burning with his anger and with heavy rising smoke,
    His lips are full of wrath, and his tongue like a devouring fire.

28 His breath is like a rampaging stream, which reaches to the rock,
    To sift the nation with the sieve of destruction,
    And with a bridle in the jaws of the people, which causes [them]
        to err.

29 You shall have a song,
    As in the night when a feast is celebrated,
    And joy of heart, as when they march with flutes,
    To go up to the mountain of the LORD, to the rock of Israel.

30 And the LORD will cause his majestic voice to be heard,
    And will manifest the coming down of his arm,
    With furious wrath and with the flame of a devouring fire.

31 For at the voice of the LORD shall Assyria be dismayed,
    When he will smite with the staff.

32 And it will come to pass that in every place,
    Where the appointed rod shall pass,
    Which the LORD shall lay upon him,
    It shall be amidst [the sound of] drums and harps,
    And in battles of brandishing weapons shall he fight them.

33 For a hearth is ordained of old,
    It is prepared for the king, deep and wide,
    Its pile is fire and much wood.
    The breath of the LORD, like a stream of brimstone will burn
        within it.

Comment:

27, 28 One of the most complete and striking theophanies in prophetic writings, conveying the awesome majesty of an aroused and angry God.

27 Behold, the name of the LORD comes from afar.

The name of the LORD is the same as the LORD Himself. The metaphors which describe the appearance of God to judge the nations are taken from nature in an angry mood. His appearance is compared to a volcano or to a rampaging stream.

28 The sieve of destruction . . .

Literally, the sieve of nothingness or of vanity; all that which is strained away is carried off by the wind, till nothing remains.

The bridle that causes to err . . .

God puts a bridle in the jaws of His enemies and causes them to err, thus frustrating their designs.

29 You shall have a song . . .

We hear an echo of pilgrims marching to the Temple to the joyful tune of flutes. The festive mood of the pilgrims seems to fit in especially with the Feast of Tabernacles.

30-33 The prophet continues his description of the angry God.

30 The majestic voice of the LORD is like the roaring of an erupting volcano, which spews forth lava and burns everything in its path.

31 The angry voice of the LORD is directed against Assyria, which He formerly appointed to be the staff of His indignation (10:5), but now He is about to use that same staff against cruel Assyria herself.

32 The punishment of Assyria shall be welcomed by the victim of her ferocious cruelty with the jubilant sound of drums and harps.

The battle of brandishing weapons . . .

The sense of this passage appears to be that Assyria's destruction will be the outcome of a fierce battle.

33 For a hearth is ordered of old . . .

"Tophet," the word translated "hearth" was in the valley of Hinnom below the hill of Zion, where human sacrifices used to be offered to Moloch (2 Ki. 23:10; Jer. 7:31). In this passage *"tophet"* means a firepit in which the king of Assyria shall be burned in a fire of wood and brimstone. This funeral pyre was prepared for him long before by the Lord Himself.

> Notes: 1. There is a striking parallel between the thought expressed here (Isa. 30:18) about God who is waiting for His people to return to Him that He might have compassion on them, and the parable of the prodigal son in Luke 15:11-32.

2. In the Qumran documents *(The Habakkuk Commentary)*, "The Teacher of Righteousness" *(Moreh Tsedek)*, a Messianic figure, is of paramount importance and may have some connection with Isaiah 30:20 and the Hebrew text of Joel 2:23 and Hosea 10:12.

Isaiah, Chapter 31

Verses 1-3 Isaiah continues to denounce the rulers of Jerusalem for their reliance on Egypt instead of God.

1   Woe to them that go down to Egypt for help,
    And rely on horses, and trust in chariots, because they are many,
    And in horsemen because they are strong,
    But do not look to the Holy One of Israel,
    Neither do they seek the LORD.

2   Yet, he too is wise and will bring evil,
    And will not set aside his words.
    He will rise up against the house of the wicked,
    And against the supporters of evildoers.

3   Now Egypt is man and not God,
    And their horses are flesh and not spirit,
    So when the LORD shall stretch forth his hand,
    Then the helper shall stumble, and he who is helped shall fall,
    And both shall perish together.

Comment:

1-3 Because the sinister efforts to secure Egyptian help for Judah continue, the prophet also continues his warnings. Obviously, the Judeans felt severely handicapped vis-a-vis the Assyrians, by their lack of cavalry and chariots, the ancient equivalent of tanks in modern warfare.

Egypt was famous for its fine horses, its horsemen and its chariots. So that is where they sought help. The fact that Judea and Egypt were confronted by a mutual enemy, Assyria, made them natural allies.

Isaiah was outraged by the fact that the leaders of Judah thought only in terms of horseflesh and manpower, failing to seek help from God.

2 He too is wise . . .

There is irony in the words of Isaiah, as if he were saying: "You think that you are so clever, but God is also wise, and He will carry out His plans without fail."

3 For Egypt is man and not God and their horses flesh . . .

In one brief passage the prophet exposes the fallacious schemes of those who depend on Egypt and their horses, which are only frail flesh and blood. When God strikes, the helper and the helped will both perish.

Verses 4-5   There is no escape from the hand of God.

4   For thus says the LORD to me:
Like as when the lion, or the young lion, growls over his prey.
And when the horde of shepherds are called out against him,
He is not frightened by their shout,
And disregards their noise,
So also will the LORD of hosts descend on Jerusalem
To fight upon mount Zion and upon her hill.

5   Like hovering birds,
So will the LORD of hosts protect Jerusalem,
And while protecting, he will save,
And passing over, he will rescue.

Comment:

4,5   In two epic similes, reminiscent of Homer, Isaiah describes the manner in which the LORD will fight for Jerusalem and protect His people: He will fight like a roaring lion and like a flock of birds which hover in the air to protect their nest.

5   Passing over he will rescue

The Hebrew word for "passing over" *(Pasoah)* is an allusion to the miracle of passover. The LORD will repeat again the miracle of passover, and rescue His people.

Verses 6-9   A Call to Repentance

6   Turn you to him, against whom you have rebelled, O sons of Israel.

7   For in that day you will cast away
Every man his idols of silver and his idols of gold,
Which your hands have made for you, for a sin.

8   And the Assyrian shall fall by a sword which is not human,
And a sword which is not man-made shall devour him.
He shall flee from a sword,
And his young men shall become bondsmen.

9   And his rock shall pass away,
And his princes shall flee from the standard.
Thus says the Lord, whose fire is in Zion,
And his furnace in Jerusalem.

Comment:

Verses 6-9

6 *"Shuvu-"* "Turn" or "turn back, repent," this is the very heart of Isaiah's message. Israel has deeply offended her LORD and can only be saved from her enemies and the consequences of her sins by turning to God. Here in the context of this particular oracle, Israel is to turn to God, because He alone, and not weak, unreliable Egypt, can save her from Assyria, the wicked empire which will fall by a sword, not wielded by man, but by God Himself.

9 **And his rock shall pass away.**

The rock is generally understood as reference to Sennacherib, the king of Assyria, who hastily abandoned his preparation for the siege of Jerusalem in 701 B.C. when his army was decimated by a terrible epidemic.

Isaiah, Chapter 32

Various prophetic utterances concerning the Messianic King, the wicked rich, the complacent women, the approaching day of judgment and redemption.

Verses 1-8 The Messianic King and a Regenerated People

1 Behold, a king shall reign in righteousness,
   And princes shall rule in justice.

2 And a man shall be like a shelter from the wind,
   And a refuge from the storm,
   Like streams of water in an arid place,

   Like a shadow of a great rock in a weary land.

3 The eyes of those who look shall not be shut,
   And the ears of those who listen shall be attentive.

4 The heart of the hasty shall understand knowledge,
   And the tongue of the stammerers shall speak clearly.

5 No longer will they call the villain "noble,"
   Nor will the crook be addressed as "honorable."

6 For the villain speaks villainy,
   And his heart devises wickedness,
   To speak perversely against God,
   To cause the soul of the hungry to crave,
   And to deprive the thirsty of drink.

7 The instruments of the crooked are wicked.
   He devises foul schemes,
   To destroy the poor with lies,
   When the needy plead for justice.

8 But the noble man plans noble things,
   And by that which is noble he shall abide.

Comment:

1-8 A beautiful vision of the future king, described in Messianic terms. He and those who rule with Him (the princes) will be characterized by perfect justice. No historical king ever fitted this description, which must be understood as a further elaboration of Isaiah's vision of the King Messiah, presented in chapter 11:1-10.

2   A man shall be a shelter . . .
The man is the king of verse one.

3,4   The spiritual restoration will affect the whole nation. The curse of blindness and unwillingness to listen to God and to understand His word, will at last be removed.

4   The heart of the hasty . . .
The rash and foolish people who form their opinions without sound judgment will learn true knowledge and wisdom.

The stammerers are apparently the vacillators who hem and haw, where clear and forthright speech is called for. They will at last learn to be clear, and without equivocation.

5-7   Isaiah inveighs against a hypocritical society where the villain— Hebrew *"nabhal"*—is called "a noble man."

Perhaps the perfect specimen of a vile person was Nabal (1 Sam. 25), a man whose very name meant "vile," and whose character was in keeping with his name. The prophet vehemently denounces the moral villainy and skullduggery which he observed among the ruling circles of Jerusalem. These are contrasted with the regenerated community, yet to be born.

8   But the noble man plans noble things.
In a few words the prophet describes the essence of the true *"nadib"*— the noble man. He thinks nobly and acts nobly. One has the strong feeling that when Isaiah describes the true noble man, the spiritual aristocrat, he unwittingly projects his own inner self. For Isaiah was a man of great integrity and nobility, qualities which shine forth from all his words and actions. This nobility of character, described and personified by Isaiah himself, represents the prophetic ideal of "the perfect gentleman."

Verses 9-20   Against the Complacent Women of Jerusalem. The Approaching Judgment and Redemption.

9   Rise up, you complacent women, listen to my voice,
 Give ear to my speech, you overconfident daughters.

10   In a little over a year you shall be troubled,
 You who are [so] confident [now],
 The grape harvest shall fail, the ingathering shall not come.

11 Tremble, you complacent women,
   Be troubled, you overconfident ones,
   Strip yourselves, make yourselves bare.

12 Put on sackcloth around your loins,
   Beat your breasts for the pleasant fields, for the fruitful vineyards.

13 For the soil of my people,
   Where thorns and briers shall come up,
   And for all the happy houses and the gay city.

14 For the palace shall be forsaken,
   The noisy city abandoned.
   The citadel and the tower shall become dens forever,
   The delight of wild asses, the pasture of flocks

15 Until the spirit be poured out upon us from on high.
   Then shall the wilderness become a fruitful field,
   And the fruitful field shall be considered a forest.

16 Then shall justice dwell in the wilderness,
   And righteousness shall abide in the fruitful field.

17 And the work of righteousness shall be peace,
   And the effect of righteousness quietness and confidence forever.

18 My people shall dwell in peaceful habitations,
   In safe dwellings in secure places of rest.

19 And it shall hail, when the forest shall come down,
   And the city shall be laid low.

20 Blessed are you, who sow beside all waters,
   Who send forth the feet of the ox and the ass [to roam freely].

Comment

9-14 From the very beginning of his prophetic ministry, Isaiah perceived that one of the main evils which was eating away the moral health of his nation was the carefree, happy-go-lucky, flirtatious and selfish life of Judean womanhood. He derided their manners and exposed their self-indulgent ways in one of his earliest oracles of woe, when he foretold the dire calamity which would one day overtake the selfish women (Isa. 3:16-26).

Those women were the wives and daughters of the ungodly rulers of Israel; they, with their menfolk, were equally responsible for the moral decay of the nation. Now Isaiah returns to the same theme and inveighs against "the complacent women and the overconfident daughters." Like their menfolk, they too are blind to the tragic reality of the situation, and do not see judgment day approaching. Yet, within a little over a year disaster will strike and the harvest of grapes and grain will fail (v. 10, 12,13). It is very likely that Isaiah uttered this prophecy in 703 or 702 B.C. just a year or so before Sennacherib invaded Judah, where he wrought great havoc before he was finally forced to retreat from Jerusalem by an act of God.

The Assyrian sword was literally hanging over the head of Judah. Many numerous and much stronger nations than Israel had already succumbed to seemingly invincible Assyria. And yet the leaders of Judah, including their women, lived as if nothing could happen to them. They ate, they drank, they made merry. Their women dressed according to the latest fashion of their day. Luxurious living was the way of life of the rich, while the poor had to pay for it with their life's blood and their wretchedness. Amos denounced a similar situation which prevailed in the northern kingdom, in Samaria.

Isaiah wrathfully demanded of the corrupt rulers of Jerusalem: "What mean you that you crush my people and grind the face of the poor?" (3:15).

Now the prophet was warning the complacent, smug, self-satisfied women of Jerusalem to wake up and repent, for the day of reckoning was at hand. But the pending disaster may be averted if they will only repent and turn to God.

15-20   The theme of this passage is the restoration which will come after the people of Jerusalem repent.

15   Until the spirit shall be poured out upon us from on high.

Before the Lord can show mercy to His people, they must first receive "the spirit from on high." Then man and nature shall experience a new birth. Justice and righteousness shall dwell not only in the fruitful fields, but even in the wilderness.

17   And the work of righteousness shall be peace . . .

Here is one of the most beautiful passages in the prophetic Scriptures. Peace, security and safety are not the results of military power nor of alliances, or victorious wars, but the fruit of righteousness.

19   It shall hail at the downfall of the forest . . .

The city shall be laid low.

A reference to Assyria, which will soon be destroyed by a great calamity. The city is Nineveh.

20   Blessed are you, who sow beside all waters . . .

This idyllic picture of a happy people, living under a just, Messianic king, cultivating their fruitful soil, at peace with God and with men, concludes this oracle.

Assyria, The Spoiler, Shall Be Despoiled

Isaiah, Chapter 33

Verses 1-12

1 Woe to thee that spoilest and thou hast not been spoiled,
That plunders and hast not been plundered.
When thou shalt cease to spoil, thou shalt be spoiled,
When thou shalt be done with plundering, thou shalt be plundered.

2 O LORD, be gracious unto us, we have waited for thee,
Be thou their arm every morning,
Our sure salvation in time of trouble.

3 At the sound of the noise peoples flee,
When thou risest, nations are scattered.

4 And your loot is gathered as the caterpillar gathers,
They leap upon it as the locusts leap.

5 The LORD is exalted, for he dwells on high,
He has filled Zion with justice and righteousness,

6 And the security of thy times shall be a store of salvation.
— Wisdom and knowledge, the fear of the Lord — this is his treasure.

7 Behold the inhabitants of Ariel cry in the street,
The messengers of peace weep bitterly.

8 The highways are desolate, the wayfarer has ceased.
He has despised the cities, he does not respect [any] man.

9 The land mourns, it languishes.
Lebanon is ashamed and dried up.
Sharon is like a desert,
Bashan and Carmel are stripped bare.

10 Now will I arise, says the LORD,
Now will I be exalted,
Now will I lift myself up.[1]

11 You conceive chaff, you will bring forth straw,
Your breath is fire which shall devour you.

12 And peoples shall be as lime burnings,
As cut down thorns, which are burned in the fire.

Comment:

Verses 1-12

Because of supposed differences in style and contents of chapter 33, it has been relegated by some critical commentators to the post-exilic period, even to as late a date as 163 B.C. (the Maccabean period).

These highly speculative assumptions preceded the discovery of the Dead Sea Scrolls, and the two manuscripts of Isaiah which date back to about the middle of the second century B.C.

However, the language and contents of this chapter are in keeping with all the other writings of Isaiah, and the events alluded to here fit in well with the history of Sennacherib's abortive effort to subdue Jerusalem in 701 B.C.

1 Woe to the spoiler . . .

An obvious allusion to the Assyrian invaders under Sennacherib. As soon as they have completed the task assigned to them by God – of punishing Judah, they themselves will be punished by him (see also Isa. 10:5-16).

2 O LORD be gracious unto us . . .

In the face of Assyria, the superpower of that day, Israel felt completely helpless. Only Jehovah could deliver His people, hence this cry to God for help.

3-6 Here is a typical Isaianic vision of an aroused Jehovah in action, roaring like a volcano and scattering the terrified nations assembled to destroy Israel.

After the debacle, the inhabitants of Jerusalem leap upon the spoil, left behind by the enemy, like so many caterpillars and locusts (v. 4).

Then will the Lord be exalted and Jerusalem will be filled with justice and righteousness. Jerusalem's true security and her defense are not mighty armies, but wisdom, knowledge and the fear of the LORD.

7-9 The present plight of Jerusalem.

Behold the inhabitants of Ariel cry in the street.

The Hebrew word *"erelam"* is translated in the KJV as "the valiant ones," but it is apparently an allusion to the inhabitants of Jerusalem, which Isaiah (29:1) has previously called *Ariel* – "the hearth" or "the altar of God."

It would appear from our text that after Sennacherib captured Lachish and many fortified cities in Judah—and, according to Assyrian record, carried away over 200,000 prisoners — Hezekiah sent "messengers of peace" to negotiate terms. However, Sennacherib with his customary brutality insulted the ambassadors, who returned to Jerusalem humiliated and weeping (v. 7).

As a result of the Assyrian depredations, the whole land is desolate, the highways are deserted, the most fertile regions of the land (Lebanon, Sharon, Bashan, and Carmel) lie idle and untilled.

10-12 In the hour of Israel's humiliation and desolation, the LORD will arise in defence of His people. Isaiah uses the most stirring terms to describe this intervention —

Now will I arise
Now will I be exalted
Now will I lift myself up.[1]

The grandiose designs of the enemies of God's people are mere chaff and straw which shall be burned like lime in a potter's kiln, or cut down like dry thorns. Their own breath, or spirit, shall be the means of their destruction. The implied thought is that evil carries within itself the seeds of its own destruction.

Verses 13-24 The effect of the LORD's intervention upon the sinners in Israel.

13   Hear, you who are far away, what I have done
     And you who are near, know my might.

14   Sinners in Zion are horror-stricken,
     Trembling has seized the hypocrites.
     Who among us can dwell with a consuming fire,
     Who among us can abide with everlasting flames?

15   He that walks in righteousness and speaks uprightness
     Who despises the gain of oppressions,
     Who withdraws his hand from holding a bribe,
     Who stops his ear from counsels of bloodshed,
     And shuts his eyes from looking upon evil.

16   He shall dwell in high places,
     His stronghold a rocky fortress
     His bread assured, his waters secure.

17   Thine eyes shall look upon the King in his beauty,
     They shall see a far-stretching land.

18   Thy heart shall ponder the terror:
     'Where is he that counts, where is he who weighs,
     Where is he that counts the towers?'

19   Thou shalt not see the fierce people,
     A people of deep speech hard to hear,
     Of an unintelligible tongue, difficult to understand.

20   Look upon Zion, the city of our solemn assemblies,
     Thine eyes shall see Jerusalem a peaceful habitation,
     A tent shall not be removed,
     Her stakes shall never be pulled up,
     Her cords shall never be broken.

21 There shall the Lord be with us in majesty,
   A place of broad rivers and streams,
   No galley with oars shall venture there,
   No splendid ship shall pass by.

22 For the LORD is our Judge,
   The LORD is our Lawgiver,
   The LORD is our King,
   He will save us.

23 Thy ropes are slack,
   They do not hold up the stand of the mast,
   They do not spread the sail.
   Then shall great spoil be divided,
   Even the lame shall take the plunder.

24 And none of the inhabitants shall say, "I am sick,"
   For the people that dwell there shall be forgiven their iniquity.

Comment:

In verse 13 the prophet addresses himself to the distant enemies ("you who are far away"), and to the people of Zion ("you who are near").

14-16 When the Lord shall appear in power and might, the sinners in Zion will be terror-stricken and wonder who will be able to abide in the presence of an indignant but righteous God.

Here is the prophet's answer to the anxious inquiry also posed in Psalms 15 and 24.

"Who shall abide in the presence of God?"

Only the man who walks in righteousness, abhors all unjust gain, whose hands are clean from bribery, who refuses to listen to wicked counsels of bloodshed or to look indifferently upon evil, only such a man "shall dwell on high." His home is like a rocky castle which shall remain secure, his daily bread and water shall be provided in abundance. Such is the reward of those who walk with God.

17, 18 Thine eyes shall look upon the king in his beauty.

Some commentators, including Delitzsch, undertand this passage to be a reference to an earthly king, who will reign over Jerusalem after the defeat of the Assyrian invaders. Others see in this a Messianic prophecy.

Actually, the prophet combines the vision of the immediate future with the more distant Messianic times. This literary device is a frequent feature of Isaiah's prophecies, sometimes called "the pregnant prophecy." Such prophecies while seemingly dealing with the immediate future, reach out into the distant future. Redeemed Israel shall look upon the glorious king and a vastly enlarged country. They will consider the terrors of the past; they shall wonder what happened to the highhanded alien officials who exacted tribute from them, who weighed and counted what the people of Israel should give to the conquerors, and which towers (strongholds) should be destroyed.

19 The fierce people who speak in a strange, unintelligible language, the foreign invader, will be no more, only a dark memory of the past.

20 Instead they shall behold a peaceful Jerusalem, secure and well-established.

21 There the Lord shall dwell with His people.

Other nations, Egypt and Assyria, have their broad rivers and streams for their protection, which no hostile ships dare trespass. Jerusalem has better protection—her Lord.

22 This verse expresses in majestic terms what Jehovah is to His people Israel: **He is her Judge, Lawgiver, King and Saviour.** What a pinnacle of faith, what grandeur!

23 Thy ropes are slack . . .

The sudden change to imagery of a ship disarrayed by a storm is rather disconcerting to some commentators, who look upon this verse as an intrusion from some other oracle. However, we have to allow for the prophet's unexpected changes of mood and imagery, to which he, like other men, was frequently subject. Here Isaiah returns for a moment from musing about the glorious future of Jerusalem to her present sad plight. In verse 21 he referred to the Lord's presence in His city, as a broad river, where no enemy flotilla, or man-of-war, would dare to intrude; now he thinks of Jerusalem as a broken down, battered ship after a storm, with her ropes slack, and unable to support mast or sail.

Then again, in rapid change of vision, Isaiah turns away from the present pathetic plight of Jerusalem to her glorious future. Isaiah sees her deliverance and the approaching "spoiling of the Assyrian spoiler." Even the lame and the halt will share in the division of the spoils.

24 In those days of divine deliverance, nobody will be sick, because the people will have their sins forgiven. The prophet expresses here the Biblical thought that sin and sickness are interrelated, as in Exodus 23:25: "And ye shall serve the LORD your God, and He shall bless thy bread, and thy water, and I will take sickness away from the midst of thee."

Note: 1. The three Hebrew verbs in Isaiah 33:10 which are applied to God are similar to those used in chapter 52:13 where they are used with reference to the Servant of the LORD, another indication which points to the unity of the first and second parts of Isaiah.

The Doom of Edom
and the Return
of the Redeemed

In chapters 34-35, which is an epilogue to the "Book of Woes," Isaiah looks beyond the downfall of Assyria to the judgment of the ungodly nations of the world. Edom, Israel's brother nation, which behaved in a most unbrotherly fashion towards Israel in the days of her severe distress, is singled out as the personification of all that is evil in humanity, and is destined to share the fate of Sodom and Gomorrah.

Like Babylon, Edom too shall become the habitation of all the eerie creatures of the wilderness. In view of the apocalyptic overtones of Isaiah 34, some critics have maintained that this chapter was a later, post-exilic addition.

A more reasonable explanation for the similarities between Isaiah 34 and some of the later prophetic writings (Zeph. 1:7, 8; 2:14, 15; Ezk. 39:4, etc.) is the assumption that the prophecies of Isaiah were familiar to the post-exilic prophets.

Chapter 35 is a glorious vision of the future redemption of Israel, and presents a striking contrast to the dismal picture of the desolation of Edom.

World Judgment and The Doom of Edom

Isaiah, Chapter 34

Verses 1-17

1   Come near, you nations, to hear,
    You peoples, attend.
    Let the earth and her fulness hear,
    The world and all that springs forth from it.

2 For the LORD has indignation against all the nations,
And fury against all their host.
He has put them under a ban,
He has delivered them to the slaughter.

3 And their slain shall be cast out,
And from their corpses shall rise a stench,
And the mountains shall melt from their blood.

4 And the host of heavens shall be dissolved,
And the heavens shall be rolled up like a book scroll,
And all their hosts shall fall down,
As the leaf falls from the vine,
And the fig falls from the fig tree.

5 For my sword has drunk her fill in heaven.
Behold it shall come down upon Edom,
And upon the people of my ban, for judgment.

6 The sword of the LORD,
It is full of blood, greased with fatness,
With the blood of lambs and goats,
With the fat of the kidneys of rams,
For the LORD has a sacrifice in Bozrah,
A great slaughter in the land of Edom.

7 And the wild oxen shall come down with them,
The bullocks with the bulls,
Their land shall be saturated with blood,
And their dust sodden with fatness.

8 For this is a day of the LORD's vengeance,
A year of retribution for the controversy of Zion.

9 And her streams shall turn into pitch,
And her dust to brimstone,
Her land shall become burning pitch.

10 It shall not be quenched by night or day,
Its smoke shall ascend forever,
None shall ever pass through it.

11 The pelican and the hedgehog shall possess it,
And the owl and the raven shall dwell in it.
And he shall stretch over it,
The line of chaos and the plummet of confusion.

12 Her electors shall have no kingdom to proclaim,
Her princes shall be mere nothings.

13　Upon her palaces thorns shall come up,
　　Nettles and thistles in its fortresses,
　　It shall be a lair for jackals,
　　An enclosure for ostriches.

14　There wild cats shall meet hyenas,
　　And satyrs shall call each other,
　　There also shall the night demon [Lilith] repose,
　　And find for herself a resting place.

15　There will the arrowsnake make her nest,
　　Lay her eggs, hatch and brood in her shadow.
　　There too shall the vultures gather,
　　Each one with her mate.

16　Search in the book of the LORD,
　　Not one of these shall be missing.
　　None shall want her mate,
　　For his mouth has commanded,
　　And his spirit has brought them together.

17　And he has cast a lot for them,
　　And his hand has allotted it to them by line,
　　They shall possess it forever,
　　And dwell there from generation to generation.

Comment:

1-4　In words which bring to mind Isaiah 1:2, the prophet now invites the whole creation to hear about God's indignation against all the nations which he predicts will result in their destruction. The judgment of the Lord is cosmic, and will shake the very foundations of the universe (cf. Isa. 13:13).

5-7　The wrath of God is directed in particular against Edom for her relentless hatred against her brother Israel. The sword of the Lord is obviously the same "heavy, great and strong sword" previously mentioned by the prophet (27:1). It will descend in full fury upon Edom.

Some commentators have attempted to substitute for "Edom" the word *"adam"* (man), spelled in Hebrew with the same consonants, but with different vowel signs (Duhm, Kissane). However, the context, and the mention of Bozrah, an Edomite city, does not favor such a reading. We find that the accepted Hebrew text is almost invariably to be preferred to dubious textual speculations and corrections.

The smaller sacrificial animals — lambs and goats, — represent the smaller nations such as Edom and Moab, while the larger beasts—oxen, bulls and bullocks — symbolize the powerful nations such as Assyria, Babylon and Egypt.

8-10 Divine retribution for all wrongs inflicted upon the people of the LORD.

The controversy of Zion

The Lord Himself appears as the champion of Zion to right her wrongs and to settle her accounts. Edom is to become a desolate land of burning pitch and brimstone, never again to be inhabited by human beings.

The description of desolated Edom situated south of the Dead Sea is fully in keeping with the mountainous and volcanic nature of the land.

11-15 Edom is to become the habitation of eerie creatures, similar to those which Isaiah predicted would one day inhabit desolate Babylon (13:20-22).

11 The line of chaos and the plummet of confusion

Isaiah employs terms taken from the story of creation to describe the fate of Edom, which will be leveled with the line of chaos *(tohu)* and the plummet of confusion *(bohu)*.

12 Her electors shall have no kingdom to proclaim

The kings of Edom were elected by a group of princes, whom Isaiah calls *"horim"* ("freemen," or "lords").

14 There shall the night demon [Lilith] repose

Among the gruesome creatures dwelling in deserted Edom, Lilith, the night monster, or night ghost, is mentioned. In later rabbinical literature, Lilith was considered as a female demon who sought to harm children, especially newborn babies.

16 Search in the book of the LORD—For his mouth has commanded

This is one of the most remarkable statements in the book of Isaiah. Since in the days of Isaiah the Old Testament canon was not yet completed, the prophet apparently was referring to his own writings as "the book of the LORD," appealing to future generations to verify his predictions by comparing them with future events, to prove that his prophecies were divinely inspired. Isaiah's appeal to future events has an even wider application and may be extended to all of the Scriptures.

Edom, desolate, deserted, still the lair of wild creatures after more than twenty-six centuries, is a mute witness to the truth of God's Word.

17 And he has cast a lot for them

What happened to Edom is no mere coincidence. God Himself has decreed that it should never be inhabited, and it has remained an eerie desert land, even to the present day.

The Return of the Redeemed to Their Homeland

Isaiah, Chapter 35

Verses 1-10

1 The wilderness and the dry land shall be glad,
And the desert shall rejoice and blossom like a rose.

2 It shall blossom abundantly and rejoice
With great joy and singing.
The glory of Lebanon shall be bestowed upon it,
And the splendor of Carmel and Sharon,
They shall see the glory of the Lord,
The splendor of our God.

3 Strengthen you the weak hands,
And make the trembling knees firm.

4 Say to them who are of a fearful heart:
"Take courage, fear not!"
Behold your God shall come with vengeance,
He will come with divine retribution and help you.

5 Then shall the eyes of the blind be opened,
And the ears of the dumb shall be unstopped.

6 Then shall the lame leap as the deer,
And the tongue of the dumb shall shout.
For in the wilderness waters shall break forth,
And streams in the desert.

7 And the desert mirage shall become a pool,
And the thirsty land springs of water.
In the lairs of jackals herds shall lie down,
It shall become an enclosure of reeds and rushes.

8 And a road shall be there,
It shall be called "The Holy Road,"
The unclean will not pass over it,
The traveler, though a fool, shall not go astray

9 No lion shall be there,
No ravenous beasts shall enter it, nor be found there,
Only the redeemed shall walk therein.

10 And the ransomed of the LORD shall return,
And shall come to Zion with singing.
Eternal joy shall be upon their heads,
They shall obtain gladness and joy,
And sorrow and sighing shall flee away.

Comment:

1, 2 Isaiah visualizes the once-captive Israel now returning to her homeland with joy and singing through the wilderness. The desert participates in their redemption and joy; it blossoms like a rose with all the splendor of Lebanon, Carmel and the fruitful valley of Sharon in springtime.

3, 4 They who became discouraged and frightened are now consoled with the assurance that soon their God will come to right their wrongs. "Take courage, fear not" is the message from God.

5, 6 The personal intervention of God on their behalf will have a regenerating effect upon their sinful nature, they who once were so blind and deaf and lame (Isa. 6:10) will now see, hear and leap for joy.

Isaiah apparently believed that the transformation will be not only spiritual, but also literal and physical, because sickness and sin are closely related in prophetic thinking (cf. Isa. 33:24; Ex. 23:25).

7 The desert mirage *(sharab)* shall become a pool . . .

The shimmering desert heat, which so often produces the illusion of abundant water, will now become a real pool of water, the deserted place a green pasture with peacefully reclining herds of domestic animals. As always, Isaiah sees nature participating in the destiny of man, which was once cursed for his sins, but blessed again through his redemption.

8-10 The Lord Himself will prepare a highway for His redeemed people, for their exclusive use. It will be a safe (well-marked) road, secure from intrusions, either by ravenous animals, or by unclean men. Only the redeemed of the Lord shall have access to it and the privilege of walking along this Holy Road of God.

Even as they once went weeping and groaning into exile, now they will return with everlasting joy and singing to Zion, the habitation of their God. Sorrow and sighing shall vanish forever.

Isaiah 35, with its evangelistic message and exalted vision of the future of redeemed Israel, is closely related to the second part of Isaiah. The closing lines of the chapter sound like a prelude to Isaiah 40:1, "Comfort ye, comfort ye my people."

Because of this, those who deny the unity of Isaiah have also attributed this chapter to the post-exilic period.

However, we consider chapter 35 as further evidence that the author of Isaiah 1-39 was the same inspired prophet who wrote chapters 40-66.

The closing four chapters (36-39) form a historical bridge linking the first part (1-39) and the second part of the book of Isaiah (40-66).

Historical Events

Chapters 36-39 are a historical supplement to the prophecies of chapters 1-35, and record some of the important events which took place during the reign of king Hezekiah and in which Isaiah himself played a prominent role.

The same events, with minor modifications and the omission of Hezekiah's prayer, are also recorded in 2 Kings 18:13-20:19.

The supplement completes the first part of Isaiah and serves as a background and a bridge to the prophecies of the second part of his book (40-66).

Chapters 36-37 describe Sennacherib's unsuccessful attempt to capture Jerusalem, and his assassination.

Chapter 38 records Hezekiah's sickness, his prayer and recovery.

Chapter 39 tells about the embassy which Merodach-Baladan, the prince of Babylon, sent to Hezekiah, and Hezekiah's folly in boastfully flaunting his wealth before the foreign visitors. The chapter closes with the ominous prediction that the descendants of Hezekiah will be carried off into Babylonian captivity.

Among Old Testament scholars there is an unresolved dispute over which of the two records (Isa. 36-39 and 2 Kings 18:13-20;19) is the original.

The references in 2 Chronicles 26:22 and 32:32 to Isaiah's historiographical activities and the prophet's habit of interspersing his oracles (e.g. 7:1-6; 8:1-4; 20:1; 22:15) with historical data, in addition to considerations of style, favor Isaiah as the author of chapters 36-39, on which the record of 2 Kings was probably based.

An Attempt at Intimidation

Isaiah, Chapter 36

Verses 1-22

1   And it came to pass in the fourteenth year of King Hezekiah, that Sennacherib, king of Assyria, went up against all the fortified cities of Judah.

2   And the king of Assyria sent Rabshakeh (the chief officer) from Lachish to Jerusalem, to king Hezekiah, with a great army. And he stood by the conduit of the upper pool in the highway of the Fuller's Field.

3   And Eliakim, the son of Hilkiah, the master of the [royal] household, and Shebna the scribe, and Joah, the son of Asaph, the recorder, went out to him.

4   And the chief officer said to them: Go say to Hezekiah, Thus says the great king, the king of Assyria, What kind of confidence is it in which thou trustest?

5   I say: This is just vain talk. Counsel and strength, these are necessary for war. Now on whom dost thou rely that thou hast rebelled against me?

6   Behold, thou hast put thy trust upon a broken reed, upon Egypt, upon which if a man lean, it will enter into his hand and pierce it; so is Pharaoh, king of Egypt, to all who trust in him.

7   And if thou wilt say to me: We trust in the LORD our God, is he not the One whose altars Hezekiah has removed and has said to Judah and Jerusalem, "only at this altar shall you worship?"

8   So now, do make a wager with my lord, the king of Assyria, and I will give thee two thousand horses, if you wilt provide the horsemen to ride upon them.

9   How then canst thou repulse even the least of my lord's servants? And yet thou trustest in Egypt for chariots and horsemen!

10   And did I now come up against this land to destroy it without the LORD, who said to me, "Go up against this land and destroy it?"

11   Then said Eliakim and Shebna and Joah to Rabshakeh: Please speak to thy servants in Aramaic, for we understand it, but do not speak to us in Judean, in the earshot of the folk who sit on the wall.

12 Then said Rabshakeh; Is it to thy lord and to thee that my lord sent me to speak these words? Or is it rather to the men who sit on the wall, who will eat their dung and drink their urine together with you?

13 So Rabshakeh stood and shouted aloud in Judean, and said: Listen to the words of the great king, the king of Assyria!

14 Thus says the king, Let not Hezekiah misguide you, for he will not be able to deliver you.

15 And let not Hezekiah make you trust in the LORD saying, "The LORD will surely deliver us. This city shall not be surrendered into the hand of the king of Assyria."

16 Do not listen to Hezekiah, for thus says the king of Assyria: Make a favorable agreement with me, and come out to me and let every man eat of his vine and every man of his fig tree and drink the water from his cistern.

17 Until I come and take you away into a land which is like your land, a land of grain and wine, a land of bread and vineyards.

18 Beware lest Hezekiah mislead you by saying, "The Lord will deliver us." Have the gods of the nations, any one of them, delivered his land from the hand of the king of Assyria?

19 Where are the gods of Hamath, of Arpad?
Where are the gods of Sepharvaim?" And have they delivered Samaria from my hand?

20 Who is there among all the gods of those lands that delivered their land from my hand, so that the LORD should deliver Jerusalem from my hand?

21 But they held their peace and answered him not a word. For the king's command was: "Answer him not."

22 Then came Eliakim, the son of Hilkiah, the master of the household, and Shebna the scribe, and Joah, the recorder, to Hezekiah, with their garments torn, and they reported to him the words of the chief officer.

Comment:

1-3 After invading Judea in 701 B.C. and capturing many fortified cities, including the important fortress of Lachish, the Assyrian king sent Rabshakeh, that is the "chief cup-bearer" or "chief officer," with a large army, demanding that Hezekiah surrender Jerusalem. The Assyrian general was met by a delegation of high Judean officials.

4-20 The Assyrian general's harangue is a classic example of psychological warfare as it was practiced in ancient times. His address is brutal, insulting and designed to intimidate the listeners.

He argues that Hezekiah's confidence in Egypt is in vain. It is no better than a broken reed, which can only hurt the one who leans upon it. Neither is the Judeans' faith in Jehovah justified, because, according to the Assyrian general, they have forfeited His favor by removing His altars from the country shrines, and insisted that He be worshipped only at the Temple in Jerusalem.

The Assyrian general ridicules the ability of Hezekiah to withstand the great might of Assyria, and offers to supply two thousand horses, if Hezekiah will find two thousand riders (v. 8). He further insists that the Assyrian invasion of Jerusalem was ordered by Jehovah Himself (v. 10).

The request of Hezekiah's representatives to the Assyrian not to speak in Judean (in Hebrew), but in Aramaic, the lingua franca of the Middle East in those days, is rudely rejected by the Assyrian general, who continues his harangue in Hebrew. He calls upon the inhabitants of Jerusalem to surrender, in exchange for the privilege of peacefully enjoying the fruits of their labors for a brief time, until they will later be resettled in another land similar to their own.[1]

The Assyrian general offers to make a favorable agreement with the Judeans to this effect. The Hebrew word for "agreement" in verse 16 is *"berachah"* (a blessing), indicating the beneficial nature of the agreement.

The Assyrian's effort to force the Judeans into surrender culminates in blasphemy when he compares Jehovah with the gods of the various conquered nations, such as Hamath and Arpad (previously mentioned in 10:9), and Samaria, which fell to the Assyrians in 722 B.C.

21-22 The people of Jerusalem listened to the Assyrian, but at the command of Hezekiah did not answer a word.

After this the royal delegation tore their clothing, in the traditional manner of mourners, and reported the message of the Assyrian commander to Hezekiah.

Note 1
>   The resettling of conquered nations in distant parts of the empire was a common practice of the Assyrians and later of the Babylonians.
>   It was a divine act of justice that about one century later, the Assyrians themselves became the victims of this policy, when they were forced to go into Babylonian captivity. They later were permitted in 539 B.C. to return to their own country by Cyrus the great emancipator of captive nations.

King Hezekiah dismayed, sends a delegation to Isaiah; Sennacherib's insolence. Hezekiah prays and God answers. The calamity of Sennacherib and his dismal end.

Isaiah, Chapter 37

Verses 1-38

1 And so it came to pass that when king Hezekiah heard it, he tore his garments and covered himself with sackcloth and went into the house of the LORD.

2 And he sent Eliakim, the master of the household, and Shebna the scribe, and the elders of the priests, covered with sackcloth, to Isaiah the son of Amoz.

3 And they said to him, thus says Hezekiah, this day is a day of trouble, of rebuke and blasphemy, for the children are come to the point of birth and there is no strength to bring them forth.

4 Perhaps the LORD thy God will hear the words of the chief officer, whom his master, the king of Assyria, has sent to taunt the living God and He will punish the words, which the LORD thy God has heard, when thou wilt make intercession for the remnant, which is left.

5 So the servants of king Hezekiah came to Isaiah.

6 And Isaiah said to them: Thus shall you say to your master: Thus says the LORD! Do not be afraid of the words which thou hast heard, with which the lads of the king of Assyria have insulted me.

7 Behold, I will put a spirit in him and he will hear a rumor and he will return to his country, and I will cause him to fall by the sword in his own land.

8 And the Assyrian went back and found the king of Assyria fighting against Libnah; for he had heard that he departed from Lachish.

9 And he heard say about Tirhakah, the king of Ethiopia, "he has come to fight thee." When he heard this he sent messengers to Hezekiah saying:

10 Thus shall you say to Hezekiah, the king of Judah, Let not thy God, in whom thou trustest, deceive you, saying, Jerusalem shall not be surrendered into the hand of the king of Assyria.

11 Behold thou hast heard what the kings of Assyria have done to all the countries, destroying them completely, and wilt thou be delivered?

12 Have the gods of those nations delivered them whom my fathers have destroyed, Gozan, Haran, Rezeph and the sons of Eden, who were in Telassar?

13 Where is the king of Hamath and the king of Arpad, and the king of the city of Sepharvaim, Hena and Ivah?

14 So Hezekiah took the letter from the hand of the messengers and read it. And he went up to the house of the LORD; and Hezekiah spread it before the LORD.

15 And Hezekiah prayed before the LORD, saying:

16 O LORD of hosts, God of Israel,
Enthroned upon the Cherubim:
Thou art the only God, of all the kingdoms of the earth.
Thou hast made heaven and earth.

17 Incline, O LORD, thine ear and hear.
Open, O LORD, thine eyes and see.
Hear the words of Sennacherib,
Who has sent to taunt the living God!

18 It is true that the kings of Assyria have devastated all the countries and their lands.

19 And have cast their gods into the fire, for they were no gods, but the work of men's hands, wood and stone, therefore they have destroyed them.

20 Now, therefore, O LORD our God, save us from his hand and let all the kingdoms of the earth know that thou alone art the LORD.

21 Then sent Isaiah the son of Amoz to Hezekiah saying: So says the LORD, the God of Israel to whom thou hast prayed about Sennacherib, the king of Assyria:

22 This is the word which God has spoken concerning him:
She despises thee, she scorns thee,
The virgin daughter of Zion,
She shakes her head behind thee,
The daughter of Jerusalem.

23 Whom hast thou taunted and blasphemed?
And against whom hast thou raised thy voice
And hast lifted up thine eyes?
Against the Holy One of Israel!

24   By thy servants hast thou taunted the Lord
     And hast said: With my many chariots
     Have I climbed the top of mountains,
     The utmost parts of the Lebanon,
     And I have felled its tall cedars,
     Its choicest cypresses,
     I have come to the farthest reaches,
     Of its forest garden.

25   I have dug [wells] and drunk,
     And have dried up with the sole of my feet
     All the rivers of Egypt.

26   Hast thou not heard?
     From way back it is I who planned it,
     From ancient days have I designed it,
     Now I brought it to pass
     That fortified cities should be laid waste,
     Into heaps of ruins,

27   And their inhabitants were helpless,
     They were dismayed and put to shame,
     They were as the grass of the fields,
     As the green herbs, as the grass on the roof,
     As the grainfield before it is green.

28   Thy sitting down, thy going out and coming in,
     And also thy raging against me I know.

29   Because thy raging against me,
     And thy roar has come to my ear,
     Therefore will I put my hook in thy nose,
     And my muzzle into thy lips,
     And I will make thee turn back,
     By the way by which thou hast come.

30   And this shall be for a sign to thee:
     This year men will eat that which is self-grown,
     In the second year that which is self-sown,
     But in the third year: sow and reap,
     Plant vineyards and eat their fruit.

31   And the surviving remnant of the house of Judah
     Shall again take root below and bear fruit above.

32   For a remnant shall go forth from Jerusalem,
     And out of Mount Zion they that shall escape.
     The zeal of the LORD of hosts shall perform this.

33 Therefore, thus says the LORD to the king of Assyria:
    He shall not come to this city,
    Nor shoot an arrow against it,
    Neither will it be assaulted with shield,
    Nor will a mound be cast up against it.

34 By the way he came, by the same way shall he go back,
    But into this city will he not enter:
    Thus says the LORD.

35 And I will shield this city to save it,
    For my own sake, and for the sake of my servant David.

36 And the angel of the LORD went forth and struck down in the
    Assyrian camp one hundred and eighty-five thousand. And when
    they rose up in the morning, behold they were all dead corpses.

37 Then Sennacherib king of Assyria departed and went forth and
    returned and resided in Nineveh.

38 And as he was worshipping in the house of his god Nisroch,
    his sons Adrammelech and Sarezer struck him down with the
    sword and escaped into the land of Ararat. And his son Esarhad-
    don reigned in his stead.

Comment:

Verses 1-38

This chapter relates one of the most dramatic episodes in the long
history of Israel, and more specifically of Judah. The miraculous intervention of God which frustrated Sennacherib's attempt to capture Jerusalem spared the Judeans the misery of exile and bondage for one more
century. Next to the deliverance from Egypt, Sennacherib's calamity
stands as a landmark of divine watchfulness over the destiny of Israel.

1-5 Dismayed by the insistence of the Assyrian general that Jerusalem
surrender to his master, Hezekiah sends a prominent delegation of the
highest state officials and priests to Isaiah asking him to intercede with
the LORD for deliverance (v. 2). The composition of the delegation
shows the high respect in which Isaiah was held by the king and the
court, as a man who stood close to God.

**3 For the children are come to birth [Hebrew: the *matrice*], and
there is no strength to bring them forth.**

This may have been a popular saying which expressed extreme perplexity and inability to cope with a situation.

6-7 The prophet's answer is reassuring: The Lord will force Sennacherib to turn back by the same way in which he came.

6 .... the lads of the king of Assyria

This is an exact translation of the Hebrew, which the KJV renders: "the servants of the king of Assyria." It is a contemptuous reference to the Assyrian messengers.

7 "Behold I will put a spirit in him"—a spirit of confusion

Verses 8 and 9 explain the circumstances which caused "a spirit of confusion" in Sennacherib's counsel. He heard a rumor or report *(she-muah"*—the same word occurs in 53:1), that Tirhakah, the Ethiopian ruler of the Nile Valley empire, was about to launch a campaign against him. Tirhakah, like his predecessors, sought to incite the subject nations to revolt against their Assyrian masters.

10-13 Sennacherib's second message to Hezekiah demanding the surrender of Jerusalem, was basically the same as the first, with the added blasphemy: "Let not thy God deceive thee."

14-21 Hezekiah's prayer.

14 And Hezekiah spread it [the letter] before the LORD

A symbolic act to demonstrate visually the enormity of the hubris hurled by Sennacherib in the face of the living God.

16 O LORD of hosts, God of Israel . . .

As if to make amends for the Assyrian's blasphemy, Hezekiah exalts his God by calling Him by His rightful name and by extolling His character. He is the Lord of hosts, the God of the whole universe, and also the God of Israel. He is the rightful King of all the kingdoms and the Creator of heaven and earth.

16 Enthroned upon the cherubim [or sitting upon] . . . .

A reference to the two figures of the cherubim over the ark in the Temple (Psa. 18:10; 80:1).

18 It is true that the kings of Assyria

Hezekiah admits that the boasting of Sennacherib, that he has destroyed all the gods and their countries, is true, but these gods were merely man-made idols and not God.

20 Now therefore, O LORD our God

Now is the time for the true God to save Jerusalem from the blasphemous Assyrian and thus prove that He alone is God.

21-35 God answers Hezekiah through his servant Isaiah. The answer comes in the form of a magnificent taunt song against Sennacherib.

22 She despises thee, she scorns thee. . . .

Jerusalem is called "the virgin daughter of Zion."

As long as God is on her side she is inviolable and virgin, and may scoff at and defy all her adversaries.

The prophet sees in vision the hastily retreating Assyrian king, while the daughter of Jerusalem "shakes her head" behind him, in contemptuous pity.

23 Whom has thou taunted and blasphemed. . . . And against whom has thou raised thy voice?

In three indignant questions Isaiah stresses the unspeakable horror of blaspheming "the Holy One of Israel."

All the vaunted exploits of the Assyrians were only possible because the Lord has used them as His instrument of wrath and punishment (cf. Isa. 10:5).

28 I know . . . .

The Lord is fully aware of all the actions and thoughts of Sennacherib, and now the time of retribution has come.

29 Therefore will I put my hook in thy nose . . . .

For many generations the Assyrians had perpetrated acts of unspeakable cruelty upon their victims, literally dragging many captive peoples into Mesopotamia, with hooks in their noses and muzzles in their lips. Now the Assyrian's turn has come. The spoiler will at last be despoiled.

30 This shall be for a sign to thee

Isaiah now directs God's message to Hezekiah.

The sign will consist of the events which will soon transpire. For two years the people will subsist on that which is "self grown" and self sown," but in the third year there will be regular sowing and reaping, planting and eating.

33-35 Jehovah promises to protect Jerusalem. The city will not experience the horrors of a long, drawn-out siege, with all its attending miseries. Incidentally, verse 33 provides us with a glimpse of the methods of siege practiced by the Assyrians and by their contemporaries, and by warriors long after them.

35 For my own sake and for the sake of my servant David

The Lord's own honor as well as His faithfulness to His servant David, are at stake.

36 And the angel of the LORD went forth . . . .

In a few brief words the prophet-historian relates the enormous calamity which befell the army of Sennacherib as a result of divine intervention. Just as in the days of Pharoah, "the angel of the Lord" slew the firstborn of Egypt, so now he slew Sennacherib's army.

36 In the morning they were all dead corpses. . . .

The redundancy of the words "dead corpses" expresses the completeness of the Assyrian disaster.

38 **They escaped into the land of Ararat,** which is now Armenia. Esarhaddon who was engaged in a military campaign, upon hearing that his brothers had murdered their father, marched on Nineveh and defeated them.

A period of about twenty years passed between Sennacherib's retreat from Jerusalem and his assassination (701-681 B.C.)

Hezekiah's Near Fatal Illness and His Miraculous Recovery

Isaiah, Chapter 38

Verses 1-22

1   In those days Hezekiah became ill unto death, and Isaiah the son of Amoz the prophet, came to him and said: thus says the LORD: Make thy will known to thy house, for thou shalt die, and not live.

2   And Hezekiah turned his face to the wall and prayed to the LORD and said:

3   Do remember, O LORD, I beseech thee, how I have walked before thee in truth and with a whole heart, and have done that which is good in thy sight. And Hezekiah wept bitterly.

4   And the word of the LORD came to Isaiah saying,

5   Go and say to Hezekiah, thus says the Lord, the God of David thy father I have heard thy prayers, I have seen thy tears, behold I will add to thy days fifteen years.

6   And I will deliver thee and this city from the hand of the king of Assyria and I will protect this city.

7   And this will be for a sign unto thee from the LORD, that the LORD will do the thing which he has spoken:

8   Behold, I will cause the shadow of the sun dial which is gone down on the sun dial of Ahaz to turn backward ten degrees. So the sun returned ten degrees, by the degrees which it went down.

9   The writing of Hezekiah, when he had been sick and recovered from his sickness.

10 I said: In the midst of my days I shall depart,
Even into the gates of Sheol.
I am deprived of the balance of my years.

11 I said: I shall not see the LORD,
The LORD in the land of the living.
I shall no longer behold man
Together with the inhabitants of the world.

12 My habitation is broken up and carried away from me
    Like the tent of a shepherd.
    I have rolled up my life like a weaver,
    He will cut me off from the loom.
    From day to night thou wilt make an end of me.

13 I waited until morning like a lion,
    So he broke all my bones.
    From day to night thou makest an end of me.

14 Like a swallow [or] a crane so have I chirped,
    I cooed like the dove,
    Mine eyes fail from looking up.
    O LORD, I am hard pressed, come thou to my rescue!

15 What shall I say?
    He has spoken to me and he has also done it,
    I shall walk softly because of the bitterness of my soul.

16 O LORD, by these things men live,
    And the life of my spirit is in them.
    Wherefore restore thou me and let me live.

17 Behold my deep bitterness has turned into my salvation,
    And thou in thy love for my soul
    Has spared it from the pit of corruption.

18 For Sheol shall not praise thee,
    Neither shall death exalt thee.
    They that go down into the pit
    Cannot hope for thy Truth,

19 The living, the living, he shall praise thee,
    As I do this day.
    The father to his children shall make known the truth.

20 O LORD, come to my help.
    We will sing in the house of the Lord to stringed musical instruments
    All the days of our life.

21 And Isaiah said, let them bake a fig cake
    And apply it to the boil
    And he shall recover.

22 And Hezekiah said: What is the sign that I shall [yet] go up to the
    house of the LORD?

Comment:
Verses 1-22

The chapter describes the grave illness of Hezekiah, his prayer for recovery and God's answer through Isaiah that the king's prayer has been heard and that he will live another fifteen years.

This incident is recorded in a parallel passage in 2 Kings 20:1-11, with only slight variations, and with the omission of Hezekiah's meditation (Isa. 38:9-20).

1 In those days. . . .

That is before Sennacherib attempted to force Jerusalem into submission.

Make known thy will to thy house . . KJV: "Set thy house in order."

The Hebrew verb *"Tsav"*—"command," is a technical term for making one's last will and testament in expectation of death.

2 . . . his face to the wall and prayed. . . .

We can imagine the dying king, surrounded by his family and highest officials. Hezekiah in his distress sought privacy in order to communicate with his God alone.

3 Hezekiah wept bitterly . . .

At the age of thirty-nine, with his people facing an invasion by the terrible Assyrians, the king felt that his death would not only be a personal disaster, but also a disaster for his people.

Verses 4-6 The Answer to Hezekiah's Prayer
4 The God of thy father David. . . .

The Lord answers the prayer of Hezekiah, not only for his own sake, but also for the sake of his ancestor David, with whom God made a covenant (2 Sam. 7:4-17).

5 I have heard thy prayers, I have seen thy tears. . . .

The verdict pronounced by Isaiah: "Thou shalt die and not live" (v. 1) was not absolute. The Lord is responsive to earnest prayer. "The effectual, fervent prayer of a righteous man availeth much" (Jas. 5:16).

6 I will deliver the city, I will protect the city

Hezekiah's prayer and tears were apparently not merely for himself, but for his beloved Jerusalem.

7-8 The sign given to Hezekiah:

In the more detailed account of this incident in 2 Kings, it was Hezekiah himself who asked the prophet for a sign from the Lord that he would truly recover. His request was granted. The sign was to be that the shadow on the steps of Ahaz would go back ten degrees or ten steps. The Hebrew word *"maaloth"* means either "steps" or "degrees."

We do not know whether Ahaz actually had a sundial, or whether the shadow of an obelisk or column, which fell on the steps of the royal palace marked the time of day for the king as he looked out of his window. What happened was an extraordinary event, which defies the laws of nature.

It is interesting to note that Hezekiah did ask for a sign, in contrast to his ungodly father Ahaz, who hypocritically refused to ask for a sign (Isa. 7:12). Hezekiah confirmed his sincerity by his request.

9-20 Hezekiah's Meditation

9 The writing of Hezekiah (in Hebrew "*michtav*")

The writing or composition of Hezekiah is a touching account of the inner thoughts and emotions of a man who looked death in the face and at the last moment received a reprieve.

10 In the midst of my days. . . .

Literally the Hebrew reads, "In the stillness of my days," apparently an allusion to the rest period, or noontime siesta in a hot climate.

I shall depart to the gates of Sheol. . . .

Sheol, often translated "grave, pit, hell, netherworld," is a place of disembodied ghosts where the dead lead a shadowy existence (See comment on Isa. 14:15 p. 198).

12 My habitation is broken up. . . .

The verse expresses the transitory nature of life and the finality of death.

13-14 In striking metaphors Hezekiah expresses the torment of his soul, his hopes and frustrations and ends with the pathetic cry:

O Lord, I am hard pressed, come to my rescue!

The Hebrew words of this cry convey the anguish of a man who is sorely harassed by his enemies or by his creditors, and looks for a friend to bail him out.

15-17 The meditation of a thankful heart

The Hebrew of this passage is not quite clear, and translators differ in their interpretation. Our translation suggests the closest meaning of the original text.

15 What shall I say?

God has spoken and has kept His promise to Hezekiah to heal him. This has made Hezekiah so deeply grateful that he is unable to express his feelings. He can only remember his bitter experience and henceforth would "walk softly" before God.

16 . . . by these things men live. . . .

The memory of God's grace will henceforth be the sustaining force of his life.

17 My deep bitterness has turned into my salvation. . . .

Here the Hebrew word for salvation is *"shalom"*: peace. In its broadest sense *shalom* means completeness, well being, health and salvation.

Thy love for my soul (v. 17)

Literally, "thy desire for my soul."

God cares for Hezekiah personally and by forgiving his sins has healed him. Forgiveness of sins and healing are closely related.

18-19 Hezekiah's view of life beyond the grave which he shares with some of the writers of the psalms and with the writer of Ecclesiastes, (see Psa. 6:5; 88:12; Eccles. 9:4, 5, 10) is limited and does not express the position of Isaiah himself.

19 The living, the living he shall praise thee. . . .

The prophet Isaiah demonstrates a far more definite faith in the resurrection than Hezekiah. To this faith Isaiah gave triumphant expression in the ringing cry:

Thy dead men shall live, together with my dead body shall they arise! (Isa. 26:19).

In the New Testament, faith in the resurrection of the body and in eternal life is one of the central themes.

20 O LORD, come to my help. . . .

Literally: the Lord to my help, "come" is implied.

We will sing to stringed musical instruments. . . .

Delivered by God from death, Hezekiah sees himself at the head of his people, as they march to the house of God, singing and playing hymns of thanksgiving to the accompaniment of stringed instruments.

From 2 Chronicles 29:25-30 it would appear that Hezekiah took a personal interest in the use of musical instruments in the Temple and the singing of the psalms of David.

21-22 The two verses are practically identical with 2 Kings 20:7 and 8 where they fit perfectly into the context. It is possible that somehow these lines were misplaced through some scribal oversight and should follow verse 6.

22 . . . what is the sign that I shall go up to the house of the Lord?

In this position, the question is out of place and remains unanswered but it fits in before verses 7 and 8.

In order to overcome the difficulty of the unanswered question some commentators have suggested the ingenious translation:

"What a sign, that I shall [really] go up to the house of the LORD!" However this does violence to the plain sense of the Hebrew text.

Hezekiah's Folly and Its Baneful Results

Isaiah, Chapter 39

Verses 1-8

1 At that time Merodach Baladan, son of Baladan, the king of Babylon, sent a letter and a present to Hezekiah, for he heard that he had been ill and was recovered.

2 And Hezekiah was glad of them, and he showed them the treasure-house, the silver, the gold, the spices, the precious oil and all his armory, and all there was among his treasures. There was not a thing in his house or his domain which Hezekiah did not show them.

3 Then came the prophet Isaiah to king Hezekiah and said to him: "What did those men say and where have they come from?" And Hezekiah said: "They have come from a far country to me, from Babylon."

4 Then said he: "What have they seen in thy house?" And Hezekiah said: "They have seen everything in my house, there was not a thing in my treasures, which I have not shown them."

5 Then said Isaiah to Hezekiah: "Hear the word of the Lord of hosts:

6 Behold the days are coming that all there is in thy house and all that thy ancestors have stored up, shall be carried off to Babylon, not a thing shall be left.

7 And of thy sons, that shall proceed from thee, whom thou shalt beget, will they take away, and they will be eunuchs in the palace of the king of Babylon."

8 And Hezekiah said to Isaiah: "The word of the Lord which thou hast spoken is good," and he said, "for there shall be peace and truth in my days."

Comment:

1 At that time. . . .

The chronology of the incident related in this chapter is vague. It is clear that Merodach Baladan's embassy came to Hezekiah after the recovery from his illness which, according to Isaiah 38:1, occurred in the fourteenth year of his reign. Hezekiah reigned twenty-nine years (715-686 B.C.), but as so frequently happened among the kings of Judah and Israel, he was co-regent during the lifetime of his father Ahaz. The "fourteenth year" may refer either to the start of Hezekiah's co-regency or to the beginning of his sole reign.

Merodach Baladan was the ruler of the Aramean tribe of Bit Jakim near the mouth of the Euphrates. In 721 he captured Babylon and reigned as king till 710, when he was driven out by Sargon II. After Sargon's death Merodach Baladan returned to Babylon and reigned there for nine months (704-703).

The question is during which period of his reign did Merodach Baladan send his embassy to Hezekiah? The answer is not certain. However, the probability is that it was during the first period of his reign, when Merodach Baladan was most anxious to win allies against Babylon among its enemies. Hezekiah seemed to be a good prospect, and his recovery from a dangerous illness was an excellent pretext for sending such an embassy.

2   And Hezekiah was glad. . . .

The embassy from Merodach Baladan greatly flattered Hezekiah's vanity. As a mark of his pleasure, Hezekiah showed them all his treasures. This was an act of great vanity and also of political short-sightedness.

3-8   Isaiah predicts that the descendants of Hezekiah will be carried off into Babylonian captivity together with all their possessions.

3   Then came the prophet Isaiah to King Hezekiah. . . .

The sudden appearance of Isaiah before the king was due to the fact that the prophet rightly suspected Hezekiah of flirting with the king of Babylon, with a view to forming a future alliance against Assyria.

5   Then said Isaiah to Hezekiah. . . .

All his life Isaiah preached against foreign alliances, either with Assyria or Syria or Egypt, considering such alliances a sin against the Lord, and a harmful policy.

6-7   Thy sons . . . and all that is in thy house shall be carried off into Babylon. . . .

7   A clear prediction that Hezekiah's house and his descendants shall be captives in Babylon. This prophecy was fulfilled about one century later. Those who question the possibility of prophetic prediction also doubt the genuineness of this passage. Some explain the reference to Babylon as arising from the circumstance that the kings of Assyria also styled themselves as "king of Babylon."

There is, however, no valid reason to reject a priori the fact that Isaiah and other prophets were able to foretell events before they came to pass.

During the lifetime of Isaiah and Hezekiah, the kingdom of Israel (or Samaria) was destroyed and its inhabitants were carried off into Assyrian exile (722 B.C.). Isaiah foresaw that Judah would likewise go into Babylonian exile, and would be enslaved by the very people with whom Hezekiah was secretly trying to ally himself.

8   Good is the word of the LORD.

This expresses Hezekiah's humble acceptance of the divine decision! "For there shall be peace and truth in my time."

Hezekiah looks upon the postponement of the predicted calamity as a partial mitigation of the disaster.

Thus chapters 36-39 of Isaiah conclude the first part of his book dealing mainly with the Syrian and Assyrian menace to Israel and Judah and form a transition to the second part of the book (chapters 40-66), anticipating the Babylonian captivity and the future restoration and redemption of Israel.

Supplement
Some Guidelines to
the Interpretation of Prophecy

Philip heard him read the prophet Isaiah and said: Understandest thou what thou readest? And he said, How can I, except some man should guide me? (Acts 8:30-31).

We can readily sympathize with the Ethiopian eunuch who could not understand what he was reading in the book of Isaiah. How often have we ourselves wished that we might have a sure guide who would help us understand prophecy?

To help the Bible reader to better understand the writings of the prophets, we have set forth a few common-sense, basic guidelines and principles.

1. The first and most important condition for the understanding of the Scriptures in general, and of the prophetic writings in particular, is to remember that the Bible differs from all other literature known to men. Here God Himself speaks to man.

It is therefore essential that we approach the study of the Scriptures with reverence and humility, and with an ear attuned to the voice of God. Any other approach, be it ever so scholarly, will not reveal the deeper meaning of prophecy. Just as in order to understand music one must have an ear for the harmony, the beauty and the message of music, just as in order to understand any form of art one must have an eye which is capable of appreciation of the form, the beauty and the meaning of the work of art, so also is it essential that our inner ear and eye be adjusted to the prophetic message. Some people are physically blind, others suffer from color blindness, but there are multitudes who are afflicted with spiritual blindness. The Psalmist prayed: "Open my eyes that I may see wondrous things out of thy law" (Psa. 119:18).

The knowledge of Hebrew, Greek and Aramaic, of archeology, of history, or the classics, while most useful, will never replace spiritual insight and comprehension. The Apostle Paul tells us that: "The natural man receiveth not the things of the Spirit of God, for they are foolishness unto him. Neither can he know them, because they are spiritually discerned" (1 Cor. 2:14).

The study of Scripture, to be fruitful, must be done in a spirit of humility, not presuming to set ourselves up as judges of the Word of God, but rather such as who are willing to submit themselves to its judgment.

The Apostle Peter writes: "God resisteth the proud and giveth grace to the humble" (1 Pet. 5:5).

2. Before proceeding with the interpretation of prophecy it is essential to determine what is the literal meaning of the prophet's message. Ask yourself the question, "What was it that the prophet sought to convey to his listeners or to his readers?" When we undersand this, we have made the first step in understanding what the particular message means to us today.

3. We need to respect the sound principle of interpretation which says: "When common sense makes good sense, seek no other sense." Bible readers (and teachers) have been known to get lost in the attractive alleys and mazes of prophetic speculation, because they disregarded the above common sense principle.

4. The historical circumstances under which the prophet lived and labored are all important factors which help us understand his message. Places, persons, nations and events to which the prophet refers set the stage for his activities and anchor them in the history of the age.

5. Although a specific historical situation usually is the occasion for the prophet's utterance or action, he is by no means limited to that particular incident or event but may make it an occasion for a pronouncement concerning events which are yet to happen, either in the near or distant future.

6. This leads us to the principle of double reference. A prophetic statement may refer to a currently existing situation and announce what God will do about it immediately. From there the prophet may proceed to predict what God will eventually do in the distant future or even in the last days. Sometimes these prophecies blend into one vision, as when one scene in a film fades out and another is superimposed upon the first. The point of transition from one vision to another is not always clearly marked. For instance in Isaiah 14:4-11, there is a taunting song against the king of Babylon and his coming downfall and destruction. However, from verse 12-17, the taunt takes on a cosmic character, describing the arch enemy of God, Lucifer. "How art thou fallen from heaven, O Lucifer, son of the morning; how art thou cut down to the ground, which didst weaken the nations!" (v. 12).

A parallel situation is found in Ezekiel 28 where from verse 2 to 10 there is a prediction about the destruction of Tyre with all its pride and wisdom. From verse 13 to 15 the oracle transcends any human being or earthly dominion, and becomes a taunting song against Satan himself:

Thou hast been in Eden the garden of God. . . .

Thou art the anointed cherub that covereth. . . .

Thou wast perfect in thy ways from the day that thou wast created, till iniquity was found in thee.

7. Prophecy is either didactic or predictive and sometimes a mixture of both. Didactic prophecy (forthtelling) seeks to lay bare or correct the moral and spiritual shortcomings primarily of Israel. Since Jehovah is eternal and His character unchangeable, therefore His judgment and His dealings with Israel are prophetic of His dealings with other nations consistent with His own righteousness and their knowledge of God (Jer. 9:25-26). The Apostle Paul emphasized this fact when he wrote: "For if God spared not the natural branches [Israel], take heed lest he also spare not thee [the Gentiles]" (Rom. 11:21).

8. In dealing with predictive prophecy it is necessary to distinguish between the prophecies which have already been fulfilled in the past, and those which still await their consummation.

Thus the predictions of the Egyptian bondage, the Assyrian invasion, the Babylonian captivity and subsequent return to the Holy Land were fulfilled.

Other prophecies were fulfilled in part and await their final consummation in the future. To this second type of predictions belong many of the Messianic prophecies. When the prophets Hosea, Isaiah, Jeremiah and others first uttered them, these were still future events which were later fulfilled with the coming of the Messiah Jesus. However, their complete fulfillment awaits the return of Christ and the establishment of His kingdom.

9. We must bear in mind that the prophets were primarily God's messengers to Israel, to teach, to rebuke, to console, to foretell His future plans for Israel. Where the prophet speaks concerning other nations, it is generally with regard to their relationship to Israel. In general it can be said that the Old Testament speaks chiefly to and about Israel, while the New Testament deals with the Church composed of Jews and Gentiles who believe in Christ as their Lord and Saviour (Eph. 2). The Church is a supranational spiritual entity. Israel is a national entity with a spiritual goal. It is therefore a mistake to confuse the Church with Israel as so many have done.

10. The point of convergence of prophecies which were of a national character and those of a universal nature, is the person of the Messiah

of Israel who is also the Saviour of all men. In His person the Kingdom of God and His salvation embraces all mankind. Within physical and national Israel there is a spiritual remnant, which is the true Israel, the Israel of God (Gal. 6:16). This is one of the central themes of Old Testament prophecy, and is continued in the New Testament. Out of this faithful remnant of Israel come Christ, His apostles and the New Testament Church, the *ecclesia*. To this Church belong both believing Jew and Gentile (Mt. 28:19; Mk. 16:15; Lk. 24:47; Gal. 3:28; John 10:16; Acts 1:8; Eph. 2; Rom. 9:24.)

11. Because the God of Israel is also the God and Father of the Lord Jesus Christ and of His Church, there are many spiritual similarities and parallels between Israel and the Church. Nevertheless historical "Israel" and "the Church"are two distinct entities which live their separate and distinct lives and should never be confused. The spiritual core of Israel, the faithful remnant is not the Church, but a part of it (Eph. 2:19-22). Conversely the Church is not Israel, nor "the New Israel" as erroneously taught for centuries by the Church of Rome and many contemporary Protestant theologians. The Church consists of believing Jews and Gentiles. The confusion of the Church with Israel has had baneful consequences for the Church and for Israel, and has caused grave misinterpretation of the Scriptures. For centuries it has colored Christian thinking about the Jews. It left the Jews with all the dire threats and predictions of judgment and desolation and exclusively misappropriated for the Church all the promises of divine redemption and mercy. There are enough distinctive and glorious promises given specifically to the Church of Christ without misapplying those which were given to Israel (Rom. 9:4, 5).

12. In interpreting prophecy one has to beware of pitfalls. One of these is the forcing of historical events into the framework of our preconceived interpretation of prophecy. However, history often has a painful way of correcting our notions.

When one reads Biblical commentaries from the Napoleonic times, he may at times find Napoleon cast in the role of Antichrist. During World War II a well-known Bible teacher in America taught that Mussolini was the Antichrist. Such examples could be multiplied *ad infinitum*.

Another dangerous pitfall is the setting of dates concerning the fulfillment of certain prophetic events, especially with regard to the second coming of Christ. This inclination has marred the reputation of some Bible teachers.

13. In interpreting prophecy we must remember that the prophets were guided by the Holy Spirit to foretell events, the full import of which they were not always fully aware themselves (1 Pet. 1:10, 11), neither when or under what circumstances their prophecies will come to pass.

They often were permitted to see the future as on a flat two dimensional canvas not realizing fully the broad valleys, the rivers and mountain ranges existing between one predicted event and another. God Himself who is the Lord of history has a way of bringing into focus prophecy which was unclear in former generations. It is easier for us, who look from the standpoint of the New Testament, to understand certain prophecies than it was in the times of the prophets. In the light of the New Testament, prophecy takes on for us a new dimension.

Our own age has brought into sharp focus certain prophecies which former generations either overlooked or misapplied. We have in mind the prophecies concerning the restoration of Israel, which have come to pass in part in our own time, namely the regathering of the Jewish people in their ancient homeland Israel (Ezk. 36:16-24; 37:10).

We of this generation have been privileged to be witnesses of the fulfillment of these prophecies. Others wait for their consummation at their appointed times. It behooves us to be humble and not too rigid in the interpretation of certain predicted events, knowing that there are certain areas of divine rule and providence which God has reserved for Himself. "The secret things belong unto the Lord our God: but those things which are revealed belong unto us and to our children forever, that we may do all the words of this law" (Deut. 29:29).

Prophecy was not given in order to satisfy the morbid curiosity of some sensation-hungry people, but to be a guide and "a light that shineth in a dark place, until the day dawn, and the day star arise in your hearts: knowing this first, that no prophecy of the scripture is of any private interpretation" (2 Pet. 1:19, 20). The purpose of prophecy is: (a) To warn men against those sins which have brought judgment and sorrow upon Israel (Rom. 11:21); (b) To guard against false prophets and doctrines (2 Pet. 2); (c) To strengthen our faith, and to comfort the believer that God will fulfill His promises of eternal redemption and the establishment of His kingdom (Isa. 65:17-25, 66:22 and Rev. 21:1-4).

General Index
Isaiah Chapters 1-39

Abimelech, 9

Abraham, 9, 138

Accadian, 10

Accession-year dating, 82

Agabus, 33

Ahab, 18, 130

Ahaz, king of Judah, 5, 38, 41, 73, 75, 145ff, 200

Albright, W. F., 84, 85n

Alcalay, R., 151

Alexander, J.A., 6, 40, 51, 97, 111n

Allis, O. T., 40, 51

Alliteration, 26, 43, 100, 128

Almah, see Virgin

Ambassadors, 211ff

Anna, 32

Arabia, prophecy against, 224ff

Archeology, 6, 16, 51, 199, 210n

Arpad, 72

Ashdod, 220

Assyria, 5, 43, 72ff, 88, 102,154ff, 170ff, 218, 262ff, 270ff

Astrology, 16ff

Astruc, J., 50

Azariah, 39, 71

Baal, 31

Babylon, 220ff

———, Kings of, 88

———, prophecy against, 190ff

Babylonians, 102

Bacon, F., 50

Balak, 16

Barnes, A., 6, 78, 79n

Bathsheba, 26

Bethsaida, 22

Biblical criticism, 3ff, 48ff

Branch of the Lord, 125ff

Calendars, biblical, 83ff

Calvin, J., 98, 139, 183

Cambyses, 215

Capernaum, 22

Chorazin, 22

Chronology, biblical, 40n, 81ff, 87ff

Cicero, 27

Co-regency, 38ff, 72

Cyrus, prophecy concerning, 22, 44, 52, 55ff.

Damascus, 5, 72, 73, 88

———, prophecy against, 208ff

Dante, 179n

Darwin, C., 49

David, 26, 31, 201

Dead Sea scrolls, 23, 67, 79, 201n, 264n, 271

Deborah, 37

Delitzsch, F., 6, 51ff, 138, 195, 201n, 228n, 273

Demosthenes, 21, 78

DeWette, 50

Documentary theory, 50ff.

Drechsler, M, 6, 51

Driver, S.R., 6, 52, 56, 59, 62n.

Duhm, B, 6, 52, 277

Ecclesiasticus, 68

Edom, prophecy against, 223ff, 275ff

Egypt, 5, 43, 72, 155, 212ff, 257ff

———, judgment and redemption, 213ff

Eichhorn, J.G., 50

Eliakim, 230ff

Elijah, 18, 38

Elisha, 18

Elisabeth, 32

Engnell, I, 52

Ephraim, 147ff, 208ff, 247ff

Eponym lists, 84

Esarhaddon, 148, 174, 215

Ethiopian eunuch, 7

Ethiopia, prophecy against 210ff

Ewald, G. H., 6, 41, 45n, 50

Feuerbach, L. A., 49

Fichte, J. G., 49

Gerizim, Mount, 73ft, 115

Gideon, 163

God, names of, 50, 101, 110, 139

———, nature of, 13, 138

Gomorrah, 194

Graf, K. H., 50

Green, W. H., 51

Gunkel, H., 56

Hamath, 72

Harnack, A., 32, 36n

Hegel, G.W.F., 49

Hengstenberg, E. W., 6, 40, 51

Herodotus, 217, 222, 225n

Heschel, A. J., 19, 28n, 156n

Hezekiah, king of Judah, 38ff, 66, 76, 127, 147, 154, 166, 220, 282ff

Homer, 49, 197, 265

Hoshea, 73

Huldah, 37

Ibn Ezra, 48, 68ff
Immanuel, 145ff, 188
Inspiration, 28n
Isaiah
———, authorship of, 3ff, 47ff, 190
———, book of woes, 129ff, 247ff
———, chronology of, 39ff, 99ff
———, family of, 37
———, Hebrew text of, 79
———, major themes of, 77ff
———, meaning of name, 38-159
———, the man, 37ff
———, text, 79
———, unity and diversity of, 56ff
———, wife of, 37
Jacob, 138
Jannaeus, A., 204
Jerusalem, 42ff, 99, 108ff, 219ff,
    225ff
———, God's purpose for, 252ff
———, rulers denounced, 249ff
———, Bible, 6, 201n
Jesus Christ, 138, 149, 154, 180ff
Jesus, meaning of name, 38, 187
Jezebel, 18
Jocz, J., 21n, 36n
John the Baptist, 32, 36, 38
Jonah, 18
Josephus, 28, 32, 36n, 44, 210n, 217,
    219n
Josiah, king of Judah, 21, 59, 126,
    155
Jotham, 38, 72, 83
Judah, 5, 71ff, 88
Kaufmann, Y., 52, 53n
Keil, C. F., 6, 40, 51
Kennett, R.H., 53
Kimchi, David, 164, 179n
King James Version, 6, 108, 115ff,
    131, 150, 151, 162ff, 198-201n,
    204, 217, 227, 233, 237, 245,
    257, 271, 289, 293
Kissane, E. J., 138, 277
Kuenen, A., 51
Lot, 103
Lucifer, 198
Luckenbill, D. D., 76n, 111n
Luther, Martin, 148
Luzzatto, Chief Rabbi of Rome,
    51, 139
Magic, 16, 21n
Magog, 166
Maher-shalal-hash-baz, 37, 154, 156ff

Manasseh, 38ff
Man, Hebrew terms for, 118
Margalioth, R., 52, 53n, 70n, 125n,
    196n
Marlowe, C., 50
Marx, K., 49
Mary, the Virgin, 32
Menahem, 72
Merodach-baladan, 296ff
Mesha, Stone of, 203, 210n
Messiah, 7, 19, 32ff, 98, 125ff, 143,
    152, 180ff, 251, 301ff
———, birth of, 161ff
———, names of, 163ff
———, nature of, 45, 163ff
Messianic kingdom, 45, 180ff, 266ff
Micah, 18, 44
Micaiah, 17
Miriam, 37, 150
Moab, 72
Moab, prophecy against, 202ff, 241
Moses, 139
Moses, law of, 29, 104ff,
———, as model prophet, 11ff.
———, song of, 186
Mussolini, B., 302
Nabal, 267
Naboth, 130
Napoleon, 302
Nathan, 26, 31
Nebuchadnezzar, 84, 102, 155, 233
Necho, 155
Nielsen, E., 52
Nietzsche, F., 49
Nineveh, 175
Obadiah, 38
Onias IV, 217
Ophir, 193
Orr, J., 51
Parable, 25ff, 128, 251ff
Parallelism, 78
Paul, Saint, 12, 33, 98, 143
Pekah, 73, 75, 99, 130, 147
Persia, kings of, 88
Philip, 7
Philistia, prophecy against, 200ff
Phillips, J. B., 124, 138
Phoenicia, decline and fall of, 231ff
Plato, 15n, 179n
Prophecy, attempts to allegorize,
    97ff
———, interpretation of, 97ff, 299ff
———, predictive, 19ff, 59, 190

Prophetic message and contents, 18ff, 25ff
Prophets, meaning of term, 9ff
———, as professional preachers, 18ff
———, characteristics of, 9ff, 11ff, 23ff, 109
———, commissioning, 136ff
———, God's methods of communicating with, 9ff, 23ff
———, methods of communication, 10, 15, 23ff
———, New Testament, 32ff
———, pagan, 16ff, 24, 28n
———, relationship with God, 9ff, 24ff, 149
———, sons of the, 18
———, true and false, 15ff
Ptolemy, Canon of, 84
Rabshakeh, 282ff
Rashi, 150ff, 156n
Rebekah, 150
Remnant, the, 71, 110, 176ff
Revised Standard Version, 33, 203n
Rezin, 72, 75, 99, 147, 157
Roman Captivity, 124
Samaria, 5, 72ff, 137
———, prophecy against, 247ff
Samaritans, 73ff
Sarah, 9
Sargon II, 73, 174, 220
Sayce, A. H., 180n
Schopenhauer, A., 49
Seed, holy, 71, 77, 142ff
Sennacherib, invasion of Judah, 99, 147, 156, 174, 178ff, 226, 282ff
———, king of Assyria, 75ff
Septuagint, 68, 150, 210, 245
Seraphim, 138ff
Shakespeare, W., 49
Shalmaneser, 73, 200
Shear-yashub, 37, 147
Shebna, 229ff

Sheol, 197ff, 294
Sidon, 72
Sirach, 68
Skinner, J., 3, 6, 52, 56
Slotki, I. W., 138, 156n, 164, 179n
Socrates, 15n, 179n
Sodom, 104, 122, 194
Sopherim, 79
Smith, G. A., 6, 56
———, W. R., 52
Spinoza, B., 48
St. Augustine, 44
St. Jerome, 4
Syria, 43
Syro-Ephraimite war, 145ff
Talmud, 34
Targum Jonathan, 163, 179n
Tarshish, 119, 233
Terebinths, 111, 143
Thackeray, H. St. J., 36n
Theocracy, 28ff
Theophany, 135ff, 263
Thiele, E. R., 45n, 84, 85n
Tiglathpileser I, 172
Tiglathpileser III, 72ff, 99, 137, 146ff, 157, 161, 172, 200
Trinity implied in Isaiah, 139, 141
Tyre, 72, 231ff
Ugaritic Tablets, 23
Uzziah, king of Judah, 38ff, 71ff, 76n, 81ff, 136ff
Virgil, 199
Virgin, "Almah", 149ff
Vulgate, 184
Wellhausen, J., 50ff
Wiseman, D. J., 85n
Women of Jerusalem censured, 123ff, 267ff
Young, E. J., 21n, 40, 51, 53n, 111n, 156n
Zacharias, 32

n: note
ff: following

Index of Biblical References

(a) OLD TESTAMENT

Genesis

1:4-26	181
1:26	141
2:21	196
3:15	152
3:17	237
3:17b	183
9:1-17	237
10:6-10	171
10:10-11	171
10:14	200
10:22	171
12:3b	218
18:1-3	138
19:25-30	102
19:31-37	203
20:7	9
24:43	150
26:3	153
28:15	153
32:20	110
32:24-30	138
39:2-3	153

Exodus

2:8	150
3:1-4	12
3:2-6	12
3:4	138
3:5	3
3:10-12	12
3:12	153
3:14-15	12
3:16	153
4:1	13
4:10	12
4:10-16	13
7:1-2b	10
7:22	17
13:17	201
15:2-18	186
19:18	139
22:21-24	106
23:8	108
23:25	274, 280
32:30-32	14
32:32	127
33:15-17	153
33:20	137, 140
40:38	153

Leviticus

3:5, 16	181
19:2	20
26:23	58
26:27-45	58

Numbers

11:25	23
12:6	23
22:	203
22:5, 13	16
24:	203
25:	203

Deuteronomy

6:16	149
13:1-5	15, 16
18:9-14	121
18:9-22	15, 16, 21
22:19	151
23:3-4	203
28:64	58
29:29	303
32:1	100

Joshua

10:10	251

Judges

3:12-30	203
4:6	161
7:	163
7:16-25	177
11:17	203
13:17-18, 22	164

Ruth

4:18 22	203

I Samuel

2:27a	10
9:9	10
12:21	65
15:22	29
25:	267
28:7	16
28:7-25	160

II Samuel

5:20	251
7:4-17	293
12:1-9	25, 31

I Kings

1:34	30
8:33-34	58
10:11	193
11:29, 30	26
13:2	21, 59
14:19	82
14:29	82
15:7	82
15:23	82
15:31	82
16:5	82
18:7	38
18:17-18	31
19:18	71
20:35	18
21:20	31
21:27	220
22:6-28	17

II Kings

1:	203
1:8	220
2:	203
2:1-18	18
3:	203
4:9	10
6:30	220
8:23	82
9:11	38
12:19	82
15:1-2	81
15:1-5	83
15:1-7	71
15:2	82
15:5	38, 83
15:19	72
15:27-31	73
15:29	161
16:5-6	73
16:9	147
17:4-6	73, 148
17:13	10
17:22-23	74
17:22-24	148
17:41	74
18:13-20:19	66, 281
19:8-13	174
20:1-11	293
20:7-8	295
20:20	66, 228

21:16a	40
23:10	263
23:15-16	21

I Chronicles

1:12	200
5:26	72
29:29	11, 30

II Chronicles

16:11	82
25:26	82
26:1-3	82
26:1-23	71
26:6-15	136
26:16-21	136, 141
26:16	72, 136ff
26:21	38
26:22	40, 281
27:7	82
28:5-8	130, 146
28:26	82
28:22, 23	5
29: 21	73
29:25-30	295
32:17-19	174
32:25-26	76
32:30	228
32:32	39, 40, 66, 281
36:22	52

Ezra

1:1-4	52

Job

32:8	28

Psalms

6:5	295
11:4	138
15:	273
18:6	138
18:10	289
24	273
45:9	193
53:1	133
68:25	150
71:22	139
73:16-20	210
73:19	198
78:12	164
78:41	139
80:1	289

Psalms

87:4	258
88:12	164, 295
89:19	139
89:10	258
103:13	165
118:22	251
119:18	299

Proverbs

1:7	181
8:22-30	181
9:10	132
30:19	150

Ecclesiastes

9:4-5, 10	295

Song of Solomon

1:3	150, 151
6:8	150

Isaiah

1:	20, 27
1:1-9	95ff
1:1	38, 40, 67, 72, 81, 136
1:1-31	96
1:2	277
1:4	42, 65
1:9	70
1:10	41
1:10-17	30, 103ff
1:11	66
1:15b	64
1:18-20	106ff
1:18	66
1:21-23	107ff
1:24	77
1:24-27	109ff
1:28-31	110ff
1:29-30	197
2:1-3	77
2:1	113ff
2:2-4	34, 44, 63, 64 113ff, 163, 195, 211, 240
2:2, 4	62
2:2-5	35
2:5	116ff
2:6-11	117ff
2:8-9	61
2:9	20
2:12-22	118ff
2:12	193
2:13	197
3:1-15	120ff
3:4	78
3:6	125
3:12	168
3:15	269
3:16-17	42
3:16-4:1	123ff
3:16-26	268
3:24-26	58
4:1	193
4:2-6	125ff
4:5	77, 139
4:6	77
5:1-3	14
5:1-6	245
5:1-7	26, 127ff
5:1-30	193
5:3-4	43
5:5-6	58
5:7	26
5:8-10	129
5:8-23	129ff
5:11-17	130ff
5:18-19	131ff
5:19	64, 65
5:20	78, 132
5:21	132
5:22-23	132
5:24	65
5:24-25	133ff
5:26-30	134
5:26	155, 192
5:26-27	201
5:30	161
6:1-4	135ff
6:1	23, 39, 69, 72, 136
6:5	15, 20, 109, 181
6:5a	117
6:5-8	139ff
6:8	23, 228
6:9-10	69, 136, 141ff
6:9-13	39
6:10	75, 280
6:11-13	142ff
6:13	71, 77, 197
7:1-6	281
7:1-2	145ff

Isaiah

7:3-9	146ff
7:3-25	31
7:3	37, 103, 147
7:9	26
7:10-17	148ff
7:12	294
7:14	146ff
7:18-25	154ff
8:1-3	37
8:1-4	156ff, 281
8:3	37
8:5-8	157ff, 210
8:9-10	158
8:10	153
8:11-15	158
8:16-18	158ff
8:18	37, 77
8:19-20	11
8:19-22	159ff
9:1	160ff
9:2-7	161ff
9:5-6	77
9:6	177, 181
9:6-7	152, 153, 219
9:7	62
9:8-10:4	166ff
9:10	197
9:20	185
10:5	263
10:5-7	210
10:5-13	77
10:5-16	271
10:5-19	170ff
10:9	284
10:12-19	190
10:13	65
10:18	197
10:20-27	176ff
10:20	65
10:20-22	77
10:21	165
10:21-22	103
10:23	70
10:24-26	210
10:28-34	178ff
11:1-5	61, 152, 180ff
11:1-9	45
11:1-10	77, 153, 267
11:1	61, 65, 127, 152, 184
11:6-9	62, 64, 182ff
11:10-16	183ff
11:10	192
11:11, 16	103
12:1-6	185ff
12:6	65
13:1	57, 190
13:1-22	190ff
13:6	77
13:9	77
13:11-13	77
13:13	273
13:14	65
13:17-22	58
13:19	57
13:19-20	22
13:20-22	278
14:1-2	194ff
14:3-23	195ff
14:4	57
14:7	60
14:4-17	300
14:21	64
14:22	57
14:24-27	199ff
14:28-32	200ff
15:1-9	202ff
16:1-14	204ff
17:1-14	208ff
17:7	65, 197
18:1-7	210ff
18:3	192
19:1-15	213ff
19:16-25	216ff
19:24-25	43
20:	26
20:1-6	219ff
20:1	281
20:2-6	38
21:1-10	220ff
21:9	57
21:11-12	223ff
21:13-17	224ff
22:1-14	225ff
22:1	11
22:4-5	42
22:12-13	42, 137
22:13	4, 74
22:15	281
22:15-25	229ff
23:1-14	231ff
23:15-18	233ff
24:1-23	235ff
24:10	65

Isaiah

24:23	65, 77
25:1-12	238ff
25:3	77
25:10	77
26:1-21	241ff
26:1	77
26:19	295
27:1-13	244ff
27:1	277
28:1-6	247ff
28:7-13	248ff
28:14-22	249ff
28:23-29	251ff
28:29	164
29:1-8	252ff
29:9-12	254
29:11-12	27
29:13	29, 69
29:13-14	255
29:14	132
29:15-24	255ff
29:18	66
29:19	65
29:21	65
29:23	65
30:1-7	257ff
30:8	27
30:8-17	259
30:9-10	41
30:10	17
30:11	65
30:12	65
30:15	65
30:16	41
30:18-26	260ff
30:22	43
30:27-33	262ff
30:31	75
31:1, 3, 6	75
31:1	65
31:1-3	264ff
31:4-5	265
31:5	77
31:6-9	265ff
31:7	43
32:1-8	266ff
32:6	77
32:9-20	267ff
32:11-14	58
32:15	197
33:1-12	270ff
33:10	66

33:13-24	272ff
33:24	280
34:1	65
34:1-2	45
34:11	65
34:1-17	275ff
34:16	27
35:1-10	279ff
35:1	60
35:2	64
35:10	60
36:1-22	282ff
36:4-21	171
36:14-21	174
36:22	231
37:1-38	285ff
37:2	231
37:23	65
37:36-38	99, 212
38:1	296
38:1-22	291ff
38:7-8	68
38:14	64
39:1	57
39:1-8	296ff
39:3	57
39:5-8	67
39:6	57
39:6-8	58, 190
39:7	57
40:1	66, 68, 280
40:1-2	57
40:3	69
40:3-5	69
40:5	64
40:12-18	60, 61
40:16	59
40:17	65
40:18-20	62
40:23	65
40:25	66
40:28	60
41:14	65, 68
41:15	60
41:16	65
41:18	60
41:19	197
41:20	65
41:23	64
41:23-25	56
41:26	64
41:29	65
42:1	69

313

Isaiah

42:1-4	52, 64
42:14	61
42:18	66
42:19	66
43:3	65
43:9a	65
43:14	57, 65
43:14-15	55
43:17	64
43:23a	59
44:9	65
44:12-19	62
44:21	66
44:23	60
44:26	57, 58
44:28	22
45:1	22
45:4	55, 69
45:11	65
45:18	65
46:5-7	62
47:1	233
47:4	65
48:3	68
48:5a	68
48:6	68
48:15	60
48:17	65
49:1-6	52, 61
49:4	65
49:7	65
50:4-9	52, 61
50:15	60
50:28	60
51:4	63
51:6	60
51:9	258
51:11	60
52:7	65
52:10	195
52:11a	57
52:13	61, 62, 274n
52:13-53:12	52
53:1-13	62
53:1	69, 70, 132, 251, 289
53:4	69
53:6	65
53:7-8	70
53:12	61
54:2-5	195
54:5	65
55:1	187
55:4-5	35
55:5	65, 195
55:126	183
55:13	197
56:7	115
56:8	61
57:20-21	116
59:3	64
59:11	64
59:20	60
60:1-22	62
60:9	65
60:14	65
60:21	65
61:1-3	61, 68, 69
61:10	60
62:5	60
62:6a	57
63:6	65
63:16b	165
65:1	70
65:8	60
65:9	61
65:12	64
65:17-25	62, 303
65:25	64, 183
66:3	59
66:4	64
66:9	66
66:10-12	110
66:19	61
66:18	64
66:22	303

Jeremiah

1:4-10	136
1:4-19	11
1:10	29
2:13	187
4:19-22	14
7:1-2	27
7:4-16	30
7:31	263
9:25-26	30, 301
17:13	187
18:9	21
20:9	12
23:5-6	126
23:9-33	15, 17
26:13	21
30:	27

Jeremiah

30:2	27
32:18	165
33:15	126
40:7	74
40:39	190
41:5	74
43:8, 13	22
44:4-6	4
44:24-30	22
48:2	241n
50:15, 28	60
50:16	190
50:29	139
51:5	139
51:6, 11	60
51:13	222

Ezekiel

1:1-28	136
1:28	12
3:16-17	12
3:22	24
16:49	104
17:1, 2	27
17:1-10	26
28:2-15	301
29:19-30	22
30:10	22
31:17-18	60
32:11	22
32:20	60
32:22	60
32:25	60
32:28	60
32:32	60
33:30-33	27
36:16-24	303
36:25	187
36:27	24
37:10	303
39:4	275

Daniel

2:2	17
12:1	127

Hosea

1:1-2	136
1:2-3	26
1:6-9	26
2:19-20	127
4:15	217
6:6	30
10:12	264

Joel

1:8	151
2:23	264

Amos

1:1	11
3:7	23
3:8	13
5:10	14
5:21-25	31
7:10-13	98
7:11	14
7:14-15	12
8:1-2	27
9:14	58

Micah

1:2	138
4:1-3	44
4:1-4	113ff, 195
4:10	58
6:6-8	30

Nahum

2:12, 13	173
3:1, 7	173

Habakkuk

2:2	27

Zephaniah

1:7-8	275
2:14-15	275

Zechariah

3:8	126
6:12	126
8:2-23	195
9:6	201
13:14	220

Malachi

3:1	152

(b) THE APOCRYPHA

Ecclesiasticus

48:25-28	68

(c) NEW TESTAMENT

Matthew

1:5-6	203
1:21	38, 187
1:23	150
3:3	69

Matthew

3:4	220
5:5	243
5:11-12	35
5:17	31
8:17	69
9:36	165
11:13	32
11:20-23	22
11:21	129
12:17-18	69
13:	26
13:4	69
14:1-11	32
15:7-8	69
15:8-9	29
21:13	115
23:13-20	129
23:23	106
23:34	33
23:37a	14
28:19	302

Mark

1:2-3	69
7:6	69
7:9-13	31
16:15	302

Luke

1:35	151
1:42-45	32
1:46-55	32
1:67-79	32
2:36-38	32
3:3-7	32
3:4	69
4:17	69
6:24-26	129
9:51-53	74
15:11-32	263n
19:9-10	187
19:41-44	227
24:44	34
24:47	302

John

1:1-14	181
1:8	36
1:14	153
1:18	137
1:23	69
1:29	32
2:25	181
3:5	187

4:9	74
4:14	187
4:24	34
7:40	33
8:48	74
10:16	302
12:38	69
12:39	69
12:40	69
12:41	69, 138
12:49	24

Acts

1:8	302
8:28-33	70
8:30-31	299
8:31	7
11:27-28	33
17:28	13
21:8-9	33
26:19	143

Romans

1:18-22	237
2:11-14	173
6:23b	111
8:21-22	183
8:22	237
9:4-5	302
9:24	302
9:27	70
9:29	70
10:16	70
10:20	70
11:5	71, 143
11:12	246
11:18, 20	98
11:21	301, 303
11:26	177

I Corinthians

1:27	132
2:14	6, 300
9:16	12
11:4-5	33
12:28	28
14:3	33
14:4	33
14:29-33	33
14:30	33
14:32-33	24
14:37	34
15:54-57	240

Galatians

3:28	302
6:7	122
6:16	302

Ephesians

2:	301, 302
2:19-22	302
6:12	238
6:14-15	182

Philippians

2:7	138

Colossians

1:15-19	25

II Timothy

3:16	28

Hebrews

11:37	40

James

5:16	293

I Peter

1:10-11	302
1:10-12	154
5:5	300

II Peter

1:19-20	303
2:	303

Revelation

1:1	96
13:8	127
14:8	199
18:2	223
21:1-4	303
21:4	240

Bibliography

Albright, William Foxwell — Archeology and the Religion of Israel. Baltimore, The Johns Hopkins Press, 1942.

Alcalay, Reuben — Complete English — Hebrew Dictionary. 4v. (Tel Aviv, 1959-61)

Alexander, Joseph Addison — Commentary on the Prophecies of Isaiah, 1846. Grand Rapids, Zondervan Publishing House, 1953.

Barnes, Albert — Notes on the Book of the Prophet Isaiah, 2v. New York, 1840.

Brenton, Sir Lancelot Lee — The Septuagint, Greek and English.

Burrows, Millar — The Dead Sea Scrolls. N.Y., Viking, 1955.

Burrows, Millar — The Dead Sea Scrolls of St. Marks Monastery. New Haven, American Schools of Oriental Research, 1950.
V.I — The Isaiah Manuscript and the Habakkuk Commentary.

Delitzsch, Franz — Biblical Commentary on the Prophecies of Isaiah. 1866. Grand Rapids, Eerdmans, 1949.

Douglas, James Dixon, ed. — The New Bible Dictionary. Consulting editors F. F. Bruce (others). (Inter-Varsity Fellowship) Grand Rapids, Eerdmans, (c1962).

Drechsler, Moritz — Der Prophet Jesaiah. Stuttgart, 1849.

Driver, Samuel Rolles — Isaiah, His Life and Times and the Writings which Bear His Name. N.Y., Fleming H. Revell Company, (1888).

Duhm, Bernard — Das Buch Jesaia. Göttingen, 1922.

Edersheim, Alfred — Prophecy and History in Relation to the Messiah; the Warburton Lectures for 1880-1884, London, Longmans, Green and Co., 1885.

Ellison, Harry L. — Men Spake from God; studies in the Hebrew Prophets. Grand Rapids, Eerdmans, (c1958).

Ewald, George H. A. — Commentary on the Prophets of the Old Testament, 5v. William & Nortgate, 1876.

Free, Joseph Paul — Archaeology and Bible History. Wheaton, Ill., Van Kampen Press, (c1950).

Gaster, Theodor Herzl—The Dead Sea Scriptures, Garden City, N.Y., Doubleday, 1956.

Harrison, Roland Kenneth — A History of Old Testament Times. Grand Rapids, Zondervan Publishing House, 1955.

Harrison, Roland Kenneth — Introduction to the Old Testament, Grand Rapids, Eerdmans, 1969.

Heschel, Abraham — The Prophets. The Jewish Publication Society of Philadelphia, 1962.

Jennings, Frederick Charles — Studies in Isaiah. N.Y., Loizeaux Bros., 1959.

Jocz, Jakob — The Spiritual History of Israel. London, Eyre & Spottiswoode, 1961.

Kaufmann, Yechezkel — The Religion of Israel from Its Beginnings to the Babylonian Exile. Translated and abridged by Moshe Greenberg. Chicago, University of Chicago Press, (1966, c 1960).

Kimchi, David — The Commentary of David Kimchi on Isaiah, edited by Louis Finkelstein (Columbia University Oriental Studies. V. XIX). N.Y., Columbia University Press, 1926.

Kissane, Edward J. — The Book of Isaiah, translated from a critically revised Hebrew text with Commentary by Rev. Edward J. Kissane, Dublin, Browne and Nolan, Limited, 1941-43.

Kittel, Rudolf — Gestalten und Gedanken in Israel, Leipzig, Quelle & Meyer, (Vorwort, 1925).

Klausner, Joseph — The Messianic Idea in Israel, London, G. Allen and Unwin, (1956).

König, Edward — Hebraisches und Aramaisches Wörterbuch zum Alten Testament, Leipzig, Dieterich, 1931.

Kramer, Samuel Noah — History Begins at Sumer. Anchor Books, 1959.

Margalioth, Rachel — The Indivisible Isaiah, N.Y., Yeshiva University, 1964.

Marti, Karl. — Das Buch Jesiah. Tübingen, 1900.

Owen, George Frederick — Archeology and the Bible. Westwood, N.J., Revell, (c1960).

Pfeiffer, Charles Franklin — ed. The Biblical World: a Dictionary of Biblical Archaeology, Grand Rapids, Baker Book House, 1966.

Pfeiffer, Charles Franklin — Introduction to the Old Testament.

Silver, Abba H. — Messianic Speculation in Israel. Beacon Press, 1927.

Skinner, J. — Isaiah (in the Cambridge Bible) 2v. 1896. Cambridge University Press, 1963. .

Smith, George Adam — The Book of Isaiah, Harper & Brothers, 1927.

Slotki, I. W.—Isaiah (Soncino Bible). 1949.

Thiele, Edwin Richard — The Mysterious Numbers of the Hebrew Kings. Rev. Ed. Grand Rapids, Eerdmans, (c1965).

Thompson, John Arthur — The Bible and Archaeology. Grand Rapids, Eerdmans, (c1962).

Unger, Merrill Frederick — Archeology and the Old Testament. Grand Rapids, Zondervan Publishing House, (1956, 1954).

Wright, George Ernest — Biblical Archaeology. Philadelphia, Westminster Press, (1957).

The Wycliffe Bible Commentary — edited by Charles F. Pfeiffer and Everett F. Harrison. Chicago, Moody Press, c1962.

Young, Edward Joseph — My Servants the Prophets. Grand Rapids, Eerdmans, 1954.

Young, Edward Joseph — Studies in Isaiah. Grand Rapids, Eerdmans, 1956.

Young, Edward Joseph — Who Wrote Isaiah? (Pathway Book) Grand Rapids, Eerdmans, 1958.

Young, Edward Joseph — The Book of Isaiah. 3v. Grand Rapids, Eerdmans, 1965-70.

The Prophet Isaiah

Victor Buksbazen

ISAIAH 40-66

The Book of Consolation

Introduction To Isaiah Part II

Jewish Tradition Concerning the Book of Isaiah

From the earliest times Jewish tradition assumed that the book of Isaiah was written by the prophet Isaiah, the son of Amoz, in accordance with the statement in Isaiah 1:1.

The Babylonian Talmud (6th century A.D.), drawing upon ancient tradition, records:

"Hezekiah and his company wrote Isaiah, Proverbs, the Song of Songs and Ecclesiastes" Baba Bathra 15a.

Here the term "wrote" is used in the sense of "copying," as in Proverbs 25:1.

"These also are the proverbs of Solomon, which the men of Hezekiah, king of Judah, copied."

Likewise ancient rabbinical literature quotes hundred of references from both parts of Isaiah without making any distinction between them. The apocryphal book of Ecclesiasticus, composed around 180 B.C. by Jesus ben Sirach strongly alludes to the unity of Isaiah in the following passage:

And Hezekiah did what was pleasing to the Lord and was strong in the ways of David, his father, which Isaiah the great prophet and faithful in the sight of God had commanded him. In his days the sun went back (cf. Isa. 38:8, also 2 Ki. 20:9-11).

With a great spirit he saw the things that are to come to pass at last and comforted the mourners in Zion (see Isa. 40:1-2). He showed what should come to pass and saw things before they came. Ecclesiasticus 48:25-28 (cf. Isa. 44:28, 45:1-4).

In the Septuagint version of Isaiah, which was begun in the third century and finished in the second century B.C., the Greek text appears as one book without any hiatus between chapters 39 and 40.

Likewise in the two manuscripts of Isaiah (IQ Isa.ᵃ and IQ

Isa.^b) found among the Dead Sea Scrolls, which date back to approximately the end of the second century B.C. there is no break between the first and second parts of the book.

It is apparent that already then the book of Isaiah was viewed as one complete entity and must have been considered as such for many centuries before the Qumran Community.

In the Gospel of Luke 4:16 ff., we read that Jesus came to the synagogue in Nazareth where he was given the book of Isaiah to read and He found the passage where it is written "The Spirit of the Lord God is upon me" (Isa. 61:1). The authorship of Isaiah was taken for granted by Jesus Himself and by the synagogue congregation.

Repeatedly our Lord and His apostles referred to the whole of Isaiah as one book (Mt. 3:3, 4:14, 12:17, Lk., 3:4, 4:16 ff., John 12:38-39, Rom. 10:16, 20).

Obviously nobody ever heard or knew in those days about a "Second or Third Isaiah."

It is interesting to note that Ezra the Scribe, (chapter 2) while listing all the people who were carried off by Nebuchadnezzar into captivity (including their horses and mules) mentions only the prophets Haggai and Zechariah, without ever mentioning an unknown, but outstanding prophet such as the writer of chapters 40-66 undoubtedly was.

After the Babylonian exile, under the influence of the kindred languages of Aramaic and Chaldean, a gradual deterioration of the Hebrew language set in.

Yet in the second part of Isaiah we have the most perfect and beautiful form of the Hebrew language extant. This is also true of the earlier writings of Isaiah.

It was only in the past two centuries that it became fashionable among some Old Testament scholars to question the genuine Isaianic origin of chapters 40-66.

Since we have already dealt with this matter in some detail in our introduction to the first volume of this study, we shall now recapitulate briefly the arguments of the critical school against Isaiah's authorship of the whole book, and see why we consider these arguments untenable.

The question concerning the authorship of chapters 40-66 of Isaiah was first seriously raised by J. C. Doederlein in 1775. He and a number of other scholars (J. B. Koppe, J. G. Eichhorn) contended that the second part of Isaiah was a collection of prophetic utterances written by an unknown prophet who lived in Babylon toward the end of the exile. This theory was finally developed into its present form by Bernard Duhm (1898), the disciple of J. Wellhausen (1844-1918), the famous co-author of the so-called Graff-Wellhausen hypothesis about the origins of the Old Testament.

Wellhausen considered the Pentateuch as a conglomerate of several independent sources known as the Jahvistic (J), 9th century B.C., the Elohistic source (E) 8th century B.C., the book of Deuteronomy which he assigned to the times of king Josiah (640-609 B.C.), and the Priestly Code (5th century B.C.). According to Wellhausen's speculations, which in time became the dominant theory of textual criticism, all the above mentioned sources were compiled into our Pentateuch, or the Five Books of Moses, around the year 350 B.C. Recent archeological discoveries, especially the Qumran Documents, have made the Graff-Wellhausen theory untenable.

Bernard Duhm, the faithful disciple of his master, applied Wellhausen's method to the book of Isaiah and by means of a series of highly speculative assumptions and "emendations" of the Massoretic text, reached the conclusion that Isaiah 56-66 was the work of "an unknown prophet" of the post-exilic period, the Third or Trito-Isaiah, who, according to Duhm, wrote these last eleven chapters, perhaps as late as 457-445 B.C.

In addition, Duhm pronounced certain sections of "First Isaiah" (ch. 13, 14, 23, 24-27, etc.) as having originated with "the second or third Isaiah," mainly because of their predictive nature, or because, according to Duhm, they did not fit in, in what he assumed to be Isaiah's theology.

Today the speculative assumptions of Bernard Duhm are almost universally accepted by liberal theologians. Anyone who does not subscribe to their theories is considered intellectually backward and hardly deserving of being considered "a scholar."

By the time Duhm and his followers were through with the dissection of the book, little was left upon which the critics could agree that it truly came down to us from the great prophet Isaiah himself. What one scholar considered "genuine," the other called "spurious."

What were the arguments of the critical school against the authenticity of Chapters 40:66? These arguments may be divided into three groups.

1. Arguments supposedly based on internal evidence.
2. Arguments based on the supposed difference in language and style between chapters 1-39 and 40-66.
3. Arguments based on the supposed difference of theological ideas.

1 The Internal Evidence.

Much was made by the critical school of the fact that Cyrus of Persia (538-530 B.C.), the liberator of the Jews from their captivity in Babylon in 538 B.C., was twice mentioned by name in Isaiah 44:28 and 45:1. How, the critics ask, could the prophet Isaiah have mentioned by name a king who was yet to be born some two centuries later? Such a prediction, according to these critics, was unparalleled in the Scriptures.

However, such predictive prophecy is not an isolated case in the Old Testament.

In 1 Kings 13:1-2 an unnamed man of God predicted to Jeroboam that in the distant future a Davidic king would be born and would be called Josiah. He would burn the bones of those who offered incense on pagan altars. Three centuries later this prophecy was fulfilled (2 Ki. 23:15-16).

There are numerous other predictions in the Old Testament, which were later fulfilled just as the prophets predicted.

Underlying this and similar arguments of the critics is their rejection of predictive prophecy as *"vaticinia post eventu,"* that is predictions inserted into the Scriptures, after the predicted event already happened.

Another argument against Isaiah's authorship of chapters 40-66, advanced by the critics is that the whole orientation of the second part of Isaiah points to a man who supposedly lived in the Babylonian Exile and not in Palestine.

And yet this argument has no real foundation in the second part of Isaiah, and is based mainly on speculation or guesswork.

There is nothing in chapters 40-66 which could not have been written in Palestine. Already in the earlier parts of Isaiah there are prophecies which predict the future captivity of Judah and, of course, of Samaria, as if it were already an accomplished fact (Isa. 1:7-9, 5:13, 14:1-4, 35:1 ff.). In Chapters 40-66 Isaiah assumes an ideal and prophetic standpoint and sees the captivity as already completed.

Yet the prophet does not indicate in any detail that he was personally acquainted with Babylon, or with the life of the captives, as for instance Ezekiel did. Babylon is more frequently mentioned in chapters 1-39 (9 times) than it is in chapters 40-66 (4 times).

There are positive indications that the author of chapters 40-66 apparently lived in Jerusalem and not in Babylon.

In chapter 40:1 he addresses himself to the people who are in Jerusalem and Zion.

In 52:11 the prophet admonishes his people to leave Babylon, saying "Depart ye, depart ye, go ye out from there."

The Hebrew word "*mee-sham*"—"from there," suggests that the prophet's geographical location was a considerable distance from Babylon.

In 62:6, the watchmen on the walls of Jerusalem are mentioned.

It would be hard to understand why the so-called Second or Third Isaiah should have so vehemently denounced Canaanite idolatry long after that practice ceased to be a live issue (Isa. 40:19, 41:7, 29, 57:5, 63:3 ff., 66:3, 17).

The internal evidence tends to support the view that Isaiah, and not some unknown prophet of the exile was the author of both the first and second parts of Isaiah.

2 The Difference in Style and Language.

It is notoriously difficult to disprove the authenticity of a book based on difference of style or vocabulary.

One must analyze all the works of a writer, without assuming in advance that certain parts of his literary heritage were not his. We know that Isaiah wrote more than what has survived in the book of Isaiah, which apparently is an anthology in two parts of his various spoken and written prophecies. The prophet himself or some of his disciples (8:16, 28:9) may have selected such prophetic utterances as were representative of Isaiah's ministry.

R. K. Harrison in his *Introduction to the Old Testament* points out:

"In antiquity it was not uncommon for books to be produced in two parts, a practice which H. St. John Thackeray attributes to the need for convenience in handling the scrolls. There is also good evidence for the contention that literary works of high caliber were frequently so planned as to yield to a natural division in the material about the middle of the work."[1]

It should be remembered that Isaiah apparently lived a long life. According to tradition he was killed by wicked king Manasseh, 686-641 B.C. during his reign of terror (2 Ki. 21:6). Accordingly his prophetic ministry covered a period of more than half a century (740-685 B.C.).

It would be reasonable to assume that during such a long time his style and vocabulary would develop and mature, reflecting his spiritual growth, the rich experiences and the new insight which the prophet gained in the course of a long and active life.

It would indeed be strange that a man at the age of seventy or eighty should express himself exactly the same way as when he was thirty or forty years old. And yet a careful analysis of Isaiah shows a striking similarity or even identity in style and vocabulary throughout the whole book.

Here are a few examples:

The Holy One of Israel: The key designation of God is common to both parts of Isaiah. In chapters 1-39 it appears twelve times. In chapters 40-66, thirteen times. The formula "The Holy One of Israel" is peculiar to Isaiah and appears only twice in Jeremiah (50:29, 51:5), in passages believed to have been influenced by Isaiah.

The LORD will say:

In Hebrew "*Yomar Yehovah*"—future.

This formula is peculiar to Isaiah and is used in both parts of his book (1:11, 1:18, 33:10, 40:1, 40:25, 41:21, 66:9).

I made it . . . I fashioned it.

(37:26, 43:7, 46:11), No parallel in other prophetic writings.

A highway

(11:16, 19:23, 35:8, 40:3, 62:10).

Peace . . . Righteousness (*Shalom, Tsedakah*)

This combination appears only in Isaiah (32:17, 48:18, 60:17).

These and similar examples of usage peculiar to Isaiah only could be multiplied in the hundreds.[2]

The prophet Isaiah seems to have had a special fondness of repeating certain words or phrases for emphasis. This is fairly common in both parts of the book (21:11, 24:16, 28:10, 13, 29:1, 40:1, 51:9, 12, 52:6, 57:19).

3 The Differences in Theological Ideas.

The holiness and majesty of God are common and are strongly emphasized in both parts of Isaiah (1:14, 5:16, 6:3, 10:17, 30:15, 27-31, 35:5, 37:23, 41:14, 43:5, 45:11, 46:9-10, etc.).

The critical school points to the fact that in the earlier portions of Isaiah the Redeemer of Israel appears as the Messianic King (9:6-7, 11:1-5), while in the second part of the book he is repeatedly called the Servant of God (42:1-7, 49:7, 52:13, 53:1-12).

Although the idea of the Messianic King is predominant in the earlier prophecies of Isaiah, yet the same idea reappears in chapter 55:3-4, while the idea of the Servant of God is not completely absent in the first part of Isaiah (22:10-25).

One of the alleged arguments against the unity of Isaiah is the supposed absence of the idea of a remnant in the second part of Isaiah, so conspicuous in the first part (4:2, 6:13, 10:20-22). Yet the thought of a remnant is also imbedded in 40-66 (56:8, 65:9, 66:19-20).

It is significant that in chapters 40-66 the prophet denounces certain idolatrous practices typical of the pre-exilic Canaanite cults (40:19, 41:7, 29, 65:3). It would be a strange thing for a prophet, who according to the critics lived during the Babylonian exile, or even later, when these particular practices no longer existed and were no longer an issue, to denounce them.[3]

It would also be most astounding that a prophet of such an exalted stature, who left a legacy of the most lofty prophetic visions and oracles, should have been completely unknown among his own generation, and completely forgotten by posterity.

It is even more unthinkable that the Jews, who guarded with such great zeal their sacred writings, should include in the canon of their Holy Scriptures the writings of "an unknown prophet" (or prophets), as Duhm and his following would have us believe.

In view of all this, we can only conclude that the arguments of the liberal critics remain unconvincing and unproven.[4]

Jewish tradition, Jesus Himself, His apostles, and the early Church attributed the whole book to Isaiah the son of Amoz.

The Division and Contents of Isaiah Part 2

The twenty-seven chapters of Isaiah part 2 are a series of messages of comfort and promises of deliverance. This part of the book can be readily divided into three equal sections, of nine chapters each. The first two end with a stern warning to the unrepentant: "There is no peace, says my God, to the wicked" (Isa. 48:22; 57:21).

The third section also ends with an ominous warning to the wicked (66:24).

The major theme of the first section (ch. 40-48) is the comforting prediction of the approaching deliverance from the Babylonian exile, through God's chosen instrument, Cyrus, the king of Persia.

The omnipotence and omniscience of Jehovah is compared with the helplessness and futility of the pagan idols.

Both national Israel and a certain individual personality, are called "the servant of Jehovah." However, Israel is described as "the deaf and blind servant" who had failed to accomplish the task which Jehovah entrusted to him. The individual servant of Jehovah is always well pleasing to Him and carries out His will. This servant is the mediator of the new covenant with Israel and brings light to the nations of the world.

In the second section (chapters 49-57) an even more glorious spiritual redemption is envisioned. Here the central figure is "the servant of the Lord," who by his suffering and vicarious death, described in chapter 53, the center of the second part of Isaiah, brings redemption to His people and to mankind.

In the third section, chapters 58-66, the universal message of redemption reaches a majestic climax. The repentant and regenerated remnant of Israel will finally become a blessing to the nations of the world, and Jerusalem will be the spiritual center of all nations. The vision of a new Jerusalem where there shall be "no sound of weeping, or cry of distress" blends with the vision of a new heaven and a new earth (Isa. 65:17-19 and 66:18-23). At this point Old Testament prophecy reaches its glorious climax. It was later beautifully amplified by John in Revelation 21:1-4.

NOTES:
1. R. K. Harrison, *op. cit.* p. 787.
2. For a detailed analysis of the vocabulary and style of Isaiah, see *The Indivisible Isaiah*, by Rachel Margalioth, Yeshivah University, N. Y., 1964.
3. Rachel Margalioth, *op. cit.* page 187.
4. Dr. Yehuda Radday of the Technion Institute in Haifa, Israel recently obtained his Ph.D. at the University of Jerusalem for a thesis on Isaiah in which computers were used "proving" that "First Isaiah" and "Second Isaiah" were written by two different persons. However, computers can work only on the data fed into them. In this case the programmer not only assumed that there were two "Isaiahs," but that one of them wrote chapters 1-39 and the other (or others), the remainder of the book. This is known in logic as "begging the question," when the proof "confirms" your basic assumption. Had the programmer assumed the essential unity of Isaiah, although written in two parts, the results would have been completely different. The computerized technique is not a serious contribution to the study of the book of Isaiah.

Isaiah, Chapter 40

Jehovah, the Omnipotent Creator of the Universe Assures His People that the Hour of Their Deliverance Has Arrived

Verses 1-11   The Prologue—a proclamation of deliverance.

1   Comfort you, comfort you, my people,
    Says your God.

2   Speak to the heart of Jerusalem
    And proclaim to her,
    That her bondage is completed,
    That her guilt is paid up,

That she has received from the LORD's hand
A double measure for all her sin.

3 A voice is calling:
Prepare a way for the LORD in the wilderness,
Make straight in the desert a highway for our God.

4 Every valley shall be lifted up,
And every mountain and hill shall be made low;
And the rugged places shall become level,
And the rough ranges a plain.

5 And the glory of the LORD shall be revealed,
And all flesh shall see it together,
For the mouth of the LORD has spoken.

6 A voice says: "Cry"
And he said: "What shall I cry?"
All flesh is grass, and its beauty as the flower of the field;

7 The grass withers, the flower fades,
Because the breath of the LORD blows upon it,
Truly the people is grass,

8 The grass withers, the flower fades,
But the word of God endures for ever.

9 Get thee up on a high mountain,
O Zion, herald of good tidings!
Lift up thy voice with strength,
O Jerusalem, proclaimer of good tidings!
Lift up thy voice, be not afraid;
Say to the cities of Judah:
"Behold your God!"

10 Behold, the Lord God shall come with might,
And his right arm will rule for him.
Behold, his reward is with him,
And his recompense before him.

11 Like a shepherd he will feed his sheep,
And will gather up in his arms his lambs,
He will carry them in his bosom,
And lead the ewes to the water.

Comment:

1 Comfort you, comfort you, my people!

Some commentators have suggested that these words constituted a call to an unknown prophet of the exile, similar to the call of Isaiah described in chapter 6. However, the very fact that the Hebrew verb *"nahamu"*—"comfort you" is in plural, contradicts such an assumption. The speaker appears to be the Lord Himself, who addresses Himself through His prophet to the faithful remnant of Israel.

The twice repeated "comfort you, comfort you" is for the purpose of emphasis, and is characteristic of Isaiah's style, as we have already pointed out in our introduction to the second part of the book.

It is significant that in rabbinic literature, one of the Messiah's names is *"Menahem"*—the Comforter. This is reflected in the words of Jesus: "And I will pray to the Father and he shall give you another Comforter, that he may abide with you forever" (John 14:16).

"My people."

In spite of all their iniquities and repeated rebellion, God continues to look upon Israel as "my people." Thus the very opening words of chapter 40 "Comfort you, comfort you, my people" have Messianic overtones.

Says your God—Hebrew "Yomar eloheihem."

The verb *"yomar"* is in future tense (Davidson's Hebrew—Chaldean Dictionary), but is used as an imperfect tense, indicative of continued action. The form *"Yomar"*—"says," is peculiar to Isaiah and appears both in the first and second parts of the book (1:11, 1:18, 33:10, 40:1, 40:25, 66:9).

2 Speak to the heart of Jerusalem

The KJV translates this passage "speak ye comfortably to Jerusalem." The Hebrew text conveys great tenderness, expressing God's deep compassion for His people.

A double measure for all her sins

It is not God who exacts a double measure for Israel's sins, but the punishment is the tragic result of Israel's disobedience. However, now Israel's appointed time of bondage, (Hebrew *"tsevaah"*), is about to end. From now on God will again turn to His people in mercy.

3 A voice is calling

The prophet hears a voice. Usually the prophet "sees," he has "visions." This time he "hears," or has "an audition."

Prepare a way for the LORD in the wilderness.

The Lord Himself, is about to lead His people through wilderness and desert, from captivity to their homeland.

4 Every valley shall be lifted up and every mountain . . . shall be made low.

When God leads, every obstacle or hindrance which stands in

332

the way of His redeemed people is swept away. It should be noticed here that the theme of a safe God-prepared highway, echoing the exodus from Egypt, is common to both parts of the book of Isaiah (Isa. 11:16, 35:7-10, 40:3-4, 41:18-19, 42:15-16).

5 And the glory of the LORD shall be revealed.

Every mighty act of redemption manifests the glory of God.

all flesh shall see. . . .

All flesh is humanity in its physical aspect.

For the mouth of the LORD has spoken.

The prophet is perfectly sure that his prediction will come to pass, because he received the message from God Himself.

6-8 The transience of human life and the eternity of God's Word.

6 A voice says: "Cry" . . .

For the second time the prophet hears a voice commanding him to proclaim to his people, that from the standpoint of God, man is like the grass, or the desert flower, which blooms in the morning and withers away before the day is past. Only the Word of God abides for ever. In this eternal, unchanging and promise-keeping God, Israel can put absolute trust.

9-11 The prophet bids the faithful remnant of Israel, personified by the feminine figures of Zion and Jerusalem as the heralds of "good tidings," to declare to the cities of Judah the appearance of their God in power and majesty.

God is visualized in the dual character of a "Strong Man of War" and of a "Gentle Shepherd," who carries His little lambs in His bosom, and tenderly leads the mother ewes with their young to the streams of water. He is the God of history and also the God of gentle compassion and mercy. One is forcefully reminded of the beautiful Shepherd Psalm (23) and of the Good Shepherd, described in the Gospel of John 10:11ff.

12-20 The great Creator and Sustainer of the Universe is contrasted with the nothingness of nations and their idols.

12 Who has measured the waters in the hollow of his hands?
Or set the limits of heaven with a span?
Or who has gathered up the dust of the earth in a bushel,
And weighed the mountains on a balance,
And the hills on scales?

13 Who directed the Spirit of the LORD,
Or who was his counsellor to instruct him?

14 With whom did he consult to gain understanding
And who has taught him knowledge,
Or instructed him in the way of discernment?

15 Behold, the nations are as a drop of a bucket,
And no more than a speck of dust on the scales,
The islands are no more than fine dust

16 Lebanon is not enough for fuel,
And its beasts are insufficient for a burnt offering.

17 All the nations are as nothing before him,
He considers them as null and non-existent.

18 To whom then will you liken God
Or what form will you attribute to God?

19 Is it to the image which the craftsman makes,
And which the goldsmith covers with gold,
And the silversmith has fitted out with silver studs.

20 (Or is it with) A block of sturdy wood, which a man chooses
And finds a skillful craftsman to make an image,
Which will not topple over.

Comment:

12 Who has measured the waters in the hollow of his hands?

In a series of questions the prophet impresses upon his people the infinite magnitude and omnipotence of Jehovah, the Maker and Sustainer of heaven and earth.

13-14 God, and He alone, is the architect of the universe. He alone is the source and fountain of all wisdom and knowledge.

15-17 Behold the nations are as a drop of a bucket. . . .

Israel, so crushed and subjugated by powerful enemies, may feel that the pagan idols are more powerful than Jehovah. Because of this the prophet seeks to impress upon his people the omnipotence and infinite grandeur of their God. In His sight all those seemingly unconquerable nations are as nothing, a mere speck of dust on the scales.

18 To whom then will you liken God?

Obviously there can be no comparison.

19-20 Is it to the image which the craftsman has cast. . .

With supreme contempt the prophet describes the pitiful, manmade idols, cast by a craftsman and adorned by the art of the goldsmith and silversmith, or the wooden artifacts of the skilled carpenter.

21-26 The omnipotence and glory of Jehovah are further demonstrated from nature and history.

21 Do you not know, have you not heard.
    Has it not been told to you from the beginning,
    Have you not perceived this from the foundations of the earth,

22 That it is he who sits above the circle of the earth,
    Whose inhabitants are like grasshoppers?

23 He stretches out the heavens like a curtain,
    And spreads them out like a tent to dwell in it.

24 Who reduces the mighty to nothing,
    And the judges of the earth to extinction,
    Scarcely are they planted, scarcely sown,
    Scarcely has their stock taken root in the ground
    Than He blows upon them, and they wither away,
    And the whirlwind carries them off like chaff.

25 To whom then will you compare me that I might be his equal?

26 Lift up your eyes above and look at the stars, who created these?
    He leads them out one by one,
    And calls them by their name,
    Because of his great might and exceeding power
    Not one of them fails (in their appointed orbits).

Comment:

21-26 In words of superb beauty the prophet reinforces his argument that the whole universe, heaven and earth and the history of mighty men and nations bear testimony to the infinite power, wisdom and grandeur of God. In His sight great and mighty men are like grass which scarcely takes root in the soil, soon withers away and is carried off by the wind. God also rules by His power and wisdom the heavens and controls the stars and planets in their courses (v. 26).

27-31 Surely Israel can trust a God who is like Jehovah.

27 Why then do you say, O Jacob, and speak, O Israel:
    "My plight is hidden from the LORD,
    And my right is ignored by my God?"

28 Do you not know, have you not heard,
    That the eternal God, the Lord,
    The Creator of the ends of the earth,
    He does not tire, nor grow weary?
    His discernment is past searching out.

29 He gives power to the weary,
    And to him that has no might, he adds strength.

30 Though youth may faint and become weary,
   And choice young men may stumble and fall,

31 Yet they who wait upon the LORD
   Shall renew their strength,
   They shall mount up on wings like eagles,
   They shall run and not become weary,
   They shall walk and never tire.

Comment:

27 Seeing that the Lord is so omnipotent, so wise and yet so gracious, how can Jacob—Israel say, or even think, that God does not care about their plight, or about the vindication of their right?

28 Do you not know, have you not read. . .

From their own experience and long history, Israel ought to know that their God is never weary and never defeated. Only man cannot always understand His ways.

29 Not only is Jehovah never weary Himself, but He gives strength to those who are completely exhausted and without strength.

30-31 Even the finest young men become tired and exhausted, but they who wait upon the LORD shall renew their strength and soar up to great heights like the eagles. They shall run and not become weary. They shall walk and never become tired.

Here is one of the most beautiful promises given to those who put their trust in God. They shall forever renew their strength. They shall always rise above seeming defeat and soar up to lofty heights. God Himself will enable them to run their course, even where much younger and stronger men stumble and fall. Their secret is that "they wait upon the Lord." Jehovah Himself is the inexhaustible fountain of their strength.

Isaiah Chapter 41

The Destiny of All Nations is in the Hands of Jehovah

1-7 The nations are summoned to a dispute.

1 Be silent before me, O you coastlands,
  Let the peoples renew their courage,
  Let them draw near and then speak.
  Let us come together before the seat of judgment.

2 Who raised up from the east,
  The one whom victory follows in his footsteps?
  Who makes nations to submit to him and subdues kings?

He scatters them with his sword like dust,
And with his bow like driven chaff.

3 He pursues them and marches on safely,
Where no journeying man has ever set foot.

4 Who has done this, and brought this to pass?
Who has called the generations from the beginning?
I the LORD, I am the first,
And with the last of them—I am he.

5 The coastlands saw it and feared,
The ends of the earth trembled.

6 They drew near and came,
Everyone helped his neighbor,
Saying to his brother, "Courage!"

7 So the craftsman encouraged the goldsmith,
And he who smites the anvil with the hammer
Said to the welder: "This is just right!"
So he fastened it with nails,
That it should not topple over.

Comment:

1 Be silent before me, O, you coastlands.

Jehovah addresses himself to the inhabitants of the coastlands, adjoining the Mediterranean and summons them to a dispute. Before the Creator and Ruler of the earth they can only appear in awe-stricken silence. Having recovered from the shock of His Presence, He bids them to come together to the place of judgment.

2 Who raised up from the east. . .

The argument is based on a future historical event, which Jehovah is making known in advance. Yet for the prophet, that even is already an accomplished fact. "The man from the east" is Cyrus, later mentioned by name (44:28, 45:1). One of the main arguments against the Isaianic authorship of chapters 40-66 by the liberal critics is based on the assumption that prophecies which mention future historical personalities by name, are either "impossible" or without parallel in the prophetic writings. Furthermore an event which is still in the future would not carry any weight with the prophet's contemporaries.

However, the very fact of being able to predict future events before they ever come to pass, is used by the prophet as proof that Jehovah alone is omnipotent and omniscient, because whatever God declares, He also brings about.

Whom victory follows in his footsteps.

Here the Hebrew term for "victory" is *"tsedek"*—"righteousness," It is used in the sense of righteousness which defeats injustice and triumphs over wrong.

Who makes nations to surrender to him and subdues kings?

The questions which Jehovah asks the nations are calculated to make them think. It is an appeal to their rational faculties.

He scatters them with his sword like dust,
And with his bow like driven chaff.

Some commentators understand that the "he" of verses 2-3 refers to God Himself. Other apply the pronoun to Cyrus. In our context the latter view seems to be more satisfactory.

4 Who has done this and brought this to pass?

Jehovah asks the question and immediately answers it Himself.
It is I who call the generations from the beginning.

Jehovah alone, and not the pagan idols, presides over the destinies of the nations from the very beginning to the sunset of their history.

5 The inhabitants of the coastlands (lit. "islands") **saw it and feared. . .**

The appearance of "the man from the east" who swept nations and kingdoms before him caused great panic among the inhabitants of the Mediterranean, which are usually referred to as "the inhabitants of the coastlands." However, instead of seeing in these events the hand of God, the nations attributed their misfortunes to the displeasure of their idols. So they sought to remedy this by producing more idols. This the prophet describes with great scorn (v. 6-7).

7 So he fastened it with nail that it should not topple over.

What a ridiculous situation to seek help from "a god" who must be fastened down with nails, that he should not fall!

8-16 Israel the servant of Jehovah will triumph in the end.

8 But thou Israel, my servant,
Jacob, whom I have chosen,
The seed of Abraham my friend.

9 Of whom I have taken hold from the ends of the earth,
And called thee from its farthest parts,
And said unto thee: "Thou are my servant."
I have chosen thee and not cast thee off.

10 Fear thou not, for I am with thee,
Be not dismayed, for I am thy God.

I will strengthen thee, yes, I will help thee
I will surely uphold thee with my victorious right arm.

11 Behold they shall be ashamed and confounded
All they who are incensed against thee,
They shall be as nothing and perish, they who strive against thee.

12 Thou shalt look for those who assailed thee, but not find them.
They shall be completely as nothing, they who make war against thee.

13 For I the LORD thy God hold up thy right arm.
Who says to thee: "Fear not, I will help thee."

14 Fear not thou worm Jacob,
And thou handful of Israel, I will help thee,
Says the LORD, and thy redeemer, the Holy One of Israel.

15 Behold I will make thee a new sharpedged, threshing-sledge with many teeth.
Thou shalt thresh mountains and grind them small,
And turn hills into chaff.

16 Thou shalt winnow them and the wind shall carry them off.
And the whirlwind shall scatter them,
But thou shalt rejoice in the LORD.

Comment:

8-10 But thou Israel, my servant . . .

From His dispute with the worshippers of the worthless idols, Jehovah now turns to Israel. This whole passage breathes a spirit of great compassion and affection. God sees Israel not as they are in reality, but as He intends them to become. Israel is called "the servant of Jehovah" by virtue of His sovereign grace and election. This election is of an indelible character, and does not depend on Israel's merits or lack of them, but rather on God's own faithfulness and integrity. If Israel disobeys Him, their disobedience brings upon them disaster and punishment. Nevertheless they remain His servant and chosen people. In subsequent chapters we shall discuss more fully the position of Israel as "the servant of Jehovah."

8 The seed of Abraham my friend.

The election of Israel goes back to Abraham "who believed in the LORD and he counted it to him for righteousness" (Gen. 15:16). God called Abraham "my servant" (Gen. 26:24). Consequently the nation which sprung from him was also "the servant of God."

9 Of whom I have taken hold from the ends of the earth. . .

The prophet speaks from the geographical position of a Palestinian, to whom Ur of the Chaldees, the original home of Abraham was "the ends of the earth."

**10 Fear not for I am with thee,
    Be not dismayed for I am thy God.**

This promise is unsurpassed in tenderness and beauty. While it was spoken primarily to Israel it is always precious to every believing heart.

I will surely uphold thee with my victorious right arm.

The Hebrew word *"af"* used in this verse, is a strong affirmation which can be translated as "surely," "certainly," "yes," or "indeed."

"Victorious right arm" *"yemin tsidki."* Here *"tsedek,"* as in verse 2 describes that righteousness which triumphs over wrong and injustice, hence "victorious right arm."

11 Behold they shall be ashamed and confounded . . .

In Biblical speech the expression "ashamed and counfounded" conveys the thought that those who are against the people of God will eventually be utterly perplexed and frustrated when they see the disastrous results of their plans.

**14 Fear not thou worm Jacob, and thou handful of Israel,
    I will help thee, says the LORD.**

In this context the term "worm" expresses great compassion and tenderness for harassed and afficted Israel. How surprising to find that the New English Bible translates this:

"Fear not, Jacob you worm, and *Israel poor louse."*

Redeemer—Hebrew *"goel,"* a kinsman, who pays up the debt in order to redeem a near but impoverished relative, who was forced to sell himself or his property to satisfy a debt. (See Lev. 25:25, 32, 48, also Isa. 59:20).

15 Behold I will make thee a new, sharpedged threshing sledge. . .

Jehovah will not only redeem Israel from bondage but use her as His instrument to execute judgment against the nations which were hostile to Him. The strident language of the prophet may sound harsh, but taking into consideration the main tenor of the book of Isaiah, it must be interpreted to mean that the prophet looks forward to the spiritual triumph of redeemed Israel over her own and God's enemies. The prophesied victory is one of truth and justice.

17-20 The present distress of Israel

17 The poor and the needy seek water, but there is none.
    Their tongues are parched with thirst,

But I the LORD will answer them,
The God of Israel will not forsake them.

18 I will open rivers in barren heights,
And fountains in the midst of valleys.
I will turn the wilderness into a pool of water
And the dry land into springs of water.

19 I will plant in the wilderness
The acacia, the myrtle and the oil tree.
I will set in the desert the cypress,
Together with the fir and the box tree,

20 That they may see and know,
That they may take it to heart and understand,
That the hand of the LORD has done this
And the Holy One of Israel has brought it to pass,

Comment:

Speaking of Israel's approaching redemption, the prophet also foresees a transformation in nature. This may be understood either literally or figuratively, or even both simultaneously. In Isaiah 55 the prophet employs similar language. In both passages the transformation of nature is closely linked with the spiritual regeneration of the people. In both passages (41:20 and 55:13) this transformation is a striking testimony to the power and glory of God. Isaiah displays an unusual familiarity with, and love for trees. Seven different trees are mentioned in verse 19 (cf. Isa. 55:13).

21-29 The worthlessness of the idols.

21 Come forward with your plea,
Present your strongest arguments.
Says the king of Jacob.

22 Let them come forward and tell us
Let them explain to us the things that shall happen,
Tell us that we may consider and know their end,
Or announce to us what will happen in the future.

23 Declare to us the things that will come hereafter,
And we shall know that you are gods.
Do good or do evil, that we may be amazed,
And thoroughly dismayed.

24 But you are nothing,
And your work is of nought,
An abomination is he that chooses you.

25 I raised up one from the north and he came,

From the rising of the sun one that calls upon my name
He will come upon rulers as upon clay,
Even as a potter treads mortar.

26 Who declared this from the beginning, that we might know?
Or made known this that we could say "He is right!"
But there was none to declare, no one to predict,
None has heard your pronouncements!

27 As the first I said to Zion, "Behold, behold them!"
I give to Jerusalem a messenger of good tidings.

28 And when I looked, there was not a man,
There was not a counselor among them,
That when I asked a question, they might give an answer.

29 Behold all of them,
Their works are sheer vanity and nought,
Their molten images mere wind and chaos.

Comment:

21-24 Jehovah resumes the dispute of verses 1-4. This time the dispute is not with the pagan nations, but with their idols. If they are gods they ought to be able to predict future events, or at least to do something which is either good or bad. But they and their "deeds" are nothing and without any substance.

25-29 Jehovah alone has proven that He is indeed God by having raised up a man from the north and east, who at His command descended upon rulers and has trodden them down like clay. The reference is of course to Cyrus, who was born in Media (in the north) and later extended his reign to Persia and to all of the Babylonian empire. "North and east" in this context are geographical positions as seen from the standpoint of the land of Israel.

25 ... He will call upon my name...
Cyrus will recognize the sovereign rule of God. Chapter 45:4-5 repeats that for the sake of Israel, Jehovah called Cyrus by name before he ever knew the Lord.

26 Who declared this from the beginning?
The fact that the arrival upon the historical scene and the meteoric rise to power by Cyrus the Great was foretold by the prophet, is proof that Jehovah alone is the true God. It should be carefully noted that the prophet himself insists that his predictions were made long before the events ever came to pass, and so validates his authenticity as a true spokesman for the Lord.

27 I give to Jerusalem a messenger of good tidings.

In stark contrast to the pagan idols who cannot foretell the future nor do anything good or bad, Jehovah has sent a messenger of good tidings, who long before the event, predicted the deliverance of His people from the Babylonian exile (Isa. 11:10-16, 21:1-10, 35:10). The whole of Isaiah 13 was a prediction of the future defeat of the Babylonian empire at the hands of the Medians.

29 Behold all of them, their works are sheer vanity and nought...

Those words sum up the prophet's thought about the idols: "they and their idols are vanity and absolute chaos, similar to that which existed before God brought order into the primeval world."

Isaiah Chapter 42

The Servant in whom the Lord Delights Contrasted with the Blind and Deaf Servant

1-4 Jehovah's faithful and obedient servant

1 Behold my servant, whom I uphold,
My chosen one, in whom my soul delights,
I have put my spirit upon him,
That he may bring forth justice to the nations.

2 He will not shout aloud, nor lift up,
Nor make his voice to be heard in the street.

3 A bruised reed he will not break,
And the smouldering wick he will not crush.
But will bring forth true justice.

4 He will not fail nor falter,
Until he will have established justice on the earth,
And for his law the islands shall wait.

Comment:

1 Behold my servant

The identity of "the servant of Jehovah," has for many centuries been the subject of a heated controversy. In this passage "the servant" clearly appears to be an individual personality, chosen and appointed by Jehovah to bring salvation to Israel and to be a light to the nations. However, further in this chapter (v. 19 ff.), "the servant of Jehovah" is distinctly Israel as a people, about whom the Lord complains that they are blind and deaf, unfaithful and hard of understanding. Many Jewish and liberal Christian commentators have maintained that "the servant of Jehovah" always refers to Israel, either as a collective body, or to "ideal Israel," or to "a faithful remnant of Israel." Nevertheless the majority of the ancient Jewish scholars have interpreted Isaiah 42:1-4 and other related passages, as referring to the Messiah.

Thus, the Palestinian Targum, an ancient Aramaic paraphrase of the Old Testament, renders "Behold my servant" as "Behold, the Messiah my servant." The difficulty in the proper identification of "the servant" is due to the fact the same adjectives are often applied both to the servant as a people, and to the servant as a person. Delitzsch explains the seeming contradiction by comparing Israel to a pyramid, the base of which is the whole of Israel, the central part is the spiritual remnant and the apex is the personal mediator of salvation, the Messiah, who is destined to accomplish that which Jehovah intended Israel to be, but was not.[1]

Usually the context of the servant passages make it quite clear whether "the servant" is collective Israel or the individual representative of true Israel, the anointed mediator and saviour. In the second part of Isaiah there are four distinct Messianic "servant of the Lord" prophecies which apply to the person of the Messiah. These are Isaiah 42:1-7, 49-1-7, 50:4-11 and 52:13-53:12.

In addition Israel also is collectively referred to as the servant in 41:8-16, 42:18-21, 43:10, 44:1-5, and v. 21. It is important that we at all times distinguish between the two types of "the servant of the Lord" prophecies or songs, as they are sometimes called.

The New Testament consistently applies the Messianic servant passages to Jesus (Mt. 12:17-20, Lk. 2:32, 4:16-18, Acts 8:30-35).

In chapter 42:1-4, the servant of Jehovah is an individual personality, as in Isaiah 11:2, is endowed with the spirit of the Lord, and is called to establish true justice for all nations. The Messianic servant of the Lord is humble, unobtrusive and compassionate (v. 2). He does not crush the weak or the broken, but heals them (v. 3). He never wavers and is not crushed by His adversaries, nor by the enormity of His task, but will in the end accomplish His divinely appointed task (v. 4).

And for his law the islands shall wait.

The implied thought here is that in the hearts of all men there is an unconscious longing for the manifestation of God's eternal law, for His truth and justice, which the servant of the Lord will reveal to all nations.

The New Testament and the early church saw in the servant passages a unique prophecy concerning Christ, remarkably fulfilled in the person of Jesus. Most Jewish and liberal Christian scholars have generally applied all these passages to national Israel. However, this interpretation does violence to the obvious sense of the text.

5-7 The servant's task.

5 Thus says God who is Jehovah,
He who created the heavens and stretched them out,
Who spread out the earth and everything which grows out of it,
Who gives breath to the people that dwell upon it,
And the spirit to them who walk upon it.

6 I the Lord have called thee in righteousness,
I have taken hold of thy hand, I have kept thee,
And gave thee for a covenant to the people.

7 To open the blind eyes, to bring out the prisoners from the dungeon,
And from the prison house them who dwell in darkness.

Comment:

5-7 Thus says God who is Jehovah

With majestic solemnity Jehovah, the Creator and Sustainer of the universe, introduces His servant declaring that He has appointed Him to be a covenant to the people Israel and for a light to the nations. The servant of this passage is to be a covenant to the people. This is "the covenant of peace" mentioned in Isaiah 54:10 and "the eternal covenant" of 61:8. It is also the new covenant promised in Jeremiah 31:31-34 and Ezekiel 16:60. The servant will heal Israel from spiritual blindness. The personal character of the servant is clear, and presents a sharp contrast to national Israel, who is still blind, and dwells in darkness in a spiritual dungeon (v. 7).

8-9 Jehovah alone is God

8 I am Jehovah, this is my name!
I will not give my glory to another,
Nor my praise to idols!

9 The first things, behold have come to pass.
And new things I declare,
Before they spring forth I let you hear about them.

8 I am Jehovah, this is my name.

Jehovah alone is Lord and therefore is the guarantor that His servant will accomplish His mission.

9 ... The former things ... the new things ...

"The former things" are the prophecies of the past which have already come to pass; "the new things" are the new prophecies which the prophet is now foretelling before the predicted events have come to pass. The acceptance of the truth of this assertion is basic to the understanding of predictive prophecy.

10-17 A new triumphal song

10 Sing unto the LORD a new song,
And his praise to the ends of the earth.
You that go down to sea, and all that which lives in it,
The islands and all its inhabitants.

11 Let the wilderness and its cities lift up their voice,
The villages where Kedar dwells,
Let the inhabitants of Sela sing for joy,
Let them shout from the top of the mountains.

12 Let them give glory to the LORD,
And declare his praise in the islands.

13 The LORD will go forth like a mighty man,
Like a man of war will stir up a battle frenzy,
He will raise a yell and a shout:

14 I have held my peace for a long time,
I have kept quiet and have restrained myself,
But now I will cry out like a woman in birth,
I shall gasp and puff at the same time.

15 I will lay waste mountains and hills,
And I will shrivel up all that which is green,
And turn rivers into islands, and dry up pools.

16 I will lead the blind by a way which they never knew,
And guide them through paths which they knew not.
The darkness I will turn into light before them.
And the crooked places straight.
These are the things that I will do, and will not forsake them.

17 They shall draw back, deeply ashamed,
All they who put their trust in idols,
Who say to molten images: "You are our gods!"

Comment:

"The new things" mentioned by the prophet in v. 9 now become the occasion for a new song, reminiscent of the triumphal hymn of Isaiah 26:14-15. The inhabitants of the coastlands and the desert oases are encouraged to sing a new song of praise to Jehovah (v. 10-12). The inhabitants of Kedar, an Arab tribe in Syria, and those who dwell in Sela, an Edomite city, are also invited to join in the praise of Jehovah. The occasion for this universal jubilation is that the LORD, who has kept silence for very long, is about to intervene with great might on behalf of Israel.

In this triumphal hymn Jehovah is compared to a mighty warrior who shouts and yells in the midst of a raging battle, and to a woman in pain about to give birth. These anthropomorphisms are intended to convey the fierceness of the divine wrath, when He finally intervenes on behalf of His people.

15 I will lay waste mountains and hills.

When God intervenes all of nature is affected, the mountains, the hills and the rivers. There is no obstacle which can stand in the path of God's plan.

16 And I will lead the blind ...

The whole purpose of God's intervention is to bring home His people, in spite of their self-inflicted blindness.

These are the things which I will do and not forsake them.

Jehovah who hitherto has punished His people so severely, will now act in mercy.

17 They shall draw back, deeply ashamed, all they who trust in idols. . .

The vindication of God's people will confound the idolators and the enemies of Israel.

18-21 The deaf and blind servant of the LORD

18 Hear, you deaf, and you who are blind, look and see.

19 Who is as blind as my servant?
And who is as deaf as my messenger, that I send?
Who is as blind as my trusted messenger,
Or as blind as the servant of the LORD?

20 You have seen much, but understood little,
You have open ears, but do not hear!

21 Yet it pleased the Lord, for the sake of his righteousness,
To magnify the law and to make it glorious.

Comment:

Without any doubt "the servant of the Lord" in this passage is collective Israel. Jehovah reproaches him that he is deaf and blind. He has seen so much, yet never really understood the significance of what he has seen. He has heard much but has proved himself incapable of comprehending the meaning of what he has heard. Like a trusted messenger (Hebrew *"meshulam"*) Israel was sent on a mission to the nations, but has proven himself unfaithful to his trust.[2]

21 **It has pleased the Lord for the sake of his righteousness. . .**

In spite of Israel's blindness and unfaithfulness, the Lord is determined to accomplish His purpose to make His law glorious and supreme in the eyes of all mankind. What Israel, as a people, has failed to accomplish, the faithful Servant, the Messiah will. In this very chapter (v. 18-21) where the servant Israel is portrayed as blind, deaf and disobedient to God, the personal Servant of God is portrayed as completely obedient and well pleasing to Jehovah (v. 1-6). The distinction between the two servants is clear and beyond the possibility of confusion.

And yet there is an umbilical cord between both types of "the servant." Both are rooted in God's choice of Israel as His people, and in His covenant with them. In the final anaylsis Christ, the Servant of Jehovah, is the perfect representative of Israel who restores the broken covenant relationship between Jehovah and His people. In this sense Israel and her Messiah are one.

22-25 **The reason for Israel's pitiful plight.**

22　But this is a people robbed and plundered.
　　All of them are trapped in holes,
　　Hidden away in dungeons.
　　They have become a prey, and there is none to deliver,
　　A spoil, and there is none to say: "Give back!"

23　Who among you will listen and pay attention against a future time?

24　Who gave Jacob for a spoil and Israel to the robbers?
　　Was it not the LORD against whom we have sinned?
　　And in whose ways they would not walk,
　　Neither were they obedient to his law?

25　Therefore did he pour out upon them his scorching wrath and the fury of war,
　　It enveloped him in flames, yet he did not know it,
　　It burned him, yet he laid it not to heart.

Comment:

22-25

Israel's pitiful situation as a plundered and robbed people is the consequence of their obstinate refusal to obey Jehovah. As a result Jehovah Himself brought upon them all their disasters. In spite of all this, Israel has failed to learn her lesson.

23 **Who of you will listen and pay attention against a future time?**

The prophet pleads with His people to learn from their own tragic history, in order to benefit from it in the future.

348

25 Therefore did he pour out upon them his scorching wrath and the fury of war.

Israel's national disasters were no mere accident but the result of divine wrath. They themselves have provoked the divine wrath, and yet in their blindness have failed to understand this basic truth.

NOTES:
1. Delitzsch *Commentary to Isaiah*, Vol. 2, pages 174-175 (Eerdmans).
2. The Hebrew adjective *"meshulam"*—"a trusted one" or "confidant," is related to the Arabic term *"muslim."*

Isaiah Chapter 43

Jehovah's Abiding Love For Israel

1-7 Jehovah will soon restore His people

1   And now, thus says the LORD, who created thee, O Jacob,
    And he, who formed thee, O Israel,
    Fear not, for I have redeemed thee,
    I have called thee by thy name, thou are mine.

2   When thou passest through the waters, I will be with thee,
    And through rivers they will not overflow thee;
    When thou walkest through the fire, thou shall not be burned,
    And the flame shall not scorch thee.

3   For I am Jehovah, thy God,
    The Holy One of Israel, thy saviour.
    I have given Egypt as thy ransom,
    Ethiopia and Seba in thy stead.

4   Because thou art precious in mine eyes, and honorable,
    And I have loved thee, therefore will I give men for thee,
    And peoples for thy life.

5   Fear not, for I am with thee,
    I will bring thy seed from the east,
    And will gather thee from the west.

6   I will say to the north: give up,
    And to the south: keep not back,
    Bring my sons from far away,
    And my daughters from the ends of the earth;

7   All those who bear my name,
    And whom I have created for my glory,
    Whom I have formed and whom I have made.

Comment:

1 And now, thus says the LORD, who created thee, O Jacob

The description of Israel's tragic plight in 42:18-25 is followed by the assurance of Jehovah's unchanging love for His people. This is a passage of singular beauty and tenderness, of exhortations, followed by comforting reassurance of God's abiding love. The alternating rebukes, dire predictions and encouragements are typical of both parts of Isaiah, and of the prophetic writings in general.

Fear not, for I have redeemed thee.

Jehovah sees Israel's restoration as an already accomplished reality. With this in view Israel need not fear, only trust her God.

2 When thou passest through the waters.

No matter what the peril, Jehovah will protect His people. The waters will not drown them, nor will the flames consume them. Israel's historical experiences and their faith in these glorious promises have helped to preserve the nation during the millennia of a perilous existence.

3 I have given Egypt as thy ransom,

The reference to Egypt has a double significance: it is a reminder of Israel's exodus from Egypt and a promise of God's readiness to intervene again on their behalf. This time the Lord will use Cyrus as His instrument of redemption.

4 Because thou art precious in my eyes, thou art honorable and I have loved thee.

A moving declaration of Jehovah's love for Israel. Mighty Babylon and Egypt may hold in contempt captive and defeated Israel, yet in God's sight they remain precious and honorable.

5 Fear not, for I am with thee.

The mystery of Israel's survival is rooted in the fact that God was and is with His people. Their survival is not due to their own merit, but to God's purpose for them: "I have created them for my glory" (v. 7). God sees His people not the way they are, but with an eye to the glorious destiny for which He has created them.

Verses 8-13   Israel, the blind and deaf servant of the Lord

8   Bring forth the blind people who have eyes,
   And the deaf who have ears.

9   Gather together all the nations,
   And let the people be assembled.
   Who among them can declare this,
   And explain the happenings of the past?

Let them bring their witnesses that they may be justified,
Or let them listen and say: this is true!

10 You are my witness, says the LORD
And my servant, whom I have chosen,
That you may know, and believe me,
And understand that I am he.
Before me there was no God formed,
And after me there will be none.

11 I, only I, am the LORD,
And beside me there is no saviour.

12 I have proclaimed, and I have saved,
And I have announced, and there was no alien god among you,
And you are my witnesses, says the LORD,
And I am God.

13 Even since that day I am he,
And there is none that can deliver from my hand;
I will do and who will undo?

Comment:

Verses 8-13

In spite of their spiritual blindness and deafness, Israel remains God's witness against the idols and their worshippers, because the future of Israel was foretold in advance by the prophets of God. No idol could do this.

There are striking similarities between the servant of Jehovah as a nation and the servant of Jehovah as a person. Both are chosen of God (42:1, 43:10). Both are beloved (42:1, 43:4). Yet the differences between the two are basic. Obedient or disobedient, "the servant" Israel is a witness to the faithfulness of God and the fact that there is no other God who is like Jehovah. Collectively Israel is a blind (v. 8) and essentially passive servant (v. 10). By contrast the individual Servant of Jehovah is God's active agent to accomplish His divine purpose for mankind. The individual Servant of the LORD, the Messiah, is the absolutely obedient messenger of God who delights to do His will (42:4).

14-21 Babylon will soon fall and Israel will be restored

14 Thus says the LORD, the Holy One of Israel,
For thy sake have I sent to Babylon,
And I will bring them all down as fugitives,
And the Chaldeans in the ships of their rejoicing.

15 I am the LORD, your Holy One,
The creator of Israel, your king.

16 Thus says the LORD, who makes a way in the sea,
    And a path in the mighty waters,

17 Who brings forth chariot and horse, army and might.
    They lie down together, never to rise again,
    They are crushed, extinguished like a wick.

18 Do not bring to mind ancient events,
    Neither consider the things of long ago.

19 Behold I do a new thing, shall you not know it?
    I will make a way in the wilderness,
    And rivers in the deserts.

20 The wild beasts shall honor me,
    The jackals and the ostriches,
    Because I cause waters to gush forth in the wilderness,
    And rivers in the desert,
    To give drink to my chosen people.

21 This people have I formed for myself,
    That they may proclaim my praise.

Comment:

14-21 Jehovah is about to perform a new miracle, surpassing in grandeur the exodus from Egypt: Babylon will be destroyed and Israel set free.

14 For thy sake have I sent to Babylon

The expression "for thy sake" (one word in Hebrew "*lemaanha*") implies the conviction that the LORD directs the destiny of nations to serve His purpose of Israel's redemption.

The Chaldeans in the ships of their rejoicing.

A difficult passage which is variously interpreted. Our translation appears to come closest to the meaning of the original text. "The Chaldeans" is the poetic and archaic name of the Babylonians.

"The ships of their rejoicing," an apparent reference to the Babylonian pleasure ships on the Euphrates, which the Persians would use to deport the fugitive Babylonians.

16 A way in the sea, a path in the mighty waters.

An allusion to the miracle of the Red Sea in the days of Moses (Ex. 14:13-31).

17 Who brings forth chariot and horse, army and might—

A further allusion to the events at the Red Sea.

18 Do not bring in mind ancient events.

Hitherto the deliverance from Egypt was the most celebrated

event in all the history of Israel, but now even greater things are about to happen.

19   Behold I do a new thing, shall you not know it?

When the hour of her deliverance arrives, with all its miraculous occurrences, Israel, in spite of being deaf and blind, will be forced to acknowledge that Jehovah has done it.

21   This people have I formed for myself,
That they may declare my praise.

This poignant declaration sums up Jehovah's ultimate purpose for Israel: they are a people whom the Creator has fashioned for the express purpose that they might glorify Him, — a high and glorious calling indeed.

Verses 22-28   The ingratitude of a nation

22   Yet thou hast not called upon me, O Jacob,
For thou hast become weary of me, O Israel.

23   Thou hast not brought me the sheep of thy burnt offerings,
Neither hast thou honored me with thy sacrifices.
I have not burdened thee with meal offerings,
Nor troubled you for incense.

24   Thou hast not bought me sweet cane,
Nor filled me with the fat of thy sacrifices.
Yet hast thou burdened me with thy sins,
And wearied me with thy iniquities.

25   I, only I, blot out thy transgressions, for my own sake,
And thy sins will I not remember.

26   Put me in remembrance, let us judge this together,
Declare thy case, that thou mayest be justified.

27   Thy first father sinned,
And thy intercessors transgressed against me,

28   Therefore have I profaned thy holy princes,
And have delivered Jacob to the ban,
And Israel to blasphemings.

Comment:
Verses 22-24

The prophet identifies himself with his people in exile. The temple, its ritual and sacrifices have become a thing of the past. No longer does God burden His people with demands for sacrifices or other ritual obligations. Yet Israel still continues to dishonor Jehovah, just as they did before their exile. With or without sacrifices, they continue to burden the LORD with their sins and iniquities, just as in the past.

25   I, only I, blot out thy sins, for my own sake.

Just as in the opening chapter of Isaiah, the prophet continues to wrestle with the false notions that in order to obtain forgiveness from God, animal sacrifices and other "religious" rites, are indispensable. In reality it is the LORD Himself, who for His own sake alone, forgives sins, irrespective of man's so-called pious acts. The Lord cannot be bribed with sacrifices. "Wash you, make you clean . . . cease to do evil," (Isa. 1:16) is implied here also.

26   Put me in remembrance, let us judge this together.
These words bring to mind Isaiah 1:18
Come now, let us reason together, says the LORD
Though your sins be like scarlet
They shall be white as snow.

27   Thy first father sinned. . .

A reference to Abraham, who although a "friend of God," nevertheless was not without sin (Gen. 15:8).

"Thy intercessors" are the prophets and teachers of Israel, "thy holy princes," the priestly hierarchy, who, like the rest of their countrymen, were carried off into exile.

28   Jacob to the ban . . . Israel to blasphemings.
Israel's suffering and tragedy is self-imposed, the result of their continued disobedience to God and spiritual myopia.

Isaiah Chapter 44

Repentant Israel promised the Spirit. The idols are taunted. Cyrus appointed the agent of deliverance.

Verses 1-5   Israel, the servant of Jehovah is reassured.
1   And now hear, my servant Jacob,
And Israel, whom I have chosen:

2   Thus says the LORD, who made thee,
And fashioned thee from the womb,
Who will help thee:
Fear not, my servant Jacob,
And thou, O, Jeshurun, whom I have chosen.

3   For I will pour water upon the thirsty land,
And streams upon the dry ground:

I will pour out my spirit upon thy seed,
And my blessing upon thy offspring.

4 They will spring up like grass,
And like willows by the streams of water.

5 One will say: I am the LORD's.
Another will call himself by the name of Jacob
And yet another will write on his hand: to the LORD,
And will surname himself by the name of Israel.

Comment:
Verses 1-5

In sharp contrast to the somber closing words of chapter 43 in which the prophet explains the reason of Israel's terrible plight, he now foretells a time of unprecedented blessing. The LORD will pour out His spirit upon His people and their offspring. Even gentiles seeing how God is blessing Israel, will attach themselves to them and bear allegiance to Jehovah.

This prophetic passage is reminiscent in tone of Zechariah 8:23. The name Jeshurun (v. 2) is synonymous with Israel and is derived from the root *"yashar,"* "to be upright.' It is therefore a title of honor and endearment. Jehovah sees His people not as they are, but as He intends them to become in the end, — a righteous and upright people.

3 I will pour water upon the thirsty land.

The Hebrew adjective *"tzame,"* "thirsty," may refer either to a thirsty land or thirsty people. However, the parallel phrase "dry ground," indicates that the word "land" is implied.

3b I will pour out my spirit upon thy seed.

The primary sense of the passage is spiritual and speaks of the future regeneration of Israel which will bring blessing to all of mankind. Their turning to God, will attract others to Jehovah and to the people of Jehovah. In contrast to Israel's former state when they were delivered to the gentiles to be treated with contempt and as an object of blasphemings (Isa. 43:28), they will in the future become an honored people, with whom non-Jews will seek to identify themselves and also with their God.

5 Another will write on his hand: to the LORD.

It was a custom among many pagans to tattoo upon their hand the name of their god, or, in the case of a slave, to inscribe the name of the owner to whom he belonged.

... **And will surname himself by the name of Israel**

The newly converted gentiles will add to their names the surname "Israel" as a mark of their admiration for the regenerated people of Jehovah.

Verses 6-8   Jehovah alone is God and Israel is His Witness

6   Thus says the LORD, the king of Israel,
And his redeemer, the LORD of hosts:
I am the first and last,
And besides me there is no god.

7   And who is like me, let him proclaim it.
Let him declare it and set it forth before me,
Since I have established the ancient people.
Let them announce future events,
And that which will yet come to pass.

8   Fear not, neither be afraid.
Have I not announced it to thee long ago and told thee?
And you are my witnesses, whether there is any god beside me.
No, there is no rock, I know none.

Comment:

Verses 6-8

Jehovah declares that He alone is God, He alone has made known to His people their future. The idols cannot do this because they are not gods.

Israel remains forever a living witness to Jehovah and to His Word.

Verses 9-20   A taunting satire against the idols, their makers, and their worshippers.

9   All the makers of idols are vanity,
And their precious works are useless,
Their witnesses see nothing and know nothing,
And so they will be put to shame.

10   Who has fashioned a god or a molten image which is of no use?

11   Behold all their makers shall be ashamed,
Let all their sculptors who are skilled above other men,
Assemble themselves, and let them stand up.
They shall be terrified and ashamed together.

12   The smith with his tongs.
He works in the coals and fashions an image with hammers.
He toils with his strong arm,

And becomes hungry and weary.
He drinks no water and is exhausted.

13 The carpenter draws a line,
He marks it out with a stylus.
He fits it with planes,
And outlines it with the compass.
Then he shapes it after the figure of a man,
According to the beauty of a human being, to dwell in the house.

14 He cuts down cedars and takes a cypress or an oak,
Which he has picked out among the trees of the forest.
He plants a fir tree and the rain makes it grow,

15 Then a man uses it for fuel,
He takes some of it to warm himself,
With some he kindles a fire and bakes bread.
He also makes a god and worships him,
He makes himself a graven image and falls down before it.

16 One part he has burned in the fire.
With one part he eats meat. He roasts a roast and is satisfied,
He warms himself and says: "Ah, I am warm, I have seen the fire."

17 With that which is left he makes a god, an idol,
He falls down to it, he worships it and prays to it.
And says, "Oh save me, for thou art my god!"

18 They do not know and do not understand,
For their eyes are glued together so that they cannot see,
And their hearts do not comprehend.

19 And none considers it in his heart,
Nor has he the knowledge or sense to say:
"I have burned the half of it in the fire,
And I have baked bread on its hot coals,
I have roasted meat and eaten it.
And shall I make an abomination with what is left,
And fall down to a chunk of wood?"

20 He feeds on ashes,
A deluded heart has led him astray.
He will not save his soul and he will not say:
"Is not that which I hold in my hand a lie?"

Comment:
Verses 9-20

With impassioned scorn the prophet describes the idol makers
and "their precious works," the idols. He mentions some of the tools

and materials which the idol makers employed in the production of their useless gods.

The prophet is amazed at the foolishness of the man who uses the same tree to bake bread, to roast meat and to make of what is left a god beseeching him: save me for thou art my god (v. 15). The only answer to this aberration is that the idol makers and worshippers are so blind and deluded that they have lost the ability to see and to understand their actions, because they have been feeding on ashes for too long (v. 20). This passage presents the prophet's strongest denunciation of the idols and the ridiculous worship of "a chunk of wood."

Verses 21-22   A call to repentance.

21   Remember these things, O Jacob and Israel
For thou art my servant.
I have formed thee, thou art my own servant, O Israel, do not forget me.

22   I have blotted out thy transgressions, like a cloud,
And thy sins like a mist.
Return to me for I have redeemed thee!

Comment:

21   Remember these things . . . do not forget me.

After exposing the idols as being utterly worthless, the prophet bids his people to remember that Israel is the servant of the Lord, and must never forget it.

22   I have blotted out thy transgressions like a cloud. . .
Return unto me, for I have redeemed thee. . .

One of the most touching declarations of God's love for His people. The cry: "Return unto me" is the very heart of the prophetic message. Alas, it remained mostly unheeded.

Verse 23   A short hymn of praise.

23   Sing, O heavens, for the LORD has done it,
Shout, you depths of the earth,
Break forth into exultation, you mountains,
The forest and all its trees,
For the LORD has redeemed Jacob
And glorified himself in Israel.

Comment:

23   This brief call upon heaven and earth to exult in the redemption of Israel is in harmony with the first chapter of Isaiah, which begins with a call to heaven and earth to be witnesses of Israel's rebellion against their maker and redeemer. Now heaven and earth are called upon to take part in the joyful celebration of Israel's redemption.

Verses 24-28   Jehovah has appointed Cyrus to fulfill His purpose.

24   Thus says the LORD, thy redeemer,
And he who has fashioned thee from the womb,
I am the LORD who made all things,
Who stretched out the heavens above,
Who spread out the earth by himself;

25   Who frustrates the signs of the lying prophets,
And makes fools of the diviners.
Who turns back the wise men,
And makes their knowledge foolish,

26   But confirms the word of his servant,
And carries out the counsel of his messenger.
Who says to Jerusalem: "She shall be inhabited again."
And to the cities of Judah: "They shall be rebuilt
And I will raise up again their ruins,"

27   Who says to the deep: "Be dry,
And I will dry up thy rivers."

28   Who says to Cyrus: "He is my shepherd
And will carry out all my will,"
Saying to Jerusalem: "She shall be rebuilt"
And to the temple: "Its foundation shall be laid."

Comment:

24   Thus says the LORD, thy redeemer.

The omnipotent creator of all things is the God who called Israel into being and also redeemed her. Actually the whole passage (v. 24-28) is one long sentence. It is logically constructed to prepare for the introduction of Cyrus as Jehovah's shepherd, and the appointed agent to perform His will.

The God of Israel brings to nought all the vain rattlings of the lying prophets (*"baddim"*—the babblers). All the vaunted knowledge of the pagan diviners is foolish nonsense (v. 25). But He confirms the message of His servant (in this instance of the prophet Isaiah, and of all His messengers, the prophets).

This God says to Jerusalem that she shall be inhabited again and the temple of Jehovah shall be rebuilt (v. 26).

27   Who says to the deep: Be dry. . .

Jehovah is about to perform another miracle. He will dry up the deep, a possible allusion to the celebrated act of Cyrus in diverting the Euphrates and the canals surrounding Babylon into an artificial lake, before he captured the great metropolis.

The Greek historian Herodotus recorded this event in his *History*, relating how Cyrus dried up the Euphrates, so that it was only one foot deep, by diverting its waters into the basin of Sepharvaim. In this way the Persian army was able to enter unexpectedly, the supposedly impenetrable city of Babylon.[1]

28 Who says to Cyrus: he is my shepherd.

Here is an unusual instance of a yet unborn king, mentioned by name about 150 years before the event. Since we have discussed this fully in the introduction to the first and second parts of Isaiah, we shall not repeat here our previous remarks.

The name Cyrus, in Hebrew *"Koresh,"* appears on ancient Persian monuments as *Kuru*, which is also the name of a river in southern Persia. It is generally assumed that the name Cyrus was derived from the name of that river.

According to Josephus,[2] when this passage of Isaiah, which mentions Cyrus as the liberator of the Jews, was brought to the attention of the king, he promptly decreed the return of the Jews to Jerusalem and gave them permission to rebuild the temple.

NOTES:
1. Herodotus, *History* 1, 187-193, Penguin edition.
2. Josephus, *Antiquities*, XI, 2.

Isaiah Chaper 45

Cyrus Appointed to Deliver Israel From Babylon

Verses 1-7 Jehovah will grant victory to Cyrus, for the sake of His people

1 Thus says the LORD to his anointed, to Cyrus,
Whom I have taken by his right hand,
To subdue nations before him,
And to render kings helpless,
To open doors before him,
And to keep the gates from being shut again.

2 I will go before thee and make the crooked places straight,
I will break the doors of brass,
And cut in pieces the iron gates.

3 I will give thee the treasures of darkness,

360

And the hidden riches of secret places,
That thou mayest know that I am the LORD,
He who calls thee by thy name, the God of Israel.

4 For the sake of my servant Jacob and for Israel my chosen one,
Have I called thee by thy name, and have surnamed thee,
Although thou hast not known me.

5 I am the LORD, and there is none other,
Beside me there is no God.
I have girded thee, though thou hast not known me.

6 That they may know from the rising to the setting of the sun,
That there is none beside me,
I am the LORD there is none else.

7 I form the light and create darkness,
I make peace and create evil,
I the LORD do all this.

Comment:

This is the only instance in Scripture in which a gentile ruler is referred to us *Mashiach*—"Anointed one," a title of honor reserved for the kings and the high priests of Israel, and for the Saviour par excellence, the Messiah (see Dan. 7:14). Here Cyrus is designated by this title as God's chosen agent who is to deliver Israel from Babylonian bondage.

Herodotus described how Cyrus conquered the supposedly impenetrable city of Babylon, the greatest and richest metropolis of Asia (see note 1, to chapter 44). In comparison with the cruel Assyrians and Babylonians, Cyrus and his dynasty were enlightened and humane rulers. After the capture of Babylon in 539 B.C., he encouraged the Jews and many other captive peoples, including the Assyrians, to return to their homeland, and even contributed generously to the rebuilding of the Temple in Jerusalem (2 Chron. 36:22, 23; Ezra 1:2, 5:13; 6:3, 4).

The Cyrus Cylinder which was excavated at the site of ancient Babylon in 1882, records.

"Marduk . . . looked through all the countries searching for a righteous ruler . . . He pronounced the name of Cyrus . . . and declared him to be the ruler of the world."

This characterization of Cyrus as "a righteous ruler" is in harmony with Isaiah 45:1a.

1 To render kings helpless before him. . .

Literally "to ungird the loins of kings," that is, to loosen their belts to which their weapons were attached, thus rendering them help-less. The opposite of this phrase is "to gird" (v. 5).

2   The doors of brass . . . the bars of iron

Herodotus, who in his worldwide travels visited Babylon, de-clared: "There are a hundred gates to the circuit of the wall, all of bronze with bronze uprights and lintels."[1]

3   The treasures of darkness . . . the hidden riches. . .

Babylon, the world center of commerce, the mistress of Mesopo-tamia, was rich beyond all calculation. Her fabulous treasures were hoarded in the secret vaults of her famous temples and palaces. Even private citizens could deposit their wealth in the temple vaults against a receipt. Thus the Babylonian temples were the forerunners of our modern banks.

4   For the sake of my servant Jacob . . . I have called thee by thy name

The victories of Cyrus were for the sake of Israel, beloved for their fathers' sake, even in their state of rebellion. Just as the As-syrians and the Babylonians were formerly used to punish Israel, so Cyrus would now be the agent of divine compassion, to set them free. Jehovah singled out Cyrus, calling him by name, as a testimony to Himself, to Israel, and to the nations of the world, that He alone is the omnipotent, omniscient and sovereign God, the God of the impossible.

7   I form light and create darkness. . .

This verse is singularly appropriate for Cyrus, because the Per-sians believed that the world is ruled by two gods, Ahura Mazda, the god of light and goodness, and Ahriman, the god of darkness and evil. Our verse declares that Jehovah is the author of both, of light and darkness, of peace and evil. The contrasting of evil as the op-posite of peace is most significant for the prophetic mind. All the events of history and their strange convolutions are ultimately trace-able to Jehovah.

Verse 8   A Brief Hymn

> Pour down you heavens from above,
> And the skies rain down righteousness.
> Let the earth open up and bring forth salvation,
> And let her cause righteousness to spring up together.
> I, the LORD, have created it.

Comment:

This brief hymn is in anticipation of the Messianic times when salvation and justice will fill the earth.

Verses 9-13 An answer to those who question the ways of the Lord.

9   Woe to him who contends with his Maker,
     A potsherd among earthen potsherds.
     Shall the clay say to the potter: "What art thou doing?"
     Or, "Thy work has no hands."

10 Woe to him who says to his father: "What hast thou begotten?"
     Or to his mother: "To what hast thou given birth?"

11 Thus says the LORD, the Holy One of Israel and his Maker:
     Would you question me concerning the things which are to come?
     Or command me concerning my sons and the works of my hands?

12 I alone made the earth,
     And the men upon it, I have created.
     My own hands have stretched forth the heavens,
     And I have ordered all its hosts.

13 I myself have also raised him up to righteousness,
     And I will make level all his ways.
     He will rebuild my city, and set my exiles free,
     Not for a price, nor for a bribe, says the LORD of hosts.

Comment:

This passage seems to be directed against some of the exiles who apparently resented that Jehovah should use Cyrus, a pagan ruler, to deliver Israel, instead of a Davidic king.

9   Woe to him who contends with his Maker

To do so is an act of hubris, of supreme arrogance. It is like a mere shard daring to talk back to the potter.

Thy work has no hands

This seems to have been a common expression still used today among some Jews, to describe something which does not make sense. The enormity of this impious act is brought out by comparing it to a child questioning his parents why they conceived him or gave birth to him.

11   Would you question me?

It is outrageous for man (finite in wisdom and knowledge) to question God concerning His ways or to tell Him how to deal with His children. Just leave these things with the God who created heaven and earth and man himself.

13   I have raised him up in righteousness

The same God who created the universe has also appointed

Cyrus to set the exiles free and to rebuild Jerusalem, "my city."
Cyrus will do it of his own free will and not for a bribe.

Verses 14-17   The nations shall turn to the God of Israel

14   Thus says the Lord:
The toil of Egypt and the wealth of Ethiopia,
Of the Sabeans, men of stature,
Shall come over to thee and be thine,
They shall go after thee and come over in fetters,
They shall fall down before thee, and implore thee:
Surely God is in thy midst and there is none other,
There is no other God.

15   Truly thou art a God who hidest thyself,
The God of Israel, the Saviour.

16   They shall be ashamed and confounded all of them,
The makers of idols shall go in confusion.

17   But Israel shall be saved by the LORD
With an everlasting salvation.
They shall never, no never, be ashamed or confounded.

Comment:

14   The toil of Egypt and the wealth of Ethiopia . . . shall come over to thee

To whom does Jehovah address Himself? A rather difficult question to answer. At first glance Israel would seem to be the addressee, but Israel never waged war against Egypt or Ethiopia. Cyrus would appear to be the more logical addressee. But neither did Cyrus himself conquer Egypt and Ethiopia. This conquest was left to Cambyses, the son of Cyrus. The only satisfactory answer is that this prophecy has an eschatological character. It is a vision of the ultimate things which will come to pass at the end of times. At that time the nations will voluntarily come over to the God of Israel. Verse 14 corresponds to the message of Isaiah 2:2-4. The history of redemption is telescoped to dramatize the ultimate purpose of God.

15   Truly thou art a God who hidest thyself

The actions of Jehovah, His seemingly strange ways are not easily discernible to him who has not learned to walk in the Lord's paths, nor to trust Him. The pagan deities were conspicuous, of monumental proportions. Not so Jehovah. He is discernible only to the eye of faith. Yet He is the Saviour of Israel and those who trust in Him shall never be ashamed.

Verses 18-25   Look unto me all the ends of the earth

18   For thus says the LORD, who created the heavens,

He is God, he formed the earth and made it, he established it.
He did not create it to be a void, but formed it to be inhabited,
I am the LORD and there is none other.

19 I have not spoken in secret, in a dark place.
I did not say to the children of Jacob: "Seek me in vain."
I the LORD speak righteousness,
I declare things which are right.

20 Gather yourselves together, come and draw near, you survivors
of the nations.
They who carry around the wood of their graven images, they
do not know,
All they who pray to a god who cannot help.

21 Come forward and declare, yes, take counsel together:
Who has declared all this from ancient time?
Who has foretold this of old?
Was it not I, Jehovah?
There was no other God beside me,
A God who is just and a Saviour,
There is none beside me.

22 Look unto me and be you saved all the ends of the earth,
For I am God and there is none other.

23 I have sworn by myself,
The word of righteousness has gone forth out of my mouth.
It will not return void,
That unto me every knee shall bow,
Every tongue shall swear:

24 Surely only in Jehovah, shall one say,
Is there righteousness and strength.
And to him shall all they who defied him come and be ashamed.

25 But in the LORD shall all the seed of Israel
Be justified and glory.

Comment:

The above passage constitutes one of the highpoints of the book
of Isaiah, and reaches out beyond Israel to embrace all of humanity
in God's infinite mercy and salvation. It is a magnificent declaration
concerning the sovereignty and majesty of the LORD and His redemptive purpose for all men.

**18 For thus says the LORD who created the heavens and formed
the earth. . .**

The purpose of the Creator is not that the earth should be pri-

mordial (wasteland—*tohu*), as at creation, but that it should be inhabited by men. However, unless men turn from their wickedness
and idol worship to the service of God, the earth would revert to
her primeval condition and become a wasteland.

19 I have not spoken in secret . . . in a dark place

Unlike the obscure and mumbling utterances of the idol-
worshipping prognosticators, the revelation of Jehovah is clear and
just; it is accessible to all men and not just to a few, who are initiated,
as in the pagan mysteries.

I did not say to the seed of Jacob: "Seek you me in vain"

Israel was not condemned to a hopeless and fruitless search for
God, as for instance the Athenians, who in their search for God,
erected an altar dedicated to the Unknown God (Acts 17:23). The
God of Israel speaks that which is just and right.

20-23 These verses constitute an invitation to all men to turn to
God and live. It is an evangelistic appeal unsurpassed in beauty and
grandeur. It is later echoed in the gospel.

20 Gather yourselves together and come

An invitation to the pagan survivors, those who will remain at the
cataclysmic end of time. The call is addressed to all idol worshippers
who carry around their wooden images and pray to a god who cannot help them.

21 Jehovah . . . a righteous God and a Saviour

In contrast to the pitiful idols who have to be carried about by
their worshippers, Jehovah is omnipotent and omniscient, the God
who makes known the future far in advance. Isaiah repeatedly emphasizes the reality of Jehovah by pointing to predictive prophecy as
an integral part of divine revelation which authenticates the true
prophet.

22 Look unto me, and be you saved, all the ends of the earth

Here is one of the climactic points of prophecy. Jehovah's love is
not limited to Israel alone, God cares for all humanity and invites
all men to "look unto me and be saved." The text contradicts all
those who maintain that the God of the Old Testament is a cruel,
narrowminded and narrowhearted God. The word of Isaiah brings
to mind the words of Jesus: "Come unto me all ye that labor and
are heavy laden, and I will give you rest" (Mt. 11:28).

23 I have sworn by myself

This is the expression of God's immutable will to accomplish His
purpose. The first line of the parallelism is followed by the second:

**The word of righteousness has gone forth from my mouth
. . . it will not return void**

The meaning here is the same as in Isaiah 55:11:

So shall my word be that goes forth out of my mouth
It shall not return unto me void.

God's word of righteousness is His eternal plan and purpose. It is
the eternal, creative inviolable Logos which abides forever.

That unto me shall every knee bow, every tongue shall swear

God's ultimate purpose is that all men should come to a saving
knowledge of Him and acknowledge Him as sovereign and supreme
Lord.

24 Only in the LORD . . . is righteousness and strength

This will be the ultimate confession of repentant humanity,
acknowledging God as righteous and the only one who is able to save.

To him shall all they who defied him come and be ashamed

(lit. were burned up against him).

They who have always defied God will in the end be compelled
to come to Him and confess with shame that they were misguided.
25 The prophet sums up his message to his people saying in essence, that in spite of all their soul-shattering experiences and sins,
Israel will in the end be justified in their faith and will glory in
Jehovah. God will not let His people down.

NOTES:
1. Herodotus, *History*, 85, Penguin ed.

Isaiah Chapter 46

The Pitiful Idols of Babylon Contrasted With
the Power and Compassion of Jehovah.

1 Bel teeters, Nebo totters,
   Their images are thrust upon beasts and cattle,
   That which you carried about
   Has now become a burden to the weary animals.

2 They teeter and totter together.
   They could not save the burden,
   And they themselves are gone into captivity.

Comment:

1 Bel teeters, Nebo totters

Bel, the equivalent of the Hebrew *baal* (lord) was the generic name for any god. When used as a proper name, it refers to Marduk, the supreme deity of Babylon. In Babylonian mythology he appears as the creator. The Greeks called him Zeus or Jupiter.

The magnificent and enormous temple of Bel stood on the banks of the Euphrates and is described by Herodotus:

> The temple is a square building, two furlongs each way with bronze gates, which was still in existence in my time. It has a solid central tower one furlong square, with a second erected on top of it, then a third, and so on up to eight. . . On the summit stands a great temple. . . In the temple there is a second shrine lower down in which there is a great sitting figure of Bel, all of gold on a golden throne, supported on a base of gold, with a golden table standing beside it. I was told by the Chaldeans that to make all this, more than twenty-two tons of gold were used. Outside the temple is a golden altar. . . The golden altar is reserved for sucklings only.[1]

Nebo comes from the same root as the Hebrew word for prophet, *nabi*. In Babylonian mythology Nebo was the son of the supreme god Marduk and is presented as the spokesman of the gods, just like Mercury, mentioned in Acts 14:12. Nebo was also the supreme god of Nineveh and was supposed to be the god of learning and wisdom. At the approach of the victorious Persians, the worshippers of these gods sought to save them by loading them on beasts of burden (camels and elephants) and on cattle (horses, asses and oxen).

2 They teeter and totter together

This describes the act of removing the idols from their temple and their final humiliation. The gods who were once carried about with great pomp in festive, annual processions of enthronement, are now pathetically helpless, a burden to the animals. The gods cannot rescue themselves nor save their worshippers.

3-4 By contrast, Jehovah instead of being carried around, Himself carries His people.

3 Hear me, you house of Jacob, and all the remnant of Israel
Who have been a burden to me from birth
And were carried from the womb.

4 Even in your old age I am the same
And to your hoary hair I will carry you.
I have made you and I will bear you,
I will carry you and will deliver you.

Comment:

What a magnificent contrast between the dumb, helpless idols who have to be carried about, and Jehovah, who has always borne

His people from their very infancy and will continue to carry and save them throughout all their exigencies until the end of their turbulent history.

5-7 The contrast between the incomparable Jehovah and the pathetic, man-made gods who cannot help anybody.

5 To whom will you liken me, or make me equal?
  To whom will you compare me and liken me?

6 You who squander gold from the bag,
  And weigh up silver on the scales,
  Who hire a goldsmith to make a god,
  And fall down before him and prostrate yourselves.

7 They hoist him on the shoulder and carry him around.
  They put him down, and he stands.
  And does not budge from his place.
  And when someone cries to him, he does not answer,
  Nor will he save him from his trouble.

Comment:

This graphic description of the handmade gods is so poignant that to elaborate on it would only detract from its force. How pitiful are "these gods"! How glorious is Jehovah.

8-13 Jehovah calls the rebels to repent.

8 Remember this, and confess your guilt,
  Lay it to heart, you rebels!

9 Bring to mind the times of long, long ago,
  That I am God and that there is none else,
  I am God and there is none like me.

10 The one who foretells the end from the beginning,
  And from ancient times that which has not yet been done,
  Who says: my counsel shall stand,
  And all my purpose will I accomplish.

11 Who calls a bird of prey from the east,
  From a far land, the man of my counsel,
  I have spoken and I will also bring it to pass.

12 Listen to me, you stubborn hearts;
  Who say: "Our vindication is far away."

13 My vindication is close at hand, not far away
  And my salvation shall not be delayed.
  And I will place salvation in Zion,
  For Israel my glory.

369

Comment:

8 Remember this and confess your guilt.

The King James Version translates this, "and show yourselves men." The Hebrew verb *"hithoshashu"* is unique and does not appear elsewhere in the Scriptures. In our context the verb apparently stems from the root *"asham"*—guilt.

Lay it to heart, you rebels

In spite of all that God had done, there were those who rebelled against God and against His dealings with Israel. They doubted whether they would ever be delivered from Babylon. To them the prophet says: God's purpose stands. He will never fail.

11 Who calls a bird of prey from the east.

To his enemies, especially the Babylonians, Cyrus must have appeared as an enormous ravenous bird who swooped down and carried off his victims one by one. He was appointed by Jehovah to carry out His plan for Israel's redemption.

12 Listen to me, you stubborn hearts!

There was apparently a rebellious and stubborn group of men who discouraged the exiles, saying that God does not care about them. The term *"tsedakah"* which usually means righteousness, has in this context the meaning of vindication, Israel and their faith in Jehovah are both vindicated.

The prophet assures God's people that their deliverance will not be long delayed. Departing from the historical situation the prophet sees Israel's glorious future. The Lord will place in Zion salvation and glory for His people Israel.

Note:
1. *Op. cit.* 179-183.

Isaiah Chapter 47

The Humiliation and Degradation of Babylon

1 Come down and sit in the dust,
O virgin daughter of Babylon,
Sit down on the ground without a throne,
O daughter of the Chaldeans,
For thou shalt no longer be called delicate and pampered.

2 Take to the millstones and grind flour;
Remove thy veil, strip thy skirt, expose the leg,
Ford rivers

3 Thy nakedness shall be uncovered.
   And thy shame shall be revealed.
   I will take vengeance,
   And will let no man intercede.

4 Our redeemer, the LORD of hosts is his name,
   The Holy One of Israel.

5 Sit thou in silence and enter into darkness,
   O daughter of the Chaldeans,
   For thou shalt no longer be called mistress of kingdoms.

6 I was angry with my people,
   I have dishonored my inheritance,
   And delivered them into thy hand,
   But thou didst show them no mercy,
   Even upon the aged hast thou laid
   An exceeding heavy yoke.

7 And thou hast said: "I shall forever be mistress."
   And hast never laid these things to heart,
   Nor considered the end.

8 Now therefore, hear this, thou pampered one.
   Who sits securely, who sayest in thy heart:
   "I am [supreme] and there is none beside me.
   I shall never be a widow, nor suffer loss of children."

9 Yet these two things shall come upon thee in a moment,
   Bereavement and widowhood, all in one day,
   They shall come upon thee in full measure,
   For all thy sorceries and the abundance of thy witchcraft.

10 Thou hast been secure in thy wickedness,
   And hast said: "Nobody sees me."
   Thy wisdom and knowledge have perverted thee,
   And thou hast said in thy heart:
   "I am [supreme] and there is none beside me."

11 Yet evil will come upon thee,
   And thou shalt not know how to charm it away,
   A disaster shall befall thee,
   And ruin shall come upon thee, before thou knowest.

12 Now then, stand fast by thy spells,
   And by all thy sorceries,
   Which thou hast practiced from thy youth.
   Perhaps these shall help thee,
   Perhaps thou shalt inspire terror.

13 Thou hast wearied thyself with many counselors
Let them now stand up and help thee,
Those astrologers, and stargazers, and monthly prognosticators,
Who foretell what will happen to thee from month to month.

14 However they shall be like the stubble,
A fire will burn them,
They will not be able to save themselves from the conflagration;
It will not be a hot ember to warm oneself.
Nor a fireside to sit by.

15 This is what will come to all those,
With whom thou hast busied thyself
To those who have traded with thee from thy youth,
Every man shall wander away in his own direction,
There will be none to save thee.

Comment:

The prophet describes vividly the coming humiliation of proud, imperial Babylon. This prophecy can be divided into four strophes: verses 1-4, 5-7, 8-11, 12-15.

1 Come down and sit in the dust. . .

The prophet sees Babylon cast down from the pinnacle of her arrogant power to the very depths of degradation.

O virgin daughter of Babylon

Because of her reputation as an invincible and inviolate city Babylon is called "virgin" (cf. Isa. 23:12). The whole chapter is similar in tone to Isaiah's lament over Egypt in chapter 19, and over Tyre and Sidon in chapter 23.

delicate and pampered. . .

Replete with the riches of the nations at the pinnacle of her great power and luxury, which was the envy of the world, Babylon is compared to a delicate and pampered lady.

2 Take to the millstones, and grind flour

But now Babylon's fate is about to undergo a drastic change. She will soon become a lowly slave forced to do the most menial tasks, just like blinded Samson who had to turn the heavy millstones (Jud. 16:21).

Remove thy veil, strip thy skirt, expose thy leg

The contrast between her former state as "mistress of many kingdoms" and her present condition of a lowly slave is described in most depressing detail.

372

Ford rivers

The ruthless conqueror who once drove others into exile without pity, will now experience the bitter taste of the homeless wanderers, forced to cross many a river in search of a refuge.

3 I will take vengeance

The God of Israel may for a time keep silence, yet He also keeps accounts, and when the hour of reckoning strikes, He balances them. "The mills of God, grind slowly," but thoroughly.

And will let no man intercede

Though the measure of Babylon's wickedness is full to the brim, yet there is no man who is willing to intercede on her behalf, nor is the Lord willing to hear such intercession.

5 Sit thou in silence, enter into darkness

In the Hebrew mind sitting in silence and darkness is associated with deep mourning.

6 I was angry with my people . . . and delivered them into thy hand.

Jehovah may rightly punish His people and deliver them into the hands of their enemies, but no nation has a right to be cruel or utterly merciless in their dealings with Israel.

Thou didst show them no mercy

While punishing Israel for her sins, Jehovah is at the same time judging the nations according to the way in which they treat Israel who are helpless strangers in their midst.

7-8 Now therefore, hear this, thou pampered one. . .

During the heyday of her glory Babylon was so confident in her power, that she never thought that her supremacy would one day come to an end. It seems that the great tyrants of history are so blinded by their temporary enormous might, that they do not suspect how fragile and vulnerable it really is. They never think that disaster may be lurking just around the corner.

9 In one day widowhood and bereavement

Widowhood symbolizes a country without her king, and in bondage to an alien master. Bereavement stands for a people which has been decimated and driven away from their homeland. Such is the fate which the prophet foresees for Babylon. It will come upon them suddenly and without warning.

10 Thou has been secure in thy wickedness

The reason for Babylon's downfall was her utter wickedness

and corruption. It expressed itself in the use of advanced technical and scientific knowledge but without any moral considerations. Their engineering skills, their irrigation systems, their military organization, their enormous temples and palaces, their works of art and their unexcelled legal system were the marvel and envy of the ancient world. Yet all this knowledge and wisdom, used for selfish purposes to enslave nations, could only lead to final disaster. Without the knowledge of God their wisdom was actually great folly. Their religion mostly consisted of stultifying witchcraft and sorcery. In the end Babylon went the way of all great empires of ancient and more recent times. Godless intoxication with their own might and accomplishments, their ruthlessness and wickedness destroyed them.

11 Yet evil shall come upon thee

Herodotus described in great detail the fall of Babylon at a time when the city felt secure behind her enormous fortifications and the river Euphrates which was cunningly channelled to encircle and protect the city with a system of great moats. Yet Cyrus' engineers managed to outwit the Babylonians and to capture the city by diverting the Euphrates.

12-15 The utter uselessness of witchcraft in the hour of need
12 Now then stand fast by the spells.

The prophet addresses himself with sarcasm to the Babylonians:

"Since you have always busied yourselves with your witchcraft, why don't you resort to it now to help you? Let all the astrologers, the stargazers and the monthly prognosticators [an apparent reference to those who predicted future events on the basis of the zodiacal signs of the month], let them now help you, or inspire terror in your enemies."

14 However they shall all be like the stubble

The futility of all these vaunted wise men will be exposed in the hour of calamity. All of them will perish in the terrible conflagration of the approaching disaster. The few who will survive will run off each in his own direction, to save their own skins. There will be none left to help Babylon.

Isaiah Chapter 48

An Exhortation to the Captivity

Verses 1-2 The captives identified and rebuked

1 Hear this, O house of Jacob,
   You who are called by the name of Israel,

And have come forth from the loins of Judah,
Who swear by the name of Jehovah,
And extol the God of Israel,
Yet not in sincerity nor with justice.

2 For they call themselves of the holy city
And rely on the God of Israel,
The LORD OF HOSTS is his name.

Comment:

1 And have come forth from the loins of Judah

An unusual description of the origins of the Judean captivity, yet not without parallel (Deut. 33:28, Psa. 68:26, where Jacob and Israel are described as "the loins" of the nation).

Yet not in sincerity nor with justice

Literally, not in truth nor in righteousness. The Judean captives are rebuked because their adherence to Jehovah is purely nominal and without deep roots in their faith or conduct. The prophet enlarges upon this theme in the following verse.

2 For they call themselves of the holy city

For the first time Jerusalem is referred to as "the holy city." This is repeated in chapter 52:1. The life and conduct of the captives is a reproach to that holy city, which is the abode of the God of Israel.

3-8 The former things and the new things

3 The former things I have declared long ago
They went forth out of my mouth and I announced them;
Suddenly I did them and they came to pass.

4 For I knew that thou art hard,
Thy neck is an iron bar, thy brow like brass.

5 Therefore have I declared these things long ago,
Lest thou shouldest say: "Mine idol has done it.
My image or cast statue, they commanded them."

6 Thou hast heard and seen all these things
Will you not acknowledge them?
From now on I announce new things to thee,
Hidden things which you did not know.

7 They were created just now and not long ago,
And before this day you have not heard about it,
Lest thou shouldest say, "I knew it."

8 Indeed thou hast not heard,
Nor didst thou know,

Nor was thine ear opened beforehand,
For I knew that thou wouldest behave altogether treacherously,
And hast been called a rebel from thy birth.

Comment:

3 The former things I have declared long ago

From all that is said in this chapter "the former things" appear to be all the events since the exodus from Egypt, including the deliverance of Jerusalem from Sennacherib.

Suddenly I did them and they came to pass

At the appointed time all the predicted events came to pass.

4 For I knew that thou art hard

The prophet explains why all the great events in the history of Israel were predicted before they ever happened, because Jehovah knew the obstinate, shameless nature of His people and that they were prone to idolatry. This characterization of Israel is extremely harsh.

6 Thou hast heard and seen all these things

Israel has not only heard beforehand but has also seen that God brought to pass His Word and so, even against their will, they are His witnesses before the whole world.

From now on I announce new things

The new things are all the things which the LORD has in store not only for Israel but for all the nations. It is the liberation and regeneration of Israel, the manifestation of the glory of God, and the redemptive work of the servant of God.

7 They were created just now and not long ago

The fulfillment of "the new things" hitherto hidden from the knowledge of the people is to begin now.

8 Indeed thou hast not heard, nor didst thou know

That which is about to happen is without parallel in the history of Israel, a new era is about to begin.

For I knew that thou wouldest behave altogether treacherously

The thought here is similar to verse 4. Certain things were not revealed to Israel because of their treacherous and rebellious nature, which would have perverted and abused this revelation.

9-11 The Lord has preserved Israel for His own sake

9 For the sake of my name I deferred mine anger
And curbed it for the sake of my praise,
That I cut thee not off.

10 Behold, I have refined thee, yet not like silver.
    I have tested thee in the furnace of affliction.

11 For my own sake, for my own sake will I act,
    For why should my name be profaned?
    I will not give my glory to another.

Comment:

9 For the sake of my name I deferred my anger

Had Jehovah acted in righteous outrage, Israel would have perished long ago. But He spared them, lest the pagan nations assume that their idols have prevailed against Jehovah.

10 I have refined thee, yet not like silver

The thought here apparently is that the Lord tested Israel but not in the fierce heat in which silver is refined. Israel's test was in the furnace of affliction, which burns but does not destroy altogether.

11 For my own sake, for my own sake, will I act

The repetition is used for greater emphasis and complements the thought of verse 9.

I will not give my glory to another

The preservation and protection of Israel are intricately connected with the honor of their faithful and covenant-keeping God.

12-16 A summons to the people to hear the message of the approaching redemption.

12 Listen to me, O Jacob and Israel my called one.
    I am he, I am the first, I am also the last.

13 It was my hand which laid the foundation of the earth.
    And my right hand has spread out the heavens.
    I call them and they stand up together.

14 Assemble yourselves, all of you and listen,
    Who among them has foretold all this?
    He whom the Lord loves will accomplish his will on Babylon
    And reveal his arm on the Chaldeans.

15 I, I have spoken and I have also called him forth.
    I have brought him and I will prosper his way.

16 Come near to me and hear this,
    From the very beginning I have not spoken in secret,
    From the time that it took place, there was I,
    And now the Lord God sent me and his spirit.

Comment:

In this passage Israel is summoned three times to hear what the

Lord has to say (vs. 12, 14, 16). The substance of the message is that the Lord will accomplish His will upon Babylon through Cyrus "whom the lord loves" (v. 14). The frequent repetition of virtually the same thoughts is probably due to the fact that the prophet addressed himself on various occasions to different assemblies. Those messages may have been later assembled and published by the disciples or friends of the prophet (see comment on Isa. 8:16-18).

16 From the time that it took place, there was I

These are Jehovah's words. Others attribute them to the prophet.

And now the Lord God sent me and his spirit

There is a difference of opinion among commentators as to the identity of the speaker. Delitzsch thinks that the speaker is the servant of the Lord. Others are of the opinion that the prophet is referring to himself. Both interpretations are not without difficulties. If it is the servant of the Lord who speaks, why is he not mentioned directly as he is in other servant prophecies? On the other hand, if it is the prophet who speaks of himself, the abruptness of the transition is most surprising. If it is the prophet who speaks, the line should read: and now the Lord God sent me *with* his spirit. In all probability the speaker is the servant of the Lord.

17-19 Disobedience to the LORD brings sorrow.

17 Thus says the LORD, thy redeemer,
The Holy One of Israel,
I am the LORD thy God, who teaches thee for thy profit,
Who leads thee by the way thou shouldest go.

18 If only thou hadst obeyed my commandments,
Then would thy peace have been like a river,
And thy righteousness as the waves of the sea.

19 Thy seed would have been like the sand
And the offspring of thy body like the grains.
His name would not have been cut off,
Nor destroyed before me.

Comment:

Here is an expression of the Lord's deep sorrow over Israel who has deprived herself of countless blessings by failing to obey the LORD, and deprived herself of the peace which He had in store for them.

The missed blessing is described in striking terms. Oh, if Israel had only obeyed.

20-22   The captives are ordered to depart from Babylon in haste

20   Go forth from Babylon, flee from the Chaldeans.
Tell it and declare it with a voice of singing,
Send it forth and make it known.
Declare it to the ends of the earth and say:
The Lord has redeemed his servant Jacob.

21   They did not thirst when he led them across the deserts,
He made the waters flow out of the rock for them,
He split assunder the rock and the waters gushed forth.

22   There is no peace,
Says the LORD to the wicked.

Comment:

20   Go forth from Babylon, flee from the Chaldeans

The exiles receive a stern command to depart from Babylon in haste. They are to make known the joyful news of their deliverance to the ends of the earth. In vision the prophet sees his people on their way back to the holy land miraculously supplied with abundant water just as in the wilderness during the exodus from Egypt.

22   There is no peace, says the LORD, to the wicked

These words express the prophet's conviction that disobedience to God can only result in disaster. It is also a warning to those Jews who in disobedience to God's command, chose to remain in Babylon, which led to their assimilation and eventual extinction. The stern warning of verse 22 ends the first section of the second part of Isaiah. The second section of the second part of Isaiah ends (57:21) with the almost identical words.

Isaiah Chapter 49

The Second Prophecy About the Servant
The Return of the Exiles

Chapters 49-57 are the second section of the second part of Isaiah (see introduction). The main theme of this section is the person of the Servant of the Lord, whose life and work are described in four prophecies or songs (42:1-7; 49:1-13; 50:4-11; 52:13-53:12).

The last of the four is the most complete and majestic portrayal of the suffering servant and describes his humiliation, his death, resurrection and exaltation.

379

1-6 The Servant of the LORD addresses Himself to the nations of the world

1 Listen to me, O coastlands,
  And pay attention, you peoples from far.
  The LORD has called me from the womb,
  From the bowels of my mother has he mentioned my name.

2 He has made my mouth like a sharp sword,
  He hid me in the shadow of his hand,
  He has made me a polished shaft,
  And concealed me in his quiver.

3 Then he said to me,
  Thou are my servant,
  Israel, in whom I will be glorified.

4 But I said: I have labored in vain,
  I have spent my strength for nought, and to no purpose.
  Yet my righteous cause is with the LORD,
  And my reward with my God.

5 And now says the LORD,
  Who formed thee from the womb to be his servant,
  To restore Jacob to him, and that Israel may be gathered to him,
  For I am honorable in the eyes of the LORD,
  And my God is my strength.

6 Then he said: It is not enough that thou shouldest be my servant,
  To raise up the tribes of Jacob,
  And to restore the preserved ones of Israel,
  I have also set thee for a light of the nations,
  To be my salvation to the ends of the earth.

Comment:

1 Listen to me, O coastlands

Who is the person who addresses himself in such a solemn fashion to the nations of the world? Some maintain that the speaker is the prophet who represents ideal Israel. Their argument is based on verse 3, where the servant is called Israel. However the servant cannot be the prophet, of whom we know practically nothing and who plays no active role, nor can it be the collective body of Israel, because the servant's mission is to restore Israel (v. 6). To this end the LORD has called His servant from his mother's womb, and has given a message, which is as sharp as a sword or as a polished shaft (v. 2), designed to penetrate and overcome the flinty hearts and stubborn minds of men.

2 And concealed me in his quiver

The LORD has prepared His servant for just such a time of deliverance as this. This is probably an allusion to the pre-existence of the servant.

3   Thou art my servant, Israel, in whom I will be glorified

The servant is destined to fulfill Israel's highest calling to bring light and redemption to the nations of the world. In the deepest sense, the servant of God and Israel are one. There is no historical personality who fits Isaiah's vision of the suffering and redeeming servant of God except Jesus of Nazareth.

4   But I said: I have labored in vain

The servant of Jehovah identifies himself with the humiliations and frustrations of his people, with their apparent ineffectiveness and failure to establish the righteousness of God in a pagan and God-defying world.

Yet my righteous cause is with the LORD

In spite of all the hostility of his people and the opposition of humanity at large, the servant of God is sustained by his unshakable faith that his righteous cause (*mishpat*—lit. judgment) is in the safe-keeping of the LORD and that it will ultimately prevail.

6   It is not enough that thou shouldest be my servant to restore the preserved ones of Israel

In addition to the restoration of Israel and "the preserved of Israel" (the remnant), Jehovah has entrusted an even greater task to His servant; he is to be a light to all nations and bring salvation to the whole earth. His destiny is not only to be the Messiah of Israel but also the Saviour of all mankind.

7-13   The LORD addresses Himself to the once despised servant, who will be exalted in the future (7-9). The vision of the returning exiles ends with a brief hymn of praise.

7   Thus says the LORD, the Redeemer of Israel, his Holy One,
To him, whose soul is despised,
To him who is abhorred of nations,
To the servant of rulers,
Kings shall see and rise up,
Princes, they shall prostrate themselves,
For the sake of the LORD who is faithful,
Because of the Holy One of Israel, who has chosen thee.

8   Thus says the LORD,
At a time of favor have I answered thee,
And in the day of salvation have I helped thee,
And I will preserve thee and give thee for a covenant of the people,
To cause thee to inherit the desolate heritage.

9 Saying to the prisoners, "Go forth."
   And to those who dwell in darkness, "Show yourselves."
   They shall feed along the ways,
   And upon all the highlands shall be their pastures.

10 They shall not hunger, nor thirst,
   Neither shall the scorching desert wind and sun strike them
   down,
   For he who has compassion on them shall lead them,
   And guide them to the springs of water.

11 And I will make all my mountains a pathway,
   And my highways shall be raised up.

12 Look, these are coming from distant lands,
   Look, and these are coming from the north and west
   And these from the land of Sinim.

13 Sing, O heavens and rejoice, O earth,
   And break forth into song, O mountains,
   For the LORD has comforted his people,
   And has had compassion upon his distressed.

Comment:

7 To him whose soul is despised . . . the abhorred of nations

These words are a prelude to the great prophecy about the despised and suffering servant in Isaiah 52:13-53:12.

As the supreme representative of Israel, the servant of the LORD shares in the contempt of the nations for Israel and in her humiliation. The mighty rulers of the ancient world held in contempt the politically and militarily "feeble Jews." But the coming of the servant of the LORD will change this. Israel will share in the exaltation and the glory of her Messiah.

Kings shall see and rise up,
Princes, they shall prostrate themselves,

It is apparent that the prophet looks forward to exaltation of the servant, which will compel the kings of the earth to pay homage to him whom God has chosen to make Himself known to all mankind. This thought is also expressed in Isaiah 52:14.

8 At a time of favor have I answered thee

The servant is the mediator who effectively intercedes before the LORD for the nations.

And I will preserve thee and give thee for a covenant of the people

The prophet makes a clear distinction between the people (Israel) and the servant of God. He is to be God's new covenant by means of which He will enter into a new relationship with Israel. The servant is the living link between God and His people.

Verses 9-10 give us a beautiful and graphic picture of the liberated nation, set free from bondage wending their way on their homeward trek.

9   Saying to the prisoners, "Go forth"

It was Jehovah who caused Israel to go into captivity, now it is Jehovah or His servant who sets His people free. Just as there is a certain blending of Israel as a people with their supreme representative, the servant or Messiah, so there is a blending between the personality of the servant and Jehovah.

10   Neither shall the scorching desert wind and sun strike them down

The scorching desert wind, in Hebrew *sharab,* also known as the *hamsin,* is one of the most dangerous natural phenomena known to the traveler of the arid deserts in the Bible lands. But the people of God shall be led safely through all the hazards of the desert, because He who has compassion on them shall be their guide and commander-in-chief.

12   Look, these are coming from distant lands

The prophet jolts our imagination with the vision of the returning exiles as they come marching through the desert from all corners of the earth.

And these from the land of Sinim

In this context the land of Sinim represents the Far East, probably China, as the remotest land in the East. Some commentators have argued against the interpretation of the land of Sinim as meaning China, on the basis that the term "China" was supposedly derived from the Tsin dynasty dating back only to 255 B. C., long after the times of Isaiah.

However, variations of the name China were known as far back as the 10th century B.C. and some of the provinces of that land were designated by that name. It is possible that merchants from China occasionally reached Babylon, the world center of commerce in those days.

The description of the return of the exiles from Babylon goes far beyond that historical event and anticipates the final ingathering of the people of God into their transformed and blessed homeland, Isaiah's "Pilgrim's Progress."

13 Sing, O heavens and rejoice, O earth

A typical brief hymn of praise, provoked by the vision of the glorious redemption which the LORD has in store for Israel and for the nations of the world (cf. Isa. 12:35; 42:10-12; 44:23, etc.).

14-26 Jehovah's tender reassurance to the captives of Zion that He has not forgotten them and that He will soon restore them and rebuild their land

14 But Zion said, Jehovah has forsaken me,
    And the LORD has forgotten me.

15 Can a woman forget her sucking baby,
    And have no compassion on the son of her womb?
    Even if she should forget,
    Yet I will not forget.

16 Behold I have engraved thee upon the palms of my hands,
    Thy walls are ever before me.

17 Thy children make haste,
    Those who destroyed thee and laid thee waste,
    Shall depart from thee.

18 Lift up thine eyes around thee and look,
    They all gather together and come to thee,
    As I live, says the LORD, thou will indeed dress thyself with them,
    As with an ornament,
    And gird them around thee like a bride.

19 Instead of thy devastated and desolate places,
    And thy land which has been destroyed,
    Now it will be too narrow for the inhabitants,
    And they who swallowed thee up,
    Shall be far removed.

20 The children who were once taken from thee,
    Shall yet say in thine ears:
    This place is too constricted for me,
    Give me space that I may settle.

21 Thou shalt then say in thy heart,
    "Who has borne me these,
    Seeing that I have been deprived of my children and barren,
    An exile, wandering to and fro?
    And who has brought up these,

Behold, I was left alone.
These, where were they?"

22 Thus says the LORD God:
Behold, I will lift my hand to the nations,
And set up my standard to the peoples,
And they will bring thy sons in their bosom,
And thy daughters shall be carried
Upon their shoulders.

23 And kings shall be thy foster fathers,
And their queens thy nursing mothers.
They shall bow down to thee to the earth,
And lick the dust of thy feet;
And thou shalt know that I am the LORD,
For they shall not be ashamed who wait for me.

24 Can the prey be taken away from the mighty one
Or the righteous captive be delivered?

25 For thus says the LORD,
Surely the captives of the mighty shall be taken away,
And the prey of the terrible shall be delivered,
And I will contend with him
Who contends with thee,
And I will save thy children.

26 And I will feed them who oppress thee with their own flesh,
And they shall be drunk with their own blood,
As with new wine.
And all flesh shall know
That I the LORD am thy Saviour
And thy Redeemer, the mighty One of Jacob.

Comment:

The second part of this chapter (vs. 14-26) is a most beautiful and moving description of Jehovah's love for his captive people in exile.

14 But Zion said, Jehovah has forsaken me

Apparently the mood of the exiles was one of gloom and depression. The thought of many was that the Lord had forgotten His people. To these the LORD sends a message of tender reassurance.

15 Can a woman forget her sucking baby?

The love of Jehovah surpasses even the tenderest love of a mother for her precious child.

16 Behold I have engraved thee upon the palms of my hands

The LORD cannot and will not forget His people. The walls of Jerusalem are ever before Him. One of the most striking verses in the Scriptures describing the intense love of God for His people.

17-24 These verses contain a dramatic description of the captives' return to Zion. The ingathering of her children from the remotest corners of the earth. There will be so many of these returning exiles that they will demand more space to settle (v. 20). One of the most remarkable statements is in v. 23, where it is predicted that kings shall be the foster fathers of Israel's children, and queens (lit. princesses) their nursing mothers. This should be interpreted not in terms of national self-aggrandizement but as the final tribute of the great of this world to the majesty of His kingdom.

23 And lick the dust of thy feet

An act of supreme homage in oriental imagery. It refers to the worship of the God of Israel and His exalted servant, the Messiah.

24-26 Some of the Israelites must have been wondering how could anyone deliver them from the awesome power of the mighty one, that is, the Babylonian empire. God assures them that He Himself will accomplish this and fight their wars (v. 25). He will punish their oppressors according to the measure of their wickedness; "They shall eat their own flesh, and drink their own blood" (v. 26).

24 Or the righteous captive be delivered?

In Hebrew "*Sh'vi tsaddik*" which the King James Version translates "lawful captive," the literal meaning "the righteous captive" is preferable, a probable allusion to the righteous remnant.

26 And all flesh shall know that I the LORD am thy Saviour

In the deliverance of Israel the honor of Jehovah is at stake.

Isaiah Chapter 50

The Third Prophecy About the Servant

1-4 Israel's separation from God not permanent

1   Thus says the LORD,
    Where is your mother's bill of divorce
    With which I have put her away?
    Or to which of my creditors did I sell her?
    Behold, you were sold for your own iniquities,
    And your mother was put away for your own transgressions.

2   Why was there no one when I came?

Why did no one answer when I called?
Have I no power to deliver?
Behold, at my command I dry up the sea,
And turn rivers to a desert.
Their fish become foul for lack of water,
And die of thirst.

3 I clothe the heavens in blackness,
And make sackcloth their covering.

Comment:

1 Where is your mother's bill of divorce?

Verses 1-3 continue the message of chapter 49:22-26 and are addressed to those exiles who felt that Jehovah had finally abandoned them and sold them into slavery. The prophet reassures them that God has not broken His covenant with Israel and that their bondage is only temporary. The prophet speaks to them in terms of their daily experiences. According to the law of Moses, when a man put away his wife he was obliged to give her a bill of divorce (Deut. 24:1). Since no such document existed, Jehovah's marriage to Israel was still binding and was never dissolved.

Using another illustration from daily life, the prophet points out that had Jehovah sold His people into bondage, as an impoverished father might sell a child to his creditors, in that case, who could have been Jehovah's creditor? This question in itself exposes the whole absurdity of such an assumption.

Behold you were sold for your own iniquities

No, Israel's bondage was not willed by God, but was self-inflicted, the result of her own wayward and sinful behavior.

Why was there no one when I came?

Jehovah further establishes the reason for Israel's present deplorable plight by pointing to the lack of any response by the people to God's constant warnings through His servants, the prophets. The same complaint is voiced in Isaiah 59:16 and also in Jeremiah 7:25-26:

And he saw that there was no man, and wondered that there was no intercessor: therefore his arm brought salvation unto him; and his righteousness it sustained him.
Since the day that your fathers came forth out of the land of Egypt unto this day I have even sent unto you all my servants the prophets, daily rising up early and sending them. Yet they hearkened not unto me, nor inclined their ear, but hardened their neck: they did worse than their fathers.

Have I no power to deliver?

Why should Israel doubt Jehovah's ability to deliver them, having experienced so much of His power and care?

Behold, at my command I dry up the sea,

The miracles which their ancestors had witnessed, when Jehovah delivered them from Egypt, should have been proof enough to remove any doubt from their minds.

The reference to the heavens being dressed in blackness and sackcloth is a further allusion to God's mighty works at Sinai (Ex. 19:16), and to His infinite power.

4-11   The servant of the LORD was prepared by Him for His mission.

4   The LORD has given me the tongue of a disciple,
That I may know how to sustain the weary with a word.
Morning by morning he wakens me.
He wakens my ear that I may listen like a disciple.

5   The LORD God has opened my ear,
And I did not rebel,
Nor did I turn back.

6   I gave my back to those who struck me,
And my cheeks to those who plucked my beard.
I did not hide my face from insults and spitting.

7   The LORD God will sustain me,
Therefore was I not overcome by insults,
Therefore also I have set my face like a flint,
And I know that I shall not be ashamed.

8   He who justifies me is near,
Who will contend with me? Let us stand up together.
Who is my adversary, let him come near to me.

9   Behold the LORD God will help me,
Who shall condemn me?
Behold they shall all mold away like a garment,
The moth shall devour them.

10   Who among you fear the LORD,
And obey the voice of his servant,
Though he walks in darkness and without a flicker of light,
Let him trust in the name of the LORD,
And lean upon his God.

11   Behold all of you who kindle a fire,
Who arm yourselves with firebrands,

Away with you into the flame of your fire,
And into the firebrands which you have kindled.
This shall come to you from my hand,
You shall lie down in grief.

Comment:

The third song about the servant of the LORD is closely related to the fourth and last in the series (Isa. 52:13-53-12). Here the servant is presented as the faithful and obedient disciple of Jehovah.[1]

4   The LORD has given me the tongue of a disciple

The word for "disciple" here is *"limmud,"* instead of the later *"talmid."* The servant affirms that he was instructed by the LORD God Himself (cf. John 7:16 and 14:24).

That I may know how to sustain the weary with a word

The message which the servant received was one of comfort for the weary (see Mt. 11:28).

5   And I did not rebel

There was complete willingness on the part of the servant to obey God's voice and to submit to His will, for He does not reveal Himself to the rebellious heart and unwilling ear.

6   I gave my back to those who struck me . . . my cheeks to those who plucked my beard

The servant readily submitted to abuse and insult in order to carry out his divinely appointed task. The experience of the servant of the Lord reminds one in a striking way of the experiences of Jesus as described in Matthew 26:27.

7   The LORD God will sustain me, therefore was I not overcome by insults

An emphatic affirmation that God will always help him, therefore no persecution could ever deflect the servant from his task. His faith and reliance upon God was the rock and the fountain of his strength and of his confidence that in the end he would be vindicated by the One who sent him.

8   He who justifies me is near, who will contend with me?

In the sure knowledge that the LORD God is the one who helps and justifies him, the servant was able to challenge all his adversaries to appear with him before the tribunal of the Supreme Judge.

9   Who shall condemn me?

The prophetic language carries a strong intimation of a court procedure. The adversaries of the servant who accuse and condemn him, are also the enemies of God, but the final word belongs to the Supreme Judge.

Behold they shall all mold away like a garment

The enemies of the servant of God have no future. They are likened to a moth-eaten garment which is about to disintegrate.

10 Who among you fear the LORD, and obey the voice of his servant

This verse is addressed to all those who "fear the LORD," a synonym for Israel's faithful remnant. The servant is mentioned just once in this passage.

Though he walks in darkness . . . let him trust in the LORD and lean upon his God

Just as the servant's ultimate source of strength is his faith and absolute trust in God, so it should be also of every believer. The words are reminiscent of Psalm 23:4:

Yea, though I walk through the valley of the shadow of death, I will fear no evil, for thou art with me.

11 All of you who kindle a fire, away with you into the flame of your fire

After a word of encouragement to those "who fear the LORD," a warning is now directed to the ungodly. It is their own mischief which will, in the end, boomerang and destroy them.

NOTE:

1. Some commentators have suggested that the original model for this particular servant passage (like the suffering servant of Isa. 52:14-53:12) was either the so-called "Second Isaiah" himself or Jeremiah; others suggested Ezekiel or Zerubbabel, or some unknown martyr as the prototype. All this is sheer guesswork without historical foundation. These speculations have this in common, they all assume a definite historical personality to be the prototype of the servant. For a detailed discussion of the subject we refer the reader to the Appendix in J. Skinner's *Commentary to Isaiah*, Vol. II, revised ed., Cambridge University Press.

There were others who assumed that the servant of the Lord represents "Ideal Israel" or her spiritual core. However, the servant of all four passages in Isaiah is unique and so exalted, that he fits no known formerly human historical personality. Only Jesus of Nazareth comes close to the majestic figure of the suffering servant. In fact, until the appearance of Jesus, ancient Jewish commentators invariably interpreted the servant passages as applying to the Messiah. The interpretation of these passages as applying to Israel collectively came into vogue much later, during the Christological controversies between the Church and the Synagogue.

We shall discuss this subject further in considerable detail in connection with Isaiah 52:13-53-12.

Isaiah Chapter 51

A Message of Comfort and Hope for Israel and the Nations

1-3 Those who do Jehovah's will, though few in number, will in the end experience the mercy of God.

1 Listen to me, you who follow righteousness,
You who seek the LORD,
Look to the rock from which you were hewn,
And to the hole of the pit from which you were dug.

2 Look unto Abraham, your father,
And to Sarah, who gave you birth,
For he was just one when I called him,
Yet I blessed him and made many of him.

3 For the LORD has comforted Zion,
He has comforted all her desolate places,
And made her wilderness like Eden,
And her desert like the garden of the LORD.
Joy and gladness shall be found in her,
Thanksgiving and the voice of melody.

Comment:

1 Listen to me, you who follow righteousness

Literally "you who pursue righteousness," that is, you who intensely search out and practice righteousness. They are the people who seek God and are anxious to do His will. Presumably there were not many such "righteous men" among the exiles, and they were in a mood of despondency. What could a mere handful of God-fearing men accomplish, surrounded as they were, by the indifference of their own countrymen and the crushing power of their pagan captors? Was there any hope for them?

2 Look unto Abraham your father and to Sarah

The believers in bondage were encouraged to remember that they were cut from the same rock and quarry as their original ancestors, Abraham and Sarah. The whole history of Israel was proof that Jehovah is the God of the impossible. There they were, an old couple, long after their childbearing age had passed, and look what God did! He made Abraham the father of Israel and of many nations.

3 For the LORD has comforted Zion

The promise is expressed in the prophetic past. What Jehovah is planning to do for His people in the future, is to the prophet an already accomplished fact. Jerusalem shall be rebuilt, and the desolate land shall become like Eden, a garden of the LORD.

Joy and gladness . . . the voice of melody

The prophet's vision reached out beyond any historical limits and becomes eschatology, a vision of the last days as he sees Israel returning, not only to their native land, but to their God.

4-8 In the end Jehovah will establish His kingdom of righteousness and salvation for Israel and all nations.

4 Attend to me, O my people,
   And give ear unto me, O my nation,
   For the law shall go forth from me,
   And my judgment shall suddenly become
   The light of the peoples.

5 My righteousness is near,
   My salvation has gone forth.
   My arm shall judge the nations.
   The coastlands shall wait for me,
   And will trust in my arm.

6 Lift up your eyes toward heaven,
   And look down upon the earth,
   For the heavens shall dissolve like smoke,
   And the earth shall wither away like a garment,
   And they who dwell upon it shall die likewise;
   But my salvation shall be for ever,
   And my righteousness shall never cease.

7 Listen to me, you who know righteousness,
   People in whose hearts is my law;
   Fear not the taunt of men,
   And be not dismayed by their insults.

8 For the moth shall eat them up like a garment,
   And the insect shall devour them like wool.
   But my righteousness shall abide for ever,
   And my salvation for all generations.

Comment:

4 Attend to me, O my people

The call is addressed to the remnant of Israel, the spiritual core of the nation.

For the law shall go forth from me

Here "the law" is not the law of Moses which was primarily revealed to and for Israel. The prophet speaks of the supreme law of which the fountainhead and spring is the Lord God Himself. This is the law and the light of all mankind (cf. Rom. 2:14-15, John 1:4).

And my judgment shall suddenly become the light of the peoples

The law, or the judgment of God, is the eternal *logos* (John 1:1). Yet its manifestation in history is sudden and unexpected. This is what the Hebrew verb *"argi-a,"* "will suddenly appear," from *"regah"* —a moment, suggests.

5 The coastland shall wait for me and shall trust in my arm

An essential part of the prophetic message is the conviction that all nations which from the beginning of time have lived in the thraldom of sin and wickedness have always, consciously or unconsciously, waited for true righteousness, the law of God.

6 Lift up your eyes toward heaven, and look down upon the earth

All that which is visible to the human eye shall one day disappear, only the mercy and the salvation of God will abide forever. Jesus, identifying Himself with His Father declared:

> Heaven and earth shall pass away, but my words shall not pass away (Mt. 24:35).

7-8 These verses repeat and reinforce the thoughts expressed in verses 4-6, with the added exhortation:

7 Fear not the taunt of men and be not dismayed by their insults

Believing in the eternal and omnipotent God, men of faith ought not to fear the taunts and insults of *"enosh"*—a weak, ephemeral being, "mere man."

9-11 The mighty arm of Jehovah is invoked to deliver Israel

9 Awake, awake, put on thy strength, O arm of the LORD.
Awake as in olden days, in ancient generations.
Art thou not he who cut up Rahab,
That pierced the dragon?

10 Art thou not he, who dried up the sea
The waters of the great deep?
Who turned the depths of the sea into a road
For the redeemed to pass over?

11 And the ransomed of the LORD shall return,
And shall come to Zion with singing.
Everlasting joy shall be upon their heads.
Sorrow and sighing shall flee away.

Comment:

9-11 "The arm of the LORD" is a metaphor for divine omni-

potence and is invoked to manifest itself in a mighty act of deliverance, as in the days of old.

9 Art thou not he who cut up Rahab?

Egypt is called Rahab, a mythical sea monster (Isa. 30:7), which is involved in the story of creation in pagan mythology. The dragon is another primeval monster representing the restless forces of the sea (Job 9:13).

10 Art thou not he, who dried up the sea

This seems to be a double allusion first to the act of creation (Gen. 1:9), and then to the exodus from Egypt. The remembrance of the mighty acts of God in creation and in history bring conviction to the prophet, that the LORD will again manifest His might and redeeming grace.

11 And the ransomed of the LORD shall return

As always, the prophet looks beyond the immediate situation toward the ultimate redemption, which is so beautifully described here. In the prophet's vision, history is the background canvas for the "ultimate days" when the Messianic King, or the suffering and exalted Servant of God, shall reign over all the kingdoms of the earth.

12-16 Seeing that Jehovah is the defender of Israel, why should His people live in constant terror of mortal man?

12   I, I myself am he who comforts you,
     Who art thou to fear feeble and mortal man,
     Or the son of man who will become as the grass?

13   And hast forgotten the LORD thy maker,
     Who planted the heavens and laid the foundation of the earth,
     And fearest all day long the fury of the oppressor,
     As he gets ready to destroy,
     And where is the fury of the oppressor?

14   He that is bent over shall speedily be released,
     And will not die in the dungeon,
     Neither shall he be short of his bread.

15   For I am the LORD thy God,
     Who stirs up the sea, so that its waves roar,
     The LORD of hosts is his name.

16   And I have put my words in thy mouth,
     And hid thee in the shadow of my hand,
     That I may plant the heavens,
     And lay the foundation of the earth,
     And that I may say to Zion: thou art my people.

Comment:

12 I, I myself am he who comforts you

Who art thou to fear feeble and mortal man?

As the mouthpiece of God, the prophet remonstrates with his people: since the omnipotent LORD Himself is their comforter and defender, why should Israel be in dread of an *"enosh,"* a feeble and mortal man?

13 And where is the fury of the oppressor?

While they live, the raging of the enemy appears to be most frightening, but when their fury is spent and they are gone, their boasting seems to be the pitiful raving of a puny man.

14 He that is bent over . . . will not die in the dungeon

Those who are now bent under the yoke of captivity will not die as prisoners, nor perish of hunger, but will soon experience the redemption of God.

15 For I am the LORD thy God, who

Jehovah, the creator and controller of all nations, is the guarantor of all His promises that they shall be fulfilled.

16 And I have put my words in thy mouth

Jehovah has entrusted His revelation to His people to make it known to the nations.

And hid thee in the shadow of my hand

A most beautiful expression of Gods' love and protection of His people, which all believers could also apply to themselves individually.

That I may plant the heavens and lay the foundation of the earth

Some interpreters have considered this passage hopelessly confused and out of harmony with the preceding thoughts (e.g. Skinner). That might be so, if the prophet had been referring to the original creation previously mentioned in verse 13. However, if we regard this as a promise of a new creation, of a new heaven and a new earth, filled with the righteousness of God, and where restored and redeemed Israel is again the people of God, then the passage makes beautiful sense. This apparently was what the prophet had in mind (cf. Isa. 65:17).

17-23 A call to prostrated Jerusalem to wake up and shake off the stupor of her enslavement and suffering.

17 Bestir thyself, bestir thyself, stand up, O Jerusalem,
    Thou who hast drunk from the hand of the LORD,

The cup of his fury, the chalice of stupor,
Which thou hast drunk and drained.

18 Of all the sons to whom she gave birth,
There is none to guide her,
Of all the sons which she has reared,
There is none to take her by the hand.

19 These twin horrors have befallen thee:
Who is there to mourn for thee?
Devastation and destruction,
Hunger and the sword,
How shall I comfort thee?

20 Thy sons are worn out,
And lie panting at every street corner,
Like an antelope in the net.
They are saturated with the fury of the LORD,
With the rebuke of the LORD.

21 Hear then this, thou afflicted,
Who art drunk, but not with wine:

22 Thus says thy LORD Jehovah
And thy God who champions thy cause.
Behold I have taken out of thy hand
The cup of stupor, and the chalice of my fury,
Thou shalt drink of it no more.

23 But I will put it into the hands of thy tormentors,
Those who said to thy soul:
Bend down, that we may pass over,
And thou hast flattened thy back to the ground,
And made it like a street to pass over.

Comment:

17 Bestir thyself, bestir thyself, stand up, O Jerusalem

Jerusalem has long lain prostrate and bewildered by the bitter cup of divine fury, which she has had to drink to the last bitter drop. Now the time has come to bestir herself and to rise up to her full dignity, as befitting the people of God.

18 Of all the sons to whom she gave birth, there is none to guide her

Jerusalem's tragedy is made even more pitiful, that in the hour of her extreme need she has none of her sons to guide her.

19-20 These two verses graphically describe the pitiful plight of Jerusalem. The scene is so dramatic that it hardly needs any comment. Devastation and destruction, hunger and the sword are the disasters which have come upon Jerusalem. We sense the horror of the unfortunate people of Jerusalem. The tone is reminiscent of the Lamentations of Jeremiah. The sons of Israel are likened to captured wild animals, which lie panting in their nets, exhausted and frightened.

21-23 Now, however, the LORD is announcing a new message for His prostrated nation. The cup of suffering and stupefaction is at last to be removed from her hand and passed on to her tormentors.

23 Who said to thy soul, bend down that we may pass over

"Thy soul" here simply means "to thee." The above words are no mere poetic license, but a description of a cruel custom, practiced by the Assyrians, the Babylonians and other Oriental conquerors, who made their captives lie down and walked over them. Such scenes were often depicted on ancient monuments.

Isaiah Chapter 52:1-12

**Let Jerusalem Array Herself in All Her Beauty
As Befitting the Dignity of a Redeemed and Holy City**

1-6 Jerusalem's redemption is at hand, for the Lord's honor is at stake

1 Awake, awake, put on thy strength, O Zion,
Put on thy beautiful garments, O Jerusalem, holy city,
For from now on shall no longer
The uncircumcised and unclean come into thee.

2 Shake thyself from the dust,
Arise and sit down, O Jerusalem,
Loosen thyself from the cords of thy neck,
O captive daughter of Zion.

3 For thus says the LORD:
You were sold for nothing,
And you shall be redeemed without money.

4 For thus says the LORD Jehovah,
At the beginning my people went down to Egypt to sojourn,
Later the Assyrian oppressed them without cause.

5 And now what do I find here?
Seeing that my people were taken away for nothing,
And they who rule over them are boasting, says the LORD,
And my name is constantly and all day blasphemed.

6 Therefore will my people know my name,
  Therefore on that day will they know,
  That I am he who speaks, behold I am here.

Comment:

1 Awake, awake, put on thy strength, O Zion

In ringing tones Zion is commanded to cast off the chains of her captivity, and to array herself in the beautiful garments of her redemption.

For from now on shall no longer the uncircumcised and unclean come into thee

This is no xenophobic sentiment, that henceforth no Gentile shall be permitted to enter Jerusalem, but a promise that the pagan who in the past came to plunder and destroy the Holy City will no longer be permitted to do so.

2 Shake thyself from the dust, arise and sit down

On the face of it, "arise and sit down" sound contradictory. What the prophet apparently is saying is that the captives should shake off the dust of defeat and humiliation, and assume the posture and dignity of the redeemed. This might be paraphrased "arise from the dust and sit down on the throne."

3 You were sold for nothing and you shall be redeemed without money

Jehovah received no payment for Israel from her captors, and He will also set them free without paying a ransom price to them.

4 At the beginning my people went down to Egypt to sojourn

The Israelites went down to Egypt at the invitation of Pharoah, but were soon enslaved by the Egyptians. However, God led them out from there. Later they were again enslaved by the Assyrians "for nothing," that is, without any moral or legal right. But Jehovah delivered them from the Assyrians, who were in turn defeated by the Babylonians (612 B. C.).

5 And now what do I find here?

What is the situation which the Lord sees in Babylon? His people are cruelly mistreated, while their captors strut and boast and constantly blaspheme His Holy Name as if their idols had vanquished Jehovah.

6 Therefore will my people know my name

"To know the name" is to know intimately the character of the person who bears the name. In this case Israel will know that Jehovah is mighty to deliver, her faithful and promise-keeping God.

7-12 The prophet's vision of the homeward march of the exiles led by Jehovah Himself.

7 How beautiful on the mountains
   Are the feet of the messenger,
   Who announces peace, proclaims good news, announces salvation,
   And says to Zion: Thy God reigns.

8 Hark, thy watchmen lift up their voice,
   They sing together,
   For they shall see, eye to eye,
   The LORD returning to Zion.

9 Break forth into joy, sing together,
   You ruins of Jerusalem,
   For the LORD has comforted his people,
   He has redeemed Jerusalem.

10 The LORD has bared his holy arm,
   Before the eyes of all nations;
   And all the ends of the earth,
   Shall see the salvation of our God.

11 Depart, depart, get out from there,
   Touch not anything unclean,
   Get out of her, make yourselves clean,
   You who carry the vessels of the LORD.

12 For you shall not depart in haste,
   Neither shall you go by flight,
   For the LORD shall go before you,
   And your rear-guard shall be the God of Israel.

Comment:

7 How beautiful on the mountains are the feet of the messenger

The prophet visualizes in spirit a fleet-footed messenger on the mountains of Judah, bringing the good tidings that the exiles, under Jehovah Himself, are returning to Zion in triumph. The apostle Paul sees in this messenger the figure of the evangelist who brings the good tiding ("the evangel") of salvation to Israel (Rom. 10:13).

8 Hark, thy watchmen lift up their voice

Meanwhile the watchmen upon the walls of Jerusalem are the first to observe the triumphant return of the exiles under the guidance of Jehovah Himself.

9 Break forth into joy, sing together, you ruins of Jerusalem

The ruins of Jerusalem are encouraged to participate in the triumphant return of those who once inhabited the glorious city.

10 The LORD has bared his holy arm

The metaphor applied to "the arm of Jehovah" is taken from an ancient warrior's stance, as he throws back his upper garment from his right shoulder, in readiness for battle.

11 Depart, depart, get out from there

With a brusque command the exiles are ordered to leave Babylon. The phrase "from there" as we have already indicated in the introduction to this volume, would appear to place the prophet somewhere far removed from Babylon. This is consistent with the view that the author of both parts of the book was Isaiah, a resident of Jerusalem.

Touch not anything unclean

As a redeemed and holy people, they must not defile themselves virtually or morally (Lev. 23:14). This applied particularly to the Levites who, according to the decree of Cyrus (Ezra 6:5), were to carry back to Jerusalem the vessels of the Temple. In a larger sense all Israel was to be the carrier of the vessels of the LORD, of His holiness, His righteousness and of His light to the ends of the earth.

12 For you shall not depart in haste

In contrast to Israel's hasty departure from Egypt from the pursuing Pharaoh, the departure from Babylon would be leisurely, in full sight of, and with the cooperation and goodwill of Cyrus, whom the LORD has previously called "my shepherd" (Isa. 44:28) and "anointed" (Isa. 45:1).

For the LORD shall go before you

Here we have a majestic portrayal of Jehovah, marching at the head of His liberated and redeemed people and at the same time safeguarding their rear from enemy attack, (see also Isa. 58:8).

Isaiah Chapters 52:13-53:12

The Suffering of the Servant of the Lord and His Future Glory

The prophecy of Isaiah 52:13-53:12 is the heart of the second part of the book of Isaiah. Here Messianic vision reaches its pinnacle.

For almost two millennia Jewish and Christian scholars have debated the question whether the prophet was speaking of himself or of Israel who suffers innocently for the nations of the world. The Ethiopian eunuch touched upon the heart of this question when he asked Philip, the early disciple of Christ: "I pray thee, of whom speaketh the prophet this, of himself, or of some other man?" Acts 8:34.

Generally there is little difference between Jewish and Christian translations of this majestic passage of Isaiah, apart from a few words of secondary importance. However, there is a profound and basic difference in the interpretation of the text. Ancient Jewish tradition has for many centuries seen in Isaiah 53 the portrait of the suffering servant of God, the Messiah, a view which still is held to this day by most Orthodox Jews.

However, at the end of the 11th century A. D., Jewish commentators began to assert that Isaiah had in mind Israel who suffers innocently for the sins of all nations.

On the other hand, Christians following Jewish tradition, have from the very beginning, maintained that Isaiah 53 is an amazing prophecy concerning Jesus, "the Lamb of God which taketh away the sins of the world" John 1:29.

Going back to the oldest Jewish interpretations of this passage, we find that Targum of Jonathan ben Uziel (2nd century A. D.), an Aramaic paraphrase of the Bible, renders Isaiah 52:13 in this way:

"Behold my servant Messiah shall prosper; he shall be high, and increase and be exceedingly strong"

The Babylonian Talmud (codified in the 6th century) also applies Isaiah's prophecy Messianically:

"The Messiah—what is his name? . . . The Rabbis say, 'the leprous one': Those of the house of Rabbi say, 'the sick one,' as it is said, 'surely he hath borne our sickness.'" San 98ᵇ

Midrash Rabbah, referring to Ruth 2:14, explains:

"He is speaking of the King Messiah: 'Come hither draw near to the Throne; and eat the bread,' that is the bread of the kingdom: 'and dip thy morsel in the vinegar.' This refers to his chastisements, as it is said, 'But he was wounded for our transgressions, bruised for our iniquities.'"

In the Yalkut Shimoni, a later Midrash (a rabbinical commentary), it is written:

"Who art thou, O great mountain?" (Zech. 4:7). This refers to the King Messiah, And why does he call him "the great mountain?" Because He is greater than the patriarchs. As it is said, "My servant shall be high and lifted up and lofty exceedingly." He will be higher than Abraham, who says, "I raise high my hand unto the Lord" (Gen. 14:22). Lifted up above Moses, to whom it is said, "Lift it up into thy bosom" (Num. 11:12): Loftier than the ministering angels, of whom it is written: "Their wheels were lofty and terrible" (Ezk. 1:18).

These are only a few of many rabbinical comments relating to Isaiah 52:13-53:12, which, with one accord, apply it to the Messiah.

What caused this radical change in the rabbinical position?

Behind this change lies the tragic Jewish experience during the Crusades. After the end of the First Crusade in 1096 A. D., when the Crusaders, in their misguided zeal, attempted to wrest the Holy Sepulchre from the Muslims, they became aware that the infidels were not only "the pagan Muslims" in far away Palestine, but also "the Christ-killing Jews" who were living in their very midst, in so-called Christian Europe. Encouraged by their fanatical leaders and frequently incited by high-ranking clerics, the Crusaders committed massacres of the Jews, especially of those who lived in France, Italy and Germany. Thousands were butchered, their synagogues burned and their possessions pillaged.

This horrible experience, which lasted for almost two centuries, left a traumatic impact on the Jews, comparable only to their later experience under Hitler. From that time on, their revulsion against everything that the Christians believed or represented, became more violent and hostile than ever before.

And since the Christians in their frequent disputes with the Jews used Isaiah 53 as one of their main arguments for the Messiahship of Jesus, the Jews felt impelled to reinterpret this prophecy in such a way as to blunt the Christian argument. Since that time the question of Isaiah 53 took on a heated polemical and emotional character.

Another compelling reason for the abandonment of the Messianic interpretation of the controversial passage was the fact that many Jews themselves became convinced that there is a cogent and strong argument for the Christian position. In fact many Jews actually converted to the Christian faith as a result of the Christian-Jewish disputations of the Middle Ages. During that period the outstanding Jewish scholar, R. Joseph Ben Kaspi (1280-1340 A. D.) warned the rabbis that "those who expounded this section of the Messiah give occasion to the heretics (Christians) to interpret it of Jesus." About this statement Rabbi Saadia ibn Danan observed: "May God forgive him for not having spoken the truth."[1]

In any case, since 1096 A. D. Jewish interpreters began to teach that Isaiah's suffering servant was not the Messiah but persecuted and suffering Israel, "who was led to the slaughter like a sheep and opened not his mouth" (Isa. 53:7).

In the light of the Crusaders' atrocities this interpretation took on a semblance of verisimility and found much favor among the majority of Jews, but not among all of them. Still the original Messianic interpretation of Isaiah 53 persisted and survived even to the present day. It is preserved in Jewish liturgy for the Day of Atonement in a prayer attributed to Eliezer Ha-Kallir (8th Century A. D.):

> "We are shrunk up in our misery even until now! Our rock hath not come to us; Messiah, our righteousness, hath turned from us; we are in terror, and there is none to justify us! Our iniquities and the yoke of our transgressions he will bear, *for he was wounded for our transgressions:* he will carry our sins upon his shoulder that we may find forgiveness for our iniquities, and *by his stripes we are healed.* O eternal One, the time is come to make a new creation, from the vault of heaven bring him up, out of Seir draw him forth that he may make his voice heard to us in Lebanon, a second time by the hand of Yinnon."[2]

From the above prayer it is obvious that the Jews of that era believed that the Messiah had already come and were praying that He may come "a second time." Some of the medieval scholars who interpreted this passage in an individual sense applied it either to Jeremiah, or to Isaiah, others to Hezekiah, and some to any righteous person who suffers innocently.

Many of the ancient rabbis were aware of the seemingly divergent elements in the Messianic prophecies. One stream of thought spoke of the suffering Messiah, (Isa. 50:5-7 and 53). The other described a triumphant Messiah who will subdue the rebellious nations and establish His kingdom (Psa. 2 and 110). To resolve this problem the rabbis have resorted to the theory of the two Messiahs, *the suffering one,* called Messiah ben Joseph, who dies in battle against Edom (Rome). He is followed by the *triumphant Messiah,* Messiah ben David, who establishes His kingdom of righteousness after defeating the Gentile nations.[8]

Another attempt to resolve the seeming contradiction of a suffering and triumphant Messiah is mentioned in Pesikta Rabbathi. According to this the Messiah ben David suffers in every generation for the sins of each generation. Other rabbinical authorities sought to find a solution to this puzzle in various ingenious ways, which however did not commend themselves to most Jewish people.

Some rabbinical authorities have postponed the solution of this and of all other perplexing questions to the coming of the prophet Elijah, the forerunner of the Messiah who will make all things clear.[4]

In the New Testament this problem is solved by the doctrine concerning the first advent of the suffering Christ followed by His second triumphant coming, (Mt. 23:29, John 14:3, Acts 1:11, 1 Thes. 4:14-17, etc.).

The chief representative of the non-Messianic, collective interpretation was the 11th century French Jewish scholar, Rabbi Shlomo Itzhaki (1040-1105), best known by his initials as Rashi. His views on Isaiah 53 were later supported by the famous commentators and scholars, Joseph Kimchi (1105-1170) and his son, David (1160-1235), and later by the renowned Jewish scholar and diplomat, Don Isaac Abarbanel of Spain (1437-1508).

In time the non-Messianic interpretation of Isaiah 53 became practically an official dogma among most Jews. Nevertheless, many learned rabbis have continued to object strenuously to this interpretation as doing violence to the literal and obvious sense of Isaiah 53. Thus Rabbi Moshe Kohen ibn Crispin (13th century) complained bitterly that those who interpret Isaiah 53 as referring to Israel do violence to it and to its natural meaning: "having inclined after the stubbornness of their own hearts and their own opinion. I'm pleased to interpret the Parasha (passage) in accordance with the teaching of our rabbis, of the King Messiah . . . and adhere to the literal sense. Thus I shall be free from forced and far-fetched interpretations of which others are guilty."[5]

Similar opinions were voiced later by other prominent rabbinical authorities. However, the collective interpretation of Isaiah 53 remains the dominant one today among the majority of the Jews. Strangely enough many liberal Christian theologians, whom Delitzsch once called, "the uncircumcised rabbis," have supported the Jewish position, sometimes out of deference to their Jewish friends, or in line with their own liberal views, which had no place for a suffering Messiah, predicted by the prophets.

Jewish arguments against the Christian interpretation of Isaiah 53 are generally based on a misinterpretation of the Christian doctrine concerning the humanity and the deity of Christ, that is the doctrine of Incarnation. The infinite majesty and omnipotence of the eternal God was contrasted by the Jewish controversialists with the physical limitations of Jesus while he was on earth in the form of a frail human being.

Here are some typical Jewish arguments against the divine nature of Christ:

1. Behold my servant, 52:13.
   If Christ is God, how can he also be called a servant?

2. He shall be exalted, 52:13.
   How can it be said of God that He *will* be exalted (future tense)? Is not God always exalted?

3. Smitten of God and afflicted, 53:4.
   If Christ is God, how can he be smitten and afflicted of God?

4. And the Lord hath laid on him the iniquity of us all, 53:6.
   If the Lord has laid upon him the iniquity of us all, then Jesus must be inferior to the LORD.

5. And he made his grave with the wicked, 53:9.
   How can God die and be buried?

6. And the pleasure of the Lord shall prosper in his hand, 53:10.
   If Jesus is God, how can it be said of him, "the pleasure of the Lord shall prosper in his hand?"

These and many more such objections completely ignore the basic New Testament view of the Incarnation, expressed so poignantly by the apostle Paul:

> Let this mind be in you which was also in Christ Jesus, who being God, thought it not robbery to be equal with God, But made himself of no reputation, and took upon him the form of a servant, and was made in the likeness of men; And being found in fashion as a man, he humbled himself and became obedient unto death, even the death of the cross (Phil. 2:58).

By ignoring the New Testament doctrine of the Incarnation, Jewish scholars have sought to make the Christian interpretation of Isaiah 53 and of other Messianic prophecies appear untenable or even nonsensical.

Some of the Jewish objections will be discussed later in the course of the exegesis of the disputed passage.

The famous Rabbi Manasseh ben Israel of Amsterdam (1604-57), who successfully interceded with Cromwell for the readmission of the Jews to England in 1655, wrote a paraphrase and a commentary in which he presented the popular Jewish position on Isaiah 52:13-53:12, according to which the Gentiles will one day confess that it was the Jews who suffered innocently for the sins of Gentile nations.

Paraphrase by **Rabbi Manasseh ben Israel** of Amsterdam:
Isaiah 52

13 Behold my servant Israel shall understand:
   he shall be exalted, extolled, and raised
   very high, at the coming of the Messiah.

14 As many of the nations were astonished at
   thee, O Israel, saying at the time of the
   captivity, Truly he is disfigured above
   all mankind in his countenance and form:

15 So at that time they shall speak of thy
grandeur; even kings themselves shall shut
their mouths in astonishment: for what
They had never been told they shall see,
and what they had not heard they shall
understand.

Chapter 53

1 Who would have believed (the nations will
say) what we see, had it been related to
them? And look upon what a vile nation
the arm of the Lord has manifested itself

2 He came up miraculously as a branch and a
root out of a dry ground, for he had no
form nor comeliness: we saw him, but so
hideous, that it did not seem to us an
appearance, for which we should envy him.

3 He was despised and rejected from the
society of men, a man of sorrows,
accustomed to suffer troubles; we hid
our faces from him, he was despised
and unesteemed among us.

4 But now we see that the sickness and
troubles which we ought in reason to
have suffered, he suffered and endured,
and we thought that he was justly
smitten by God and afflicted.

5 Whereas he suffered the sicknesses and
sufferings which we deserved for our
sins; he bore the chastisement which
our peace and felicity deserved; but
his troubles appear to have been the
cure of ourselves.

6 All we like sheep went astray: we
followed every one his own sect,
and so the Lord seems to have trans-
ferred on him the punishment of us all.

7 He was oppressed and afflicted: he
was taken by us as a lamb to the
slaughter and as a sheep before its
shearers, depriving him of life and
property: and he was dumb and opened
not his mouth.

8 From prison and these torments he is
now delivered: and who would have
thought of this his happy age when
he was banished from the holy land?
Through the wickedness of my people
(each nation will say) this blow
came upon them.

9 He was buried with malefactors, and
suffered various torments with the
rich, without having committed crime
or used deceit with his mouth.

10 But it was the Lord (the Prophet says)
who wished to make him sick and afflict
him, in order to purify him: if he
offer his soul as an expiation he shall
see seed, he shall prolong his days,
and the will and determination of the
Lord shall prosper in his hand.

11 For the trouble which his soul suffered
in captivity, he shall see good, shall
be satisfied with days: by his wisdom
my righteous servant Israel shall justify
the many, and he will bear their burdens.

12 Therefore I will give him his share of
spoil among the many and powerful of
Gog and Magog, because he gave himself
up unto death for the sanctification
of my name; and was numbered with the
transgressors from whom he received
injuries.[6]

This paraphrase is most interesting for it shows clearly the self-righteousness and self-infatuation of the rabbis who taught that Israel is completely righteous and suffers innocently merely because of Gentile wickedness. Rabbi Manasseh commenting further on his paraphrase of Isaiah 53:6 explains:

" 'But all we like sheep went astray, etc.' That is, they (the Gentiles) will not only acknowledge the ill-treatment and bodily inflictions they had made Israel suffer, but at the same time their errors, attributing their wickedness thereto; for many will say, we all, that is Ishmaelites and Edumeans, (who in rabbinical parlance are the Mahomedans and the Christians), like sheep went astray, each in his own way following a new sect, just as the prophet Jeremiah says (16:19),

'And the Lord made to fall on him, that is Israel, the wickedness of us all.' That is, we (the Gentiles) erred; they followed the truth; consequently they suffered the punishment, which we deserved.

"We deprived them of their property as tribute and afflicted their bodies with various kinds of torture, yet he opened not his mouth, etc. The experience of this is seen every day, particularly in the cruelties of the Inquisition, and the false testimony raised against them to take their wool and rob them of their property."

It would be difficult to conceive of a greater misinterpretation of the text or distortion of the obvious sense of the disputed passage.

The Division of Isaiah 52:13-53:12

Having previously considered the differing Jewish and Christian interpretations of Isaiah 53, we shall now proceed with the translation of the Hebrew text and will seek to interpret its natural and obvious sense.

The passage under discussion may be divided into five sections, each consisting of three verses.

First Section: Isaiah 52:13-15

Jehovah introduces His faithful servant and announces that he will accomplish the divine purpose and shall in the future be highly exalted.

Second Section: Isaiah 53:1-3

The confession of penitent Israel

Third Section: Isaiah 53:4-6

The servant of Jehovah suffered for the sins of his people.

Fourth Section: Isaiah 53:7-9

Although without sin, the servant submitted himself to humiliation, suffering and death without opening his mouth.

Fifth Section: Isaiah 53:10-12

The servant's offering was God-ordained in order to bring forgiveness and redemption to many. Yet the servant shall rise from the dead, have a lasting following and rejoice in the results of his completed work.

The heart of the issue in this hotly contested passage, is the question whether the prophet considered Israel as the servant of Jehovah, as most modern Jews and liberal Christians do, or whether the prophet gave us a word-portrait of a God-appointed individual who suffers innocently for the sins of his people, just as the oldest Jewish tradition and the early Church have always maintained.

It is obvious to us that only the second position is consistent with

408

the common sense meaning of the text. Repeatedly, the prophet refers to the servant of Jehovah in the singular: "he," "him," "his" or "thee." Furthermore, the prophet's portrait of the servant is utterly irreconcilable with Isaiah's frequently expressed scathing opinions about Israel.

Whereas Israel is castigated as a blind and disobedient servant (Isa. 24:18-20) who refuses to obey the Law (42:24), the servant of the Lord as a person is presented as humble and silent under extreme suffering and torture (53:7). The Jewish people have always loudly protested against their tormentors. Whatever the virtues of Israel may be, silence under suffering was never one of them.

We shall see in greater detail the essential differences between Israel as a servant and the suffering servant of God—the Messiah of Isaiah 53.

It is clear that in this great prophecy Israel is not the innocent sufferer for the redemption of the nations, but is herself the object of salvation by the servant of God. This remarkable chapter compels us to reflect upon the life and destiny of Jesus in the light of the New Testament. However, as soon as we try to force it to fit Israel as a people, the comparison falls apart.

Because of the striking parallel between the suffering Messiah of this amazing prophecy and its remarkable fulfillment in the person of Jesus, Isaiah 53 has been excluded from the Sabbath readings of the Prophets in the synagogue, known as the Haftorah. Some have called Isaiah 53 "the secret chapter," or "the guilty conscience of the synagogue."

The 13th century rabbinical scholar, Rabbi Moshe Kohen ibn Crispin, probably most clearly enunciated the traditional Messianic interpretation of Isaiah 53 in these words:

> "This prophecy was delivered by Isaiah at the divine command for the purpose of making known to us something about the nature of the future Messiah, who is to come and deliver Israel . . . in order that if any one should arise claiming to be himself the Messiah, we may reflect and look to see whether we can observe in him any resemblance to the traits described here: if there is a resemblance, then we may believe that he is the Messiah Our Righteousness; but if not, we cannot do so."[7]

NOTES:
1. S. R. Driver & Adolf Neubauer, *The Suffering Servant of Isaiah,* p. 203.
2. *Op. cit.,* p. 445.
3. Sukkah 246, Soncino Edition.
4. Baba Metzia 6.
5. S. R. Driver & Adolf Neubauer, *The Suffering Servant of Isaiah,* p. 199f.
6. *Op. cit.,* pp. 437-440.
7. *Op. cit.,* p. 114.

Isaiah Chapters 52:13-53:12

The Text

Section I

52:13-15 Jehovah introduces His servant

13 Behold my servant shall deal wisely,
   He shall be lifted up, he shall be exalted and shall be very high.

14 Even as many were appalled at thee,
   So marred was his figure beyond any man's
   And his form from that of the sons of men,

15 So shall he sprinkle many nations,
   Kings shall shut their mouths before him,
   Because that which has not been told to them, they shall see,
   And that which they never heard, they shall comprehend.

Comment:

In this section, which is a prelude to the prophecy of Isaiah 53, Jehovah Himself introduces His servant, the Messiah.

13 **Behold** (Hebrew: *hinneh* or *hen*). This is the prophet's favorite exclamation when he draws attention to a matter of great importance.

Behold my servant

As we have already observed, the crux of the dispute between Jewish and Christian commentators revolves around the question, "Who is the servant?" Is it Israel, as most contemporary Jewish and many liberal Christian scholars insist, or does the prophet visualize a God-appointed individual who willingly takes upon himself the sins of his people, and dies for them in order to redeem them? We have already pointed out that this passage cannot be applied to Israel as a nation or to ideal Israel because the prophecy clearly refers to an individual, and because the portrait drawn by the prophet is incompatible with historical Israel, or with his opinion of this people.

However, when we compare Isaiah 53 with the life of Jesus, the prophecy springs to life and takes on the reality of a historical personality. Nevertheless there is a real link between national Israel and the suffering servant of God. Both Israel and her Messiah were called to be God's servant, but Israel failed to accomplish her divine mission; whereas, the Messiah, the obedient servant of God, did accomplish the mission which the Father entrusted to Him.

Furthermore, the suffering servant of God personified that which Israel was intended to be: "a light to lighten the nations." Thus in a sense Israel and her Messiah are one.

410

Shall deal wisely

The KJV translates this "shall prosper." The Hebrew verb "*yaskil*" means "to act wisely or prudently." "To prosper" is the result of wise or prudent action.

He shall be lifted up . . . exalted and shall be very high

The three verbs are used to convey the absolute height to which the servant of God shall attain. It will be absolute and beyond any comparison.

The first two verbs, "lifted up and exalted," are the same which Isaiah used about the LORD whom he saw sitting upon the throne "high and exalted" (Hebrew: *ram ve-nissa* Isa. 6:1).

14 Even as many were appalled at thee

Jehovah addresses Himself directly to His servant in the pronoun of the second person as "thee." The word "appalled," (Hebrew: *shamem*), means "devastated." It expresses deep, bewildered amazement, caused by the transformation of the once marred and distorted (beyond human resemblance) visage of the servant, to the now exalted personage.

So marred was his figure beyond any man's

This is a parenthetical sentence in which the prophet explains the reasons why so many were appalled at this appearance. We have here a glimpse into the depth of the intense suffering of the Messiah, which transfigured His whole image beyond human semblance.

15 So shall he sprinkle many nations

Here the prophet compares the previous physical appearance of the servant, which was marred and distorted, to his exalted, high-priestly position of the one who cleanses many from the defilement of their sins. To sprinkle, in Hebrew "*yazzeh*" (from the verb *nizeh* —to sprinkle or to be sprinkled) is often used in the Old Testament to describe the ritual cleansing of a leper by means of the sprinkling of the blood of a sacrifice (Lev. 14:7), or the veil in the Tabernacle (Lev. 4:6).

In this connection it is interesting to note that in the Talmud, one of the names of the Messiah is "*Nagua*"—"the leprous one" (Sanhedrin 98b). This is based on Isaiah 53:4 and 8. The servant of Jehovah, once shunned like a leper now brings cleansing to the nations, not through the blood of animals, but by his own.

Some Jewish interpreters translate "*yazzeh*," not as "sprinkle," but "startle" (Slotki). This translation is possible, but "sprinkle" is more suitable, because of the content and the other passages where this verb is also so translated (Lev. 4:6, 14:7).

Kings shall shut their mouths before him

The convincing and convicting force of the Messiah's message shall be so great that the great among men will stand before Him in mute awe and reverence, because that which they will hear from His lips, was never heard before and the matchless life which they will see was never seen before. This is elsewhere described in Isaiah:

Kings shall see and arise,
Princes they shall worship,
Because of Jehovah, who is faithful,
And the Holy One of Israel who has chosen thee (49:7).

Isaiah 52:13-15 forms a prologue to the great Messianic vision of chapter 53 and sums up its entire message.

Section II

53:1-3 The confession of a penitent people

1 Who has believed the message which we have heard?
And the arm of the LORD, to whom was it revealed?

2 For he grew up like a tender plant before him,
And as a root out of a dry ground,
He had no form nor beauty,
And when we looked at him, there was no attractive appearance,
That we should desire him.

3 He was despised and shunned by men,
A man of afflictions and acquainted with suffering,
He was as one from whom men hide their face,
He was despised and we esteemed him not.

Comment:

1 Who has believed the message which we have heard?

It is essential that we understand who it is that asks the above question.

The majority of modern Jewish and some non-Jewish interpreters put the question in the mouth of the Gentile nations who in the last days will see the exaltation of the once despised Jews.

Although most flattering to the national ego, this interpretation is inconsistent with the prophet's known views about his people and with the language of his prophecy.

Repeatedly the prophet denounced his people for being deaf and blind to the will of their God (42:19-20, 43:24).

According to the prophet, they do not deserve the name Israel, and their allegiance to Jehovah is insincere (48:1). He characterizes

412

his nation as "an obstinate people with a neck like an iron sinew and their forehead is like brass" (48:4).

The whole history and national character of Israel is completely out of harmony with the prophet's portrait of God's obedient servant who takes upon himself the sins of his people to redeem all men. In view of all this, the only reasonable answer to the question, "who has believed in the message which we have heard?" is that it is asked by repentant Israel or by their godly remnant when they will finally recognize their past rebellion against God and against His servant, the Messiah. In reality the sense of the question is a self-accusation by the people that so few of them have believed.

The word, "our report" in Hebrew "*shmuatenu*," literally means "that which we have heard," or "our message." This refers to the cumulative witness of the prophets who for many generations have prophesied about the coming of the divinely appointed Saviour to deliver His people from their sins.

And the arm of the LORD to whom was it revealed?

"The arm of the LORD" is a figure which describes the power and wisdom of God manifested in His redemptive acts in history.

2 For he grew up like a tender plant before him

The prophet points to the unostentatious and humble beginnings of the servant, who was like a tender plant bursting forth from the dry ground. The Hebrew word for "root" is "*yonek*," a suckling; or horticulturally speaking, "a twig" or "a stalk."

In 11:1 the prophet proclaimed:
There shall come forth a shoot
From the root stock of Jesse,
And a twig out of his roots shall bear fruit.

The connection between the Messiah proclaimed in the first part of Isaiah and the suffering servant of God in the second part is here strongly suggested.

And as a root out of a dry ground

In the prophetic writings the Messiah is often called a root or branch. This is a reference to his Davidic descent (Isa. 11:10).

Out of a dry ground—Hebrew, "*me-eretz tziah*." Under Herod the Davidic dynasty became all but extinct. The attrition of time, and finally the murderous jealously of Herod, so called "the Great," have done their worst, almost wiping out all known or potential claimants to the throne of David. In this sense "the root of Jesse" vegetated and finally sprung up in "dry ground."

Spiritually speaking, Israel in the first century before Christ and long after became "a dry land." No longer were there the prophets to proclaim to Israel the will and the Word of Jehovah. It was the age of the great pharisaic scholars, legislators and interpreters of the Law of Moses according to their own human understanding. It was the age of Jewish scholasticism, acute, occasionally even brilliant, but spiritually not very creative. It was an age somewhat reminiscent of the later medieval scholasticism of the Church.

"*Eretz tziah*"—a dry land—may have originally suggested the name Zion, which means "a dry hill or place." This would point to the fact that the grandeur of Zion and all that it represents was not inherent in the land itself, which was dry and barren, but came from God who has chosen Zion as His habitation.

And when we looked at him, there was no attractive appearance

There was nothing in the outward circumstances of the servant's advent to make him attractive to his people or to the world. There was no pomp or circumstance, no earthly splendor, usually attendant upon the arrival of earthly princelings, nothing to excite the imagination of his countrymen or of the world. Israel's vision of the Messiah was focused on his majestic appearance as king and conqueror, who will subdue the enemies of Israel, impose his peace upon the nations and establish his and Israel's glorious kingdom. Foremost in the minds of the Jewish people were those passages of the Scripture which predicted divine judgment and the downfall of the Gentiles and the establishment of a kingdom where:

The wolf shall dwell with the lamb,
And the calf and the young lion shall lie down together,
They shall no longer hurt nor destroy in my holy mountain.
For the earth shall be filled with the knowledge of God
As the waters cover the sea.
And the root of Jesse shall stand for a standard for the nations . . .
(Isa. 11:5, 10; 65:22-25)

These ideas have always exercised an enormous fascination for the Jewish people, even to the present time. It was Israel's "vision splendid," which she transmitted to all mankind. However there was scant recognition of the fact that before this Messianic kingdom could become a reality, the Messiah must first suffer, die and rise again from the dead. This aspect of the Messianic mission hardly registered on the national consciousness of Israel. Nor did they ever become deeply aware of the fact that the mission of the Messiah was to bring His people and the nations to repentance and to faith in Him as the divinely appointed Redeemer.

It was with this in mind that the risen Christ on the way to Emmaus chided the two disciples:

O foolish ones, and slow of heart to believe all that the prophets have spoken. Ought not Christ to have suffered these things, and to enter into his glory? And beginning at Moses and the prophets, he expounded the scriptures, the things concerning himself (Lk. 24:25-27).

A Messiah without earthly splendor, humble and humiliated, who is tormented and dies upon a shameful cross as a vicarious and voluntary sacrifice for the redemption of Israel and mankind, has always been and still remains offensive to Jewish thinking.

3 He was despised and shunned by men

In earlier rabbinic literature the Messiah was recognized, at least in part, as a sufferer. In the Jewish prayer book there are frequent allusions to Isaiah 53 and to the suffering of the Messiah, but later contemporary Judaism has sought to eliminate, or at least to play down, all such allusions to a suffering Saviour.

The legend of the two Messiahs was invented in an effort to reconcile the two Biblical strands of thought: one which speaks of a suffering Messiah, and the other which foresees his victorious reign. One is Messiah ben Ephraim (also sometimes called Messiah ben Joseph). He is the suffering Messiah who dies in battle against Armilius (Rome). Then comes the second, Messiah ben David, who is victorious over Rome (all pagan powers), and restores the kingdom of Israel and establishes peace among the nations of the world.[1] This was the feeble effort to reconcile the two distinct phases of the coming of the Saviour, first as "the Lamb of God" who sacrifices Himself for the redemption of all men, and His second coming as King of kings, to establish His glorious Kingdom.

The prophet by inspiration and also from his own knowledge of his people foresaw all this, and so spoke of the servant as already despised and rejected by men. The Hebrew word for "men" is *"ishim,"* the poetic form for the regular *"anashim,"* a reference not to the ordinary rank and file men (*hoi polloi*), but to men of stature. Such men shunned him. The very fact of His humble origin and of His dwelling in Nazareth, an obscure town in Galilee, not even mentioned in rabbinical literature, outside the New Testament, was in the eyes of His contemporaries an almost insurmountable obstacle (John 1:46, 7:41).

A man of afflictions and acquainted with suffering

We translated the Hebrew word *"machoboth"* as "afflictions," which is nearer to the original than the KJV's "grief." "The afflictions" could be either physical or spiritual.

415

Jewish controversalists have maintained that since Jesus never suffered personal affliction during his life time, nor was ever sick himself, therefore, the above words could not apply to him. However, this is not a reasonable argument. Like all the prophets, Jesus identified Himself with His people. He was afflicted in their afflictions, and felt all the maladies of His people with a keen personal sensitivity, even as Isaiah did centuries before:

> From the sole of the foot even to the head,
> There is not a sound spot,
> Only wounds and bruises and running sores,
> Which have not been pressed out nor bound up,
> Nor softened with oil (Isa. 1:6).

The servant came to suffer with and for His people and to lay down His life for them.

He was as one from whom men hide their face,
He was despised and we esteemed him not

People are loathe to look at a man whom they hate immensely; in all the history of Israel no other was more intensely hated and despised than the person of the servant of God. The prophet rightly called him "a man of affliction and acquainted with suffering." For hundreds of years, His name was not even mentioned among Jews except by such circumlocutions as "that man" or "the hanged one." The words "he was despised" are repeated twice in this sentence to emphasize its intensity. The Hebrew name of Jesus, *"Yeshua"* (Saviour), has been deliberately distorted into *"Yeshu,"* the initial letters of which were supposed to spell out a Hebrew sentence which means, "Let his name and his memory be blotted out." This aversion to him has even increased with the passing of time.[2] However with the growing social, moral and religious ferment among the Jewish people, this attitude is gradually changing to a more positive stance.

Section III

53:4-6 The vicarious suffering of Jehovah's servant

4 And yet he surely did bear our diseases
  And our afflictions he did carry.
  But we considered him stricken,
  Smitten of God and afflicted.

5 But he was wounded for our transgressions
  He was crushed for our iniquities,
  The chastisement which secured our peace was upon him,
  And by his stripes healing has come to us.

6 All we have gone astray like sheep,

Every one of us turned to his own way,
But the LORD caused to fall on him
The iniquity of us all.

Comment:

4 And yet he surely did bear our diseases

Repentant Israel continues its great confession as they look upon God's servant, their once despised Messiah. Now they acknowledge that He did not suffer for His own sins, but that He carried upon His shoulders the burden of their sins and the pain of their transgressions. His suffering was expiatory and vicarious in nature. The word, "*nasa*" to "bear," in this sentence is also used in connection with the sacrifices of expiation (Lev. 5:1, 17; 16:22, 20:19, 20).

But we considered him stricken, smitten of God and afflicted

The three expressions: "stricken" (Hebrew "*nagua*") refers to a loathsome disease such as leprosy; "smitten of God" a divine retribution for a heinous sin, and "afflicted" as one might be afflicted by the punishment for one's crime: all these describe the terrible consequences of sin. The Talmud calls Jesus a transgressor, and the renowned 12th century scholar, Maimonides, states that Jesus deserved the violent death which he suffered.

5 But he was wounded for our transgressions

"But he" is the emphatic assertion that the real cause of His suffering was not, as Israel falsely assumed, for His own sins, but for the transgressions of His people. The word "wounded," "*mecholal*" literally means "he was pierced." Only an inspired prophet could use a word which so literally corresponds to that which actually happened to the righteous servant of God, the Messiah Jesus. "Wounded (or pierced) for our transgressions and crushed for our iniquities" expresses fully the vicarious character of the suffering of the servant of God—the innocent for the guilty.

In spite of the assertions of the rabbis and of some non-Jewish theologians that vicarious suffering is morally objectionable and unacceptable, this is exactly what the Scriptures teach. This is also what history and life itself teaches us.

The whole sacrificial system symbolizes substitution, of the innocent for the guilty. No sacrificial animal, however perfect, could by itself make atonement for sin. In the last analysis the sacrifice was merely symbolic and pointed to the fact that the sinner deserved to die, and that it was the servant of God, who voluntarily took upon himself the sins of all men. This is why John the Baptist pointed to Jesus as "the Lamb of God which taketh away the sins of the world" (John 1:29).

417

Sin brings in its wake suffering and death, not only upon the sinner, but frequently also upon the innocent, just as the voluntary sacrifice of an "innocent" person may bring healing and salvation to the guilty.

The chastisement which secured our peace was upon him

"*Musar shlomenu*," the "chastisement which secured peace." Forgiveness, to be real, must be obtained at a price. A righteous God, in order to forgive sinners, must base it on moral ground. Otherwise forgiveness would be morally objectionable and spiritually meaningless, as there would be no difference between righteousness and wickedness. But God is not only merciful but also righteous. And so the righteous servant of God took upon Himself the chastisement or the punishment which secures our peace.

And by his stripes healing has come to us.

This line complements the preceding. "By his stripes," 'that is, by the vicarious suffering of the servant, we may secure peace—*shalom*—that is, complete reconciliation with God, harmony within our souls, and peace with men. Healing in this context is primarily the healing of the soul from the sickness of sin. Yet in addition to the spiritual healing, physical and emotional healing may also be included. In our age it is recognized that physical ailments frequently have an emotional and psychic background. Our hospitals are often filled with such patients. The servant who brings to sinful man peace with God and healing to his soul also brings healing from a multitude of diseases.

6 All we have gone astray like sheep

"All we"—"*kullanu*"—is an emphatic assertion concerning all men, without exception, that they have an innate bent to stray or wander away from the path of righteousness. Straying is characteristic of sheep.

Every one of us turned to his own way

The emphasis is here upon "his own way"—not God's way. Sheep are not accountable for wandering off and becoming lost, because they have no understanding or judgment. But when men who are endowed with a God-given mind and with a conscience yet behave like sheep, they cannot be held blameless. They are committing sin.

But the LORD caused to fall on him the iniquity of us all

Men are by their own nature inclined to wander off like sheep into their own ways, even though this may lead them to destruction. Yet God in His mercy has appointed His righteous servant, the Good Shepherd, to guide them to the path of life.

53:7-9 The ordeal and death of Jehovah's servant

7 He was tormented and he submitted himself,
And opened not his mouth.
As a lamb which is led to the slaughter,
And as a ewe sheep before her shearers is dumb,
So he also opened not his mouth.

8 From prison and from judgment he was removed,
Yet who of his generation pondered this?
That he was cut off from the land of the living,
For the transgression of my people the stroke fell upon him.

9 And his grave was appointed with the wicked,
And with a rich man in his death,
Although he had committed no violence,
Neither was there any deception in his mouth.

Comment:

7 He was tormented and he submitted himself

Our translation differs from the KJV which reads: "He was oppressed and he was afflicted." We believe that our translation comes closer to the original text and is in agreement with many of the more recent translations. The whole sense of this sentence is the voluntary, humble and quiet submission of the ill-treated servant of God to his tormentors.

And opened not his mouth

This prediction is in harmony with the story of the trial of Jesus and His silence before His accusers (Mt. 26:62-63, 27:12).

As a lamb which is led to the slaughter

The references in the New Testament to Jesus as the Lamb of God have their roots in the story of the passover lamb, and the sprinkling of its blood on the door posts of the Israelite households in Egypt (Ex. 12:3, 4, 7). It is also a reference to the lamb-like submission of the Messiah to His tormentors and to His sacrifice.

This kind of submissive behavior can in no way be attributed to Israel as a nation. Whatever the virtues of Israel are, suffering in silence and submission to her tormentors is not one of them. Whenever the Jews were able, they resisted with all their might and when they were unable to do this because of unfavorable circumstances, they protested vigorously and vociferously against their oppressors. In fact, they never considered suffering in silence as a virtue. Even in the infamous extermination camps and in the ghettoes of the Nazis, they resisted whenever they were able, or sent messages of protest and alarm to the rest of the world. This was an understandable and natural reaction on the part of the Jews, but is completely at odds with the description in Isaiah 53 of the behavior of the servant of God.

8 He was removed from prison and from judgment

"From prison," Hebrew *"me-otzer,"* literally a place of restraint or prison. One marvels at the accuracy of the prophecy in so many details when we compare them with the events described in the Gospels in connection with the passion of Jesus.

Yet who of his generation pondered this?

Little thought was given to the importance of the death of Jesus by His contemporaries. Life went on as before. Probably there were too many events taking place during that turbulent period in the history of Israel for anyone to ponder too much about the significance of the death of an unknown Galilean teacher. Only some of His disciples and a number of His other followers believed in His subsequent resurrection. Yet by all odds the coming of Jesus, His death and resurrection, was the most important event in the history of mankind. Since then, world history has been divided into two epochs, B. C.—before Christ and A. D.—Anno Domini—the year of our Lord Jesus Christ.

That he was cut off from the land of the living

He was cut off from life prematurely. He lived a short life, about thirty-three years. With the crucifixion, the earthly career of Jesus came to an end, at least this was what His adversaries had hoped. But in fact, His impact on mankind had only begun. He lives on in the minds and hearts of countless millions. He cannot be erased from the consciousness of men. "His Truth goes marching on."

Well did Jesus say:
And I, if I be lifted up from the earth will draw all men unto me (John 12:32).

For the transgression of my people the stroke fell upon him

Jewish interpreters put these words and the rest of Isaiah 53, in the mouth of the Gentile nations, who one day will realize that all along the Jews suffered innocently and have voluntarily taken the punishment which was due to each of the Gentile nations.

To bolster their argument they maintain that the last two words in the above sentence "upon him" is in Hebrew a plural, *"lamo,"* "upon them." The regular singular "upon him" should be *"lo,"* (*lamed vav*). Yet *"lamo"* is repeatedly used both as plural and as a singular (Job 20:23, 22:2 and again in Isa. 44:15), "He makes it a graven image and falls down before it (*lamo*)." The argument is specious.

The term which is used in our sentence, "my people," can only refer to Israel for whom the righteous servant of God suffers and dies.

9 And his grave was appointed with the wicked
And with a rich man in his death

Again we are astounded at the accuracy of the prophetic prediction which found its fulfillment in the events of the crucifixion. Jesus' body, considered by Jewish and Roman officialdom as that of a rebel, would normally have been assigned together with the two other criminals who died on the two other crosses, and would have been buried, where criminals usually were buried, in an unmarked grave, except for divine intervention. "The rich man," Joseph of Arimathea (Mt. 27:57), intervened with the Roman authorities and had Jesus buried in a private grave in his garden, "wherein never man before was laid" (Lk. 23:53).

Although he had committed no violence

The complete innocence of the servant, who has committed no crime in deed or in word is here emphasized. There was nothing in the life of Jesus to justify such a cruel and extreme sentence.

Section V

53:10-12 The future glory of the servant of Jehovah

10 Yet it pleased the LORD to crush him
° To afflict him with grief,
If his soul shall make a trespassing offering,
He shall see seed, prolong his days,
And the purpose of the LORD shall prosper in his hand.

11 He shall see of the travail of his soul and shall be satisfied.
By his knowledge shall my righteous servant justify many,
And their iniquities he shall bear.

12 Therefore will I give him a portion among the great,
And with the strong will he divide spoil;
Because he poured out his life unto death,
And was numbered among the trangressors.
Yet he bore the sin of many,
And made intercession for the transgressors.

Comment:

10 Yet it pleased the LORD to crush him

All the things which happened to the servant of Jehovah were, in the final analysis, the result of Jehovah's will. It was Jehovah's will to crush him, it was His will to afflict him with grief, in Hebrew, "*hecheli*," the same word which is used in verses 3 and 4.

If his soul shall make a trespass offering

"*Asham*" is a trespass offering distinct from every other sacrifice. It was made by the individual person in compensation for any wrong committed by him. It discharged the person from guilt and set him free (Lev. 5:15). The central idea of the trespass offering was satisfaction demanded by a just God.

Thus the servant of God made himself a sacrifice in restitution for the sins of every man, individually.

He shall see seed, prolong his days

"He shall see seed" refers to those who are redeemed by His sacrifice. "He shall prolong his days" refers to His resurrection and the life which only began after His crucifixion. Jewish commentators have maintained that "seed" refers exclusively to physical offspring, that is children, but in reality it refers also to spiritual seed, a following (Psa. 22:30, Isa. 65:25, Mal. 2:15).

And the purpose of the LORD shall prosper in his hand

It was the whole counsel of God, which the servant accomplished, because of His willingness to offer Himself as a trespass offering. This purpose of God continues to prosper through the ages. The servant of Jehovah was appointed to restore Israel so that they might in the end become a light to the nations and carry the salvation of God to the ends of the earth (Isa. 49:6).

11 He shall see of the travail of his soul and shall be satisfied

The servant shall look upon His travail and the sorrows which His earthly life brought upon Him and will be well satisfied with the results of His sacrifice.

By his knowledge shall my righteous servant justify many

"My righteous servant" is used here in an emphatic form, to express the absolute righteousness of God's chosen servant. Through the knowledge of Him, others were made righteous. The knowledge of Him is not just mental, but a personal experience of Him in the living communion with the servant of God. It is justification by faith in Him.

And their iniquities he shall bear

This action goes beyond the finished work of the Messiah and points to His continuous work of mediation (Heb. 8:6).

12 Therefore will I give him a portion among the great

"*Barabim*" means "among the great ones" and also "among

many." Here the prophet further elaborates the thought in Isaiah 52:15:

So also shall he sprinkle many nations,
Kings shall shut their mouths before him.

The completed work of the servant of Jehovah will affect not only Israel but also the nations of the world (see 49:7). The prophet foresees the time when the great men of history shall pay homage to the servant of God, the Messiah.

Because he poured out his life unto death

His impact upon the nations and the homage which the mighty and the great will pay Him will be the consequence of His pouring out His life; although at the time of His crucifixion, He was considered a transgressor by those who sat in judgment over Him.

Yet he bore the sin of many

Far from being a transgressor, the servant of God was the Saviour of transgressors and interceded for them at the very moment when He was being put to death by them (Lk. 23:34).

With Chapter 53, which is the heart and the center of the Book of Consolation, Messianic prophecy reaches its majestic pinnacle.

Delitzsch, to whom all who ever commented on Isaiah in the course of the last century owe a great debt, writes in his commentary:

The Servant of Jehovah goes through shame to glory and through death to life. He conquers when He yields; He rules after being enslaved; He lives after He has died; He completes His work after He Himself has been apparently cut off. His glory streams upon the dark ground of the deepest humiliation. . ."[3]

We can only add that apart from the Lord Jesus Christ, it would be impossible to understand this majestic chapter in Isaiah, and it would forever be a dark mystery without solution. However, in the light of His life it has become the brightest star of Hebrew prophecy, the star of hope and salvation for all men.

NOTES:
1. Sukkah 246, Soncino Edition
2. Modern Hebrew dictionaries and official documents still spell the name Jesus as "Yeshu" instead of the correct "Yeshua".
3. Franz Delitzsch, *The Prophecies of Isaiah*, Vol. 2, p. 341, Eerdmans Publ. Co.

Isaiah Chapter 54

Zion's Glorious Future

1 Sing, O barren, thou who didst not bear,
   Burst forth into singing, shout aloud,
   Thou who hast never been in labor,

For more are the children of her who was forsaken,
Than the children of the married wife, says the LORD.

2 Enlarge the place of thy tent,
Stretch the curtains of thy habitation, spare not!
Lengthen thy cords and fasten thy stakes.

3 For thou shalt spread out to the right and to the left,
And thy seed shall possess the nations,
And inhabit the desolate cities.

4 Fear not for thou shalt not be ashamed,
Be not dismayed for thou shalt not be put to shame.
Thou shalt forget the shame of thy youth,
And the reproach of thy widowhood thou shalt remember no
more.

5 For thy Maker is thy Husband,
The LORD of hosts is his name,
And thy Redeemer is the Holy One of Israel,
The God of all the earth shall he be called.

6 For as a forsaken wife, grieved in spirit,
The LORD has called thee back,
As a wife of youth who has been rejected,
Says thy God.

7 For a short moment have I forsaken thee,
But with great compassion will I gather thee.

8 In a burst of anger I hid my face from thee, for a moment,
But with everlasting kindness will I have compassion on thee,
Says the LORD, thy Redeemer.

9 For this to me is like the waters of Noah,
For as I have sworn that the waters of Noah,
Should never again flood the earth,
So have I sworn not to be angry with thee,
Nor to rebuke thee.

10 For the mountains may depart,
And the hills be removed,
But my loving kindness shall not depart from thee,
And my covenant of peace shall not be removed,
Says the LORD who has compassion on thee.

11 O, thou afflicted, tossed with tempest and not comforted,
Behold, I will set thy stones in antimony,
And thy foundations with sapphires.

12 I will make thy battlements of rubies,

And thy gates of sparkling stones,
And all thy borders shall be of precious stones.

13 Thy sons shall all be taught by the LORD,
And great shall be the prosperity of thy sons.

14 Thou shalt be established in righteousness,
Thou shalt be far removed from oppression,
For thou shalt not fear,
And from terror, for it shall not come near thee.

15 Behold, they shall gather against thee, but not by me,
Whoever gathers against thee shall fall by thee.

16 Behold, I have created the smith,
Who blows the fire of coals,
And forges a weapon according to his craft,
I also created the ravager to destroy.

17 No weapon which is fashioned against thee shall succeed,
And every tongue which rises against thee in judgment
Thou shalt confute.
Such is the heritage of the servants of the LORD,
And their vindication is from me, says the LORD.

Comment:

After portraying the majestic personality of the Servant-Redeemer in Isaiah 53, the prophet resumes his message about redeemed Israel, interrupted in Chapter 52:12. Chapter 54:1-3 begins with a triumphant song of Zion, now restored to the favor of her Lord.

1 Sing, O barren, thou who didst not bear

During her captivity Israel was like a rejected wife: childless, desolate and grieved in spirit. But now that the LORD is about to look with favor upon her she is to break forth in joyful song.

**For more are the children of her who was forsaken,
Than the children of the married wife**

The returning exiles from all the corners of the earth will be more in number than the children of Zion before her dispersion.

3 For thou shalt spread out to the right and to the left

The repatriates will not only repopulate the desolate cities but will build new ones to accommodate the rapid increase in population, a prophecy reminiscent of Israel's present day situation.

4-10 Jehovah's anger was only for a brief moment but now He will turn His face toward His people with great compassion.

4 Thou shalt forget the shame of thy youth . . . the reproach of thy widowhood

"The shame of thy youth" refers to Israel's early experience in Egypt. "The reproach of thy widowhood" is probably an allusion to the anticipated Babylonian exile, which lasted seventy years, "a brief moment" in the eyes of God.

8 In a burst of anger I hid my face from thee for a moment, But with everlasting kindness will I have compassion on thee

Jehovah's essential relationship to Israel is that of "everlasting kindness" which may occasionally be disturbed or frustrated by the rebelliousness and waywardness of His people. Yet in the end Jehovah's mercy always prevails.

9 For this to me is like the waters of Noah

Jehovah's love for His people is as immutable as His promise to Noah never again to visit the earth with a flood. Israel may be punished by Jehovah for her sins, but never with the ultimate punishment of complete annihilation.

10 For the mountains may depart . . . but my loving kindness shall not. . .

Jehovah's "covenant of peace" with Israel (*b'rith shalom*) is eternal; it may be broken by Israel, but never by Him. The LORD always waits for His people to repent so that He may renew His eternal covenant of peace.

11-17 This is one of the most beautiful and touching declarations of God's love for His people and of His glorious plan for their ultimate destiny.

11 O, thou afflicted, tossed with tempest and not comforted

In moving words of deep pathos the prophet describes Israel's present miserable condition and her bright future which God has purposed for His people.[1]

Behold, I will set thy stones in antimony

The prophet sees the new Jerusalem, a holy city descending from heaven and made of the most dazzling colors and adorned with the most precious stones which nature affords. There is a blending of the earthly with the heavenly. The Revelation of St. John 21:10-27 elaborates on Isaiah's vision. The new Jerusalem is St. Augustine's "City of God." In the prophet's vision it is the Kingdom of God, whose citizens are all taught by God Himself (v. 13).

14 Thou shall be established in righteousness

The secret of the glory, the beauty and the security of the holy

Jerusalem is seen in the fact that she is built on the foundation of righteousness. Such a city need fear no foe and no terror.

15 Behold, they shall gather against thee, but not by me

Israel may be threatened and assailed by foes, but their actions are not according to the will of God and so will never succeed.

16 Behold, I have created the smith . . . (and) the ravager to destroy

The thought here is that the smith who forges the weapons of destruction, and also the ravager himself who uses them are both the creations of God. They are all in His hand, and He can use them according to His will.

17 No weapon fashioned against thee shall succeed

Israel's destiny is in God's hand; therefore, no matter what the weapon may be, it will never succeed. This, no doubt, is the ultimate secret of Israel's indestructibility. No weapon, no false accusation, no libel or policy of extermination will ever succeed against Israel. History has repeatedly borne out this remarkable prophecy.

Such is the heritage of the servants of the LORD
And their vindication is from me, says the LORD

God watches over His people because they are His servants and witnesses. He watches over them and protects them. Their vindication, in Hebrew, "*tsidkatham*," literally, "their righteousness," is not in themselves, but comes from God whose purpose they serve, knowingly or not, willing or not.[2]

NOTES:

1. The quotation from Isaiah 54:11 is inscribed on the Statute of Liberty at the entrance to the New York Harbor as a part of the sonnet by Emma Lazarus.

2. Since the days of the early Church, most Christian commentators have applied this and many other prophecies of a similar character to the Church, on the theory that national Israel has been rejected by God once and for all and that now the Church is "The New Israel." All the promises of future blessing and glory have systematically been applied to the Church and all the dire predictions of judgment and punishment were left for the Jews. Unfortunately this gross distortion of the obvious sense of the prophetic message has had a baneful effect both on the Church and on the Jewish people. The Church has been deprived of a proper understanding of the Scriptures, and tended to develop a Pharisaic self-righteousness and superiority in her attitude toward the Jews. This inevitably produced the awful blight of so-called "Christian Anti-Semitism."

On the other hand, the Jews were further alienated from the Messiah of the prophets and "the wall of separation" which Christ came to break down was built up even higher.

Isaiah Chapter 55

The Invitation to a Spiritual Feast

1 Ho, everyone who is thirsty come to the waters,
And he that has no money, come, buy and eat!
Come buy wine and milk without money and without cost.

2 Why do you spend money on that which is not bread,
And your toil on that which does not satisfy?
Listen attentively to me and eat that which is good,
And let your soul delight itself in fatness.

3 Incline your ear and come to me,
Listen and your soul shall live;
And I will make an everlasting covenant with you,—
The trustworthy mercies of David.

4 Behold, I have appointed him for a witness to the peoples,
A prince and a commander to the peoples.

5 Behold thou shalt call a nation which thou didst not know,
And a nation which knew thee not
Shall come running to thee because of the LORD thy God,
And for the Holy One of Israel, who has glorified thee.

6 Seek you the LORD while he may be found,
Call on him while he is near.

7 Let the wicked man forsake his way,
And the evil man his thoughts,
Let him return to the LORD and he will have mercy on him,
And to our God, for he will abundantly pardon.

8 For my thoughts are not your thoughts,
Neither are your ways my ways, says the LORD.

9 For as the heavens are higher than the earth,
So are my ways higher than your ways,
And my thoughts than your thoughts.

10 For just as the rain and the snow descend from heaven,
And do not return until they have watered the earth,
Causing it to bring forth and bud,
And to give seed to the sower and bread to the eater;

11 So shall also my word be which proceeds out of my mouth,
It shall not return to me void,
But will accomplish that which I please,
And prosper in that for which I sent it.

12   For you shall go out with joy,
      And shall be led forth in peace jubilantly,
      The mountains and the hills shall break forth before you into
      singing,
      And all the trees of the field shall clap their hands.

13   Instead of the thorn shall come up a cypress tree,
      And instead of the brier shall come up a myrtle tree.
      And this shall be to the LORD for a name,
      For an everlasting sign which shall never be erased.

Comment:

1 Ho, everyone who is thirsty come to the waters

Here is one of the most glorious and beautiful chapters in the book of Isaiah. It is a chapter in which an invitation is extended to all who are hungry and thirsty for righteousness, to come to a feast which God has prepared for them. All they have to do is to accept His gracious invitation.

The water, wine, milk and bread of which the prophet speaks are the various aspects of the Word of God. Water is essential to life, without it life is impossible. Wine is exhilarating, and in the lands of the Bible was frequently used to nourish and to strengthen the sick. Milk is basic to growth and health. Bread is "the staff of life." All these are offered by a gracious God, freely and without any cost.

**2 Why do you spend money on that which is not bread
And your toil on that which does not satisfy?**

Here is a timeless question addressed to all men of every generation. Men have always toiled and spent their substance and strength on that which did not truly satisfy their deepest hunger and needs, because without the light of God's Word they never understood themselves nor their true needs. And so they lived and died frustrated and disappointed.

Listen attentively to me and eat that which is good

True happiness does not depend primarily on the abundance of things possessed as so many seem to think, but in communion with God. "Man shall not live by bread alone" is a truth which is often scorned and yet remains eternally true.

And let your soul delight itself in fatness

"Fat" in our modern culture is something to be avoided at all cost. The diet of Western man often consists of too much fat with all the resulting health problems. But we must think in terms of Biblical man and his civilization. The Israelite was, in general, an

429

abstemious person who lived mainly on vegetables, grain and fruit, with an occasional addition of fish or meat for festive occasions. He needed a certain amount of fat for health. This came mostly from olives and olive oil. So "to delight oneself in fatness" was something highly desirable. The prophet is telling us that the Word of God provides all the essential elements of a wholesome and balanced diet to sustain body and soul in glowing health.

3   Listen and your soul shall live

Life, and not mere vegetation, depends on communion with God and in listening attentively and obeying His Word.

And I will make an everlasting covenant with you,—
The trustworthy mercies of David

The trustworthy mercies of David, — in Hebrew, "*Hasdei David haneemanim.*" The prophet harkens back to the everlasting covenant with God made with David when He promised him:

Thine house and thy kingdom shall be established forever before thee, thy throne shall be established for ever (2 Sam. 7:16). This was "the everlasting covenant" with David.

Since David died many centuries before, the reference must be understood in a Messianic sense. Messiah, who is the scion of David, is the agent through whom God carries out His redemptive will. He is the Word of God Incarnate who lives eternally. The same view is also expressed by the Apostle Peter in Acts 2:29-31.

4   Behold, I have appointed him for a witness to the peoples
And prince and a commander to the peoples

The purpose of the eternally living David is to be a witness, a prince and a commander to the nations, a task which is identical with the mission of the servant of God (Isa. 42:1, 49:6, 52:15). Now the prophet Isaiah merges the two images of the Messiah into one, that of Servant and King (Isa. 11:10).

5   Behold thou shalt call a nation which thou didst not know. . .

"Thou shalt call" is a reference to Israel, who through her supreme representative, the King-Messiah, has brought about the emergence of a new nation, The Church of Christ, composed of Jews and Gentiles. This new nation found shelter under the wings of the Shechinah-Glory, through the life and work of the Messiah Jesus.

6-7   A call to return to the LORD
6   Seek the LORD while he may be found

Repeatedly the Scriptures appeal to Israel and through her to all men to return to God, while there is yet time. "Today, if you will hear his voice, harden not your hearts" (Psa. 95:7-8, also Isa.

61:2 and Lk. 4:19). We still live in "God's acceptable year" which may one day come to an end.

7 Let the wicked man forsake his way and the evil man his thoughts

The wickedness of men is manifested in his thoughts and in his actions. These he must abandon as a precondition for repentance.

Let him return to the LORD

The idea of repentance, in Hebrew, *"teshuvah,"* is based on the word, "return"—*shuv*. It is the dominant note and heart cry of the prophets: forsake your evil ways and return to God.

For he will have mercy on him . . . He will abundantly pardon

The vision of a compassionate God, who is anxious for the prodigal to repent and return to Him, is at the very heart of the Scriptures. Nowhere is it more beautifully expressed than in the parable of the prodigal son (Lk. 15:11-32).

8-9 The infinite transcendence of God's thought and ways above man's

8 For my thoughts are not your thoughts

Man can never fathom the depths and the greatness of God, except to the extent to which He has revealed Himself to him, through His Word, especially through the Incarnate Word, Christ. God is not only omnipotent and all wise, but also full of compassion and forgiveness, when man turns to Him in repentance.

9 For as the heavens are higher than the earth
So are my ways higher than your ways

In this striking figure the infinite transcendance of God over man is expressed. There just is no comparison between man's thoughts and ways and God's.

10-11 The sure and unfailing Word of God
10 For just as the rain and snow descend from heaven

Just as sure as the winter rain and snow bring new life to earth providing bread for the eater and seed for a new harvest:

11 So shall my Word be . . . it shall not return to me void

The Word of God has the same effect on the soul of man as the rain has on earth. Only the Word of God has the power to revive and to provide food for the hungry and fainting soul. Only those who have been fed by the Word of God are able to feed others. Jesus said:

Whosoever drinketh of this water shall thirst again: But whosoever drinketh of the water that I shall give him shall never thirst; but the water that I shall give him shall be in him a well of water springing up into everlasting life (John 4:13-14).

There is an explicit promise here that God's Word will everlastingly perform its appointed mission of bringing new life to man regardless how inauspicious and unpromising the momentary situation may seem.

12-13 Transformed nature shall joyfully participate in Israel's redemption.

12 For you shall go out with joy

In the historical situation the immediate reference appears to be to Israel's redemption from exile. But as usual the prophet's vision reaches out beyond the immediate circumstance and looks toward the greater redemption which will one day encompass all of humanity and nature itself. The same thought was voiced later by the Apostle Paul (Rom. 8:2).

And shall be led forth in peace jubilantly

The Hebrew term *"tubalun"* is related to *"yovel"* from which comes our "jubilee." This was celebrated with a festive procession. Unlike the redemption from Egypt, where there was haggling with Pharaoh and which was followed by the pursuit of his armies, this time the God-appointed, benevolent ruler (Cyrus) will permit Israel to depart with joy and jubilation. It is characteristic of Isaiah, the great nature lover, that he sees the hills and the mountains rejoicing and the trees clapping their hands. This is more than mere poetic license. It is the expression of a deep conviction that man and nature are somehow united in a mystical bond of Divine destiny. Our own generation has become more and more conscious of this bond and of the interdependence between them, than any previous generation.

13 Instead of the thorn shall come up a cypress tree
And instead of the brier shall come up a myrtle tree

At first glance it may seem just a beautiful figure of speech, related to the return of the exiles to their homeland and its subsequent transformation. But the prophet looks beyond that and sees human thorns and briers, unsightly and useless, fit only for the fire, transformed and regenerated by the grace of God through His living Word turned into tall, beautiful, useful and majestic cypress trees, and into fragrant myrtle trees which refresh and bless all those who come near them.

And this shall be to the LORD for a name
For an everlasting sign which shall never be erased
Regenerated men and women are an undeniable proof and ev-

idence of the transforming power of God. Their lives are a living testimony of God's amazing grace, a testimony which cannot be denied.

Such a transfigured life will bring glory to the name of God.

Isaiah Chapter 56

Encouragement for the Eunuchs, for Gentile Converts and a Rebuke of the Wicked and Self-Indulgent Rulers

1 Thus says the LORD:
Keep justice and follow righteousness.
For my salvation is near,
And my righteousness shall soon become manifest.

2 Blessed is the man who does this,
And the son of man who holds fast to it,
Who keeps the sabbath from being profaned,
And withholds his hand from doing evil.

3 Let the foreigner, who has attached himself to the LORD,
Not say: "The LORD has surely separated me from his people."
Neither let the eunuchs say: "Behold I am a dried up tree."

4 For thus says the LORD
To the eunuchs who keep my sabbath,
And have chosen to do that which pleases me,
And to hold fast to my covenant.

5 To them shall I give within my house and my walls,
A lasting memorial, better than sons and daughters,
An everlasting name that will never be erased.

6 And the sons of foreigners
Who attach themselves to the LORD to serve him,
To love the name of the LORD and to be his servants,
Who keep the sabbath from being profaned,
And to hold fast to my covenant.

7 Them will I bring to my holy mountain,
And make them rejoice in my house of prayer.
Their burnt offerings and their sacrifices
Shall be acceptable upon mine altar;
For my house shall be called:
"A house of prayer for all peoples."

8 Thus says the LORD God who gathers the scattered of Israel,
I will yet gather to him others
Besides those already gathered.

Comment:

1-8 Those who adhere to God's covenant with Israel and live a righteous life will experience His salvation. This promise applies also to proselytes and eunuchs.

1-2 In view of the aproaching salvation every Israelite is admonished to live righteously and to adhere to His covenant.

2 Blessed is the man . . . who keeps the sabbath . . . and withholds . . . from . . . evil

Essential to God's covenant with Israel, besides circumcision is the observance of the Sabbath and the avoidance of all evil.

3-7 The prophet directs a special word of hope to proselytes and eunuchs.

3 Let the foreigner . . . not say: "The LORD has surely separated me from his people."

Neither let the eunuchs say: "Behold I am a dried up tree."

According to Deuteronomy 23:1 a person who has been physically emasculated could not be a member of the congregation of Israel.

The same prohibition also applies to the Ammonites and Moabites because of their hostile treatment of the Israelites when they were wandering through their territories on their way back from Egypt to the Promised Land (Dt. 23:4). A noticeable exception was Ruth the Moabitess, the ancestor of King David. However, it is possible that the prohibition applied only to men and not to women.

In any case the two groups developed a natural sense of inferiority. In the case of the Jewish eunuchs, the prophet refers to involuntary emasculation inflicted on them by their pagan captors when they selected them for service in their harems.

"The foreigners" in this verse apparently refers to those Gentiles who were attracted to the worship of Jehovah and became proselytes adhering strictly to the ritual and ethical ordinances of Israel, following justice and righteousness, also observing the Sabbath.

The Sabbath was singled out by the prophet, because it is a visible profession of Jehovah as Creator and Lord of their lives.[1]

5 To them (the eunuchs) shall I give within my house and my walls

A lasting memorial better than sons and daughters

They were not to consider themselves "as dried up trees." Because of their devoted service to the LORD, they shall have a more lasting memorial (*yad veshem*, literally, "a hand and a name") than sons and daughters.[2]

7 Them will I bring to my holy mountain

These proselytes and eunuchs will not only be admitted to full membership in the household of Israel, but their offerings and sacrifices will be acceptable to the LORD, just as those of any other God-fearing Israelite.

For my house shall be called: "A house of prayer for all peoples"

King Solomon in his dedicatory prayer of the Temple (1 Ki. 8:41-43) looked forward to the day when foreigners from distant lands would come to worship the LORD on Mt. Zion. Now the prophet explicitly states that God's Holy Temple will be a universal house of prayer for all peoples. Jesus quoted those words when He drove out the merchants from the Temple (see also Mt. 21:13 and Lk. 19:46).

8 I will yet gather to him others, besides those already gathered

The thought here is that in addition to the ingathering of scattered Israel, the Lord will add others to His flock from among the nations, those who would come freely to worship Him. This verse enlarges verse 7, and reminds us of the words of Jesus:

> And other sheep I have which are not in the fold, them also must I bring, and they shall hear my voice. And there shall be one fold and one shepherd (John 10:16).

Thus says the Lord God. . .

These words are a solemn declaration that Jehovah intends to break down the middle wall of partition between God-fearing Jews and Gentiles, a promise which was fulfilled in Christ and later confirmed by the Apostle Paul:

> For he is our peace who has made both one and has broken down the middle wall of partition between us (Eph. 2:14).

9 All beasts of the field come to devour,
All you beasts in the forest!

10 His watchmen are all blind and ignorant,
They are dumb dogs, which cannot bark,
They rave, they lie down and love to slumber.

11 These greedy dogs which cannot be satisfied,
And such are the shepherds;
They have no ability to understand
Each one has turned to his own way,
Each of them seeks his own gain, all of them without exception.

12 "Come, and I will fetch wine, (they say),

And we will fill ourselves with strong drink,
And tomorrow will be just as today,
Only much bigger and better."

Comments:

9-12 The rapid transition from the vision of an enlarged Israel to a denunciation of her watchmen as blind, dumb and greedy dogs, is startling. Some commentators have even assumed that this is a separate prophecy, unrelated to the rest of the chapter. However, it should be remembered that such unexpected changes in the prophetic mood occur frequently in Isaiah. It is not always possible to account for these changes. After expressing great compassion for those (including the proselytes and eunuchs) who have been humiliated and wronged by foreign tyrants, the prophet now, as God's spokesman, expresses his indignation against the blind, self-indulgent and greedy leaders of Israel.

9 All beasts of the field come to devour

The beasts of the fields and the forest are the foreign oppressors of Israel, abandoned by her own leaders and about to become the prey of her rapacious neighbors, "the beasts of the fields."

10 His watchmen are all blind and ignorant
They are dumb dogs, which cannot bark

Just as Jeremiah did (later ch. 23), so our prophet denounces in scathing terms Israel's watchmen of his own day. They were blind and ignorant of what ailed their people and what was happening around them. Instead of being seers and prophets, they were dumb dogs, which cannot bark to warn people.

They rave, they lie down and love to slumber.

There is a play on words in the Hebrew text: the prophet declares that the leaders of Israel, instead of being *"chozim"*—"seers," are *"hozim"*—"ravers and babblers"; lazy dogs which love to slumber when they should be alert and watchful.

11 These greedy dogs which cannot be satisfied and such are the shepherds

With each stroke of his quill the prophet adds another feature to the character of Israel's watchmen and shepherds. They are greedy and insatiable dogs. All of them, without exception, seek their own gain. They have lost their capacity for moral or spiritual discernment.

12 "Come and I will fetch wine, (they say)
And we will fill ourselves with strong drink"

The last stroke in this dismal picture of Israel's shepherds portrays them as drunkards and debauchers of the people. Apparently, in a land so rich in vineyards, alcoholism was one of the major problems which plagued the nation, especially the "upper class."

"And tomorrow will be just as today only much bigger and better."

Here is a picture of complete moral degradation, utterly unbecoming of God's people, called to be "a holy nation." The drunken scene, similar to that previously described in Isaiah 28:1-8 would fit better into some pagan Bacchanalia, than into the life of God's chosen shepherds.

NOTES:

1. For the relationship of the Sabbath to the Lord's Day, we recommend our book, *The Gospel in the Feasts of Israel* published by The Spearhead Press, Collingswood, N. J.
2. It is interesting to note that the Mt. Zion memorial to the six million Jewish victims of Hitler is known as *"Yad va-shem,"* literally "a hand and a name" (Isa. 56:7), a common expression for a lasting memorial.

Isaiah Chapter 57

A Rebuke of the Godless, Encouragement of the Faithful

1 The righteous perish and nobody takes it to heart,
   The godly are removed and none understands
   That the righteous is removed from the evil to come.

2 He shall enter into peace, they shall repose on their beds.
   Each one who walks in integrity.

Comments:

1 The righteous perish and nobody takes it to heart

As a result of the wicked rule of the ungodly, mentioned in the previous chapter (56:9-12), the godly and the righteous perish. The prophet's scathing words may reflect the situation in Judah under the reign of Manasseh of whom we read: "Manasseh shed innocent blood very much, till he had filled Jerusalem from one end to another" (2 Ki. 21:16).

Yet the prophet has a word of consolation for the righteous who perish innocently.

. . . the righteous is removed from the evil to come

Terrible judgment is coming upon the evildoers, but at least the godly shall be spared the coming evil.

2 He shall enter into peace, they shall repose in their beds

The grave is here called a bed—*mishkav*, a fitting description of the ancient graves hollowed out in rocky caves. The godly people who walked in uprightness and died as martyrs will enter into the peace of God. The thought of immortality is implied but not expressly stated.

3-13 A scathing denunciation of the widespread practice of idolatry and immorality among the Israelites.

3 But as for you, come on here, you sons of witches,
The spawn of the adulterer and the harlot.

4 Whom are you mocking?
Against whom do you open wide your mouths and stick out your tongue?
Are you not children of wickedness, a brood of falsehood?

5 You who burn with lust under the oaks,
And under every spreading tree,
Who slaughter children in the valleys,
Under the clefts of the rocks.

6 Among the smooth stones of the valley there is thy portion,
These, these are thy lot,
To these hast thou poured out a libation,
And offered a meal offering,
Should I be appeased by such doings?

7 Upon a high and lofty mountain
Hast thou set thy bed,
And there hast thou gone up to offer sacrifices.

8 And behind the doors and the doorposts,
Didst thou set up thy signs,
There hast thou exposed thyself and gone away from me,
Thou hast made thy bed wide,
And hast come to terms with them,
Thou hast loved the bed of anyone
Who beckoned thee with his hand.

9 And thou wentest to Moloch with ointment, richy perfumed.
And hast sent thy procurers to far away lands,
Even down to Sheol itself.

10 Thou hast wearied thyself out with all thy traveling,
Yet hast never said, "This is useless,"
But as soon as you recovered you were not affected.

11 Of whom were you so afraid and in terror, as to deny me,
And hast not remembered me, nor given me any thought?

Is it because I have kept silence for so long,
That thou hast ceased to fear me?

12 I will now declare thy "righteousness,"
And thy actions, but they shall not profit thee.

13 When thou criest, let thy bunch of idols save thee.
But all of them shall be carried off by the wind,
A breath shall blow them away.

Comments:

3 But as for you, come on here, you sons of witches

The prophet addresses himself in extremely harsh words to the Jewish idolators. Not only they but their ancestors were adulterers and harlots. They come from a long line of sinners.

4-9 A description of the moral perversity and sexual licentiousness of the idol worshippers.

4 Whom are you mocking?

The mockery by the wicked of the godly is extremely vulgar. They contort their faces, stick out their tongues, thus showing their utter contempt for God and for His servants.

5 You who burn with lust under the oaks . . . who slaughter children in the valleys

Sexual promiscuity and the sacrifice of children on pagan altars were all part of Semitic idolatry. Some of the temples employed "sacred prostitutes," who acted as priestesses and priests of the gods, especially of Ashtereth or Astarte, the Semitic Venus. The cult of Moloch demanded the sacrifice of children. This murderous cult was practiced by King Manasseh in the Valley of Hinnom, below Mt. Zion (2 Chr. 33:6).

6 Among the smooth stones of the valley there is thy portion

Certain smooth stones of the riverbeds, polished by the swift running waters, were anointed with oil and became the objects of pagan worship. The famous black rock in Mecca, still venerated by the Mohammedans, was, according to an ancient tradition, long before the Muslim era, such an object of pagan worship.

"The smooth stones of the valley" is a play on words, in Hebrew —*"be-chalked nachal chelukeich."* Israel had a part in these heathen rites. To these stones they offered libations and meal offerings. What a degradation for a people who were privileged to know Jehovah and were called to be His witnesses, to fall down to wood and stones to worship them.

It was to avoid infection with such moral and spiritual perversion that God pronounced judgment on the original population of Canaan.

In spite of this, many Israelites succumbed to idolatry which was inextricably mixed up with sexual license in the guise of religion.

Should I be appeased by such doings?

Should the holy and righteous Lord be satisfied by all this perversion?

7-8 Further details concerning the sexual licentiousness of paganism. The text is so grimly eloquent in itself that it hardly needs further elucidation.

9 And thou wentest to Moloch with ointment, richly perfumed

The word *Moloch* is in Hebrew the same as the word, "king"— *"melech"* (so translated in KJV) only the vowels were changed *melech* to *Moloch,* to indicate the deep aversion to the bloodthirsty pagan idol.

Idolatrous Hebrew women would anoint themselves and use costly perfumes while serving the worshippers and pagan priestesses of Moloch.

And hast sent thy procurers to far away lands

Not content with local deities, the Israelites sent their messengers to far away shrines, even to Sheol itself to find more idols to worship.

10 Thou hast wearied thyself out with all thy traveling

In search of strange gods the idolators of Israel never wearied, and never considered that all this pagan worship was less than useless, but as soon as they caught their breath, they remained unaffected and carried on as before.

11 Of whom were you so afraid and in terror, as to deny me?

Jehovah is asking His people this question, as if to say, What have I done to you that you forgot me?

**Is it because I have kept silence for so long
That thou hast ceased to fear me?**

The apostate Israelites took the silence of their God for indifference, rather than attribute it to His longsuffering.

12 I will now declare they "righteousness"
And thy actions, but they shall not profit thee

Here is an example of divine irony.

What they consider as their "righteousness" will not help them when their actions will be brought to light. Man's "righteousness" or moral code is starkly contradicted by his actions, even by the standards of his own light.

13 When thou criest, let thy bunch of idols save thee

The unfaithful of Israel have accumulated a whole collection of gods. The prophet sarcastically says that since they have put their trust in these useless idols, let them now, in the hour of their need, come to their rescue. But all these idols are completely worthless, a breath of wind will carry them off.

13b-21 Redemption and everlasting peace are only in Jehovah.

13b   But he who has made me his refuge
       Shall possess the earth and inherit my holy mountain.

14   And he shall say:
       Build up, build up, prepare a highway,
       Remove the roadblocks from the path of my people.

15   For thus says the High and Exalted One,
       Who inhabits eternity, whose name is Holy:
       I dwell in the high and holy place,
       And with him who is of a broken and humble spirit
       To revive the spirit of the humble,
       And to quicken the hearts of the contrite.

16   For I will not contend for ever,
       Nor will I always be angry.
       For the spirit would pine away before me,
       And the souls which I have made.

17   For the iniquity of his greed, was I angry and smote him,
       I hid my face and was wroth,
       But he continued in his wilful way.

18   Yet have I considered his ways and I will heal him,
       And will bring comfort to him and to his mourners,
       I create the fruit of the lips.

19   Peace, peace to him who is so far and to him who is near,
       Say the LORD, he who will heal him.

20   But as for the wicked, they are like the troubled sea, that cannot rest,
       And its waters cast up foam and filth.

21   There is no peace, says my God, to the wicked.

13b-15 The worthlessness of the idols is starkly contrasted with the holiness and mercy of Jehovah.

13b But he who has made me his refuge
     Shall possess the earth and inherit my holy mountain

Help and salvation are only in Jehovah. Those who trust Him

shall, in the end, inherit the earth and enjoy the fellowship and blessing of God. One is reminded of the words of our Lord:

"Blessed are the meek, for they shall inherit the earth" (Mt. 5:5).

14   And he shall say: Build up, build up, prepare a highway

The speaker is the Lord who will command the nations, who are His chosen instruments, to prepare a highway and to remove the roadblocks from the path of His people. While the above words may refer to the return of the exiles to their homeland, they also have a much wider significance. God is always able and willing to prepare a way of escape for His people, no matter how bleak and hopeless their situation may appear. The same thought and in almost the same words is expressed in Isaiah 40:3 (see also 1 Cor. 10:13).

15   I dwell in the high and holy place
And with him who is of a broken and humble spirit

The glory of the Lord is manifested not only in His holiness and majesty, but above all in the fact that He condescends to receive those who are of a broken and humble spirit. The Psalmist expresses the same thought in Psalm 51:17.

16   For I will not contend for ever, nor will I always be angry

In relation to Israel the Lord is not only a God of justice and judgment, but also a God of mercy. If the Lord should always chide and punish, the spirit and the soul of man could not endure it.

17   For the iniquity of his greed, was I angry and smote him.

The nature of man is essentially greedy and self-seeking. This is what provokes divine anger. Yet in spite of the afflictions which result from His anger, some continue perversely because of the inherent wickedness of their hearts.

18   Yet have I considered his ways and I will heal him

Although God knows what is in men's hearts, yet is He willing to heal them in distress and to comfort them in affliction. This quality of divine mercy surpasses human compassion. Its supreme manifestation was Christ. God's final word to man is not anger and punishment, but mercy and healing.

19   I create the fruit of the lips (saying:)
Peace, peace to him who is far and to him who is near

"The fruit of the lips" is a figure of speech for "the words which fall from the lips."

"*Shalom, shalom*"—"peace, peace," is the daily greeting used nowadays in Israel. It conveys the idea of complete or perfect peace. This peace the Lord has in store not only for those who are of the household of Israel but for those of the Gentiles, who were once far from God but have come near to Him through the Messiah of Israel. The Apostle Paul put it this way:

> He (Christ) came and preached peace to you (Gentiles) who were once far off, and to them who were near (that is, to the Jews) (Eph. 2:17).

20 But as for the wicked, they are like the troubled sea, that cannot rest

A striking comparison of the heart of the wicked to the restless and stormy sea which keeps on casting up foam and filth.

21 There is no peace, says my God, to the wicked

This is God's judgment concerning the ungodly (*reshaim*). By the inherent sinfulness of their nature, the wicked are condemned to constant turmoil and to self-destruction.

Isaiah Chapter 58

Piousness Without Compassion is Unacceptable to the Lord

1 Shout at the top of thy voice, hold not back,
  Lift up thy voice like a trumpet,
  And tell my people their transgressions,
  And the house of Jacob their sins.

2 Yet they seek me day by day,
  And delight to know my ways,
  Like a nation which acts righteously,
  And has not forsaken the judgment of their God:
  They inquire of me about righteous judgments,
  And delight to draw near unto God.

3 "Why do we fast and thou seest not?
  Why do we afflict ourselves and thou payest no heed?"
  Behold on the day of your fast you pursue your pleasure,
  And enforce all your labors.

4 Behold, you fast for strife and contention,
  And to deal blows with a vicious fist.
  Such a day of fasting will not cause your voice to be heard above.

5 Is this the fast which I have chosen?
  A day in which a man afflicts his soul,
  And bows down his head like a reed,
  And puts sackcloth and ashes under himself?
  A day which is acceptable to the LORD?

6 Is not rather this a fast which I have chosen:
To loose the fetters of wickedness,
To undo the bands of the yoke,
To let the oppressed go free,
And to break every yoke?

7 Is it not rather a day to distribute thy bread to the hungry,
And to bring home the poor wanderer?
When thou seest the naked to cover him,
And that thou hide not thyself from thy own flesh?

8 Then shall thy light break forth as the dawn,
And thou shalt be healed quickly,
And thy righteousness shall go before thee,
And the glory of the LORD shall be thy rearguard.

9 Then wilt thou call and the LORD will answer,
Thou shalt cry and he will say: "Here I am,"
If thou wilt remove the yoke from the midst,
If thou wilt cease to point a finger and to speak wickedness.

10 If thy soul will go out in compassion and bestow thy bread on
the hungry
To satisfy the afflicted soul,
Then shall thy light shine forth in darkness,
And the dusk will be like noonday.

11 And the LORD will guide thee continually,
And satisfy thy soul in drought,
He will strengthen thy bones,
And thou shalt be like a well-watered garden,
And like a spring, whose waters never fail.

12 Then shall thy own rebuild the old ruins,
And raise up the ancient foundations,
And thou shalt be called "a breach mender"
And "restorer of ruined paths for habitation."

13 If thou wilt withhold thy foot from the sabbath,
To do thy pleasure on my holy day,
But wilt call my sabbath a delight,
And the LORD's holy day a day to be honored,
And honor it by not pursuing your own affairs,
Or doing whatever pleases you, nor talking business on it.

14 Then shalt thou delight thyself in the LORD,
And I will cause thee to ride upon the high places of the earth,
And I will feed thee with the heritage of thy father, Jacob,
For the mouth of the LORD has spoken this.

Comment:

1 Shout at the top of thy voice, hold not back

Literally, "with a full throat, spare not."

Lift up thy voice like a trumpet

The Hebrew word for "trumpet or horn," is *"shofar"*—a ram's horn used by the priests to call the people to a solemn assembly, or by a military commander to sound the signal for alarm or for action.

In like manner the prophet is commanded to sound the trumpet to warn his people of the imminent danger of apostasy, in spite of all the superficial manifestations of piety.

2 Yet they seek me day by day and delight to know my ways

Even while they greviously offend God and provoke Him to wrath, the people act as if they are truly seeking God and delight to know His ways. They are not even conscious of their hypocrisy, because they have convinced themselves that to know the LORD and to serve Him is simply a matter of a scrupulous observance of certain religious procedures.

They inquire of me about righteous judgments
And delight to draw near unto God

They are anxious to know about all the right procedures and even to draw near to God in some way which does not effect a complete change of heart, or impose on them the demand of a new relationship to their fellowmen, and does not affect their personal possessions. This great intellectual curiosity about "God's righteous judgments" has in time produced an involved, voluminous and speculative literature, the Talmud, which dealt with all the minutiae of proper religious behavior and procedures and rites, affecting the daily life of "the good Jew" from morning till evening and from cradle to grave. However, it did little to change the hearts of men. We recall the words of Jesus when asked about the most important commandment of the Law, and His answer, "Thou shalt love the Lord thy God with all thy heart and with all thy soul and with all thy mind. This is the first and the greatest commandment."

"And the second is like unto it, thou shalt love thy neighbor as thyself. On these two commandments hang all the law and the prophets" (Mt. 22:37-40).

3 "Why do we fast and thou seest not?"

Believing that they were scrupulous in seeking to do the will of God, they felt aggrieved and wronged that God did not hear their prayers and did not take notice of their fasting, without realizing that their religious life did not affect their moral behavior.

445

3b-5 The Lord's answer to the complaint of the people

3b Behold on the day of your fast you pursue your pleasure

Their fasting is not the result of true contrition, but mere compliance with the Law and tradition. In reality their thoughts were far removed from God and absorbed with their own business and pleasure. Even on their fast day, they exacted from their servants all the labors which had been imposed on them.

4 Behold you fast for strife and contention and to deal blows with a vicious fist

Their behavior was outwardly pious, but in reality their conduct was ungodly and cruel. Such was the Lord's severe indictment against His people. The moral and social scene described by the prophet is extremely dark. However, we must be careful not to transfer the situation described by the prophet to the Jewish people of today. The holy and righteous God is the judge of all men. He judges men according to His infinite mercy and justice, whether they be Jews or non-Jews. The prophet makes the point that physical fasting, devoid of repentance and mercy, will not be heard by God.

5 Is this the fast which I have chosen . . . a day which is acceptable to the LORD?

Having made abundantly clear that the Lord despises all sham piety, the prophet now proceeds to describe to those who are His what the Lord does desire.

**6 To loose the fetters of wickedness, to undo the bands of the yoke. . . .
And to break every yoke**

It is a ringing challenge not only to Israel but to men of all generations to be done with outward appearances and to set free those who are crushed and oppressed and to break every yoke.

**7 Is it not rather a day to distribute thy bread to the hungry
And to bring home the poor wanderer?**

The deeds of mercy which are acceptable to the Lord are spelled out in ringing and challenging detail. Isaiah's pronouncement reminds us of the words of Christ in which He identified Himself with all the sufferers and distressed:

> I was hungry and ye gave me meat . . . Thirsty and ye gave me drink . . . a stranger and ye took me in . . . naked and ye clothed me . . . sick and ye visited me . . . in prison and ye came unto me (Mt. 25:35-36).

There is more of Isaiah in the Gospels than we generally realize.

For Christ was saturated with the knowledge and the spirit of the prophets.

8 Then shall thy light break forth as the dawn and thou shalt be healed quickly

God's favor and blessing are contingent upon a man seeking to do what is acceptable to Him. "Thy light" is contrasted with the darkness of a sinful heart and mind. "Thy healing" is physical health and renewal of strength which comes from living in harmony with God. "Thy righteousness" is the righteousness of obedience to the will of God. It is the righteousness of faith. Faith and action must go together.

11 And the LORD will guide thee continually, and satisfy thy soul in drought. . .
And thou shalt be like a well-watered garden. . .

One of the most beautiful promises to the true servant of God: The Lord's continuous guidance and a never-failing spring of divine resources. Here again we recall the words of Jesus spoken to the woman of Samaria:

Whosoever drinketh of the water that I shall give him, shall never thirst, but the water that I shall give him shall be in him a well of water springing up into everlasting life (John 4:14).

12 Then shall thy own rebuild the old ruins. . .
And thou shalt be called "a breach mender" and "restorer of ruined paths". . .

The blessings of God will also be poured out not only on the penitent person alone, but on the penitent nation. This will manifest itself in the reclamation of the ancient ruins, so that they will become known as a nation of "breach menders" and "restorers of ruined paths."

13 If thou wilt withhold thy foot from the sabbath to do thy pleasure on my holy day

The importance of the keeping of the Sabbath is repeatedly emphasized by the prophet, as a visible acknowledgment of the sovereignty of Jehovah, as Lord of our lives and of our time. The Sabbath was of particular importance to Israel in exile as a unifying and sanctifying force, and has remained such throughout the ages.

But wilt call my sabbath a delight and the LORD's holy day a day to be honored

When the children of Israel shall observe the Sabbath not merely as a burden, the Sabbath will become a delight to them. It has been said by a Jewish sage: "More than the Jews kept the Sabbath, the Sabbath kept the Jews."[1]

14 Then ... will I cause thee to ride upon the high places of the earth

The honoring of the Sabbath and of the LORD who sanctified the Sabbath will bring exaltation and honor to Israel from the nations of the earth, also restoration and enjoyment of their ancestral heritage.

For the mouth of the LORD has spoken this

A most solemn declaration that the promise does not originate from a human source but from the very mouth of God.

1. For a fuller discussion of the relationship of the Christian to the Sabbath, see *The Gospel in the Feasts of Israel* by Victor Buksbazen, published by The Spearhead Press, W. Collingswood, N. J.

Isaiah Chapter 59

Israel's Sins Stand Between Her and Jehovah

1 Behold the hand of the LORD
Is not so short that it cannot save,
Neither is his ear so dull that it cannot hear.

2 But your iniquities, these have separated you from your God,
And your sins have caused his face to hide from you,
So as not to hear.

3 For your hands are stained with blood,
And your fingers with inquity.
Your lips have spoken lies,
And your tongues have uttered wickedness.

4 There is none who sues justly,
And none is judged faithfully.
They trust in vanity and speak lies.
They conceive mischief and bring forth iniquity.

5 They hatch adders' eggs and weave a spider's web,
He who eats of their eggs will die,
And that which is crushed hatches a viper.

6 Their webs shall not be made into a garment,
Neither shall men cover themselves with their works.
Their works are works of evil,
And violence is in their palms.

7 Their feet run to do evil,
And they hasten to shed innocent blood.
Their thoughts are thoughts of iniquity,
Desolation and ruin are in their paths.

8 They know not the way of peace,
Neither is there justice in their tracks.
They have perverted their paths,
Whosoever follows them knows no peace.

9 This is why justice is far from us,
And righteousness does not reach us,
We wait for light, and behold darkness
For brightness, — but we walk in gloom.

10 We grope along the wall like the blind
And feel our way like sightless men.
We stumble at noonday as if it were twilight
And like the dead we dwell in the dark.

11 We all growl like bears
And we keep moaning like doves.
We look for justice, but there is none.
For salvation, but it is far from us.

12 For our transgressions against thee are many,
And our sins bear witness against us,
For our transgressions are with us
And we know our iniquities.

13 Rebelling and denying the LORD
And turning away from following our God,
Speaking oppression and revolt,
Conceiving and uttering words of falsehood from our hearts.

14 And justice has been turned back,
And righteousness stands afar off,
For truth has stumbled in the broad street,
And fairness cannot enter.

15 So truth is missing,
And he who avoids evil is plundered,
And the LORD saw this and it appeared evil in his eyes
That there was no justice.

16 For he saw that there was no man,
And he was amazed that there was no intercessor,
Therefore, his own arm brought him salvation,
And his righteousness sustained him.

17 He clothed himself with righteousness as a breast plate,
The helmet of salvation on his head.
He put on the garment of vengeance for his clothing,
And wrapped himself with zeal as with a robe.

18 According to their deeds so will he repay.
Wrath to his adversaries, retribution to his enemies
To the inhabitants of the islands he will repay as they deserve.

19 And they, from the west, shall fear the name of the LORD
And from the east, his glory
For distress shall come like a pent-up stream
Driven by the spirit of the LORD.

20 And the Redeemer shall come to Zion,
And to those in Jacob who turn away from transgression,
Says the LORD.

21 And as for me: this is my covenant with them, says the LORD.
My spirit which is upon thee,
And the words which I have put in thy mouth
They shall not depart from thy mouth,
Nor from the mouths of thy seed,
Nor from the mouths of thy seed's seed,
Says the LORD, from now on and for ever.

Comment:

1-8 Israel's sinful condition has separated them from their God.

1 Behold, the hand of the LORD is not so short

The reason why God does not come to Israel's rescue is not His inability to help (the hand too short), nor is it His indifference (a dull ear).

2 But your iniquities, these have separated you from your God

The enormous sins of the people have formed a barrier between them and their God.

3 For your hands are stained with blood

From a general indictment the prophet proceeds to point out specific sins. The first is the shedding of innocent blood. The same accusation is mentioned in chapter 1:15. Their fingers are defiled with iniquity, an allusion to wicked manipulations and schemes.

Their lips speak lies, their tongues are used for wickedness. There is no truth in daily communications between the people.

4 There is none who sues justly and none is judged faithfully

The judicial process is perverted by the litigants and by the judges.

They conceive mischief and bring forth iniquity

When the mind is perverted, what comes out of it can only be iniquity.

5 They hatch adders' eggs and weave a spider's web

In these two figures the prophet aptly describes the prevailing corruption among the people. Adders' eggs are poisonous and dangerous, and no garment can be made of the flimsy web of a spider (v. 6).

7   Their feet run to do evil, and they hasten to shed innocent blood

Just as they are slow in doing justice (v. 4), they are quick to do evil and to shed innocent blood.

8   They know not the way of peace . . . they have perverted their paths

In effect the prophet accuses his compatriots that they have perverted and twisted their path and lost the way of peace. The Hebrew term for peace—*shalom,* as we have already pointed out, is a much more encompassing term than our word "peace." *Shalom* means harmony between man and his neighbor, peace within and peace with God. Isaiah accuses his people that they have so perverted all social, personal and national relationships that "*shalom*" has become impossible. The prophet draws a bleak picture of the moral scene, which is strongly reminiscent of Isaiah's first chapter.

9-11   The lamentable consequences of moral corruption

9   This is why justice is far from us

Under the conditions so vividly described by the prophet there can be no justice, but constant frustration and disappointment.

We wait for light, and behold darkness

One feels the constant sense of frustration of the helpless victims of injustice who wait for a glimmer of light amidst the night of darkness which refuses to pass.

10   We grope along the wall like the blind

The prophet further enlarges on what he said in verse 9. Without the guidance of the God-revealed righteousness, the people are like the blind who grope along the walls. This is a striking picture familiar to the inhabitants of Jerusalem where blindness was such a frequent and pathetic occurrence.

11   We all growl like bears and we keep moaning like doves

In a double metaphor the prophet compares the complaining and lamenting people, the victims of their own domestic oppressors, to the growling of bears which in the days of Isaiah must have been quite numerous in the land, and to the mournful cooing of doves.

12-15   The confessions of a repentant people

12   For our transgressions against thee are many

A righteous remnant in Israel was keenly aware of the sinful condition of their people and confessed to God on behalf of their

451

compatriots. It is also possible that the prophet himself, identifying himself with his people, confesses their sin. All sins which a man commits against men are basically sins against the holiness and righteousness of God Himself (Psa. 51:4).

13 Rebelling and denying the LORD

From specific transgressions the prophet goes on to the roots of the sinful conditions which are in the hearts and minds of the people: rebelling and denying God, ceasing to follow Him, scheming rebellion in their hearts and speaking all kinds of falsehoods.

14 And justice has been turned back and righteousness stands afar off

The prophet sees justice, righteousness, truth and fairness as living persons, who were assaulted by wicked men, wounded in the main street (*rehov*), and forbidden to enter the city.

15 So truth is missing

The prophet continues his metaphors and sees truth as a missing person, and those who do not join the wicked majority, or their leaders, as exposed to plunder and injustice.

And the LORD saw this and it appeared evil in His eyes

15b-18 The outraged God intervenes to punish the wicked and to restore justice.

16 For he saw that there was no man

The LORD waited for a man worthy of the name, who would come and restore righteousness and punish the wicked, but there was none.

Therefore, his own arm brought him salvation

As there was no man to stand up for the cause of justice, the LORD Himself decided to intervene. "The arm of the LORD" symbolizes God in His mighty acts of salvation (Isa. 53:1).

17 He clothed himself with righteousness as a breast plate

The Lord is presented as a mighty man of war, attired as a warrior to do battle with the enemies of righteousness. He is depicted as ancient warrior with the breastplate (*shirion*), or coat of mail, for protection from the swords and darts of His enemies. His head is covered with the helmet of salvation, and the garment of vengeance covers His body. For His outside tunic, He wears His zeal (cf. Eph. 6:10-17).

18 According to their deeds so will he repay:
Wrath to his adversaries, retribution to his enemies

It now become apparent that the adversaries and enemies of

God are not only the wicked of Israel, but also "the inhabitants of the islands," the heathen nations who are the enemies of His people and also of His righteousness.

The Apostle Paul dealing with this same theme said that God is no respecter of persons, but judges the Jews according to the divine revelation which they have received, and the Gentiles who are outside the Law according to their innate sense of right and wrong (Rom. 2:11-15).

19-21 The consequences resulting from God's judgment upon the nations and upon Israel.

19 And they, from the west, shall fear the name of the LORD
And from the east, his glory

"To fear the name of the LORD," is not abject terror but a reverential awe before the majesty, omnipotence and holiness of God.

For distress shall come like a pent-up stream driven by the spirit of the LORD

God manifests Himself in history and in nature in cataclysmic acts which reveal Him as creator and sustainer of the universe and as judge of all men and nations.

20 And the Redeemer shall come to Zion

When judgment shall come upon the nations of the world, the Lord will send the Redeemer to Israel. The advent of the Redeemer is not further defined as to time and circumstance, except that He will come "to those who turn away from transgression," that is, to a repentant remnant.

21 And as for me: this is my covenant with them, says the LORD

God's covenant with them, that is, His people, is the promise that the Spirit of God manifested in His revelation to Israel shall remain with His people throughout the coming generations. The "covenant" has nothing to do with the merits or disobedience of Israel. It is an act of the sovereign will and grace of God. Israel is destined to remain forever His witness whether in obedience or disobedience, the custodian of His Word.[1]

NOTE:
1. It should be emphasized that this and the following chapters (60-62) are addressed to Israel and not to the Church of Christ, as many Christian commentators have falsely maintained. To apply this to the Church and not to Israel is to obfuscate and distort the plain sense of the Scriptures. This unfortunate practice of confusing Israel with the Church started in the early Christian centuries and was later followed by most of the Reformers and commentators. This misinterpretation had its roots in the teaching that Israel by rejecting Christ has forfeited her election and promises of future blessings, which were inherited by the Church, "the New Israel."

Isaiah Chapter 60

The Glory of the New Jerusalem

1 Arise, shine; for thy light has come,
And the glory of the LORD is risen upon thee.

2 For, behold, the darkness shall cover the earth,
And deep darkness the peoples:
But upon thee the LORD will arise,
And his glory shall be seen over thee.

3 And nations shall walk toward thy light,
And kings toward the gleam of thy rising.

4 Lift up thine eyes round about, and look:
They are all assembled and are coming to thee,
Thy sons shall come from afar,
And thy daughters are carried on the side.

5 Then shalt thou see and be radiant,
And thy heart shall throb and swell,
For the abundance of the sea shall be turned over to thee,
And the wealth of the nations shall come to thee.

6 The caravans of camels shall cover thee,
The young camels of Midian and Ephah;
They shall all come from Sheba:
They shall carry gold and frankincense;
And shall proclaim the praises of the LORD.

7 All the flocks of Kedar shall be gathered together for thee,
The rams of Nebaioth shall serve thee,
They shall be offered up acceptably upon mine altar,
And I will adorn my beautiful house.

8 Who are these which fly like a cloud,
Like doves to their dovecotes?

9 For the coastlands are waiting for me,
The ships of Tarshish are in front,
To bring thy sons from afar,
Their silver and gold is with them,
For the sake of the name of Jehovah, thy God,
And the Holy One of Israel, who has glorified thee.

10 And the sons of strangers shall rebuild thy walls,
And their kings shall minister unto thee;
For in my wrath have I smitten thee,
But in my favor I had compassion on thee.

11 And thy gates shall be continuously open,
Never shut by day or by night,
To bring to thee the wealth of the nations,
Led by their kings.

12 For that nation and that kingdom
Which shall refuse to serve thee shall perish;
And those nations shall be completely destroyed.

13 The glory of Lebanon shall come to thee:
The cypress, the boxwood and the larch
To adorn the place of my sanctuary;
And I will make the place of my feet glorious.

14 And the sons of thy oppressors shall come to thee bowing down;
And all they who despised thee shall bow down to the soles of thy feet,
And they shall call thee "The City of the LORD,"
"Zion of the Holy One of Israel."

15 Instead of being forsaken and hated,
Without anybody passing through,
I will make thee an eternal excellence,
A joy to generation after generation.

16 And thou shalt suck the milk of nations,
And the breast of kings shalt thou suckle.
And thou shalt know that I the LORD am thy Saviour,
And that the Mighty One of Jacob is thy Redeemer.

17 Instead of brass, I will bring gold,
And instead of iron, I will bring silver,
Instead of wood, there will be brass,
And instead of stones—iron:
I will appoint peace for thy magistrates,
And righteousness for thy administrators.

18 Violence shall no more be heard in thy land,
Nor desolation and destruction within thy borders,
But thou shalt call thy walls Salvation,
And thy gates Praise.

19 The sun shall no more be thy light by day,
Nor shall the brightness of the moon give light to thee.
But the LORD shall be thy everlasting light,
And thy God shall be thy glory.

20 Thy sun shall no more go down,
Neither shall thy moon wane,
For the LORD shall be for an everlasting light to thee,
And the days of thy mourning shall come to an end.

21 Thy people shall all be righteous,
    They shall inherit the land forever,
    The branch which I planted,
    My handiwork to glorify me.

22 The smallest shall become a thousand,
    And the least a mighty nation:
    I, the LORD, will hasten it in due time.

Comment:

Chapters 60-62 continue the theme of restored and redeemed Jerusalem, introduced in the last two verses of chapter 59.

1 Arise, shine; for thy light has come

Zion, the personification of Israel, is commanded to arise from the former gloom of depression and to radiate the light and the glory of God. The Hebrew verb, *"zarah,"* is used to describe the rising of the sun. The light of the glory of God, is in later literature called "The *Shechinah.*"

2 For behold darkness shall cover the earth . . . but upon thee the LORD will arise

This verse enlarges further upon the previous one.

This writer once watched in Jerusalem the rising of the sun in the east, behind Mount Zion, gradually dispersing all around the darkness of the night. The prophet, a native of Jerusalem, must have seen this sight often and applied its significance to Zion—Israel and her role among the nations.

3 And nations shall walk toward thy light and kings toward the gleam of thy rising

The sun of righteousness and God's favor shining upon redeemed Israel will attract nations from distant lands to walk toward her light. Israel is to be, so to speak, the Pied Piper of the nations for God. It is the same vision described by the prophet elsewhere (Isa. 2:2-5).

4 Lift up thine eyes round about and look: they are all . . . coming to thee

The prophet bids his people to share in his vision of the nations come to her, bringing back Israel's exiled sons and daughters. The phrase, "thy daughters are carried on the side," refers to the oriental custom of mothers carrying their children on the hip.

5 Then shalt thou see and be radiant and thy heart shall throb and swell

A moving description of the reunion of Israel with her long-lost sons and daughters, an emotional experience seen today in Israel and elsewhere.

6 The caravans of camels shall cover thee

One of the results of Israel's restoration to divine favor will be a great increase in commerce with all her neighbors.

"The young camels" translated by the KJV's as "dromedaries," are actually young camels and not the one-humped camels. In this verse a number of descendants of Ishmael are mentioned: Ephah is a Midianite tribe (Gen. 25:4), the son of Keturah and Abraham. Most commentators believe that Sheba is modern Yemen.

They come bringing their most precious gifts, gold and frankincense, proclaiming the praise of Jehovah. The most significant aspect of this prophecy is the reconciliation of the Arab tribes with Israel and their worship of Jehovah. This prophecy, together with Isaiah 19:23-25, indicates that in Isaiah's time there was a live hope and desire that Israel and her Arab neighbors might be reconciled and worship together one God. The reference to gold and frankincense brings to mind the story of the wise men from the East who brought gifts to the newborn child, Jesus, of gold, frankincense and myrrh (Mt. 1:11).

7 All the flocks of Kedar . . . the rams of Nebaioth

Kedar and Nebaioth are mentioned in Genesis 25:13 as sons of Ishmael. The hope of the future conversion of the children of Ishmael to Jehovah is enlarged upon here, also their reconciliation with Israel.

And I will adorn my beautiful house

Some commentators have assumed that the mention of "the beautiful house" refers to the second temple, as having been already rebuilt. But such a supposition is without foundation. The prophet's words are apparently predictive that the Temple will one day be rebuilt, in God's own time.

8-9 The return of the sons of Israel from the east

8 Who are these which fly like a cloud, like doves. . .

The comparison here is with the swift flight of flocks of doves to their cotes. Israel's children are similarly endowed with a homing instinct.

9 For the coastlands are waiting for me . . . to bring thy sons from afar

"The islands" or "coastlands" are usually a reference to the people along the shores of the Mediterranean. In verse 4, the prophet predicted the return of the exiles from the east. Now he predicts the same about the exiles from the west.

Tarshish was a city at the extreme end of the Western Mediterranean. "The ships of Tarshish" is a term applied to the large, sea-going ships. Like the exiles from the east, they, too, will be returned by their former captors bringing gifts of gold and silver as a tribute to Jehovah.

For the sake of the name of Jehovah, thy God

10-22 Israel's restoration and return to her homeland will be an act of God's favor which will result in the conversion of the nations.

10 And the sons of strangers shall rebuild thy walls, and their kings

The rebuilding of the walls of Zion by the sons of strangers will be motivated by their desire to honor Jehovah and also as compensation for the wrong which they have done to Israel in former days. This action brings to mind the compensation or the "*Wiedergutmachung*" which the West Germans have in recent years paid to the Jews for the wrongs committed against them under the rule of Hitler.

For in my wrath have I smitten thee
But in my favor I had compassion on thee

The same thought was previously expressed by Isaiah in 54:7-8. God's wrath for Israel is a passing phase, but basically, God's intention toward them is one of favor and compassion.

11 And thy gates shall be continuously open, never shut. . .

The constant influx of people from all the nations, crowding the city of Jerusalem, either bringing tribute to Jehovah, or trading with Israel, will be so great that constantly open gates will become essential.

12 For that nation and that kingdom

The words sound harsh or even vindictive, but the thought expressed in them is that every nation or government which opposes God, will have no future and will eventually perish. It complements the thought, "the meek shall inherit the earth."

13 The glory of Lebanon shall come to thee

The famous trees of Lebanon mentioned here which were used in the building of the first and second temples were Lebanon's glory (1 Ki. 5:10 and Neh. 2:8).

And I will make the place of my feet glorious

The vision here is of Jehovah who inhabits the heavens, but has chosen Zion as the resting place of His feet. This parallels another vision of God, in Christ, who came down to earth to dwell among men (John 1:14).

The prophet Ezekiel called the Temple: "The place of the soles of my feet" (Ezek. 43:7).

14 And they shall call thee "The City of the LORD" "Zion of the Holy One of Israel"

The homage paid to Jerusalem by the nations of the world is the result of her repentance and her restored favor with God, manifested by His presence in the Temple.

15 Instead of being forsaken and hated

Regenerated Zion's relationship to the nations will undergo a radical transformation. No longer will she be shunned or hated but will become a place of eternal excellence, the spiritual center of the world.

16 Thou shalt suck the milk of the nations . . . the breast of kings

A figure of speech descriptive of Zion's most favored position among the nations and their rulers. The same thought is expressed in 49:23, 26.

17 Instead of brass I will bring gold

Jerusalem's material prosperity and splendor will be matched by her spiritual transformation.

I will appoint peace for thy magistrates and righteousness for thy administrators

Israel shall be governed by rulers and judges who will personify peace and righteousness.

18 Violence shall no more be heard in thy land, nor desolation...

A beautiful vision of the new Jerusalem, free from violence and desolation.

But thou shalt call thy walls Salvation and thy gates Praise

Again, salvation and praise are personified as the very foundation and bulwarks of restored Jerusalem.

19 The sun shall no more be thy light by day

The effulgence of God's presence, the *Shechinah*, will be so intense that it will outshine the sun and the moon.

In the book of Revelation this theme is enlarged upon with these words:

And the city had no need of the sun, neither of the moon to

shine in it, for the glory of God did lighten it, and the Lamb is the Light thereof (Rev. 21:23ff.).

20 Thy sun shall no more go down, neither shall thy moon wane

The prophet elaborates in some detail the vision of verse 19.

And the days of thy mourning shall come to an end

In the city of God there will be no sorrow or mourning.

21 Thy people shall all be righteous, they shall inherit the land forever

Israel will become a nation of righteous people. It is most significant to note the prophetic idea of perfect Israel: not a nation of philosophers—the Greek idea; nor a nation of invincible warriors—the Roman ideal; but a nation of *"tsadikim,"* men who are righteous in the sight of God. Only such a people shall in the end inherit the earth.

The branch (or twig) which I planted, my handiwork to glorify me

Branch or twig, Hebrew *"netser,"* appears in Isaiah 11:1 and 14:19. Israel's highest calling and destiny is to glorfy God. The same thought is expressed in Isaiah 43:21:

This people have I formed for myself;
That they might tell of my glory.

22 The smallest shall become a thousand, and the least a mighty nation

It is not just the thought of numerical increase which is expressed here, but the vision of regenerated Israel who will reproduce herself spiritually by her wonderful power to attract the nations to the worship of her God.

I, the LORD, will hasten it in due time

A solemn asurance that the LORD Himself will hasten the day of fulfillment, in the fullness of time.

Isaiah Chapter 61

The Mission of the Servant of the Lord
and Israel's Glorious Destiny

1 The spirit of the LORD God is upon me,
For the LORD has anointed me
To bring good tidings to the humble,
He sent me to bind up the broken-hearted;

460

To proclaim liberty to the captives,
And to open the prison to them who are bound.

2 To proclaim the year of the LORD's favor,
And a day of vengeance of our God,
To comfort all who mourn;

3 To appoint deliverance to the mourners of Zion,
And to give to them a garland instead of ashes,
The oil of gladness instead of mourning,
A garment of praise instead of a failing spirit,
And they shall be called "the oaks of righteousness,"
The planting of the LORD for his glory.

4 And they will rebuild the ancient ruins,
They will raise up the former desolations,
And restore the ruined cities
That were wasted for many generations.

5 And strangers shall stand and feed your flocks,
And the sons of aliens shall tend your farms and your vineyards.

6 But you shall be called, "the priests of the LORD,"
And they will speak of you as "the ministers of our God."
You will feed on the wealth of the nations
And revel in their splendor.

7 Instead of shame, you will receive a double share [of honor]
And for humiliation, they will rejoice with their portion
And so in their land shall they possess double,
Everlasting joy shall be theirs.

8 Because I the LORD love justice,
I hate robbery with iniquity,
And I will recompense them faithfully
And will make an everlasting covenant with them.

9 And their offspring shall be renowned among the nations,
And their posterity among the peoples,
All they who will see them shall recognize them,
That they are the seed whom God has blessed.

10 I will rejoice exceedingly in the LORD,
My soul shall be joyful in my God,
For he has clothed me with the garments of salvation,
And covered me with the robe of righteousness,
As a bridegroom puts on a priestly diadem,
And as a bride adorns herself with her jewels.

11 For as the earth brings forth her growth,
And as a garden causes its plantings to spring forth

So shall the LORD Jehovah cause righteousness and praise
To spring forth before all the nations.

Comment:

1 The spirit of the LORD God is upon me for the LORD has anointed me

Again the question arises who is the speaker of these and the following words? Jewish commentators apply these words to the prophet himself. But no prophet ever spoke of himself in this manner. These can only be the words spoken by the servant of the LORD, previously mentioned in 42:1, 50:4, 5. The mission described in verses 1-3 is of such a sweeping nature that only God Himself is able to perform it, using the servant as His agent. The mission of the Anointed One is further described in detail:

To bring good tidings to the humble

The anointed servant of God is to bring good tidings to the humble, a term which usually describes God's faithful remnant. The good tidings is that their enslavement is about to end.

He sent me to bind up the broken-hearted

This means to bring comfort and healing to those who suffer for righteousness' sake.

To proclaim liberty to captives

This is an immediate reference to the captives of Israel, but in a larger sense, it points to the deliverance from the bondage of sin.

And to open the prison to them who are bound

This line complements the former, enlarging upon the fact that besides being captives in bondage, some of them were also confined in prison.

2 To proclaim the year of the LORD's favor

Shnath-ratson la-Jehovah—the year of the LORD's favor—is that glorious time when God shall turn His face in mercy toward His people (see 60:10).[1]

And a day of vengeance of our God

In contrast to the year of God's favor toward His remnant, this will also be the day of reckoning for the ungodly.

To comfort all who mourn

Those who mourn for righteousness will be comforted through the presence and the work of the servant (see Mt. 5:4).

**3 To appoint deliverance to the mourners of Zion
And to give to them a garland instead of ashes**

To "appoint" and to "give" are synonymous expressions; the first is general, the second more specific. The word "deliverance" is not in the original text, but is implied.

In the Hebrew text there is a play on words: *"pe-ar"*—"a garland"; *"aipher"*—"ashes." Those who wore the ashes of mourning shall obtain a garland of joy. The following two lines are supplementary and express the same thought.

And they shall be called "the oaks of righteousness"

A term which conveys a meaning similar to 'the pillars of righteousness."

The planting of the LORD for his glory

The line is similar in sense to 60:21.

4-7 The ruins of the Holy Land will be rebuilt.

4 And they will rebuild the ancient ruins

"They" refers to the children of Israel who will return and rebuild their ruined cities.

5 And strangers shall stand and feed your flocks

A similar thought is expressed in 60:10, indicating that the converted Gentiles out of love for the LORD and for His people will work in harmony with the children of Israel as farmers and vinedressers and in the rebuilding of the land.

6 But you shall be called, "the priests of the LORD" . . . "the ministers of our God"

In Exodus 19:6, the children of Israel were called to be "a kingdom of priests and a holy nation." In appreciation of the material help and service of the converted Gentiles, the redeemed Jews will minister to them as "the priests of the LORD." The expression, "our God," points significantly to the sharing of a common faith, and the worship of the same God. The term, *"meshorthei"*—"ministers"—means servants who perform higher functions. The prophet sees Israel as the God-appointed minister to the nations of the world.

You will feed on the wealth of the nations and revel in their splendor

The word, translated "revel" ("boast" in KJV), literally means "to take in exchange." The thought here is that Zion—Israel—will share her spiritual wealth with the nations, and in exchange will participate in everything which is great and noble among the nations. We have translated *"kavod"*—usually translated "glory" as "splendor." It comes from a root which means "heavy or weighty." It refers to all that which is truly meaningful and glorious.

7 Instead of shame, you will receive a double share [of honor]

At first glance the Hebrew text sounds incomplete, but the meaning of it is clear. For her shame and humiliation which her oppressors inflicted on her, she will now receive a double portion of joy in her own land.

8 Because I the LORD love justice, I hate robbery with inquity

Robbery with "inquity" instead of the Massoretic "*olah*"—"burnt offering." We read the same consonants as "*avlah*"—"injustice or inquity," which makes better sense, following the Septuagint, the Targum and several Hebrew manuscripts which read this word in the same way. God is just and hates all injustice. Israel will be recompensed faithfully for the wrong done to her.

9 And their offspring shall be renowned among the nations

Redeemed and restored Israel and her posterity shall be acknowledged by the nations as God's people, whom He has blessed and distinguished in a singular way.

10 I will rejoice exceedingly in the LORD,

These words and the following lines are a brief hymn of praise, which the prophet puts into the mouth of the redeemed.

As a bridegroom puts on a priestly diadem . . . a bride . . . her jewels

The prophet compares Israel adorned with the garments of salvation to a bride and bridegroom in their festive wedding attire. The "priestly diadem" refers to the Biblical custom according to which the bride put on a special wedding turban and adorned herself in her jewelry. After the destruction of the Temple in 70 A. D., this ancient custom became defunct in sign of mourning.

11 For as the earth brings forth her growth . . . a garden . . . its plantings

God's promises to Israel are as sure as the laws of nature, just as the seed planted in the soil will under favorable conditions bring forth new growth and plant life. The thought is similar to Isaiah 55:10.

So shall the LORD Jehovah cause righteousness and praise to spring forth before all the nations

Even as the earth brings forth her growth in due season so also shall the LORD cause righteousness and glory to sprout forth before all nations. "*The LORD Jehovah*" is a most emphatic use of God's name.

NOTE: The Gospel of Luke records that Jesus read the above words of Isaiah 61:1-2 in the synagogue of Nazareth and indicated that He came to fulfill this messianic prophecy and program.

464

Isaiah Chapter 62

The Salvation and Glory of Zion

1 For Zion's sake I will not be silent,
And for Jerusalem's sake I will not rest
Until her righteousness shines forth like the dawn,
And her salvation like a blazing torch.

2 And nations shall see thy righteousness,
And all the kings thy glory:
And thou shalt be called by a new name
Which the mouth of the LORD shall design.

3 And thou shalt be a crown of splendor in the hand of the LORD
And a royal diadem in the palm of thy God.

4 Thou shalt no more be called, "Forsaken,"
Neither shall thy land be called, "Desolate,"
But thou shalt be called [Hephzi-bah] — "I Delight in her"
And thy land "Married," [Beulah]
For the LORD delights in thee
And thy land shall be married.

5 For as a young man marries a virgin,
So shall thy sons marry thee,
And as a bridegroom rejoices over the bride,
So shall thy God rejoice over thee.

6 Upon thy walls, O Jerusalem,
Have I set watchmen.
They shalt never keep silence by day or by night,
You who remember the LORD take no rest.

7 And give him no rest until he establish,
And make Jerusalem a praise in the earth.

8 The LORD has sworn by his right hand,
And by his strong arm
Never again will I give your grain to your enemies for food,
Nor will strangers drink your wine,
For which you have toiled.

9 But they who harvest it, shall eat it
And praise the LORD.
And they who gather it, shall drink it
In the courts of my sanctuary.

10 Pass through, pass through the gates,
Clear the way of the people.

Cast up, cast up a highway,

Remove the stones,
Raise a signal over the peoples.

11 Behold the LORD has proclaimed to the ends of the earth,
Say to the daughter of Zion:
"Behold, thy salvation is coming;
Behold, his reward is with him,
And his recompense before him."

12 And they shall be called, "The holy people,
The redeemed of the LORD."
And thou shalt be called, "The sought out,
A city not forsaken."

Comments:

1-7 The glorious promises concerning the future of Israel in chapters 60-61 are continued.

1 For Zion's sake I will not be silent . . . for Jerusalem's sake I will not rest

The question has been raised who is the speaker of the words, the Lord or the prophet. The message itself and especially verse 6 makes it clear that it is the LORD Himself who speaks, solemnly assuring Zion that He will not keep silent until her righteousness shines forth like the dawn. Righteousness is here synonymous with the vindication of Israel before the nations of her world.

2 And nations shall see they righteousness and all the kings thy glory

The nations which once despised Israel will now see what God has done for His people and Israel's glory, which will reflect the glory of Jehovah Himself. Just as in the past Jacob wrestled with the angel of the LORD and was named Israel—a prince with God; so again as a mark of Israel's new dignity she will receive a new name, which the LORD Himself will designate, a name which will be appropriate to her new stature as a regenerated and holy people.

**3 And thou shalt be a crown of splendor in the hand of the LORD
And a royal diadem in the palm of thy God**

Instead of bringing dishonor and disgrace upon God's name about which Ezekiel bitterly lamented (Ezk. 36:17-20), Israel will now become God's masterpiece. The crown and royal diadem symbolize royal and high-priestly dignity. The Hebrew word *"tsnuf"* or *"mitsnephet"* is the head-dress of the high priest (Ex. 28:4) and of the king (Ezk. 21:26). Out of her lowly beginning in history the LORD is shaping a kingdom of priests.

4 Thou shalt no more be called, "Forsaken" . . . "Desolate"

"Forsaken" and "Desolate" were the designations of Zion in the days of her humiliation and degradation, but when restored to divine favor, she will be called *Hepzi-Bah*, that is, "My delight-is-in-her" and "Married"—*Beulah*.

For the LORD delights in thee and thy land shall be married
These words explain clearly the reason for Zion's new names.

5 For as a young man marries a virgin so shall thy sons marry thee
After the introductory word *"ki"*—"for as," each of the five following words in the Hebrew text begins with the alliterative *"b"* in each root word. This is a rather engaging mark of Isaiah's style. The sense of these words is that Zion's sons will marry and possess their land, just as a young man marries and possesses his beloved.

And as a bridegroom rejoices over the bride, so shall thy God rejoice over thee
Israel in her redeemed state and splendor is figuratively called, "The Bride of God," just as the new Jerusalem is referred to in Revelation 21:2 and 22:17 as "The Bride of Christ, beloved and precious to the LORD."

6 Upon thy walls, O Jerusalem have I set watchmen
Ancient and medieval cities had their appointed watchmen, whose primary duty was to warn the citizens against any impending attack by the enemy. So also the LORD has set watchmen on the walls of His holy city, Jerusalem, whose duty is to guard the city against her spiritual enemies, against wicked and ungodly men and against spiritual and moral corruption. These watchmen were the prophets of God, who must never be silent or at ease, but keep on pleading with God on behalf of Jerusalem, that is, Israel.

7 ... until he establish and make Jerusalem a praise in the earth
The watchmen and the remembrancers of God must never cease their intercessions until Jerusalem becomes what God intended her to be: "a praise in the earth," the "holy city of God."

8 The LORD has sworn by his right hand and by his strong arm
The right hand and the strong arm of God are figurative of God's power, manifested in His redemptive actions on behalf of Israel.

Never again will I give your grain to your enemies for food
The LORD will not permit that Israel should again be robbed of the fruits of her labors, or to become a prey of the nations.

**9 But they who harvest it, shall eat it and praise the LORD. . .
In the courts of my sanctuary**
These words complement naturally the preceding lines. To eat

467

and to drink with praise in the courts of God's sanctuary does not imply that all food and drink must be consumed in the sanctuary, but alludes to the requirements of the Law concerning the festal meals in the Temple and the double tithe for the Levites, for the widows, the orphans and the poor (Dt. 14:22-27, 29).

10-12   A call to the nations to prepare the way for the returning exiles

10   Pass through, pass through the gates, clear the way of the people

The question has been raised to whom this command is directed —and about which gates the prophet was speaking. Some have thought that "the gates" might be those of Jerusalem (Young). However, it seems that it is more likely that the prophet had in mind any place wherever the Jews were held captive, including Babylon. The above verse parallels the command given to the exiles in 48::20-21 and 52:11-12.

Raise a signal over the peoples

The thought here and the words are similar to those in 49:22, where God lifts a signal for the peoples of the world that they should bring back the captive sons and daughters of Zion.

11   Behold the LORD has proclaimed to the ends of the earth. . . thy salvation is coming. . .

God has proclaimed (*hishmeea*), that they, that is the nations, should announce to the daughter of Zion that her salvation is coming. This salvation (*Yeshuah*) is personified, thus suggesting a personal Saviour (*Yeshua*-Jesus).

Behold his reward is with him and his recompense before him

This salvation or Saviour brings His reward of redemption with Him and His recompense before Him (see comment on 40:10 and 48:20).

12   And they shall be called, "The holy people, The redeemed of the LORD"

God's basic plan for Israel is that they should be a holy people (Ex. 19:6). This will become a reality when they will be redeemed and regenerated.

And thou shalt be called, "The sought out, a city not forsaken"

Just as they were once forsaken and desolate (v. 4), now they shall be a sought-after people, a city which will be the spiritual center and the attraction of all nations.

Isaiah Chapter 63

Jehovah, the Avenger and Redeemer

1 Who is this, that comes from Edom,
   In crimsoned garments from Bozrah, resplendent in his attire,
   Swaying in his great strength?
   It is I who speak in righteousness, the mighty to save.

2 Why is thine apparel so red?
   And thy garment like his who treads the wine press?

3 I have trodden the press by myself,
   And of the peoples there was none with me.
   I trod them in my wrath, and trampled them in my fury.
   Their life sap spurted on my garments,
   And all my apparel was stained.

4 For a day of vengeance was in my heart,
   And my year of redemption has come.

5 And I looked and there was none to help,
   And I was amazed that there was none to uphold;
   Therefore, my own arm brought me salvation,
   And my fury, it upheld me.

6 And I trod down the peoples in my wrath,
   And made them drunk with my fury.
   And I caused their lifeblood to flow down to the earth.

7 I will mention the loving acts of the LORD,
   The praises of the LORD according to all that
   Which the LORD has done for us,
   According to all that which the LORD has bestowed on us,
   And all the great goodness toward the house of Israel,
   Which he has bestowed on them,
   According to his compassion and his great kindness.

8 And he said: Surely they are my people,
   Children who will not deal falsely,
   So he was their Saviour.

9 In all their afflictions he was afflicted,
   And the angel of his face saved them.
   In his love and his pity he redeemed them,
   And he took them up and carried them all the days of old.

10 But they rebelled and grieved his holy Spirit,
   So he turned against them and became their enemy,
   And he waged war against them.

11 Then his people remembered the days of old, of Moses:
    'Where is he who brought them up from the sea,
    With the shepherd of his flock,
    Where is he who put within their midst his holy Spirit?'

12 Who caused his glorious arm to walk at the right hand of Moses
    Who split the waters before them,
    To make himself an everlasting name?

13 Who led them through the abyss,
    Like a horse in the wilderness,
    Without stumbling?

14 As the cattle go down into the valley,
    The Spirit of the LORD caused them to rest,
    Thus didst thou lead thy people,
    To make for thyself a glorious name.

15 Look down from heaven and see
    From thy holy and glorious habitation,
    Where is thy zeal and thy mighty acts,
    The yearning of thy innermost heart and thy compassion,
    Are they now withheld from us?

16 For thou art our Father,
    Though Abraham does not know us,
    And Israel does not acknowledge us,
    Thou, O Jehovah, art our father,
    Our Redeemer, is thy name from everlasting.

17 Why, O LORD, dost thou cause us to err from thy ways,
    And hardenest our hearts from thy fear?
    Return, for the sake of thy servants,
    The tribes of thine inheritance.

18 Thy holy people possessed [the land] but for a little while,
    Our adversaries have trampled down thy sanctuary.

19 We have become as they over whom thou hast never ruled,
    As they over whom thy name has not been called.

Comment:

1-6 Jehovah, the avenger of His people

The chapter presents an awesome vision of Jehovah. The prophet sees Him as a warrior marching from Edom in red-bespattered clothing and asks anxiously:

1 Who is this, that comes from Edom in crimsoned garments from Bozrah

Edom, although a brother nation, personifies the unrelenting hostility of the pagan world toward Israel (see Isa. 34:5ff., Jer. 25:22ff., 49:17ff., etc.). In later rabbinical literature Edom became symbolic of Rome and all oppressive, pagan power.

Bozrah was once a great city in Edom, on the east shore of the Dead Sea. The name Edom, the other name of Esau (Gen. 36:8) comes from *"adom"*—"red," suggesting blood. Bozrah is related to the word, *"Bazir"*—"a vintage." It is interesting to note that during the Roman rule the coins of Bozrah had a winepress for their emblem.

Swaying in his great strength?

"Tsoch" is translated in the KJV as "travelling" or "marching." The Hebrew term means "to sway" and is descriptive of a mighty man, as he marches. To the prophet's anxious question "Who is this?" comes the answer:

It is I who speak in righteousness, the mighty to save

The speaker introduces Himself as Jehovah, the perfectly righteous God who is mighty to save, that is, who is able to accomplish His righteous purpose.

2 Why is thine apparel so red?

Literally, why is there red (*adom*) in Thy apparel? A clear allusion to Edom.

3-6 God answers the prophet's question:

3 I have trodden the press by myself
And of the peoples there was none with me

The judgment which Jehovah executed over Edom, He accomplished by Himself without any human assistance.

I trod them in my wrath and trampled them in my fury
Their life sap spurted on my garments and all my apparel was stained

Jehovah trampled a winepress, but the grapes were the grapes of His wrath. Their life sap (*nitscham*) spurted and reddened His clothing. The extreme wrath of God is here described.

4 For a day of vengeance was in my heart and my year of redemption has come

In order that Israel might be redeemed, Edom the eternal enemy of Israel and of her God must first be obliterated. The vengeance of God is "for a day,"—a short period of time; but His redemption is "for a year,"—a long, or indefinite time.

5 And I looked and there was none to help

A virtual repetition of 59:6 (see comment) and 63:3a.

Therefore my own arm brought me salvation . . . my fury . . . upheld me

The divine arm and fury symbolize His power to perform redemptive acts. His fury refers to His holy nature which is outraged by the iniquity of men.

6 And I trod down the peoples in my wrath and made them drunk in my fury

These figurative expressions are descriptive of the staggering effect of divine punishment, which makes people reel like drunks. Some manuscripts read instead of "I made them drunk" rather "I broke them," a change of one letter in the Hebrew text, a *"b"* instead of a *"k"* (*"Ashabreim"* instead of *"Ashakreim"*).

And I caused their lifeblood to flow down to the earth

The prophet continues the comparison of the red grape juice from the winepress with the lifeblood (*nitzcham*), which flows down to the earth.

The political and physical end of the Edomite kingdom actually came during the Maccabean period, when the Edomites were compelled to become Jews. Later their land became a desert with few inhabitants.

63:7-64:12 A penitential confession by the prophet on behalf of Israel and a prayer for forgiveness and their restoration to God's favor.

7-9 The prophet recalls Jehovah's compassion for Israel in the days of old.

7 I will mention the loving acts of the LORD

The word, "loving acts" (*chasdei*) is in the plural, indicating specific acts of God's mercy and undeserved favor which Jehovah bestowed upon Israel in the course of their history. This is the prophet's act of thanksgiving and praise of the LORD.

8 And he said: Surely they are my people, children who will not deal falsely

Having shown Israel so much loving kindness, Jehovah had the right to expect gratitude rather than treachery. On that assumption He became their Saviour, rescuing them repeatedly from many perilous situations.

9 In all their afflictions he was afflicted and the angel of his face saved them

Here is one of the most disputed lines in Isaiah, resulting from the uncertain spelling of the short negative *"lo"*—"no" or "not," which has a negative meaning; the same word *"lo"* with a long *"o"* has a positive sense and means "to him."

In our verse *"lo"* is spelled in the negative way, but has an asterisk over the aleph, indicating that the negative sense should be ignored. In the KJV there is a marginal note: omit "not."

There are fifteen such passages in the Hebrew Old Testament where the word *"lo"* was misspelled. It is written *"no"* (*ketib*), but should be read (*keri*) in a positive sense. We have followed the obvious sense of the text, which states that God does care and shares our afflictions. This is in stark contrast to the ancient Greek concept of god, as being completely indifferent to the affairs of men, a god who is "without passion or compassion."

"The angel of his face" (or Presence)—*malach panav*. This angel personifies the presence of God with His people to save and protect them. He is the supreme manifestation of God. This angel is mentioned on a number of occasions (Ex. 14:19; 23:20-23; 32:12, 14, 15 etc.). In later rabbinical literature, "The Angel of His Face" became another name for the Messiah.

And he took them up and carried them all the days of old

As a father picks up his little child and carries it when it is weary and unable to walk by itself, so did Jehovah act with Israel.
10-14 Israel's rebellion caused Jehovah to turn away from her.
10 But they rebelled and grieved his holy Spirit, so he turned against them. . .

Instead of being profoundly grateful to Jehovah who had done so much for them, they rebelled against Him and grieved His Spirit (the Hebrew word *"yitsvu"* means to cause a cutting pain)—they cut Him to the quick. As a result, Jehovah turned against them and acted as if He were their enemy, even to the point of fighting against His people, yet with the ultimate purpose of bringing them to their senses.[1]

11 Then his people remembered the days of old, of Moses

This is one of the especially perplexing sentences in Isaiah. In Hebrew, it begins with the word—*"vaizkor"*—"he remembered." The question arises to whom does "he" refer: to Jehovah or to Israel? It should be noted that the Hebrew text reads: "Moses his people." Some manuscripts amended the Hebrew text to read: "Moses, his servant" (*"abdo"* instead of *"ammo"*). Our translation gives the most feasible sense. It means that the people having experienced a period of great calamities finally woke up to the fact that all their misfortunes and miseries were the direct result of their disobedience and unfaithfulness. So Israel is asking agonizing questions:

"Where is he who brought them up from the sea with the shepherd of his flock"

This is a reference to the crossing of the Red Sea under the leadership of Moses and Aaron, a central event in the history of Israel.

"Where is he who put within their midst his holy Spirit?"

The Holy Spirit rested on Moses and those whom Jehovah chose to lead His people.

12 Who caused his glorious arm to walk at the right hand of Moses

"The glorious arm" of God is the personified might of God in action, so that what Moses did was not in his own strength, but through the enabling might of God.

Who split the waters . . . to make himself an everlasting name

The crossing of the Sea brought Jehovah a name which would last forever.

13 Who led them through the abyss, like a horse in the wilderness without stumbling

"The horse in the wilderness" is another figure of speech which expresses the personal care of God for His people, just as a man might lead his horse by the halter through a dangerous land in order that it should not stumble.

14 As the cattle go down into the valley, the Spirit of the LORD caused them to rest

A further picture of God's loving care for His people.

15-19 A cry to God to renew again His favor and personal protection of Israel

15 Look down from heaven and see, from thy holy and glorious habitation

After extolling Jehovah's great mercies in the past, the prophet now pleads with God for His renewed favor. In his despair he all but accuses Jehovah of having closed His heart to Israel and of having abandoned her in her dire distress.

Where is thy zeal . . . thy compassion . . . are they now withheld from us?

The pathos of verses 15-19 is unsurpassed in all of Isaiah. Only a prophet who had so completely identified himself with his people would dare plead with God in such grief-stricken and almost reproachful terms.

16 For thou art our Father though Abraham does not know us

Although in a physical sense Abraham and Jacob (Israel) are

474

the people's ancestors, they are now gone and do not remember their offspring any longer. Yet in the truest sense, it is Jehovah who is everlastingly their God. He is their Creator, their Father and their Redeemer. Thrice Jehovah is called here, "our Father" and once, "our Redeemer." It seems that the idea that Jehovah is the Father of His nation Israel is deeply rooted in the consciousness of Israel:

Israel is my son, my firstborn (Ex. 4:22).
When Israel was a child I loved him and called my son out of Egypt (Hosea 11:1, also Jer. 3:4).

To this day the Jewish prayerbook refers to God as "our Father." Yet the awareness that God is the Father of the individual Israelite, although implied, is either absent or muted.

17 Why, O LORD, dost thou cause us to err from thy ways?

This sounds like half plea and half reproach. The deeper sense of it is that the constant showing of His wrath without letup causes the people to become disheartened and to fall into a mood of "What's the use, no matter what we do we are going to be punished." This is further expressed in the next line:

And hardenest our hearts from thy fear

The incessant punishments of the past have only resulted in a hardening of Israel's heart so the prophet pleads with Jehovah to renew His compassionate relationship with His people, to be their Father again. The relationship between Israel and Jehovah has a strong element of family drama: a disobedient and rebellious son and a father who has been deeply hurt and disappointed. Yet the more the child is punished, the more it becomes hardened and rebellious. The prophet pleads that the Father deal more gently with His son, Israel.

18 Thy holy people possessed [the land] but for a little while

This is another involved sentence which bristles with difficulties. It is partly due to the unusual structure of the sentence and partly to the Hebrew word "*mitsar*" "a very short time." The best sense seems to be the one suggested above, in which "the land" is implied as the object. Israel possessed the land for a comparatively short time during the reigns of David and Solomon. This was followed by a series of repeated invasions which culminated in the Assyrian and Babylonian captivities and the destruction of "thy sanctuary." The prophet refers to Israel as "thy holy people" or "the people of thy holiness" by virtue of the fact that Jehovah has set them apart for Himself. Theirs is an imparted holiness.

For thou art a holy people unto the LORD thy God. The Lord thy God has chosen thee to be a special people unto himself (Dt. 7:6).

19 We have become as they over whom thou hast never ruled

The lamentable situation of Israel is such as though Jehovah had never been their God and their King.

NOTE:

1 It is interesting to note that in verses 8-10 God is called a compassionate Father who carries His people, as Saviour (the Angel of His Face) and Redeemer (v. 8 and 9), and Holy Spirit (v. 10). This is an indirect reference to God in His triune nature.

Isaiah Chapter 64

Israel Pleads With the Lord and Confesses Her Sins

1 Oh, that thou wouldst tear the heavens apart and come down,
That the mountains might melt away before thy presence.

2 As fire kindles dry twigs and makes water bubble up,
So make thy name known to thy enemies,
That the nations might tremble before thee.

3 When thou didst awesome things,
For which we did not look,
Thou camest down and the mountains melted away before thy presence.

4 Since the times of old, no man has heard, nor perceived by ear,
Neither has eye seen a God besides thee,
Who works for him that waits for thee.

5 Thou didst meet him who rejoices to work righteousness,
Who remembers thee in thy ways.
Behold, thou hast been angry with us, and we sinned,
We have continued long in these ways,
That we might be saved.

6 All of us have become as one who is unclean,
And all our righteousness is like a filthy rag.
We all fade away like a leaf,
And our iniquities carry us away like the wind.

7 And there is none who calls upon thy name,
Who bestirs himself to take hold of thee.
For thou has concealed thy face from us
And hast consumed us through our iniquities.

8 But now, O LORD, thou art our Father,
We are the clay, and thou art our potter.
We are all the work of thy hand.

9 Be not, O LORD, angry with us to the utmost,
   And do not remember iniquity forever.
   Behold, consider, we beseech thee, we are all thy people.

10 Thy holy cities have become a wasteland,
   Zion is a wilderness; Jerusalem, a desert.

11 Our holy and beautiful house,
   Where our fathers praised thee is burned by fire,
   And all that which was our delight is in ruins.

12 Wilt thou, O LORD, in spite of all these things, restrain thyself?
   Wilt thou be silent and afflict us to the utmost?

Comment:

1-3 A plea for Jehovah's renewed mercy

1 Oh, that thou wouldst tear the heavens apart and come down

In the Hebrew text this verse closes chapter 63, but in the English version it is more appropriately placed at the beginning of chapter 64. Israel's situation is so desperate and hopeless that only God's personal intervention can save her. The cry that God might tear apart the heavens and come down to earth is probably the most passionate outburst of the human soul. And so once, at a time when the cup of suffering and woe was full, God heard and answered that cry and actually came down to earth.

That the mountains might melt away before thy presence

The twofold reference to the mountains melting away and to the fire burning the desert brushwood indicates that the prophet thinks of the theophany at Mount Sinai with all its terrifying phenomena. In her present desperate situation Israel again needs such divine intervention to save her from her enemies and to make known to the nations who hold the name of Jehovah in contempt that He alone is the omnipotent God.

3 When thou didst awesome things, for which we did not look

This verse partly complements and partly repeats the preceding verse.

4 Since the times of old, no man has heard, nor perceived by ear

From extolling the fearful and unexpected miracles of the past, the prophet now expresses his faith in what Jehovah will yet do for those who wait for Him. It will be more amazing than anything He has done before and beyond what men can even perceive. The Apostle Paul refers to this passage of Isaiah in a free paraphrase:

> As it is written: Eye has not seen, nor ear heard, neither have entered into the heart of man, the things which God has prepared for them that love him (1 Cor. 2:9).

5 Thou didst meet him who rejoices to work righteousness

This is another difficult passage. The Hebrew word, *"pagatha"* —"thou hast met," usually has a hostile connotation. But here it is used in a positive sense, that God graciously meets those who rejoice in doing justice and remember Him, as they walk in His ways.

Behold thou hast been angry with us, and we sinned

The prophet is contrasting God's favorable dealing with those who rejoice to walk in His ways with His anger toward the obdurate sinners. Lack of repentance is in itself a sign of divine anger.

We have continued long in these ways that we might be saved

This is a difficult text. The KJV translates it, "In those is continuance and we shall be saved." This leaves the meaning obscure. In the first part of the sentence we translated *"olam"*—which usually means "ancient" or "everlasting" as "we have continued a long time in these ways," which makes better sense. Disobedience to Jehovah brought on disaster.

6 All of us have become as one who is unclean

The prophet delves deeply into the moral and spiritual degradation of his people, comparing their state to a plague of leprosy. According to Leviticus 13:45, anyone afflicted with this dread disease was kept in isolation and wherever he went was obliged to cry "unclean, unclean" to prevent others from becoming contaminated by him.

And all our righteousness is like a filthy rag

This is one of the prophet's most scathing descriptions of what people usually call "righteousness." In the sight of the Holy God even their so-called righteousness is nothing but a filthy, cast-away rag. We sense the same moral outrage and disgust which Isaiah voiced in the opening chapter of his book.

We all fade away like a leaf, and our iniquities carry us away like the wind

Without spiritual health the nation is devoid of staying power; it fades away like a leaf and is carried away by the wind.

7 And there is none who calls upon thy name . . . to take hold of thee

Spiritual indolence and indifference have taken a hold of the nation, so that there is no one to storm the heavens for mercy and forgiveness. This is because God has concealed His presence from the people and has permitted their own degeneracy to take its natural course.

8-12 A broken-hearted prayer to God for compassion in view of all of the calamities which have befallen the nation.

8 But now, O LORD, thou art our Father, we are the clay and thou art our potter

Having unsparingly uncovered the sinfulness of his people, the prophet casts himself and his people on the mercy of God. He is their Creator. He is their Father. They are merely clay in the potter's hand. He can make them or break them, according to His will.

9 Be not, O LORD, angry with us to the utmost

Israel has been punished sufficiently. God cannot hold against them their iniquities forever, else they must perish.

Behold, consider, we beseech thee, we are all thy people

Israel may have become a prodigal son; nevertheless, they are still God's people.

10-12 A lament over Israel and her desolate country

10 The holy cities have become a wasteland. Zion is a wilderness; Jerusalem a desert

A heart-broken and dramatic description of 'the holy cities" which have become a wilderness.

11 Our holy and beautiful house . . . is burned by fire
And all that which was our delight is in ruins

The Temple which was the visible emblem of Jehovah's presence amidst His people, all their delight, their pride and joy is now in ruins. All this was surely a sign that Jehovah had abandoned His people.

12 Wilt thou, O LORD, in spite of all these things, restrain thyself?

Can God continue not to be moved by the extreme calamity of His people? Can He be silent and continue to afflict them? With these tormented questions, Isaiah closes his plea for divine mercy for Israel.

Isaiah Chapter 65

Jehovah's Reply to Israel's Pleadings

1 I was sought by them who did not ask for me,
I was found by them who did not seek me;
I said: "Here I am, here I am" to a nation,
Which was not called by my name.

2 All day long have I spread out my hands
   To a rebellious people,
   Who walk in a way which is not good,
   Following their own thoughts.

3 This people that angers me constantly to my face,
   Who sacrifice in the gardens and burn incense upon bricks.

4 Who sit in the graves and spend nights in the vaults,
   Who eat the flesh of swine,
   And the broth of foul things is in their vessels.

5 Who say: "Keep to thyself, do not come close to me,
   For I am holy to thee."
   These are a smoke in my nostrils, a fire which burns all day.

6 Behold, it is written before me;
   I will not be silent until I repay,
   And I will pay them back in their laps.

7 Your iniquities together with the iniquities of your fathers,
   Who burned incense on the mountains,
   And blasphemed me on the hills, says the LORD;
   I will first measure out their reward into their laps.

Comment:

1-7 The cause of Israel's pitiful plight

The last chapter ended with a heartbreaking description of Israel's pitiful plight ending with a challenge to Jehovah: "Wilt thou be silent and afflict us to the utmost?" (64:12).

Now Jehovah answers the people:

1 I was sought by them who did not ask for me
I was found by them who did not seek me

The question arises who are they who did not seek Jehovah and yet found Him? The majority of Jewish commentators are of the opinion that God addresses Himself to the same people, that is the Jews, in both verses 1 and 2. On the other hand Christian commentators usually apply verse 1 to the Gentiles and verse 2 to the Jews, which seems to be the meaning.

The expression "I was found by them" (in Hebrew, *nidrashti*) is the reflective passive form of the verb—"*darash*"—"to seek, to inquire after."

I said: "Here I am, here I am" to a nation which was not called by my name

Jehovah made Himself known to a nation which originally was not called by Him. The expression, nation—*goi*, is usually applied to a non-Jewish nation, although it should be noticed that on a number of occasions Israel, too, is called, *"goi."* Israel is generally called, *"am"*—"a people."

2 All day long have I spread out my hands to a rebellious people

This is the tragedy of Israel: while God constantly pleaded with His people to follow Him in faith, their response was rebellion and defiance. By contrast, many of the Gentiles to whom God has not specifically made Himself known as He did to Israel, nevertheless have found Him. The conversion of Gentiles to Jehovah happened from time to time in the pre-Christian era but later became a widespread reality through the Messiah of Israel and His apostles. Paul refers to these two verses in the above sense in Romans 10:21.

On the basis of the above two verses and also some other passages, many theologians, including some of the Reformers, concluded that God has rejected Israel and that believing Gentiles or the Church are now "The Israel of God" or "The New Israel." This misinterpretation has continued through the centuries even to the present time, obscuring the true meaning of the Scriptures concerning the relationship between historical Israel and the Church.

In this passage the prophet is merely emphasizing the sharp contrast between rebellious Israel with whom Jehovah has pleaded for many generations and those Gentiles who one day will of their own free will come to Him, although they have not been instructed and wooed by the prophets, as Israel has been.

3-5 A detailed description of Israel's idolatry

3 This people that angers me constantly to my face
Who sacrifice in the gardens and burn incense upon bricks

The idolatry described here resembles the Canaanite and other Semitic cults. The burning of incense on bricks or brick altars may have been of Babylonian origin.

4 Who sit in the graves and spend nights in the vaults

This was one of the ancient necromantic cults specifically forbidden in Scripture (see Dt. 18:11, 1 Sam. 28:3 ff.).

Who eat the flesh of swine

The meat of swine was forbidden to Israel as ritually impure (Lev. 11:7ff, Dt. 14:8).

And the broth of foul things is in their vessels

The broth, here written (*ketib*), *"parak,"* should be read, *"marak"* —a "broth" or thick soup.

"Foul things," Hebrew *"piggulim"* refers to the foul creatures alluded to in Isaiah 66:17 and to the creeping or crawling creatures, forbidden in Leviticus 11:41-47.

5 "Keep to thyself, do not come close to me, for I am holy to thee"

The utter perversity of the apostate people who practice these abominable cults is apparent in the fact that they consider themselves holy or sanctified by these idolatrous rites, or as the KJV puts it "holier than thou." That which is their shame, they consider as their pride.

These are a smoke in my nostrils, a fire which burns all day

All their evil and immoral practices constantly provoke God to anger and bring about His retribution.

6 Behold, it is written before me; I will not be silent until I repay

And I will pay them back in their laps

God keeps strict account of the misdeeds of the wicked (and of the righteous also). There is a common belief held among the Jews, even to the present day, that God keeps balance sheets of the deeds and misdeeds of His people and judges them accordingly (especially on the Day of Atonement). The Lord will not rest until He settles accounts with the evildoers. "To repay in their laps" is a figure of speech, meaning to punish in full measure.

7 Your iniquities together with the iniquities of your fathers

The iniquities of Israel have a long history and go way back to their ancestors. Before a righteous God can again be merciful to His people, He must first measure out punishment to the wicked. He cannot be merciful to unrepentant sinners, without compromising His holiness and righteousness.

8-16 Nevertheless Jehovah will preserve a faithful remnant after punishing the rebels.

8   Thus says the LORD: as when new wine is found in a cluster
And one says: "Destroy not, for there is a blessing in it,"
So will I do for the sake of my servants not to destroy all.

9   And I will bring forth a seed from Jacob
And from Judah an heir of my mountains.
And mine elect shall inherit it,
And my servants shall dwell there.

10   And Sharon shall be a fold for flocks,
And the valley of Achor a place for herds to lie down,
For my people who have sought me.

11 But you, forsakers of the LORD, who forget my holy mountains,
Who prepare a table for Gad, [the idol of Fortune],
Who fill a mixed potion for Meni, [the idol of Destiny]:

12 I will destine you to the sword,
And you shall bow down to the slaughter,
Because when I called, you answered not.
When I spoke, you did not hear,
But did that which was evil in mine eyes
And chose that in which I had no pleasure.

13 Therefore, thus says the LORD:
Behold, my servants shall eat, but you shall hunger,
Behold, my servants shall drink, but you shall thirst.

14 Behold, my servants shall sing for joy of heart,
But you shall cry for grief of heart and wail from a broken spirit.

15 And you shall leave your name for a curse for mine elect:
"Thus may the LORD God slay thee."
But his servants he shall call by another name.

16 So that he who blesses himself on earth,
Shall bless himself by the God of Truth,
And he who swears on earth,
Shall swear by the God of Truth.
Because past troubles shall be forgotten,
And hidden from mine eyes.

Comment:

8-16 Jehovah promises that although He will exact severe punishment from those who defied Him, He will not completely obliterate His people, but preserve for Himself a remnant.

8 ... as when new wine is found in a cluster

Just as the vinedresser may preserve a cluster, after the grapes have been pressed out, for the sake of the little wine which may still bo lcft, so will the LORD spare a remnant of the nation for the sake of His faithful servants. Thus the idea of a remnant emerges again just as in the earlier writings of Isaiah (1:9, 10:20-23, 11:11-16).

9 And I will bring forth a seed from Jacob

This preserved seed of Jacob, the remnant, shall again repossess the land and inhabit it.

10 And Sharon shall be a fold for flocks and the valley of Achor ... for herds

Sharon is the fertile valley stretching from the Carmel mountains in the north, down to Yaffa (Tel Aviv) in the south. The valley of

Achor runs from the lower regions of the river Jordan to the plains of Jericho in the South. The prophet, therefore, is predicting that Israel's remnant shall again inhabit their land from north to south.

11 But you, forsakers of the LORD, who forget my holy mountains

In verses 11-16, the prophet predicts an unhappy end to the idolatrous majority among the people. To forget "the holy mountains of God" refers to the abandonment of God's holy Temple for the spurious cults of the various idols mentioned below.

Who prepare a table for Gad [the idol of Fortune]
Who fill a mixed potion for Meni [the idol of Destiny]

Gad and Meni were the gods of Fortune and Destiny, worshipped among the Semitic peoples and identified later by the Greeks and Romans with Jupiter and Venus. The prophet declares that Jehovah alone is the sole controller of the destiny of men and nations. To worship "good luck" or "good fortune" idols is a denial of the sovereignty of the LORD. It is hardly necessary to mention that the ancient cults of Gad and Meni have their modern counterparts in astrology, chiromancy, card reading, fortune telling, etc.

12 I will destine you to the sword

Alluding to the idol Meni, Isaiah uses the verb *"manithi"*—"I will destine"—as a warning that God will destine those who worship Meni to the sword. The reason for their unhappy future will be the result of their oblivion to Jehovah's voice and their neglect of His pleadings.

13-14 The dismal contrast between the sinful majority and the Godly remnant is graphically depicted.

15 And you shall leave your name for a curse for mine elect

Literally for a swear word or curse. The name of the ungodly shall be used as a grim warning when it will be said: "So may the LORD God slay thee" (as He did those wicked men).

But his servants he shall call by another name

It will be a new name of honor and distinction, suitable to their new status as servants of the Lord (cf. Gen. 32:28 - Jacob - Israel).

16 So that he who blesses himself on earth shall bless himself by the God of Truth

Just as the name of the ungodly shall be used as an execration, so shall the name of God's servants be used for a blessing, remember what the God of Truth, literally the God of Amen, has done for His faithful ones (see 2 Cor. 1:20).

484

Because past troubles shall be forgotten and hidden from mine eyes

The unhappy past shall be crowded out by the new, glorious events which shall replace them.

17-25 Jehovah will create a new universe and a glorious new Jerusalem

17 For, behold, I create a new heaven and a new earth,
And past events will not be remembered nor brought to mind.

18 But rejoice and be glad forever,
For, behold, I create Jerusalem a joy
And her people a rejoicing.

19 And I will rejoice in Jerusalem, and have joy in my people;
And the voice of weeping and the voice of crying
Shall no longer be heard in her.

20 From then on there shall no longer be an infant of days
Nor an old man will not live out his days,
For the youth shall die a hundred years old,
And the sinner of a hundred years shall be accursed.

21 And they shall build houses and inhabit them,
They shall plant vineyards and shall eat their fruit.

22 They shall not build and another inhabit,
They shall not plant and another eat,
For the days of my people shall be like the days of the tree,
And my chosen ones shall enjoy for a long time
The labors of their hands.

23 They shall not labor in vain,
Nor give birth for terror,
For they are the seed of the blessed of the LORD,
And their offspring with them.

24 And it shall be so that before they will call, I shall answer.
And while they are still speaking, I shall hear.

25 The wolf and the tender lamb shall feed together as one,
And the lion shall eat straw like the ox,
And the serpent's food shall be dust.
They shall do no harm nor destroy,
In all my holy mountain says the LORD.

Comments:

17-25 The glory of the new universe and the perfect happiness of the new Jerusalem

485

17 For, behold, I create a new heaven and a new earth

Just as in the beginning God created a perfect heaven and earth, so now, after having executed judgment upon the ungodly, the Lord will recreate a new heaven and earth, a new cosmos, a completely new order of things.

18 For behold I create Jerusalem a joy and her people a rejoicing

The glory of this new world will be Jerusalem and her people, in whom God Himself will have joy.

19 And the voice of weeping and the voice of crying
Shall no longer be heard in her

One of the wonderful aspects of the new Jerusalem will be the absence of tears, of sorrow and suffering.

In Revelation 21:1-4, the same theme is enlarged upon in detail, surpassing in splendor the original vision of Isaiah:

> And I saw a new heaven and a new earth,
> For the first heaven and the earth were passed away;
> And there was no more sea,
> And I, John, saw the holy city, new Jerusalem
> Coming down from God out of heaven,
> Prepared as a bride adorned for her husband
> And I heard a great voice out of heaven saying:
> "Behold the tabernacle of God is with men and he will dwell with them.
> And they shall be his people, and God shall be with them and be their God.
> And God shall wipe away all the tears from their eyes;
> And there shall be no more death, neither sorrow, nor crying,
> Neither shall there be any more pain;
> For the former things are passed away."

20 From then on there shall no longer be an infant of days

A prominent aspect of the new era will be the longevity of men and the absence of premature death. This brings to mind the Genesis story of the long-lived men before sin and moral decay set in.[1]

21 And they shall build houses and inhabit them
They shall plant vineyards and shall eat their fruit

The long enjoyment of their labors and security from hostile ravages will be another of the blessings which God shall bestow upon His people.

22 For the days of my people shall be like the days of the tree

The people shall be as long-lived and sturdy as the trees. Perhaps the prophet had in mind the great oak tree and the gnarled olive of the Holy Land, famous for their longevity.

23   They shall not labor in vain nor give birth for terror

The fear of enemy invasion and destruction was an ever present danger for the inhabitants of Israel and Judea. In the new era all this will be a thing of the past. They and their offspring will live in perfect security, protected by the Lord Himself.

24   And it shall be so that before they will call, I shall answer

The greatest of blessings of redeemed Israel will be the readiness, indeed, the eagerness of Jehovah to answer their prayers, even before they formulate their prayers or express their needs.

25   The wolf and the tender lamb shall feed together as one

The prophet reverts to his early vision of perfect peace in the animal world, paralleled by peace among the nations, who will be led by a little child (Isa. 11:6-9). It is a Messianic vision of the king- dom of God presided over and guided by the King Messiah (Isa. 11:1-5, 10).

The wolf and the tender lamb (Hebrew—*toleh*), a lamb which is so young and delicate that it has to be carried. The meaning of this passage is not merely of harmony, but of a total transformation of human and animal nature. This will cause the wolf not to feed upon the helpless lamb, just as the transformation of the lion will cause it to eat straw like the ox, and the serpent to feed upon dust. The passage may be understood both in its literal as well as in its figurative sense. In such a transformed world there shall be no war, no destruction among the nations, even as the prophet Isaiah earlier saw in his vision:

They shall not hurt nor destroy
In all my holy mountain.
For the earth shall be filled with the knowledge of the LORD
Even as the waters cover the sea (Isa. 11:9).

1. It is interesting to note that among the blessings of the new era immortality is not mentioned. However, it is not completely absent from the prophet's thought. In his earlier writings Isaiah exclaims triumphantly:
He will swallow up death forever.
And the LORD God shall wipe away tears from all faces (25:8).
and again:
The dead shall live, their dead bodies shall arise (26:19).
Neither is the hope of immortality absent from other sacred writings in the Old Testament (see Job 19:25-27; Psa. 17:15, 49:15, 73:24; Dan. 12:2 and indirectly Ezk. 37:7-10).
Yet the dominant theme of the Old Testament is that the LORD blesses His saints with favors here on earth, with peace, long life, godly children, good harvests, above all with the abiding presence of a prayer-hearing and

prayer-answering God. No doubt, however, the hope of immortality must have been present in the people's minds, but it seldom finds expression. With the passing of the centuries, the experiences of invasions, enemy oppression, exile, and every kind of injustice and suffering, personal and national longing for eternal life where the just shall receive their rewards, and all the wrongs will be set right, greatly increased. This hope finds full expression in the apocryphal writings, in the book of Enoch, the Wisdom of Solomon and in the book of Baruch. In the New Testament, in the Gospels and the Epistles, the resurrection and eternal life through the Risen Christ are central themes. The Apostle Paul voices this faith in his ringing declaration:

If in this life only we hope in Christ, we are of all men most miserable (I Cor. 15:19).

For a fuller discussion of this subject see the author's pamphlet, *Immortality in Jewish Thought*, published by The Spearhead Press.

Isaiah Chapter 66

A Man-Made Temple Cannot Contain an Infinite God, Nor Can the Sacrifice by the Wicked Please a Holy God

1 Thus says the LORD, the heavens are my throne,
And the earth my footstool.
Where is the house which you could build me?
And where is the place of my rest?

2 For all these things were made by my hand,
And so came into being, says the LORD.
Yet to such a man shall I look:
To him who is poor and of a contrite spirit,
Who trembles at my word.

3 He who slaughters an ox is, as if he had slain a man.
He who sacrifices a lamb is, as if he had broken a dog's neck.
He who brings a meal offering is, as if he offered a pig's blood.
And he who makes an offering of incense is, as if he blessed an idol.
All they have chosen their own ways,
And their souls delight in their abominations.

4 Therefore I also will choose their mockeries,
To bring their fears upon them.
Because when I called, none answered.
When I spoke, none did hear,
But did that which was evil in mine eyes,
And chose that in which I do not delight.

Comment:

1 Thus says the LORD: the heavens are my throne . . . the earth my footstool

Since the whole universe is the handiwork of God and the earth merely His footstool, how can puny man build a temple for this infinite God?

2   Yet . . . I look to him who is poor and of a contrite spirit

Nevertheless, this transcendent and infinite God condescends in His mercy to take notice of a man who is humble and of a contrite spirit.

The Hebrew word, *"ani"*—"poor," is closely related to the word, *"aniv"*—"humble," and both are occasionally used interchangeably, that is, "poor in spirit" or "humble." In the Sermon on the Mount there is an echo of Isaiah 66:2:

> Blessed are the poor in spirit, for theirs is the kingdom of heaven (Mt. 5:3).
> Blessed be ye poor, for yours is the kingdom of God (Lk. 6:20).

Who trembles at my word

"Who trembles at my word" refers to a man who stands in absolute awe and in obedience to God's Word.

3   He who slaughters an ox is, as if he had slain a man

The expression, "as if," is absent from the Hebrew text, but is clearly implied.

Four lawful sacrifices are paired and contrasted with four unlawful and disgusting sacrifices, used in pagan rites. The sense of it is that even the sacrifices commanded by the Law are to the Lord just like pagan offerings, if the one who brings the sacrifice is wicked, a theme which Isaiah preached right from the beginning of his book (see 1:11ff.).

4   Therefore I also will choose their mockeries to bring their fears upon them

Just as the ungodly have chosen their wicked ways to defy and to outrage God, so He also will choose their outrageous acts to punish and to bring upon them the very fears which they tried to avert by their pagan rites.

The word *"tauleihem"*—their "mockeries" or "frivolous acts"—is derived from a word which describes a spoiled child, what in contemporary speech might be called "a brat." This is how the wicked, apostate and self-willed children of Israel appeared to Jehovah.

Because when I called, none answered

This is a repetition of 65:12.

5-9   A message of comfort for the faithful but despised remnant.

5   Hear the word of the LORD, you who tremble at his word,
Your brethren who hate you,

And have cast you out for my name's sake, have said:
"Let the LORD be glorified that we may see your joy."
But they shall be put to shame.

6 Hark, a sound of uproar from the city.
Hark, a tumult from the temple,
It is the voice of the LORD,
Who executes retribution to his enemies.

7 Before she was in labor, she gave birth.
Before the pangs of birth came upon her,
She brought forth a son.

8 Who has heard such a thing?
Who has seen anything like this?
Is a land brought forth in one day?
Is a nation born at once?
But as soon as Zion was in labor,
She gave birth to her children.

9 Shall I bring to birth and not cause to bring forth?
Or shall I bring forth and shut the womb?
Says thy God.

Comment:

5 Hear the word of the LORD, you who tremble at his word

The message is addressed to the despised remnant who cling to the word of God.

Your brethren who hate you and have cast you out . . .

The faithful remnant and the apostate people are both a part of Israel, they are therefore called "your brethren." The term "to cast out" later became a technical term for excommunication from the synagogue. It was used in this sense in the Gospels:

They shall put you out of the synagogues: yea the time is coming that whosoever kills you will think that he does God a service (John 16:2 see also Mt. 24:9 and Lk. 21:12).

"Let the LORD be glorified so that we may see your joy"

A taunting remark, addressed by the ungodly to the faithful. As if to say: "If you consider your persecution as suffering for the sake of God, then let us see how you enjoy it." But these wicked will be ashamed when God delivers His saints and settles accounts with those who despised them.

6 Hark, a sound of uproar from the city

This verse describes the punishment about to fall upon the ungodly city and on the Temple. This prophecy was dramatically fulfilled when the Babylonians and later the Romans invaded Jerusalem and razed the Temple.

7-9 After the punishment of the wicked, the LORD will rapidly replenish the population of Jerusalem.

7 Before she was in labor, she gave birth

Verses 7-9 express amazement at the speedy rebirth of the nation and the land.

9 . . . Shall I bring forth and shut the womb?

The LORD who brought about the rebirth of the nation will not leave His work unfinished but will complete it. The promise ends with the solemn assurance, "says thy God."

10-14 A message of comfort to the mourners of Jerusalem

10 Rejoice with Jerusalem and be glad for her,
All you who love her.
Rejoice with her exceedingly, all you who mourn for her.

11 That you may suck consolation from her breast and be fully satisfied,
That you may drink in deeply and delight yourselves
With the abundance of her glory.

12 For thus says the LORD:
Behold, I will extend to her peace like a river,
And like an overflowing stream the glory of the nations.
And you shall suck and be carried on the side
And dandled on the knee.

13 Like a man whom his mother comforts, so shall I comfort you.
And you shall find comfort in Jerusalem.

14 When you shall see this, your heart shall rejoice,
And your bones shall flourish like grass.
And the hand of the LORD shall be known toward his servants,
But he shall be indignant against his enemies.

Comment:

10 Rejoice with Jerusalem . . . all you who love her

The prophet commands those who love Jerusalem and have mourned for her in her degradation to rejoice with her in her glory. The verbs "*simhu*" and "*gilu*" are synonymous expressions of rejoicing.

11 That you may suck consolation from her breast and be fully satisfied

Here the mourners and lovers of Jerusalem are compared to an infant, long deprived of its mother's milk and comfort. The infant, which is the faithful remnant, will soon be restored to its mother's breast, Jerusalem. It will drink in hungrily and with delight the nourishing abundance of its mother, (the word, "*ziz*" literally means an "udder," a figure of abundance). Jerusalem is here movingly personified as a loving mother who embraces all her returning children and feeds them from her breast.

12 . . . Behold, I will extend to her peace like a river

Jerusalem, which in the past has suffered endless ravages of war and disaster will at last become that which her name signifies, "The City of Peace." Peace will flow toward her like a river, whose waters never cease to roll.

And like an overflowing stream the glory of the nations

Jerusalem will become a spiritual center and will draw towards her "the glory of the nations," that is, the best among the nations and the best of what they possess. "The glory of the nations" should be understood concretely, that is, the best of everything which the nations possess both in spiritual and material values. All this they will bring to Jerusalem as a tribute to Jehovah, the God of Jerusalem and of her people.

And you shall suck and be carried on the side and dandled on the knee

In the prophet's vision Israel is no longer despised among the nations, but beloved for the sake of her God. The carrying of children on the side was practiced in antiquity among the Semitic nations. The children of Israel will be brought back from exile, carried and fondled by their former captors and hosts because of their new reverence and love for Jehovah. The same thought is expressed in greater detail in 49:22 and 60:4ff.

13 Like a man whom his mother comforts, so shall I comfort you . . . in Jerusalem

The prophet now leaves the figure of the hungry infant craving to be comforted by its mother and introduces in its place the figure of a mature but troubled man who seeks comfort, understanding and compassion from his mother. In a similar manner, God will comfort His faithful servants. Incidentally it is rare in the Old Testament to find God compared to a loving mother. Usually He is compared to a compassionate father (Psa. 103:13; Isa. 63:16, 64:8).

14 When you shall see this, your heart shall rejoice

The abundant grace of God in restoring the children of Israel to Jerusalem will fill the hearts of His people with joy.

And your bones shall flourish like grass

"The bones" in Old Testament usage represent the whole physical structure of man, his body, and well being which are affected by joy or sorrow (see Psa. 35:10, 51:8; Isa. 58:11).

And the hand of the LORD shall be known toward his servants . . . and . . . enemies

The LORD shall manifest Himself to His servants in love, but toward His enemies in indignation. This is a line which forms a natural transition to the next passage.

15-17 Divine judgment upon the nations.

15 For behold the LORD shall come with fire,
And his chariots will be like a whirlwind,
To assuage his anger with fury,
And his rebuke with flames of fire.

16 For with fire will the LORD contend
And with his sword against all flesh;
And many shall be the slain of the LORD.

17 They that sanctify themselves and purify themselves,
[To attend] the gardens, one following the other, standing in the middle,
Eating the flesh of swine, of vile things and rats,
They shall all come to an end together, says the LORD.

Comment:

15-16 The wrath of God against all sinners will be manifested in fire and the whirlwind, especially against the sinners of Israel.

17 They that sanctify themselves and purify themselves (to attend) the gardens

This describes the pagan rites practiced by some apostate Jews, which were preceded by special ceremonies of "sanctification and purification," performed in groves dedicated to various idols.

. . . one following the other, standing in the middle

The Hebrew text is not completely clear but seems to refer to a magic circle formed by the participants of an occult pagan rite.

Eating the flesh of swine, of vile things and rats

The eating of swine and of all the other "vile things" was forbidden to the children of Israel as an abomination (Lev. 11:4-31). The prophet predicts that they who do these things shall be destroyed (see also Isa. 65:4).

18-24 The manifestation of God among the nations and their tribute to Him.

18 But [I know] their works and their thoughts,

[The time] will come when I will gather together all nations and tongues
And they shall see my glory.

19 And I will set a sign among them,
And I will send those who escaped to the nations: to Tarshish, to Pul and Lud,
Who draw the bow: to Tubal and Javan and to the far islands,
Who have never heard my name, nor seen my glory,
And they shall declare my glory among the nations.

20 And they shall bring all your brethren from among the nations,
As an offering to the LORD.
On horses and chariots, on litters and mules,
On dromedaries to Jerusalem, my holy mountain, says the LORD.
Even as the children of Israel bring their offering
In a clean vessel into the house of the LORD.

21 And also from among them will I take for priests, for Levites, says the LORD.

22 For even as the new heavens and the new earth, which I make
Shall endure before me, says the LORD,
So shall your seed and your name endure.

23 And it shall come to pass, that from one new moon to another,
And from one Sabbath to another, all flesh shall come
To worship before me, says the LORD.

24 And they shall go out and see the corpses of men,
Who rebelled against me;
For their worm shall not die,
And their fire shall not be quenched,
And they shall be an abhorrence to all flesh.

Comment:

18 But [I know] their works and their thoughts

The words "I know" are implied. Although the ungodly may delude themselves that their works and their hidden thoughts are unknown to God, they shall be judged for them.

"The time," another implied word, will come when God shall make Himself known to all nations.

19 And I will set a sign among them

The word, "sign"—"*oth*," indicates a miraculous manifestation of divine providence or power. This sign will finally convincce the nations that Jehovah alone is God.

And I will send those who escaped to the nations

The survivors will be the remnant of faithful Israel. Them will Jehovah send to the nations which do not know Him as yet, nor have yet seen His glory. The nations mentioned are: Tarshish, at the extreme western end of the Mediterranean, presumably Spain; Pul and Lud are North African tribes mentioned by Ezekiel (27:10 and 30:5). They were warriors renowned for their prowess with bows. These African tribes were closely associated with the Egyptians. Javan is the ancient name of Greece (Ionia). Tubal and Meshech are mentioned in Ezekiel 32:26, 38:2, 3 and 39:1. These tribes lived in the area south of the Black Sea. "The far islands who have not heard my name" refers to all the nations around the east and north coasts of the Mediterranean and beyond.

And they shall declare my glory among the nations

This is Israel's highest calling which Jehovah has entrusted to her:

The people which I formed for myself,
That they may declare my glory (Isa. 43:21).

20 And they shall bring all your brethren from among the nations

"All your brethern" refers to the scattered of Israel. Israelites have lived abroad almost from times immemorial. They were the descendants of those who from time to time were carried away into slavery by the numerous invaders, or voluntarily settled abroad as traders, craftsmen, or specialists in various fields and professions. These exiles shall be brought home again by their brethren with the cooperation of converted Gentiles who will put every means of transportation at their disposal. This they will do out of love and reverence for Jehovah, the God of Israel. Parallel passages are found in Isaiah 60:4ff. and Zephaniah 3:10.

Even as the children of Israel bring their offering in a clean vessel into the house of the Lord

The bracketing together of Gentiles who believe in Jehovah with the children of Israel indicates a new dispensation in history, the ingathering of believing Jews and Gentiles into a new fellowship, a prophetic anticipation of the Church which later became a reality through the Messiah of Israel, the Saviour of Jews and Gentiles (Eph. 2:10-16).

The motley collection of animals and conveyances enumerated in this verse expresses the eagerness of the believing Gentiles to hasten the return of the remnant to their homeland when prompted by the Spirit of God.

21 And also from among them will I take for priests and for Levites. . .

The question arises: to whom does the expression "of them also will I take" apply? Some have thought that the reference applies to the formerly exiled Jews. But this would in any case be the normal privilege of the descendants of Aaron and Moses. What the prophet has in mind here is a completely new order of things: the inclusion of Gentiles in the service of the LORD, without regard to race or descent. The only condition implied is the acceptance of the LORD in faith and a willingness to serve Him.

22 For even as the new heavens and the new earth, which I make shall endure before me, says the LORD, so shall your seed and your name endure

The survival and eternal existence of restored Israel is a basic element in the prophetic message (Jer. 31:35-37, 33:25-26).

23 And it shall come to pass, that from one new moon to another . . . shall all flesh come

Formerly only the Israelites used to appear before the LORD, at the appointed times, according to the lunar calendar, that is, "from month to month." But in the new dispensation not only the Jews, but Gentiles also will participate in the worship of God. Here is one of the highlights of prophetic vision: that the LORD will one day include in His kingdom also the Gentiles, without rejecting or casting away His people, Israel, as some prejudiced theologians have taught for centuries, and still do today. Among such theologians, we record with sadness, belong even some illustrious men such as Luther, Calvin and a host of others.

24 And they shall go out and see the corpses of men who rebelled. . .

As the pilgrims from distant lands return from their pilgrimage to Zion, they shall, on their way home, look upon "the slain of the LORD," that is, the bodies of those who rebelled against Him (verse 16).

For their worm shall not die, and their fire shall not be quenched

Isaiah probably had in mind the valley of Hinnom in Jerusalem, where human sacrifices were offered to the pagan gods, and in later times refuse was cast away, and the bodies of unclaimed, or unknown criminals were disposed of. All this was in time decomposed by worms or burned by fire (see 2 Chron. 28:3, Jer. 7:32, Neh. 11:30). This location gave rise to the rabbinical tradition of Gehinnom, which means "the valley of Hinnom" or "Gehenna." This is reflected in the apocryphal books (Judith 16:17 and Wisdom 7:17), and is also mentioned in Mark 9:43-48.

And they shall be an abhorrence to all flesh

"Abhorrence," in Hebrew *"deraon,"* is a word which occurs in the Old Testament only twice, here in Isaiah and in Daniel 12:2 both in a similar context.

The sight of the decomposing bodies of the rebels against the LORD will be a horrible reminder of divine judgment to all humanity.

Because of the Jewish distaste to end the book of Isaiah on such a dismal and downbeat note, the Hebrew Bible repeats verse 23 after verse 24, in order to end the prophecy on a note of universal hope:

"All flesh shall come to worship before Me, says the LORD."

Similar repetitions occur at the end of the books of Lamentations, Ecclesiastes and Malachi.

Postscript

It is customary among the Jewish people to pronounce a benediction, the *"shehiyanu,"* on the occasion of a memorable event or a significant personal experience.

Having now finished the work on Isaiah I feel a compelling need to thank God for permitting me to complete this labor of love, which I undertook ten years ago. If it were not for His mercy and the good help and constant encouragement of my dear wife, Lydia, I would never have been able to accomplish this.

When I started the work on Isaiah, I only had a general and vague idea of the magnitude of the task to which I had set my hand. But as one progressed, the enormity of the undertaking loomed ever larger before my eyes. Increasingly one became aware of his own inadequacy. Had I known from the beginning what I learned later, I might not have dared to start out. Nevertheless, the Spirit of the Lord kept spurring me on and encouraging me to fiinish what I started out to do.

As the work progressed I felt a strange thrill and exhilaration as I came face to face with the majestic personality of the great prophet. He made the luminous person of Israel's Redeemer and Messiah, Jesus, so much more real and meaningful to me.

At times one had to wrestle agonizingly with difficult and rarely used terms or phrases obscured by time and unknown historical allusions. Many words and expressions lent themselves to various translations and interpretations. We consulted the best translators and commentators and benefited from many of them, but where we could not agree with the bewildering variety of opinions and ideas, we were guided by the original Hebrew text and translated it as clearly as possible, always seeking to reach out beyond the words themselves to the very heart and mind of the prophet.

It should be remembered that only the Bible in the original languages was inspired by the Holy Spirit, but no translation, however excellent or popular, can make this claim. Every Bible scholar will readily admit that even with his best efforts there always remains an element of the incomprehensible, the obscure, and the mystical which eludes complete comprehension. Our own work is no exception. We are reminded of the words of St. Paul:

> For now we see in a mirror, darkly; but then face to face: now I know in part; but then shall I know even as I am known (1 Cor. 13:12).

The commentary was not primarily written with a view to the Old Testament specialist or scholar, but rather for the general reader, who wants to have an intelligent grasp of what the Spirit of God revealed to Isaiah and what He has to say to him today through the prince of the prophets. I hope and earnestly pray that you, dear reader, may recapture some of the thrill of soul-stirring experiences which was granted to this writer while preparing both volumes on Isaiah.

The completion of this commentary coincides with my seventieth birthday and with my retirement from the active, almost lifelong ministry as General Secretary of The Friends of Israel.

"To God be the glory, great things He has done!"

Victor Buksbazen

Collingswood, New Jersey
1973

General Index

Isaiah Chapters 40-66

Abarbanel, Don Isaac, 404
Abraham, 339, 354, 391, 457, 474ff.
Achor 482f.
Ahriman, 362
Ahura Mazda, 362
Ashtereth, 439
Astarte, 439
Augustine, 426
Baba Bathra, 323
Babylon, fall of, 352ff., 370ff.
Babylonian Talmud, 323, 401
Bel, 367
Ben Sirach, Jesus, 323
Bozrah, 469ff.
Buksbazen, V, 448n.
Calvin, J., 496
China, 383
Crispin, Moshe Kohen ibn, 404, 409
Cromwell, O., 405
Crusaders, 402
Cyrus Cylinder, 361
Cyrus of Persia, 326, 329, 337f., 342, 350, 359ff., 361, 370, 374, 378, 400, 432
Danan, Saadia ibn, 402
David., 323, 413, 430, 434, 475
Dead Sea scrolls, 324
Delitzsch, F., 349n., 378, 404, 423n.
Divinity of Christ disputed, 404
Doederlein, J. C., 324
Driver, S. R., 409n.
Duhm, B., 325ff.
Edom, 469ff.
Egypt, 350ff., 364f., 388, 394, 398
Eichhorn, J. G., 324
Ethiopia, 349, 364f.
Eunuchs encouraged, 433ff.
Exodus from Babylonia, 379, 382f., 398f., 425
Exodus from Egypt, 332, 350f., 376, 388, 394, 398, 400

Ezra the Scribe, 324
Gad, 483, 484
God, avenger and redeemer, 469ff.
——, calling for compassion, 443ff.
——, calling for repentance, 358, 369f., 442
——, comforting Israel, 331ff., 350ff., 354ff., 384f., 391ff., 491ff.
——, contending with Israel, 386f., 441f., 449ff., 479ff.
——, as creator and sustainer, 333ff., 365ff., 376
——, rebuking the godless, 437ff.
——, as restorer, 350ff., 377f., 384ff., 423ff.
——, as tester of mankind, 336ff.
Haifa, 330n.
Ha-Kallir, Eliezer, 403
Harrison, R. K., 327, 330n.
Herod, 413
Herodotus, 360ff., 368f.
Hezekiah, 323
Hinnom, valley of, 439, 496
Idolatry, 332ff., 336ff., 353ff., 363f., 367ff., 374ff., 439ff., 479ff.
Isaiah, divided authorship of, 323ff.
——, division and contents, 329ff.
——, internal evidence for unity, 326ff.
——, vocabulary of, 327ff.
Israel, as servant, 338ff., 343ff., 350ff., 354ff., 379ff., 402. 409
——, restoration of, 331ff., 341f., 349ff., 360ff., 381ff., 397ff., 423ff., 454ff., 460ff.

———, Manasseh ben, 405ff.
Itzhaki, Shlome, 404
Javan, 494ff.
Jeroboam, 326
Jerusalem, 327, 329ff., 343, 359, 360ff., 375, 396ff., 426f., 437, 456, 459, 465ff., 485ff., 491ff.
———, the new, 330, 454ff., 459, 467, 485ff.
Jesus Christ, 324, 329, 332, 343, 389, 393, 400ff., 414ff., 431, 435, 441f., 445ff., 468, 488
———, as messiah, 343ff., 381, 402, 414ff., 447, 495
———, as servant, 343, 381, 389, 422, 423, 430
Joseph of Arimathea, 421
Josephus, 360
Jupiter, 368, 484

Kaspi, Joseph Ben, 402
Kedar, 346, 457
Keturah, 457
Kimchi, D., 404
Kimchi, J., 404
Koppe, J. B., 324

Lazarus, Emma, 427n.
Lebanon, 455, 458
Luther, M., 496

Maimonides, 417
Manasseh, 327, 439f.
Marduk, 368
Margalioth, R., 330n.
Meccca, 439
Medians, 343
Meni, 483, 484
Meshech, 494ff.
Messiah, 328, 322, 343ff., 350, 361, 381, 386, 394, 400ff., 410ff., 416ff., 427n., 430, 462, 487, 495
Messianic king, 328, 394, 401f., 430, 487
Midrash Rabbah, 401

Moloch, 439f.
Moses, 470, 473
———,law of, 325, 387, 392
Nazareth, 324
Nebaioth, 457
Nebo, 368
Nebuchadnezzar, 324
Neubauer, A., 409n.
Noah, 426
Qumran, 324
Radday, Y., 330n.
Rahab, 394
Ruth, 434
Sarah, 391
Seba, 349
Sela, 346
Septuagint, 323
Servant, identification of, 343ff., 390n., 401ff., 410ff .
———, work of, 329f., 343ff., 379ff., 388ff., 410ff., 415ff., 427, 460ff.
Sharon, 482f.
Sheba, 457
Sidon, 372
Sinai, 388
Sinim, 383
Skinner, J., 390n., 395
Solomon, 323, 435, 475
Tarshish, 454, 458, 495
Thackeray, H. St. J., 327
Trees, 341, 358, 429, 432, 455, 458, 461, 463, 485, 486
Tubal, 494ff.
Tyre, 372
Ur of Chaldees, 340
Uziel, Jonathan ben, 401
Venus, 439, 484
Welhausen, J., 325
Yalkut Shimoni, 401f.
Young, E. J., 468
Zeus, 368
Zion, future of, 370, 384, 391, 398, 423ff., 435, 453, 465ff.

n: note
ff: following

Index of Biblical References

(a) OLD TESTAMENT

Genesis

1:9	394
14:22	401
15:8	354
15:16	339
25:4	457
25:13	457
26:24	339
32:28	484
36:8	471

Exodus

4:22	475
12:3, 4, 7	419
14:13-31	352
14:19	473
19:6	463, 468
19:16	388
23:20-23	473
28:4	466
32:12, 14, 15	473

Leviticus

4:6	411
5:1	417
5:15	422
5:17	417
11:4-31	493
11:7ff.	481
11:41-47	482
13:45	478
14:7	411
16:22	417
20:19	417
20:20	417
23:14	400
25:25	340
25:32	340
25:48	340

Numbers

11:12	401

Deuteronomy

7:6	475
14:8	481
14:22-27	468
14:29	468
18:11	481
23:1	434
23:4	434
24:1	387
33:28	375

Judges

16:21	372

Ruth

2:14	401

1 Samuel

28:3ff.	481

2 Samuel

7:16	430

1 Kings

5:10	458
8:41-43	435
13:1-2	326

2 Kings

20:9-11	323
21:6	327
21:16	437
23:15-16	326

2 Chronicles

28:3	496
33:6	439
36:22-23	361

Ezra

1:2	361
2	324
5:13	361
6:3, 4	361
6:5	400

Nehemiah

2:8	458
11:30	496

Job

9:13	394

19:25-27	487
20:23	421
22:2	421

Psalms

2:	403
17:15	487
22:30	422
23:	333
23:4	390
35:10	493
49:15	487
51:4	452
51:8	493
51:17	442
68:26	375
73:24	487
95:7-8	430
103:13	492
110:	403

Proverbs

25:1	323

Isaiah

1:1	323
1:6	416
1:7-9	326
1:9	483
1:11	328, 332
1:11ff.	489
1:14	328
1:15	450
1:16	354
1:18	328, 332, 354
2:2-4	364
2:2-5	456
4:2	329
5:13	326
5:16	328
6:1	411
6:3	328
6:13	329
8:16	327
8:16-18	378
9:6-7	328
10:17	328
10:20-22	329
10:20-23	483
11:1	413, 460

11:1-5	328, 487
11:2	344
11:5	414
11:6-9	487
11:9	487
11:10-16	343
11:10	413, 414, 430, 487
11:11-16	483
11:16	328, 333
12:35	384
13:	343
14:1-4	326
14:19	460
19:23	328
19:23-25	457
21:1-10	343
21:11	328
22:10-25	328
23:12	372
24:16	328
24:18-20	409
25:8	487
26:14-15	346
26:19	487
28:1-8	437
28:9	327
28:10	328
28:13	328
29:1	328
30:7	394
30:15	328
30:27-31	328
32:17	328
33:10	328, 332
34:5ff.	471
35:1ff.	326
35:5	328
35:7-10	333
35:8	328
35:10	343
37:23	328
37:26	328
38:8	323
40:1	326, 328, 332
40:1-11	330
40:1-2	323
40:3	328, 442
40:3-4	333
40:10	468

40:12-20	333	44:28	323, 326, 337, 400
40:19	327, 329	45:1-4	323
40:21-26	335	45:1-7	360
40:25	328, 332	45:1	326, 337, 361, 400
40:27-31	335	45:4-5	342
41:1-7	336	45:8	362
41:7	327, 329	45:9-13	363
41:8-16	338, 344	45:14-17	364
41:14	328	45:11	328
41:17-20	340	45:18-25	364
41:18-19	333	46:1-2	367
41:20	341	46:3-4	368
41:21	328	46:5-7	369
41:21-29	341	46:8-13	369
41:29	327, 329	46:9-10	328
42:1-4	343, 344	46:11	328
42:1	351, 430, 462	47:1-15	370ff.
42:1-7	328, 344, 379	48:1-2	374
42:4	351	48:1	412
42:5-7	345	48:3-8	375
42:8-9	345	48:4	413
42:10-12	384	48:9-11	376
42:10-17	346	48:12-16	377
42:15-16	333	48:17-19	378
42:18-21	344, 347, 348,	48:18	328
42:19ff.	343	48:20	468
42:19-20	412	48:20-21	468
42:22-25	348	48:20-22	379
42:24	409	48:22	329
43:1-7	349	49:1-6	380
43:4	351	49:1-7	344
43:5	328	49:1-13	379
43:7	328	49:6	422, 430
43:8-13	350	49:7	328, 412, 423
43:10	344, 351	49:7-13	381
43:14-21	351	49:14-26	384
43:21	460, 405	49:22	468, 492
43:22-28	353	49:22-26	381
43:24	412	50:1-4	386
43:28	355	50:4-5	462
44:1-5	344, 354	50:4-11	344, 379, 388
44:6-8	356	50:5-7	403
44:9-20	356	50:29	328
44:21-23	358	51:1-3	391
44:15	421	51:4-8	392
44:21	344	51:5	328
44:24-28	359	51:9	328
44:23	358, 384	51:9-11	393
		51:12	328

51:12-16	394		59:6	471
51:17-23	395		59:16	387
52:1	375		59:20	340
52:1-6	397		60:1-22	454
52:6	328		60:4ff.	492, 495
52:7-12	399		60:10	462, 463
52:11	327		60:17	328
52:11-12	468		60:21	463
52:12	425		61:1-11	460
52:13	328, 401, 404, 408		61:2	431
52:13-15	410		61:1	324
52:13-53:12	344, 379, 382, 389,		61:8	345
	390, 400, 408		62:1-12	465
52:14	382		62:6	327
52:15	423, 430		62:10	328
53:1	452		63:1-19	469
53:1-12	328		63:3ff.	327, 471
53:1-3	412		63:7-64:12	472
53:4	405		63:16	492
53:4-6	416		64:1-12	476
53:7	402, 409		64:8	492
53:7-9	419		64:12	480
53:9	405		65:1-7	479
53:10	405		65:3	329
53:10-12	421		65:4	493
54:1	427		65:8-16	482
54:1-17	423ff.		65:9	329
54:7-8	458		65:12	489
54:10	345		65:17	395
55:1-13	428		65:17-19	330
55:3-4	328		65:17-25	485
55:10	464		65:22-25	414
55:11	367		65:25	422
55:13	341		66:1-4	488
56:1-8	433		66:2	489
56:7	437		66:3	327
56:8	329		66:5-9	489
56:9-12	435, 437		66:9	328, 332
57:1-2	437		66:10-14	491
57:3-13	438		66:15-17	493
57:5	327		66:17	327, 482
57:13-21	441		66:18-23	330
57:19	328		66:18-24	493
57:21	329, 379		66:19-20	329
58:1-14	443		66:24	329
58:8	400		**Jeremiah**	
58:11	493		3:4	475
59:1-21	448		7:25-26	387

7:32	496
16:19	407
25:22ff.	471
31:31-34	345
31:35-37	496
33:25-26	496
49:17ff.	471
50:29	328
51:5	328

Ezekiel

1:18	401
16:60	345
21:26	466
27:10	495
30:5	495
32:26	495
36:17-20	466
37:7-10	487
38:2, 3	495
39:1	495
43:7	459

Daniel

7:14:	361
12:2	487, 497

Hosea

11:1	475

Zephaniah

3:10	495

Zechariah

4:7	401
8:23	355

Malachi

2:15	422

(b) THE APOCRYPHA

Judith

16:17	497

Wisdom

7:17	497

Ecclesiasticus

48:25-28	323

(c) THE NEW TESTAMENT

Matthew

1:11	457
3:3	324
4:14	324
5:3	489
5:4	462
5:5	442
11:28	366, 389
12:17	324
12:17-20	344
21:13	435
22:37-40	445
23:29	403
24:9	490
24:35	393
25:35-30	440
26:27	389
26:62-63	419
27:12	419
27:57	421

Mark

9:43-48	497

Luke

2:32	344
3:4	324
4:16ff.	324, 344
4:19	431
5:16ff.	324
6:20	489
15:11-32	431
19:46	435
21:12	490
23:34	423
23:53	421
24:25-27	415

John

1:1	393
1:4	392
1:14	459
1:29	401, 417
1:46	415
4:13-14	432
4:14	447
7:16	389
7:41	415

10:11ff.	333
10:16	435
12:32	420
12:38-39	324
14:3	403
14:16	332
14:24	389
16:2	490

Acts

1:11	403
2:29-31	430
8:30-35	344
8:34	401
14:12	368
17:23	366

Romans

2:11-15	453
2:14-15	392
8:2	432
10:13	399
10:16, 20	324
10:21	481

1 Corinthians

2:9	477
10:13	442
13:12	498
15:19	488

2 Corinthians

| 1:20 | 484 |

Ephesians

2:10-16	495
2:14	435
2:17	442
6:10-17	452

Philippians

| 2:58 | 405 |

1 Thessalonians

| 4:14-17 | 403 |

Hebrews

| 8:6 | 422 |

Revelation

21:1-4	330, 486
21:2	467
21:10-27	426
21:23ff.	460
22:17	467

Bibliography

Albright, William Foxwell — Archeology and the Religion of Israel. Baltimore, The Johns Hopkins Press, 1942.

Alcalay, Reuben — Complete English — Hebrew Dictionary. 4v. (Tel Aviv, 1959-61)

Alexander, Joseph Addison — Commentary on the Prophecies of Isaiah, 1846. Grand Rapids, Zondervan Publishing House, 1953.

Barner, Albert — Notes on the Book of the Prophet Isaiah, 2v. New York, 1840.

Brenton, Sir Lancelot Lee—The Septuagint, Greek and English.

Burrows, Millar — The Dead Sea Scrolls, N.Y., Viking, 1955.

Burrows, Millar — The Dead Sea Scrolls of St. Marks Monastery. New Haven, American Schools of Oriental Research, 1950.
V.I. — The Isaiah Manuscript and the Habakkuk Commentary.

Calvin Commentaries, Isaiah. Reprinted Associated Publisher and Authors, Inc. Grand Rapids.

Delitzsch, Franz — Biblical Commentary on the Prophecies of Isaiah. 1866. Grand Rapids, Eerdmans, 1949.

Douglas, James Dixon, ed. — The New Bible Dictionary. Consulting editors F. F. Bruce (others). (Inter-Varsity Fellowship) Grand Rapids, Eerdmans, (c1962).

Drechsler, Moritz — Der Prophet Jesaiah. Stuttgart, 1849.

Driver and Neubauer — The "Suffering Servant" of Isaiah According to the Jewish Tradition. Hermon Press, New York, reprinted 1969 First Edition Oxford and London, 1877.

Driver, Samuel Rolles — Isaiah, His Life and Times and the Writings which Bear His Name. N.Y., Fleming H. Revell Company, (1888).

Duhm, Bernard — Das Buch Jesaia. Göttingen, 1922.

Edersheim, Alfred — Prophecy and History in Relation to the Messiah; the Warburton Lectures for 1880-1884, London, Longmans, Green and Co., 1885.

Ellison, Harry L. — Men Spake from God; studies in the Hebrew Prophets. Grand Rapids, Eerdmans, (c1958).

Ewald, George H. A. — Commentary on the Prophets of the Old Testament, 5v. William and Nortgate, 1876.

Free, Joseph Paul — Archaeology and Bible History. Wheaton, Ill., Van Kampen Press, (c1950).

Gaster, Theodor Herzl — The Dead Seat Scriptures, Garden City, N.Y., Doubleday, 1956.

Ginsberg, H. L., Editor — The Book of Isaiah, The Jewish Publication Society of America, 1973.

Harrison, Roland Kenneth — A History of Old Testament Times. Grand Rapids, Zondervan Publishing House, 1955.

Harrison, Roland Kenneth — Introduction to the Old Testament, Grand Rapids, Eerdmans, 1969.

Heschel, Abraham — The Prophets. The Jewish Publication Society of Philadelphia, 1962.

Jennings, Frederick Charles — Studies in Isaiah. N.Y., Loizeaux Bros., 1959.

Jocz, Jakob — The Spiritual History of Israel. London, Eyre and Spottiswoode, 1961.

Kaufmann, Yechezkel — The Religion of Israel from Its Beginnings to the Babylonian Exile. Translated and abridged by Moshe Greenberg. Chicago, University of Chicago Press, (1966, c. 1960).

Kimchi, David — The Commentary of David Kimchi on Isaiah, edited by Louis Kinkelstein (Columbia University Oriental Studies. V. XIX). N.Y., Columbia University Press, 1926.

Kissane, Edward J. — The Book of Isaiah, translated from a critically revised Hebrew text with Commentary by Rev. Edward J. Kissane, Dublin, Browne and Nolan, Limited, 1941-43.

Kittel, Rudolf — Gestalten und Gedanken in Israel, Leipzig, Quelle and Meyer, (Vorwort, 1925).

Klausner, Joseph — The Messianic Idea in Israel, London, G. Allen and Unwin, (1956).

König, Edward — Hebraisches und Aramaisches Wörterbuch zum Alten Testament, Leipzig, Dieterich, 1931.

Kramer, Samuel Noah — History Begins at Sumer. Anchor Books, 1959.

Margalioth, Rachel — The Indivisible Isaiah, N.Y., Yeshiva University, 1964.

Marti, Karl. — Das Buch Jesiah. Tübingen, 1900.

Owen, George Frederick — Archeology and the Bible. Westwood, N.J., Revell, (c1960).

Pfeiffer, Charles Franklin — ed. The Biblical World: a Dictionary of Biblical Archaeology, Grand Rapids, Baker Book House, 1966.

Pfeiffer, Charles Franklin — Introduction to the Old Testament.

Silver, Abba H. — Messianic Speculation in Israel. Beacon Press, 1927.

Skinner, J. — Isaiah (in the Cambridge Bible) 2v. 1896. Cambridge University Press, 1963.

Smith, George Adam — The Book of Isaiah, Harper and Brothers. 1927.

Slotki, I. W. — Isaiah (Soncino Bible). 1949.

Thiele, Edwin Richard — The Mysterious Numbers of the Hebrew Kings. Rev. Ed. Grand Rapids, Eerdmans, (c1965).

Thompson, John Arthur — The Bible and Archaeology. Grand Rapids, Eerdmans, (c1962).

Unger, Merrill Frederick — Archeology and the Old Testament. Grand Rapids, Zondervan Publishing House, (1956, 1954).

Wright, George Ernest — Biblical Archaeology. Philadelphia, Westminster Press, (1957).

The Wycliffe Bible Commentary — edited by Charles F. Pfeiffer and Everett F. Harrison. Chicago, Moody Press, c1962.

Young, Edward Joseph — My Servants the Prophets. Grand Rapids, Eerdmans, 1954.

Young, Edward Joseph — Studies in Isaiah. Grand Rapids, Eerdmans, 1956.

Young, Edward Joseph — Who Wrote Isaiah? (Pathway Book) Grand Rapids, Eerdmans, 1958.

Young, Edward Joseph — The Book of Isaiah. 3v. Grand Rapids, Eerdmans, 1965-70.